Mistake, Fraud and Duties to Inform in European Contract Law
edited by Ruth Sefton-Green
0 521 84423 1

Security Rights in Movable Property in European Private Law
edited by Eva-Maria Kieninger
0 521 83967 X

Pure Economic Loss in Europe
edited by Mauro Bussani and Vernon Valentine Palmer
0 521 82464 8

The Enforceability of Promises in European Contract Law
edited by James Gordley
0 521 79021 2

Good Faith in European Contract Law
edited by Reinhard Zimmermann and Simon Whittaker
0 521 77190 0

Precontractual Liability in European Private Law

This volume analyses thirteen cases, from the perspective of sixteen national European legal systems, in order to explore the legal nature of the precontractual phase and the liability which may follow a break-off of precontractual negotiations. The precontractual phase is difficult to characterise and analyse in either legal or practical terms. The negotiating parties have begun their journey together, but they are not yet in the relationship - the contract - which is their aim. The negotiations may fail after a lengthy period in which either party may have incurred significant expenses and invested time and effort. The break-off of the negotiations may come as a shock to one party where the negotiations were far advanced, or at least where there was nothing to suggest that they were not likely to lead to their fruition in the contract. The disappointed party is therefore likely to seek a remedy.

JOHN CARTWRIGHT is Professor of the Law of Contract at the University of Oxford, and Professor of Anglo-American Private Law at the University of Leiden. He is also a Solicitor.

MARTIJN HESSELINK is Professor of European Private Law at the University of Amsterdam and Director of the Centre for the Study of European Contract Law.

The Common Core of European Private Law

For the transnational lawyer, the present European situation is equivalent to that of a traveller compelled to cross legal Europe using a number of different local maps. To assist lawyers in the journey beyond their own locality, the Common Core of European Private Law Project was launched in 1993 at the University of Trento under the auspices of the late Professor Rudolf B. Schlesinger.

The aim of this collective scholarly enterprise is to unearth what is already common to the legal systems of European Union Member States. Case studies widely circulated and discussed between lawyers of different traditions are employed to draw at least the main lines of a reliable map of the law of Europe.

Books in the series

Precontractual Liability
edited by John Cartwright and Martijn Hesselink
978 0 521 51601 3

Environmental Liability and Ecological Damage in European Law
edited by Monika Hinteregger
978 0 521 88997 1

The Enforcement of Competition Law in Europe
edited by Thomas M.J. Möllers and Andreas Heinemann
978 0 521 88110 4

Commercial Trusts in European Private Law
edited by Michele Graziadei, Ugo Mattei and Lionel Smith
978 0 521 84919 7

Precontractual Liability in European Private Law

Edited by
John Cartwright and Martijn Hesselink

CAMBRIDGE
UNIVERSITY PRESS

CAMBRIDGE UNIVERSITY PRESS
Cambridge, New York, Melbourne, Madrid, Cape Town, Singapore,
São Paulo, Delhi, Dubai, Tokyo, Mexico City

Cambridge University Press
The Edinburgh Building, Cambridge CB2 8RU, UK

Published in the United States of America by Cambridge University Press, New York

www.cambridge.org
Information on this title: www.cambridge.org/9780521183949

First published 2008
First paperback edition 2010

A catalogue record for this publication is available from the British Library

Library of Congress Cataloguing in Publication data
Cartwright, John, 1957-
Precontractual liability in European private law / John Cartwright,
Martijn Hesselink.
p. cm.
Includes bibliographical references and index.
ISBN 978-0-521-51601-3 (hardback)
1. Contracts, Preliminary–Europe–Digests. 2. Liability (Law)–
Europe–Digests. I. Hesselink, Martijn Willem, 1968- II. Title.
KJC1732.A52 2008
346.2402′2–dc22 2008049678

ISBN 978-0-521-51601-3 Hardback
ISBN 978-0-521-18394-9 Paperback

Contents

General editors' preface

This is the ninth book in the series *The Common Core of European Private Law* published within the *Cambridge Studies in International and Comparative Law*. The Project was launched in 1993 under the auspices of the late Professor Rudolf B. Schlesinger.

The methodology used in the project is still unparalleled. By making use of case studies it goes beyond mere description to detailed inquiry into how most European Union legal systems resolve specific legal questions in practice, and to thorough comparison between those systems. It is our hope that these volumes will provide scholars with a valuable tool for research in comparative law and in their own national legal systems. The collection of materials that the Common Core Project is offering to the scholarly community is already quite extensive and will become even more so when more volumes are published. The availability of materials attempting a genuine analysis of how things are is, in our opinion, a prerequisite for a fully-fledged and critical discussion on how they should be. Perhaps in the future European private law will be authoritatively restated or even codified. The analytical work carried on today by the almost 200 scholars involved in the Common Core Project is a precious asset of knowledge and legitimisation for any such normative enterprise.

We must thank the editors and contributors to the already published volumes, and those who are working hard to achieve future results. With a sense of deep gratitude we also wish to recall our late Honorary Editor, Professor Rudolf B. Schlesinger. We are sad that we have not been able to present him with the scholarly outputs of a project in which he believed so firmly.

No scholarly project can survive without committed sponsors. The Italian Ministry of Scientific Research is funding the project, having recognised it as a 'research of national interest'. The International University College of Turin with the Compagnia di San Paolo and the Consiglio Nazionale del Notariato allow us to organise the General Meetings. The European Commission has partially sponsored some of our past general meetings, having included them in their High Level Conferences Programme. The University of Torino, the University of Trieste, the Fromm Chair in International and Comparative Law at the University of California and the Hastings College of Law, the Centro Studi di Diritto Comparato of Trieste, have all contributed to the funding, and/or the success of this Project.

Our home webpage is at www.iuctorino.it. There you can follow our progress in mapping the common core of European private law.

General Editors
MAURO BUSSANI (University of Trieste)
UGO MATTEI (University of Turin and University of California, Hastings College of Law)

Honorary Editor
RUDOLFO SACCO (University of Turin)

Late Honorary Editor
RUDOLF B. SCHLESINGER (Cornell University - University of California, Hastings)

Preface

This volume is designed to form another piece in the jigsaw of the map of private law in Europe – a map which is being drawn, piece by piece, through the results of the various projects undertaken by the Common Core group.

This project was first conceived at the meeting of the Contracts sub-group of the Common Core group in Trento in 1996, although it took a number of years for the project to take shape. The work of our national reporters and other contributors, and our own editorial work to produce this volume, have therefore been carried out over a number of years. We describe the Common Core method, and the particular approach which we have taken to our own project, in the Introduction.

It seemed particularly appropriate for this project to be undertaken under the joint editorship of a Dutch lawyer and an English lawyer; not simply because this ensures that both the 'civil law' and the 'common law' are represented in the editorial team (this does not mean that we wish to reinforce the caricature of the so-called civil law/ common law divide, on which we comment in the Conclusions) but because, of all the legal systems represented within our project, Dutch law and English law represent the extremes of principle. Amongst the 'civil law' systems, Dutch law is known for having a particularly strong view of the liability which one negotiating party may incur towards the other once the negotiations have reached an advanced stage, accepting that in principle this might even extend to remedies designed to compensate the innocent party for her failure to obtain the contract under negotiation. By contrast, amongst the 'common law' systems, English law is known for having a particularly strong view of the *absence* of liability which the negotiating parties may incur towards each other, even where negotiations have reached a very advanced stage. We have been able to use these extremes of principle as (we believe) useful reference points for our discussion and analysis of all the jurisdictions, and have commented on them in particular in the Conclusions.

We should like to thank those who have contributed to our project, both by offering their advice and comments in the early days when the project was in its conception, and by their active participation in the writing of the project itself. The members of the Contracts sub-group gave very helpful advice at the meetings in 1996 (when the project was first proposed) and 1997 (when we had prepared a first draft of what became the final questionnaire); and our national reporters have of course provided the core material for our project. We thank them for their hard work in preparing their reports, both their original reports and revisions to the reports which became necessary during the further discussion on the scope of the project once we collected together the results of the questionnaires. We also thank them for their understanding in allowing us a wide editorial discretion in finalising their reports for publication, and their patience – and particularly the patience of our more assiduous reporters who worked very quickly in preparing their reports and in answering all our questions and requests for revision – in waiting for the final publication of this volume. The editing of the reports was finally completed towards the end of 2007, although some of our contributors' national reports were finalised some time before that.

We are also particularly grateful to Nili Cohen for having agreed to write a chapter which gives a most interesting alternative perspective on our topic from the point of view of Israeli law, and to Eleonora Melato and Francesco Parisi for having agreed to write a stimulating chapter giving a view of our topic, and of some of our particular cases, from the perspective of law and economics scholars.

We must also thank Ugo Mattei and Mauro Bussani for their support in relation to our project and, through their organisation of the Trento Common Core group, for having given us the opportunity to undertake the project at all.

Finally, Martijn Hesselink would like to thank John Cartwright for having undertaken much of the work involved in editing the national reports for this volume.

JOHN CARTWRIGHT
MARTIJN HESSELINK

Contributors

The case studies have been prepared:
for Austria by Willibald Posch, University of Graz
for Denmark by Ole Lando, Copenhagen Business School
for England by John Cartwright, University of Oxford and University of Leiden
for Finland by Matti Rudanko, Helsinki School of Economics
for France by Olivier Deshayes, University of Amiens, and Grégory Maître, University of Sceaux - Paris-XI
for Germany by Stephan Lorenz and Wolfgang Vogelsang, University of Munich
for Greece by George Arnokouros, member of the Athens Bar
for Ireland by Raymond Friel, University of Limerick
for Italy by Alberto Musy, University of Piemonte Orientale, Novara
for the Netherlands by Martijn Hesselink, University of Amsterdam
for Norway by Lasse Simonsen, University of Oslo
for Portugal by Luís Menezes Leitão, University of Lisbon
for Scotland by Martin Hogg and Hector MacQueen, University of Edinburgh
for Spain by Francisca Hernanz, member of the Madrid Bar
for Sweden by Christina Ramberg, University of Gotheburg, and Johnny Herre, Stockholm School of Economics
for Switzerland by Peter Loser, University of Basel

From the common law to the civil law: the experience of Israel by Nili Cohen, University of Tel-Aviv

A law and economics perspective on precontractual liability by Eleonora Melato, Washington University in St. Louis, Law School, and Francesco Parisi, University of Minnesota Law School and University of Bologna, Department of Economics

Introduction, Comparative observations and Conclusions by John Cartwright, University of Oxford and University of Leiden, and Martijn Hesselink, University of Amsterdam

Abbreviations

General abbreviations

art(s).	article(s)
cf.	compare
ch.	chapter
CISG	United Nations Convention on Contracts for the International Sale of Goods
ed(s).	editor(s)
edn	edition
ff.	and following page(s)
m	million
n(n).	note(s)
no.	number
p(p).	page(s)
PECL	Principles of European Contract Law
reg(s).	regulation(s)
s(s).	section(s)
vol(s).	volume

Introduction and Conclusions

AJCL	*American Journal of Comparative Law*
DCFR	Draft Common Frame of Reference, Interim Outline Edition
ECR	European Court Reports
ELJ	*European Law Journal*
Harv. Int'l LJ	*Harvard International Law Journal*
MLR	*Modern Law Review*
OJ	*Official Journal of the European Communities*

RabelsZ	*Rabels Zeitschrift für Auslandisches und Internationales Privatrecht*

Case studies: abbreviations by country

Austria

ABGB	Allgemeines bürgerliches Gesetzbuch (General Civil Code of Austria)
BGBl	*Bundesgesetzblatt* (Government Gazette)
JBl	*Juristische Blätter* (law journal)
LJZ	*Liechtensteinische Juristen-Zeitung*
OGH	Oberster Gerichtsthof (Austrian Supreme Court)
ÖJZ	*Österreichische Juristen-Zeitung* (law journal)
RdW	*Recht der Wirtschaft* (law journal)
SZ	Entscheidungen des österreichischen Obersten Gerichtshofes in Zivilsachen (decisions of the OGH in private law and administration of justice)

England

AC	Law Reports, Appeal Cases
All ER	All England Law Reports
All ER (Com)	All England Law Reports, Commercial Cases
All ER (D)	All England Direct Law Reports
B	Baron
Ch	Law Reports, Chancery Division
CLR	Commonwealth Law Reports (Australia)
CP	Law Reports, Common Pleas
DLR	Dominion Law Reports (Canada)
EGLR	Estates Gazette Law Reports
Ex	Exchequer Reports, Welsby Hurlstone & Gordon
EWCA Civ	Court of Appeal (Civil Division)
FSR	Fleet Street Reports
J	Justice
KB	Law Reports, King's Bench Division
LJ	Lord Justice
LR	Law Reports

MR	Master of the Rolls
QB	Law Reports, Queen's Bench Division
P & CR	Property, Planning and Compensation Reports
RPC	Reports of Patent, Design and Trade Mark Cases
SI	Statutory Instrument
WLR	Weekly Law Reports

Finland

KKO	*Korkein oikeus* (Yearbook of the Finnish Supreme Court)
VahL	Vahingonkorvauslaki (Damages Act, 1974)

France

al.	alinéa (paragraph within a provision of the Code)
Bull Civ	Bulletin civil de la Cour de cassation (reports of the civil chambers of the Cour de cassation)
CA	Cour d'appel
CCC	*Contrats, concurrence, consommation* (legal periodical)
C.civ.	Code civil (French Civil Code)
Civ (1, 2, 3)	Cour de cassation, Chambre civile (first, second, third chamber)
Com	Cour de cassation, Chambre commerciale
D	*Recueil Dalloz* or *Dalloz Sirey* (legal periodical, in three sections: 'chron.' is chronique, 'som.' is sommaires, 'IR' is informations rapides)
DH	*Dalloz, Recueil hebdomadaire de jurisprudence* (legal periodical)
Gaz Pal	*Gazette du Palais* (legal periodical)
ICC	International Chamber of Commerce
J-Cl	*Juris-classeur* (legal encyclopaedia, 1950, updated annually)
JCP	*Jurisclasseur périodique, édition générale* (legal periodical, also known as *La Semaine Juridique*)
JCP éd E	*Jurisclasseur périodique, édition entreprise et affaires* (legal periodical)
obs	observations
PA	*Les Petites Affiches* (legal periodical)

Req	Chambre de requêtes of the Cour de cassation
Rev.	*Revue*
RJDA	*Revue de jurisprudence de droit des affaires* (legal periodical)
RRJ	*Revue de la Recherche Juridique* (legal periodical)
RTDCiv	*Revue Trimestrielle de Droit Civil* (legal periodical)
RTDCom	*Revue Trimestrielle de Droit Commercial* (legal periodical)

Germany

AcP	*Archiv für die civilistische Praxis* (law journal)
BGB	Bürgerliches Gesetzbuch (German Civil Code)
BGH	Bundesgerichtshof (Federal Supreme Court)
BGHZ	Entscheidungen des Bundesgerichtshofs in Zivilsachen (official report of the Bundesgerichtshof)
DB	*Der Betrieb* (law journal, Düsseldorf)
DTZ	*Deutsch-Deutsche Rechts-Zeitschrift* (law journal, Munich)
GWB	Gesetz gegen Wettbewerbsbeschränkungen (Act Against the Restraint of Competition)
JuS	*Juristische Schulung* (law journal, Munich)
JZ	*Juristenzeitung* (law journal, Tübingen)
LM	Lindenmaier and Möhring, *Nachschlagwerk des Bundesgerichtshofs in Zivilsachen* (decisions of the BGH)
MünchKomm	*Münchener Kommentar zum Bürgerlichen Gesetzbuch* (4th edn, München, 2001) (with name of author of article appended)
NJW	*Neue Juristische Wochenschrift* (law journal)
NJW-RR	*Neue Juristische Wochenschrift – Rechtsprechungs-report* (supplement to law journal with case reports in private law)
RG	Reichsgericht
Rn.	Randnummer (paragraph)
sent.	sentence
Soergel	T. Soergel, *Bürgerliches Gesetzbuch mit Einführungsgesetz und Nebengesetzen* (12th edn, Stuttgart, 1988) (with name of author of article appended)

Staudinger	J. von Staudinger, *Kommentar zum Bürgerlichen Gesetzbuch mit Einführungsgesetz und Nebengesetzen* (13th edn, Berlin, 1993) (with name of author of article appended)
UWG	Gesetz gegen den unlauteren Wettbewerb (Unfair Competition Act)
WM	*Wertpapiermitteilungen, Zeitschrift für Wirtschafts- und Bankrecht* (law journal)
ZeuP	*Zeitschrift für Europäisches Privatrecht* (law journal)
ZRP	*Zeitschrift für Rechtspolitik* (law journal)

Greece

AP	Areios Pagos (Greek Supreme Court in Civil and Criminal Matters)
Arm	*Armenopoulos* (law journal)
ECR	European Court Reports
EEN	*Efimeris Ellinon Nomikon* (law journal)
EllD	*Helliniki Dikaiosini* (law journal)
GCC	Greek Civil Code
NoV	*Nomiko Vima* (law journal)

Ireland

A & E	Adolphus and Ellis' Reports
All ER	All England Law Reports
App Cas	Law Reports, Appeal Cases
ChD	Law Reports, Chancery Division
Eq	Equity
ER	English Reports
FSR	Fleet Street Reports
HL	House of Lords
Hob	Hobart's Reports
ILRM	Irish Law Reports Monthly
ILTR	Irish Times Law Reports
IR	Irish Reports
IRCL	Irish Reports, Common Law
LR	Law Reports
LR Ir	Law Reports (Ireland), Chancery and Common Law
NI	Northern Ireland Law Reports
P	Pacific Reporter (United States)

QB	Law Reports, Queen's Bench Division
QC	Queen's Counsel
RPC	Reports of Patent, Design and Trade Mark Cases
VR	Victorian Reports (Australia)
WLR	Weekly Law Reports

Italy

App.	Corto d'Appello (Appeal Court)
Cass	Corte di cassation
c.c.	Codice civile (Italian Civil Code)
CI	*Contratto e Impresa* (legal periodical)
Cons. Stato	Consiglio di Stato
Corte Cost.	Corte Costituzionale (Constitutional Court)
Cost.	La Costituzione della Repubblica Italiana (Italian Constitution)
c.p.	Codice penale (Criminal Code)
c.p.c.	Codice di procedura civile (Code of Civil Procedure)
DL	*Diritto del Lavoro* (legal periodical)
D.Lgs.	Decreto legislativo (legislative decree)
Enc. Dir.	*Enciclopedia del diritto* (legal encyclopaedia)
Enc. Giur.	*Enciclopedia giuridica* (legal encyclopaedia)
Foro it	*Il foro italiano* (legal periodical)
GC	*Giustizia civile* (legal periodical)
Giur com	*Giurisprudenza commerciale* (legal periodical)
GI	*Giurisprudenza italiana* (legal periodical)
L	Legge (law)
lav.	lavoro (employment)
Novissimo Dig	*Novissimo Digesto Italiano* (legal encyclopaedia)
pen.	penale (criminal)
PRET	Pretura (District Court)
RCDP	*Rivista critica di diretto privato* (legal periodical)
RCP	*Responsabilità civile et previdenza* (legal periodical)
r.d.	Royal Decree
RDC	*Rivista di diritto civile* (legal periodical)
RDCo	*Rivista di diritto commerciale* (legal periodical)
Riv. Giur. Sarda	*Rivista giuridica Sarda* (legal periodical)
RTDPC	*Rivista trimestrale di diretto e procedura civile* (legal periodical)
sez.	Sezione (Section of the Corte di cassation)

S.U.	Sezione Unite (United Sections of the Corte di cassation)
TAR-T	Tribunale amministrativo regionale (regional administrative court)
TRIB-T	Tribunale (Court of first instance)

Netherlands

AA	*Ars Aequi* (legal periodical)
BW	Burgerlijk Wetboek (Dutch Civil Code)
ERPL	*European Review of Private Law*
HR	Hoge Raad des Nederlanden (Supreme Court)
NJ	*Nederlandse Jurisprudentie* (law journal)
NJB	*Nederlands Juristenblad* (law journal)
WPNR	*Weekblad voor Privaatrecht, Notariaat en Registratie* (law journal)

Norway

JT	*Juridisk Tidskrift* (law journal, Sweden)
JV	*Jussens Venner* (law journal)
NIR	*Nordiskt Immateriellt Rättsskydd* (*Nordic Intellectual Property Law Review*)
NJA	Nytt Juridisk Arkiv (Swedish Supreme Court Reports)
RG	Rettens Gang (law reports of lower courts)
Rt	Norsk Retstidende (Norwegian Supreme Court Reports)
TfR	*Tidsskrift for Rettsvidenskap* (law journal)

Portugal

BMJ	*Boletim do Ministério da Justiça* (law reports)
CC	Código Civil (Portuguese Civil Code)
CJ	*Colectânea de Jurisprudência* (law journal)
RC	Relação de Coimbra (Appeal Court of Coimbra)
RL	Relação de Lisboa (Appeal Court of Lisboa)
ROA	*Revista da Ordem dos Advogados* (law journal)
STJ	Supremo Tribunal de Justiça (Supreme Court)

Scotland

AC	Law Reports, Appeal Cases
affd.	affirmed

CSOH	Court of Session, Outer House
D	Dunlop's Session Cases
Edin LR	*Edinburgh Law Review*
F	Fraser's Session Cases
FC	Faculty of Advocates, Collection of Decisions (law reports)
GWD	Greens Weekly Digest (case summaries)
HL	House of Lords
M	Macpherson's Session Cases
R	Rettie's Session Cases
S	Shaw's Session Cases
SC	Session Cases
Sh Ct Rep	Sheriff Court Reports
SLT	Scots Law Times

Spain

BOE	Boletin Oficial del Estado (law reports)
CC	Código Civil (Spanish Civil Code)
RCL	Repertorio cronólogico de legislación (legislation)
RJ	Repertorio de jurisprudencia (law reports)
STS	Sentencias del Tribunal Supremo de Justicia en Materia Civil (decisions of the Supreme Court)

Sweden

CA	Avtalslagen (1915:218) (Contract Act)
JB	Jordabalken av den 17 december 1970 (Real Estate Code)
JT	*Juridisk Tidskrift* (law journal)
NJA	Nytt Juridisk Arkiv (Swedish Supreme Court Reports)
PA	Lag om offentlig upphandling (1992:1528) (Procurement Act)
prop.	Regeringens proposition (approximates to a Government Bill)
SGA	Köplagen (1990:931) (Sale of Goods Act)
SOU	Statens Offentliga Utredningar (official reports of legislative and investigation commissions)
TSA	Lag om skydd för företagshemligheter (1990:409) (Trade Secrets Act)

Switzerland

BaslerKommentar	H. Honsell, N. P. Vogt and W. Wiegand (eds.), *Kommentar zum Schweizerischen Privatrecht, Obligationenrecht I, Art. 1–529 OR* (3rd edn, Basel, 2003) (with name of author of article appended)
BernerKommentar	*Berner Kommentar, Kommentar zum schweizerischen Privatrecht* (Bern) (with name of author of article appended)
BGE	Entscheidungen des Schweizerischen Bundesgerichtes (reports of the Federal Court)
CommRomand	L. Thévenoz and F. Werro (eds.), *Commentaire Romand, Code des Obligations I* (Basel, 2003)
E.	Erwägung (consideration)
Intro.	Introduction
OR	Schweizerisches Zivilgesetzbuch mit Obligationenrecht (Swiss Code of Obligations)
SemJud	*La Semaine Judiciare* (legal periodical)
UWG	Bundesgesetz gegen den unlauteren Wettbewerb (Unfair Competition Act)
ZBGR	*Schweizerische Zeitschrift für Beurkundungs- und Grundbuchrecht* (legal journal)
ZBJV	*Zeitschrift des Bernischen Juristenvereins* (legal periodical)
ZGB	Schweizerisches Zivilgesetzbuch (Swiss Civil Code)
ZSR	*Zeitschrift für Schweizerisches Recht* (legal periodical)
ZürcherKommentar	*Zürcher Kommentar, Kommentar zum Schweizerischen Zivilgesetzbuch* (Zürich)

From the common law to the civil law: the experience of Israel

LSI	Laws of the State of Israel
CA	Civil Appeal
PD	Piskei Din (Israeli Supreme Court reports in Hebrew)

Note on translations of foreign language statutory provisions

Some reporters have used published English translations of statutory texts:

In the Austrian reports, translations of Code articles (with amendments in brackets where necessary) are taken from M. Winiwarter (trans.), *The General Civil Code of Austria* (rev. P.L. Baeck, New York, 1972).

In the Finnish reports, quotations in English from the Sale of Goods Act are taken from an official translation made in the Finnish Ministry of Justice.

In the German reports, translation of the reformed provisions (§§241, 280, 311, 437 BGB) are by Werner Lorenz. Other translated BGB provisions are taken from S.L. Goren, *The German Civil Code* (Littleton, 1994).

In the Swiss reports, quotations from articles of the Swiss Code of Obligations of 1912 (OR) are taken from Swiss-American Chamber of Commerce, Swiss Code of Obligations, English Translation (4th edn, Zürich, 2002) and quotations from articles of the new Code of Obligations and the Swiss Civil Code (ZGB) of 1912 are taken from Wyler and Wyler, *The Swiss Civil Code, English Version* (Zürich, 1987).

1 Introduction

JOHN CARTWRIGHT AND MARTIJN HESSELINK

A. The Common Core Project

1. *Aim and method*

a. Aim

The present volume forms part of a project that started in Trento in 1993 and has produced, so far, ten similar volumes.[1] The aim of the Common Core Project has been defined, and refined, by the general editors of the project, Mauro Bussani and Ugo Mattei, on several occasions.[2] The main aim is legal cartography, that is, to draw a reliable map of private law in Europe:[3]

> the Common Core Project is seeking to unearth the common core of the bulk of European Private Law ... The search is for what is different and what is already common behind the various private laws of European Union Member States ... Such a common core is to be revealed in order to obtain at least the main lines of one reliable geographical map of the law of Europe.

The research project is meant to be neutral, without any specific agenda for or against further Europeanisation of private law, whether or not

[1] Zimmermann and Whittaker, *Good Faith in European Contract Law*; Gordley, *The Enforceability of Promises in European Contract Law*; Bussani and Palmer, *Pure Economic Loss in Europe*; Werro and Palmer, *The Boundaries of Strict Liability in European Tort Law*; Kieninger, *Security Rights in Movable Property in European Private Law*; Sefton-Green, *Mistake, Fraud and Duties to Inform in European Contract Law*; Graziadei, Mattei and Smith, *Commercial Trusts in European Private Law*; Pozzo, *Property and Environment*; Möllers and Heinemann, *The Enforcement of Competition Law in Europe*; Hinteregger, *Environmental Liability and Ecological Damage in European Law*.

[2] Notably, in M. Bussani and U. Mattei, 'The Common Core Approach to European Private Law' (1997/1998) 3 *Columbia Journal of European Law* 339 and M. Bussani and U. Mattei, 'Preface: the Context', in Bussani and Mattei, *The Common Core of European Private Law* (2002), pp. 1–8.

[3] Bussani and Mattei, 'The Context', above n. 2, p. 1.

through codification. As Bussani and Mattei put it, 'We are not drafting a city plan for something that will develop in the future and that we wish to affect. This project seeks only to analyze the present complex situation in a reliable way.'[4] This also means that the legal systems of the Member States are treated on an equal basis; no relations between legal systems, hierarchical or in terms of 'legal families', are assumed.

This neutral stance distinguishes the present project from other international research projects in the area of European private law, such as the projects undertaken by the Commission on European Contract Law (Lando Group),[5] the Study Group on a European Civil Code (Von Bar Group),[6] the Accademia dei Giusprivatisti Europei (Gandolfi Group),[7] and the European Research Group on Existing EC Private Law (Acquis Group),[8] who all aim to draft common rules ('principles') of private law for Europe; and also from the Study Group on Social Justice in European Private Law (Social Justice Group) which, without drafting rules, pursues a well-defined political aim.[9]

b. Method

As to the methodology, the Trento Common Core Project has had two main sources of inspiration. First, was the Common Core Project that Rudolph Schlesinger directed at Cornell University in the 1960s.[10] From Schlesinger's project the Trento Project borrowed its functional approach and its specific case-based method. Schlesinger thought that legal rules are best described by their function and that a good way of

[4] Ibid. p. 2.

[5] See Lando and Beale, *Principles of European Contract Law, Parts I and II, prepared by the Commission on European Contract Law*; Lando, Clive, Prüm, Zimmermann, *Principles of European Contract Law, Part III, prepared by the Commission on European Contract Law*. On the aims see art. 1:101 PECL. On the working method, see 'Introduction', in *Principles of European Contract Law, Parts I and II*.

[6] See von Bar, *Principles of European Law: Benevolent Intervention in Another's Affairs*; Hesselink, Rutgers, Bueno Díaz, Scotton, Veldman, *Principles of European Law: Commercial Agency, Franchise and Distribution Contracts*; Barendrecht et al., *Principles of European Law: Service Contracts*; Drobnig, *Principles of European Law: Personal Security*. See also www.sgecc.net.

[7] Gandolfi, *Code Européen des contrats - Avant-projet*.

[8] See Research Group on the Existing EC Private Law (Acquis Group), *Principles of the Existing EC Contract Law (Acquis Principles), Contract I (Pre-contractual Obligations, Conclusion of Contract, Unfair Terms)*.

[9] Study Group on Social Justice in European Private Law, 'Social Justice in European Contract Law: a Manifesto' (2004) 16 *European Law Journal* 653.

[10] Schlesinger, *Formation of Contracts: a Study of the Common Core of Legal Systems*.

comparing legal systems is by inquiring how different legal systems solve the same practical cases ('factual approach').

The second source of inspiration is Rodolfo Sacco's work on the methodology of legal comparison, in particular his theory of legal formants.[11] Sacco distinguishes several legal formants that together form a legal system. The originality of Sacco's theory compared to theories and descriptions of 'sources of law' lies in the fact that Sacco rejects the assumption that different legal formants of one legal system always point in the same direction (that is, give the same answer to a question of law). Instead, within his 'dynamic' approach to comparative law legal formants are regarded as being in a competitive relationship with one another.

Ugo Mattei and Mauro Bussani have merged these two approaches to legal comparison into one method, 'the common core method'. The Trento Common Core Project seeks to provide a reliable map of European private law by comparing the way in which the national systems of the different Member States deal with the same practical cases relating to some of the main topics in some of the main areas of private law. The national reporters are encouraged not to take for granted that their legal system provides one determinate and coherent answer to the questions under consideration. On the contrary, they are asked, in principle, to discuss the answer given by each of the legal formants separately.

Legal formants are formally distinguished into three levels.[12] On a first level ('operative rules') the national reporters are asked to indicate how the case would be solved according to case law, legislation, legal doctrine, custom and usage, and whether all these formants are concordant, both from an internal point of view, and from a diachronic point of view. On a second level ('descriptive formants') the reporter is to indicate the reasons why lawyers feel obliged to adopt the solutions mentioned on the first level. Finally, on a third level ('metalegal formants') the reporters are invited to indicate any other elements that might affect the solutions mentioned at level I, such as policy considerations, economic factors, social context and values, and the structure of the legal process. However, the 'Instructions about how to answer the

[11] Sacco, *Introduzione al diritto comparato*, p. 43ff.; R. Sacco, 'Legal Formants: a Dynamic Approach to Comparative Law' (1991) 39 AJCL 1–34, 343–401.

[12] 'Instructions about how to answer the questionnaires', published as Annex 1 in Bussani and Mattei, 'The Common Core Approach to European Private Law', above n. 2.

questionnaires' also point out that it will often be possible to group together answers on levels II and III and for different questions.[13]

2. *Methodological criticism*

Since the beginning of the Trento Common Core Project in 1993 many prominent theorists of comparative law have visited the yearly general meetings of the Project. On these occasions they have been invited to express their views on the aims and method of the project. These views have been published by the general editors.[14]

a. Functionalism

The first line of criticism is a specific instance of the general attack on functionalism in comparative law. Until quite recently the functional method was the dominant method of comparison. A classical statement of functionalism was given by Konrad Zweigert and Hein Kötz:[15]

> The basic methodological principle of all comparative law is that of *functionality* . . . The proposition rests on what every comparatist learns, namely that the legal system of every society faces essentially the same problems, and solves these problems by quite different means though very often with similar results.

A first criticism of the functional method has been that there is more to law than its function; law is a cultural expression just like, for example, a song or a work of architecture.[16] A second, more undermining criticism is that there is no such thing as the objective function of a legal rule or doctrine which can be scientifically established. Therefore, the findings and conclusions of any comparative research are dependent on the way in which the functional question was formulated. In other words, a comparatist necessarily imposes his or her own functional categories on the law of a foreign country.[17] This criticism was formulated by Günter Frankenberg in 1985.[18]

[13] Ibid.

[14] Bussani and Mattei, *Making European Law: Essays on the 'Common Core' Project*; Bussani and Mattei, *The Common Core of European Private Law*.

[15] Zweigert and Kötz, *Introduction to Comparative Law*, p. 34 (emphasis in original).

[16] See, e.g., Legrand, *Que sais-je? Le droit comparé*, p. 119: 'La comparaison des droits sera *culturelle* ou ne sera pas.'

[17] Cf. generally Said, *Orientalism*.

[18] G. Frankenberg, 'Critical Comparisons: Re-thinking Comparative Law' (1985) 26 *Harv Int'l LJ* 411.

However, the element in Zweigert and Kötz's version of functionalism that aroused the strongest criticism was probably their claim that legal systems, such as those in the European Union, answer the needs of legal business in the same or in a very similar way; and that this idea could provide a useful starting point for legal comparison ('*praesumptio similitudinis*'):[19]

[A]s a general rule developed nations answer the needs of legal business in the same or in a very similar way. Indeed it almost amounts to a '*praesumptio similitudinis*', a presumption that the practical results are similar. As a working rule this is very useful . . . the comparatist can rest content if his researches through all the relevant material lead to the conclusion that the systems he has compared reach the same or similar practical results, but if he finds that there are great differences or indeed diametrically opposite results, he should be warned and go back to check again.

Among the many critics of this is Pierre Legrand:[20]

Ainsi le respect de l'altérité ne se présente pas comme le résultat d'une comparaison des droits: il en est le pré-requis . . . Il incombe donc au comparatiste de protester vigoureusement contre l'axiomatisation de la ressemblance, contre l'impérialisme du Même, tout particulièrement lorsque l'illusion simplificatrice devient tellement excessive qu'elle conduit à suggérer que le chercheur qui constaterait avoir mis au jour des différences entre divers droits devrait revoir ses conclusions.

Other functionalists have tried to limit the damage by severing the functional method from the *praesumptio similitudinis*. See, for example, Jaakko Husa:[21]

The idea [i.e. the idea of presumed similarity] is, to me, an unnecessary auxiliary to hardcore functional method. Why is it not always important to treat any 'results' of comparative study with natural built-in suspicion? This does not have anything to do with the fact whether or not the comparison shows similarities or differences . . . Functionalism is better without this overstretched universality presumption; the hardcore of functional method in comparative law does not support similarity-presumption, on the contrary, it encompasses both similarities and differences.

However, it is doubtful whether this rescue operation can be fully successful. The problem seems to lie deeper. As Frankenberg said,

19 Zweigert and Kötz, *Introduction to Comparative Law*, p. 40.

20 Legrand, *Que sais-je? Le droit comparé*, pp. 36–8.

21 J. Husa, 'Farewell to Functionalism or Methodological Tolerance?', *RabelsZ* 2003, 419, 424–5.

'The sameness of the problems produces the relative sameness of results.'[22]

How does the criticism of functionalism affect the Common Core Project? As to the first criticism (law is culture), most participants in the Project are well aware that the law consists of more than mere black-letter rules. Moreover, as has already been said, the 'Instructions about how to answer the questionnaires' ask the national reporters to go beyond what are traditionally regarded as the sources of law and to address also the deeper levels of their 'descriptive formants' and 'metalegal formants', which include such things as economic and/or social factors, social context and values. Indeed, the three-level method that has been adopted looks rather like the '*comparaison à étages*' that Pierre Legrand proposes as an alternative to functionalism.[23]

The reply could, of course, be given that in their national reports most reporters do not go much beyond the black-letter rules (understood as code, statutes and case law) of their systems. But then, could such an attitude not be regarded as typical of the national '*mentalité*' of the reporter? Is a cultural comparatist allowed to tell a national reporter that he has too narrow a conception of his own law; that his national law comprises much more than he, as local lawyer, has always thought? Any other answer seems to imply that there exists such a thing as a national legal system or national legal culture of a given country 'out there', that can be described in a better way by the comparatist than by a national reporter who has been asked explicitly to dig deep into the deepest layers of his own legal culture. As Bussani and Mattei say, 'the common core project wishes to compare rather than to preach how we should compare'.[24]

The second criticism (functional categories are imposed on foreign systems), does not seem to apply fully to the Common Core Project either. First, this is because the questionnaires are agreed upon by all the national reporters together, therefore functional categories and formulations of the facts of the cases are not imposed upon another legal

[22] Frankenberg, 'Critical Comparisons', above n. 18, p. 436.

[23] See Legrand, *Que sais-je? Le droit comparé*, p. 28: 'La positivité de surface d'un droit dissimule des strates qui restent essentielles à un riche entendement de ce positivisme même. En effet, ce sont ces structures cognitives – cette mentalité – qui soutiennent le droit positif, dans lesquelles ce droit positif se trouve ancré. Ce sont ces étais que le comparatiste doit mettre au jour à travers une "comparaison à étages", et c'est là la spécificité de la contribution qu'il peut apporter à l'éclairement du droit.'

[24] Bussani and Mattei, 'The Context', above n. 2, p. 2.

system. Secondly, within the Project reporters are encouraged to report whether a certain perceived problem is actually considered to be a problem in the national legal system. However, it must be acknowledged that the way in which the facts of the cases and the questions are formulated, and the way in which the cases are selected (which cases belong to a particular subject) are crucial. Moreover, a very basic question is what counts as an (interesting) subject of study. In this regard, it has to be acknowledged in particular, that the names of the sub-groups of the Project ('Contract', 'Tort' and 'Property') and of the specific projects that have been finalised so far,[25] are highly conceptual ('good faith', 'the enforceability of promises', 'pure economic loss', 'the boundaries of strict liability', 'security rights in movable property', 'mistake, fraud and duties to inform', 'commercial trusts').

Finally, the *praesumptio similitudinis* is certainly not a part of the Common Core method. Not only have the general editors emphasised time and again that they are interested in producing reliable maps, but also the editors of the projects are as keen on finding differences ('look, here French and Spanish law are clashing!') as similarities ('you see, in this case the odd ones out are France *and* England'). Of course, the deeper criticism of the *praesumptio* does apply to the Common Core method: the sameness of the problems produces the relative sameness of results. The fact that the reporters and editors of a questionnaire have agreed on the way in which cases and questions have to be formulated in a given questionnaire implies that they have limited their investigations to a 'common frame of reference' which excludes potentially important differences in the way that they and their co-nationals look at the world.

Twenty years after his seminal article on comparative legal method, Günter Frankenberg came to Trento and commented upon the Common Core Project and its method.[26] His main methodological criticism is inspired by fact scepticism.[27] The 'Trentinos', he argues, are guilty of 'reductionism' and 'sterilization of facts'. That is a somewhat surprising reproach to make to someone who is trying to draw a map. Are not maps always sterilised? Does that make them less useful? Or does that make them biased in the sense that they are only useful for tourists who

[25] Above n. 1.

[26] G. Frankenberg, 'How to Do Projects with Comparative Law: Notes of an Expedition to the Common Core' (2006) 2(2) *Global Jurist Advances* Article 1.

[27] Ibid. Section V.

want to travel to the same destinations, using the same roads, as those who drew up the map? Moreover, the critique of reductionism and sterilisation of facts seems to suggest that there is a better way to find the common core; that it exists 'out there' and that the Trento method is not the best way to find it. Again, the question is: what would be a better method of giving an impression of the existing similarities and differences in the private laws of Europe?

b. Neutrality, scientific method and the politics of comparative law

A second line of criticism is directed against the Project's proclaimed 'critical neutrality'. The general editors of the Project have consistently argued that the Common Core Project is neutral towards the general question of whether private law in Europe should be further harmonised and the specific question of the desirability, feasibility and possible content of a European Civil Code:[28]

> [W]e still believe that the most important cultural difference between the 'Common Core Project' and other remarkable enterprises – such as the Unidroit Principles, the Lando Commission, or von Bar's Study Group – is that they may be seen as doing city planning rather than cartographic drafting . . . the 'common core' research may be a useful instrument for legal harmonization, in the sense that it provides reliable data to be used in devising new common solutions that may prove workable in practice. Be that as it may, the latter goal has nothing to do with the common core research itself, which is devoted to produce reliable information, whatever its policy use might be.

Observers have pointed out that one of the general editors has published a provocative article in which he rejects the soft approaches towards private law harmonisation in Europe, such as the drafting of principles and a 'Common Frame of Reference', and calls for a 'hard code now'.[29] Moreover, it can be added that the Common Core Project participates, together with (among others) the Study Group on a European Civil Code and the Acquis Group, in the Joint Network on European Private Law (CoPECL),[30] a 'network of excellence', funded by the European Commission, which has the task of preparing for the

[28] Bussani and Mattei, 'The Context', above n. 2, p. 4.

[29] See Frankenberg, 'How to Do Projects with Comparative Law', above n. 26. The article is U. Mattei, 'Hard Code Now!', (2002) 2(1) *Global Jurist Frontiers* Article 1.

[30] See www.copecl.org.

European Commission a 'Common Frame of Reference' that may one day provide the basis for an (optional) European Code of Contracts.[31]

What should we make of such criticism? First, it should be pointed out that the Common Core Project also includes opponents of a European Civil Code. Indeed, some editors have explicitly rejected the idea.[32] Secondly, the general editors are right to the extent that, in theory, it is at least conceivable that one could conduct a project like the Common Core Project with exactly the opposite aim: to show as many differences as possible with a view to making a case against a European Civil Code – there are too many differences; it will be impossible to reach agreement; or with all these different traditions the code would be applied differently; or it may be possible but it would destroy cultural diversity.

The reality, however, is different. It is probably fair to say that most participants are not hostile, in principle, to the idea of further private law harmonisation in European, even in the shape of an (optional) European Code. This is not surprising. The project has brought together through the years hundreds of enthusiastic scholars (often young) from all Member States and far beyond. Not only did they share an initial curiosity towards what might be the common core of their legal systems; also, over the more than ten years that the project has been conducted, it has contributed to shaping a non-nationalistic but common European culture of legal scholarship, as this (somewhat immodest) account by the general editors describes:[33]

> in the process of drafting the map we are changing the landscape of European private law by affecting the mode of thought of one of the most important formants of professional law: i.e. legal doctrine . . . In the course of these years that we have spent more or less intensely worrying about the same methodological problems, the same difficulties in communication due to the lack of common taxonomies, the same need to make our own law, including its more tacit assumptions, understandable by all the other members of our group, we have actually changed, we have augmented our comparative sensitivity and perhaps we have learned to think a bit more like European lawyers rather than like Italians, French, Greeks or Scottish.

[31] Communication from the Commission to the European Parliament and the Council: a more coherent European contract law; an action plan: COM(2003) 68 final (12.2.2003) (OJ 2003 C63/01).

[32] See R. Zimmermann, 'Roman Law and European Legal Unity' in Hartkamp *et al.*, *Towards a European Civil Code* (3rd edn), pp. 21–39; R. Sefton-Green, 'Cultural Diversity and the Idea of a European Civil Code' in Hesselink, *The Politics of a European Civil Code*, p. 71.

[33] Bussani and Mattei, 'The Context', above n. 2, p. 3.

It is not surprising that such a cosmopolitan community tends to reject legal nationalism and to be curious and even enthusiastic towards attempts to construct a truly common European private law.

The criticism of the neutrality of the Common Core method raises the further question whether other methods of legal comparison might be (more) neutral, objective or scientific. Several critics of the Project (or of functionalism in general) seem to imply that their own methods are more appropriate for academic comparative legal studies.[34]

This brings us to the broader debate on scientific method that has been going on among philosophers of science. Today, the possibility of drawing categorical distinctions between knowledge and opinion, between science and non-science, and of a 'scientific method' which can lead to objective, true and scientific knowledge, seems to be very doubtful.[35] Historical and sociological approaches to science and knowledge, which focus on what scientists actually *do* when they are producing scientific knowledge, seem to be more promising than prescriptive theories of scientific method.[36] What are the implications for the debate on the method of legal comparison, in particular for the debate on the Common Core approach? First, of course, that the general editors' initial claim of objective and neutral cartography is indeed implausible. However, the emphasis of critics on that metaphor seems unfair. The project has been going on for more than a decade and all the participants seem to have moved well beyond such naive scientism. In the meantime we have learned much more about both legal comparison and European private law. Indeed, with hindsight most of the initial contributions to the debate on the Europeanisation of private law actually were rather naive.[37]

[34] See, e.g., Legrand, *Que sais-je? Le droit comparé*, p. 28 (emphasis in original): 'Nonobstant les objections prévisibles des "résonneurs" du droit, la complexification de l'objet de la comparaison juridique s'impose en raison de ce que seule la compréhension *approfondie* ou l'interprétation *dense* d'un aspect quelconque d'un droit étranger et du croisement de ce droit avec l'expérience juridique du comparatiste lui-même peut justifier l'entreprise comparative pratiquée dans le milieu universitaire, laquelle ne mérite d' être sanctionnée par la communauté savante que dans la mesure où elle veut bien accepter de s'intellectualiser. Quant à elle, la connaissance fouillée dont je me fais le défenseur ne saurait pouvoir être obtenue que si le comparatiste intervenant comme observateur d'autres droits se montre prêt à s'émanciper de la dimension positive ou dogmatique du droit, éphémère et contingente, c'est-à-dire friable, pour situer le phénomène juridique dans un contexte culturel.'

[35] See, e.g., such different authors as Feyerabend, *Against Method*; Rorty, *Philosophy and the Mirror of Nature* and Derrida, *L'Université sans condition*.

[36] See, e.g., Latour, *Science in Action* and Shapin, *The Scientific Revolution*.

[37] See, e.g., Hartkamp *et al.*, *Towards a European Civil Code* (1st edn).

However, the more important implication seems to be that there is no such thing as the right or proper or scientific method of legal comparison, which could be contrasted with methods that are wrong and unscientific. When looking at what comparatists actually do, the picture seems to be more or less as follows. During the last decade or so there has been a debate concerning the proper method of legal comparison. This debate has been closely linked to the debate on the desirability of legal harmonisation and unification with a specific focus, in Europe, on the idea of a European Civil Code. In a nutshell, functionalists tend to favour legal harmonisation or unification, whereas culturalists tend to reject it or be sceptical about it. And, vice versa, universalists and europhiles tend to favour a functional method of comparison, whereas legal nationalists and eurosceptics tend to emphasise the cultural dimensions of law.

Two examples may illustrate this. First, Hein Kötz, co-author with Konrad Zweigert of the most famous statement of the functional method[38] (which has been the focal point of critics of functionalism)[39] has subsequently written an introduction to European contract law which aims at contributing to a common European contract law.[40] Secondly, Pierre Legrand, who advocates a culturalist approach to legal comparison,[41] has undertaken a virulent attack on the idea of a European Civil Code.[42]

David Kennedy has pointed to the politics of comparative law. He argues that doing comparative law is an act of international governance.[43] He contrasts early idealist comparative lawyers with today's

[38] Zweigert and Kötz, *Introduction to Comparative Law*. See above, text to n. 15.

[39] See, e.g., Frankenberg, 'Critical Comparisons', above n. 18; Legrand, text to n. 20 above.

[40] Kötz, *European Contract Law*, Part I, Preface, p. v ('If Europe is to be economically unified in a Single Market, there is no doubt that its private law will also have to be unified, at least to some extent . . . But all that is needed to constitute European private law is to recognise it. For this purpose we need books, books which disregard national boundaries and, freed from any particular national system or sytematics, are addressed to readers of different nationalities. Of course national rules must be taken into account, but only as local variations on a European theme. To the extent that the actual solutions on a particular topic are found to be sufficiently alike, it makes sense to speak of a European common law').

[41] See, e.g., Legrand, *Que sais-je? Le droit comparé*; Legrand, *Fragments on Law-as-Culture*.

[42] P. Legrand, 'Against a European Civil Code' (1997) 60 MLR 44. See also P. Legrand, 'A Diabolical Idea' in Hartkamp *et al.*, *Towards a European Civil Code* (3rd edn).

[43] D. Kennedy, 'The Politics and Methods of Comparative Law' in Bussani and Mattei, *The Common Core of European Private Law*, pp. 131–207.

professionals of comparative law. Somewhat more than a century ago, at the International Congress of Comparative Law in 1900 in Paris, early comparatists such as Lambert and Saleilles had quite explicit political goals. They promoted comparative law in the name of cosmopolitan, internationalist, humanist and socially progressive political visions.[44] Moreover, the early comparatists meant comparative law to be applied: they promoted broad projects of unification and harmonisation of law. In contrast, later comparatists such as Schlesinger, Von Mehren, Zweigert and Kötz adopted the professional project of mapping and explaining similarities and differences as an escape from the politics of ideology.[45] However, Kennedy argues, the escape from politics remains a hope:[46] 'by holding firm to neutrality, continuing to the enumeration of similarities and differences, the profession is able to obscure the ongoing contribution it makes to global governance - but it does not eliminate it'.

B. The precontractual liability project

1. General

In 1996, during the yearly meeting of the Common Core group in Trento, the Contracts sub-group decided to dedicate a questionnaire to 'precontractual liability'. The following year, the editors presented a questionnaire which was discussed and amended during a two-day discussion. After the approval from the general editors, the editors started the search for national reporters. Eventually, we found reporters for all the then Members States of the European Union except Belgium and Luxembourg, together with Norway and Switzerland.

In 2001, when we had received reports from all our reporters, the editors drafted a first comparative report and formulated specific questions to the reporters. The same year, the reporters and editors came together in Trento for a one-day meeting in order to discuss the first results. After the reporters had answered the questions from the editors, their reports were edited (with a view to clarity and uniform style) and sent back to the national reporters for checking and further revision. In the meantime the editors drafted the general conclusions. The work which is presented in this volume was therefore done over a number of years. Although some later materials have been added

[44] Ibid. p. 134. [45] Ibid. p. 137. [46] Ibid. p. 138.

during the final editing, or by reporters who did not finalise their reports until 2007, most of the national reports were completed by the end of 2005.

2. *The questionnaire*

a. Precontractual liability

The questionnaire was intended to cover all types of cases which in any of the European systems are regarded as dealing with liability for conduct (including omissions) during the precontractual stage. Precontractual *liability* was the focus of the study. It was therefore not concerned mainly with other effects of precontractual misconduct, such as the invalidity of any contract which is formed.[47] Indeed, in most cases discussed in this volume no contract is formed at all; usually the party seeks a remedy for the very reason that her hopes of a contract have been dashed as a result of the breakdown of the negotiations, and the losses which she seeks to cover may be the failed expectation of the contract itself, as well as other losses such as expenditure incurred during the period when the negotiations were on foot. We have included, as the last case in the volume, a quite different set of facts where a contract is concluded, for the very reason that we wished to see to what extent the principles which emerge from the answers to the other cases in the book are limited to the case where there is no contract. But in this volume we are generally concerned only with liability which arises during the precontractual[48] stage itself.

The national reporters were therefore asked to discuss each case, addressing the questions: (a) whether party A was liable in damages (this may be in tort, contract, restitution, *culpa in contrahendo* or on the basis of any other doctrine); (b) if so, to what extent she was liable (in particular, reliance or expectation interest); (c) whether party B had any other remedies (such as a court order to continue negotiations, to conclude the contract or to perform the contract); and (d) whether some of the remedies might be cumulated.

[47] Cf. the volume by Ruth Sefton-Green, *Mistake, Fraud and Duties to Inform in European Contract Law* (2005), which has a more significant focus on the (in)validity of the contract for certain types of precontractual misconduct and mistake.

[48] Hence our deliberate use of the word 'precontractual' rather than 'pre-contractual'. The latter may tend to suggest that it is referring to the period before a contract which was in fact concluded.

b. Legal formants

We decided not to adopt the formal distinction and separate discussion of legal formants. Does this choice imply a theoretical position with regard to Sacco's theory of legal formants? Maybe it does. The reason why we decided not to follow the model was that both the national reporters and the general reporters found it too artificial and unworkable. Most national reporters appear to have thought that this method was not the best way to present their national system and tradition as they know it. These are not external reports made by outsiders, but internal reports from insiders. And as reporters, most of us thought that our national legal system should be presented as being coherent. The relevant players (legislator, courts, scholars, teachers) treat their system as being coherent, even though from the outside this assumption may be questionable. Moreover, there have been much more radical versions of (internal and external) critiques of coherence[49] and it seemed odd to privilege (and reify) Sacco's moderate version.

Still, what we retained of Sacco's approach is that national reporters were invited specifically to report on inconsistencies (both between sources of law or legal formants and within them individually), and also to report on deeper/higher levels of their national tradition where they could contribute to explaining rule choices.

3. The cases

The present book contains the discussion of 13 cases. The original questionnaire, prepared by the editors and answered by the reporters, contained 19 cases. In part, the reduction is deceptive because we have sometimes amalgamated two or three cases into a single case, where the facts were very close and we first drafted variant facts as separate cases in order to allow the reporters to focus their answers on the separate variations; but in editing them we have been able to merge the answers in a way which highlights more clearly the variations. For example, case 7 (the breakdown of merger negotiations) contains three separate situations within each of which it is necessary to consider variations of the facts; this began as three separate cases, which we have edited into one. However, the reduced number is also a result, in part, of our decision not

[49] See Kennedy, *A Critique of Adjudication (fin de siècle)*, who regards Sacco as 'a classic external critic in that he believes that "legal formants" determine legal rules through the vehicle of indeterminate legal dogmatics' (p. 387, n. 41).

to include certain cases in the finished volume because they would either add little to the rest of the cases, or were marginal to the topic and we needed to keep a close eye on the overall length of the volume. For example, we originally included a case which read:

> A is the owner of a shop which sells carpets. Whilst one of A's employees is showing a range of carpets to B, who is considering ordering a new carpet, the employee moves some rolls of carpet and carelessly knocks one over, injuring B. What liability (in contract, tort, restitution, or any other form of liability), if any, does A have to B? Would it make a difference if the roll of carpet fell not on B but on C, B's seven-year old daughter who was accompanying him?

Of course, this case corresponds to the famous *Linoleumrollenfall* case decided in Germany by the Reichsgericht in 1911.[50] We have already said that the questionnaire was intended to cover all types of cases which in any of the European systems are regarded as dealing with liability during the precontractual stage; and this case is naturally seen as such by the German reporters and, for similar reasons, the Austrian and Swiss reporters, since (as our German reporters put it in their answer to the case) it was the starting point of the tort-related category of *culpa in contrahendo*; its reasoning continues to be followed, establishing *culpa in contrahendo* as a means to overcome certain flaws in the German law of tortious liability. This case gave rise to an interesting discussion amongst our reporters; one went so far as to say:

> Is this case not brought to bend the knee for a German peculiarity? The Germans treat such a case as a case of *culpa in contrahendo* which in German law is contractual liability. They want it to be covered by rules on contract liability which impose vicarious liability which the German tort law does not do. It is submitted that this is a simple tort case outside of the scope of precontractual liability.

In the end, we decided not to devote a whole case within the published volume to this set of facts, but we think it important to draw attention to it as one of the marginal cases which shows the risks of conceptualising our topic: if we ask reporters to describe cases within 'precontractual liability', the Austrian, German and Swiss reporters would presumably include it; whereas all other reporters see no link because of their own perceptions of the boundaries of the topic.

We did, however, include within the volume (as the final case) one which might also be thought to be marginal: the case of

[50] RG, Urt. v. 7.12. 1911.

misrepresentation or silence about a harvester's capacity during the negotiations for its sale, where the negotiating parties have in fact concluded the contract. We thought it important to include this case, because it was relevant, for each jurisdiction, to test whether and (if so) how the formation of the contract affected the jurisdiction's analysis of the precontractual stage.

Obviously, from a methodological point of view these may be important choices which may significantly influence the conclusions. Indeed, from certain vantage points, what has been omitted may be as interesting as what has been included. For example, omitting cases on the ground that they add little to the rest of the cases, or are marginal to the topic, forms an important step in (further) defining the topic; and this in turn contributes to 'normalising' the subject matter as a coherent (common European) category with certain well-defined borders. The difficulty over the *Linoleumrollenfall* case is a particularly good example of this.

The drafting and selection of the original cases was based on preliminary comparative research.[51] That research provided us with a preliminary idea of what the main issues might be. The cases are hypothetical cases; they were constructed by us. But the construction and selection of hypothetical facts did not occur at random. Rather, we tried to formulate the cases and questions in such a way that they would reveal the factors that seem to be decisive in the Member States when deciding whether a party should be liable for her conduct (including omissions) during the precontractual stage. We tried to formulate the facts and, in particular, the questions as neutrally as possible. This meant, among other things, that we tried to avoid formulations which would point to (or fit better with) a certain solution (to avoid 'leading questions') or a certain legal system (to avoid Member State-specific terminology).

Again, we are well aware that 'the main issues' is a very problematic concept and that neither neutral language nor crude facts exist. Also, some of the cases look rather similar to actual reported cases, as some reporters comment in their discussions.

4. *The national reports*

The national reports on each case are presented in the alphabetical order of the names of the countries: Austria, Denmark, England,

[51] See M.W. Hesselink, 'Precontractual Good Faith' in Beale *et al.*, *Cases, Materials and Text on Contract Law*, ch. 2, section 2 (pp. 237–93).

Finland, France, Germany, Greece, Ireland, Italy, the Netherlands, Norway, Portugal, Scotland, Spain, Sweden, Switzerland. This was a deliberate choice. It deviates from some of the other projects within the Common Core Project. For example, the project on good faith[52] organised its reports according to 'legal families', starting with German law as the parent of the apparently most important legal family for that topic; and the project on the enforceability of promises[53] is also organised by families, starting with French law.

We thought that the presentation of our results according to legal families would not be helpful; not only because this would contradict the egalitarian ideology of the project, as formulated by the general editors[54] – 'our project equally focuses on all the European systems under review, it treats them as equally as possible and places no emphasis on systems that are or could be considered leading or paradigmatic, or hegemonic' – but also, and more importantly, because the main object of our research was to discover whether such legal families actually exist in terms of the way in which they answer legal questions within the scope of this project. Indeed, one way of seeing the Common Core Project is as a deconstruction of the idea of legal families.[55] In particular, we hoped to find out whether alliances are consistently the same with regard to different cases and different questions, in the way that the idea of legal families would suggest. The issue will be addressed extensively in the Conclusions.

Finally, in order to assist the reader we decided to edit the reports to quite a significant degree (and we are grateful to our reporters for their tolerance and understanding in this respect). Editing included, amongst other things: bringing the reports to a similar level and style as far as the English language is concerned; bringing the size of the reports to similar proportions; and introducing a common terminology for some of the main issues. Again, we are well aware that these editorial choices (especially the introduction of a common terminology which, of course, can never be neutral), which all contribute to an impression of greater uniformity, are likely to have some influence on our comparison.

[52] Zimmermann and Whittaker, *Good Faith in European Contract Law*.
[53] Gordley, *The Enforceability of Promises in European Contract Law*.
[54] Bussani and Mattei, 'The Context', above n. 2, p. 5.
[55] Many introductions into comparative law have been based on the idea of legal families. See, e.g., David and Jauffret-Spinosi, *Les grands systèmes de droit contemporain*; Zweigert and Kötz, *Introduction to Comparative Law*.

2 Case studies

Case 1: Negotiations for premises for a bookshop

Case 1

A, who has a bookshop on High Street hears that C, a nationwide chain of bookshops, is negotiating with B to buy for €1.2m large premises that B owns and which are located opposite to A's shop. A fears competition from C, and so starts negotiations with B for the purchase of the premises, pretending he wants to move his shop to larger premises and that he is prepared to pay €1.5m. This makes C withdraw from the negotiations and C decides to buy another shop on Market Street at the other end of town. After that A breaks off his negotiations with B. Ultimately B succeeds in selling the premises for only €1m. What liability (in contract, tort, restitution or any other form of liability), if any, does A have to B?

Discussions

Austria

The General Civil Code of Austria of 1811 (ABGB) contains no specific provision dealing with precontractual liability or *culpa in contrahendo* in general, since this concept was 'discovered' by the German scholar Rudolf von Jhering[1] some 50 years after the Austrian codification. Nevertheless, precontractual liability has become an acknowledged concept in Austria.[2]

[1] 'Culpa in contrahendo oder Schadensersatz bei nichtigen oder nicht zur Perfection gelangten Verträgen' (1861) 4 *Jherings Jahrbücher für die Dogmatik des bürgerlichen Rechts* 1.

[2] G. Frotz, 'Die rechtsdogmatische Einordnung der Haftung für culpa in contrahendo' in Faistenberger and Mayrhofer, *Gedenkschrift Franz Gschnitzer*, p. 163; Welser, *Vertretung ohne Vollmacht – Zugleich ein Beitrag zur Lehre von der culpa in contrahendo* and 'Das

The ABGB makes no clear distinction between contractual liability and non-contractual (or delictual) liability. Nevertheless, there are a number of differences which make it more favourable to a victim to bring a claim that is based on contractual liability rules, rather than on tortious grounds.[3] Since contractual liability provides these considerable advantages[4] for the victim, 'contract shopping' is attractive. Thus, in order to expand contractual liability rules to the precontractual stage, the doctrine of *culpa in contrahendo* was created and achieved significant importance in practice. A general principle of precontractual liability or *culpa in contrahendo* has been deduced from a number of provisions of the ABGB by the Austrian Supreme Court (OGH).[5] It follows from the current situation of a well-established and

Verschulden beim Vertragsschluss im österreichischen bürgerlichen Recht', ÖJZ 1973, 281; cf. also R. Welser, 'Die culpa in contrahendo im österreichischen Recht', LJZ 1984, 101 and R. Welser, 'Die vorvertraglichen Pflichten in der Rechtsprechung des OGH' in Wagner-FS 65 Jahre (1987) 361. For a recent comprehensive commentary on the judge-made rules on *culpa in contrahendo* with, however, rather complacent arguments, see R. Reischauer in Rummel, *Kommentar zum ABGB* I Vor §§918–933, N. 14ff. For a report in English on precontractual liability in Austrian law, see W. Posch in Hondius, *Precontractual Liability*, pp. 41–52.

3 Vicarious liability (according to §1313a ABGB the *respondeat superior* rule applies only to violations of contractual duties by servants. In the absence of a contractual relationship between master and victim, liability can only be imposed on the master, according to §1315 ABGB, if the victim proves either that the servant is 'incompetent' or that the master has knowingly employed a dangerous person); burden of proof of fault (under the rules of contractual liability the burden of proof is reversed and lies on the person breaching a contractual duty thereby causing damage to another (§1298 ABGB), whereas §1296 ABGB imposes the burden of establishing the defendant's fault, in an extra-contractual injury case, on the victim); the scope of liability ('pure economic loss' is only recoverable if contractual liability rules apply. The law of extra-contractual liability offers no protection to a person suffering losses, such as wasted expenses, caused by negligent misstatements by another person).

4 Unlike German law, the Austrian Code makes no distinction with regard to prescription. The common prescription period for delictual and contractual claims for compensation is three years.

5 §874 ABGB: 'In any case, any party who has induced a contract by fraud or coercion is liable for damages [to another person who] suffered thereby'; §878 ABGB, third sentence: 'A person who, when entering into the contract was or should have been aware of [the] impossibility [of its performance], is liable to the other innocent party for any damage suffered by him through his reliance upon the validity of the contract, [provided that the other party was not aware thereof himself]; §932 ABGB: if a person is at fault for breach of warranty, he will be liable for damages (however, as of 1 January 2002 this provision has been replaced by a new provision on damages; the relevant provision is now §933a ABGB). Until 1 July 2001 there was, in addition to these three articles, another provision in force that served as a basis for analogy. §866 ABGB stated that a person having attained the age of 18, 'who fraudulently represents that he

still expanding judge-made doctrine of *culpa in contrahendo* that the answer to the question of whether A is liable to B under Austrian law lies within the discretionary power of the judge.

There is near absolute certainty here that an Austrian judge will decide in favour of B and award damages on the ground of *culpa in contrahendo* for his higher costs: the difference between the price he would have received from C and the price he actually received for his premises after C had withdrawn from the negotiations. It appears that A was never seriously negotiating with B. A's opening and breaking off the negotiations with B amounts to 'chicanery', the exercise of a right that can only have the purpose of harming another person. In addition to this, the principles of fair dealing have been grossly violated by A.

However, it may not be necessary for B to resort to the judge-made rules of *culpa in contrahendo* to obtain this remedy. B may also claim his 'reliance interest' on the basis of purely tortious (delictual) principles of compensation under §1295(2) ABGB which reads: 'A person who intentionally injures another in a manner in violation of public morals is liable therefor; however, if the injury was caused in the exercise of legal rights, the person causing it shall be liable therefor only when the exercise of this right obviously has the purpose to cause damage to the other'. §1295(2) ABGB was inserted into the Austrian Civil Code in 1916 and mirrors a provision of the German Civil Code (§826 BGB). The idea behind this rule is to allow the recovery of pure economic loss in a case of serious violation of fairness, within the principles of non-contractual liability. It can, however, be difficult to bring clear and convincing evidence of the tortfeasor's wrongful intention to cause damage by exercising a right.

Denmark

Danish law has no relevant statutory provisions. The Danish courts are reluctant to award damages for precontractual behaviour.[6] There are very few cases in which damages have been awarded, and there appear to be no cases dealing with the situation where a person enters into negotiations with no real intention of reaching an agreement (which

is able to conclude a contract, and in doing so deceives another who cannot easily make inquiries in regard thereto, is liable for damages suffered thereby'. This provision became obsolete as a result of the reduction of the age of capacity from 19 to 18 years.

6 Andersen, Madsen and Nørgaard, *Aftaler og Mellemmænd*, p. 108 (Andersen); Lando in Hondius, *Precontractual Liability*, pp. 111–24; Simonsen, *Prækontraktuelt Ansvar*.

will be called 'cheat contracting') or continues negotiations with no real intention of reaching an agreement ('cheat continuing'). However, there are provisions in Danish law that impose liability for falsely pretending to have legal capacity or authority as an agent.[7]

This case is an example of cheat contracting. Danish courts would probably classify A's behaviour as a tort but do not attach great importance to the distinction between tort and contract. On the whole, Danish courts tend to be moderate in awarding damages. A court might award damages but probably less than €0.2m and certainly not €0.5m.

England

A is liable to B for damages in the tort of deceit. Under the tort of deceit a claimant can recover damages if he can show that the defendant fraudulently made a false representation to him, with the intention that he act on it; and that he did act on it and suffered loss.[8] It appears that A has made a statement to B which he knows to be untrue: he starts negotiations 'pretending he wants to move his shop to larger premises and that he is prepared to pay €1.5m'. He intends this to induce B to break off his negotiations with C and so to suffer loss. A is therefore liable to B.

In the tort of deceit the defendant compensates the claimant for all the loss he suffers in consequence of his reliance on the fraudulent statement, whether or not it is loss that the defendant could have foreseen.[9] The only limitations are that the claimant must establish a causal link between the statement and the loss; and he cannot claim for loss which he could have taken reasonable steps to reduce or eliminate after he discovered the fraud. The measure of recoverable loss in deceit is the sum by which the claimant's wealth is diminished as a result of his reliance on the statement. On the facts this would be €0.2m if a court accepts that, on the balance of probabilities, B would have been able to sell the shop to C for €1.2m but has lost that opportunity and now could only reasonably obtain the lower price of €1m.[10] If the court

[7] Guardianship Act §§45(2), 46(2) and 65(2) and Contract Act §25. In the former case the minor or incapacitated person has to reimburse the other party no more than his reliance costs; in the latter case the false agent has to compensate the other party's expectation interest.

[8] *Bradford Third Equitable Benefit Building Society v. Borders* [1941] 2 All ER 205, 211; J. Cartwright, *Misrepresentation, Mistake and Non-Disclosure*, ch. 5.

[9] *Smith New Court Securities Ltd v. Scrimgeour Vickers (Asset Management) Ltd* [1997] AC 254.

[10] If the claim had been one for damages for breach of contract, the damages would instead be calculated to put the claimant in the position in which he would have been if the statement had been true: here €0.5m, the difference between what A would

is not satisfied about these figures (for example, if the likely figure at which the sale to C would have been finalised is lower, or if the court believes that B's ultimate acceptance of the price of €1m to sell to a third party is not the best he could reasonably achieve in the circumstances) the court's substitute figures would be taken in making the calculation. In addition to this basic measure of loss, other consequential losses may be recoverable: for example, any continuing business losses during the period of delay if the bookshop was in the meantime making a loss, or any loss of return B would have made on investment of the sale price which he was delayed in receiving. But against this B would have to give credit for any further profits he has made from the bookshop in the period of delay, if the shop was still profitable.

It is essential for B's case that he prove that A made a false statement during the precontractual negotiations about his intentions to conclude the contract. In the absence of such a statement B would have no remedy because in English law there is no general duty of good faith in negotiating, and no other basis on which B would have any remedy on these facts.[11]

Finland

A would probably be liable to B for the reliance interest (negative interest) according to the rules of *culpa in contrahendo*. In Finnish law, there seem to be no other remedies available to B.

In Finnish academic writing, *culpa in contrahendo* is usually not treated as an independent doctrine but rather as a part of tort law. This doctrine has never been adopted in Finland as a separate basis for liability, but is employed more commonly as a kind of *terminus technicus* in order to deal with liability situations related to the formation of contracts.[12] The distinction between the 'positive' and 'negative' interest is considered in Finnish academic writing to be one of the cornerstones upon which

have promised to pay had there been a contract (€1.5m) and the actual sum received (€1m): *Robinson v. Harman* (1848) 1 Ex 850, 855. But A did not make any contractually binding promise to buy the bookshop, and so no damages on the contract measure are recoverable.

[11] See also the English report on case 2 for further discussion of the possible bases of liability during the negotiation phase (contract, the tort of negligence, estoppel and restitution).

[12] On *culpa in contrahendo* in Finnish contract law see, e.g., Hemmo, *Sopimus ja delikti*, p. 198.

the special status of contractual relationships is based. The positive interest is the measure with which the sphere of recoverable damages is defined in (valid) contracts, and the negative interest is to serve the same purpose in tort situations (or if the contract proves to be invalid).[13] The measure used in *culpa in contrahendo* situations is mainly that of the negative interest. As the terminology shows, the doctrine derives from German contract law, but it is applied in Finland in an independent manner.

The formation phase of the contract is considered to be problematic as to the basis of damages liability.[14] It cannot be easily placed within the sphere of contract or tort law, because precontractual situations bear resemblance to both categories. This distinction is, however, of importance because the rules pertaining to the different categories vary in aspects of recoverable damages and the basis of liability. The main differences between contract and tort liability rules in Finnish law relate first to the recoverability of pure economic losses, and secondly to the burden of proof concerning fault, which is usually one of the general prerequisites of liability in both contract and tort law. In contract law, the burden of proof lies on the defendant – he must prove the absence of fault – but in tort law, the injured person has the burden of showing the defendant's fault.[15] The Finnish Damages Act of 1974[16] is the general norm of tort liability. According to an express provision on the scope of application of the Act, it does not apply to liability based on contract.[17] Pure economic loss is, as a general rule, recoverable only under the law of contract. In tort law, according to the Damages Act, the right of recovery of pure economic loss requires that the damage be a result of a criminal offence or of an act of a public

[13] On positive and negative interests see e.g. Hemmo, *Sopimusoikeus* II, p. 279.

[14] See Hemmo, *Sopimus ja delikti*, p. 198.

[15] The other main prerequisites of liability, namely the existence of damage and a sufficient causal relationship (the term often used by academic writers is 'adequate' causality) between the action of the liable person and the damage, must be proved by the plaintiff (the injured person) in both contract and tort law. The adequate causality is mainly defined in terms of *foreseeability*, i.e. the possibility of the defendant realising the risk of damage connected to his action.

[16] Vahingonkorvauslaki (VahL). The liability in contract, on the contrary, is not generally regulated by written law provisions, but is mainly based on general principles developed in court practice and in academic writing. The pivotal statute in general contract law, Oikeustoimilaki (Contracts Act, 1929), contains provisions on formation of contracts, representation and invalidity of contracts. However, there are no express provisions on liability in connection with the formation of the contract.

[17] Ch. 1 sect. 1 VahL.

authority, or otherwise that there are very weighty reasons for compensation.[18] These restrictions, of course, do not apply in the law of contract.

In the formation phase of the contract, the regulation of risk allocation may have more in common with contractual relations than with an ordinary non-contractual causation of damage between two parties having no relation with each other but based on mere chance. So there may be some grounds for the compensation of pure economic loss, too. But because there are no existing contractual obligations between the parties, the burden of proof of fault should perhaps as a general rule be distributed rather as in tort situations than following contract rules.[19] Under some circumstances, however, there may be some grounds for a contract-law-like reversal of the burden of proof.[20]

It has to be decided whether A was at fault – whether he has acted in a blameworthy manner. In *culpa in contrahendo* this usually means an action against good practice in negotiating and concluding a contract. If that prerequisite is fulfilled (and, of course, if the causal relationship from fault to damage is proved) the defendant is usually liable. Starting negotiations with no real intention to conclude the contract can be seen as contrary to good contracting practice and blameworthy. So A's motives in negotiating with B (fear of competition from C, pretending to be prepared to buy B's premises for €1.5 m) are wrongful and form a basis for liability.

As already stated, the standard of compensation applied in connection with *culpa in contrahendo* is usually the negative (reliance) interest. According to this measure, in addition to the negotiation costs, also the lost profits (*lucrum cessans*) from contracts not concluded because of reliance on the formation of the contract with the party responsible for *culpa in contrahendo* are in principle recoverable.[21] In this case, the lost profit covers the difference between the price offered by C (€1.2m) and that actually received by B (€1.0m), making €0.2m. The lost profit from B's contract with A, on the contrary, pertains only to the positive (expectation) interest that is usually not recoverable in *culpa in contrahendo* cases.

[18] Ch. 5 sect. 1 VahL. [19] Hemmo, *Sopimus ja delikti*, p. 207. [20] See, e.g., case 2.

[21] See, however, Hemmo, *Sopimusoikeus* I, p. 152 on specific questions concerning the causation (foreseeability) of indirect losses in cases of *culpa in contrahendo*. Some problems may also arise concerning the existence of recoverable loss and the contributory negligence of the injured person (failure to enter into an alternative transaction to limit his losses).

A's liability requires, of course, that B can prove his damage. This requirement is met only if B succeeds in proving that €1.2m was a real price that was available to him and that this was lost only because of A's intervention causing C's withdrawal from the negotiations with B. B may also have to prove that no other transaction could be made at a higher price than €1m.

If the damage is proved and other general prerequisites of liability are fulfilled, A seems to be liable to B for the reliance interest, covering the lost profit from the contract with C (€0.2 m).

France

French statutory law contains no specific provision on precontractual liability. Nevertheless, since precontractual liability is commonly considered as tortious,[22] it falls under the broad articles 1382 and 1383 of the Civil Code, dealing with tortious liability for fault. Liability under these articles requires the fulfilment of three cumulative conditions: fault, harm and a chain of causation between the two.

The *fault* consists in the breach of a legal duty. According to the majority of writers, a person is at fault if he violated a 'general norm of behaviour'.[23] In principle, the gravity of the fault does not matter: even the slightest fault may lead to liability.[24] In the context of breaking off

[22] There has been a discussion among academic writers about whether precontractual liability is contractual or tortious. The precontractual period is very specific, for it occurs before the contract is concluded, without the parties being complete strangers to each other. On the one hand, no contract should mean no contractual liability. On the other hand, tortious liability supposes most of the time a harm caused by one person to another without any specific relationship between them: the harm does not usually occur because of such a relationship. Some writers, especially Jhering and Carbonnier, were in favour of contractual liability applying. However, in the end, their arguments did not convince the majority of writers and the courts: see P. Mousseron, 'Négociations précontractuelles et responsabilité civile délictuelle', RTDCom 1998, 248ff.

[23] See Viney and Jourdain, *Les conditions de la responsabilité*, no. 450; Flour and Aubert, *Les Obligations*, vol. 2, *Le fait juridique*, no. 85f.

[24] This general rule of tort applies to precontractual liability, although the issue has often been debated. A party to contractual negotiations is not prohibited from breaking off negotiations before the contract is concluded. He may be held liable, but only if the specific circumstances reveal a fault. At first courts required a serious fault as a condition of liability, although the criterion of seriousness was not very easy to use. Some thought it was established by an intention to harm, others by an abuse of rights (*abus de droit*), others by bad faith. Finally, the condition of bad faith, which seems to have been the winning criterion for a long time, has been recently rejected

negotiations, there are three main wrongful types of behaviour. First, it is wrongful to enter or maintain negotiations without a real intention to conclude the contract, as in the present case. Secondly, the fault can occur during the negotiations because one of the parties behaved wrongfully towards the other party, for example by providing a third party with confidential information obtained during the negotiations.[25] Lastly, the fault may consist in a sudden breach of the negotiations when the other party had good reason to think the contract was to be concluded. This kind of fault depends on the circumstances of the breach of negotiations. For example, it is usually considered wrongful for an engaged man or woman to break his or her promise the day before the wedding.[26] All these definitions and examples are very general: the existence of fault is left to the judge's interpretation, according to the particular circumstances of the case. The author of a wrongful break-off of negotiations can escape liability by giving a 'legitimate reason'[27] for not having concluded the contract. Case law is not very clear about this last point. The judicial demand for a 'legitimate reason' varies according to the courts and to the cases. The Cour de cassation seems to ask for such a reason in its most recent decisions:[28] the absence of reason therefore plays an important part in determining the liability of the defendant. If a reason is given, the judge will have to determine whether it justifies the breaking-off of the negotiations.[29]

Secondly, the other party must have suffered *harm*. Its content has been debated among academic writers, as well as in recent case law.[30] Four categories of harm have been identified.[31] First, the harm includes

by the Cour de cassation: Com 22 Feb. 1994, RTDCiv 1994, 849. In that case, the Cour de cassation speaks of a 'blameworthy levity' (*légèreté blâmable*). On this point, see Mousseron, 'Négociations précontractuelles et responsabilité civile délictuelle', above n. 22, p. 260.

25 See case 12. 26 See case 5.

27 '*Motif légitime*', the phrase used for example in Com 7 Jan. 1997, D. 1998, J., 45.

28 Ibid.; Com 14 Dec. 2004, no. 02-10157; Mousseron, 'Négociations contractuelles et responsabilité civile délictuelle', above n. 22, p. 256.

29 P. Chauvel, in his commentary on Com 7 Jan. 1997, D. 1998, J., 45, gives several examples of possible legitimate reasons, with judicial references. In addition we can give the example of a major modification in the expectations of one of the parties, such as an unpredictable increase in the cost of accomplishing the task required by the other party: Civ 3, 6 May 1996, decision no. 841, Lexilaser.

30 See O. Deshayes, 'Le dommage précontractuel', RTDCom 2004, 187.

31 This categorisation is only descriptive, and is not unanimously admitted by all academic writers. See Mousseron, 'Négociations contractuelles et responsabilité civile délictuelle', above n. 22, p. 264ff.

all the negotiation fees and expenses borne by the other party.[32] Secondly, it includes the loss of opportunity, which covered, until recently, both the loss of a chance of concluding and benefiting from the negotiated contract and the loss of a chance of concluding a replacement contract with another party during the negotiations.[33] Thirdly, the victim of the breach can obtain compensation based on what French law calls '*préjudice moral*', such as the wrong caused to the reputation of the victim.[34] Fourthly, a residual category includes

[32] One author has suggested dividing these fees and expenses into two parts. One part would include the 'general costs', which are always incurred by a competitor just to stay in business by negotiating with others. This should not be included in the damages awarded to the victim. The other part is composed of all the costs specifically incurred in the negotiations, and may be taken into account when calculating the damages. See J. Schmidt-Szalewsky, 'La sanction de la faute précontractuelle', RTDCiv 1974, 54 and the references mentioned in the French report on case 6. This distinction has not yet been adopted by the Cour de cassation but seems supported by a growing number of courts of appeal. See Aix-En-Provence, 16 Sep. 1993, Jurisdata no. 045651, where the costs incurred by an advertising agent were not considered as recoverable by way of damages because of a professional usage in this area. Also see Angers, 25 Nov. 1992, Jurisdata no. 048656 and Lyon, 29 Sep. 2000, Jurisdata no. 132246.

[33] This duality of the loss of opportunity is discussed among writers. Whereas the loss of a chance of concluding a replacement contract is unanimously considered as compensable, the compensation of the loss of a chance of concluding the negotiated contract is criticised. See P. Chauvel, commentary on Com 7 Jan. 1997, D. 1998, J., 50, no. 27 and B. Fages, 'Négociations, La rupture des pourparlers' in Fages *et al.*, *Lamy Droit du contrat*, étude no. 110. The Cour de cassation seemed to ignore this opinion until recently. In an important and widely commented-upon decision, the Cour de cassation decided that 'the circumstances creating a fault in the exercise of the freedom to break off the negotiations do not cause the harm consisting in the loss of a chance to benefit from the negotiated contract': Com 26 Nov. 2003, RTDCiv 2004, 80 (J. Mestre and B. Fages); JCP E 2004, 738 (Ph. Stoffel-Munck); JCP 2004, I, 163 (G. Viney). After this decision, academic writers thought that the loss of a chance of concluding the negotiated contract was no longer compensable under French law. At first this prediction seemed to be contradicted by more recent decisions, left unpublished by the Cour de cassation: see Com 14 Dec. 2004, no. 02-10157 and Civ 3, 30 Mar. 2005, no. 04-10662. But since then it has been firmly confirmed by another widely commented-upon decision which quoted almost word for word the sentence used in the 2003 case: Civ 3, 28 June 2006, RTDCiv 2006, 754 (J. Mestre and B. Fages); JCP G 2006, II, 10130 and JCP E 2006, 1524 (O. Deshayes). Presenting this case in its annual report for 2006, the Cour de cassation observes that the solution is a consequence of the right of negotiators to break off negotiations freely. Because the fault lies in the circumstances of the breaking-off and not in the breaking-off itself, it can never cause the loss of a chance to benefit from the contract. The annual reports of the Cour de cassation are available at www.courdecassation.fr.

[34] See, e.g., Tribunal de commerce de Paris, 27 Apr. 1996, Jurisdata no. 047078. '*Préjudice moral*' is not very easy to determine with precision. It corresponds to various types of non-economic harm (pain and suffering, harm caused to a personal right such as the

various types of harm, such as the harm caused in competition or by divulging confidential information obtained during the negotiations.

In French law, the harm resulting from a precontractual breach only entitles the aggrieved party to damages and never to the conclusion of the envisaged contract. The compensation is supposed to be full, according to the '*principe de réparation intégrale*': 'the aim of liability (either in tort or in contract) is to restore the equilibrium destroyed by the harm, and to place the victim in the situation in which he would have been if the harm had never happened'.[35] In consequence, the damages must include the whole of the losses suffered, as long as they are certain.[36] Furthermore, French law does not accept the principle of mitigation of loss; it also rejects the concept of punitive damages.[37]

Finally, the harm suffered must have been caused by the fault. The issue of *causation* does not raise great difficulties, and is often 'forgotten' by the courts, which have a habit of simply holding that 'the fault caused the harm'. In fact, causation is usually obvious, apart from the case where the harm is not immediately linked to the fault, which is quite unusual in precontractual liability as long as we focus on the liability of one party in the negotiations towards the other.[38]

In this case, A has initiated negotiations with B in order to stop C from competing with him, by preventing him from buying B's

right of privacy, the loss of commercial reputation, etc.), and its assessment is left to the judges' discretion. Some writers (Viney and Jourdain, *Les conditions de la responsabilité*, no. 253ff.) consider that this type of harm is very close to the concept of punitive damages.

35 Civ 2, 20 Dec. 1966, D. 1967, 169. See Viney and Jourdain, *Les effets de la responsabilité*, no. 57ff.; Mousseron, 'Négociations contractuelles et responsabilité civile délictuelle', above n. 22, p. 264ff.

36 The *principe de réparation intégrale*, which means that the harm suffered and the damages awarded should correspond, raises a particular difficulty when evaluating the damages awarded for loss of opportunity. The opportunity is not certain, and the evaluation is not easy, because the damages cannot match the value of the future contract which has not been concluded because of the wrongful breaking-off of negotiations. The Cour de cassation timidly speaks of applying a coefficient of decrease (*coefficient de minoration*) to this value, in order to take into account the absence of certainty in the conclusion of the contract, see Com 31 Mar. 1992, Bull Civ IV, no. 145; Com 4 Dec. 1990, decision no. 1455, Lexilaser.

37 Viney and Jourdain, *Les effets de la responsabilité*, no. 4f.

38 On the question of causation, see Viney and Jourdain, *Les conditions de la responsabilité*, p. 151ff., pointing out that defining causation is difficult. The condition of causation remains important when the victim claims for damages against a third party who played a part in the failure of the negotiations. Furthermore, the chain of causation between fault and harm might be uncertain, but in the present case the question is solved by examining the issue of loss of opportunity.

premises. Such conduct is wrongful. A entered into the negotiations without any intention to conclude the contract, which is one of the situations of fault discussed above.[39] B certainly suffers harm as a consequence of that fault, because he lost an opportunity to sell his premises at a fair price, and certainly incurred costs as a result of the negotiations. Thus, fault, harm and causation are established, leading to A's precontractual liability under article 1382 of the Civil Code.

B is entitled to ask for damages on the ground of A's liability for his wrongful conduct. These damages comprise two separate components. First, B can recover the costs he incurred during the course of the negotiations, such as the cost of evaluation of his premises. Secondly, B is certainly entitled to compensation for his loss of opportunity.[40] The precise amount of the damages is difficult to evaluate, because it is fixed by the judge.[41] B finally sold his premises for €1m after A withdrew his offer. A's offer cannot be considered as a serious one, so it cannot be used to quantify B's damages. Without A's manoeuvres in bad faith, B may have sold his premises to C, but there is no certainty that the sale would have taken place. In consequence he lost an opportunity to sell his premises at a price of €1.2m. Therefore, the damages awarded for this loss of opportunity will probably exceed €0, because the loss is real, but will not be as much as €0.2m, because the sale was not certain.

Germany

The doctrine of *culpa in contrahendo* was 'discovered' by Rudolf von Jhering.[42] He derived it from the few and rather specific Roman law sources establishing liability for void contracts, claiming as their rationale that a party entering into contractual negotiations, when lacking capacity to conclude a valid contract, acted in a culpable way in misleading the other party. By initiating contractual negotiations, Jhering concluded, a party was leaving the ambit of purely negative duties to refrain from an act (*culpa in faciendo*) and was entering the sphere of positive diligence (*culpa in non faciendo*).

[39] Rennes, 8 July 1929, DH 1929, 548; Paris, 13 May 1988, *arrêt Vittel*, JurisData no. 025708.

[40] On this question, see Viney, *Introduction à la responsabilité*, no. 198, p. 361, and above n. 35. See also Com 2 Nov. 1993, Bull Civ IV, no. 380.

[41] Civ 1, 3 June 1997, JurisData no. 002562.

[42] 'Culpa in contrahendo oder Schadensersatz bei nichtigen oder nicht zur Perfection gelangten Verträgen' ('Culpa in contrahendo or damages in situations where contracts are void or did not reach the stage of perfection') (1861) 4 *Jherings Jahrbücher für die Dogmatik des bürgerlichen Rechts* 1.

Jhering's seminal article immediately gave rise to further scientific investigations of his basic ideas, the draftsmen of the German Civil Code thus being well aware of this new theory. Nevertheless, they incorporated the doctrine of *culpa in contrahendo* into the codification in no more than a sparing and fragmented fashion.[43] It was therefore up to the courts and academic writers to establish *culpa in contrahendo* as a general ground of liability. Since the 1920s it has been consistent practice of the courts that from the moment of entering into contractual negotiations, a special relationship (*Sonderrechtsverhältnis*) is created between the negotiating parties by virtue of the law (*gesetzliches Schuldverhältnis*) imposing on both parties duties of protection and loyalty (*Schutzpflichten*). The imputable violation of such a *Schutzpflicht* may entail liability according to the rules governing contractual relations.[44]

These principles have recently been codified. In 2001, the German legislator combined the implementation of Directive 1999/44/EC[45] into German law with a major revision of the BGB. The main purpose of the reform was (1) to reform the law of impairment of the performance of an obligation (*allgemeines Leistungsstörungsrecht*) together with the law of sale (*Kaufrecht*) and (2) to integrate well-established institutions of judge-made law into the Code such as frustration of contract (*Störung der Geschäftsgrundlage*)[46] and *culpa in contrahendo.*[47] Accordingly, precontractual liability now has a statutory basis. It is governed by §280 (1) BGB in combination with §§241(2), 311(2), (3) BGB:

§280 BGB:

(1) If the debtor fails to comply with a duty incumbent upon him under the obligations entered into, the creditor may demand compensation for the damages done. This does not apply if the debtor is not responsible for the failure to comply with the duty.

§241 BGB:

(2) An obligation may obligate each party, having regard to its substance, to take into consideration the rights, legally protected interests and (other) interests of the opposite party.

§311 BGB:

(2) An obligation with duties under §241(2) will also arise from

43 Cf. §§122, 179, 307, 309 BGB.

44 Larenz, *Lehrbuch des Schuldrechts, Bd. I, Allgemeiner Teil*, p. 104ff.; Medicus, *Schuldrecht, Allgemeiner Teil*, p. 56ff.; P. Gottwald, JuS 1982, 877.

45 Directive 1999/44/EC of the European Parliament and of the Council of 25 May 1999 on certain aspects of the sale of consumer goods and associated guarantees.

46 Cf. §313 BGB.

47 Lorenz and Riehm, *Lehrbuch zum neuen Schuldrecht*, para. 1ff.

1. the beginning of contractual negotiations,
2. initiating the conclusion of a contract whereby one of the parties, having regard to a possible contractual relationship, either grants the other party the possibility of affecting his rights, legally protected interests and other interests, or entrusts the other party with them, or
3. similar business contacts.

(3) An obligation with duties under §241(2) may also arise in relation to persons who are not meant to become contracting parties. Such an obligation will come about especially where the third party takes special advantage of confidence thus exercising considerable influence on the contractual negotiations or the conclusion of the contract.

The legislator did not intend with these provisions either to change the judge-made rules of *culpa in contrahendo* or to impede their further development by case law. Therefore, §§241(2), 280(1) and 311(2) BGB must be construed with reference to the case law preceding the reform.

In general neither the beginning nor the continuance of contractual negotiations may impose any duty on a party to enter into a contract.[48] It is a firmly established principle of German law that parties must be free to break off negotiations without fear of liability if the institution of contract is to be maintained as an instrument of self-determination (*Grundsatz der Vertragsabschlußfreiheit*). The ordinary course of the bargaining process places a legal obligation upon a party only from the point at which he has made a binding offer, whereas both parties are only bound after there is acceptance. The fact that under German law an offer is normally binding upon the offeror unless he has excluded the binding effect[49] is one reason why the present problem appears to be less significant than in other legal systems.[50] Once negotiations have ripened into an offer, it depends solely upon the offeree to bring about a contract. But if the offeror expressly declares that he does not consider himself bound, the other party has little or no reason to rely on the proposed contract and spend money in expectation of it. Furthermore, German law recognises the possibility of a 'contract to make a contract' (*Vorvertrag*). An actionable right to demand the conclusion of the main contract will not arise until the negotiations of the parties have reached the point of an agreement on the essentials of the main future contract. Therefore, the situations where the law will come to the

[48] BGH, decision of 22 Feb. 1989, NJW-RR 1989, 627; BGH, decision of 28 Sep. 1977, WM 1977, 618, 620; BGH, decision of 17 May 1962, WM 1962, 936, 937.

[49] Cf. §145 BGB.

[50] For a comparison of French and German law, see S. Lorenz, ZEuP 2 (1994), 218, 227ff.

rescue of a party who is still in the process of negotiation without having been able to reach the stage of a binding offer or a *Vorvertrag* are rather exceptional. A party is entitled to rely on the conclusion of a future contract only if the other party is in breach of his duty to bargain *bona fide*,[51] that is, if he has (1) entered into, (2) continued with or (3) terminated contractual negotiations in contravention of the standards of good faith.[52] A party breaches his duty to bargain in good faith by the mere fact of entering into contractual negotiations if he starts negotiations without any reasonable chance for the opposite party to make a bargain (objective test) or without any intention at all to contract with the other party (subjective test). The law will not condone a party conducting sham transactions. The same applies *mutatis mutandis* if a party continues negotiations, having given up any intention to contract with the other party. Furthermore, by terminating contractual negotiations a party is in breach of his duty to bargain in good faith if in the course of the events he made the other party believe a contract would certainly come about, but then, without good reason or from ulterior motives, refuses to go ahead.[53] A party must not induce the other to incur expenses he could have regarded as necessary in the circumstances by encouraging his hopes that a contract would come about even though, from an objective point of view, this hope is completely futile,[54] no matter whether the legitimate expectations of the other party had been raised culpably or not.[55] Nevertheless, this is not a case of strict liability as argued by some writers, since the *culpa* necessary for a claim in *culpa in contrahendo* is established by the fact of terminating negotiations without any good reason.[56]

It should, however, be borne in mind that a party is never held liable on the ground of *culpa in contrahendo* by the fact only that the other party made (even substantial) investments in reliance on the conclusion of a future contract. It is a firmly established practice of the Bundesgerichtshof that *culpa in contrahendo* must not be used as an

51 Cf. §§241(2), 311(2) No. 1 BGB.

52 BGH, decision of 10 Jan. 1996, WM 1996, 738.

53 BGH, decision of 22 Feb. 1989, NJW-RR 1989, 627; BGH, decision of 12 June 1975, NJW 1975, 1774; BGH, decision of 14 July 1967, NJW 1967, 2199; Markesinis, Lorenz and Dannemann, *The German Law of Obligations*, vol. I, *The Law of Contracts and Restitution*, p. 69.

54 BGH, decision of 12 June 1975, NJW 1975, 1774; BGH, decision of 10 July 1970, NJW 1970, 1840.

55 BGH, decision of 22 Feb. 1989, NJW-RR, 1989, 627, 629.

56 Cf. MünchKomm-*Emmerich*, Vor §275 para. 164.

inroad to the principle of freedom of contract by indirectly putting pressure on a party to conclude a contract:

> Within the scope of freedom of contract, until there is a bargain, every party has a perfect right to refrain from entering into the envisaged contract. Expenses incurred in the expectation of a future contract are basically at a party's own risk. A party owes compensation to another party on the ground of *culpa in contrahendo* only if he refuses the conclusion of a contract without a valid reason, although, pursuant to the course of negotiations, a bargain was certainly to be expected and the other party in relying thereon has incurred expenses necessary for the conclusion of the contract.[57]

A party liable on the ground of *culpa in contrahendo* has to make up for the aggrieved party's reliance interest (*Vertrauensschaden*). The scope of liability mirrors its rationale which is not to be found in a party's refraining from a bargain but in his creation of legitimate expectations within the other party that a contract would be brought about. The aggrieved party has to be put into the position he would have been in if he had known of the other party's unwillingness to make a commitment. This means there must be compensation for the necessary expenses incurred by the party legitimately expecting the conclusion of a contract.

Where a party at the start of the negotiations had no intention whatsoever to conclude a contract, he must make up for the total reliance loss. In the case of a party terminating contractual negotiations without good reason, compensation is limited to those expenses incurred after the conditions for liability were met, that is, there must be a causal connection between the aggrieved party's expectations and his expenditure.[58]

In the case of breaking off contractual negotiations, the significance of *culpa in contrahendo* within the German legal system follows from the fact that in most cases a person terminating contractual negotiations cannot be held liable in tort. German law does not provide for torts by the means of an all-embracing statute. As a rule it rather protects from wrongful interference a discrete group of selected legal interests such as life, body, health, freedom and property in goods.[59] These provisions do not cover pure economic loss (*reiner Vermögensschaden*). Damages of

[57] BGH, decision of 29 Mar. 1996, NJW 1996, 1884, 1885; cf. also BGH, decision of 22 Feb. 1989, NJW-RR 1989, 627; BGH, decision of 7 Feb. 1980, BHGZ 76, 343, 349; BGH, decision of 12 June 1975, NJW 1975, 1774; BGH, decision of 6 Feb. 1969, WM 1969, 595, 597.

[58] BGH, decision of 22 Feb. 1989, NJW-RR 1989, 627, 628.

[59] §823 BGB.

this kind can only be claimed in tort provided the defendant caused them wilfully in a manner contrary to public policy.[60] However, breaking off contractual negotiations, even without any good reason, will not normally satisfy such stringent conditions. Not a single relevant decision can be found.[61]

Here, A is liable on the ground of §§280(1), 311(2) No. 1 BGB (*culpa in contrahendo*). A party entering into contractual negotiations without any intention to bargain at all is in breach of his duty to bargain in good faith. If A was aware of the fact that, as an outcome of their negotiations, B would have to accept a lower price for the premises, he is liable in tort for wilfully causing damage to B in a manner contrary to public policy (§826 BGB).

Whether the claim is in *culpa in contrahendo* or in tort, A must put B into the position he would be without B's mock negotiations (reliance interest). As B would have sold the premises for €1.2m if A had negotiated in good faith, A must recompense the difference between this sum and the purchase price at which B ultimately sold the premises (€1m), i.e. the sum of €0.2m.

Greece

The Greek Civil Code of 1940/46 (GCC) contains explicit provisions regarding general precontractual liability. Article 197 GCC on the responsibility arising from negotiations states that:

> in the course of negotiations for the conclusion of a contract the parties shall be reciprocally bound to adopt the conduct which is dictated by good faith and business usage.

And the first paragraph of article 198 GCC states:[62]

> a person who in the course of negotiations on the conclusion of a contract has by his own fault caused damage to the other party shall be liable for compensation even if the contract has not been concluded.

The specific nature of precontractual liability in Greece is disputed. The prevalent approach considers precontractual liability to form a

60 §826:1 BGB.

61 Cf. W. Lorenz in Hondius, *Precontractual Liability*, pp. 159–77, at p. 165.

62 The second paragraph of this article provides that with regard to the prescription period one must apply the relevant provision in the law of delict by analogy (art. 937§1), which provides for a limitation period of five years from the time the injured party has knowledge of the injury.

separate, third type of liability, alongside the other two types, namely contractual and delictual. Thus, under Greek law precontractual liability is considered to be a *sui generis* type of liability and this is supported by the autonomous regulation of precontractual liability in the GCC.[63] Nevertheless, among those who acknowledge precontractual liability as a separate type of liability, there are still divergences: some emphasise the contractual affinity of precontractual liability (quasi-contractual),[64] others stress the delictual nuances (quasi-delictual),[65] whereas still others stand indecisively somewhere in between.[66] Since articles 197 and 198 GCC do not provide a complete liability system and many issues remain unregulated (such as the capacity of the parties, compensation of immaterial damage, liability for another's fault, and the degree of fault required), whether the pendulum leans towards the contractual or delictual nature of precontractual liability will determine which body of law (contract or tort) fills the gaps. In legal literature the issue remains unclear but it seems that contract law is considered to be the most suitable body of law to complement the provisions on precontractual liability. Case law is of the unequivocal opinion that precontractual liability is a third source of liability, alongside the contractual and delictual, and it considers to be appropriate the application of the contractual provisions by analogy.[67]

According to article 197 GCC, precontractual liability arises if a party conducts negotiations in a manner that is contrary to good faith and business usage. *Areios Pagos* has stressed that good faith consists of, according to common understanding, the expected sincerity in the transactions of a reasonable man; whereas business usage indicates the fair and usual conduct of the relevant business with an emphasis on the obligation to inform.[68]

[63] M. Karasis in Georgiadis and Stathopoulos, *Commentary on the Greek Civil Code*, vol. I, p. 319.

[64] Pouliadis, *Culpa in contrahendo und Schutz Dritter*, p. 201; M. Karasis, 'Comments on article 198 para. 2 GCC', EEN 1976, 811, 813; Court of Appeals of Athens 5246/1998 EllD 1998, 1353.

[65] G. Koumandos in Georgiadis and Stathopoulos, *Commentary on the Civil Code*, n. 9; Court of Appeals of Athens 11518/1986 EllD1988, 916.

[66] Kambitsis, *Precontractual Liability*, p. 62ff.; D. B. Bosdas, 'Precontractual Liability', *Arxeion Nomologias*, 1968, 337, 338.

[67] AP 344/1982 NoV 30, 1465; AP 756/1981 EEN 49,491; Court of Appeals of Athens 4265/1983 EllD 25, 819; First Instance Court of Thessaloniki 1278/1998 Arm 1998, 543.

[68] Particularly AP 344/1982 NoV 1982, 1465; see also Court of Appeals of Athens 5857/1990 EllD 1993, 1629; Court of Appeals of Thessaloniki 1136/1990 Arm 1990, 941;

Moreover, precontractual liability is based on fault (article 198 GCC). The majority of case law has invariably identified fault at the precontractual stage with behaviour which is contrary to good faith and business usage, in other words with the same premise of article 197 GCC on what constitutes unlawfulness. This view has been criticised in the legal literature as insufficiently distinguishing the unlawful behaviour from the requirement of fault; yet that issue can be traced back to the discussion on the objectivity of fault.[69]

Under Greek law, remedies for precontractual liability are limited to damages; specific performance[70] or restitution are not awarded here. However, specific performance or restitution may be invoked on the appropriate legal bases, other than precontractual liability. For instance, a party may ask for restitution of a benefit conferred upon another party on the basis of unjust enrichment provisions. One must also note that, irrespective of whether one considers precontractual liability as being of contractual or delictual nature, the remedies would not differ, with the exception that damages for immaterial loss can be awarded only if precontractual liability is considered of delictual nature. Compensation for immaterial loss is not, however, generally recognised.

Damages in precontractual liability are limited to the reliance interest. Support for this view in the case law and legal literature derives mainly from the argument that the negotiating party cannot obtain what the contracting party would have obtained had the contract been concluded (namely the expectation interest).[71] However, the reliance

Court of Appeals of Athens 5382/1988 EllD 1990, 155; Court of Appeals of Thessaloniki 550/1983 Arm 1984, 279; Court of Appeals of Thessaloniki 221/1980 Arm 1980, 792.

[69] G. Koumandos in Georgiadis and Stathopoulos, *Commentary on the Civil Code*, n. 50; M. Karasis in Georgiadis and Stathopoulos, *Commentary on the Greek Civil Code*, vol. I, p. 320; Pouliadis, *Culpa in contrahendo und Schutz Dritter*, pp. 165–7, also with extended reference to case law.

[70] In the legal literature there is limited support for the remedies of specific performance or compensation *in natura* in the case of precontractual liability; in particular, these remedies could be employed to oblige a party to fulfil the formality that impedes completion of a contract. Yet this remains an exceptional view that has not been followed by case law recognition. See Deligiannis, *Legal Consultations 1960–1966*, p. 110; Kambitsis, *Precontractual Liability*, pp. 135–6. But see also G. Koumandos in Georgiadis and Stathopoulos, *Commentary on the Civil Code*, n. 80.

[71] For this point see the Supreme Court decisions: AP 309/1996 EllD 38, 83; AP 628/1995 NoV 45, 598; AP 1505/1988 NoV 38, 62; AP 1303/1984 EllD 1985, 402; AP 756/1981 EEN 1982, 491; Stathopoulos, *General Contract Law*, vol. A1, pp. 62, 63; M. Karasis in Georgiadis and Stathopoulos, *Commentary on the Greek Civil Code*, vol. I, pp. 320–1;

interest includes not just positive (i.e. expenses) but also negative (i.e. loss of opportunity/profit) damages.[72] Yet some writers argue that the provision on precontractual liability (article 198 GCC) does not draw a distinction between reliance and expectation interest but it rather requires full compensation of damage as long as the damage is causally linked to the conduct which is contrary to good faith.[73] On that basis, it is generally admitted that the reliance interest may in effect be higher than the expectation interest, a claim that has found recognition in case law.[74] Accordingly, in certain cases of precontractual liability it is claimed that compensation may be composed of *quasi-expectation* interest.[75] Finally, the view has also been expressed that the expectation interest must be awarded when one party walks away from negotiations when they have been successfully concluded, the conclusion of the contract being imminent, and all that is left is the formal

Pouliadis, *Culpa in contrahendo und Schutz Dritter*, p. 168, n. 52; Kambitsis, *Precontractual Liability*, p. 124ff.

72 Art. 298 GCC. With regard to the quantum and type of damages, Court of Appeals of Thessaloniki 2325/1990 Arm 1991, 14 is an exemplary case: the claimant was induced to believe that he had concluded a contract of commercial agency to represent in the Greek market the products (spirits and liquors) of a foreign producer. The latter claimed later that no contract had been concluded; meanwhile the claimant had undertaken the promotion of the products. The court found the defendant precontractually liable and awarded to the claimant the expenses he had incurred in conducting the negotiations and promoting the products, and the lost revenue of his regular occupation for the time he spent in the negotiations and promotion; but the court declined to remedy the loss of expectation interest (i.e. the loss of revenue from the commercial agency for the agreed contractual time) or any immaterial damage. The court therefore awarded both aspects of reliance interest, i.e. positive and negative damage, and turned down the claim for the compensation of the expectation interest and immaterial damage.

73 G. Koumandos in Georgiadis and Stathopoulos, *Commentary on the Civil Code*, nn. 77–8; M. Karasis, 'Precontractual Liability', NoV 26, 594–5; Barbalias, 'Precontractual Liability according to Articles 197 and 198 of the Greek Civil Code', NoV 1974, 733, 737; Court of Appeals Thessaloniki 221/1980 Arm 1982, 792; cf. AP 1303/1984 NoV 1985, 993; Kambitsis, *Precontractual Liability*, p. 126.

74 See Court of Appeals of Athens 2698/1978 Arm 1978, 551 (note by Kornilakis), which accepts that the reliance interest is not limited by the expectation interest. In that case it was stated that if the contract under negotiation is not concluded, then the reliance interest may in fact be higher than the expectation interest, as long as this is justified by the causal link between damage and conduct contrary to good faith. It must be noted that, unlike other provisions of the Civil Code (e.g. 145§1, 231§2 GCC), article 198 GCC does not make an explicit reference to any such limitation, and from that one may draw an additional argument against limiting the reliance interest to the quantum of the expectation interest.

75 M. Karasis in Georgiadis and Stathopoulos, *Commentary on the Greek Civil Code*, vol. I, p. 321; also M. Karasis, 'Precontractual Liability', NoV 26, 594–5.

endorsement of it.[76] This last point remains an exceptional view and has not been followed by the Greek courts.

Turning to the case in hand, in principle the parties are free to discontinue negotiations and the obligation to conduct them in good faith does not mean that the parties *must* reach an agreement. However, the parties must seriously intend to negotiate and lack of such intention indicates bad faith. A does, indeed, act in bad faith by not conducting negotiations in earnest; instead, he conducts negotiations deceptively and with the intention and knowledge of causing damage to B. Therefore, A's behaviour contravenes the requirement of article 197 GCC that negotiations must be conducted in good faith.

Article 198 GCC provides that a person who in the course of negotiations and by his own fault causes damage to another person is liable for compensation even if the contract was not concluded. In this case a Greek court would award damages to B on the basis of the provisions of article 198 GCC as long as: (a) the damage occurred due to conduct that took place during the negotiation stage; (b) A was at fault; (c) there is a causal link between the damage and the unlawful act; and (d) B can prove all the above.[77] A's fault consists of the fact that he entered into negotiations with the sole aim of disrupting negotiations between B and C, which also amounts to conducting negotiations in bad faith. B must prove that A never entertained a serious intention to conclude a sales contract and that he only intended to cause the negotiations between B and C to fail. As a result of A's conduct, B lost the opportunity to sell his premises for €1.2m (the offer made by C). B can seek compensation for the damage thereby caused.

Due to A's unlawful behaviour, B loses an opportunity to sell his premises for €1.2m and he is instead forced to sell his premises for the

[76] Gazis, *Legal Consultations 1956–1999*, p. 303: 'whenever according to due conduct by the negotiating parties the contract would be concluded but for a negation to sign the agreed document or not complying with a formality requirement, it is accepted that the non-performance constitutes the damage and expectation interest is due' (legal consultation delivered in 1969). Further on, at p. 310, he characterises reliance interest as being a dogmatic construction, concluding at p. 318: 'This view [i.e. compensation of expectation interest] must be deemed to be correct irrespective of the fact that it has not until now concerned our jurisprudence. This is so because article 198 para.1 refers to restitution of damage without limiting it to the reliance interest. Whether compensation comprises the reliance or the expectation interest is a question of causal link alone' (legal consultation delivered in 1977).

[77] Court of Appeals of Athens 4913/1991 EllD 1992, 881; Court of Appeals of Athens 1204/1986 EllD 1988, 913.

lower price of €1m. Therefore B may claim from A the difference between the actual sale and the lost opportunity, which is €0.2m. Such compensation places B in the position he would have been in had he never entered into or relied upon the negotiations with A. B cannot request the difference (€0.5m) between the actual sale and the price they (A and B) were actually negotiating, which represents the expectation interest that places B in the position he would have been in had the negotiations between A and B resulted in a valid contract. In the case of precontractual liability, the Greek courts do not award such compensation.[78] B will also be compensated for the expenses and costs related to conducting the negotiations.

Ireland

A is liable to B under the tort of deceit, probably in the amount of €0.2m.

In general, the freedom to enter into a contract implies the freedom not to enter into a contract. Thus, there is no liability where contractual negotiations between the parties have been unsuccessful and result in no contract being established. There is no requirement in Irish law to negotiate a contract in good faith. Contractual principles apply only where a completed contract has been concluded. This rule, if applied in an absolute sense, would lead to potential injustice. Accordingly there are exceptions to the rule, although they arise outside of the law of contract. The principal legal actions lie in the law of tort, restitution or quasi-contract. The remedy in tort is that of damages, an amount of money to compensate the plaintiff for any loss which has been suffered. The remedy in restitution is the return of any benefit which the defendant has unjustly received from the plaintiff. The remedy in quasi-contract is the reimbursement of costs incurred by the plaintiff as a result of the defendant's activities.

Precontractual liability in tort arises either through the deceit or negligence of the defendant. From the facts of this case, the most appropriate action is that of deceit. An action for deceit requires that there has been an untrue representation of fact made fraudulently by the defendant with the intention of inducing the plaintiff to rely upon the representation and which was in fact relied upon by the plaintiff, resulting in damage.[79] All five elements of the action are crucial.

[78] See, *inter alia*, AP 628/1995 EEN 1996, 545.

[79] McMahon and Binchy, *Irish Law of Torts*, p. 967ff.; Quill, *Torts in Ireland*, p. 271ff.

There must be an untrue statement of fact. In general, a statement of intention is not a statement of fact.[80] Thus, a statement that X intends to buy a property is not a statement of fact and X is free to change his or her intention without any exposure to liability. However, in *Edgington v. Fitzmaurice*[81] the court ruled that a statement of a person's intention is a statement of fact where the statement which was made by the defendant was not true at the time the statement was made.

Merely making an untrue statement of fact in itself is not sufficient unless it was fraudulently made with the intention that the statement would induce the plaintiff to rely on that statement. A statement is fraudulent where it is made by the defendant knowing it to be untrue or without any belief as to its truth.[82] The latter includes situations where the defendant is reckless as to the truth of the statement. It follows that an honest, albeit unreasonable, belief that the statement is true will relieve a defendant of responsibility.[83] The motive of the defendant is not relevant to a finding of fraud, nor need it be shown that the defendant personally benefited from the fraud.[84]

The defendant must have intended to induce the plaintiff to rely on the statement, although this does not require that the statement be made directly to the plaintiff. Liability arises where the statement is indirectly transmitted to the plaintiff as a result of the defendant's actions.[85] However, the intended manner of reliance must correspond with the reliance placed upon it by the plaintiff. No liability arises where the plaintiff pursues a course of action fundamentally different from that which the defendant had intended, albeit in reliance on the statement.[86]

For the plaintiff to succeed he or she must show that they relied upon the representation and that this reliance caused damage. The representation need not be the sole motivation for the plaintiff's actions but it must have materially influenced the plaintiff.[87] This is usually proved through circumstantial evidence. Under the Civil Liability Act 1961, section 34(1), a court may reduce any award of damages to a plaintiff based on contributory negligence. This may arise where the plaintiff

[80] *Edgington v. Fitzmaurice* (1884) 29 ChD 459. [81] Ibid.
[82] *Derry v. Peek* (1889) 14 App Cas 337.
[83] *Delaney v. Keogh* [1905] 2 IR 267; *Barbour v. Houston* (1885) LR Ir 475.
[84] *Northern Bank Finance Corp v. Charlton* [1979] IR 149.
[85] *Peek v. Gurney* (1873) LR 6 HL 377.
[86] Quill, *Torts in Ireland*, pp. 251–2; *Smith v. Chadwick* (1884) 9 App Cas 187.
[87] *Edgington v. Fitzmaurice* (1884) 29 ChD 459, 466.

was reckless in relying on the representation of the defendant,[88] although it is exceptionally rare.[89]

Injury arising from reliance upon the representation usually takes the form of economic loss. Damages are relatively difficult to calculate. The measure of the loss is to restore the plaintiff to the position he would have been in if the representation had not been made.[90] The difficulty is therefore that the court must return to the precontractual negotiations at the time the representation was made, remove it from the equation and then discover what would have transpired in the absence of this representation. The outcome of this should then be compared with the present position of the plaintiff and damages awarded to the extent necessary, if any, to compensate the plaintiff for any loss.

In the case at hand, A has clearly made a representation as to his intention which was untrue at the time it was made. The representation was made fraudulently with the intention that it would be relied upon by B. In fact, B did rely upon the representation and this resulted in damage to B. The damage is in the form of a sale of the property for less than might have been obtained had the representation not been made. This would be in the amount of €0.2m.

Italy

This case concerns precontractual liability under article 1337 of the Codice Civile, which provides protection against unjustified withdrawal during negotiations (*ingiustificato recesso dalle trattative*), and imposes a general duty of good faith during the negotiations (*buona fede nelle trattative*).

Recesso ingiustificato dalle trattative: the unjustified withdrawal from negotiations can be seen as one of the oldest and most developed features of Italian case law concerning precontractual liability.[91] Article 1337 provides a duty of fair play before reaching an agreement, such as

[88] *Gill v. McDowell* [1903] 2 IR 463.

[89] McMahon and Binchy, *Irish Law of Torts*, p. 973.

[90] *Northern Bank Finance Corp. v. Charlton* [1979] IR 149.

[91] Benatti, *La responsabilità precontrattuale*; Faggella, *I periodi precontrattuali e la responsabilità precontrattuale*; Loi and Tessitore, *Buona fede e responsabilità precontrattuale*; Turco, *Interesse negativo e responsabilità precontrattuale*; Patti, *Responsabilità precontrattuale e contratti standard*; Richter, *La responsabilità precontrattuale*; Monateri, *La responsabilità contrattuale e precontrattuale*; Musy, *Il dovere d'informazione*; Palmieri, *La responsabilità precontrattuale nella giurisprudenza*.

during negotiations, under the principle of good faith (*buona fede*). The Supreme Court has interpreted the article to mean that:

> precontractual liability occurs only when, during negotiations and before reaching an agreement, the parties have behaved so as to induce reasonable reliance in the conclusion of the contract. Moreover, the unjustified breach of such relationship has to consist in conduct contrary to good faith.[92]

Italian case law requires that two conditions be met in order to invoke precontractual liability: the negotiations have given rise to one party's reasonable reliance (*affidamento*) in the conclusion of the contract; and the other party has not shown any reasonable excuse (*giusta causa*) capable of justifying the withdrawal from the negotiations.[93]

Buona fede nelle trattative: the question is whether or not the party behaved in accordance with the principle of good faith, a concept which plays a central role in precontractual liability. Italian law distinguishes two kinds: subjective good faith,[94] where the party's positive intention conceals his dishonesty,[95] and objective good faith, which implies a general limit to the parties' freedom to trade, according to duties of fair play (*correttezza*), reliability (*serietà*) and co-operation between the parties (*solidarietà*).[96] The Italian Supreme Court has consistently given an objective interpretation of the duty of good faith under article 1337,[97] although the damaged party cannot invoke precontractual liability where he suffered the loss through his own fault,[98] he had knowledge of the matters pointing against the conclusion of the contract,[99] or when he failed to take reasonable care to ascertain the facts.[100]

92 Cass 25 Nov. 1976, n. 4448; Cass III, 25 Oct. 1973, n. 2757.

93 Most recently Cass, sez. II, 14 June 1999, n. 5830; TRIB-T. Milano, 5 May 1997. Examples of justification are when the party creating the reliance refuses to sign a contract whose terms are different from the agreement reached, or where there is no agreement on the essential elements of the contract.

94 C.M. Bianca, 'La nozione di buona fede quale regola di comportamento contrattuale', RDC 1983, I, 205; G. Criscuoli, 'Buona fede e ragionevolezza', RDC 1984, I, 709.

95 See, e.g., arts. 128 and 1147 c.c.

96 In particular arts. 1175, 1358, 1336, 1375, 1460 c.c. See F. Benatti, 'Culpa in contrahendo', CI, 187, 293.

97 Cass 30 Aug. 1995, n. 9157; Cass 30 Mar. 1990, n. 2623; Cass 11 Sep. 1989, n. 3922; Cass 18 Jan. 1988, n. 340; Cass 17 Jan. 1981, n. 430; Cass 14 Apr. 1975, n. 1411.

98 Cass, sez. II, 14 Mar. 1985, n. 1987. See P.G. Monateri, 'Concorso di colpa e affidamento nella responsabilità precontrattuale', RCP 1985, 761.

99 Cass 29 Nov. 1985, n. 5920.

100 Cass 14 Mar. 1985, n. 1987; Cass 11 Oct. 1994, n. 8295. The care required of a professional may be higher: Trib. Foggia, 31 Dec. 1993. See M. Bessone, 'Rapporto precontrattuale e dovere di correttezza (osservazioni in tema di recesso dalla

In this case, A's liability arises from his misconduct during the negotiations: first, for having induced B to rely on his offer to purchase the premises at a higher price, thus inducing C to withdraw his own offer; and then for breach of good faith in having broken off the negotiations immediately after C's withdrawal. As a consequence, B not only failed to obtain the price he hoped for from A, but also lost the contract with C at €1.2m, having in the end sold the premises for only €1m. Recoverable damages for precontractual liability are said[101] to consist only in the negative interest (*interesse negativo*).[102] In this case, they will therefore be €0.2m. Punitive or exemplary damages are not awarded, although recently it has been said that in certain cases[103] malicious conduct or gross negligence could lead to an increase in the level of damages awarded. Since the measure of damages is left to the evaluation of the trial judge,[104] a punitive element in the award of damages could be used by the judge within the exercise of this discretion.

Netherlands

In *Baris/Riezenkamp* (1957)[105] the Hoge Raad decided that parties starting negotiations enter into a legal relationship that is dominated by good faith, which requires them to take each other's interests into account. Although this was a case about mistake, it is generally regarded as the starting point for the development of the broader doctrine of precontractual good faith. The ground-breaking case with regard to liability for breaking off negotiations is *Plas/Valburg* (1982).[106] Since this

trattativa)', RTDPC 1972, 962, 965ff.; Trimarchi, *Rischio e responsabilità*, emphasising how the level of care has to be related to current practice.

101 The correspondence between precontractual liability and negative interest has been emphasised by Luminoso, *La lesione dell'interesse negativo*. Recent decisions confirm the constant line of Italian case law, e.g. TRIB-T. Udine, 22 Apr. 1996; Cass 30 Aug. 1995, n. 9157; Cass 13 Dec. 1994, n. 10694; Cass 26 Oct. 1994, n. 8778; Cass 25 Feb. 1994, n. 1897; Cass III, 30 Mar. 1990, n. 2623; Cass II, 11 Sep. 1989, n. 3922.

102 Positive interest (*interesse positivo*) is related to the due fulfilment of the contract. It cannot be awarded, in order to respect the principle of freedom to withdraw from negotiations.

103 Especially in cases related to defamation or environmental protection, as App. Milano, 23 Dec. 1986; Corte Cost., 30 Dec. 187, n. 641; TRIB-T. Napoli, 18 Sep. 1989; TRIB-T. Roma, 24 Jan. 1989; TRIB-T. Milano, 27 Jun. 1991; TRIB-T. Roma, 24 Nov. 1992.

104 As stated in Cass, sez. lav., 15 Dec. 1999, n. 14109.

105 HR 15 Nov. 1957, NJ 1958, 67, note Rutten.

106 HR 18 June 1982 (*Plas/Valburg*), NJ 1983, 723, note Brunner; AA 32 (1983) 758, note Van Schilfgaarde.

case, the Hoge Raad has distinguished three stages in the negotiating process. At the first stage, both parties are entirely free to break off negotiations. At the second stage, a party is still free to break off negotiations, but if he does so he has to pay the expenses the other party has incurred. Finally, at the third stage the parties are no longer free to break off negotiations. This is the case when the other party may reasonably believe that some contract of the type the parties were negotiating about will be concluded or if other circumstances of the case make breaking off unacceptable.[107] If a party breaks off at that third stage he is liable in damages, which may even amount to the expectation interest. Also he may be ordered to continue negotiations. However, in a more recent case, *De Ruiterij/Ruiters* (1996),[108] the Hoge Raad has limited its *Plas/Valburg* doctrine. In that case it held that a party is not liable in all cases where the other was justified in expecting the imminent conclusion of a contract, because in determining whether there is liability the interests of the party breaking off the negotiations must also be taken into account; moreover, a change of circumstances during the negotiations may also provide a justification. This decision, of course, raises the question whether a (new) better offer from a third party may justify breaking off negotiations even in that stage. In the third stage, breaking off is in itself contrary to good faith. In other words, in opposition to other systems, under Dutch law an advanced stage of negotiations can actually cause a party to lose his right to break off negotiations. Thus, Dutch law has replaced the clear-cut distinction between contract and no-contract by a gradual process where at a very advanced stage of negotiations, a party can claim to be put financially into the position as if a contract were concluded.[109] As to the nature of liability: the Hoge Raad has based its 'three stages rule' on tort and good faith alternatively, and sometimes on both.[110] In the most recent decisions, the Hoge Raad has based liability directly on good faith.[111] The drawback of such a 'third way' approach to liability would be in most systems that the code only provides for two regimes of liability (contract and tort) and therefore acceptance of a new third regime by the courts would lead to

[107] See HR 23 Oct. 1987, NJ 1988, 1017, note Brunner (*VSH/Shell*).

[108] HR, 14 June 1996, NJ 1997, 481, note HJS (*De Ruiterij/Ruiters*).

[109] Cf. Van Schilfgaarde, note on *Plas/Valburg*, above n. 106.

[110] For a decision based on tort see, e.g., HR 13 Feb. 1981, NJ 1981, 456, note Brunner (*Heesch/Reijs*).

[111] See, e.g., HR 16 June 1995, NJ 1995, 705, note Stein.

considerable uncertainty. However, in the Netherlands this approach is possible since the Dutch Code provides for a single regime for any type of liability.[112] As to the extent of liability, if a party breaks off negotiations in the so-called second stage, as discussed above, he must reimburse the other party's expenses. A party who breaks off negotiations in the third stage, where breaking off is no longer allowed, is liable for the expectation interest. This was first accepted in the *Plas/Valburg* case. The principle has been repeated in every later case on breaking off negotiations.[113] However, it should be added that there have not yet been many cases where expectation damages actually were awarded. The Dutch rule can be explained by the fact that in the so-called third stage, which begins at the moment the other party could reasonably expect that a contract would be concluded, breaking off itself is unlawful (contrary to good faith). The damage caused by this unlawful act (that is, the breaking-off) is the non-conclusion of the contract, since at that stage of the negotiations, the contract would have been concluded if the negotiations had not been broken-off. Thus, the fact that Dutch courts accept expectation damages when negotiations are broken off in the third stage is just a logical consequence of considering their breaking-off itself at a certain point unlawful (contrary to good faith).[114]

As has been said, in the 'third stage' even the expectation interest can be recovered. However, from case law it is not clear when the reliance interest can be recovered. It seems likely that when the negotiations have reached the third stage the defendant is liable also for the reliance interest (that is, the claimant is entitled, in the alternative, to either the expectation interest or the reliance interest). Indeed, it has been argued[115] that it is only at that stage that liability for the reliance interest should arise, as in most other European countries. Moreover, a recent case has raised some controversy among observers.[116] In that case the Hoge Raad formulated, as a general

[112] See arts. 6:95ff. and 3:310 BW.

[113] See, e.g., HR 24 Nov. 1995, NJ 1996, 162.

[114] The *Plas/Valburg* case has been commented upon by several foreign authors, such as Farnsworth, Sacco and Van Ommeslaghe. Most of them disapprove of the Dutch rule. See, e.g., P. Van Ommeslaghe, Rapport Général, in *La bonne foi, Travaux de l'Association Henri Capitant, Tome XLIII 1992* (Paris 1994), p. 34.

[115] M.W. Hesselink, 'De schadevergoedingsplicht bij afgebroken onderhandelingen in het licht van het Europese privaatrecht', WPNR (1996), 6248 (pp. 879–83), 6249 (pp. 906–10).

[116] HR 12 Aug. 2005, NJ 2005, 467 (*CBB/JPO*).

standard for determining liability, that the parties are free to break off the negotiations, unless breaking off would be unacceptable. This general standard contains two novelties. First, the Hoge Raad expresses and emphasises, for the first time, the freedom in principle to break off negotiations (and it underlines that the standard is a severe one, which 'requires restraint' of the courts). Secondly, the Hoge Raad no longer mentions what has become known as the 'second stage'. This omission has brought some academic writers to the conclusion that the second stage is no longer recognised and also that the reliance interest is not recoverable unless breaking off was unacceptable (because of justified detrimental reliance or other circumstances).[117] However, others argue that the omission was due to the fact that, when the case came before the Hoge Raad, the only issue was about the expectation interest.[118] Another explanation might be that in the *Plas/Valburg* case, the liability for expenses did not depend on whether the defendant was still allowed to break off the negotiations.[119]

In this case, it is not likely that B will be able to recover his loss from A on the basis of the doctrine of breaking off negotiations. There are no indications that the negotiations reached the 'third stage', and so there is no liability for the expectation interest (lost profit, i.e. €0.5m). As discussed above, it is uncertain whether at some stage in negotiations breaking-off leads to liability for the reliance interest. Therefore, in this case there is probably no liability under this doctrine for B's lost opportunities.

However, A may be liable for entering into or for continuing negotiations without having a real intention of reaching an agreement with B. One could argue that under these circumstances, A has committed a tort (*onrechtmatige daad*) by conducting negotiations with B.

[117] T. Harlief and R.P.J.L. Tjittes, 'Kroniek Vermogensrecht', NJB 2005, 1605–6; C.E. Drion, 'Vooraf', NJB 2005, 1781; R.P.J.L. Tjittes, 'De afbraak van de aansprakelijkheid voor afgebroken onderhandelingen' in van Kooten and Wattendorff, *Hartkampvariaties*, p. 139ff.

[118] G.J. Knijp, 'Plas/Valburg geldt nog altijd', NJB 2005, 2375–6.

[119] There is yet another possible, albeit admittedly rather speculative, reading. If indeed the second stage was abolished in this case that would make it easier for the Hoge Raad to turn the formerly third stage (and now new second stage) into a stage where, without changing the test for liability, the recoverable damages would be limited to the reliance interest. On this reading the recent case may have paved the way for a more radical change in the direction of the European common core (a 'Europe-friendly interpretation').

If so, he may be liable (even though there was no detrimental reliance by B on the imminent conclusion of the contract) because of A's positive (but not disclosed) intention not to conclude a contract with B. However, there does not seem to be any specific authority for this claim in Dutch law. Liability should be based on the general tort clause.[120] If this liability can be established, B will probably be able to recover the damage which he suffers as a result of the loss of prospective buyer, C – that is, €0.2m.

Norway

Since A entered into negotiations with B without a genuine intention of purchasing the premises, he is liable to pay damages to B based on the reliance interest.

It is probably more correct to consider such precontractual liability as a unique type of liability in Norwegian law. Precontractual liability is designed to protect the basic expectations of the parties with respect to good faith and fair dealing in the precontractual period. However, contractual aspects could also apply, for instance, when a 'letter of intent' has been issued, or in the regulations relating to tenders.

Recent Supreme Court cases show that conduct during the precontractual period can provide a basis for claiming damages.[121] In the *Kina Hansen* case[122] the presiding judge[123] summed up legal developments in Norway to the present time in this way:

> Under which legal regulation this situation should be judged is not clearly determined in Norwegian law. With respect to the conditions governing the right to damages in cases of reliance interest, there is little material to refer to in previous cases, and no clearly defined legal doctrine. However, blameworthy behaviour during contract negotiations should have been displayed – such as acting in bad faith, or in a dishonest or misleading manner. In a recently published thesis, unreasonable or irrelevant reasons for breaking off negotiations are discussed as possible grounds for liability: see Lasse Simonsen, *Precontractual Liability*, 1997, especially p. 226ff.[124]

120 Article 6:162 BW.

121 See Rt 1998, 761, the *Kina Hansen* case, Rt 1995, 543, the *Selsbakkhøgda housing cooperative* case, and Rt 1992, 1110, the *Stiansen* case.

122 Rt 1998, 761.

123 See p. 772. In Norway the term used is the first voting judge (*førstvoterende*).

124 Bad faith is used here to translate the Norwegian term '*illojalitet*', which indicates a blameworthy act.

Entering into precontractual negotiations presupposes a genuine possibility of the parties' reaching a binding agreement.[125] Whenever one party has no such intention, but has other motives for the negotiations, there is no such possibility. B has the right to be placed in a financial position similar to that which he would have been in if A had not entered into negotiations with him – according to the so-called reliance interest. In other words, B should be placed in a situation where he would be able to pursue his negotiations with C without the interference of A.

The loss suffered by B involves the eventual sale of the premises for €1m whereas, without A's interference, he would have been able to obtain €1.2m, or at least there would have been a strong likelihood of obtaining this price. This consequential loss (*disponeringstapet*) 'comprises' an unrealised gain with respect to a third party.[126]

From the perspective of reliance interest, there are two necessary causal elements. First, the loss must be due to the unlawful act. In the present case, there is a question as to the likelihood that B would have sold the premises at a price of €1.2m if A had not interfered. According to common theory, a strong likelihood must be shown. Secondly, only foreseeable losses can be recovered. In the present case, however, it seems possible for A to predict the loss, as he presumably knew of the price negotiations between B and C.

Portugal

A is liable to B under the doctrine of *culpa in contrahendo*, which is established in article 227 of the Código Civil.[127] It is against the principles of good faith to enter into negotiations without any intent to conclude a contract.[128] In this case, the negotiations caused B the loss of a better contract, so the amount of damages would be established by reference to the difference in the value of the contracts.

According to the traditional view, and still the opinion of the majority of writers, the liability based in *culpa in contrahendo* is limited to the reliance interest and therefore cannot involve the expectation

125 Simonsen, *Precontractual Liability*, p. 192. 126 Ibid. p. 343ff.

127 'Anyone who negotiates with another to conclude a contract has the duty, either in the negotiations or in its formation, to act according to the rules of good faith or he will be liable for losses due to his fault'.

128 The rule of good faith requires the parties always to behave with the intention of concluding the contract. See Cordeiro, *Tratado de Direito Civil Português*, I-1, p. 399.

interest.[129] A new approach, however, holds that even in *culpa in contrahendo* the liability should involve the expectation interest.[130]

A must therefore pay damages of at least €0.2m (reliance interest), although this could be higher if a court accepted the view that the expectation interest can be awarded. B has no other remedies in this case.

Scotland

A has carried out negotiations in bad faith, having no genuine intention to contract. A 'pretended he wants to move his shop to larger premises and that he is prepared to pay €1.5m'. Such a pretence may constitute fraudulent misrepresentation under Scots law, entitling B to damages in delict. The classic definition of fraud in Scots law is provided by the Institutional Writer, Erskine, who describes this intentional delict as 'a machination or contrivance to deceive'.[131] It may readily be appreciated from Erskine's understanding that, as one leading commentator on the law of contract has put it, 'fraud has a wide definition'.[132]

Before B could successfully claim damages he would have to overcome two hurdles. First, B would be required to show some sort of positive act by A which caused the misrepresentation. The classic example is misrepresentation by words, but conduct alone has been sufficient to amount to a finding of misrepresentation.[133] The facts suggest that some positive words or conduct have been used by A to convey the pretended intention, and that this requirement has therefore been met. The second obstacle to an award of damages is that B would need to show that the misrepresentation was made with the requisite mental intent. To succeed in a claim for fraudulent misrepresentation B would need to show either (i) that A positively knew the statement was false or (ii) that A positively believed the statement was

[129] See Telles, *Direito das Obrigações*, p. 77; Varela, *Das Obrigações em geral* I, p. 271; Jorge, *Direito das Obrigações*, p. 166; Costa, *Responsabilidade civil pela ruptura das negociações preparatórias de um contrato*, p. 78; Da Silva, *Estudos de Direito e Processo Civil (Pareceres)*, p. 73 and Leitão, *Direito das Obrigações*, I, p. 317. For court decisions, see RC 13 Feb. 1991 in CJ 16 (1991), 1, 71.

[130] See Cordeiro, *Da Boa Fé no Direito Civil*, p. 585, and *Tratado de Direito Civil Português*, I-1, 407. There is already a court decision supporting this doctrine: RL 29 Oct. 1998 in CJ 33 (1998), 4, 132.

[131] Erskine *Institute*, 3.1.16.

[132] McBryde, *The Law of Contract in Scotland*, para. 14–09.

[133] *Gibson v. National Cash Register Co Ltd* 1925 SC 500; *Patterson v. H Landsberg & Son* (1905) 7 F 675.

false even though he did not positively know it was false (liability only arising if in fact untrue) or (iii) that A made the statement with reckless indifference to the veracity of the remarks and that the statement related to a matter of importance between the two parties. The facts of this scenario suggests that this requirement is also met, as A appears to have made the pretence knowing it to be false.

It therefore appears that a damages claim for fraudulent misrepresentation could be made out. The measure of such a damages claim is designed to restore B to the position he would have been in had the wrongful act not been committed. In this case, one must ask: had A not made the false representations about his contractual intent, would B have concluded a contract of sale with C (or indeed any other party) for €1.2 m? Proof of such a counterfactual outcome might be difficult. Were causation of loss impossible to prove on the balance of probabilities, a claim for damages for misrepresentation would fail. However, a possible alternative claim might lie for B's loss of a chance of avoiding the €0.2m losses.[134] Such a claim would be measured by the value of the chance lost: for instance, the loss of, say, a 75 per cent chance of avoiding the €0.2m loss would be valued at 75% x €0.2m, i.e. €0.15m.

No other remedies for B are readily apparent on these facts, it not having yet been established incontrovertibly that there is a general duty in Scots law to negotiate in good faith.[135]

Spain

In Spanish law, precontractual liability (*culpa in contrahendo*) in its proper sense is based on article 1902 of the Civil Code (tort), under which any damage intentionally or negligently caused in violation of the general principle *neminem laedere* gives rise to liability. Under this provision, the abrupt and unjustified breaking-off of negotiations can give rise to liability for damages caused by it, the conceptual foundation (justification) being the general principle of good faith,[136] which requires a certain standard of behaviour during continued

[134] For a recent delictual loss of a chance case, see *Paul v. Ogilvy* 2001 LT 171, commented upon in M. Hogg, '*Paul v. Ogilvy*: a Lost Opportunity for Lost Chance Recovery' (2003) 7 Edin LR 86.

[135] See generally on obligations of good faith in Scots law, Forte, *Good Faith in Contract and Property*.

[136] Cf. art. 1258 CC.

negotiations.[137] Academic writers and case law have established four criteria to determine whether there is liability:[138] the existence of a reasonable situation of confidence concerning the conclusion of the contract; the absence of justification for the break-off of negotiations; the proof of damage to one of the parties; and a causal link between the damage and the confidence inspired. The cases where such a liability has been admitted concerned expenses which were made in anticipation of the conclusion of a contract, such as the giving up of a business or travel expenses.[139]

A is negotiating in bad faith. But the damage which occurs is not a consequence of B's confidence in A's will to contract, but of C withdrawing from the contract. For this reason, A would not be held liable on the foundations of *culpa in contrahendo* stricto sensu. But A's liability could be established on the doctrine of abuse of right.[140] Based on this rather old theory one could say that, even if A has the right to negotiate as he wants, he is not to do it in a way which is contrary to the sense of the right itself and certainly not in a way that causes harm to others. Article 7.2 of the Civil Code establishes liability if any act or omission which clearly goes beyond the normal limits of exercising a right causes harm to a third party. In this case, we could argue that negotiating without any intention of concluding a contract but only to prevent someone else from concluding the contract is an abuse. However, it is not beyond doubt that negotiating itself can be considered as the exercise of a right.[141]

Sweden

A is liable to compensate B in the sum of €0.2m.

Due to the form requirements for sales of real estate (the agreement has to be in writing and contain, *inter alia*, the price and a declaration by the seller that the ownership of the property is transferred to the buyer), there is some uncertainty as to whether there can be liability on the basis of *culpa in contrahendo*. Neither party is bound by an agreement

137 STS, 26 Feb. 1994, RJ 1994\1198; Díez-Picazo and Gullón, *Sistema de Derecho Civil*, vol. II, p. 81.

138 STS, 14 June 1999, RJ 1999\4105.

139 STS, 16 May 1988, RJ 1988\4308; Tribunal Superior de Justicia de Baleares, 10 Mar. 1997, AS 1997\1007.

140 'Abuso de un derecho': art. 7.2 CC and art. 1902 CC: STS, 14 Feb. 1944, RJ 1944\293; Sentencia de la Audiencia Provincial de Barcelona, 23 Sep. 1993, AC 1993\2109, SEXTO.

141 Audiencia Provincial de Barcelona (cited above n. 140).

for the sale of real estate until it fulfils the form requirements. However, as A negotiated with B with the sole intention of preventing the sale of the property to C, there is some support in the case law and legal doctrine for liability.[142]

In NJA 1973.175, where the parties were negotiating a sale of real estate and the owner incurred costs for changes of the property in accordance with the wishes of the prospective buyer, the Supreme Court found that the buyer could not be liable 'only because of the promise to buy the property'. As the circumstances in the case showed that the prospective buyer had not undertaken to bear the cost of the changes regardless of whether the contract was concluded or not, the Supreme Court found that the owner was not entitled to damages. It is evident from the facts of the case that the prospective buyer had a real intention to buy the property when initiating the negotiations. Had that not been the case, the statement by the Supreme Court cited above gives some support for liability.[143]

In NJA 1990.745, the parties had for more than a year been negotiating a contract. The intention was that one of the parties (L) would become a distributor of goods on condition that the other party (S) acquired a final licence agreement for the goods. As the negotiations had developed so far that both parties intended to conclude the agreement if the licence agreement was concluded, the Supreme Court found that S had an obligation to consider L's interests. S could therefore be liable for damages if S acted in a disloyal manner, by for instance not informing L about significant matters for the successful completion of the negotiations. The Supreme Court found that S had not acted in such a disloyal manner. However, S was considered to have an obligation to inform L as soon as possible when the decision had been made not to conclude the agreement with L. This obligation was not fulfilled as S informed L about the decision almost a month after the decision. As L had not incurred any significant costs during this period, the Supreme Court found that S was not liable for damages.[144]

[142] Grauers, *Fastighetsköp*; Hellner, *Kommersiell avtalsrätt*; J. Kleineman, 'Avtalsrättsliga formföreskrifter och allmänna skadeståndsrättsliga ansvarsprinciper', JT 1993–94, 433; J. Kleineman, 'Skadeståndsgrundande uppträdande vid avtalsförhandlingar', JT 1991–92, 125; Ramberg and Ramberg, *Allmän avtalsrätt*.

[143] J. Kleineman, 'Avtalsrättsliga formföreskrifter och allmänna skadeståndsrättsliga ansvarsprinciper', JT 1993–94, 442ff.

[144] J. Kleineman, 'Skadeståndsgrundande uppträdande vid avtalsförhandlingar', JT 1991–92, 135ff.

These cases show that one can become liable for damages when misleading another party with fault (that is, either intentionally or carelessly). Due to the circumstances in the present case, A would probably be considered to have acted with fault, as his act was intentional. Therefore, A is liable for damages. B is entitled to compensation for all costs incurred during the negotiations with A. If B could prove with some degree of certainty that C would have purchased the property, A is also liable for the difference between the price C would have paid and the price finally received for the property, €0.2 m.

Switzerland

The Swiss Code of Obligations of 1912 (OR) contains no specific provision dealing with precontractual liability in general. But the concept of *culpa in contrahendo*, developed by Rudolf von Jhering,[145] is found in some special provisions, first in the former Swiss Code of Obligations of 1881, and later in the new Code of Obligations and the Swiss Civil Code (ZGB) of 1912.[146] Moreover, the concept of *culpa in contrahendo* has generally been accepted by courts and academic writers.[147] On the one hand, *culpa in contrahendo* is based on a general analogy with the special provisions. On the other hand, it is based on the concept of good faith and fair dealing according to ZGB 2, a provision which applies throughout Swiss private law.[148]

From the moment when the parties start negotiations or, even earlier, when they prepare the ground for the contract, a relationship of reliance (*Vertrauensverhältnis*) exists between the parties that leads to a legal relationship (*Rechtsverhältnis*) with duties of protection and loyalty

145 'Culpa in contrahendo oder Schadensersatz bei nichtigen oder nicht zur Perfection gelangten Verträgen' (1861) 4 *Jherings Jahrbücher für die Dogmatik des bürgerlichen Rechts*, 1.

146 Among these provisions are liability of the party acting under error (OR 26), liability for wilful deception and duress (OR 28 and 29 together with OR 31 III), liability of a principal who does not ask for the return of his power of attorney (OR 36), liability of the unauthorised agent (OR 39) and liability of a ward or a minor alleging to be capable of concluding contracts (ZGB 411 II).

147 See BGE 120 II 331, 336; BGE 134 III 390, 395ff.; ZürcherKommentar-Schönenberger/Jäggi, OR 1 n. 566ff.; BernerKommentar-Kramer, OR Einleitung n. 133ff.; BernerKommentar-Kramer, OR 22 n. 4ff.; BaslerKommentar-Bucher, OR 1 n. 78ff; CommRomand-Thévenoz, OR Intro. 97–109 n. 19ff.; Piotet, *Culpa in contrahendo et responsabilité précontractuelle en droit privé suisse*; Gonzenbach, *Culpa in contrahendo im schweizerischen Vertragsrecht*; Gauch *et al.*, *Schweizerisches Obligationenrecht Allgemeiner Teil*, n. 948ff.; Tercier, *Le droit des obligations*, n. 572ff.

148 ZGB 2 I: 'Every person is bound to exercise his rights and fulfil his obligations according to the principles of good faith'.

(*Schutz- und Loyalitätspflichten*) for both parties.[149] There are different opinions on the legal basis of the *culpa in contrahendo*, because of the different modalities (*Haftungsmodalitäten*) of tortious liability and contractual liability: several differences (the rules of vicarious liability, burden of proof and limitation periods) make it more favourable for a victim to bring a claim based on contractual liability rules (non-performance of obligations) than on tortious liability rules.[150] In accordance with an emerging opinion in academic writing, the Swiss Federal Court holds that *culpa in contrahendo* is neither contractual nor tortious but a liability by virtue of law,[151] a liability *sui generis* with its own rules. For each modality of the liability there has to be a pragmatic decision whether contractual rules or tortious rules should apply by analogy in order to find an appropriate solution. In the field of vicarious liability and of the proof of fault, the contractual rules apply in favour of the victim. By contrast, the Federal Court applies the short period of prescription of one year (which is criticised by the prevailing opinion of academic writers).

The extent of the liability is generally limited to the negative interest (reliance interest).[152] But this rule is not without exceptions. In some provisions[153] the judge is authorised to award more damages in the interest of equity. According to writers, the judge should apply these provisions in other situations by analogy and award damages up to the positive interest (expectation interest).[154]

[149] BernerKommentar-Merz, ZGB 2 n. 264; BernerKommentar-Kramer, OR Einleitung n. 134ff.

[150] *Vicarious liability*: a contracting party is fully liable for the acts of auxiliary persons (OR 101), whereas in tort the liability is limited to acts of employees and servants (not independent auxiliaries) and the principal is not liable if he proves that he has taken all precautions appropriate under the circumstances to prevent damage of that kind (OR 55); *burden of proof of fault*: in tort the victim has to prove the fault of the wrongdoer (OR 41), but in contract the party breaching his duties has to prove that he was not at fault (OR 97); *limitation periods*: in contract ten years (OR 127), but the claim based on tort is barred after one year from the date when the victim has knowledge of the damage and the wrongdoer, and in any event, after ten years from the tortious act (OR 60).

[151] '*Gesetzliche Haftung*': BGE 101 II 268, BGE 104 II 94. The theory was established by Peter Jäggi in ZürcherKommentar-Schönenberger/Jäggi, OR 1 n. 592. For details on the theory and its origins see Loser, *Vertrauenshaftung im Schweizerischen Schuldrecht*, nn. 1145ff., 1149.

[152] BGE 130 III 345, 349. Cf. Koller, *Obligationenrecht Allgemeiner Teil*, § 28 n. 36.

[153] OR 26 II, OR 39 II.

[154] Cf. Koller, *Schweizerisches Obligationenrecht Allgemeiner Teil*, § 28 n. 37; Loser, *Vertrauenshaftung im Schweizerischen Schuldrecht*, nn. 238ff., 1241ff.

In recent years the Federal Court and academic writers have developed the concept of *culpa in contrahendo* and generalised it together with some other liabilities to a non-contractual (but with similarities to a contractual) liability – so-called liability based on reliance (*Vertrauenshaftung*).[155] The liability based on reliance contains not only the traditional cases of *culpa in contrahendo* but also other forms of liability, for example, the responsibility of the principal for apparent authority, even if specific performance is awarded.[156] Moreover, a person can be held liable who is not the future party of a contract but has in some way (for example, by false information) influenced the contracting parties. According to this principle, an expert, for instance an assessor of the value of a house, may be liable if his client uses the appraisal report a second time later on while concluding another contract.[157] And the creditor of a company that has gone into bankruptcy was allowed to sue the parent company of the group, because it had induced the reliance that it would ensure the fair and correct behaviour of all group companies (group standard).[158]

155 BGE 134 III 390; BGE 133 III 449; BGE 130 III 345; BGE 121 III 350; BGE 120 II 331. Recently and in detail see Loser, *Vertrauenshaftung im Schweizerischen Schuldrecht* (with an English summary of the theory in nn. 1369ff.); see also BernerKommentar-Kramer, OR Einleitung n. 150f.; BaslerKommentar-Bucher, OR 1 n. 69aff.; BaslerKommentar-Wiegand, OR vor 97–109 n. 11; Chappuis and Winiger, *La responsabilité fondée sur la confiance – Vertrauenshaftung;* Gauch *et al.*, *Schweizerisches Obligationenrecht Allgemeiner Teil*, n. 982aff.; Schwenzer, *Schweizerisches Obligationenrecht Allgemeiner Teil* n. 52.01ff.; Tercier, *Le droit des obligations*, n. 1094ff.; H.-P. Walter, 'Die Vertrauenshaftung: Unkraut oder Blume im Garten des Rechts?', ZSR 2001 I, 79ff.; Werro, *La responsabilité civile*, n. 305ff.; C. Widmer 'Vertrauenshaftung – Von der Gefährlichkeit des Überflüssigen', ZSR 2001 I, 101ff. This liability may apply when a party (A) to a special relationship (mainly in connection with a future or already existing contract) induces and then breaks the reliance of the other party (B) to his detriment. The sanction can consist in a remedy through which the reliance of B is fulfilled or in a remedy that awards only the negative interest. The reliance is mostly based on assumptions regarding the present, fact or law; sometimes the assumptions have regard to the future behaviour of A.

156 BGE 120 II 197. The Federal Court has also used this new concept to award damages in the expectation measure if a contract fails for lack of formality, although the victim knew the invalidity (BGE, 28 Jan. 2000 no. 4C.280/1999 in SemJud 2000 I, 549). And in a claim against a committee of an athletic competition, the Federal Court awarded damages for the expenses of an athlete who was not allowed to participate in the competition, after the committee changed the rules for participation (BGE 121 III 330). For an overview on the different scopes of application of the liability based on reliance see Loser, *Vertrauenshaftung im Schweizerischen Schuldrecht*, nn. 259ff., 1377ff.

157 BGE 130 III 345.

158 BGE 120 II 331. In a recent case (BGE 133 III 449), however, the Federal Court set out its reasoning: there is generally no protection of the reliance that the counterparty will fulfil a 'promise' without a binding contract. For further details on this concept, see Loser, *Vertrauenshaftung im Schweizerischen Schuldrecht*, nn. 971, 979ff.

In particular, this last type of liability based on reliance (*culpa in contrahendo* or liability of 'third persons') has given rise to criticism against the new concept.[159] The critics are less opposed to the liability itself than to the theoretical grounds of the liability. It is argued that the liability (especially of 'third persons') should be based on tort rather than on a new concept between tort and contractual liability. The background of the debate, on the one hand, relates to the question whether the modalities of tortious liability (which are less favourable to the victim as mentioned above) are appropriate.[160] On the other hand, there are different opinions on the scope of tortious liability in Swiss law (OR 41). Some authors reject the prevailing opinion that Swiss tort law protects special interests defined by the law, and that damages for pure economic loss are awarded only in case of the violation of a special norm (*Schutznorm*).[161]

It should be noted that a reform of the Swiss law of liability has been planned. According to the reform project *culpa in contrahendo* and any other form of liability based on reliance would be integrated into tort law.[162] On the other hand, most differences between tort and contractual liability would be eliminated. The reform project, however, has been criticised, and it is not clear whether and to what extent it will be implemented.

On the facts given, A is liable on the ground of *culpa in contrahendo*. He has started negotiations with B without any intention to conclude a contract with B but with the sole purpose of inducing B not to conclude a contract with C. B's reliance was based on an assumption related to

[159] Cf. Schwenzer, *Schweizerisches Obligationenrecht Allgemeiner Teil*, n. 52.01ff.; Werro, *La responsabilité civile*, n. 314ff.; C. Widmer, 'Vertrauenshaftung – Von der Gefährlichkeit des Überflüssigen', ZSR 2001 I, 101ff.

[160] Despite the critics the Federal Court adopts the short limitation period of tortious liability (one year) for the liability based on reliance and for *culpa in contrahendo*: see BGE 134 III 390, 397ff.

[161] For the prevailing opinion with a narrow scope of tortious liability, compare BGE, 26 Sep. 2001 no. 4C.193/2000 E. 4a; and BGE, 30 Oct. 2002 no. 4C.202/2002 E. 4.1; BGE 133 III 323, 330; less clear BGE 130 III 345, 347. OR 41: 'Whoever unlawfully causes damage to another, whether wilfully or negligently, shall be liable for damages. Equally liable for damages is any person who wilfully causes damage to another in violation of *boni mores*'.

[162] Draft-OR 46; cf. P. Loser, 'Kritische Überlegungen zur Reform des privaten Haftpflichtrechts – Haftung aus Treu und Glauben, Verursachung und Verjährung', ZSR 2003 II, 133ff. For the Draft Rules and a Commentary see *Revision und Vereinheitlichung des Haftpflichtrecht, Vorentwurf eines Bundesgesetzes/Erläuternder Bericht* (Bern, Bundesamt für Justiz, 2001; also at http://bj.admin.ch).

the present fact; that is, A's willingness to bargain and his serious intention to conclude the contract. The reliance is broken because the assumption was wrong. A is to blame for wrong information. He has breached his duty to negotiate in good faith.[163]

A must compensate B's negative interest: he must put B into the position he would be in without the unfair negotiations. B would have sold the premises for €1.2m and now had to sell for €1m. A must pay the difference: €0.2m.

Wilful behaviour gives the right to damages in the expectation measure, according to some provisions.[164] The extension of this rule to cases of broken-off negotiations is not appropriate, because it would conflict with the freedom to conclude the contract. The possibility of compensation in the expectation measure, according to prevailing opinion, is limited to situations where a contract has been concluded (even if it is not valid).[165]

Editors' comparative observations

At first sight, this set of facts gives rise to a common solution amongst the jurisdictions – a 'common core'. All jurisdictions provide B with the remedy of damages, based on the 'reliance' interest. However, the solutions are in fact more nuanced: there is variation not only in the technical legal basis of A's liability, but also in the identification of the 'trigger' for liability (the key facts which give rise to the liability) and in the calculation of the 'reliance interest'.

Basis of liability: in giving their answers to this first case within the volume, most reporters have taken the opportunity of giving some account of the general approach of their jurisdiction to precontractual liability. The contrasts between the jurisdictions will become clearer as they are applied to the later cases, but already some lines can be drawn. A clear majority have a general principle of precontractual liability, although its legal basis varies. Some jurisdictions have an explicit and specific legislative rule for precontractual liability (Germany, Greece,

[163] BernerKommentar-Kramer, OR 22 n. 12, 14ff.; Hartmann, ZBJV 2003, 516ff.; Loser, *Vertrauenshaftung im Schweizerischen Schuldrecht*, n. 620.

[164] OR 26 II, OR 39 II.

[165] Cf. Koller, *Schweizerisches Obligationenrecht Allgemeiner Teil*, § 28 n. 37; Loser, *Vertrauenshaftung im Schweizerischen Schuldrecht*, nn. 616ff., 628, 1241. *Contra* Widmer, *Umfang des Schadenersatzes bei nicht zur Perfektion gelangten Verträgen*, 78, 178ff. (relevance of the causation if the contract would have been concluded).

Italy and Portugal); some regard the general principle of precontractual liability as part of the law of tort, and therefore base its legislative authority on the general legislative provision governing tort (Finland, France, Spain); some see it as an implicit principle, deduced either from other rules within the legislative texts (Austria and Switzerland; this was also the position in Germany before the 2001 reform of the BGB) or, in the case of non-codified jurisdictions, from general principles of law (Denmark, Norway and Sweden). By contrast, the reporters for England, Ireland and Scotland make clear that there is no generally accepted principle of precontractual liability (the Scottish reporters rather tantalisingly say 'not yet') and therefore they have to turn to other specific bases of liability for the pre-contract phase (contract, tort, restitution).

In applying these rules, all the jurisdictions would find A liable for his conduct described in the facts. England, Ireland and Scotland find A liable in tort. Most of those which have a general principle of precontractual liability find that A has broken his precontractual duties. But on the facts, in order to impose liability the Netherlands would turn to the law of tort (and not the general precontractual duty); Spain would turn to the doctrine of abuse of rights (rather than the general precontractual duty under the law of tort); and Austria and Germany would both consider that A might be liable in tort *as well* as for *culpa in contrahendo*. These differences point to the fact that the reporters do not all identify the same 'trigger' for liability on the facts.

'Trigger' for liability: as we shall see in the following cases, there are various different possible events during the precontractual phase that might give rise to liability on one negotiating party in favour of the other. The way in which a party *starts* the negotiations might give rise to a claim; or the way in which he *conducts* himself *during* the negotiations; or the way in which he *breaks off* the negotiations. Or there might be some particular *state of mind* which triggers the liability (such as the fact that some act by one party during the negotiations, which causes loss to the other party, was done with the *intention to cause harm* or – if it can rather loosely be said to be a state of mind – was done *negligently*). Or there might be a *misrepresentation* by one party, which causes the other to make a mistake and therefore suffer loss. The reports on case 1 already show some difference between the jurisdictions as to their focus on the various possible 'triggers'.

The clearest division is between the jurisdictions that accept a general principle of good faith in negotiations, and those that do not. England, Ireland and Scotland regard the key fact here as being A's misrepresentation about his intentions to conduct serious negotiations with B. And, more than that, it is crucial to the result that A's misrepresentation was fraudulent. This places the claim within a specific tort: fraudulent misrepresentation, or *deceit*. Amongst the other jurisdictions, however, there is some difference of emphasis. Most focus on the fact that A *started* the negotiations in bad faith (Austria, Denmark, Finland, France, Germany, the Netherlands, Norway, Portugal and Switzerland) although some find alternative bases: the *intention to cause harm* (Austria, Germany and Greece – the first two as additional claims in delict, the last as part of the assessment of the breach of the duty of good faith); the bad faith *conduct* of the negotiations (Greece, Italy, the Netherlands, Spain and Sweden); the bad faith *breaking-off* of the negotiations (Austria and Italy). Some of these bases are taken together by some reporters, and therefore a firm distinction between them (such as between A having started and having continued the negotiations in bad faith) is not always made – generally, it appears, because these reporters are not addressing themselves to a particular question such as 'did A begin the negotiations in bad faith' but the more general legal question 'was A in breach of his duty to negotiate in good faith'.

Remedy: all jurisdictions award damages to B, to compensate him for his 'reliance interest' losses. In most cases the reporters identify this as being €0.2m, as reflecting the value of the loss of the sale to C. Some reporters explicitly include B's wasted costs in the recoverable damages, but it is not clear that any reporters would exclude the wasted costs, as long as they are causally related to the wrong which gives rise to the liability.

However, the reporters take slightly differing views about the figure of €0.2m as damages. Some jurisdictions will take an (apparently scientific) approach to the calculation of the actual loss that flows from B's loss of the sale to C. Several jurisdictions will investigate the likelihood of the sale having proceeded with C at the price of €1.2m, and, indeed, whether the price of €1m ultimately secured by B is the best price he could (reasonably) have obtained, before being satisfied about the calculation; and where there is a doubt will reduce the damages by reference to the *chance* of the sale to C. In the case of some jurisdictions, however, the precise assessment of damages is said to be difficult to predict, even if there is no uncertainty about the sale to C, because of the judge's discretion in the assessment (Denmark, France, Italy). France falls in both categories: it has a rule of assessment of damages which takes into account the chance of the loss of a replacement contract; but then the actual assessment of the figure is less certain because of the trial judge's power to assess the loss. It should be noted that these matters are not in any jurisdiction a peculiarity of the law governing precontractual liability. Although perhaps the question of chance might commonly arise in such claims (because inevitably a negotiating party's losses will very often comprise the benefits he might have secured had the negotiations not been conducted by the other party in bad faith), the issues raised here are just highlighting differing views amongst the jurisdictions about how to value and compensate loss.

There is only one possible exception to the solution of 'reliance' damages in this case: in Portugal there is some support in the legal literature (and in one decided case) for the award of damages on the 'expectation' measure for *culpa in contrahendo*, although the reporter's own preferred position is to maintain the traditional approach of 'reliance' damages, which therefore keeps him in line with all the other jurisdictions.

Case 2: Negotiations for renewal of a lease

Case 2

B was A's tenant under a three-year lease of a warehouse; the lease was due to come to an end at the end of 1999, and in July 1999 the parties began negotiations for the renewal of the lease. Before opening negotiations with A, B had explored the possibility of moving to another warehouse, and had found a possible alternative warehouse which he could have rented from X, but since it was at the same rent and would have involved expenses in moving to the new warehouse, he told X that he was not interested in concluding that lease. Earlier in 1999, A had already decided to sell the warehouse, in order to realise its capital value, and had begun negotiations with C for the sale which continued alongside the negotiations with B for the lease renewal. As A knew, C intended to buy the property with a view to leasing it to another company, D, but to induce C to pay a higher price, A started and continued the negotiations with B in order to demonstrate the potential profitability of the warehouse by way of rental income. During the negotiations B continued to use the warehouse as a major distribution point, and made no further effort to find an alternative warehouse. One week before the end of the lease, A told B that he was not prepared to renew the lease, because he had agreed to sell the warehouse to C; and that C would not be offering to grant a lease because he would be leasing it, from 1 January 2000, to D. The evidence of the negotiations with B for the renewal of his lease induced C to pay a significantly higher price than A could otherwise have expected to have received for the warehouse. Having had to move at short notice, B has to rent a temporary warehouse from 1 January 2000 at a high rent, in an inconvenient place, and he may have difficulties with his distribution arrangements. What liability (in contract, tort, restitution, or any other form of liability), if any, does A have to B?

Discussions

Austria

Since the answer to the question of whether A is liable to B under the general principle of precontractual liability or *culpa in contrahendo* lies within the discretionary power of the judge,[1] an absolutely clear and unequivocal decision is difficult to predict. However, it can be presumed that an Austrian judge will decide in favour of B and award damages for the higher costs he incurs.

Whether A is liable for the loss suffered by B resulting from the higher rent he has to pay for continuing his business in an inconvenient place depends on whether A's conduct amounts to chicanery (the exercise of a right that can only have the purpose of harming another), or whether the rules of dealing in good faith would have required A to notify B of his intention not to renew the lease with B.[2] The position of the court was originally rather restrictive but has changed in more recent decisions. Therefore, a judge will most likely resort to the doctrine of *culpa in contrahendo*, thereby allowing the recovery of B's pure economic loss as 'reliance interest' under the rules of contractual liability. Under tort rules, B's pure economic loss would only be recoverable from A if A had caused that loss wilfully and in a way that amounts to a violation of good morals (*gute Sitten*).

The facts of this case indicate that the major problem in cases of this type lies in the difficulty of drawing the line between freedom of contract and bargaining in good faith. Indeed, freedom to negotiate is a cornerstone of contract law and it includes the freedom to break off negotiations, but it may collide with the mutual reliance on the honesty of the negotiating parties that stems from the duty to bargain in good faith. It is a matter of discretion to decide, in a given factual situation, how far the freedom to break off negotiations goes and at which point the creation of the negotiating partner's confidence in the perfection of the deal attains dominance, so as to put the disappointed partner in the position of a victim under the judge-made rules of *culpa in contrahendo.*

[1] See Austrian report on case 1. [2] Cf. OGH 6 July 1976, SZ 49/94.

A is therefore liable for the higher costs that B incurred as a result of the necessity to lease a temporary warehouse.[3] There is no liability for loss of X's contract, since that predates B's negotiations with A (so no causal link), nor is there any claim here for unjust enrichment.

Denmark

The facts do not appear to show that A has committed more than 'cheat continuing',[4] since A and B may very reasonably start negotiating. Had they reached agreement before A sold the warehouse, B would under Danish law be protected and could not have been evicted.

A Danish court would probably award damages but would not give B the full cost difference between moving into X's inexpensive warehouse and into the more expensive temporary warehouse.[5]

England

A is probably liable to B for damages in the tort of deceit. If he had not already surrendered the lease of the warehouse, he would have had a statutory right to a new lease, but this is now too late.

Under the tort of deceit a claimant can recover damages if he can show that the defendant fraudulently made a false representation to him, with the intention that he act on it; and that he did act on it and suffered loss. The false representation may be by words or conduct, or may be a positive statement which, though literally true, is misleading because of the context or because of what it omits to say. But there is generally no liability in deceit for non-disclosure; it is not sufficient, for example, that the defendant stood by and knowingly allowed the claimant to persevere in his misunderstanding. So the question here is whether B can show a false representation by A. A engaged in and continued the negotiations with B without having any real intention of concluding them: his motive was to demonstrate to C the profitability of the warehouse. There is no evidence that he ever made any express statement to B that he was serious about the negotiations; but it is likely that a court would find either some express statement made by A

[3] Federal Landlord and Tenant Law (Mietrechtsgesetz) of 1981 provides protection against eviction for many commercial leases; however, according to §1(2) N. 1 this statute does not apply to warehouses.

[4] On the terminology 'cheat continuing' (contrasted with 'cheat contracting'), see the Danish report on case 1.

[5] For further comments on the general approach of Danish courts to an award of damages, see the Danish report on case 1.

during the negotiations which was false by virtue of his not having intended the negotiations to be pursued, or an implied representation by A as to his seriousness in the negotiations. If such a claim can be established, the damages payable by A would be the additional costs B incurs in consequence of his reliance on the fraudulent representation: this would include the additional costs of the alternative temporary warehouse and any other quantifiable losses flowing from the disruption to his distribution arrangements.[6]

If he cannot show a misrepresentation and establish a claim in the tort of deceit, B will have no remedy.

He cannot succeed here in the tort of negligence because, although it is established that one party during negotiations for a contract may owe a duty of care to the other party in relation to the accuracy of statements made during the negotiations,[7] the duty does not require one party to look to the other's interests in the conduct of the negotiations themselves: there is no duty of (effectively) good faith in pre-contractual negotiations through the tort of negligence. No such duty has ever been established in the English cases, and would be contrary to the general position that each party to contractual negotiations is entitled to pursue his own interest, so long as he avoids making misrepresentations.[8]

There is no contract between A and B on which a claim to damages could be based. The negotiations for the renewal of the lease do not result in a concluded agreement for the renewal and there is no other contract on the facts, such as a contract to continue the negotiations or not to break off the negotiations without good reason: English law does not generally recognise such contracts.[9] Nor on the facts is there any contractual undertaking by A not to negotiate with C:[10] A has made no express promise, and a court would not imply such a promise simply

[6] An award of *exemplary* damages may be made in a claim in tort (including, in principle, the tort of deceit) if the case fulfils the general requirements for such an award, such as where the defendant's conduct was calculated to make a profit for himself which may well exceed the compensation payable to the claimant: *Kuddus v. Chief Constable of Leicestershire Constabulary* [2002] 2 AC 122. However, no award of exemplary damages for the tort of deceit has yet been made in any reported case.

[7] *Esso Petroleum Co Ltd v. Mardon* [1976] QB 801.

[8] *Walford v. Miles* [1992] 2 AC 128, 138. See the English report on case 6. The Supreme Court of Canada has explicitly rejected a general tortious duty of care between parties negotiating a contract: *Martel Building Ltd v. Canada* (2000) 193 DLR (4th) 1.

[9] See discussion in the English report on case 6.

[10] Such a contract is in principle possible: see the English report on case 6.

from the continuation of lengthy and apparently serious negotiations with B.

In certain, defined circumstances a person may be 'estopped'[11] from denying a proposition to be true; his legal position is then affected by the 'estoppel', so that his rights and duties are given effect on the assumption that the proposition in question is true. One species of estoppel is promissory estoppel, where a person who has made a representation (or promise) is estopped from refusing to give effect to the representation; in effect, his promise is enforced even though the promise was not made within a contract. The doctrine of promissory estoppel is still very narrow in scope in English law, and generally applies only to prevent one party to a contract from going back on a promise to the other party that he will not enforce his rights under the contract.[12] Promissory estoppel has been applied as a much wider doctrine in some other common law jurisdictions, in effect to allow a promise by X to Y, on which Y relied, to be enforceable even though there is no concluded contract between them. This is discussed below, in relation to case 8. But it will in any event not apply here, since on the facts there is no sufficient positive representation by A that he will continue with negotiations and conclude a contract with B. There is therefore no basis on which B could claim that A's breaking-off of negotiations was in contravention of any promissory estoppel.

Another species of estoppel is proprietary estoppel, which is restricted to the context of rights in property, typically real property, although this doctrine, or other related equitable doctrines, may apply also to personal property rights.[13] If P misleads Q into believing that he

[11] 'The word "estoppel" only means "stopped". You will find it explained by Coke in his Commentaries on Littleton . . . It was brought over by the Normans. They used the old French "estoupail". That meant a bung or cork by which you stopped something from coming out. It was in common use in our courts when they carried on all their proceedings in Norman-French': *McIlkenny v. Chief Constable of the West Midlands* [1980] QB 283, 316–17 (Lord Denning MR). For further discussion of estoppel, see Spencer Bower, *Estoppel by Representation*; J. Cartwright, 'Protecting Legitimate Expectations and Estoppel in English Law', Report to the XVIIth Congress of the International Academy of Comparative Law, Utrecht, July 2006, (10.3) *Electronic Journal of Comparative Law* (December 2006), at www.ejcl.org/103/article103-6.pdf.

[12] *Combe v. Combe* [1951] 2 KB 215. The doctrine can also apply outside the context of a contract, but still only to prevent one party who has other, non-contractual legal rights against the other from going back on a promise not to enforce them: *Durham Fancy Goods Ltd v. Michael Jackson (Fancy Goods) Ltd* [1968] 2 QB 839 (rights arising under statute).

[13] *Western Fish Products Ltd v. Penwith District Council* [1981] 2 All ER 204, 218 (Megaw LJ).

has, or will obtain, a right in P's property, and Q relies to his detriment on P's representation so that the court judges it inequitable to deny him a remedy, then he may be awarded a remedy which (at the court's discretion) may even extend to an order to transfer to him the property right that he believed he had or would obtain.[14] Here, if A had led B to believe that he was being granted, or would be granted, the renewal of the lease, this could fall within the doctrine of proprietary estoppel since a lease is a property right.[15] But there is no sufficient representation on the facts here.

B therefore has no claim based on estoppel, either promissory or proprietary estoppel.

Nor does B have a claim in restitution to recover A's profit in his contract with C as a result of continuing the negotiations with B whilst not intending to carry them through to a contract. For a claim in restitution in English law, it must be shown that the profit A has made (his 'enrichment') cannot justly be retained, having been made at B's expense. This generally requires the profit to have been made by receipt from B, or in consequence of a breach of a duty owed to B, in circumstances where A cannot justly retain it.[16] But here the profit was received not directly from B, and although A has made his profit in consequence of having committed the tort of deceit against B, this does not appear to give rise to a claim in restitution.[17]

Under statute, however, there are special rules for the termination and renewal of leases of premises occupied by the tenant for the purposes of his business. There are certain exceptions (such as leases not exceeding six months), but the lease under which B holds the warehouse appears to fall within the statute. Under Landlord and Tenant Act 1954, Part II, a tenancy continues automatically beyond the end of its contractual period until terminated in accordance with the Act (which requires the landlord to serve particular notices on the tenant), and the tenant has the right to the grant of a new tenancy. If the landlord serves

14 *Crabb v. Arun DC* [1976] Ch 179; Burn and Cartwright, *Cheshire and Burn's Modern Law of Real Property*, pp. 814–25, 841–6.

15 *J.T. Developments Ltd v. Quinn* (1990) 62 P & CR 33.

16 Goff and Jones, *The Law of Restitution*, esp. ch 1.

17 There are some suggestions in the books that there may be a claim in restitution for profits made by committing the tort of deceit (see, e.g., Goff and Jones, *The Law of Restitution*, para. 36-005) but this is controversial (see Cartwright, *Misrepresentation, Mistake and Non-Disclosure*, para. 5.43) and in any event the cases on which the claim is based do not cover the situation here.

the prescribed notice to terminate the tenancy, he can only resist the grant of a new tenancy (if the tenant applies to the court for it) if he can establish one of a list of grounds set out in the Act for obtaining possession. None of the grounds for possession appears to be established here: they include such things as serious breaches of tenancy obligations by the tenant; or that the landlord requires possession of the premises either to demolish or reconstruct them, or to occupy them himself.

However, on the facts given, B appears to have surrendered his tenancy of the warehouse, since he has moved out and now made alternative arrangements. Even if he had ceased to occupy the warehouse for business purposes after the end of the lease, he could still have exercised his right under the Act to a new lease.[18] But once the tenancy has been surrendered, such as by delivering possession up to the landlord, this remedy is no longer available.[19]

Finland

A may be liable to B for damages under the rules of *culpa in contrahendo*. The provisions of tenancy law applicable to the agreement between A and B[20] are not relevant for the assessment of A's acts in connection with the termination of the contract and the negotiations for a new agreement with B. Nor do damages provisions of the relevant Act contain any special elements in addition to the ordinary contract law rules.

A's and B's negotiations are to be considered as a precontractual situation rather than a contractual one. However, the existing contractual relationship between them must perhaps be taken into account to some extent. It accentuates their close relationship and makes a difference not only from common tort situations but also from ordinary contract negotiations between parties having no existing contract between them. But this special feature is not in itself sufficient to change the applicable damages standard to the contractual positive interest. Otherwise, the idea of a fixed-term contract would be rendered nugatory, and the tenant would in any case be entitled to continue the

[18] Landlord and Tenant Act 1954, s. 24(3). [19] Ibid. s. 24(2).

[20] There are three separate acts, Tenancy Act (Huoneenvuokralaki) and Act on Ground Rent (Maanvuokralaki) concerning respectively house tenancies and tenancies of land to private persons, and Act on the Lease of Business Premises (Laki liikehuoneiston vuokrauksesta). The last of these governs the agreement between A and B. In fixed-term contracts the Act does not restrict the right of the landlord to terminate the contract at the end of the contract period.

lease (or to be put in an equivalent economic position). The contract law elements have to gain in weight from the special circumstances in this case, but this must be achieved by some other means than the application of the positive interest. As commonly in *culpa in contrahendo* situations, costs and other economic losses should in principle be recoverable, and in addition the burden of proof of fault might be placed on the defendant.[21]

The crucial question for imposing liability on A concerns the possible elements of fault in his behaviour. The prevailing principle is freedom of contract negotiations, including freedom to break off negotiations with no need to give good reasons and without incurring liability to the other party.[22] On the other hand, there are commonly accepted limits to this freedom.

It is possible for a party's withdrawal from negotiations to give rise to liability. In Finnish discussions on *culpa in contrahendo*, views have been offered that freedom of negotiations should reach its utmost limit where the reliance of a party on the conclusion of the contract has become worth protecting. This point should be reached only in extreme (and very rare) cases, when that party has very good grounds to believe that the formation of the contract is immediately at hand, lacking no more than just the formal confirmation. In order to impose reliance-based liability on the party who withdraws from negotiations, he must have been at fault in giving some basis to the other's reliance. Withdrawing from negotiations should under these circumstances be sanctioned with liability, in most cases of the negative interest.[23] Nothing that is indicated about A's behaviour in this case, however, seems to reach the level of fault that should be sanctioned with reliance-based liability, taking into account that this test should be satisfied only in very special circumstances. On the contrary, it seems that the general principle of freedom of negotiations should prevail.

Further limits to the freedom of negotiations are derived from the fact that a party is not entitled to enter into negotiations with no true intention to conclude a contract. Trying merely to make out the cost

[21] For a general discussion of *culpa in contrahendo* in Finnish law, see the Finnish report on case 1.

[22] Von Hertzen, *Sopimusneuvottelut*, p. 266.

[23] Ibid. p. 276. See also *Oikeustoimilakitoimikunnan mietintö* (Committee Report on the Revision of the Contracts Act, Komiteanmietintö [Government Committee Reports] 1990:20), p. 129, in which even compensation of the positive interest is regarded as possible in extreme cases.

level of contract performance is an acknowledged example of an improper motive for starting competitive bidding or contract negotiations.[24] In this case (since A 'had already decided to sell') getting a better position in negotiations for selling the warehouse to C seems to be A's only motive in negotiating with B. This kind of motivation could also be considered improper, as not intending to conclude a contract. So the burden of proof concerning fault is not an issue, and A's fault can be taken to be proved. Even if this were not so, it appears that B would still succeed because of the burden of proof lying on the defendant, A.

The general conditions for liability (fault, damage, causal relationship between fault and at least some of the losses) seem to be established. So A is in principle liable for B's damage that he has caused. But there are still questions about what damages are an 'adequately' causal consequence of A's acts, whether B's losses are of recoverable categories, and what impact his possible contributory negligence would have on A's liability.

B has suffered several kinds of (economic) losses due to the ending of the lease. Some of these losses are not causal consequences of A's wrongful acts, because B had no right to continue the contract. We have to ask whether there are any damages that could have been avoided if A had followed good practice in relation to B. B could not expect to avoid expenses from moving to another warehouse but in this case he may have suffered some other losses that he would have been able to avoid if he had been adequately informed about A's true intention. These losses are in principle recoverable to the extent that B could not have avoided them (i.e. to the extent they cannot be considered to be consequences of B's contributory fault).

In addition to removal costs, B's losses in the case consist of a higher rent of the new warehouse and possible costs arising from its inconvenient place, as well as possible costs and lost profits because of difficulties with the distribution arrangements. All these losses are of recoverable categories, because *culpa in contrahendo* rules allow compensation of economic losses. We have to consider the role of A's fault and, respectively, B's contributory fault as causal factors leading to these losses. As pointed out above, the blameworthy elements in A's behaviour focus on his improper motives in commencing negotiations with B and in not informing B that A did not intend to continue the lease. Because A had already decided to sell the warehouse when B was

[24] See, e.g., Hemmo, *Sopimus ja delikti*, p. 209.

in contact with X, B would perhaps have rented X's warehouse if informed about A's decision. Of course, it cannot be stated with certainty that A had an obligation to give the information to B at that time. But certainly A broke his duties of disclosure and good faith at the latest when misleading B about his intentions by starting negotiations with him. At that time, it is true, B may already have lost his opportunity to contract with X. B, in turn, may have committed contributory fault in not making further effort to find another warehouse during the negotiations with A.

If B, when negotiating with X, had known about A's decision to sell (which was already made at that time) he would presumably have rented X's warehouse and avoided the losses due to higher rents, and perhaps even those arising out of an inconvenient place and distribution arrangements. The removal costs, however, would have been avoidable only to the extent that they exceeded costs from moving to X's warehouse. The losses thus avoidable are in principle recoverable. Whether they are in fact recoverable depends on whether A's not disclosing his decision to B at that time was blameworthy. We can perhaps make the assumption that A's behaviour was blameworthy from the beginning of his misleading negotiations with B, at the latest. So B's losses are recoverable to the extent they were avoidable by that time: the compensation would therefore cover the difference between a possible warehouse that might have been available then, and the actual one rented by B. Also the removal costs, damages caused by the inconvenient place of the new warehouse and the difficulties with distribution arrangements are recoverable only to the extent they could have been avoided by B if informed properly about A's intentions. The costs pertaining to X's warehouse cannot as such be taken as the standard, because we cannot take it for granted that A had an obligation to inform B of his intentions at the time of B's contact with X.

As concerns B's removal costs and damages caused by the inconvenient place of the new warehouse and the difficulties with distribution arrangements, all these items of damage may be caused rather by B's own than A's fault – or they might perhaps have accrued in any case, due to B's removal. As A is not obliged to continue the lease, he is in principle not liable for such damages. Liability could be established only as far as a causal relationship to A's blameworthy behaviour described above can be traced.

B had a duty to limit his loss (the principle of contributory fault). As a party to a fixed-term contract, he should have taken into account the possibility of having to move at the end of the term. The wording of the case gives the impression that he was at fault in this respect ('makes no further effort to find an alternative warehouse'). So A's possible liability would be limited on the basis of B's contributory fault to the extent that B could have avoided losses by properly trying to restrict them. If it can be shown that B should have accepted X's offer, then no losses exceeding those pertaining to moving to X's warehouse would be recoverable.

A made a profit in contracting with C at 'a significantly higher price'. A profit made by the tortfeasor in connection with the tortious act is in itself no basis for imposing tort (or contract) law liability on him towards the injured party. According to rules of unjust enrichment (*condictio sine causa*), there has to be a profit of one person corresponding to a loss of another, both arising from one and the same origin (as well as some additional preconditions for liability).[25] In this case A's profit and B's loss do not correspond. This doctrine is therefore no additional basis for A's liability to B.

France

The non-renewal of a commercial lease in France is subject to specific legal rules set out formerly in a Decree of 30 September 1953, now codified in the Commercial Code. These rules, which are mandatory,[26] make the question asked somewhat irrelevant in a French context.

Article L. 145-9 of the Commercial Code indicates that the question of the renewal or the termination of the lease must be examined at least six months before its end. If the notice to quit is given less than six months before the end of the lease, it is considered void, and the contract is renewed by default. In that case, disagreement between the two parties about the price of the lease and other clauses should be resolved by the courts. In the present case, the notice is given by A one week before the end of the lease, and is therefore void. In consequence, A would not be allowed to evict his tenant.

25 On unjust enrichment in Finnish law, see, e.g., Aurejärvi and Hemmo, *Velvoiteoikeuden oppikirja*, p. 226.

26 This means the parties cannot derogate from these rules by contract. None of the parties can ignore the statutory protection if the other does not agree. Consequently, the fact that B has left the premises cannot be considered as a renunciation of the protection, unless he was aware of the protective rules he benefited from. In that case, he could not ask for compensation under art. 1382 C.civ., because the statutory provisions exclude this article.

Furthermore, the reasons for giving the notice to quit must be set out,[27] and if it does not give proper reasons the notice is void and the lease is renewed. As it appears that A did not explain his reasons to B, we can assume that his notice is not only late but is also unexplained and consequently, as one might say, doubly void. Had A explained his reasons to B, it is unlikely these reasons would be valid, because A started the negotiations without a real intention to contract, which is contrary to the duty of good faith.[28]

Article L. 145–14 of the Commercial Code states that, if the notice is given by the landlord in accordance with the rules,[29] he must pay an indemnity to the tenant. This indemnity depends on the consequences of the notice. If the notice causes the loss of the tenant's customers,[30] the indemnity includes the value of the tenant's business as well as the costs of reinstallation.[31] If the tenant does not lose his customers by moving his business to another place,[32] on the other hand, these costs are the only component of the indemnity.

In conclusion, French law is not likely to be faced with situations such as the one described in this case, because the applicable rules are very protective of the tenant, therefore preventing the landlord from committing an abuse of his right to give notice to quit.

Germany

A is liable on the grounds of §§280(1), 311(2) No.1 BGB (*culpa in contrahendo*). Where a party enters into contractual negotiations without any intention to bargain at all but with the sole purpose of inducing a third party to reconsider its initial bargaining position, then that party is in breach of his duty to bargain in good faith. It is true that B could not rely

[27] The tenant, unlike the landlord, is not compelled to give any reason for the non-renewal of the lease.

[28] Article 1134 al. 3 C.civ.

[29] There are some exceptions, where the landlord is not compelled to compensate the tenant for his loss. According to art. L. 145–17 of the Commercial Code, no indemnity is to be paid if there is a 'serious and legitimate reason' not to pay it, such as a serious fault of the tenant, or if the object of the lease is to be destroyed.

[30] Customers are the core element of what French law calls *fonds de commerce*, which can be roughly translated by 'business', but has a more specific and technical meaning.

[31] Com 14 Dec. 1988, Bull Civ IV, no. 182.

[32] French legal opinion is divided about this distinction in the computation of the indemnity. Some consider that the value of the business is to be paid in all cases: see Ripert and Roblot, *Droit Commercial*, vol. 1, no. 461. Others support the distinction, e.g. Pédamon, *Droit Commercial: commerçants et fonds de commerce*, no. 346ff. This last opinion has been confirmed by the courts (see above n. 31).

on a bargain as A did not promise the renewal of the lease; but the law will not condone a party conducting sham negotiations: A's breach of duty is established by the mere fact of feigning serious negotiations.

A is liable in tort only if he wilfully caused damage to B in a manner contrary to public policy (§826 BGB). These conditions are met in the present case if A started or continued the mock negotiations being aware that B might suffer economic loss (for example, if A knew that B had the opportunity to lease other premises).

A is not liable in restitution as he is not enriched at B's expense.

A must compensate (both under the *culpa in contrahendo* claim and the tort claim) B's reliance interest: he must put B into the position B would have been in if he had known that the renewal of the lease would not come about. The plaintiff, however, will always rely on the *culpa in contrahendo* claim as its requirements are easier to establish.

There is, however, no causal relationship between A's initiating sham transactions and the fact that B did not enter into a contract with X, since B had rejected X's offer to lease his premises before entering into negotiations with A. Therefore A is only liable for B's economic loss resulting from the lease of a temporary warehouse (higher rent and loss of profits) if B, as long as he negotiated with A, could have prevented these losses by entering into the lease of a permanent warehouse with another party.

Greece

Before commencing the negotiations with B, A had decided not to lease the warehouse to B but rather to sell it to C. Thus, he entered into the negotiations with B with no intention of concluding a contract. Instead, negotiations with B were used solely as a means of exerting pressure on C, the prospective buyer. In doing so, A misled B into believing that they were negotiating in earnest for the conclusion of a lease contract. Article 197 GCC requires that the parties to negotiations adopt conduct which is dictated by good faith and business usage. It is a good faith obligation that the parties enter into negotiations, irrespective of their outcome, with the earnest intention of exploring the possibility of reaching an agreement with the other party.[33] Negotiations for their own sake or for a motive alien to reaching an agreement, such as to gain time or to exert pressure on a third party, and lacking an earnest

[33] See Kambitsis, *Precontractual Liability*, p. 91: 'It is a basic obligation of the parties that they enter into negotiations seriously contemplating the notion of concluding a contact.'

reason, are therefore contrary to good faith and provide to the injured party a right to compensation. A's behaviour is clearly contrary to good faith and, if the other conditions of article 197 GCC are met, he should compensate B for the damage which has occurred.

Article 198 GCC provides that a negotiating party who through his fault causes damage to the other party shall be liable to pay compensation. A Greek court would find that A's fault lies in his conduct, which is contrary to good faith and business usage. Under Greek law the sole remedy in precontractual liability is compensation in damages; there is no remedy which can compel a party to continue negotiations or to conclude the contract or to prevent the conclusion of another contract. Compensation comprises the reliance interest, in other words B must be compensated for the damage he suffered when relying on the fact that negotiations were conducted in earnest; the compensation must place him in the position he would have been in had the negotiations never taken place. Reliance interest includes negative and positive damage; that is, not only the expenses B incurred in conducting the negotiations, but also the loss of opportunity/profit.[34]

Thus, according to articles 197 and 198 GCC, in the case of negotiations which are contrary to good faith, B may recover damages from A for the costs he incurred in participating in the deceptive negotiations, the loss he incurs in having to pay a high rent due to the need to move at such short notice after the abrupt breaking-off of negotiations, and the loss incurred due to the inconvenience of the temporary warehouse and the disruption of the distribution agreements. B must prove that all these losses are causally linked to A's unlawful conduct. The loss with regard to the temporary warehouse will be calculated for the length of time B must reasonably be expected to make use of it. However, the lost opportunity for B presented by X's warehouse cannot be compensated because it occurred before the commencing of negotiations and therefore lacks a causal link with the negotiations conducted in bad faith.[35] B has no claim as regards the benefit which A obtained in selling

[34] For further discussion of the principles of liability under arts. 197 and 198 GCC, see the Greek report on case 1.

[35] Also, the conduct resulting in the damage must have occurred during the negotiation stage: AP 261/1996 EllD 1996, 1560; AP 1324/1994 EllD 1996, 639; AP 1303/1984 NoV 1985, 993; AP 756/1981 EEN 1982, 491; Court of Appeals of Peiraius 718/1996 EllD 1998, 152; Court of Appeals of Thessaloniki 3/1994 Arm 1994, 1132; Court of Appeals of Thessaloniki 65/1994 Arm 1994, 1134. The decision of Court of Appeals of Athens 689/1979 NoV 28, 289 states that a claim for compensation must be declined when

the warehouse to D for the higher price induced by the negotiations between A and B. Finally, on the basis of a claim for precontractual liability, B most probably has no claim to damages for immaterial loss.[36]

Ireland

No liability arises in this situation. There is no general duty to negotiate in good faith unless a special relationship exists between the parties. An ordinary contract negotiation between landlord and tenant does not constitute a special relationship.

An argument may be made that an action lies under the tort of deceit, but for a variety of reasons, the claim is likely unsustainable, and even should it succeed, the quantification of damages may not be significant.

The tort of deceit requires an untrue representation of fact, made fraudulently by the defendant with the intent to induce the plaintiff's reliance on the representation and the plaintiff actually having relied on the representation must have suffered material harm as a result.[37]

It is not clear from the facts whether A expressly represented to B that a new lease would in fact be concluded subject only to agreement on the quantum of rent or some other term. Moreover, it seems highly unlikely in the circumstances that A would make such a representation since the aim is to use the negotiations as a bargaining tool with C, but not to conclude the agreement with B. If A did in fact make such a representation, then an action in deceit may be possible.

If the court is satisfied that the representation has been made it must still be proven that it was fraudulently made. Barring an admission against interest by the defendant, this places a burden on the plaintiff, one that will be difficult to satisfy in an Irish court. The plaintiff may attempt to discharge the burden by adducing circumstantial evidence that the defendant never intended to complete the contract despite the

that damage occurs at a stage after the end of the negotiations between the parties for lack of causal link. The chronological delimitation of the stage of negotiations is of clear significance for issues of liability.

36 Court of Appeals of Thessaloniki 2325/1990 Arm 1991, 14. Damages for immaterial loss are not awarded on the basis of the provisions of the Civil Code on precontractual liability. For such damages to be awarded the law must specifically provide for it (art. 299 GCC), as for instance in the law of delict (art. 932 GCC). Exceptionally, Court of Appeals of Athens 11518/1986 EllD 1988, 917 has accepted, following part of the legal literature, that immaterial damage may be compensated in a claim for precontractual liability due to the affinity of precontractual and delictual liability. See G. Koumandos, in Georgiadis and Stathopoulos, *Commentary on the Greek Civil Code*, n. 84.

37 See generally, Quill, *Torts in Ireland*, pp. 271–80.

representation to the contrary. However, even if the circumstantial evidence is compelling, as a matter of practice Irish courts generally hesitate to make findings of fraud or deceit in commercial cases. A simple question to the defendant,[38] even where the defendant has made an admission against interest, when met with a positive response would likely be sufficient to damage the plaintiff's case irreparably. The aim would be for the defendant to establish that his intention to sell the building to C was not absolute. If there was any possibility, no matter how remote or unlikely, that A might enter into a new lease with B (say, for example, if negotiations with C were to break down) then the negotiations are not fraudulent.

In the unlikely event that the court finds that there is a fraudulent misrepresentation, the plaintiff must establish that he has relied upon the statement to his detriment. In *Northern Bank Finance Corp. v. Charlton*[39] the court ruled that a defendant will be liable for all the direct consequences of the deceit and not merely those consequences which would have been reasonably foreseeable. The only possible damage arising here would be the economic loss arising from relocating to temporary premises. The liability would only extend to the difference in rent between that which one might reasonably have been expected to pay for a long-term rental and the higher short-term rental actually being paid.[40] Thus, if the rent being paid for the temporary premises is €120,000 p.a., and it can be established that when negotiations commenced between A and B it would have been possible to secure premises for €110,000 p.a., then the loss would be €10,000 p.a. Even then, it would be calculated pro rata for the period of time necessary to negotiate a lease on permanent premises.

It is unlikely that the loss could be quantified for the inconvenience factor mentioned above since any relocation arising from the natural expiration of the original tenancy would in any event bring with it additional inconvenience. The inconvenience arises from the natural termination of the lease, and not from the deceit. Without more specific details nothing further can be said on this particular element of the claim.

It would be unlikely that there would be any benefit from pursuing such a problematic action for deceit in the circumstances.

[38] 'Were there any grounds under which you might not have completed the sale with C?'

[39] [1979] IR 149. [40] *Leyden v. Malone* (unreported, Supreme Court) 13 May 1968.

Italy

This case can be considered only from a theoretical point of view, because the Italian law governing leases (*locazione*) does not allow a lease of three years.[41] But, apart from that obstacle, A would be liable to pay damages to B under article 1337 of the Civil Code (precontractual liability).[42] A's behaviour leads to precontractual liability because the facts (including the length of the negotiations themselves) show that A withdraws from an advanced state of negotiations; and A's conduct with C seems to fall far below the standard of good faith required during negotiations for the renewal of the lease.

The negotiations carried on by A with B, without disclosing the simultaneous negotiations with C, was conduct capable of inducing reasonable reliance in B about the renewal of the lease. That was moreover shown by the fact that B has kept in use A's warehouse as his major distribution point. A seems not to have given any reasonable justification (*giusta causa*) of his conduct.

Furthermore, A's conduct seems to fall far below the standard of good faith required by way of fair dealing in commercial relations. By using the negotiations with B in order to gain a higher price from C, A seemed already to know how difficult and expensive it might be for a person (such as B) to find a warehouse similar to the one under the lease. But the failure to disclose to B the simultaneous offer to buy made by C, and the failure to communicate to B within a reasonable time his decision to sell to C, shows that A was playing an unfair game capable of giving rise to precontractual liability. The Italian Supreme Court has expressed different opinions as to the burden of proof of good faith. Many decisions hold that it is unnecessary for the claimant to prove that the other party had a specific intention to damage him. On the other hand, a recent dissenting decision places on the damaged party the burden of proving the bad faith of the withdrawal.[43]

B's damages (which for precontractual liability consist only in the negative interest) will correspond to his losses flowing from the new location of the warehouse at a higher cost (his higher rental costs); his removal costs and negotiation expenses; and possibly B's loss of profits

[41] Legge 9 Dec. 1998, n. 431 and Legge 27 July 1978, n. 392. The minimum time of 'four-plus-four years' (for dwellings) or 'six-plus-six years' (for commercial buildings) are implied terms of the contract.

[42] For further discussion, see the Italian report on case 1.

[43] Cass II, 1 Feb. 1995, n. 1163.

due to the different location (there is doubt about recoverability of pure economic loss).

Netherlands

Contract: B may try to establish that a contract was concluded because agreement was actually reached. Under Dutch law a contract, like any other juristic act, is concluded not only when both parties intended to be bound,[44] but also when one party intended to be bound and was justified in relying on the impression given by the other party, by words or conduct, that the other intended to be bound as well.[45] Hence B may try to establish that at a certain point there actually was an agreement on a new lease (consensus was reached with regard to price, duration and other main issues). Alternatively, he may try to establish that, although A never had a true intention to be bound, B was justified in relying on the impression given by A that he actually had: A's declarations or conduct made B believe that some sort of agreement (such as an agreement in principle) had actually been reached, and the parties only had to negotiate further on the details. In either case there would be a contract under Dutch law.

If the conclusion of a contract is established, in principle B will have a choice between a variety of remedies. The two most relevant seem to be an order of specific performance and damages. Specific performance will in principle be ordered unless performance has become impossible.[46] Since A has already sold and transferred the property in the warehouse to C, who has let it to D, performance has become virtually impossible. Although in theory A could buy the warehouse back and pay D to leave the premises, it will most likely be held that specific performance is impossible or contrary to good faith.[47] Damages, however, will, in principle, be a viable option. If an agreement is established, A will be in default from the day the new lease starts: 1 January 2000. No notice (*ingebrekestelling*) will be necessary since the date of the new lease will be regarded as 'fatal'.[48] A will be held liable for all loss caused by the non-performance,[49] which includes damages for delay.[50] This includes loss as a result of the high rent, the inconvenient place, the difficulties with his distribution arrangements, and other loss of profit that may

[44] Article 3:33 BW: declaration of intent. [45] Article 3:35 BW: reliance principle.
[46] Article 3:296 BW. [47] Articles 6:2 BW; 6:248 BW. [48] Articles 6:81 BW; 6:83 BW.
[49] Article 6:74 BW. [50] Article 6:85 BW.

have occurred as a result of the fact that B could not use A's warehouse as a major distribution point.

The application of the reliance principle is not always easy to predict, because everything depends on the circumstances of the case. In principle, whether or not there was justified reliance is a question of fact which is for the lower courts to decide. As a result, if the lower courts decide to award damages they are less likely to risk their judgment being reversed (*cassatie*) by the Hoge Raad if they simply hold that there was an agreement of some kind.

Breaking off negotiations: another possibility for B may be provided by the doctrine of 'breaking off negotiations'. On the basis of the *Plas/Valburg* doctrine,[51] B could attempt two lines of argument. First, he could argue that A broke off the negotiations at the moment when they had reached the 'third stage', that is, at the moment that A had induced B's justified reliance on the imminent conclusion of the contract. It is important to note that this reliance should be distinguished from the reliance mentioned above.[52] If A, by his declarations or other conduct, has made B believe that a contract *was* concluded (agreement was reached) there is a binding contract. However, if B did not think that a contract was actually concluded but believed (and it was reasonable for him to do so) that conclusion of a contract of the kind the parties were negotiating was imminent, A may be liable if he broke off at that stage. However, the remedies may be quite similar.[53] Both expectation damages and an order to continue negotiations (or even to conclude a contract) can, in principle, be obtained. Were the negotiations in the third stage? This depends on whether B thought that a contract would soon be concluded and whether he was justified in doing so as a result of A's conduct. On the facts as presented, this is certainly not excluded. If so, in principle, all his loss which is mentioned in the statement of facts may be recovered, as being part of his expectation interest. For reasons similar to those mentioned above (under *Contract*) a court order to continue negotiations or actually to conclude a contract is not likely to be given.

[51] Discussed in relation to case 1.

[52] Critical of this distinction: M.W. Hesselink, 'De schadevergoedingsplicht bij afgebroken onderhandelingen in het licht van het Europese privaatrecht', WPNR (1996), 6248 (pp. 879–83), 6249 (pp. 906–10).

[53] Indeed it has been argued that under Dutch law it is not necessary to conclude a contract to obtain contract remedies: Hesselink, above n. 52.

When the 'second stage' of negotiations is reached (the stage where expenses may be recovered) is not clear from case law (nor whether it still exists, after the Hoge Raad's recent *CBB/JPO* decision).[54] If this second stage was reached and if B had expenses, they may be recovered. However, the statement of facts does not say anything about the expenses of the negotiations.

As discussed in relation to case 1, it is uncertain whether at some stage in negotiations breaking-off leads to liability not only for the other party's expenses of negotiation (as in the 'second stage') but also for damages for his reliance interest, including lost opportunities to conclude contracts with third parties. In this case, B had an opportunity to conclude an equally interesting contract with X. In this case, before opening negotiations with A, B had explored the possibility of moving to another warehouse, and had found a possible alternative warehouse which he could have rented from X, but since it was at the same rent and would have involved expenses in moving to the new warehouse, he told X that he was not interested in concluding that lease. If X's warehouse was still available for some time during the negotiations between A and B, and if B can establish that he did not consider renting X's warehouse in justified reliance on the imminent conclusion of a contract with A (or if under Dutch law liability for the reliance interest arises at an earlier stage of negotiations), B may recover the difference in rent and the other damage he now suffers (inconvenient place, and possible difficulties with his distribution arrangements). However, the statement of facts does not say anything about such a possibility.

Tort (delict): A seems to have conducted negotiations with B for the sole purpose of obtaining a better price from C. One could argue that, under these circumstances, A has committed a tort (*onrechtmatige daad*) by conducting negotiations with B. If so, he may be liable for B's losses within the reliance interest (discussed above) even though there was no detrimental reliance on the imminent conclusion of the contract, the reason being A's positive (but not disclosed) intention not to conclude a contract with B.[55]

Restitution: before 1992 Dutch law did not contain a general action for unjust enrichment.[56] However, the new Code introduced such a general action, which is conceived as a claim in damages.[57] It could be argued that A is unjustifiably enriched at the expense of B since he

[54] Discussed in relation to case 1. [55] At 6:162 BW.
[56] See HR, 30 Jan. 1959, NJ 1959, 548 (*Quint/Te Poel*). [57] Article 6:212 BW.

unjustifiably makes a profit at his expense. Thus, one could argue that A should make restitution of the profit he made (the extra price he obtained when selling the warehouse to C) as a result of conducting negotiations with B. However, there has not yet been any case law on unjustified enrichment in precontractual situations. There is a famous old case which explicitly rejects restitution in a precontractual situation,[58] but that case was decided before the new Code and therefore before the general action for unjustified enrichment was introduced. Moreover, that case concerned a different kind of restitution: the restitution of expenses made in performance of the prospective contract.

Conduct of parallel negotiations: under Dutch law, a party, in principle, is not only free to conduct parallel negotiations, but is also free not spontaneously to inform the other party (of course, he is not free to lie when asked). For that reason, the mere fact that A started negotiations with C without telling B does not make him liable to B.[59]

Norway

Since A entered into negotiations with B without the intention of renewing the contract, he is liable to pay damages to B based on the reliance interest. B has no claim to the profit made by A as a result of his actions.

When a party enters into negotiations with an intention other than that of arriving at a contractual agreement, it is a prime example of behaviour giving grounds for liability. B can request that his financial situation be restored to what it would have been if A's unlawful act had not taken place. In the present case, this implies that he should be placed in the situation in which he would have been had he not entered into fruitless negotiations. In other words, he can claim damages based on the reliance interest.

The question is whether B, if he had immediately started to look for what warehouse facilities were generally available, rather than entering into negotiations, would have been in a better financial position than he is at the moment. He was offered by X the option of renting a warehouse at a cost identical to that which he was paying A. If B had

[58] See HR, 12 Mar. 1926, NJ 1926, 777 (*Goudse Bouwmeester*).

[59] Cf. M.W. Hesselink, 'Cour de Cass., 26.11.2003 – "*Perte de Chance*" (Expectation Interest) and Liability of a Third Person in Case of Breaking Off Negotiations' (2005) 13 ERPL 443.

realised that A had no intention of extending the tenancy, there is reason to believe that X's alternative would have been accepted. Although B's dealings with X predated the opening of negotiations with A, if it is likely that B declined the offer from X because A gave the impression of wanting to renew the contract, there would be a sufficient causal link between the additional costs incurred by B after the expiry date of the rental period and A's lack of good faith.

Only foreseeable losses are covered by the reliance interest, but B's losses, such as a temporary higher rent and difficulties with his distribution arrangements, appear to be within this foreseeable limit.

However, the present case gives rise to the question whether the right to damages should be *reduced* as a consequence of conditions falling within B's responsibility – the question of mitigation of harm. B has run a risk by continuing negotiations until the termination of the contract without securing an alternative location. Whether this risk is a ground for a reduction of damages has to be decided, among other things, on the basis of the likelihood of an extension of the contract with A. The legal basis for this evaluation is to be found in the Damages Act (1969), section 5–1, no. 1, first paragraph, and no. 2, which can be used both within and outside contract law.[60]

Portugal

A is liable in damages to B, at least for the reliance interest, under the doctrine of *culpa in contrahendo* (article 227 of the Código Civil). B has no other remedies.

It is clear under Portuguese law that conducting negotiations without any intent to conclude a contract but exclusively to obtain benefits from a third party is against the rules of good faith. Therefore, the liability of A is indisputable.

What can be disputed is the extent of the damages B may claim since, as discussed in relation to case 1, it might be arguable that liability under *culpa in contrahendo* covers the expectation interest. However, it is

[60] Damages Act, section 5–1, no. 1, first paragraph: 'If the offended party or the claimant has contributed to the situation through his own error, compensation can be reduced or lost, if this is reasonable, given his actions, their significance for the damage that occurred, the extent of the damage, and the general circumstances.' And no. 2: 'A contributing factor is also the situation which the offended party or the claimant, within reason, has failed to rectify, or to reduce the risk of damage resulting therefrom, or, according to his ability, failed to limit.'

certain that B cannot recover the profits A obtained in consequence of his wrongful act because the profit does not correspond to the loss suffered by B.

B has no other remedies in this case. A court order to continue negotiations, to conclude the contract or to perform the contract is not acceptable under the Portuguese legal system which considers this kind of behaviour as non-coercible. The only similar remedy granted by Portuguese law is *execução específica*, which is a constitutive action with the same legal effects as the contract not performed.[61] However, this action is only admissible when there is a promise of contract and in this case we have only negotiations between A and B.

Scotland

Had B not already quit the premises, then under Scots law he would have been entitled to remain as the tenant, so avoiding the need to bring a damages claim. In Scots law, a lease does not automatically terminate at the expiry date (known as the 'ish' or 'term date'). The lease will terminate at this date only if either party has served on the other a notice to quit, having given the correct minimum period of notice. If no 'notice to quit' is served, or if it is not served in accordance with the specified minimum period of notice, then the lease will continue in force by virtue of the doctrine of 'tacit relocation'. Where tacit relocation applies, a lease is automatically renewed by operation of law for a further period of time, the actual period being dependent upon the nature and length of the lease undertaken by the parties. In the instant case, the minimum period of notice is 40 days,[62] and as notice has not been given before this time the lease could have been tacitly renewed for a further period of one year.

However, as B has quit the premises, he has lost the right to have the lease extended under the doctrine of tacit relocation. B's clearest alternative remedy is now to claim damages for A's fraudulent misrepresentations concerning the possibility of a new lease being granted. It seems clear that B has been deceived by A's misrepresentation into believing that a new lease can be negotiated, whereas A had in fact no intention of granting a new lease. Such behaviour could found a claim for damages for fraudulent misrepresentation in the law of delict. Such a damages claim would be designed to put B into the position he would

[61] Article 830 CC. [62] Sheriff Courts (Scotland) Act 1907, ss. 35–8.

have been in had the delict not occurred (thus protecting his reliance interest). Had A not represented that he was willing to negotiate for a new lease, B would be likely to have begun searching for new premises much earlier. Damages might again therefore reflect the difference between the high rental which had to be paid and the lower rental that would have been available with longer notice, and any effect on distribution. The costs of removal would not be claimable, as these would have been incurred in any event.

A further alternative claim, for damages in respect of a breach of the lease by A, seems unlikely given that B has quit the premises without protest, thus preventing the operation of tacit relocation which would otherwise have provided A with a contractual right to remain in the premises and a right to damages if his lawful occupation was disturbed by the landlord.

Spain

The basic question is to know whether B was entitled to believe that A was willing to conclude the contract. It is clear that A conducted the negotiations with B in bad faith (this has to be proved by B, as good faith is presumed). It seems quite clear that, by negotiating until one week before the end of the lease, A made B believe that the contract would be renewed, leaving the duration and the exact term of the renewed lease to be settled. Even if the fixed-term contract ends after three years and there is no tacit reconduction,[63] B, negotiating with A in good faith, need not expect that his right to use the warehouse will end. In this situation there is a reasonable situation of confidence, especially as there was a contract of lease already in place and A allowed B to continue to develop his business. In such a relationship, good faith imposes on A the duty to tell B at least in good time that he has another partner, so that B would be aware of the insecurity of the renewal of the lease. A must pay the losses flowing from the short-term notification (higher rent and difficulties with distribution arrangements, loss because of inconvenient place) as they are clearly caused by his behaviour.[64] The removal costs are not payable, as they would still have arisen if A had behaved correctly and had given information to B on time. B is not entitled to recover A's profit on selling to C at a higher price, as there is

[63] Cf. arts. 1565 and 1566 CC.

[64] For loss, see Tribunal Superior de Justicia de Baleares, 10 Mar. 1997, AS 1997\1007, SEPTIMO.

no unjust enrichment (although C might possibly obtain a reduction in the price, given A's behaviour contrary to good faith).[65]

Sweden

A has not given a notice of termination in accordance with the legal requirements and therefore the rental agreement is automatically prolonged.[66]

If the rental agreement was concluded in writing and B has taken possession of the premises, B's right under the contract will be valid against C even if B's right is not reserved in the agreement between A and C.[67] Even if the rental agreement did not fulfil these requirements, A has an obligation to B to make a reservation for B's right in the agreement with C.[68] If A does not fulfil this duty and the rental agreement therefore is not binding against C, B is entitled to damages for all losses due to A's breach. The sole purpose of these rules is to protect the lessee. B's right to damages and the amount of damages are therefore not dependent upon whether or not he insisted on the existing statutory protection.

As the parties have a contract for lease of non-residential premises for three years, that is, for a specified period, and the contractually agreed time exceeds nine months, a notice of cancellation has to be given nine months before the expiry of the contract. If such a notice is not given, the agreement is automatically prolonged for an indefinite and undetermined time.[69] To be valid as such, the notice of cancellation, *inter alia*, has to be in writing and state the reason why the agreement is not prolonged.[70] Such cancellations are used also when the only purpose is to renegotiate the rent.

As A has not given B a valid notice of cancellation in due time, the agreement is prolonged to last for an indefinite and undetermined time. If the rental agreement is binding also between B and C, C has to give a notice of cancellation to B. If C does not have a valid ground for not prolonging the agreement,[71] B is entitled to damages amounting to one year's rent.[72] He is also entitled to compensation for other losses

[65] Articles 1101, 1258 CC.

[66] Doctrine: Grauers, *Fastighetsköp*; Grauers, *Nyttjanderätt*; Holmqvist, *Hyreslagen. En kommentar*; J. Ramberg, 'Pre-contractual Liability according to Swedish Law' in Hondius, *Precontractual Liability*.

[67] Jordabalken av den 17 Dec. 1970, Real Estate Code (JB), Ch. 7 §13. [68] Ch. 7 §11 JB.

[69] Ch. 12 §§3 and 4 JB. [70] Ch. 12 §§8 and 58 JB. [71] Cf. Ch. 12 §57 JB.

[72] Ch. 12 §58b JB.

resulting from the breach. However, he is not entitled to any claim in restitution to recover the profits A has made from the breach.

Had A given B a valid notice of cancellation within the stipulated time, the agreement would have expired before 1 January 2000. If A had a valid ground for not prolonging the agreement,[73] A is not liable to compensate B. Otherwise, B is entitled to damages.[74] The only rule that could be applicable in this case is that the lessor 'has a good reason for not continuing the lease'. However, a sale to another party does not in itself constitute such a 'good reason', nor that the buyer's purpose in buying is that he wishes to lease the premises to another party.

Switzerland

A is liable on the ground of *culpa in contrahendo*. He started negotiations with B in July 1999 without serious intention to conclude a contract with B but with the main purpose of inducing C to reconsider his bargaining position. There might have been some chance of a contract with B because it was not certain that C would buy the warehouse at a reasonable price. But A should have disclosed his essential reservation. A is to blame for wrong information. Therefore A has breached his duty to negotiate in good faith.[75]

There is no liability in tort alongside the liability for *culpa in contrahendo* (except for a party with the intention to cause harm).[76] According to the minority opinion of academic writers, *culpa in contrahendo* is liability in tort.[77] For the prevailing opinion, behaviour constituting *culpa in contrahendo* might automatically also be tortious behaviour,[78] but the tort liability has no importance.

A must compensate B in the measure of his negative interest, by putting B into the position he would have been in if he had never relied on A's serious intention to conclude a contract. The standard of comparison is a warehouse B would have rented between July and the end of 1999. The loss consists of the higher rent and of other loss because of increased difficulties in his distribution arrangements.

[73] Cf. Ch. 12 §57 JB. [74] Ch. 12 §§57 and 58b JB.

[75] BernerKommentar-Kramer, OR 22 n. 12, 14ff. [76] OR 41 II.

[77] See general discussion in the Swiss report on case 1.

[78] The duties of protection and loyalty might be understood as special norms for the protection of the other party (*Schutznormen*). Thus, their violation gives rise to liability on the ground of *culpa in contrahendo* and liability in tort. Compare Loser, *Vertrauenshaftung im Schweizerischen Schuldrecht*, n. 1101; BGE, 26 Sep. 2001 no. 4C.193/2000 E.4a.

Given the uncertainties, the judge may assess the damages according to OR 42 II.[79]

The rent of A's warehouse is not the standard of comparison. This would be compensation of the expectation interest, and B had no right to the renewal of the contract. Nor is the rent of X's warehouse the standard of comparison. At that time A was not in breach of his duties, and so there is no causal link.

Editors' comparative observations

With the possible exception of Ireland, all jurisdictions provide B with a remedy, although the legal basis of the remedy varies.

Protection for tenants: the particular context (the contract of lease) is significant in a number of jurisdictions in which the business tenant is protected by statute against the wrongful termination of the lease. In all four jurisdictions which adopt this approach on the facts of this case (England, France, Scotland and Sweden), there appears to be an underlying policy that the tenant should be entitled to a new lease (or a continuation of the old lease) unless the landlord has good reason to refuse it. This protects the business tenant who may have built up goodwill associated with the premises and who may suffer loss of custom and other losses or costs if he is required to move at the end of the contractual term, when there is no good reason for the landlord to require him to vacate the premises. The reasons which those jurisdictions regard as sufficient will vary (and may include, for example, the tenant's misconduct or the landlord's overriding need for the premises) but in none of these jurisdictions would A as landlord have a sufficient reason on the facts given: the sale of premises at a higher value to a third party is not a good reason. However, the strength of this rule varies between jurisdictions: in France, for example, the lease continues even where B has left the premises unless he has consciously renounced the statutory protection – and then he has no right to any compensatory damages. But in England, once B has delivered up the premises it is too late to insist on a new lease and he is left to his general claim to damages (described below).

[79] OR 42 II: 'If the exact amount of damages cannot be established, the judge shall assess them in his discretion, having regard to the ordinary course of events and the measures taken by the damaged party.'

Damages: all jurisdictions which give B a claim in damages against A take a broadly similar approach to the scope of recoverable damages. Although A has made a profit from his negotiations with B in having secured a better price in the sale to C, all jurisdictions (with the possible exception of the Netherlands, which is uncertain on this issue) reject B's claim to recover A's enrichment. The facts give rise only to claims for B's losses, and so generally there is no remedial disincentive to A's (mis)conduct in such a case beyond his liability to compensate B (although in English law exemplary (punative) damages might sometimes be available to deal with such a case).

The losses suffered by B on the facts given (his additional costs associated with renting a temporary warehouse at short notice and the business losses which might flow from this disturbance to his distribution arrangements) are all within the 'reliance' or 'negative' interest. Most jurisdictions would, in any event, limit the recoverable loss to the 'reliance' interest: an exception is the Netherlands, where expectation damages can be recovered either if there is held to be a concluded contract between A and B to grant the new lease, or if (without there yet being a concluded contract) the negotiations are held to have reached a sufficiently late stage when they are broken off (the third of the 'three stages' of negotiations).

The claim to 'reliance' damages is either based on the general principle of precontractual liability (*culpa in contrahendo*) or in tort. Jurisdictions characterise A's wrongdoing – the 'trigger' for his liability – in different ways, and this impacts upon the basis on which they award damages here. England and Scotland, not having a general principle of precontractual liability, have to find a specific wrong, and do so in A's false statement about his intention to conclude a contract (the tort of deceit). So would Ireland, but the Irish reporter doubts whether there is a fraudulent misrepresentation on the facts. And Germany will find (in addition to *culpa in contrahendo*) liability in tort arising from A's intention to cause economic loss to B; the Austrian reporter also contemplates a claim in tort, but prefers *culpa in contrahendo*. Jurisdictions which recognise a general principle of precontractual liability (either autonomous or within the law of tort)[80] find the trigger for A's liability in different facts: some focus on the fact that A created a misleading impression from the beginning about his seriousness in conducting the

[80] For the different approaches of the several jurisdictions to this issue, see the Editors' comparative observations on case 1.

negotiations (Austria, Finland, Germany, Greece, the Netherlands, Norway, Portugal, Switzerland) and/or conducted the negotiations with B in bad faith by failing to inform B about the parallel negotiations with C (Denmark, Italy), although reporters differ as to how firmly they separate these stages of the negotiations on these facts. Some, however, hold that it is A's breaking-off the negotiations at an advanced stage that gives rise to his precontractual liability (Italy, the Netherlands, Spain). Some jurisdictions find more than one basis (and more than one 'trigger') for A's liability: the most notable case is the Netherlands, which might find liability here in contract, tort, precontractual liability and restitution, in each case focusing on different aspects of A's conduct to identify the relevant 'trigger' for liability.

There are, however, some disagreements about the precise scope of damages recoverable within the 'reliance' interest here: in particular, some jurisdictions (in particular, Norway) would use the earlier loss of an alternative contract with X to quantify B's loss, although others (such as Germany, Greece and Switzerland) appear to take a stronger approach to causation and exclude the contract with X on the basis that, predating the negotiations between A and B, it cannot be linked causally to the later breakdown of those negotiations. Many reporters note that B's removal costs would not be recoverable, since they would have been incurred anyway (no causal link), and Finland and Norway consider the possibility of reducing B's damages by reference to his own fault in not taking steps to find alternative accommodation.

Amongst those jurisdictions that protect the tenant against wrongful termination within the rules particular to leases, England and Scotland solve this case by awarding damages in the law of tort, since the lease rules do not apply here (and, in any event, B could choose to claim damages in tort rather than the renewed lease if he so preferred). But France and Sweden solve the case exclusively by an application of the lease rules, so nothing can be learnt from this case about their approach to damages (in tort, or for precontractual liability/*culpa in contrahendo*) on such a set of facts.[81]

[81] In the original version of the questionnaire, cases 1 and 2 were reversed. But since some jurisdictions did not answer this case on the basis of precontracual liability at all, we decided to reverse the order for presentation in the published volume so that the reader can obtain a better general picture of the reporters' views about precontractual liability in reading what is now case 1 first. In reality, taking all the jurisdictions together, it is necessary to read the reporters' answers to both case 1 and case 2 to see the broad picture.

Case 3: Mistake about ownership of land to be sold

Case 3

B enters into negotiations with A about a piece of land that B wants to buy from A on which to build a house. A thinks he is the sole owner of the land. When the parties have reached agreement they make an appointment to sign the sale contract on 2 December. On 1 December A finds out that the land of which he thought he was the sole owner by inheritance from his father is in fact owned jointly by him together with his two sisters who do not agree to the sale of it. A therefore does not sign the sale contract. B has incurred expenses in negotiations (estate agents' fees, travel tickets to visit the land) and has had an architect make drawings for the house. What liability (in contract, tort, restitution, or any other form of liability), if any, does A have to B?

Discussions

Austria

Under Austrian law there would be no liability, either under the rules of contractual or delictual liability, or under those of *culpa in contrahendo*. The expenses B has incurred lie within his sphere of risk, since it was his decision to buy travel tickets and to consult an architect at a time when it was not clear that the contract would be concluded. A's conduct does not amount to chicanery,[1] nor have the rules of dealing in good faith been violated by A. In a decision of 1976 the OGH refused to grant recovery on the grounds of *culpa in contrahendo* in a decision concerning a similar factual situation.[2]

[1] See Austrian report on case 1. [2] OGH SZ 49/94.

The principles of precontractual liability have changed slightly since 1976, in that the negotiating party's obligation to give information about his change of mind has become more strictly interpreted by the OGH. But in this case it is clear that A's conduct was not such that B could realistically have formed the impression that the contract with A would certainly be concluded.

Denmark

Under Danish law a seller is strictly liable for lack of title to the object sold. If B can prove that there was an agreement between A and B,[3] the contract is valid and A is liable in damages for breach of contract. It is doubtful whether a court would award the architect's fee, since it may hold it unwise for a party to hire an architect before the sales contract is perfected.

England

B's only arguable remedy is in the tort of negligence, for the loss suffered by his reliance on A's careless statement about his ownership of the land.

It has been accepted by the courts that one party may owe another party a duty of care in relation to statements made during the negotiations: and this can apply to a vendor of land making statements to a possible purchaser.[4] A claim in tort should not hinge on whether the parties ultimately concluded a contract, although cases based on the duty to take care in making the statement during the negotiations have typically involved claims based on loss resulting from entering into the contract rather than, as here, losses suffered in anticipation of a contract which did not materialise.[5] If a court finds that A did owe B such a duty, we do not know whether A has breached the duty: it depends on whether he failed to take such care as a reasonable man would have done in his circumstances to discover that any statements he has made about his title to the property were false. We do not know whether it was reasonable for him (as a non-lawyer) to believe that he owned the property. If there is a duty that is broken, B could recover from A such of

[3] See Danish report on case 11.

[4] *Gran Gelato Ltd v. Richcliffe (Group) Ltd* [1992] Ch 560, 569.

[5] *Esso Petroleum Co Ltd v. Mardon* [1976] QB 801; *Gran Gelato Ltd v. Richcliffe Group Ltd* [1992] Ch 560. See, however, *Box v. Midland Bank Ltd* [1979] 2 Lloyd's Rep 391 (bank manager, making statement about likelihood of acceptance by head office of customer's application for a loan, owed duty to customer).

his losses, within the scope of the duty, as are of a kind that A could reasonably have foreseen he might suffer as a result of the breach of duty. These would include the expenses that B has incurred in the negotiations, but would only include the costs of employing the architect if on the facts A should have expected that B would employ an architect at this stage.

There are no other remedies available. There is no contract between A and B: even though they have reached agreement on the terms of the sale contract, they do not intend the contract to be binding until 2 December when they sign the sale contract; and anyway in English law a contract for the sale or other disposition of an interest in land must be in writing, signed by both parties.[6] There is no evidence of any separate, collateral contract which might already have been concluded about A's title to the property, and no such contract will be implied: under standard conveyancing practice in England a seller will during the course of the negotiations for the sale of land give information to the buyer about such things as his title to the land.[7] But these representations will not generally be contractually binding outside the sale contract itself. There is no basis for an estoppel, nor a claim in restitution (A has not been enriched). There can be no claim in the tort of deceit, since any misrepresentation A may have made about his rights in the property is made honestly: we know he did not discover the defect in title until 1 December.

This case again illustrates the general reluctance of English law to impose liability during the precontractual phase. In the case of a sale of real property it is well established that, up to the moment of the formal contract, either party is generally free to withdraw unless they have entered into some specific obligation to continue, such as a contract which grants an option for the other party to enter into the main contract of sale, and in effect binds the party granting the option not to withdraw the offer of a contract. And although a misrepresentation made during the negotiations can give rise to liability (in tort) for damages, the courts may be reluctant to impose such liability where the contract is not concluded since it would undermine the party's freedom to withdraw from the negotiations.

6 Law of Property (Miscellaneous Provisions) Act 1989, s. 2.

7 The facts of this case are in practice relatively unlikely to occur, at least if the parties are legally represented: it would be normal for the seller not only to make statements about his title during the negotiations, but also to supply evidence of it.

Finland

The sale of land is one of the most important types of contract in Finnish law that are subject to a specified form. This also gives an extraordinary character to precontractual liability questions. The Finnish Code of Real Estate (Maakaari 1995) has express provisions on the legal status of a pre-contract (*pactum de contrahendo*).[8] Applying these provisions to this case seems to impose precontractual liability on A, on the basis of some kind of *culpa in contrahendo*. This liability would cover B's negotiation expenses and reliance-based investment costs (such as the architect's drawings).

The Code of Real Estate (Ch. 2), section 1, sets the requirements for form and contents of a contract of sale of land. The contract has to be concluded in a written form, signed by the seller and the buyer, and confirmed by a notary public. The minimum contents of the contract (matters that have to be agreed upon in the written document) are also prescribed. Infringement of these requirements renders the contract invalid.

Section 7 prescribes that the same form and other requirements that are applicable to a contract for the sale of land apply also to a pre-contract for the conclusion of that contract. Also the minimum content of a pre-contract is defined, including the date on which the final contract is to be concluded and any conditions to be fulfilled. The price can be left to be agreed upon later, according to the standards specified in the pre-contract. The period of validity of the pre-contract, if not otherwise agreed, is five years. The provision also states the main entitlement of a party arising out of the pre-contract: the right to demand the conclusion of the final contract on the terms agreed upon, or a claim for damage caused by the breach of the pre-contract. The compensation covers the positive (expectation) interest.

Section 8 contains a definition of damages arising out of withdrawal from making the final agreement that are recoverable on the basis of a pre-contract not drafted in the prescribed form. The compensation covers reasonable expenses from advertising, visiting the property and other necessary measures pertaining to the conclusion of the contract. If any deposit has been paid the receiving party has to refund the part of it exceeding the amount of these expenses. So, in line with compensation rules applicable to cases of invalidity of contract, the negative

[8] On the pre-contract, especially concerning a contract for the sale of land, in Finnish law, see Hemmo, *Sopimusoikeus* I, p. 161.

(reliance) interest standard is applied if the pre-contract is not drafted in the proper form.

Application to this case of these provisions of the Code of Real Estate will render A liable to B for his reliance interest covering all the losses mentioned in the facts: the estate agent's fees, travel tickets and the architect's fees. A's liability does not depend on proof of his fault. The only means by which A might avoid liability would be by *force majeure*, though this question remains uncertain. What is clear is that the reasons indicated in the facts for A's not signing the final contract are not sufficient to relieve him of liability.

It is clear that B has no right to require A to sign the final contract. In that sense, the pre-contract can be said to be invalid as not drafted in the proper form. It cannot lead to the intended result, because otherwise the form requirement for a contract for the sale of land would lose its meaning.

France

The facts described in this case are rarely likely to occur in France. The question is, however, of theoretical interest.

It appears likely that no contract has been concluded: therefore loss may be compensated only in tort.[9] Article 1382 or 1383 of the Civil Code will be applicable here if the three conditions of fault, harm and causation are established.[10]

A's behaviour does not constitute intentional fault (article 1382) since he was not aware at the time of the negotiations that the land was co-owned by him and his sisters. However, he may have committed a fault of imprudence or negligence (article 1383) because he would probably have discovered the real situation regarding the property if he had looked for proof of his title to it: registration at the land registry or a deed dividing up the estate between the heirs (an *acte de partage*), which is necessary for the contract to be binding on third parties. However, the Cour de cassation has not taken this view: in a case in 1976, it was decided that no fault was committed by the seller unless his *intentional* fault could be shown.[11]

If A is at fault, the estate agent's fees, travel expenses and architect's fees would be compensated. Moreover, despite theoretical objections,

[9] J. Schmidt-Szalewski, French report, in *Formation of Contracts and Precontractual Liability*, p. 95.

[10] See the French report on case 1.

[11] Civ 1, 12 Apr. 1976, Bull Civ I, no. 122.

a French judge is likely to award damages for the loss of opportunity to buy the house.[12] The amount of damages awarded will depend on the estimated chance of the sale being concluded had the fault not been committed. *Dommage moral* may also be admitted here, but since the assessment of damages is global, the question is not of practical interest.

B may also claim the enforcement of the contract. Because the contract of sale is, under French law, consensual,[13] the sale contract can be formed before the contract is officially signed. The sale of someone else's property is not valid[14] but A is not trying to sell someone else's land. He is partly the owner of the land. In such cases courts have decided that the contract is valid as between the seller and buyer but of no effect[15] against co-owners[16] (in our case, A's sisters). The solution to this contradiction lies in the termination of the joint ownership. A and his sisters are not obliged to remain joint owners.[17] If he agrees on this point with his sisters, A can have the entire property rights in the land. Being then the sole owner, he is bound by the contract made with B, although no signature has been given; the contract is then fully valid[18] and can be officially signed. In case of conflict B can ask the judge to recognise that the contract is fully valid and have this judicial decision recorded in the land registry. He will then have proof of ownership that is binding on third parties.[19] If A's sisters (or, in case of conflict, the judge) are not willing to give the land to A, the contract between A and B can have no effect.[20] It is retroactively considered as null.[21] A is then liable in tort as set out above.

[12] See the French report on case 1.

[13] See case 11. The analysis here assumes that neither party raises an argument about the lack of evidence to prove the contract.

[14] C.civ., art. 1599.

[15] French writers and courts refer to a theory of '*opposabilité*'. On this theory see Ghestin, Billiau and Jamin, *Les effets du contrat*, p. 417ff.; J. Duclos, *L'opposabilité, essai d'une théorie générale*.

[16] Civ 1, 9 May 1978, JCP 1979, II, 19257, note Dagot; Civ 1, 15 June 1994, RTDCiv 1995, 411, obs Patarin.

[17] See C.civ., art. 815.

[18] Bergel, Bruschi and Cimamonti, *Les biens*, no. 491; M. Donnier, J-Cl-Civil, art. 815 to 815–18, fasc. 30, 1992, no. 76ff.

[19] Under the theory of *opposabilité* mentioned above n. 15.

[20] See, e.g., Civ 1, 12 Apr. 1976, Bull Civ I, no. 122.

[21] Bergel, Bruschi and Cimamonti, *Les biens*, no. 491; M. Donnier, J-Cl-Civil, art. 815 to 815–18, fasc. 30, 1992, no. 76ff.

Germany

A is not liable. He has no liability on the ground of §§280(1), 311(2) No. 1 BGB (*culpa in contrahendo*). In the first place, his termination of the negotiations is supported by a good reason. Secondly, the projected contract requires a specific form. According to §311b(1) sent. 1 BGB a contract whereby one party binds himself to transfer a piece of land requires notarial authentication. A legal transaction which is not in the form prescribed by law is void.[22] In the case of a proposed sale of an interest in real property, therefore, a party breaking off negotiations may be held liable in reliance damages on the ground of *culpa in contrahendo* only in very exceptional circumstances. Otherwise the policy behind the formal requirement, which is meant to protect the parties from hasty and inconsiderate decisions in a matter where a valuable object is at stake, would be frustrated. The party breaking off negotiations would indirectly be put under pressure to enter into the contract if he or she had to compensate the other party's reliance interest. For this reason it is standard practice[23] of the Bundesgerichtshof that an action based on *culpa in contrahendo* only lies if the conduct of the party ultimately refusing to sign the notarial instrument was particularly repugnant so that the result would be 'absolutely unbearable'. The court's reasoning rests upon 'abuse of the law'. In a recent judgment it was made clear that in the case of a contract subject to formal requirements, the conduct of the party breaking off negotiations amounts to abuse of law only if he has deliberately failed in his duty to bargain in good faith.[24] A, however, did not make B believe by design that the proposed contract would be concluded in due form.

A is not liable in tort, either, since he did not wilfully cause damage to B.[25]

Greece

The general obligation under articles 197 and 198 GCC to negotiate in good faith imposes a number of particular obligations on the parties, such as obligations to conduct negotiations in earnest, to protect the

[22] §125 BGB and see case 11.

[23] BGH, decision of 16 Feb. 1954, NJW 1954, 1241; BGH, decision of 3 Dec. 1958, NJW 1959, 626; BGH, decision of 27 Oct. 1967, NJW 1968, 39; BGH, decision of 12 June 1975, NJW 1975, 1774; BGH, decision of 7 Feb. 1980, NJW 1980, 1683; BGH, decision of 19 Nov. 1982, NJW 1983, 563; BGH, decision of 29 Mar. 1996, NJW 1996, 1884.

[24] BGH, decision of 29 Mar. 1996, NJW 1996, 1884.

[25] §826 BGB.

interests of the other party and to provide the other party with the necessary information.[26] It is a basic assumption that a party (the seller) negotiating the sale of an object actually owns this object, unless otherwise agreed upon by the parties. A seller who is negotiating the sale of an object which he does not own, if he does not inform the prospective buyer of this fact, is liable to the prospective buyer for negotiations in bad faith.[27] B justifiably assumes that the land under negotiation belongs to A and the latter is negligent in believing that he is the sole owner. A's behaviour is at fault and, on the basis of the above provisions, gives rise to a claim for compensation due to precontractual liability.[28]

Proprietary rights in immovable property are registered in public records which are accessible to all those who may be interested. On account of this, the question may arise whether the buyer is guilty of contributory negligence[29] in not verifying the property status of the land by checking the public registries. The case law on precontractual liability answers this question in the negative; the buyer is not negligent in failing to verify the property status of the land of his own volition. In other words, the negotiating party is not contributorily negligent in not checking the reliability of the statements made by the other party when one would expect that it is reasonable to rely on them.[30]

[26] *Areios Pagos* has determined the obligation of the negotiating parties to provide information as follows: 'Each party is under a duty to communicate to the other party real facts which are significant for that party to form a decision and that party could not ascertain the information from elsewhere. In any case that obligation does not extend to issues which the negotiating party should and could have ascertained by personal diligent research', AP 344/1982 NoV 1982, 1465–6. The seller must take the initiative to inform, and does not require specific questions by the buyer (Court of Appeals of Athens 11518/1986 EllD 1988, 916). For the obligation to inform see also Deligiannis, *Legal Consultations 1960–1966*, p. 72.

[27] Kambitsis, *Precontractual Liability*, p. 92.

[28] Court of Appeals of Athens 11518/1986 EllD 1988, 916 concerned a similar case: the seller, who had become owner of an immovable by inheritance, did not communicate to the prospective buyer in the stage of negotiations that the validity of the will, which transferred ownership to him, was disputed in court and he was therefore considered to be precontractually liable towards the buyer.

[29] Article 300 GCC.

[30] In one case the property to be sold was burdened with a mortgage and the court rejected the seller's claim that the buyer's fault in not checking the public registers before the purchase limited the former's precontractual liability as it amounted to contributory negligence; the court held that the buyer could rely on the seller's statements without being contributorily negligent, thus the seller was solely precontractually liable (Court of Appeals of Athens 2065/1971 Arm 1971, 1071). However, a later case of the Court of Appeal on facts similar to those here stated vaguely that liability under the provision of

In precontractual liability, the Greek courts compensate the reliance interest of the aggrieved party by way of full compensation for the damage causally linked to the conduct of negotiating in bad faith. Therefore A must compensate B for the estate agent's fees and the travel tickets to visit the land. However, B will most probably not be compensated for the expenses incurred in commissioning an architect to make drawings for the house which B intended to build on the land. This expense is not directly connected with the negotiations: in other words, an inner link (adequate causal connection) is missing between the conduct of the negotiations and the loss suffered as regards the architect's expenses.[31]

Ireland

B has no claim against A with respect to the failure to complete the contract.

A contract for the sale of land, or any interest therein, is unenforceable unless it is evidenced in writing and signed by the person against whom it is being pleaded. This is one of the few areas in the Irish legal system which requires formalities and comes from Statute of Frauds (Ireland) 1695, section 2. The Statute has undergone little modification since its enactment. It is silent as to what constitutes sufficient writing, but the courts have developed a sophisticated body of case law in this whole area. The requirement of written evidence is known as a memorandum.[32] The memorandum must contain four crucial elements:[33] the parties,[34] the property,[35] the price[36] and any specific

precontractual liability may be limited on the basis of contributory negligence (Court of Appeals of Athens 11518/1986 EllD 1988, 918).

[31] See, e.g., a case where the seller of land during the negotiations for the sale neglected the productivity of olive trees in view of the impending sale; the loss he suffered after the prospective buyer abandoned negotiations was not compensated. The court found the prospective buyer to be precontractually liable but denied the seller's claim for compensation for the reduced productivity of the olive trees because of a lack of any causal link between the loss and the buyer's fault (First Instance Court of Arta 79/1995 Arm 1996, 1319). On causal link see also Court of Appeals of Thessaloniki 221/1980 Arm 1980, 792. For a strict (and rather mistaken) interpretation of the requirement of causal link see AP 1565/2000 *Chronika Idiotikou Dikaiou* 2001, 220 (with note by Iatrou).

[32] There must be an intention to create authentic documents (*McQuaid v. Lynam* [1965] IR 564); although there is no requirement to establish an intent to create a memorandum: *Murphy v. Harrington* [1927] IR 339.

[33] It must, of course, accurately reflect the agreement: *Crane v. Naughten* [1912] 2 IR 318.

[34] *Law v. Roberts* [1964] IR 292.

[35] *Waldron v. Jacob* (1870) IR 5 Eq 131.

[36] Or some method of ascertaining the price: *Smith v. Jones* [1952] 2 All ER 907.

particulars.[37] The memorandum need not be a single document but can consist of a number of documents joined together to satisfy the four crucial elements,[38] for example a cheque has been held to be sufficient written evidence as to the price, when combined with other documentation.[39] Similarly, the definition of a signature has been given a broad interpretation by the courts.[40] Initials, rubber stamps, even headed paper have been held to constitute a signature within the meaning of the Statute.[41]

If there is no memorandum sufficient to comply with the Statute of Frauds then the contract between A and B is unenforceable. Accordingly, B has no claim under the purported contract for expenses already incurred. Neither does B have any claim in tort, since A's belief does not fall within the action for deceit.[42]

Italy

A's conduct during negotiations seems to lead to precontractual liability under article 1338 of the Civil Code which concerns the negotiating party's duty to communicate to the other party any grounds for the invalidity of the contract that he knows or ought to have known.

Current academic writing distinguishes article 1338 from article 1337, as applying in cases where the parties have concluded an invalid contract or entered into negotiations as a result of the deliberate or negligent failure of one party to provide information. In a recent decision, the Italian Supreme Court appears to have agreed with this, saying that 'article 1338 differs from 1337 because it provides protection for the party's reliance on the validity of contract, and not for reliance on contract conclusion. Recoverable damages will cover all consequences for having relied on the validity of the contract, and not on its conclusion.'[43]

The invalidity (*invalidità*) of a contract has then been interpreted as any situation that prevents the contract from having any effect.[44] Italian case law has mainly referred to article 1338 in cases concerning

[37] *Law v. Roberts*, above n. 34.
[38] *Tradax (Ireland) v. Irish Grain Board* [1984] IR 1.
[39] *Doherty v. Gallagher* (unreported, High Court), 1975.
[40] The key issue is that the signature attests to authenticity: *McQuaid v. Lynam* [1965] IR 564.
[41] *Casey v. Intercontinental Bank* [1979] IR 340.
[42] See the Irish report on case 1.
[43] Cass 26 May 1992, n. 6294.
[44] Sacco and De Nova, *Il contratto*, I, 592; F. Benatti, 'Culpa in contrahendo', CI, 187, 293.

the public administration in order to clarify its duty of information:[45] despite the important role played in the evolution of precontractual liability,[46] few decisions have expressly cited this article.[47]

Moreover, there have been questions about what is meant by saying that a party 'ought to have known' about grounds of invalidity. The solution seems to rely on the duty of reasonable diligence under the Codice Civile. Article 1338 certainly has to be read in the light of articles 1578, paragraph 2, and 1821, paragraph 1, about the duty to inform and knowledge of circumstances.[48]

Italian academic writers and case law are divided over the interpretation of article 1338. The Italian Supreme Court generally excludes precontractual liability when the grounds of invalidity consist in a breach of imperative laws.[49] Italian case law usually cites the principle *nemo tenetur ignorare legem* as a case of negligence of the negotiating parties. Mistake of law (*errore di diritto*) is set against the duty of diligence provided by article 1338. Both parties are then seen to be equally negligent, and in consequence this has often been held to exclude parties' justified reliance on the conclusion of the contract.[50]

On the other hand, the prevalent view of writers[51] and some dissenting case law[52] consider that mistake of law, as mistake of fact, can be excusable. The increasing complexity of written law and the absence of any specific distinction in the Codice Civile does indeed support a more flexible position, which would lead to a duty on one party to inform the other party that has relied without fault (*senza sua colpa*) on the validity of the contract.[53] Real importance can then be given to the evaluation of the actual degree of care shown by the party suffering the loss in relation to the nature of the law of which he was ignorant.

According to this interpretation of article 1338, in the present case A's ignorance (and consequently his silence about the grounds that would have made the contract void) does not seem to correspond to the

[45] TRIB-T. Torino, 30 Oct. 1990; App. Torino, 9 Dec. 1992.

[46] Musy, *Il dovere d'informazione*; S. Rodotà, 'Il tempo delle clausole generali' RCDP 1987, 709.

[47] Cass 26 May 1992, n. 6294; TRIB-T. Roma, 14 May 1980; Cass 17 Nov. 1978 in GC 1979, I, 33; TRIB-T. Verona, 31 May 1980.

[48] F. Benatti, 'Culpa in contrahendo', CI, 187.

[49] Cass, S.U., 4 Oct. 1974, n. 2603.

[50] Cass, sez. I, 6 Mar. 1998; Cass, sez. III, 26 June 1998, n. 6337.

[51] Sacco, *Il contratto*, p. 924; Visintini, *La reticenza nella formazione dei contratti*, p. 272; Benatti, *La responsabilità precontrattuale*, p. 304.

[52] TRIB-T. Roma, 14 May 1980; TRIB-T. Pescara, 4 Mar. 1978.

[53] Sconamiglio, *Dei contratti in generale*, p. 223.

minimal degree of care required in a sale of land.[54] Since it appears that the land belongs at the same time to A and his sisters because of inheritance, A is liable for negligence, having been ignorant of the law. Italian hereditary succession law[55] generally follows the principle that the heir must expressly accept the deceased's estate,[56] a rule which applies also when law directly attributes (by intestate succession) part of the estate to an heir.[57] A seems not to have any defence against the rule *ignorantia legis not excusat*.

As in any case of precontractual liability B is entitled to ask in theory for damages corresponding to the *interesse negativo*. But in this case the amount could be reduced considering B's negligence in relation to the *ignorantia legis*.

Netherlands

Under Dutch law A is probably liable to compensate the expenses incurred by B in the negotiations (estate agents' fees, travel tickets to visit the land) and for having had an architect make drawings for the house. Since *Plas/Valburg*, the Hoge Raad has held that even before the 'third stage' in negotiations is reached a party may be liable to compensate expenses ('second stage').[58] It is very likely that in this case A will be liable (on the basis of tort or precontractual good faith) to compensate B's expenses in the negotiations, especially since in all likelihood a Dutch court would hold that the 'third stage' in negotiations was reached: the day before the parties are supposed to formally sign the contract A withdraws from the deal. At that moment B was justified in expecting that a contract would actually be concluded on 2 December. For that reason, B may even be able to recover the lost profit, if there was any (for example, if the agreed price was below the market price), as part of the expectation interest. Whether the cost of having an architect make drawings for a house to be built on the land is recoverable depends on whether this loss can be said to have been caused by A's reprehensible conduct. Dutch law contains a very open and normative causation test: the question is

[54] Cass, sez. II, 25 Nov. 1997, n. 11811. [55] Libro II c.c.

[56] See arts. 459, 490, 512, 649 c.c. For case law see in particular Cass, sez. II, 23 Aug. 1999, n. 8832; Cass, sez. II, 4 May 1999, n. 4414; App. Roma, 14 Jan. 1999; Cass, sez. II, 7 Feb. 1998, n. 1301; TRIB-T.Napoli, 4 Apr. 1996.

[57] See art. 586 c.c. and art. 42 Cost.

[58] On the question whether the 'second stage' still exists, after the recent *CBB/JPO* case, see the Dutch report on case 1.

whether the damage can reasonably be attributed to the event.[59] Even though, for the application of this test, foreseeability is not decisive, it would certainly help B's case if he can establish that A knew that he had hired an architect. Especially in the latter case, it seems likely that the damage will be fully attributed to A's acting contrary to good faith which may be found in either his carelessly taking up and conducting negotiations without having full authority to sell the property, or his breaking them off at such a late stage.

Norway

The case raises the question of two different kinds of liability: compensatory damages in contract and precontractual liability.

First, there is the question whether A can be held responsible for events resulting from a breach of contract. This presupposes that a contract has been entered into. Property purchases in Norway are subject to the Sale of Property Act of 3 July 1992, no. 93. According to section 1-3, there are no specific formality requirements for the sale of property.[60] Therefore, if it can be proved that the parties have agreed to the sale of property, or that a reasonable person in the position of the parties would have considered an agreement to have been formed, there is a binding agreement. The fact that the parties have agreed to sign a written purchase contract at a later date does not appear to be sufficient to change this situation. The situation would be different, on the other hand, if there was not yet agreement with respect to certain points prior to the signing of the contract document.

If one assumes that a contract has been entered into, A will be liable for losses suffered by B if the agreement cannot be fulfilled. Under the Sale of Property Act, section 4-17, the rules governing the right to damages due to defects in title apply. Expenses incurred by B with respect to the negotiations and for the preparation of architectural drawings could be claimed under a provision in the Sale of Property Act, section 4-14. According to this, liability would exist unless the failure is due to an impediment beyond his control. Admittedly, this concerns regular expenses which would also have been incurred if the contract

[59] Article 6:98 BW.

[60] 'Agreement with respect to the sale of real property can be made in writing or orally. If the agreement has been made orally, it should be put into writing when this is requested by one of the parties.'

had been concluded. It could therefore be argued that the breach of contract has not caused the expenses. However, the expenses might be claimed within the expectation interest. The aim is to cover the loss of income, which is assumed to be at least equal to the expenses incurred.[61]

If there is no binding contract, the question arises as to whether A has incurred precontractual liability. The answer is not clear. According to the presiding judge in the *Kina Hansen* case[62] liability requires that 'blameworthy behaviour during contract negotiations should have been displayed – such as acting in bad faith, or in a dishonest or misleading manner'. According to this statement, one must at least blame A for having been mistaken about his rights to the property. Whether negligence alone is sufficient to incur liability or whether a more serious level of blame is required remains, however, an open question. As it concerns a legal mistake (regarding property rights), this might be a reason for placing a somewhat more stringent duty on A. However, in the *Kina Hansen* case the judge said:[63] 'I can hardly see that the bank can be considered as acting in bad faith or improperly towards Hansen.' The concepts 'bad faith' and 'improperly' clearly indicate that the person causing damage must be seriously blameworthy before he incurs precontractual liability.

Portugal

A is liable to B according to the rules of precontractual liability (article 227 of the Civil Code), and could be required to pay all the expenses which B incurred, including the architect's fees. Although his fault was not intentional, he was negligent in conducting negotiations without knowing the ownership of the land. Precontractual liability can also arise in cases of negligence, so the liability of A is clear. B could also however be at fault, in which case his contributory negligence could exclude or reduce his damages.

There is no other liability in this case, unless the agreement to sell the property were established in a written document. An agreement to sell land must be in writing under article 410, no. 2 of the Civil Code. In that case, A's liability could also be based on contract.

[61] Probably the burden of proof on this issue is on the defendant: it is not up to the plaintiff to show that his venture would have been profitable but up to the defendant to show that it would have been unprofitable.

[62] Rt 1998, 761, 772. [63] See p. 772.

Scotland

The facts of this case are unlikely to arise in Scotland. Negotiations for the sale of land in Scotland are usually conducted through legal agents (solicitors) or, less often, through non-legally qualified estate agents. The facts of this case disclose that B used an estate agent. It is standard practice for such an agent to undertake at an early stage of the negotiations a title examination to ascertain that the seller has full and proper title to the subjects of sale. Such an examination, properly carried out, would have prevented the losses from arising. However, the consequences of such an examination being negligently carried out are considered below.

Whilst, as discussed below, it might be possible for B to compel A to convey his one-third share of the land to B, B is unlikely to want ownership of a mere one-third of the property. A damages claim is more likely to be sought. Such a claim would proceed on the basis that A had misrepresented that he was the sole owner of the property, and that, as a result of such misrepresentation, B has incurred wasted expenditure in negotiating. Although A has made no explicit statement that he is the sole owner of the property, it may be argued that A, by entering into negotiations for the sale of the land without disclosing that he is not the sole owner, has impliedly held out that he is the sole owner. It seems from the facts that in this case A did not intend to mislead B, and thus any misrepresentation is likely to be considered negligent. It could be argued that before entering into negotiations to sell property it is incumbent upon A to check that he is indeed the owner: failure to do so may be argued to be negligent. Such a claim, for pure economic loss for negligent misrepresentation, lies in delict. The case law indicates that the circumstances where such a claim is permitted in law are limited. However, where the claim has been made directly by one negotiating party to another, the relationship is likely to be close, or proximate, enough to found liability.[64] B would need to show that A's implied representation as to title had been reasonably relied upon by B. Evidently, if B's estate agent had disclosed that A did not have full title to the land, then reasonable reliance on such representation could not continue after the time of

[64] *Hedley Byrne & Co Ltd v. Heller & Partners Ltd* [1964] AC 465, approved in Scotland in *John Kenway Ltd v. Orcantic Ltd* 1979 SC 355 and *Eastern Marine Services (and Supplies) Ltd v. Dickson Motors Ltd* 1981 SC 355.

such disclosure and any losses incurred thereafter would not be recoverable against A. The possible liability of B's estate agent is discussed below.

Any claim for pure economic loss against A will lie in delict, the object of damages being to put B into the position he would have been in had the misrepresentation not been made. Here, had B not been misled into believing that A had good title to the whole of the land, B would not have begun negotiations with A and would have avoided all the losses which followed from such negotiations, including the costs of visiting the land, and costs related to the instruction of the estate agent and the architect.

As stated above, it is likely that an estate agent or solicitor would have carried out a title search on behalf of B to ascertain whether A was the owner of the property being offered for sale. If B's estate agent has failed to undertake such a title search, or had undertaken it negligently, then a claim would lie in contract for damages against him. It is likely that this would be the preferred course of action here, as it is easier to establish a remedy for pure economic loss (which is the nature of the claim here) in contract against the estate agent than in delict against the seller. Crucially, however, no damages would lie against the estate agent for any losses incurred by B in the period of time before which the estate agent would be expected to have carried out the title search, as such losses would have been incurred anyway. From the list of suggested losses given in the facts, the only items which are likely to have been incurred prior to the time when a title examination would have occurred would be travel costs incurred in visiting the land. Such losses might still lie against A in delict, however.

An alternative, but clearly less desirable, claim would be for B to seek to compel A to convey his one-third share of the land to B. It would not be possible under Scots law to compel A's two sisters to convey the remainder of the land to B. In terms of the Requirements of Writing (Scotland) Act 1995,[65] contracts for the sale of land require to be constituted in writing. The facts disclose that no written contract was concluded between the parties, and thus *prima facie* there is no enforceable contract of sale. However, there is a notable exception to the requirement of writing rule[66] under which, even if the requirements of writing have not been met, a party seeking to deny the enforceability of the contract may be personally barred from

[65] Section 1(2)(a)(i). [66] Section 1(3), (5).

doing so. The requirements for pleading this form of personal bar are: (i) one of the parties to the contract must have acted or refrained from acting in reliance on the contract (party B); (ii) the action or inaction must have been known to the other party (party A); (iii) party B must be able to demonstrate that he has been affected to a material extent by his (in)action in reliance on the contract; and (iv) party B must show that he will be affected to a material extent if party A is permitted to withdraw. On the given facts, it may be problematic for B to meet all of these requirements. In particular, the requirement that B show that his action in commissioning the architect and the estate agent were undertaken in reliance on the agreement may be hard to meet, as the commissioning of an estate agent and architect will normally occur before an agreement (albeit informally made) was reached.

It is conceivable that A might be sued by B in delict for some of the losses, but that B might choose to sue his estate agent for the remainder of the losses (for instance, those occurring after the point at which a proper examination of title ought to have occurred). Double recovery for the same losses would not be permitted. If B seeks to compel A to transfer his one-third share to B, it is conceivable that a damages claim might still lie for certain losses on the basis, for instance, that the architect's plans constitute wasted expenditure, B being unable to build on a plot of which he is only a co-owner.

Spain

In Spanish law, contracts for the sale of land are valid by mere consent, if the objects of the contract (the land and the price) are determined and the cause (*causa*) is licit.[67] The requirement of a formal document[68] is only a formality *ad probationem* and not *ad solemnitatem*,[69] and so a party is entitled to demand that the public document be made if he can prove the existence of the agreement.[70] Furthermore, based on just a promise to buy or to sell, the contracting parties can ask for performance of the contract.[71]

If B can prove that he and A reached an agreement, he is entitled to demand the performance of the contract. According to Spanish case law, the fact that A was not sole owner by inheritance is not an excusable error,[72] as he must have known about the existence of

[67] Articles 1261, 1278, 1445ff. CC. [68] Articles 1280, 1 CC ('public document').
[69] STS, 16 May 1996, no. 401/1996, RJ 1996\4348.
[70] Article 1279 CC. [71] Article 1451 CC. [72] Article 1266 CC.

his two sisters and the rights in inherited property are normal and generally known (or at least, using due diligence, easily knowable) circumstances.[73] For this reason there is a valid contract between A and B. Based on A's incapacity to fulfil the contract, B can rescind the contract and claim damages.[74] He is to be put in the same situation as he would have been had the contract never been concluded (*interés negativo*), which means that all expenses of negotiation and the architect's expenses can be recovered, as all of those costs were foreseeable.[75] A might exclude the costs of the architect from his liability, if he manages to prove that he did not, and could not, know of B's intention to build on the land, although this seems very unlikely.

Even if he cannot prove that there has been a contract of sale, but proves an agreement to conclude a future contract, B can claim the same damages.[76]

Sweden

A is not bound by his oral promise to sell and is not liable to compensate B. A binding agreement for sale of real estate requires the agreement to be in writing. The written agreement should contain, *inter alia*, the price and a declaration by the seller that the ownership of the property is transferred to the buyer. Neither party is bound by an agreement for sale of real estate until it fulfils the form requirements.[77] A is not liable in contract since the form requirements are not met.[78]

There may be a ground for liability due to *culpa in contrahendo*, even if the main rule is that a promise to buy or sell real estate could not lead to liability.[79] The actions or omissions that could amount to a case of *culpa in contrahendo* in real estate transactions have to be serious. A person inheriting real estate has to apply for the registration of the title to the property within a certain time.[80] The certificate of registration of title should contain the name of the owner(s) of the property. If no

[73] STS, 27 May 1992, RJ 1982\2605. [74] Article 1124 CC. [75] Article 1107 CC.

[76] Article 1451, 1124 CC; STS, 29 July 1996, no. 680/1996, RJ 1996\6408, TERCERO and CUARTO.

[77] Real Estate Code (Jordabalken av den 17 Dec. 1970 (JB)), Ch. 4 §1.

[78] Grauers, *Fastighetsköp*; Hellner, *Kommersiell avtalsrätt*; J. Kleineman, 'Avtalsrättsliga formföreskrifter och allmänna skadeståndsrättsliga ansvarsprinciper', JT 1993–94, 433; J. Kleineman, 'Skadeståndsgrundande uppträdande vid avtalsförhandlingar', JT 1991–92, 125; Ramberg and Ramberg, *Allmän avtalsrätt*.

[79] NJA 1973.175. [80] Ch. 20 §1 JB.

application has yet been made when A initiated the negotiations and A then thought that he was the sole owner, this could probably not amount to such negligence that could result in liability. If A was considered to have acted negligently and therefore B would be entitled to damages, there is no support for any liability for damages outside the reliance interest. B would therefore be entitled to damages for expenses incurred during the negotiations. However, it is highly uncertain whether any damages would be awarded for A's costs of the architect, as these would probably be regarded as too remote according to the principles of adequate causality.

Switzerland

A is not liable on the basis of a contract. Although it is possible to conclude an oral contract, if the parties reserve a certain form it means that the form is constitutive and the parties intend not to be bound before such form requirements are met.[81] The other party would have to prove the opposite: that the written form serves only to make the proof of the contract easier. This is not possible in the case of a land sale because a formal public deed is required by law.[82]

If a party refuses to fulfil the form requirements he will be treated as having broken off serious negotiations. But in Swiss law, breaking off serious negotiations makes a party liable only in exceptional situations.[83] A's fault is not simply in breaking off the negotiations, but because he has negotiated without reservation although he knew or ought to have known that there was an obstacle to the sale of the land.[84] In a similar case the Federal Court of Switzerland held a bank liable on the ground of *culpa in contrahendo* because its local branch had negotiated a loan contract which required the approval of the head office; the

[81] OR 16 I. [82] OR 216 II.

[83] See Loser, *Vertrauenshaftung im Schweizerischen Schuldrecht*, nn. 635ff., 642. Especially for contracts with form requirements: Gonzenbach, *Culpa in contrahendo im schweizerischen Vertragsrecht*, p. 98ff.; Schmid, *Die öffentliche Beurkundung von Schuldverträgen*, n. 834; Hartmann, 'Der Abbruch von Vertragsverhandlungen als Enttäuschung von Vertrauen-Bemerkungen im Anschluss an das Bundesgerichtsurteil 4C.152/2001 vom 29. Oktober 2001', ZBJV 2003, 536; BGE, 29 Oct. 2001 Nr. 4C.152/2001 (in SemJud 2002 I, 164ff.), E. 3b. *Contra* Schwenzer, *Schweizerisches Obligationenrecht Allgemeiner Teil*, N 31.43; Widmer, *Umfang des Schadenersatzes bei nicht zur Perfektion gelangten Verträgen*, p. 181ff. See general discussion in the Swiss report on case 4.

[84] See P. Tercier, 'La *culpa in contrahendo* en droit suisse' in *Premières journées juridiques yougoslavo-suisse* (Zürich, 1984), pp. 225, 229: 'Ce n'est pas tant le refus de conclure qui est en soi critiquable . . . , c'est le fait de tromper la confiance d'autrui par une attitude qui suscite l'espoir infondé que le contrat sera certainement conclu.'

bank managers could have realised with due diligence that the approval was necessary and they could have informed the other party about that requirement. The Federal Court did not exclude the liability just because the bank managers did not act wilfully: even negligent acts can lead to liability.[85] Thus, the duty to negotiate in good faith not only prohibits negotiating without the serious intention to conclude a contract; it also obligates the party to disclose objective and subjective obstacles to the contract that the party is able to recognise.[86] This rule applies also for contracts that require a special form.[87]

A is therefore to blame that he negligently did not inform himself about the ownership of the land and that he did not disclose this information to B. A has violated his duties to negotiate in good faith.

A has to compensate B for the negative interest (i.e. reliance interest), to put B into the position in which he would have been if he had known of the obstacle to the contract and had not relied on the contract. A must compensate B for the expenses incurred in the negotiations.

The architect's expenses are also part of the negative interest because B would not have had the architect make the drawings if he knew about the obstacle. But these expenses can be compensated only if they were incurred *in bona fide*.[88] The expenses must have been reasonable in the circumstances. But the contract was not certain, and B should have realised that A might change his mind. Therefore, A must compensate for the architect's expenses as far as they served for the decision to conclude the contract; they are expenses incurred in the negotiations. But the judge can reduce the compensation according to OR 44[89] if the expenses were incurred to allow B to use the land. The expenses of performance of the contract, or the use of the object of the purchase, incurred before the contract is concluded, are generally at the party's own risk.[90]

[85] BGE 105 II 75, 80ff.; BGE, 3 Feb. 2003 no. 4C320/2002 E. 3.3.

[86] Cf. BGE, 5 Mar. 2001 no. 4C.356/2000 E. 5b; BGE, 8 June 1998 (in SemJud 1999, 113ff.), E. 3.

[87] Cf. BernerKommentar-Kramer, OR 22 n. 16; BGE, 30 Jan. 2001 no. 4C.253/2000 E. 3.

[88] There is an express limitation of compensation for expenses *in bona fide* in the provisions on betrothal according to ZGB 92 (cf. case 5). This rule should be applied if a contract has not yet been concluded.

[89] OR 44 I: 'The judge may reduce or completely deny any liability for damages if the damaged party consented to the act causing the damage, or if circumstances for which he is responsible have caused or aggravated the damage, or have otherwise adversely affected the position of the person liable.'

[90] BernerKommentar-Becker, OR 26 n. 6ff.; ZürcherKommentar-Oser/Schönenberger, OR 39 n. 10ff.

Editors' comparative observations

This case shows a significant difference of approach across the jurisdictions under consideration. Some provide B with a remedy, others do not; and even within jurisdictions that agree on there being (or not being) a remedy, the reasons are not unanimous. In assessing the reports on this case it is important to consider the influence of the context – given that the jurisdictions take into account in differing ways, and to different degrees, the fact that a contract for the sale of land might for reasons of policy have special requirements of form – and to disentangle this from the more general question of on what basis, if at all, A should be liable.

Context: negotiations for the sale of land: a key feature of the case is that it involves negotiations for a contract for the sale of land. Jurisdictions differ on whether there are requirements of form for the validity of such a contract. Those for which there is no such requirement rest their analysis on a similar basis to that in other cases of failed negotiations (see, for example, the discussion of this in the Dutch, French and Norwegian reports). However, amongst those which have a formal requirement some hold that it has an impact on the negotiation stage to the point of overriding the normal rules of precontractual liability/*culpa in contrahendo*, whilst for others the formality requirement only excludes the enquiry based on possible contractual liability (given the absence of a formal contract here) but leaves open the possibility of invoking the non-contractual bases of liability. The clearest example of the formal requirements overriding the normal rules is Finland, where the Code of Real Estate becomes the basis on which the analysis of A's (precontractual) liability is assessed, thereby removing the usual enquiry as to whether A was at fault, or in bad faith, in order to impose liability on him for having withdrawn from the negotiations. But in the application of their rules governing the negotiation stage some other jurisdictions (Germany, Norway and Sweden) also take into account the fact that the negotiations are for a contract which has a requirement of form for its validity, on the ground that to impose non-contractual liability might undermine the policy of the statute which set the formal requirement; and England, which does not in any case have a general principle of precontractual liability, is even more cautious in assessing the precontractual stage where the negotiations are for a contract for the sale of land.

Precontractual liability/culpa in contrahendo: amongst the jurisdictions which have a general principle of precontractual liability (whether autonomous or within the law of tort) the reports on this case point to differences in the application of the principle. Some jurisdictions focus on the absence of A's intention to inflict damage on B – the fact that A is, at most, negligent – as a distinguishing factor from other cases in this study, and therefore cannot find him liable: for example, Austria and Germany, which have a claim in tort (in addition to *culpa in contrahendo*) where the defendant intentionally inflicts economic harm, emphasise the absence of intention here as one of the reasons for there being no liability for *culpa in contrahendo* either. Norway also appears to be reluctant to impose liability for simple negligence. However, other jurisdictions find A liable on the basis of his negligence (France (although there is some conflict there with case law, which appears not to hold negligence to be sufficient in a case such as this), Greece, Italy, the Netherlands, Portugal and Switzerland). The trigger for liability is sometimes said to be A's failure to inform B of the problem over his title to the property (Greece, Italy and Switzerland) or A's failure to refrain from the negotiations until he has ensured that he has authority to sell the property (the Netherlands). Since A did not in fact know of the problem over his title, the breach of the duty to inform is itself based on negligence – his failure to inform himself, and thereby to have information which he should have passed to B (see, for example, the Greek report).[91] The Netherlands and Switzerland both find the trigger (also) in the fact that without good reason A broke off the negotiations at such a late stage, although in the case of Switzerland it is not just the breaking-off that counts, but doing so in circumstances where he was negligent about his title. The approach of the Netherlands, by contrast, is to regard simply the breaking-off as the key, because it happens in the 'third stage'[92] of negotiations, when even the expectation measure of damages might be awarded for precontractual liability.

'Negligence': fundamental to the analysis of this case, therefore, in many jurisdictions, is the fact that A did not intend to harm B, but may have been negligent. The actual results of the case can vary depending on how the different jurisdictions view the place of negligence in their rules of precontractual liability, as well as how they interpret A's

[91] For a broader enquiry into the duty to inform, see the companion volume in this series, Sefton-Green, *Mistake, Fraud and Duties to Inform in European Contract Law*.

[92] For the three 'stages' of negotiations, see the Dutch report on case 1.

conduct on these facts. It is important not to place too much importance on differences which flow from this last point; again, it is often the particular context of a contract for the sale of land and where the problem is one of A's title to the land, that directs reporters to decide whether or not A was negligent on the facts, often dependent on the local practice as to when and how title to land is normally investigated.

The fact that A may be (at most) negligent is also significant for England, Ireland and Scotland. In these jurisdictions there is no general principle of precontractual liability; and on these facts there is no contractual claim because of the failure of the required form for contracts for the sale of land.[93] So the enquiry has to move to the law of tort, in order to find a particular basis of claim, which again[94] focuses on whether A has made a misrepresentation. Since A was not fraudulent, the tort of deceit cannot be invoked: at most, this is a case of negligent misrepresentation. The trigger for liability (if any) is therefore the false statement that A might be held impliedly to have made about his title (these jurisdictions do not even begin to contemplate that A's silence could have been sufficient – that he might have been under a duty to inform about his title). But a misrepresentation is not a sufficient trigger on its own; it has to be a misrepresentation recognised as actionable within the rules of a particular tort (here, the tort of negligence). The reporters have interestingly differing views about how easily the tort of negligence can be invoked in such a case (Ireland is silent about it, apparently assuming that negligence could not be sufficient here).

Contract: jurisdictions which have formal requirements for the validity of this type of contract cannot rest A's liability on contract. However, those jurisdictions which do not have such a requirement are sometimes able to hold that, since the agreement was here concluded – and as long as the signing of the written document on 2 December should not be interpreted as undermining the parties' agreement on the terms of the contract – the contract can itself be a source of liability. This is an approach taken by Denmark, France, Norway and Spain, although each of these then has to sort out how their law of contract

[93] There are, however, differences here: in Ireland the statutory requirement is evidential, whereas in England and Scotland it goes to the validity of the contract. But in none of the three jurisdictions is the formality satisfied, nor can any exception to the formality requirement be invoked, on the facts, although the Scots reporters consider whether A might be barred from denying the enforceability of the contract.

[94] See also, e.g., the English, Irish and Scots reports on cases 1 and 2.

and/or law of property will solve the difficulty arising from the co-ownership of the land with A's sisters, particularly if (as in the case of France) the remedy under the contract might be the specific enforcement of the contract itself, rather than just damages.

Scope of recoverable loss: in those jurisdictions which would impose liability on A there is some disagreement about the scope of recoverable loss. Apart from those cases where the claim can be founded on contract, and the Netherlands (where the claim might be for the breaking-off of negotiations in the third stage, giving rise to expectation damages), the remedy is reliance damages, which is generally agreed to include B's expenses in the negotiations. Some jurisdictions, however, are doubtful about the architect's fees, either because they are the kind of precontractual expenses which should be at the spending party's own risk (Denmark and Switzerland; an explanation also given by the Austrian reporter who, however, would not find liability in any event), or there might be difficulties in showing a sufficient causal link (or they might be too remote) (England, Greece, Spain and Sweden). On the other hand, Italy and Portugal contemplate the possibility that B's damages might be reduced to take account of the fact that he was also at fault.

Case 4: An architect's preparatory work for a contract which does not materialise; parallel negotiations

Case 4

A is a manufacturer of computer hardware who wants a new building designed in which to house his operations for the production of hardware. In February he approaches B, a specialist architect, and B begins negotiations with a view to his being engaged as architect for the project. B's policy is not to undertake more than one commission at a time, nor is he prepared to compete in competitive tendering; and in the hope of concluding a contract with A for his services he does preparatory work on plans and specifications for the building he would propose to design, without yet concluding any contract with A. A had also, at the same time, begun negotiations with C, another architect, but did not tell B. A year later, A contracts with C to be the architect on the project, having negotiated with C as well as with B throughout the period. B discovers this only after C's contract with A is concluded. No contract is at any stage concluded between A and B, but B complains that he would never have undertaken the preparatory work (because of his policy on tendering and single-project work) had he known of the negotiations with C. What liability (in contract, tort, restitution, or any other form of liability), if any, does A have to B arising out of A's parallel negotiations? Would it make any difference if A knew of B's policy on tendering and single-project work?

Discussions

Austria

In the case where he does not know of B's policy, it is doubtful whether A would be liable on any basis. In the alternative situation, however, where A knew of B's policy on tendering and single-project work, an Austrian judge may impose liability for reliance interest damages on A under *culpa in contrahendo* principles.

In the first situation, it is once more difficult to confirm or deny whether a duty to inform the negotiating partner has been violated. On the basis of the Austrian court practice no general statement can be made, especially with regard to the hypothetical facts of standard cases: it is the 'usual practice of dealing in good faith' that has to be observed. It depends on the facts what 'dealing in good faith' might be under the circumstances.

There is a precontractual duty to keep the other party informed of certain matters in a business relationship, whenever it is clear for the negotiating partner that the other party must have a significant interest in having knowledge of them. This may be assumed with some certainty in the alternative case (where A knows of B's policy). In that case, B must be put into the position he would be in had he not legitimately relied on A's seriousness in negotiating for the contract. The (reliance interest) damages will include the costs incurred by B as well as (if it can be shown that B would have concluded another advantageous contract), the (hypothetical) profit he would have made under it.

Denmark

In a case reported in *Ugeskrift for Retsvæsen*[1] a building enterprise was approached by the landowners to make a sketch of how to build a house, which it made without concluding a contract with the owners. The court held that the building enterprise had not done more work on the sketch and the tender than those who prepare tenders usually do and that as a professional party it should have made it clear to the other party if it expected to be paid for what it was doing. Consequently, the owners were not liable. Here also the defendant had conducted parallel negotiations with another contractor who was awarded the job.

However, in another case where a contractor had not made his bid conditional on payment of any costs for making a tender for a building, but where the owners had only shown the contractor a very loose sketch of the building they wanted to have built, and where the contractor therefore had prepared drawings supporting his tender which went beyond the normal preparation of a tender, the court awarded the

[1] 1996–309.

contractor compensation for his efforts.[2] Whether the compensation was awarded on a contract, tort or *quantum meruit* basis is difficult to say.

In the present case a Danish court would probably award the architect compensation if the owner knew or ought to have known that the architect had to do more than was normal for preparing a tender. It probably makes no difference that A had conducted parallel negotiations with C and that A knew of B's policy on tendering and single-project work.

England

A has no liability to B arising out of the parallel negotiations. The mere fact that A conducts parallel negotiations with another party does not give rise to any claim: A has not undertaken expressly to B not to enter into such other negotiations,[3] and there is no basis in the facts for any such implied undertaking. There is therefore no claim for breach of contract based on the parallel negotiations. Nor is there any tort (since there is no express or implied statement on which a claim in deceit, for example, could be based) or estoppel. There is no claim in restitution. Where a party has undertaken preparatory work at the other party's request, which confers a benefit on the other party, it is sometimes possible to base a claim for restitution on the value of the benefit which has been conferred;[4] but here there is no such claim because it is not clear that B's work goes beyond the normal preparatory work which would be at his own risk; he was not asked by A to undertake it; and it does not appear that the result of the work confers any valuable benefit on A. The fact that the work was done in the context of parallel negotiations is not relevant: the only question for a restitution claim is whether A has been unjustly enriched at B's expense; and here he has not.

Even if A had known of B's policy on tendering and single-project work, B would have no claim on the facts stated. He has no duty to negotiate in good faith, and so the mere fact that he is negotiating with C knowing that B would not be prepared to continue his own negotiations does not give rise to any liability unless he has made a contractually binding promise to B that he will not negotiate with third parties

[2] See *Ugeskrift for Retsvæsen* 1981-572.

[3] Which could be enforceable if the undertaking had contractual force: see the English report on case 6.

[4] See the English report on case 8.

or made any misrepresentation about the negotiations which could found a claim in tort. On the facts, he has not made any such promise or misrepresentation, although the court would look closely at the communications between the parties to check that nothing said by A to B could be taken by B as making such a promise or misrepresentation. If that could be found, B would have a claim to damages to compensate for his losses as a result of continuing with the negotiations: in both contract and tort the recoverable losses would extend to the costs incurred in preparing the plans, and (if he can prove it) the lost profit on other projects which he has not been able to work on by being kept in the fruitless negotiations with A.[5]

This case again shows the reluctance of English law to impose liability in the precontractual phase, in the absence of a promise or misrepresentation. If one party wishes to restrict the other's freedom to negotiate with third parties, or to be free to withdraw without compensating him for the costs he incurred during the negotiations, he should stipulate for it expressly. The fact that one party *knows* of the other's reluctance to negotiate in such circumstances is not of itself a ground for remedy: there is no general duty of good faith in the negotiations. It is for the party who wishes to impose restrictions on the negotiations to do so; but a court will scrutinise the facts carefully to ensure that there is no promise or misrepresentation which might give rise to a remedy.

Finland

This case is an application of the principle of freedom of negotiations in Finnish law. A incurs no liability for breaking off negotiations with B in order to sign a contract with C. This is clearly the result if A did not know about B's policy on tendering and single-project work and A did not delay in informing B after concluding the contract with C, or when this outcome had become likely enough.

Under some circumstances, however, B would perhaps be entitled to compensation. This is the case at least if A caused additional costs to B by being slow in informing him about his withdrawal from negotiations. The liability could be established also if A did know about B's

[5] For the recovery of damages in tort for lost potential profits, see *East v. Maurer* [1991] 1 WLR 461. The same basic measure would be recoverable in contract on the facts assumed here, since there is no promise by A that he would contract with B; only that he would not contract with a third party. So the profits of the contract which B hoped to conclude with A are not themselves within the scope of the claim.

policy on tendering and single-project work. The latter case, however, may not in itself be a sufficient basis to make an exception from the principle of freedom of negotiations. It may only give an indication of A's wrongful (disloyal) behaviour in relation to his counterpart, depending on the circumstances. Fault, or wrongfulness, is a general precondition of liability in damages. In these cases the basis of liability can be found in a kind of *culpa in contrahendo* thinking.

The compensation to be paid to B, if any, would cover his negative interest consisting of expenses of his preparatory work for the contract. If A has been at fault only in delaying in giving information to B about the contract to be concluded with C, A's liability would be restricted to the additional costs thus caused to B.

France

A enters into negotiations with B and with C for the same contract. B complains that he would not have undertaken the preparatory work had he known of the negotiations with C. In the absence of a contract to negotiate, the harm is only compensable in tort. A's liability is subject to proof of three conditions: fault, harm and a causal relation between the fault and the harm.[6]

The fact that A did not tell B that he was undertaking parallel negotiations is not a fault per se. A professional, whatever his field of specialty, must know that the free market in which he exercises his activity involves economic competition. Courts do not hesitate on this question: case law has firmly established that no liability arises out of parallel negotiations.[7] But although negotiating with more than one person at a time for only one contract is not a fault per se, the judge may find additional arguments to highlight a fault: for example, when a negotiator has no intention, from the very beginning, of concluding the contract but lets the negotiations go on.[8] Analysis of recent cases shows that fault is often found when a negotiator created an appearance which led to the belief that the contract was being

[6] See the French report on case 1.

[7] Com 15 Dec. 1992, RJDA 1993, no. 296, RTDCiv 1993, 577, obs J. Mestre; Bordeaux, 11 June 1997, JCP éd. E, 1997, I, 617, no. 1, obs P. Mousseron; Com 26 Nov. 2003, JCP éd. E, 2004, 738, note Ph. Stoffel-Munck, RTDCiv 2004, 80, obs J. Mestre and B. Fages.

[8] See Civ 2, 4 June 1997, RTDCiv 1997, 92, obs J. Mestre. In this case, a negotiator let the negotiations go on with a first candidate while engaging in negotiations at a much lower price with another, showing that he had no intention of concluding the contract with the first party.

concluded.[9] Whether this belief is considered reasonable[10] depends on the importance of the preparatory work, the length of the negotiations (one year here!) and whether the parties are professionals or non-professionals. If A was not aware of B's policy on tendering and single-project work, and in the absence of other elements, A has not committed a fault. The solution might be different had A known about B's policy. Though A's knowledge of B's single-project policy does not by itself require him to tell B about parallel negotiations, it makes A aware of the importance of the negotiations for B. The judge might therefore find that A is responsible for not having sufficiently stressed the fact that the contract was not yet concluded.

B suffered economic loss since he has carried out useless and costly preparatory work. He also lost the opportunity to conclude another contract. Indeed, he would probably have negotiated with somebody else if A had told him that he was undertaking parallel negotiations. To evaluate this harm the judge will have to determine the value of the lost opportunity according to the probability of another contract being concluded.[11]

The harm is directly caused by A's fault (if his fault is established), because it is shown that B would not have done the preparatory work had he known about the parallel negotiations.

Germany

A is not liable. There being no contract, contractual liability is out of the question. A is not liable on the ground of §§280(1), 311(2) No. 1 BGB (*culpa in contrahendo*) for breaking off contractual negotiations. A neither started the bargaining process without any intention at all to bring about a contract, nor did he terminate the negotiations without any good reason. It is immaterial whether A was familiar with B's business policy. The special relationship (*Sonderrechtsverhältnis*) created between negotiating parties by virtue of the law (*gesetzliches Schuldverhältnis*) does

[9] Paris, 4 Apr. 1997, Juris-data no. 021076; Paris, 10 Mar. 2000, JCP 2001, II, 10470; Com 11 July 2000, Juridisque Lamy, arrêt no. 1548, PA 2001, no. 57, p. 19, note Y. Dagorne-Labbé, CCC 2000, no. 174, obs L. Leveneur. See also Com 10 Oct. 2000, Juridisque Lamy, arrêt no. 1668; Com 20 June 2000, Juridisque Lamy, arrêt no. 1337.

[10] The Cour de cassation recently decided that the negotiator who 'bets' on the success of the negotiations has to bear the entire weight of the expenses incurred in the belief of the contract being concluded. In a way, one could say that the negotiator commits a fault when anticipating the success of the negotiations. See Com 12 Jan. 1999, Juridisque Lamy, arrêt no. 97.

[11] Com 7 Apr. 1998, D.1999, Jur 514, note P. Chauvel.

not entail a duty to refrain from or to inform the other party about parallel negotiations, as such a duty would be at variance with the basic mechanisms of a market economy. It is a firmly established practice of the courts that, as long as a party bargains in good faith, expenses of the other party incurred in the anticipation of a future contract - however substantial - are basically at this party's own risk, even though his negotiating partner knew of or caused the outlay. Otherwise *culpa in contrahendo* would undermine the principle of freedom of contract.

A is not liable in tort. He neither violated one of the special legal interests protected by §823(1) BGB, nor did he wilfully cause damage to B (cf. §826 BGB).

B has no claim in restitution since B's preparatory works did not enrich A at the expense of B.

Greece

Whether the party who is conducting parallel negotiations with more than one party must inform each party of such parallel negotiations is not entirely clear under Greek law, much depending on the specific circumstances and the agreement between the parties. Case law has scarcely dealt with the issue, whereas the majority of the legal literature appears to be rather opposed to such an obligation.[12] In all probability a Greek court would not consider A's conduct to be contrary to good faith. As everybody is free to participate in economic life by conducting negotiations which may or may not lead to a contract, it is equally plausible that one may be conducting negotiations with more than one person at the same time (or in sequence) without there being a need to inform the other party about it. This conduct, in essence, lies at the heart of the freedom to negotiate. This is so unless for some specific reason one must expect that in the particular circumstances it is consistent with good faith for the party conducting parallel negotiations to inform the other party about them, particularly when the parallel negotiations can be to the detriment of the other party. A, not being aware of B's business policy by conducting parallel negotiations, does not in all probability exhibit any conduct which is contrary to good faith.

[12] See *inter alios* M. Karasis, in Georgiadis and Stathopoulos, *Commentary on the Greek Civil Code*, vol. I, p. 320, who seems not to extend the obligation to inform as far as this. On the other hand, Filios, *Law of Obligations, General Part*, p. 379 seems to favour an obligation to inform in these circumstances.

However, if A had been aware of B's policy to undertake single projects and not to participate in competitive tendering, then he should have informed B that he was conducting parallel negotiations. The duty to inform in this particular case arises from the good faith requirement that the parties, once they initiate negotiations, protect the other party's interests at least so far as to avoid causing damage to that party. In such a case, by failing to inform the other party despite knowing B's commitment to single projects, A's conduct would probably be contrary to the requirement under article 197 GCC to negotiate in good faith.

The party who is precontractually liable according to articles 197 and 198 GCC must compensate the other party for the damage comprising the reliance interest. This is the unanimous approach in Greek case law. Article 198 GCC calls for full compensation of positive and negative loss. Yet, even if A were to be held precontractually liable, the preparatory work B conducts in the hope of concluding the contract with A would not be compensated, because in spite of B's particular negotiation policy the negotiations with A did not require (nor did A himself ask or encourage) B to initiate the work. In other words, there is an insufficient causal (internal) link between the damage and A's injurious conduct. B cannot aggravate the damage by extremely meticulous conduct or by adopting exceptionally cautious steps. The necessary costs required by the nature of the negotiations can be compensated, but not extravagant expenses. Thus, other normal expenses that B incurred in conducting the negotiations and preparatory work will be compensated. The loss of opportunity will also be compensated, if B can prove that during negotiations he turned down other offers of work. Non-material damage[13] can only be compensated when B bases his claim on delict.[14]

[13] Damages for non-material loss are not awarded on the basis of the provisions of the Civil Code on precontractual liability. For such damages to be awarded the law must specifically provide for it (art. 299 GCC), as e.g. in the law of delict (art. 932 GCC). Exceptionally, the Court of Appeals of Athens 11518/1986 EllD 1988, 917 has accepted, following one view in the legal literature, that damages for non-material loss may be awarded in a claim for precontractual liability due to the affinity of precontractual and delictual liability: see G. Koumandos, in Georgiadis and Stathopoulos, *Commentary on the Greek Civil Code*, n. 84.

[14] Articles 914, 932 GCC. Case law and academic writing generally accept the concurrency of the provisions on delict; but see D.B. Bosdas, 'Precontractual Liability', *Arxeion Nomologias* 1968, 337, 341, who argues that the provisions on precontractual liability preclude the provisions on delict.

Ireland

The liability of A to B depends on whether there is a contract with respect to the preparatory work or whether B can make a claim in restitution.

If B expressly made it clear to A that he would have to pay for preparatory work whether or not the final contract was concluded then this would constitute a contract in itself for which A would be liable. Further, if A was aware of B's policy, B might argue that there was a collateral contract with A covering the expenditure incurred. Simply put, this would be a contract collateral to the principal contract for which A was in negotiations: a contract whereby A agreed to pay B the costs incurred in preparing to tender for the main contract.[15] Such a finding would be unlikely in the current climate of the courts.

In Irish law, where the parties have not entered into a contract, their relationship is governed by the law of tort, restitution or quasi-contract. Liability in tort is confined to actions for deceit or negligent misrepresentation.[16] Liability in restitution or quasi-contract arises where the plaintiff has incurred expenditure in the belief that there was, or would be, a contract with the defendant. The law of quasi-contract is relatively complex. The principal function is to allow recovery in *quantum meruit*. In *Fanning v. Wicklow County Council*[17] building work was completed in the mistaken belief that a contract had been concluded between the parties. No contract had in fact been concluded but the builder was allowed to recover *quantum meruit* for the value of the benefit bestowed upon the defendant. *Quantum meruit* also operates where the parties are not contractually bound on a particular issue. Thus, in *Devaney v. Reidy*[18] an architect was engaged in planning regulation work which one would expect of a member of this profession. Despite the silence of the contract, the architect was awarded compensation for these efforts. *Quantum meruit* is particularly useful where negotiations have taken place with respect to a contract that ultimately is never agreed upon. Thus, in *British Steel Corporation v. Cleveland Bridge & Engineering Co.*[19] the court held that benefits which had been bestowed upon the defendant by the plaintiff should be compensated for. In that case, the plaintiff, at the

[15] *Blackpool and Fylde Aero Club Ltd v. Blackpool Borough Council* [1990] 1 WLR 1195.

[16] Generally, see Quill, *Torts in Ireland*, p. 271ff.; in particular, see the Irish report on case 1.

[17] (Unreported, High Court), 30 April 1984, O'Hanlon J.

[18] (Unreported, High Court), 10 May 1974. [19] [1984] 1 All ER 504.

request of the defendant, and before a completed contracted had been concluded, supplied certain parts to the defendant.

There is also authority for the proposition that *quantum meruit* can be used to compensate the plaintiff for the cost of preparatory work requested by the defendant. This is significant since it breaks the requirement to show benefit to the defendant. In *Folens v. Minister of Education*[20] the plaintiff entered into negotiations with a government department, the Department of Education. The negotiations were to secure the publication of a children's encyclopaedia in the Irish language. With the approval of the Department, the plaintiff undertook preparatory work with respect to the subject matter of the contract. At some later stage, the Department decided not to proceed with the ultimate contract and the plaintiff sought to recover the expenses incurred to date. The plaintiff succeeded in quasi-contract. The test outlined by McWilliam J was simple. If the plaintiff had been told that the Department wanted this preparatory work done but that, in the event of the contract not proceeding, then there would be no payment, the plaintiff would not have embarked upon the work at its own risk. Thus, the preparatory work must (a) have been requested by the defendant and (b) have been undertaken by the plaintiff in the expectation of payment for expenses incurred. If the work was volunteered by the plaintiff, or if the plaintiff did not expect payment, then no action lies. The application of these rules to the case at hand requires determinations of fact. Did A request the preparatory work? Did A believe that he might be compensated for the work if the ultimate contract did not succeed? It appears that the better view would be that B undertook the preparatory work at his own initiative in the hope of securing the final contract. Therefore A has no liability to B.

Italy

B seems to have little practical chance of recovering damages for his work under precontractual liability where he does not know of B's policy.

The two main questions are, first, whether B can prove that his reliance was justified, and secondly, whether A was in breach of good faith in the negotiations. As to the first question, academic writers and case law seem to provide different solutions. On the one hand, in academic writing the negotiation of onerous building projects is seen as a prime

[20] [1984] ILRM 265.

example of justified reliance.[21] But there is no relevant case law on the point. Article 2237 of the Civil Code makes provision for the client's withdrawal (*recesso ad nutum*) in a contract with a professional: 'the client is free to withdraw from the contract, but it has to pay the professional the expenses and the work already done', and case law has always considered the client's freedom to withdraw as one of the main principles of contracts with professionals,[22] justified by the fiduciary relationship existing between him and the professional.[23] However, the Italian Supreme Court has underlined the professional's right to recover his expenses and the price of the work done. In this case, however, B's preparatory work was not based upon any contract with A, and so B could recover his losses only if the judge is prepared to apply an extensive interpretation of extra-contractual liability for unfair dealing in commercial relations. However, given the lack of academic writing and case law on the breach of the duty to inform during negotiations with professionals, the result of B's action is not certain.

A could be liable if it is proved that he was aware of B's policy of tendering and single-project work. His conduct then appears contrary to the requirement of good faith in negotiations.[24]

However, if A acted in accordance with good faith it seems difficult for B to prove that he reasonably relied upon A's proposal. B made no statements during negotiations, and it seems unwise not to have communicated to A his particular project policy. B's conduct appears to have been at his own risk. But since the question would be for the judge to evaluate, a successful claim of precontractual liability is not impossible.

Netherlands

Parallel negotiations: under Dutch law there is no specific rule or doctrine on account of which conducting parallel negotiations with third parties without informing the negotiating party might be held to be contrary to good faith or otherwise lead to liability. Therefore, under Dutch law it must be held that a party, in principle, is not only free to conduct

[21] See Benatti, *La responsibilità precontrattuale*; Monateri, *La responsabilità contrattuale e precontrattuale*.

[22] TRIB-T. Milano, 6 June 1998; PRET. Milano, 26 May 1998; TRIB-T. Milano, 16 Mar. 1994; Cass, sez. II, 12 Nov. 1976, n. 4181.

[23] Cass, sez. lav., 11 June 1999, n. 5775; Cass, sez. II, 15 May 1996, n. 4501; PRET. Milano, 5 Mar. 1997.

[24] For a general account of good faith, see the Italian report on case 1.

parallel negotiations, but is also free not to inform the other party spontaneously (of course, she is not free to lie when solicited). For that reason, the mere fact that A started and conducted negotiations with C without telling B, in principle, does not seem to make him liable towards B. The answer would probably be the same if A knew of B's policy on tendering and single-project work. However, it should not be fully excluded that a judge might, under certain circumstances, find an agreement (a contract) between A and B to the effect that A would not conduct any parallel negotiations with third parties. Such a contract would then be based on either an implicit agreement[25] or the reliance principle (B was justified in relying on A's respect of B's policy).[26]

Breaking off negotiations: whether A may be liable for breaking off negotiations with B depends on what stage the negotiations had reached, quite apart from the parallel negotiations. If A broke off his negotiations with B when they had reached a stage where he was no longer allowed to do so (that is, after induced justified reliance),[27] he may be liable, even to the extent of the expectation interest, which in this case would include loss of the profit B would have made under the contract. Whether this stage was reached is not clear from the statement of facts. It is stated that the negotiations lasted for a year, but this fact is not alone conclusive. Moreover, it is not on this account (breaking off negotiations) that A would be liable for B's expenses for a year's preparatory work as (unlike B's loss of profit) that loss cannot be said to be caused by the breaking-off of the negotiations.

A may be liable at an even earlier stage. The Hoge Raad has held that even before the stage is reached where a party is no longer allowed to break off, he may nevertheless be liable to compensate expenses if he breaks off. Under what circumstances this liability may arise is not clear. However, it is clear that where A knew of B's policy he could easily have avoided B incurring his expenses: if he had informed B of the negotiations he was conducting with C, B would probably have given up the negotiations with A and therefore not suffered any damage. This may be a relevant argument in establishing whether A is liable. Also, within the context of fraud[28] and mistake[29] (that is, the cases where a contract *was* concluded, but one party wishes to step out of it on account of an allegedly incorrect or insufficient informational basis) a party's precontractual duty to inform, which is based on a

[25] Article 3:37 BW: declarations may also be silent. [26] Article 3:35 BW.
[27] See the Dutch report on case 1. [28] Article 3:44(1), (3) BW. [29] Article 6:228 BW.

general duty of precontractual good faith,[30] depends on what he knew or could know about the relevance of the information for the other party. It should be remembered, however, that a recent case (*CBB/JPO*) has raised some doubt as to whether the Hoge Raad still recognises the 'second stage'.[31]

Norway

There are several possible reasons for a claim against A.

The initial approach is to examine whether a contract has been agreed upon with respect to the work already carried out, that is, to part of the work only. This can be called a 'partial contract'.[32] If the parties have explicitly entered into such a partial contract, which is not uncommon, the question is straightforward. However, in case law there has been a tendency to presume the existence of such a partial contract. This rationale for claiming damages has a special significance in view of precontractual liability, partly because a specific basis for liability for compensatory damages (such as bad faith) is not required, and partly because partial, and not full, compensation, is paid.

If A has *asked* B to do the preparatory work, the basis for argument would be that B as a business person has the right to regular payment for the work. If, on the other hand, the work has been carried out on B's *own initiative*, in the expectation of being awarded the contract, the argument is reversed. The risk of the work being wasted rests, naturally, with B. The facts do not, however, describe the situation in detail, and it is therefore difficult to arrive at a definite conclusion. An intermediate situation arises in the case where B, more or less on his own initiative, has commenced preparatory work, and has allowed A to derive advantage from it during the negotiation period. Is this sufficient reason to claim for unjust enrichment? Norwegian law has not developed a doctrine of unjust enrichment. Any answer to the problems mentioned above will therefore be somewhat uncertain. However, the basis must be such that if B wittingly gives A access to the material he is working on during the negotiation period, this does not in itself constitute the right to claim against A.

If no partial agreement is present, the question of precontractual liability applies in its purest form. On the facts as stated, it is doubtful whether A would be responsible on the basis of precontractual liability.

[30] HR 15 Nov. 1957 (*Baris/Riezenkamp*), NJ 1958, 67, note Rutten.
[31] See the Dutch report on case 1. [32] Simonsen, *Precontractual Liability*, p. 399ff.

According to Norwegian law, there are certainly no prohibitions against entering into parallel negotiations.[33] On the facts given, there are no indications that A has misled B into believing that the negotiations were exclusive. The question is, however, whether A should have informed B that he was also negotiating with others. This would have provided a better opportunity for B to evaluate the risk these negotiations entailed. There is no case law on this question. Negotiating parties have no general duty to inform: specific reasons must exist for there to be such a duty. One such reason is that negotiations are in an advanced state; in other words, that one is approaching the final stage of the negotiation period. Another reason is that the other party has acted in the belief that he would secure the future contract. However, such a situation has to be justified or to arise naturally. That B, because of his policy, has not accepted other work or participated in competition for contracts, and consequently has become particularly vulnerable to a breach of contract, appears to be a situation that he alone should be responsible for. As no contract has been entered into, each party should have realised that the other party also could be involved in negotiations with others. If B had wanted to guard himself against parallel negotiations, the normal procedure would have been to state in a letter of intent a prohibition against such negotiations for a specified period of time. It is doubtful whether A's awareness of this situation is sufficient to require a duty to inform. If B's policy on tendering and single-project work is considered a typical personal risk, A's knowledge of it does not appear to affect the question of liability.

Portugal

In this case A would not be held liable to B. There is no rule in Portuguese law that prevents parties from conducting negotiations with more than one person in order to choose the best contract. This kind of behaviour is considered normal in the negotiations to conclude a contract; it is not contrary to good faith and does not give rise to liability.

[33] Simonsen, *Precontractual Liability*, p. 222: 'Beyond agreed situations it seems fairly clear that no general obligation not to conduct separate negotiations exists. The exploitation of business competition is such a fundamental part of the market mechanism that this right will not normally be considered to limit entry into other contract negotiations'; G Woxholth, *Avtaleinngåelse, ugyldighet og tolkning*, p. 210ff.: 'If a main rule should be established, it would be that parallel negotiations do not involve precontractual liability.'

It would not make any difference if A knew of B's policy on tendering and single-project work. Only if a lock-out agreement had been concluded between A and B would it be possible to establish the liability of A, which would be based not in precontractual liability but in the contract. The simple fact of A knowing about B's policy is not sufficient to establish a duty on him to inform B about parallel negotiations, as they are normal in the process of establishing a contract.

Scotland

In Scots law it is generally accepted that parties negotiating a contract are at arm's length, in the sense that each party is permitted to look to his own interests and comes under no obligation to reveal information to the other or to negotiate in good faith. Positive bad faith may, on the facts of the case, amount to a misrepresentation,[34] or may constitute illegal coercion of the other party or exploitation of a special relationship of trust, both of which are prohibited by Scots law. Prior to the moment of agreement, and therefore the point of legal commitment, Scots law holds that parties are in general terms entitled to break off negotiations for whatever reason and to withdraw.

By and large Scottish courts are reluctant to sustain claims for damages based on failed precontractual negotiations.[35] There are a number of cases, beginning with *Walker v. Milne*,[36] where recovery for wasted expenditure incurred during contractual negotiations was awarded. Recent interpretation of this line of cases by the Court of Session has held that they are to be seen as cases where recovery was permitted where one party had represented to the other that a binding contract existed but, for reasons of failure to comply with a requirement of form, it did not.[37] The availability of this common law remedy for the recovery of wasted expenditure is not affected by the statutory personal bar provided for in Requirements of Writing (Scotland) Act 1995. Where the common law remedy is sought, financial compensation for the wasted costs will be awarded, whereas where statutory personal bar is allowed, enforcement of the contract will occur.

In the present case it seems quite clear that neither party was under the impression that an enforceable agreement existed between them.

[34] As in case 1.

[35] H.L. MacQueen, 'Good Faith in the Scots Law of Contract: an Undisclosed Principle?' in Forte, *Good Faith in Contract and Property*.

[36] (1823) 2 S 379.

[37] This line of cases is discussed in more detail in relation to case 8.

That being so, the common law remedy for wasted expenditure outlined above would be unavailable to B. Rather, the misunderstanding revolves around the exclusivity of the negotiations. A does not appear to have knowledge of B's unusual conditions regarding commissions and tendering. Without being positively informed of B's conditions, and without these conditions being held customary, there would be no duty of inquiry upon A to find out the terms on which B enters into negotiations. In these circumstances there can be no liability in damages upon A.

If A knew of B's policy on tendering and single-project work it would suggest that A, in beginning parallel negotiations with C, is thereafter negotiating in bad faith with B. However, in order to found an action in damages, such continued negotiations would have to be argued to be a misrepresentation, whether fraudulent or negligent. This would clearly have to be implied from A's conduct in continuing the negotiations. The tenability of such a claim is questionable.

Spain

Liability in this case depends on whether A is acting in good faith or not. Considering that it is quite normal to start negotiating with more than one partner in order to select the best offer, A's conduct cannot be qualified as contrary to good faith nor as an abuse of his right to negotiate. The mere fact of starting negotiations does not by itself constitute a relation of confidence strong enough to impose a duty to inform about parallel negotiations, especially as this is a rather usual fact.[38]

But generally, according to Spanish legislation, it seems that preliminary works and projects by an architect are to be paid for.[39] The work done has therefore to be analysed and qualified: it might be considered as *estudio previo* (preparatory studies) or even an *anteproyecto* (pre-project) in the sense of the legislation. But in that case, B has to prove that A told him to do the preliminary work, for which he now asks to be paid; in other words, that there existed a contract concerning the preparatory work that B did. However, if A actually did use the

[38] Cf. STS, 14 June 1999, RJ 1999\4105; Audiencia Provincial de Valladolid, 9 Nov. 1998, AC 1998\8974.

[39] Real Decreto 2512/1977, 17 June 1977, RCL 1977\2113; cf. STS, 24 June 1991, RJ 1991\4578.

preliminary work B had done, he is liable on the grounds of unjust enrichment (*gestion de negocios ajenos*).[40]

If A knew about B's policy on tendering and single-project work he undoubtedly had the duty to inform B about his parallel negotiations, as this fact was of decisive importance for B. Since this policy concerned the precontractual phase itself, the knowledge of the policy automatically creates a precontractual duty to inform, based on the principle of good faith, as one cannot negotiate in good faith knowing that the other party, if he knew about the parallel negotiations, would not negotiate at all. For this reason A would be liable on the basis of article 1902 of the Civil Code for all expenses and losses B suffered.

Sweden

A is not liable to pay damages if he did not know about B's policy. If A had such knowledge, it is likely that B would be entitled to compensation.

The main rule is that the parties negotiate at their own risk and cost, that a party can be engaged in parallel negotiations regarding the same object without informing the parties he is negotiating with, and that either party is free to discontinue the negotiations at any time. When the negotiations have reached a certain stage, a party can have an obligation to consider the other party's interests.[41] B exposes himself to huge commercial risks by adopting the policy on tendering and single-project work as he could not always count on finalising a contract for all offers or negotiations he is involved in.

In NJA 1978.147, the parties during negotiations agreed that in the ongoing renovation of a building, premises should be reserved for the other party (T) and designed in a way that would suit a supermarket. According to the agreement, T had the intention to rent or buy the premises, but neither the rent and time for the lease, nor the price, were agreed upon. Later on, T discontinued the negotiations, the main reason being a market survey showing that an establishment might prove not to be profitable, especially considering the range for the rent or price for the premises indicated by the other party. According to the Supreme Court, the parties were under the obligations to co-operate

[40] Article 1893 CC; STS, 19 Jan. 1998, RJ 1998\304.

[41] NJA 1990.745: see the Swedish report on case 1; Hellner, *Kommersiell avtalsrätt*; J. Kleineman, 'Skadeståndsgrundande uppträdande vid avtalsförhandlingar', JT 1991–92, 125; Ramberg and Ramberg, *Allmän avtalsrätt*.

with the intention to reach a final agreement and take the other party's interest into consideration. Therefore, T had to devote himself in good faith to the final decision regarding the establishment of the supermarket and keep the other party informed about the development. However, T had grounds to believe that the other party could take care of his own interests in a commercial relationship of this type. As T had not acted contrary to these obligations, the Supreme Court found that T was not liable to compensate the other party for the costs incurred in the design of the premises. If A did not know about B's policy, it follows from NJA 1978.147 that A is not liable to compensate B for the costs incurred in the preparatory work.

A party might be considered at fault if he is not acting in accordance with ethical principles in business. However, in a competitive setting, only qualified unethical behaviour by the discontinuing party can make a party liable.[42] Since A had reason to believe that B could take care of his own interests, and since it was in B's interest to secure compensation for his preparatory work, A's behaviour would probably not be qualified as at fault. If A knew about B's policy, A may be considered at fault in not informing B about the parallel negotiations with C and thus be liable to compensate B for *culpa in contrahendo*. In this case, A would have to inform B about the parallel negotiations. As he did not do so and therefore did not give B a chance not to participate in the negotiations, he might be liable to compensate B for his negotiation costs and his costs of the preparatory work.

Switzerland

A is not liable on contractual grounds. No express contract has been concluded, but contracts for the compensation of an architect's preparatory work can also be concluded implicitly. But the courts act with restraint. In the present case a judge would not assume an implied contract because A has not requested B to make the drawings.[43]

A is not liable on the ground of *culpa in contrahendo*. Parallel negotiations generally are not against good faith as long as the party negotiates seriously. The party must always expect that the other party is assessing other alternatives. Parties are therefore not obliged to disclose

[42] Cf. NJA 1990.745 and J. Kleineman, 'Skadeståndsgrundande uppträdande vid avtalsförhandlingar,' JT 1991–92, 125, 140.

[43] Cf. BGE 119 II 43; Gauch, *Der Werkvertrag*, n. 448.

the parallel negotiations. In the present case A has not violated his duty to negotiate in good faith.

Thus, A is only to blame for having broken off serious negotiations. But a party can only rely on the contract in good faith if the other party has committed himself by an offer. In Swiss law an offer is binding; the reliance is protected in a positive way (*positiver Vertrauensschutz*); and revocation of the offer is excluded after the other party has knowledge of the offer.[44] Another possibility to secure the expectations of a future contract is to conclude a preliminary contract (*Vorvertrag*). But a preliminary contract is only concluded if the parties have agreed with regard to all essential points.[45] The requirements of these two possibilities are not fulfilled in the present case. The prevailing academic opinion refuses to protect expectations in other situations because freedom of contract has priority.[46] The negotiating party must always realise that the other party might change his mind. The mere fact that the negotiations have lasted a long time, or that the defendant knows what the plaintiff has invested in the negotiations, are not sufficient for liability.[47]

On the other hand some authors propose a different solution, under which a party breaking off the negotiations may be liable if he made the other party believe that a contract would certainly come about.[48] This opinion is supported by a judgment of the Federal Court of 1995[49] in which, in a claim against a committee of an athletic competition, the court awarded damages for the expenses of an athlete who was not allowed to participate in the competition. According to the applicable rules of participation, it seemed certain that the athlete should have been allowed to participate. Shortly before the competition the committee changed the rules. As a consequence the athlete no longer

[44] OR 9. [45] BernerKommentar-Kramer, OR 22 n. 93, 97.

[46] Cf. BernerKommentar-Kramer, OR 22 n. 13; Merz, *Vetrag und Vertragsschluss*, n. 132; Schwenzer, *Schweizerisches Obligationenrecht Allgemeiner Teil*, N 47.08; Gauch, Schluep, Schmid and Rey, *Schweizerisches Obligationenrecht Allgemeiner Teil*, vol. I, n. 991ff.; Gauch, *Der Werkvertrag*, n. 452f.

[47] BGE, 29 Oct. 2001 no. 4C.152/2001 (in SemJud 2002 I, 164ff.), E. 3; BGE, 3 Feb. 2003 no. 4C320/2002 E. 3.3.

[48] Cf. Piotet, *Culpa in contrahendo et responsabilité précontractuelle en droit privé suisse*, 128; Koller, *Schweizerisches Obligationenrecht Allgemeiner Teil*, § 28 n. 10; ZürcherKommentar-Schönenberger/Jäggi, OR 1 n. 587 (break-off at an improper time); Gonzenbach, *Culpa in contrahendo im schweizerischen Vertragsrecht*, 96ff.; Widmer, *Umfang des Schadenersatzes bei nicht zur Perfektion gelangten Verträgen*, 155, 184; Loser, *Vertrauenshaftung im Schweizerischen Schuldrecht*, n. 642.

[49] BGE 121 III 330.

fulfilled the requirements. The Federal Court held the committee liable for the wasted expenses (*nutzlose Aufwendungen*) because there was no good (material) reason (*wichtiger Grund*) for the committee to change the rules. The committee was in a similar situation to the party who breaks off negotiations although it seemed certain a contract would come about. Therefore, in Swiss law breaking off serious negotiations without a good reason can exceptionally lead to liability.[50] But due to the lack of court decisions, the prerequisites for liability are not clear. And in the present case the conditions for the liability are obviously not met.

Even if A knew of B's policy on tendering and single-project work he is not liable on the ground of *culpa in contrahendo*. According to court decisions there is no duty to disclose the parallel negotiations just because of the knowledge of B's expenditure.[51] A has therefore not negotiated in bad faith.

Even if one takes the opposite opinion, put by some authors, it does not seem certain that A must compensate the whole of B's work. On the one hand, B must prove that he has missed out on other contracts because of his preparatory work.[52] In this connection the judge may assess the damages in his discretion.[53] On the other hand, it is questionable whether B has done his preparatory work in good faith.[54] The work served not to conclude the contract but to prepare its performance: this justifies a reduction of the compensation.[55]

Editors' comparative observations

This case gives rise to two separate issues: the negotiating party who carries out preparatory work in the hope of concluding the contract (and, when the contract does not materialise, has the loss of both the

[50] In BGE, 29 Oct. 2001 no. 4C.152/2001 (in SemJud 2002 I, 164ff.), E. 3 the Federal Court held that in exceptional cases liability may arise because of the break-off of negotiations, for example if the defendant had made the plaintiff believe that a contract is certain to come about. Confirmed in BGE, 17 Nov. 2005 no. 4C.247/2005 E.3.

[51] See BGE, 29 Oct. 2001 no. 4C.152/2001 (in SemJud 2002 I, 164ff.) E. 3a; BGE, 3 Feb. 2003 no. 4C320/2002 E. 3.3; BGE, 16 June 2004 no. 4C.56/2004 E. 2.3/2.4. *Contra* S. Hartmann, 'Der Abbruch von Vertragsverhandlungen als Enttäuschung von Vertrauen-Bemerkungen im Anschluss an das Bundesgerichtsurteil 4C.152/2001 vom 29 Oktober 2001', ZBJV 2003, 531.

[52] Lost profit (*entgangener Gewinn*).

[53] OR 42. Cf. BGE, 3 Feb. 2003 Nr. 4C320/2002 E. 4, where the court recognised the wasted expenditure and time.

[54] *In bona fide*: cf. the Swiss report on case 3.

[55] OR 44.

hope of that contract and of any other contract he might have entered into during the negotiations); and the fact that the other party, who ultimately breaks off the negotiations, was conducting parallel negotiations with someone else. The case is set in the particular context of a party, B, who has a particular policy of not undertaking more than one job at a time, and not competing in competitive tenders; and it offers a variation: whether it makes any difference whether or not the party breaking off the negotiations, A, knew of this policy. There is agreement amongst the jurisdictions on some matters, but disagreement on others.

Precontractual expenditure: all jurisdictions start their analysis from the same point: that precontractual expenditure by a professional such as B (an architect, negotiating for a design contract) is generally at the spending party's own risk. On the facts, the negotiations had been continuing for a year (and B's expenditure had been growing over that period). But the only jurisdictions to suggest that this might make a difference are Finland (which suggests that there might have been an obligation on A to inform B once the parallel negotiations with C had reached a stage of being likely to be concluded) and the Netherlands (which can contemplate the possibility that the negotiations had reached a sufficiently advanced stage to give rise to A's liability for breaking them off (the length of the negotiations is not there conclusive but is relevant to answering this point) but which (paradoxically) may not cover the architect's expenditure). All other jurisdictions take the position that, unless it is possible to construct some other basis of liability which does not immediately appear from the facts (either a contract between A and B for the precontractual work to be done, or that A either requested the work to be done or has obtained a benefit from it, which might in several jurisdictions give rise to claims for unjust enrichment), the basic position (B's expenditure is at his own risk) is maintained. A number of reporters observe that this position is reinforced by general commercial understandings of the risk allocation of precontractual expenditure, and the fact that B's own expenditure here is in pursuance of an unusual, personal policy about the negotiations of which he cannot expect A to bear the risk when the negotiations are broken off, at least in the case where A does not know of the policy. There is less agreement between the jurisdictions as to how to deal with the case when A does know of B's policy (see below).

Parallel negotiations: similarly, all reporters start their analysis of the parallel negotiations from the same point: in principle no wrong is committed by a party who begins parallel negotiations without informing the other: no tort, no liability in contract, no *culpa in contrahendo*, no basis of a claim for unjust enrichment. Again, reporters often emphasise that such parallel negotiations are normal commercial practice and so B should have expected that A might be exploring other contracts; and the fact that B was a professional is again invoked to emphasise that he should have understood this normal commercial practice. The policy which B maintains about not participating in competitive tendering of itself makes no difference in any jurisdiction, because it is an unusual policy which B should have communicated if he wished to disturb the normal risk allocation of the negotiations.

A's knowledge of B's policy: where, however, A knows of B's unusual policy about tendering and single-project work, the picture becomes less unanimous, both in the result and in the reasoning. Jurisdictions can be divided broadly into three.

There are those which say that A's knowledge makes no difference because the mere bad faith of A – if, with knowledge of B's policy, it can be said to be in bad faith for A to continue the negotiations so as to increase B's potential loss, and to conduct the parallel negotiations – cannot act as a trigger for his liability. England, Ireland and Scotland take this position, maintaining their general approach seen throughout this study that, without any contractual undertaking by A to pay and/or not to negotiate with others, and without A committing any tort (such as by fraudulent or negligent misrepresentation), there is no basis on which B can rest any claim to a remedy. Bad faith during the negotiations does not of itself give rise to a remedy in these jurisdictions.

However, all the other jurisdictions do accept in principle[56] that there is some kind of duty of good faith in the negotiations, and therefore ask whether A's bad faith satisfies their test. But they disagree in the result. The majority (Austria, Finland, France, Greece, Italy, the Netherlands, Spain and Sweden) hold A liable. B has an interest in knowing that A is conducting parallel negotiations with C, since he would not be prepared to negotiate with A if he knew it, and the risk of his precontractual expenditure being wasted is increased by the fact that A might in fact contract with C. But it is A's knowledge of this that is seen as being crucial in the jurisdictions which impose liability on him; although the liability is not for the parallel negotiations themselves, but for failing to inform B about them. But other jurisdictions

[56] See, e.g., the reports on case 1.

(Denmark, Germany, Norway, Portugal and Switzerland) would say that the mere fact that A knows about B's policy does not impose on him this duty to inform. The general approach here is to say that if B wishes to impose a restriction on A's normal freedom to negotiate with others, or if he wishes to pass to A the risk of B's precontractual expenditure, it is not sufficient just to inform A of the policy, but to go further, such as to obtain A's agreement to compensate if the contract does not materialise.

Measure of the remedy: in those jurisdictions where A would be required to pay damages,[57] most say that if A is in breach of his duty to inform B of the parallel negotiations, he then becomes liable not only for B's expenses in the negotiations, but also for the potential loss of other contracts (if they can be proved: this might in some jurisdictions[58] be treated as a quantification issue, for the loss of the *chance* of another contract). However, some (Greece, Switzerland) would say that the general preparatory work, which was under the normal principles of risk allocation begun by B at his own risk, remains so and is therefore excluded from the damages calculation, or that at least the compensation has to be reduced; or (Finland) emphasise that since the duty which A has broken is to inform of his parallel negotiations, he cannot be liable for all of B's losses but only for those incurred after A failed to inform B in fulfilment of his duty.

[57] Or, at least, *might* be liable to pay: some jurisdictions are rather tentative about the basis of liability (e.g. Austria, Finland and the Netherlands).

[58] See in particular the French report above.

Case 5: A broken engagement

Case 5

In 1997 A and B became engaged to be married. The wedding was planned for June 2000. At the beginning of the engagement B gave A a diamond engagement ring which cost him €750. In April 2000, B paid a (non-returnable) deposit of €1,500 to the caterers who were to prepare the food for the wedding reception; and in May he made a (non-returnable) advance payment of rent (amounting to €2,000) on a flat which he and A were to rent as their first home together after their marriage. The day before the wedding was due to take place, A told B that she no longer wished to marry him. What liability (in contract, tort, restitution, or any other form of liability), if any, does A have to B?

Discussions

Austria

The ABGB includes two provisions on engagements and the consequences of the unjustified breaking-off of negotiations. For some authors the engagement is a form of precontractual obligation, but the majority opinion is that the 'betrothal' is a preliminary contract to a marriage with certain characteristic features, such as its lack of enforceability.[1]

§1247 ABGB states in its second sentence that, 'if one betrothed party promises or makes a present to the other party, in view of the future marriage, such donation can be revoked if, without any fault on the part of the donor, the marriage does not take place'. And §46 ABGB

[1] Koziol and Welser, *Bürgerliches Recht*, vol. 1, p. 404ff.

provides that 'the party to a betrothal which has been breached without reasonable cause has the right to assert his or her claim for any actual damage which can be proved to have been caused by the breach'. Therefore, on the basis of these provisions, the disappointed B may make a claim for the return of any gift that he made to the other (the ring), and for compensation of the damage he suffered as a result of his disappointed reliance on the coming into existence of the marriage (the catering deposit and the deposit on the flat). The former is by its nature a claim for unjust enrichment, the latter a claim for civil liability as a result of a specific form of breach of a contractual duty stemming from the preliminary contract of marriage. The consequences of this non-enforceable agreement (*pactum de contrahendo*) for a future marriage are similar to those resulting from *culpa in contrahendo*.

§46 ABGB may appear rather old-fashioned. The concept of 'actual damage' (*wirklicher Schaden*) in this provision aligns with the concept of 'reliance damage': all the losses that would not have occurred had the betrothal not been broken off are recoverable, provided that there is no reasonable explanation (*gegründete Ursachen*) for the breaking of the engagement. The OGH has held that all the expenses incurred in preparation for the marriage, including the costs incurred for the future home of the couple, are recoverable. Furthermore, although there is no express provision in the Code, there is some case law (although not very recent) which gives the parents of the disappointed partner the right to claim compensation for losses arising from the breaking of the engagement.[2]

Although betrothals have lost their traditional importance in contemporary Austrian society, the breaking of an engagement by one partner entitles the loyal disappointed partner to claims for the return of gifts and compensation for the damage he, or she, actually suffered. These claims do not appear to be a reaction to the breach of a contractual duty, but rather to the violation of justified reliance of the loyal, engaged person. Therefore the claim for damages is a non-contractual one.

Denmark

The general rule is that neither of the parties has any claim against the other in case of a broken engagement. However, rings must be returned

[2] OGH 7 Dec. 1960, SZ 33/135; 2 Feb. 1967, SZ 40/15.

whichever party broke the engagement. Liability for a broken promise to marry will only be imposed in case of fraudulent behaviour, for instance if a party pretends to be willing to marry in order to profit from his or her consent.

In the present case B can claim the ring back, but has no other claim against A.[3]

England

A has no liability to B by virtue of having broken off the engagement. Under Law Reform (Miscellaneous Provisions) Act 1970, section 1, an agreement to marry does not have effect as a contract giving rise to legal rights, and therefore the breach by one party of the engagement does not constitute a breach of contract. If the engagement ring was given on the condition, express or implied, that it should be returned if the marriage did not take place, A will be required to return it. However, under section 3 of the 1970 Act, in the absence of evidence of such a condition being imposed it is presumed that the gift of an engagement ring is an absolute gift. On the facts as given, therefore, A is entitled to keep the ring.

Until 1970 an engagement was technically a contract which would give rise to a claim for breach of contract (generally referred to as an action for 'breach of promise of marriage') against the party who unilaterally broke off the engagement. However, this action was already little used by the time it was abolished by statute on the recommendation of the Law Commission[4] who thought that the consequences of a broken engagement should no longer depend upon the parties' respective fault. The principal difficulties which required solutions were the property disputes arising between the parties to the engagement, and for this the 1970 Act[5] provides that the law governing property disputes between husband and wife should apply. The abolition of the contract of engagement is also consistent with the general approach of English law to the relationship between husband and wife, in which it is normally presumed that domestic arrangements do not give rise to contractually binding agreements.[6]

B's ability to recover for the payments he has made to the caterers and the advance rent on the flat therefore do not depend on A's

[3] See I. Lund-Andersen, *Familieret* 1990, 142.

[4] Law Commission Report No. 26, *Breach of Promise of Marriage* (London, 1969), para. 10.

[5] Section 2. [6] *Balfour v. Balfour* [1919] 2 KB 571.

wrongful conduct in having broken off the engagement (since there is no legal wrong committed) but on B demonstrating some other ground of recovery, such as the fact that he was acting as A's agent in making the payments (or, at least, that the payments were made by B acting for A and B jointly) so as to create a liability in A to reimburse her share of payments made. Whether such a case can be established will depend on a detailed consideration of the transactions that B entered into with the caterers and the intended landlord, facts which we have not been given.

Finland

Until 1988, the Finnish Marriage Act contained special rules on engagement to be married, such as returning the gifts given to one's betrothed in the event of cancellation of the engagement. These legal provisions were, however, repealed in 1988. Nowadays questions of the legal relationship between the betrothed couple fall under the general rules of civil law, such as contract and damages law.[7]

Thus, the possible liability of a person withdrawing from an engagement depends on the general conditions of liability for damages or restitution of gifts. As to the liability for damages, the question of fault is crucial. In a case like this, we have to pose the question whether the person, here A, has acted in a manner contrary to good practice in this kind of situation. It is an internationally acknowledged principle that an engagement to be married, due to its strong personal character, is an agreement that can be freely terminated. Thus, acting this way cannot in itself be a basis for any liability. The long duration of the engagement, as in this case, makes no difference in this respect.

But this does not mean that no liability can under any circumstances arise out of one's conduct in connection with terminating an engagement. For example, being slow in informing the other party of one's intention not to marry can cause him or her unnecessary expense in continuing to make preparations for the wedding. This may constitute fault and make the terminating party liable for damages to the other party that could have been avoided if the relevant information had been available to him or her. The liability can be said to have its basis in the *culpa in contrahendo* doctrine and to cover that part of the injured party's negative (reliance) interest that is caused by the lack of information. As

[7] See, e.g., Aarnio and Helin, *Avioliittolain muutetut säännökset* [*The Revised Provisions of the Marriage Act*], p. 18.

regards fault, the long duration of the engagement, as a general rule, does not have a clear impact on a party's liabilities.

Basing an action on *culpa in contrahendo* in situations like this would, however, in some cases cause serious practical problems concerning evidence. Which party would have the duty to bring evidence on the question of fault? If we apply the contract law rule, the burden of proof is reversed: it would lie on the defendant. In this case, A would have to prove that she was not slow in informing B about her plans. If, on the contrary, the general damages law rule is applied, the burden of proof would lie on the plaintiff: B would then have to prove the existence of fault in A's conduct. Because it is likely that only circumstantial evidence could be brought about A's intentions, the burden of proof question would probably have a decisive role in the case. There are no established rules about burden of proof in engagement situations. However, the exceptional character of damages claims based on an engagement would perhaps make courts more willing to impose the burden of proof on the plaintiff. In this case this could diminish in a decisive way B's real possibility of getting compensation.

In this case, if elements of fault in A's conduct can be found, such as in not informing B of her intentions in time, that have caused B's damage or a part of it, A can in principle be held liable for that damage. The damages which might be recoverable are within the negative interest and consist of the deposit paid by B and the advance payment of rent (the latter only if B had no use of the flat when the marriage was cancelled).

As to whether A must return the diamond engagement ring given by B as an engagement gift, we have to refer to general rules on the validity of legal acts under false assumptions. The pivotal rule is in the Finnish Contracts Act (Oikeustoimilaki, 1929), section 33: 'A promise that should in other respects be held valid should not be executed if it has been made under circumstances which would render it contrary to good faith[8] for a person knowing about the circumstances to refer to the promise and the addressee of the promise must be supposed to have known about them.' It is most likely that the question of A's liability for returning the engagement ring would be considered on the basis of this provision, and it is very probable that the contract[9] would be declared void, because the expectation of a marriage, which motivated a party to

[8] Literally: contrary to honour and unworthy.

[9] The case KKO 1969 I 1 shows that Contracts Act, s. 33 is applicable to a gift.

conclude a contract but was later not fulfilled, has been held[10] to satisfy the criteria set out in section 33 for the contract to be void. In addition, it seems likely that A knew that the expected marriage was B's motive in giving her the gift.

Declaring the gift void would make A liable to return it to B. The long duration of the engagement and A's possession of the ring cannot have a clear impact on her liability for returning the ring. It has also to be emphasised that, in contrast with damages liability, the defendant's fault is not a legal prerequisite for declaring the gift void or for the liability to return it.

France

In principle, French law recognises a person's right (or, rather, *liberté*) to break off his or her engagement.[11] This right is allowed provided that there is no abuse in its exercise. In case of abuse, the person who broke off the engagement would be held liable under article 1382 of the Civil Code. The validity of the termination depends upon several factors, all focused on one main idea: it is abusive if it occurred while the other engaged party had a reasonable belief[12] that the marriage would take place.

Three factors are relevant. First, the duration of the engagement must be taken into account, since a long period is likely to found the belief that the marriage will occur. The engagement between A and B lasted three years, which is a very long time, especially nowadays. One can therefore conclude that the marriage between A and B was quite certain, B having strong reasons to believe it would occur. Secondly, the suddenness of the breaking-off must be examined: the closer it is to the wedding day, the stronger the belief that the marriage will actually take place.[13] In our case, A broke off the day before the wedding, which is very close to the ceremony. Furthermore, the fact that B has spent money in organising the couple's future life is further evidence of his

[10] KKO 1977 II 76: a seller of real estate had expected that the buyer was going to marry him a short time after the sale. As this expectation, which the buyer knew about, was not fulfilled, the contract was considered to have been made under circumstances which rendered it contrary to good faith for the buyer to enforce it, taking into account also the low consideration agreed upon. Therefore the contract and the official registration of the buyer's ownership of the real estate were declared void.

[11] Civ 1, 22 Oct. 1970, Bull Civ I, 215. The engagement itself is *not* a contract, and so tort rules apply here.

[12] '*Croyance légitime*'. See the French report on case 7, n. 19, for a discussion about the similarities and differences between this concept and the idea of reliance.

[13] Civ 2, 2 July 1970, Bull Civ II, 178.

belief that he was to marry A. Thirdly, breaking off the engagement may be justified by a legitimate motive,[14] such as a disagreement about the choice of the legal rules governing matrimonial property.[15] As no motive is reported, we can assume there is no reasonable ground for the breaking-off.

A is therefore likely to be held liable for breaking off her engagement with B under article 1382 of the Civil Code.

Under this ground of liability, French law allows the victim[16] to recover two types of damages. First, B can obtain damages for the distress suffered consequent upon his engagement being broken. The amount of this head of damages ('*dommage moral*')[17] is left to the discretion of the judges. Secondly, the victim can recover the sums spent in view of the wedding ceremony[18] as well as the couple's future life. Therefore, B would be able to recover the costs he had borne both for the price paid to the caterers and for the advance payment of rent he made on the flat.

The issue of the restitution of the engagement ring must be examined separately, for it is not connected to tortious liability in French law, nor is it caught by the subsidiary action of unjust enrichment. According to article 1088 of the Civil Code, the engagement ring bought by the engaged person, as any other present made under the belief the wedding was to take place, can be recovered if the wedding is not celebrated.[19] Though the text is comprehensive, case law has established that it does not apply to wedding presents that are considered as presents according to usage.[20] Such '*présents d'usage*' can be kept by the formerly engaged person, whatever the circumstances of the breaking-off of the engagement. According to the facts, it seems that the ring corresponds to such a definition, because it is usual to offer a ring when

[14] There is a controversy among academic writers about the existence of this third condition.

[15] '*Régime matrimonial*'. See Civ 1, 19 July 1966, Bull Civ I, no. 443.

[16] It seems that French courts award damages more easily to engaged women than to engaged men: see J. Rubellin-Devichi, RTDCiv 1989, 278, no. 2; Bénabent, *Droit de la famille*, no. 50; Civ 1, 15 Mar. 1988, Rép. Defrénois 1988, art. 34309, no. 73, 1012.

[17] This can be roughly considered as an equivalent for the English pain and suffering. See Paris, 12 Mar. 1987, D.1987, IR, 142.

[18] Bénabent, *Droit de la famille*, no. 50; Civ 2, 2 July 1970, D.1970, J, 178.

[19] Paris, 3 Dec. 1976, D. 1978, J, 339.

[20] See Civ. 1, 30 Dec. 1952, D. 1953, J, 161. A '*présent d'usage*' is a present that is considered as a usual gift, according to the circumstances in which it was given, as long as it matches the engaged person's means.

an engagement occurs, and because B seems to have the means of affording the cost of such a ring (€750). Therefore, it is likely that A can keep the ring.

Germany

The BGB contains special provisions in relation to the withdrawal from an engagement. Under §1298 BGB the withdrawing person must compensate all losses of the other party (and his parents and third persons who acted *in loco parentis*) caused by expenses incurred or by obligations undertaken in expectation of marriage, provided these were appropriate in the circumstances and there was no serious ground for withdrawal. The burden of proof of a serious reason lies with the person withdrawing from the engagement. It is generally acknowledged that the liability imposed on the withdrawing party by §1298 BGB is liability for the other party's reliance interest (*Vertrauensschaden*).[21] Therefore A has to compensate for the catering costs as well as for B's advance payment of rent.

If the marriage fails to take place, under §1301 BGB each engaged person may claim the restitution of the gifts made in consideration of the engagement, provided these were not gifts in discharge of a moral debt. Hence B is entitled to the return of the diamond ring as well, regardless of who broke the engagement.[22]

The prevailing opinion in the courts and in legal writing holds §1298 BGB to be a special case of *culpa in contrahendo*, whereas §1301 BGB is regarded as a special provision of the law of unjust enrichment.[23] There is no doubt that the Code's provisions towards engagement regulate the failure of a marriage conclusively, and so B has no additional claims in contract, tort, restitution or any other form. Although only a few cases have been reported in recent times, it would be utterly inappropriate to deem the provisions of §§1298 to 1301 BGB as nothing more than 'law in the books'.

Greece

In marital relationships it is rather unsuitable to speak of negotiations in good faith, at least within the legal meaning of the term!

[21] Gernhuber and Coester-Waltjen, *Lehrbuch des Familienrechts*, §8 V 1 (p. 79).

[22] Cf. MünchKomm-Wacke, §1301 Rn. 1.

[23] BGH, decision of 18 May 1966, BGHZ 45, 258 (262); Gernhuber and Coester-Waltjen, *Lehrbuch des Familienrechts*, §8 VI 1; Staudinger-Lorenz, Vorbem. zu §812ff. para. 35; Palandt, *Bürgerliches Gesetzbuch* §1301 para. 3.

Nevertheless, marriage is a contract and the engagement period resembles the precontractual stage although, according to Greek law, the engagement itself is also considered to be a contract (thus, liability emanating from the engagement is contractual).[24] Greek family law contains a specific set of provisions dealing with 'precontractual liability' issues in marital affairs. These provisions are limited to determining some financial aspects between the engaged couple where the engagement comes to an end. These specific provisions of family law override the general provisions on precontractual liability in the Greek Civil Code.[25]

Article 1348 GCC provides that when the marriage is called off each party may recover from the other, on the basis of unjust enrichment provisions, anything that was provided as a donation to or a token of the engagement. Hence, B may recover the diamond ring from A on the basis of the unjust enrichment provisions in the Civil Code.[26]

Also, article 1347 GCC provides that if one of the engaged persons unilaterally breaks off the engagement without sufficient grounds, that person must provide compensation to the other party or to his or her parents for the expenses incurred or other measures taken in anticipation of the marriage, taking into account any special circumstances which may exist. In this case, A unilaterally broke off the engagement without sufficient reason and therefore, according to article 1347 GCC, A must compensate B for the expenses he incurred in the preparations for the wedding. The compensation includes the sums paid by B, namely the non-refundable deposit of €1,500 to the caterers and the advance rent of €2,000.

Ireland

A must return the engagement ring to B if requested to do so. A may also be liable for some or all of the non-refundable caterer's deposit and the advance rent payment if (1) the amounts involved are considered substantial with respect to B's earnings and (2) B has received no benefit from these payments.

Family Law Act 1981, section 2, removes an agreement to marry (an engagement) from the law by clearly stating that no action shall lie for

[24] Article 1346 GCC.

[25] G. Daskarolis, 'Dissolution of the engagement and precontractual liability' EEN 28, 699ff.; Kambitsis, *Precontractual Liability*, p. 77.

[26] Article 904ff. GCC.

breach of such an agreement. However, the legislation recognises that where an engagement is terminated, financial and property disputes may arise between the parties and it therefore provides a mechanism by which these can be resolved. Gifts made by one of the parties to the other (including the engagement ring) are presumed, in the absence of evidence to the contrary, to have been conditional gifts which should be returned at the request of the donor if the marriage does not take place for any reason other than the death of the donor.[27] Where the marriage fails to take place due to the death of the donor, then it will be presumed that the gift was given unconditionally unless there is evidence to the contrary.[28]

The Act also provides for the recovery of substantial expenditure on the termination of the engagement, in certain situations. Section 7 operates where a party to an engagement incurs substantial expenditure arising from the engagement from which that party did not benefit by reason of the termination of the engagement. In such instances, the court may make an order against the other party as it sees just and equitable in the circumstances, including an award for the recovery of expenditure incurred. There are three crucial elements: first, that 'substantial expenditure' had been incurred; secondly, that the party lacked any benefit from the expenditure; finally, that the reason for this lack of benefit was as a result of the termination of the engagement.

The question of what constitutes substantial expenditure was determined in *MM v. DM*.[29] Here the court held that 'substantial' had to be determined in relation to the resources of the parties themselves, that is, substantial in comparison to their earnings. Where the expenditure is not regarded as substantial then the party incurring such expenditure is not entitled to any court order.

The party must have received no benefit arising from the expenditure. In *MM v. DM*, a party who had paid a substantial amount for a honeymoon failed in her claim since, although the marriage had not gone ahead, the parties had both gone on the holiday together. Since there had therefore been a benefit, no order could be made under the relevant section.

Finally, it is clear that the failure to benefit must have arisen from the termination of the engagement. For example, suppose that one party has paid several thousand pounds for a honeymoon. The wedding is then called off but both parties agree to continue with the honeymoon

[27] Family Law Act 1981, s. 4(1)(a); see generally Shatter, *Family Law*, p. 143ff.

[28] Family Law Act 1981, s. 4(1)(b). [29] [1996] IFLR 187.

as a holiday. However, the paying party is unable to go on the holiday because they have fallen ill. Such a scenario fulfils the first two requirements but a court is not entitled to given any order since the failure to benefit did not arise due to the termination of the engagement.

Italy

According to Italian law A must return the ring, but it would be very unlikely that B would recover damages for loss caused by the broken engagement unless he could prove a formal written promise of marriage by the two of them.

Italian law[30] provides three specific rules for promises of marriage. First, the promise is considered as an imperfect obligation, since the parties cannot be forced to fulfil it according to the principle of freedom in marriage.[31]

Secondly, breach of promise is expressly recognised as giving rise to the parties' right to ask for the specific restitution of goods given in anticipation of the marriage. Case law holds that 'the duty of restitution concerning engagement presents finds its own limit only in the nature of goods if they can deteriorate or be consumed, or if it is proved that they have been received for reasons other than the expected wedding'.[32] Generally, in academic writing[33] and some decisions,[34] this rule is considered as concerning usual gifts (*liberalità d'uso*), and it is the end of the relationship (and not the cause of the gift) that is the legal reason for invoking restitution.[35]

Finally, article 81 of the Civil Code provides for damages. The Supreme Court has said that the degree of particularity of article 81 excludes the application of the general principle of precontractual liability under article 1337 in the case of a breach of promise of marriage.[36] Under article 81, damages can cover expenses that have been

[30] See arts. 79, 80, 81 c.c.

[31] Article 79 c.c. For academic writing see A. Candian, 'Gli sponsali come fonte negoziale di aspettativa', T 1951, 457.

[32] Cass, sez. I, 8 Feb. 1994, n. 1260.

[33] G. Oberto, 'Doni prenuziali e donazioni obnuziali' *Famiglia e dir.* 1996, 371; F. Gatti, 'I doni fatti a causa di ella promessa di matrimonio: natura giuridica e limite alla restituzione', RDC 1995, II, 33; V. Riganò, 'La restituzione dei doni scambiati tra fidanzati a causa della promessa di matrimonio e il c.d. fidanzamento' *Nuova giur. Civ* 1995, I, 296.

[34] Cass, 2 Feb. 1983, n. 3015.

[35] Trabucchi, *Promessa di matrimonio*, 50.

[36] Cass, sez. II, 10 Aug. 1991, n. 8733. This is generally followed by other judges and by writers.

made, and obligations incurred, as a result of the anticipated wedding.[37] But according to article 81, paragraph 1, damages can be awarded only where there was a formal bilateral (*vicendevole*) promise in a public deed (*atto pubblico*) or private document (*scrittura privata*) between adults or authorised minors; or if the wedding has already been brought to public knowledge by 'wedding publication'. Furthermore, according to article 81, paragraph 2, breach of promise can always be justified for proper reasons (*giustificato motivo*) in which case no damages are assessed. The recent reform of Italian family law has provided[38] that the amount of damages should be decided according to the parties' economic situation.

Both the actions for restitution and for damages have a limitation period of one year from the day of the refusal, according to article 81, paragraph 3.

Netherlands

A is probably liable towards B.

Article 1:49 BW (family law) says explicitly that engagements to be married are not binding, that breaking such promises does not lead to liability, and that stipulations to the contrary are void. However, section 2 of the same article also says that if the parties had already committed the formal act of asking to be married by the state authorities (*acte van huwelijksaangifte*),[39] losses may be recovered. However, recovery of loss of profit is explicitly excluded. Therefore, since the engagement was broken one day before the marriage it seems likely that the formal act has been done and that therefore B can recover all his damage from A, that is, the cost of the ring, the deposit paid to the caterers and the rent. The claim must be made within 18 months after the *acte van huwelijksaangifte*.

Norway

According to Norwegian law, a promise of marriage is not binding.[40] However, depending on the circumstances, a breach of promise of marriage can nonetheless be a basis for different types of claim. With respect to the damages B might claim from A, it is necessary to distinguish between the engagement ring and the various other expenses incurred.

[37] Cass, sez. I, 21 Feb. 1966, n. 539. [38] Art. 3 L. 19 Feb. 1975, n. 151.
[39] See art. 1:43. [40] Arnholm, *Privatrett IV*, pp. 26 and 27.

Engagement ring: in principle, a breach of promise of marriage might be a basis for a claim for compensation against the party who opts out. However, the relationship must clearly have been undertaken in bad faith if that is to be considered. Strictly personal reasons for opting out of the engagement must, of course, be considered relevant. If, on the other hand, there had been no genuine intention of entering into marriage, it would be an obvious case of liability. Such situations could, for instance, occur when the intention of the engagement was to effect a transfer of assets. Such a case would border on fraud. In the present case, there is no information indicating any element of bad faith on A's part.[41] The relationship has lasted for three years, and hence it is obvious that a claim for compensation is not relevant.

One may further ask if the ring should be returned, based on the doctrine of failed contractual assumption.[42] In the present case, it seems reasonably clear that such a claim would be futile, considering the nature of the gift (a strictly personal one), its value, and the time frame (approximately three years) for the planned wedding.[43] There is no precedent in Supreme Court practice with respect to gifts. From the lower courts may be mentioned RG 1955, 523 (the Eidsivating Court), in which a dispute was decided in the claimant's favour and gifts he had given his fiancée were to be returned, for instance, a fur coat valued at NOK2,800 and a fur stole valued at NOK600 (1954 NOK value). The garments had been purchased less than six months prior to the breaking-off of the engagement. The judgment was not unanimous.

Expenses: with respect to the expenses incurred in the wedding preparations, as well as the rental repayment, the situation is somewhat more complex. In cases in which *debts* are involved, one can distinguish three levels of questions: first, it has to be decided

41 From Norwegian case law Rt 1915, 30, the Appeal Court of Kristiania can be mentioned. A woman claimed compensation for monetary loss resulting from a broken engagement, e.g., she had travelled on several occasions and had resigned from her job in the belief that the marriage was approaching. However, no compensation was awarded to her.

42 According to the Contract Act, s. 36, a contract or a promise can be put aside if it would seem unreasonable to adhere to the contract or promise. Norwegian law admits this kind of reasoning: in Rt 1984, 497, 504 it is generally expressed that, in cases of the termination of cohabitation, it should be possible to consider claims based on general enrichment and restitution principles.

43 K. Strøm Bull in 'Vederlagskrav overfor ektefelle eller samboer [Compensation with respect to spouse or partner]' TfR 1985, 499, discusses, for instance, the question of the return of engagement gifts at 542ff. She provides an informative account of court practice and the interpretation of the law in Nordic legal literature.

who is responsible to others, for instance, in respect to creditors (the external situation). This problem is decided on the basis of legal agreements. Secondly, a decision has to be made with respect to the division of debt between the two parties (the internal situation). This problem should be kept separate from that relating to creditors. Thirdly, the question arises whether the termination of the relationship brings about a change in the division of debt between the two parties. The present case pertains to *payments already made*, not to future indebtedness. The external situation is therefore clear. When it comes to the internal situation, the fact that B made all the payments is not decisive. One should ask if this reflected a conscious division of expenditure or if it was due to chance. If the latter situation were the case, it would seem reasonable to have both parties cover their personal share of the expenses. It is not clear how far the courts would be willing to assume that the parties intended to divide the expenditure between them.[44]

If it is assumed that both parties intended that B meet the cost of the wedding, the question arises whether this arrangement appears in a new light once A breaks off the relationship. The situation does not involve a financial gain on A's part, and there are consequently no enrichment or restitution concerns. We are left with items of actual expenditure. (These might possibly involve a certain financial gain on B's part, a gain which ultimately should be deducted from his possible claims against A.) If A were seen as acting in a blameworthy manner, a claim for compensation would be a suitable procedure (see above). Such, for instance, would be the situation if A originally had decided to call off the engagement at an earlier date, but for various reasons neglected to mention this until the day before the wedding. A blameworthy action is constituted by A's delay in waiting until the very last day to inform B. A's failure to fulfil her duty to inform would give B the right to claim compensation for all expenses he could have avoided had A informed him in due time. Whether B, based on an *objective* ground, without respect to blame or bad faith on the part of A, could demand that A bear part of the expenses, is rather uncertain. The general view is that there is always a risk attached to personal events such as weddings. If one of the parties has taken upon himself to meet the expenses personally, he also bears the risks involved.

[44] With respect to the allocation of responsibility for the debt of spouses and partners, see T. Sverdrup, JV 2000, 268–9.

Portugal

A would be liable to B for breaking the engagement, and would have to give the ring back to him and to pay all the expenses which B incurred.

According to article 1591 of the Civil Code the engagement to be married neither gives the parties the right to claim the marriage nor the right to any compensation that is not established by statute, even if the parties agreed on a penalty clause.[45] However, the statute establishes claims based in restitution (article 1592) and in a specific liability (article 1594).[46]

Referring to restitution, article 1592 states that if the marriage does not take place due to incompetence or the will of one of the spouses, he or she has to give back to the other all the gifts he or she received for the engagement and in anticipation of the marriage. Therefore, the engagement ring must be returned to B.

Referring to the liability, article 1594 states that if one of the intended spouses breaks the engagement without a good reason, he or she has to pay damages to the other spouse, his or her parents or third parties who incurred expenditure on their behalf, in order to compensate for all the expenses and debts which they had incurred in the expectation of the wedding. The damages can, however, be reduced by the court by reference to the benefits that can be obtained from the expenditure irrespective of the marriage taking place. Therefore, A would have to reimburse the money paid to the caterers. The deposit of the rent, however, would only be fully reimbursed if B could not take any benefit from it. Legal writers state that this liability is based in the engagement, which is regarded as a contract.[47]

Scotland

At common law an engagement to marry was a contract, and wrongful failure by either party to implement this contractual undertaking gave

[45] Due to the limitations of the statute, case law does not accept any other liability for breaking the engagement. Therefore the other spouse can claim compensation neither for pain and suffering nor for losses based in tort or contract. See STJ 14 Mar. 1990, in BMJ 395, 591.

[46] These rules are applied in practice, although there are not many cases. See, e.g., Sentença T. Círculo Ponta Delgada 21 Dec. 1979 in CJ 1980, 5, p. 241 and STJ 14 Mar. 1990 in BMJ 395, 591.

[47] See Coelho, *Direito da Família*, p. 190; De Lima and Varela, *Código Civil Anotado*, IV, p. 64.

rise to an action in damages. Similarly, a promise to marry could amount to a legally enforceable unilateral promise, breach of which also gave rise to a right to damages. Damages included not only compensation for pecuniary loss arising from the breach, for example the cost of preparations for the wedding, but also for *solatium* to compensate for the emotional strife suffered by the ex-fiancé(e).[48]

However, the law was amended by Law Reform (Husband and Wife) (Scotland) Act 1984, section 1(1).[49] The extent of this provision is wide. First, an engagement is no longer a legally enforceable contract. Therefore, any contractual remedies for breach are no longer competent in Scottish courts. Secondly, by stipulating that a promise or agreement to marry does not create *any* rights or obligations it would appear that the section excludes delictual liability as well as contractual liability for breach of promise. Thus, to draw on the example used by Professor Thomson,[50] if a man deliberately lied when he promised to marry a woman she would appear to have no right to sue him in delict on the ground of his fraudulent misrepresentation. Similarly, there would be no right to sue in negligence, if the promise was made carelessly; for example, if, without taking reasonable care to discover whether he had the capacity to marry the promisee, a man gives a promise to marry which he cannot fulfil. Thus, in contrast with the parallel English legislation, which only prevents agreements to marry operating as contracts,[51] the Scottish legislation prohibits delictual as well as contractual liabilities.

The 1984 Act does not address itself to any of the issues surrounding related contracts or gifts which might arise between engaged couples. Thus, where a marriage does not take place and a dispute arises over the ownership of a house purchased with a view to a marriage, the solution will be governed by the general principles of the law of property. In *Grieve v. Morrison*,[52] an engaged couple bought a house, title to which was taken in joint names. Part of the price was met from the free

[48] *Hogg v. Gow* 27 May 1812 FC.

[49] 'No promise of marriage or agreement between two persons to marry one another shall have effect under the law of Scotland to create any rights or obligations; and no action for breach of any such promise or agreement may be brought in any court in Scotland, whatever the law applicable to the promise or agreement.'

[50] Thomson, *Family Law in Scotland*, p. 8.

[51] Law Reform (Miscellaneous Provision) Act 1970; see the English report on this case above.

[52] 1993 SLT 852.

proceeds of a sale of the woman's previous house. When the marriage did not take place the woman failed to recover the proceeds because she had not established that the transfer of the proceeds to purchase the new house was made in consideration that the marriage would take place. Instead, the court ordered a division and sale under which both parties obtained half the free proceeds from the sale of the new house. On the other hand, in *Shilliday v. Smith*,[53] where a woman paid for repairs and improvements to an intended matrimonial home owned by her fiancé, the Court of Session allowed an action by the woman in unjustified enrichment to recover the sums provided by her.

In relation to the contracts entered into by B with the third parties (for the wedding reception and the lease of the intended matrimonial home), an initial question to be asked is: has B bound himself solely to these contracts, or has he acted as A's agent and thus bound her jointly along with him? If B has bound himself alone, then he is solely liable under them. In such a case, a damages claim is unlikely to lie against his ex-fiancée. To determine whether A has been bound or not would require further examination of the negotiations between B and the third parties. If A has been jointly bound then the liability of A and B to the third parties is likely to be deemed to be 'joint and several', meaning that the third party may look to both for their respective contribution or to either for the whole amount due under the contract. In such a case B would be entitled to relief from A in respect of her share and might raise an action of relief in respect of one-half of each deposit he has paid (and any other sums which might become due). If the contracts have not been frustrated by the cancellation of the wedding (which is unlikely), then B will be likely to seek to avoid the contracts, if provision is made in them for cancellation, or, if not, to repudiate them and face a damages claim (if any) from the third parties.

Where B has acted as A's agent to bind her to contracts with third parties, his action against her is an action of relief in contract law between joint debtors. The amount of recovery would be one-half of the forfeited deposits. If B has acted as A's agent, then if B repudiates the contracts with the third parties and is faced with a damages claim by the third parties, A will be bound to contribute a one-half share of any such damages.

There are no special rules in relation to gifts between engaged parties. If the gift is intended to be made outright then it need not be

[53] 1998 SC 725.

returned if the engagement is ultimately broken off. However, if the gift is made expressly or impliedly conditional on the marriage taking place it must be returned if the condition fails. For examples of outright gifts Professor Thomson cites birthday presents, whereas for conditional gifts he cites the donation of family jewellery.[54]

With particular reference to the present case, the law has not adopted an unequivocal view in relation to the gift of an engagement ring. In one sheriff court case,[55] it was held that the gift of an engagement ring is made unconditionally, but in another[56] it was thought that the ring was returnable if the wedding did not take place, unless the donor had unjustifiably called off the impending marriage. Given that engagements no longer give rise to any legal rights or obligations between the parties, it is thought that it would be better to view the gift of an engagement ring as made outright.[57]

Spain

In Spanish law an engagement is seen as an unenforceable promise to marry which, in case of its being broken, can give rise to liability for 'unjust impoverishment' (*empobrecimiento injusto*).[58] This liability only arises where there is no reason (*causa*) for the breaking of the promise.[59] As no facts are mentioned in this case, it seems that there is no reason for cancelling the wedding. In consequence, A is liable for expenses incurred and for contracts concluded in view of the marriage. There is no liability for the cost of the engagement ring, as the ring was bought not as a marriage gift, but as an engagement gift, and the engagement was concluded and lasted. There is liability, though, for the various deposits which were clearly made in preparation of the wedding or in anticipation of the marriage. The scope of the liability will be fixed considering the circumstances of the case.[60]

Sweden

The ring is a completed gift for which B is not entitled to any compensation. As a presumption, A and B have to share the costs for the reception and the rent of the flat.

[54] Thomson, *Family Law in Scotland*, p. 9, n. 34. [55] *Gold v. Hume* (1950) 66 Sh Ct Rep 85.
[56] *Savage v. M'Allister* (1952) 68 Sh Ct Rep 11.
[57] Thomson, *Family Law in Scotland*, pp. 9–10.
[58] *Audiencia Provincial de Almeria*, 24 Oct. 1994, AC 1994\2380. [59] Article 43 CC.
[60] Cf. *Audiencia Provincial de Almeria*, 24 Oct. 1994, above n. 58, Tercero in fine.

In earlier days there was a provision in Swedish law regulating the consequences of, and responsibilities arising from, 'a broken promise to marry'. This provision was discarded many years ago and in current law no legal responsibility arises from breaking off an engagement. However, a breach of an engagement can still give rise to certain legal effects, even though there are no rules regarding this in the Marriage Code.[61] *Inter alia*, general principles of contract law are applicable to questions concerning the cancellation of gifts between the parties and, in some exceptional cases, concerning liability for damages for one of the parties.[62]

A promise of a gift, such as a promise to give the other party an engagement ring, can be revoked without any consequences as long as the gift has not been handed over to A. If the gift has been handed over to A, it might have been given under the condition that the parties marry. In order for B to reclaim the ring, A must have understood, or ought to have understood, the condition. In most cases, a transferred gift in the form of an engagement ring given to the other party could not be revoked. Thus, A does not have any obligation to return the ring or compensate B for the value of the ring.

If the costs of the reception and the rent are based on agreements between A and B, the presumption would be that these costs should be borne equally by A and B.[63] This presumption could, however, be rebutted due to the circumstances in the particular case, for example if A was unaware of the contract to rent a flat. A fact of no relevance is which party caused the cancellation of the wedding.

Switzerland

According to Swiss law a promise to marry gives rise to a contract[64] that is governed by special legal rules. The provisions regarding 'betrothal' were revised in 2000.

The contractual promise to marry is in opposition to the general rule that the spouses freely decide on their marriage in the moment of the

[61] Äktenskapsbalken av den 14 maj 1987, Marriage Code; Agell, *Äktenskap, samboende, partnerskap*; Ramberg and Ramberg, *Allmän avtalsrätt*.

[62] Agell, *Äktenskap, samboende, partnerskap*.

[63] Cf. §2 of Lag (1936:81) om skuldebrev (Promissory Notes Act) which can be used as an analogy for debts also outside the scope of application of the Act.

[64] Werro, *Concubinage, mariage et démariage*, n. 166; BaslerKommentar-Huwiler, ZGB 90 n. 3ff.

solemn marriage act.[65] Therefore ZGB 90 holds that betrothal does not give rise to an action for specific performance of the marriage. Each party has the right to withdraw from the betrothal at any time.

There is a special provision for the return of presents after the dissolution of the betrothal. By ZGB 91 I:

> In case of the dissolution of the betrothal each party can claim the return of the presents made to the other, with the exception of the usual occasional presents; where the agreement to marry is terminated by the death of a party, the return of the presents cannot be claimed.

This new provision is more favourable to the defendant because there is no duty to return the usual occasional presents. The content of this term depends on the financial situation of the parties.[66] If A and B did not have a very high standard of living, A is obliged to return the diamond ring.

There is also a special provision regarding the liability to compensate other expenses. By ZGB 92:

> Where one party in view of the promised marriage has, in good faith, made special arrangements, he or she can, at the repudiation of his or her promise of marriage, demand adequate compensation, provided this does not appear to be unfair considering the circumstances as a whole.

The deposit for the caterers and the payment of rent are in general 'arrangements' within the meaning of the provision (according to legal writers,[67] examples of 'arrangements' are the purchase of furniture, the booking of a honeymoon and the renting of a new flat). But the duty to contribute requires that the arrangements be made in good faith. There is no good faith if the amount of the expenses was not reasonable in relation to the financial situation of the parties. Moreover, the plaintiff cannot necessarily claim full compensation. The judge has the discretion to determine the amount that is the 'adequate' contribution. According to the earlier provision there was no liability in the case of a good (material) reason for the dissolution. The new rule is more flexible: in addition to the reason for the dissolution the judge has to take into account the consequences of the dissolution and other circumstances. In view of the wide discretion of

[65] Hegnauer and Breitschmid, *Grundriss des Eherechts*, n. 3.07.
[66] Cf. ZürcherKommentar-Escher, ZGB 632 n. 2ff.; BaslerKommentar-Huwiler, ZGB 92 n. 13.
[67] BaslerKommentar-Huwiler, ZGB 92 n. 11.

the court, A might be liable for part or the full amount of the expenses (€3,500).

Editors' comparative observations

This case raises two separate issues in relation to an engagement which is broken off by the fiancée the day before the wedding is due to take place: whether she must return the engagement ring; and whether she is liable for the expenses her fiancé had incurred in relation to (a) the wedding itself (the cost of the wedding reception) and (b) their future married life (an advance of rent on their intended home together). A majority of jurisdictions give remedies in each case, but the reasoning varies.

The case demonstrates how many jurisdictions modify their general approach to precontractual liability in the light of the very particular social policies they think are appropriate to the case of failed engagements.

Engagement ring: a majority of jurisdictions have special rules which make express provision either for gifts generally, or for engagement rings in particular, in the case where the engagement is broken off. Sometimes the general rule is that the ring (or other gifts) must be returned (Austria, Denmark, Germany, Greece, Ireland, Italy, Portugal, Switzerland); sometimes it can be kept (England, France). In France and Switzerland the answer depends on whether it was an unusual gift in relation to the donor's means. The reasoning is sometimes seen as a particular case of the rules on unjust enrichment; but in some cases is based on a presumption of the parties' intention when the ring was first given, either that the gift was conditional on the marriage taking place (Ireland) or that it was unconditional (England). And jurisdictions which either do not have special rules for broken engagements (Finland, Norway, Sweden), or although the case of a broken engagement is regulated they do not have a special rule for *presents* between the engaged couple (the Netherlands, Scotland, Spain), resort to general principles of unjust enrichment, contract and property law which are sometimes similar to the special provisions of other jurisdictions in asking whether the gift can in the circumstances be held to have been either conditional or unconditional. The point on which all systems are clear is that the answer for the ring does not in principle depend on the fault of the party who breaks off the engagement: the trigger for liability to restore the ring (or, in some cases, such as the Netherlands, its value) is simply the breaking-off of the engagement. However, in Austria if the donor who seeks restitution was (unlike in the present case) himself at fault he will not be able to claim restitution of the ring.

Expenses: again, the answer to whether A is liable to reimburse B's expenses sometimes depends on special statutory rules applicable to the breaking-off of an engagement; sometimes it is governed by the general rules applicable to the precontractual phase of a contract. But in jurisdictions which have special rules, they are generally seen as a particular application of the system's rules on *culpa in contrahendo* (by contrast to the special rules for the return of the ring, above, which were seen as a particular application of the rules on unjust enrichment). Most commonly, jurisdictions which have a general rule of precontractual liability or *culpa in contrahendo* will give B a remedy based on the fact that A's breaking-off of the engagement was unjustified. This is the case for Austria, Germany, Greece, Italy, the Netherlands, Portugal, Spain and Switzerland (special statutory rule) and Finland, France, Norway (general application of precontractual liability, *culpa in contrahendo* or tort). However, Denmark applies a more limited rule for broken engagements which requires fraudulent behaviour; and Italy and the Netherlands only allow the liability to be imposed where there has been a formal announcement by the parties of their intention to marry.

It should be noted that Germany, Greece and Portugal have express provision that the liability for expenses on the wrongful ending of an engagement extends to the parents of the disappointed partner, no doubt reflecting a social reality that it is the parents, rather than the engaged son or daughter, who will in fact have incurred the costs of the planned marriage. The Austrian statutory provision does not cover parents' losses but has been extended to them by (not very recent) case law.

Jurisdictions which have not accepted a general principle of precontractual liability differ on the outcome of this case. In England statute has removed contractual liability for the breaking-off of an engagement, and no tort is committed; Scotland has a wider statutory provision excluding tort liability even in principle; but Ireland has a special statutory provision under which expenditure can sometimes be recovered.

A number of reporters (England, Norway, Scotland, Sweden) consider whether A's liability might in fact arise based on either B's acting as her agent in having incurred them (or his share of them), or on the basis of at least some implied agreement between A and B for A to reimburse B's costs.

Case 6: An express lock-out agreement

Case 6

A and B are negotiating for the sale by A to B of A's business. At the start of the negotiations, A agrees that 'for a period of three months he will not negotiate with any third party nor consider any proposal from a third party with a view to concluding a contract for the sale of the business'. During the negotiations between A and B the price is agreed (as €2m) although there is no contract concluded because of other outstanding matters, including the question of whether B will continue to employ the whole of A's workforce. After two months, A receives a proposal for the sale of the business from C, who agrees to take on the whole workforce and to pay a higher price (€3m). A then breaks off the negotiations with B and, after conducting negotiations with C, concludes a contract with C for the sale of the business. During the negotiations, B had incurred accountants' and lawyers' fees in investigating the state of the business. The real value of the business, as established by independent experts, is €3m. What liability (in contract, tort, restitution, or any other form of liability), if any, does A have to B? Would it make a difference if A had instead agreed that 'he will negotiate with B in good faith and only break off the negotiations for a proper reason'?

Discussions

Austria

According to §861 ABGB, people are bound to an agreement only if they have either expressly or impliedly consented to its terms. So as a general rule in Austrian law, no person owes any duty to conclude a contract merely because of the fact that negotiations have already taken place and the other party has started to rely on the contract being concluded.[1] Even breaking off the negotiation process in the very last minute and without giving any reason does not usually give rise to liability.[2]

In exceptional cases, however, liability for breaking off negotiations may arise from the doctrine of *culpa in contrahendo*. The explanation for precontractual liability in these cases lies in (a) reasonable and legitimate reliance of the one party that the partner will not break off the negotiation process and (b) lack of a good cause for breaking off by the other party.[3]

According to the prevailing view, the reliance of a party to negotiations is reasonable if two conditions are fulfilled.[4] First, the major points (the *essentialia negotii*)[5] of the envisaged contract have to be already agreed upon. Secondly, the reliance on the successful completion of the negotiations has to be foreseeable for the other party. Examples of foreseeable reliance are anticipated performance or the incurring of expenses which are apparently of use only if the contract is concluded. If, however, the party did not act in reasonable reliance on the successful completion of the negotiation process, this does not automatically mean that the party breaking off is not liable at all. In such a case, a duty of care may exist and its breach may give rise to liability.

Once there has been reliance by the other negotiating party, only a good cause may justify the breaking-off, thereby excluding liability. As in the stage of negotiations there is no contractual duty that is binding on the parties; the requirements for a proper reason for breaking off negotiations have to be more relaxed than those allowing the cancellation of a contract that has already been concluded. Thus, not only mistake or subsequent impossibility, but also the mere fact that going ahead with the contract in question would be unreasonable for the party breaking off under the present circumstances, constitute proper reasons for the breaking-off.[6]

In the present case, an agreement is reached only on the price, but not on other outstanding matters such as the continued employment of the whole workforce. As not all major points are settled, B's reliance

[1] OGH 28 May 1991, JBl 1992, 118; Koziol, *Österreichisches Haftpflichtrecht* II, p. 74.
[2] OGH 28 May 1991, JBl 1992, 119; 24 Oct. 1995, RdW 1996, 306.
[3] Koziol, *Österreichisches Haftpflichtrecht* II, p. 78.
[4] R. Reischauer in Rummel, *Kommentar zum ABGB* I, Vor §§918–933 N. 17.
[5] E.g. the price of a good or the exact description of a service.
[6] OGH 28 May 1991, JBl 1992, 120.

that a final agreement is going to be reached is not reasonable and legitimate. Consequently, A is not liable to B for breaking off the negotiations. Because of this focus that Austrian law puts for the existence of an agreement on the *essentialia negotii*, the specific wording of the stipulations – that A would not negotiate with third parties – does not matter.

However, had A and B agreed on all central issues, including price and employment of the workforce, then A's liability would depend on whether B incurred any expenses, which A could foresee, as a result of his reliance on the contract becoming perfected. Here, it was definitely foreseeable for A that B would incur accountants' and lawyers' fees when investigating A's business. In consequence, A would be liable under the doctrine of *culpa in contrahendo*, because B's reliance was reasonable and legitimate. A could only avoid liability for breaking off negotiations with B if he succeeds in advancing a proper reason for his conduct. According to the OGH, a reason for breaking off is regarded as proper if continuing the negotiations with B would be clearly unreasonable in the given circumstances.

In the present scenario, however, even though A has found a better opportunity elsewhere, continuing with the negotiations with B may not be found to be clearly unreasonable. Consequently, it is doubtful whether there is a 'proper reason' for his conduct. Only if there is not would A be liable to B for *culpa in contrahendo*.

Nevertheless, even in the absence of an agreement on the central issues, A may be held liable under Austrian law if the judge finds that A's conduct amounts to a breach of his precontractual duty of keeping his partner informed of any foreseeable obstacles to the conclusion of an intended contract. If generously construed, the wording of both stipulations (not to negotiate with third parties, and to negotiate with B in good faith and only break off for a proper reason) could give rise to such a duty to inform. As a result, A might be found to have had a duty to inform B about his negotiations with C. If the judge so finds, he would have to impose liability on A for breaching his duty to keep B informed under the (expanding) doctrine of *culpa in contrahendo*. In any case, A would only be liable for B's reliance interest, that is, accountants' and lawyers' fees; recovery of expectation interest losses would not be available. The imposition of a duty to inform the partner of all circumstances that may endanger or prevent reaching a final agreement must not be excessively assumed. That makes the result of a claim in the present case unpredictable.

Whether another remedy would be available to B is doubtful. He might have a claim in tort only if A is to blame for a violation of §1295(2) ABGB. That means that A must have acted against *bonos mores* (good morals, *Handeln gegen die guten Sitten*). Breaking off negotiations after having agreed not to break them off for three months except for a proper reason comes close to a violation of *bonos mores*. As B has suffered pure economic loss, A's clear intention to cause damage to B is a requisite for imposing liability on A pursuant to §1295(2) ABGB. This condition may not be fulfilled in the present case, and it may not be possible to prove it.

Another remedy that may be cumulated with *culpa in contrahendo* could be found in regular contractual liability. The agreement not to break off negotiations could be regarded as a separate contract between A and B on how to proceed with the negotiations and breaking off the negotiations within a period of three months, or without a proper reason,[7] would then amount to a violation of this separate contractual stipulation. The primary remedy under Austrian law would be an order to continue negotiations. However, as the contract with C has already been concluded, this may be inappropriate, so B could claim damages. As B suffered loss because of his relying on A's performance of the 'contract to negotiate', he is entitled to reliance damages, that is, the accountants' and lawyers' fees he incurred.

B might claim both remedies, that is *culpa in contrahendo* and contractual liability cumulatively, but in both cases he will receive no more than reliance damages. It is most likely that damages would be claimed on the basis of *culpa in contrahendo*, but this is not easy to predict with certainty.

Denmark

A has contractually bound himself not to negotiate with others and this 'letter of intent' is binding. A Danish court would probably reimburse B his lawyers' and accountants' fees but, as there was no contract to sell A's business to B, not his expectation interest in such a contract.

A promise by A to negotiate in good faith and only to break off the negotiations for a proper reason would probably entail a duty to discontinue or break off the negotiations with B as soon as A gets a serious offer from C. A better offer is certainly a good reason for breaking off negotiations.

[7] Whether there is 'a proper reason' for breaking off the negotiations, as referred to by A, is not entirely clear.

England

A may be liable to B for having broken his contractual promise not to negotiate with a third party, nor to consider any proposal from a third party, for a period of three months. An agreement under which one party promises for a specified period of time not to negotiate with anyone except the other party is capable of being an enforceable contract (a 'lock-out agreement'), as long as there is consideration for the promise:[8] that is, as long as B did something or made a counter-promise to A in return for (as the price of) A's promise not to negotiate with third parties. Although there is no express consideration on the facts stated here, a court would look carefully into the facts to see whether there was something which showed that, expressly or impliedly, A was to receive something in return for his promise to restrict the negotiations to B; and the courts are reluctant to find that an agreement between commercial parties fails for lack of consideration.[9] Assuming that a court could find that B had provided consideration for A's promise, A would be liable for damages for breach of contract, which are normally calculated to protect the injured party's expectations, that is, to put the claimant, so far as money can do it, in the same position as if the contract had been performed rather than breached.[10] Here, the figure for damages would be €1m if the court were satisfied on the balance of probabilities that, if A had not broken off the negotiations and sold the business to C, B would have concluded a contract with A for €2m (and so by A's breach of contract B has been deprived of obtaining a business worth €3m for which he would have paid €2m), although there must be some doubt about what a court would in fact find here if there is evidence from experts, and from the offer from C, that the real value was substantially higher.[11] B will not

[8] *Walford v. Miles* [1992] 2 AC 128, 139.

[9] *Pitt v. PHH Asset Management Ltd* [1994] 1 WLR 327 (promise by party in B's position that, if the negotiations ended in agreement, he would enter into the formal transaction within two weeks, could be sufficient consideration for a lock-out agreement).

[10] *Robinson v. Harman* (1848) 1 Ex 850, 855 (Parke B).

[11] In *Walford v. Miles*, above n. 8, the trial judge made clear that the breach of a lock-out agreement would give rise to an assessment of damages for the loss of opportunity, although no assessment was in fact made because the Court of Appeal and the House of Lords held that there was no binding lock-out contract. (There was also an award for wasted expenditure, not challenged on appeal, but based on a claim for misrepresentation rather than breach of the lock-out agreement; this is irrelevant in our case). In *Pitt v. PHH Asset Management Ltd*, above n. 9, there was a successful claim for

be able to maintain a claim for the losses incurred by way of accountants' and lawyers' fees in addition to the claim for the lost value of the business, since those are costs that he would always have incurred in order to obtain the business. A claimant may, instead of claiming damages calculated on the expectation measure, claim his wasted expenditure; but if the wasted expenditure would not have been recouped even if the contract had been performed, the damages are limited to the sum which would have been recouped.[12] Here, on the basis that the lost value of the business is likely to have been significantly higher than the accountants' and lawyers' fees, it will be in B's interest to claim and prove the lost expectation, rather than the wasted expenditure.

If B cannot establish a claim in contract (for example, because he cannot show that he gave consideration for A's promise not to negotiate with third parties), he will have no claim to damages. The wasted expenditure might be recoverable in a tort claim, but on the facts A has committed no tort unless he was fraudulent in making a statement about his intention not to negotiate with others. The only such statement which A appears to have made was at the beginning of the negotiations but it was two months later before he received C's proposal, so there is no basis for a claim in the tort of deceit.

If A's promise had been to negotiate in good faith and only to break off the negotiations for a proper reason, B would have no claim. The House of Lords in *Walford v. Miles*[13] held that a lock-out agreement is acceptable but a 'lock-in' agreement is not. English law does not recognise as a contract an agreement (even an express agreement) to negotiate in good faith because it lacks certainty. Lord Ackner said that a court cannot know, in the event of a dispute following the breakdown of the negotiations, whether a proper reason existed for the termination of the negotiations; that is, the 'good faith' is subjective and the court has no means of determining whether the duty to negotiate in good faith has been broken; and, moreover, that:

> the concept of a duty to carry on negotiations in good faith is inherently repugnant to the adversarial position of the parties when involved in negotiations. Each party to the negotiations is entitled to pursue his (or her) own interest, so long as he avoids making misrepresentations.[14]

breach of a lock-out agreement, but the assessment of damages in the case is not reported.

[12] *CCC Films (London) Ltd v. Impact Quadrant Films Ltd* [1985] QB 16.

[13] Above n. 8. [14] *Walford v. Miles*, above n. 8, 138.

This is the most extreme view in the cases but no later cases have yet formally tempered it.[15]

This case highlights the English courts' hostility to imposing duties between contracting parties during the negotiations. Even where one party has expressly undertaken towards the other an obligation of good faith in negotiating, the courts will not give effect to it. The decision of the House of Lords in *Walford v. Miles* is the strongest and most recent decision in this regard, and Lord Ackner's approach was there based explicitly on the importance of allowing the negotiating parties the freedom to withdraw up to the moment the contract is concluded. This is not, of course, to say that there cannot be contractual or other obligations during the negotiations. A party who makes an offer can by granting an option bind himself contractually not to withdraw the offer; or (as this case shows) he can contractually bind himself not to negotiate with others, but only as long as such a contract is sufficiently certain in its terms, including, in particular, that there is an express time limit fixed for the 'lock-out'.[16]

Finland

Because of A's promise not to negotiate with any third party for a fixed period this might be a case of concurrent bases of liability. First, A has evidently broken standards of good behaviour in contract negotiations, and therefore it is a case of *culpa in contrahendo*. And secondly, A has broken his promise to B, which constitutes a basis for contractual liability. The measure of damages to be compensated in *culpa in contrahendo* is the negative interest (reliance value), which covers B's expenses from the preparations for concluding the contract. This means that A is liable for the fees that B had incurred. A's contractual liability, in turn, covers B's positive interest (expectation value), that is, the value to B of A's promise not to negotiate with anyone else during the agreed period.

[15] More recently, there have been indications of a reluctance in the Court of Appeal to allow an *expressly* negotiated clause between *commercial* parties to fall foul of *Walford v Miles*; see *Petromec Inc v. Petroleo Brasilieiro SA* [2006] 1 Lloyd's Rep 121 [116]–[121]. However, this has not yet been reviewed in the House of Lords.

[16] In *Walford v. Miles*, above n. 8, there was no time fixed for the 'lock-out' which was therefore unenforceable: to imply a 'reasonable time' would bring back the difficulties of certainty in deciding whether the reasonable time had elapsed, and would indirectly import the duty to negotiate in good faith: see Lord Ackner at 140.

It may, however, be difficult to prove the scope of B's positive interest, or even whether there is any loss suffered by B that would be covered by the positive interest. In principle, B's costs of preparing for the contract cannot be compensated on the basis of the positive interest.[17] But if B could prove that if the promise had been performed it would have yielded B a result worth at least these costs, they should be compensated on the basis of the positive interest. This would cover also the possible positive surplus value of A's promise to B exceeding the costs he had incurred.

But as indicated above, it may be difficult to show causation of damage, a prerequisite of liability. The required 'adequate' causality means usually 'foreseeability': a party is liable if he actually knew or at least should have realised the inherent risk of damage of the relevant type in his action. Also there may be an issue in relation to the obligation of the injured person to limit the damage (the contributory negligence principle).

In making his preparations for a contract that is only under negotiation, a party has to take into account the possibility that no contract will ever be achieved. This implies some degree of carefulness in incurring costs that would become useless if no contract is concluded. Only insomuch as a party can show that he had reasonable grounds to make his investments in reliance on the contract will his reliance be protected by compensation of his costs. Even a promise not to negotiate with anyone else nor to consider any proposal from a third party does not in itself give any guarantee of achieving a contract.

Among the issues that affect the prospects of a contract in this case is the major unsettled question of the employment of A's workforce. The fees A had incurred seem to be indispensable costs for assessing the profitability of the contract. Costs like these are usually incurred at one's own risk and should be borne by oneself even in cases where the negotiations are broken off. Perhaps B could have the costs imposed on A by proving that he would not have undertaken the preparations if A had not given his promise.

Even B's positive interest (expectation value) pertaining to A's promise not to negotiate with others does not cover the value of the intended contract between A and B (€2m), and certainly not the value of

[17] See the general outlines of the positive and negative interests in the Finnish report on case 1.

the contract concluded between A and C (€3m). Performing what A promised to B would not necessarily have brought about the final contract between them. Thus, B cannot claim any lost profits that would have accrued from the contract. But if B could show that without A's promise he would have sought other partners at an earlier stage and could have concluded contracts with them, B could perhaps claim the value of any such contracts.

If A had promised only to 'negotiate with B in good faith and only break off the negotiations for a proper reason' his liability ought to be judged differently. In this case there would not have been any fixed period reserved for negotiations only with B. Liability for breaking off the negotiations could be based only on *culpa in contrahendo*, meaning usually behaviour contrary to good practice in contract negotiations. This general standard would here be supplemented by the promise to follow the 'good faith' standard and 'only break off the negotiations for a proper reason'. Getting a clearly better offer from a third person is a commonly accepted reason for withdrawing from contract negotiations. A's behaviour would have fulfilled both the general and the promised standards of good practice. So, it would not have been a case of *culpa in contrahendo* (or breach of promise), and A could not have been held liable to B for breaking off the negotiations.

France

A agrees with B not to undertake negotiations with a third party for the sale of his business during a period of three months. The price of the sale of the business is set at €2m between A and B but the contract of sale is not yet concluded because of uncertainty on outstanding points. It should be noted that in France the question as to whether the workforce is going to be employed by the buyer of the business is answered by law and cannot, thus, be regarded as an outstanding point. Indeed, article L.122-12 of the Code du travail, implementing European Directive 2001/23/EC, obliges the buyer to employ *all* of the seller's workforce.

The problem arises from the fact that A breaks off the negotiations with B before the end of the three-month period and concludes the contract with C.

The negotiation agreement between A and B is, under French law, of a contractual nature. Writers and courts use the expression '*avant-contrat*' to stress that the agreement is a contract by itself but is aimed at concluding another contract - the main contract (*contrat principal*). The existence of a contract obliges B to sue under contract law.[18] The conditions of contractual liability resemble those of tortious liability: fault, harm and causation.[19]

There is certainly contractual fault here since A breached the contract in negotiating with C before the end of the three-month period. The harm is apparently of two types: the economic loss (lawyers' and accountants' fees) representing the expenses incurred during the negotiations, and the loss of the opportunity to conclude the contract. 'Precontractual negotiations may not be regarded as leading certainly to the conclusion of the contract; therefore, the breach of negotiations entails a mere "loss of chance" to conclude the contract and make benefits.'[20] Courts[21] will compensate this loss if the lost chance was 'real' and 'serious', conditions whose fulfilment is hard to determine in the present case. B had little chance to conclude the contract at €2m since another buyer already proposed €3m. In fact, we know now that the real value of the business is €3m. Is the harm directly linked to the fault?[22] At first sight the answer seems positive, and it certainly is as far as the loss of opportunity to conclude the contract is concerned. But a closer look reveals that the question is quite hard to answer as to the expenses. Some writers argue that, in any event, these expenses would have been borne by B had the negotiations not been wrongly broken off; they therefore conclude that A does not have to pay for damages independent of the fault.[23] Others disagree.[24] A theoretical approach undoubtedly leads to the conclusion that the expenses are not 'caused' by the fault. Courts, however, seem to be very in favour of awarding compensation.[25]

[18] This is the consequence of a jurisprudential principle, the *principe du non-cumul des responsabilités contractuelle et délictuelle*. On this question see Viney, *Introduction à la responsabilité*, p. 403ff.

[19] For a discussion of the general principles of tortious liability, see the French report on case 1. There is very little interest in distinguishing contractual and tortious liability in this case. See, e.g., P. Chauvel, note on Com 7 April 1998, D.1999, 514, no. 4.

[20] Schmidt-Szalewski, *Formation of Contracts and Precontractual Liability*, p. 95.

[21] Com 3 May 1979, Bull Civ, IV, no. 137; Com 2 Nov. 1993, Bull Civ, IV, no. 380.

[22] See general solutions given in the French report on case 1.

[23] B. Lasalle, 'Les pourparlers', RRJ 1994–93, 825ff., esp. 851–2; Com 30 Nov. 1991, Bull Civ IV, no. 288. See French report on case 1.

[24] Ph. Le Tourneau, 'La rupture des négotiations', RTDCom 1998, 479ff., esp. no. 27; F. Violet, note on Paris, 10 Mar. 2000, JCP 2001, II, 10470, no. 2.

[25] Com 7 Jan. 1997, D.1998, J., p. 45, note P. Chauvel, esp. nos. 31 and 32; Civ 3, 9 Oct. 1972, Bull Civ III, no. 491. See O. Deshayes, 'Le dommage précontractuel', RTDCom

Would it make a difference if A had only agreed to 'negotiate in good faith' and 'break off the negotiations only for a proper reason'? The contractual duty in fact, adds nothing to the legal duty to negotiate in good faith. Under articles 1382 and 1383 of the Civil Code, A's behaviour could not be regarded as a fault. Free to undertake parallel negotiations, A is free to break off negotiations with B. He would not therefore be liable.

Germany

A cannot assert a claim resulting from a sales contract, since the parties have not reached agreement upon all the outstanding matters they deemed necessary. According to §154(1) BGB, consent upon individual points does not, as a rule, bind the parties, as long as they have not agreed upon all points upon which according to even only one party agreement had to be reached.

A is, however, in breach of his contractual duty not to negotiate for a period of three months with any third party. German law, as a rule, requires a party in breach of a *contractual duty* to recompense the other party's expectation interest (*Erfüllungsinteresse*). Nonetheless, B is not entitled to expectation damages, there being no causal relationship between A's breach of contractual duty and B's economic loss. Since A, after the expiry of the three-month period, would not have been barred from selling the business to C at its market value of €3m, B cannot demonstrate (the onus of proof lying on him) that without A's breach of duty he would have secured A's business and thereby made a profit of €1m. As to damages, therefore, the duty not to negotiate for a certain period is immaterial under German law unless the debtor has promised the payment of a sum of money in case he does not perform his obligation or does not perform it in a certain manner[26] or has granted a right of pre-emption[27] or an option to the promisee. In this case the only consequence of A's breach of duty is to entitle B to break off further negotiations immediately.

A is not liable on the ground of §§280(1), 311(2) No. 1 BGB (*culpa in contrahendo*) for breaking off contractual negotiations, since he did not

2004, 182ff; one could say that liability in such a case is really a means of punishing the author of the fault. The damages represent a sort of punitive damages (which French law, as a general rule, does not recognise).

[26] §339 BGB. [27] §463ff BGB.

make B expect that a contract would (almost) certainly come about. Hence, B's expenses (accountants' and lawyers' fees in investigating the state of the business) are at his own risk.

A is not liable in tort. He has not injured one of the special legal interests protected by §823(1) BGB nor wilfully caused damage to B.[28] And he is not liable in restitution: A is not enriched at the expense of B.[29]

It is immaterial whether A had agreed that he would negotiate with B in good faith and only break off the negotiations for a proper reason. Under German law such an agreement would be purely declaratory in character, the duty of bargaining in good faith as the basis of the institution *culpa in contrahendo* already being established by virtue of the law.[30]

Greece

A and B had agreed to conduct exclusive negotiations for the sale of a business from the former to the latter for a period of three months and in that time not to consider any other proposal. It must be stressed that this is an agreement for exclusive negotiations for a limited period of time and not an agreement to conclude the contract. The most proper way to construe such an agreement between the parties would be to consider it as a specification to the precontractual obligation to conduct negotiations in good faith and according to business usage. The parties to the negotiations are indeed free to determine specifically the content of the obligation to act in good faith.[31] Therefore, by breaking off negotiations upon considering C's proposal and entering into negotiations with him merely two months after the beginning of the negotiations between A and B, A behaves in a manner which is contrary to good faith according to article 197 GCC as construed by the additional agreement between the parties. Had such an agreement not been in existence, then A's conduct would probably not violate the requirement of negotiating in good faith.

Accordingly, on the basis of article 198 GCC, B is entitled to compensation, which will be limited to the reliance interest comprising of positive and negative damage. B will recover the expenses he incurred for the expert's fees. He will not recover the price difference between the agreed price and the estimated real value of the business. This sum represents

[28] Cf. §826 BGB. [29] Cf. §812(1) BGB. [30] §§241(2), 311(2) BGB.

[31] But they may not agree to exclude liability from the negotiations. Of course, they may agree that their contact does not constitute negotiations. See G. Koumandos, in Georgiadis and Stathopoulos, *Commentary on the Greek Civil Code*, n. 61; Kambitsis, *Precontractual Liability*, p. 147; Gazis, *Legal Consultations 1956–1999*, p. 259.

the amount he would have profited from had the contract been concluded, which represents the non-compensatable expectation interest.[32]

As for the meaning of an agreement between the parties 'to negotiate in good faith and only break off negotiations for a proper reason': according to article 197 GCC, in the course of the negotiations the parties must behave in a manner that is consistent with good faith and trade usage. As the stages of negotiation progress, so the obligations of the parties intensify. Still, the obligation to conduct negotiations in good faith never becomes an obligation to conclude the contract; the parties can, in principle, freely disengage from negotiations.[33] But as the negotiations advance, either party may only break off negotiations for a proper reason. A proper reason is broadly understood to be any reason that is consistent with the bargaining. Any reason inherent in the negotiation process is always consistent with good faith; for instance, if no agreement can be reached on some specific points or a better offer is made. Nevertheless, what amounts to a proper reason varies according to the circumstances.[34] In a case where negotiations have significantly progressed and an agreement has been reached on all major points, but a formality remains to be complied with and one party reassures the other that the conclusion of the contract is certain, then it would be contrary to good faith to break off negotiations if a better offer comes along (that is, not a proper reason).[35] In view of all the above, under Greek law an agreement between the parties in such general terms to 'negotiate in

[32] See AP 1565/2000 Chronika Idiotikou Dikaiou 2001, 220 (with note by Iatrou).

[33] M. Karasis, in Georgiadis and Stathopoulos, *Commentary on the Greek Civil Code*, vol I, p. 320: 'The principle of good faith does not create an obligation to conclude a contract. The breaking off of the negotiations, even without a reason, does not constitute *ipso facto* conduct which is contrary to good faith and business usage; the case is different if a party is culpable and the other party has the impression that the conclusion of the contract is a certainty.' That a party may break off negotiations without invoking a proper reason, except if a party has promised otherwise, is established in Court of Appeals of Athens 2403/1962 NoV 12, 101.

[34] Gazis, *Legal Consultations 1956–1999*, p. 301, states that if a party breaks off negotiations after having given the impression that the contract will be concluded or negotiations have lasted for a long time or they have been costly for the other party, then a party is liable if he breaks off negotiations without invoking a proper reason; in that case he considers that a better offer is not such a proper reason. Also at p. 309 he says that an honest and fair party does not abandon negotiations without a proper reason (*αποχρώντα λόγο*).

[35] Thus, in a case where an agreement had been reached between the negotiating parties and one party reassured the other that the signing of the contract was imminent and all that was left was a mere formality, a better offer was not considered to be a proper

good faith and only break off the negotiations for a proper reason' does not substantially add to the rights and obligations of the parties during the precontractual stage. Thus, if such a term had been stipulated, A would not be liable for precontractual fault, given the fact that the negotiations were not significantly protracted and, besides the price, other outstanding matters remained undecided. Given the progress of negotiations in these circumstances a better offer most probably constitutes a proper reason for breaking off negotiations.[36]

Ireland

A's promise not to negotiate with a third party is unsupported by consideration. Therefore A will not be liable to B. However, if B can establish that the promise is in fact a collateral contract, then it may be enforceable and B can claim reliance damages with respect to expenses incurred.

For any agreement to be enforceable it must be supported by consideration[37] or made under seal. Precontractual promises[38] are generally not enforceable as they lack the necessary consideration.[39] However, this principle is not without exception. The obvious injustices that may arise in such cases are dealt with by a variety of common law responses.[40] First, where a benefit has been transferred to one party in the belief that a contract will be concluded, restitutionary remedies may be available.[41] However, this is unlikely to

reason for breaking off the negotiations (First Instance Court of Thessaloniki 1278/1998 Arm 1998, 543).

36 See Court of Appeals of Thessaloniki 65/1994 Arm 1994, 1134, where a party was considered to have lawfully and without liability broken off negotiations when the other party protracted the stage of negotiations for an unnecessarily extended time. The loss the latter suffered from the end of the negotiations was deemed to be his own fault because for ten months he delayed the conclusion of the contract.

37 *Eastwood v. Kenyon* (1840) 11 A & E 458.

38 *Dickinson v. Dodds* (1876) 2 ChD 463 (offer to sell, stated to be open for a fixed period: could still be withdrawn within the period because no binding contract yet). Precontractual promises include: promises to negotiate a contract, promises to keep an offer open for a specified amount of time, and promises not to negotiate with third parties, the so called 'lock-out' promise.

39 Courts have tended to give varying interpretations as to what constitutes consideration: in *Pitt v. PHH Asset Management* [1994] 1 WLR 327, a 'lock-out' promise was held valid as it was supported by consideration consisting of, *inter alia*, a promise to exchange contracts within a specified period.

40 *Interfoto Picture Library Ltd v. Stiletto Visual Programmes Ltd* [1989] QB 433.

41 *British Steel Corporation v. Cleveland Bridge and Engineering Co. Ltd* [1984] 1 All ER 504.

enable a plaintiff to seek recovery of expenditure incurred.[42] Secondly, the doctrine of promissory estoppel may also be applied. Under this doctrine, a promise which is relied upon by an individual to their detriment may be enforceable despite the absence of consideration where it is just to do so. On a conservative view, the doctrine only applies where there is a pre-existing contractual relationship between the parties. However, there has been no definitive response from the Irish courts although there are some dicta which indicate that the doctrine might apply even in the absence of such a pre-existing contractual relationship. However, the doctrine will not operate to create a cause of action where none previously existed and therefore has limited application in situations such as this. Thirdly, liability might arise in tort if one party intentionally deceived the other party as to the possibility of completing a contract when in fact there was no such possibility. However, no tort action arises simply by virtue of a change of mind. Finally, the most promising form of action for precontractual liability may be that of the collateral contract. The consideration in a collateral contract is the putative main contract itself. In *Blackpool and Fylde Aero Club v. Blackpool Borough Council*,[43] the court compensated the plaintiff for expenses incurred in a tender process where the plaintiff's tender had negligently been omitted from consideration. The court effectively held that there was a collateral contract between the parties that the tender would be considered by the defendant. The consideration for this collateral contract was engaging in the tender itself. The difficulty in the collateral contract doctrine is the nebulous nature of its application. How are we to distinguish between precontractual promises which are collateral contracts and those which are not? Much of course depends on the individual facts of each case. What is clear is that the promise must go beyond the facts of *Dickinson v. Dodds*.[44] We are looking for something extra. A's original promise is exactly within the ambit of *Dickinson* since it is nothing more than a promise to give B an exclusive option to purchase. Without consideration it is unenforceable. However, if A were to amend the promise so as to include that negotiations are to be in good faith and termination would only be for proper cause, this might be sufficient to bring the promise into the category of an enforceable collateral

[42] Although under US law a less rigorous approach is taken: *Earhart v. Low William Co.*, 600 P 2d 1344 (Cal 1979).
[43] [1990] 1 WLR 1195. [44] Above n. 38.

contract. Damages for collateral contracts are limited to reliance damages only and do not include expectation loss.[45]

Italy

It is likely that A would incur precontractual liability according to the principle of good faith in negotiations (article 1337 of the Civil Code). A has given B reason to rely on their negotiations. Having agreed to negotiate with B exclusively for a determined period (and a period which is not too long), A has shown himself to be willing to limit his own freedom to negotiate in favour of B. Despite the lack of agreement on major points of the contract, A is bound by his promise because it was expressly related to the conduct he should adopt during the negotiations.

Italian case law has accepted that withdrawal is justified where the negotiations have become less attractive[46] or the withdrawing party had received a better offer.[47] But in the present case it does not seem that C's offer could be taken as a satisfactory reason justifying A's withdrawal. Although judges have shown sensitivity about employment matters in the precontractual phase,[48] it is very unlikely that A would escape liability. As a consequence, A has to reimburse B's expenses (equivalent of *interesse negativo*).[49]

If the promise to negotiate exclusively with B for three months was explicitly inserted within the letter of intent the case could be analysed as a 'lock-out' contract: in this case, however, the remedy is expectation damages for breach of contract, rather than a case of precontractual liability, because the lock-out clause is a contract binding on A.

On the other hand, if A agreed that 'he will negotiate with B in good faith and only break off for a proper reason', no time limit would have been established as a real limit of the good faith of the party in the negotiations. However, the solution as regards precontractual liability will not change. Indeed, article 1337 has been so interpreted by the courts. It is for the judge to balance B's unsatisfied expectations against A's conduct, to determine whether it consists of a breach of good faith in negotiations. In particular, in assessing the amount of damages the judge could bear in mind C's promises to take on the whole of A's workforce

[45] *Walford v. Miles* [1992] 2 AC 128.
[46] App. Roma, 20 May 1955. [47] App. Venezia, 6 July 1955.
[48] As shown by PRET, P. Pinerolo, 2 Mar. 1982, concerning precontractual liability of a firm ceasing trading.
[49] See the Italian report on case 1.

and the much higher price offered by C. According to Italian case law, this could at least be considered a reason to reduce A's liability.[50]

Netherlands

A and B have concluded a binding contract. A broke this contract by starting negotiations with a third party (C) within the three months' period, and by considering its proposal. A is therefore liable to compensate all B's damage.[51] A is immediately in default because proper performance is no longer possible.[52] With the acquisition of the business B would have made €1m profit. The question is whether the non-acquisition may be regarded as a consequence of the breach of the lock-out agreement.[53] That agreement did not contain any explicit lock-in agreement; that is, A was under no contractual obligation to reach an agreement with B. Nor is there any indication that the negotiations were in the 'third stage' where breaking-off is no longer allowed and where the liability may extend to the expectation interest.[54] On the contrary, there remained some important outstanding issues. On the other hand, however, without the breach the business would not have been sold to C and would still have been available for acquisition by B. Therefore, it can be said that, as a result of A's breach, B has lost the chance to buy A's business for a price considerably (€1m) less than its market value. Similarly, it can also be questioned whether the accountants' and lawyers' fees that B has incurred in investigating the state of the business are losses caused by A's breach. However, it seems unlikely that the broad and normative (not merely factual) Dutch test of causation (what damage can be reasonably attributed to the event (i.e. the breach)?) would be interpreted in such a strict way by the Dutch courts that the breach of this contract entails no remedy whatsoever.

If the parties had only agreed that A would 'negotiate with B in good faith and only break off the negotiations for a proper reason' the result would probably have been different. Whether A would be liable under these circumstances would depend on the interpretation of the agreement. The meaning of a written contract depends on the meaning that the parties could reasonably be expected to give to it in the circumstances.[55] In principle, interpretation of contracts is a factual matter

[50] Cass Civ, 29 Nov. 1985, no. 5920 in GI 1985, I, 1. [51] Article 6:74 BW.
[52] Article 6:81 BW. [53] On causation, see art. 6:98 BW.
[54] See Dutch report on case 1.
[55] HR, 13 Mar. 1981, NJ 1981, 635, note Brunner; AA 1981, 355, note van Schilfgaarde.

that the highest court (Hoge Raad) will not go into. Although the agreement is fairly vague it explicitly says that A is allowed to break off the negotiations for a proper reason. In this case B had more than one proper reason. First, C agrees to take on A's whole workforce. If A cares about his workers it may be crucial to him that the new owner of his business takes on the whole workforce, whereas in the negotiations with B this question had remained open. Secondly, A agrees to pay a higher price (€3m). The difference in price is substantial: 50 per cent more. Therefore, it seems, under the alternative agreement A would probably not be liable.

Norway

Agreement to negotiate exclusively: no binding contract for the sale of the business exists – the agreement with respect to price is not sufficient – and the question then becomes whether A is subject to precontractual liability. A appears to have committed an obvious breach of duty with respect to B, which therefore should constitute liability. Determining the degree of liability, however, could give rise to certain problems.

According to Norwegian law, the parties can agree to follow certain rules during the negotiations, for instance, with respect to precontractual agreements. Such agreements are 'binding as far as they go'.[56] The agreement between the parties imposes on A 'a period of three months during which he is not to negotiate with any third party nor [to] consider any proposal from a third party with a view to concluding a contract for the sale of the business', which naturally also excludes other offers during this period. This binding agreement has been deliberately broken by A, and he is liable.

In the first instance, B can claim the accountants' and lawyers' expenses, in accordance with the *reliance interest*. Admittedly, the requirement to show cause and effect between the unlawful act and the

[56] Cf. Rt 1992, 1110, the *Stiansen* case, at 1114, which refers to a letter of intent with respect to a contract for the construction of buildings. In the rules of tendering, which are typical precontractual agreements, this has been stated on several occasions. One such occasion is referred to in Rt 1997, 574, the *Lrlingeklausul* case, at 577 where the presiding judge states: 'The participants – if they have put time and money into submitting a tender – have the right to rely on the owner basing his negotiations and decisions on the agreed terms.' In Rt 1998, 1951, the *Klubben* case, at 1957, it was said: 'The municipality of Ulvik invited tenders for snow removal in the district. This implied that the municipal authorities in their choice to whom to grant contracts, also committed themselves to follow the rules for tendering.' In neither case were the invitations to submit tenders subject to the EU/EEA regulations.

loss might be a problem. The unlawful act occurs after the bulk of the expenses have been incurred, and nothing indicates that A originally had any other intention but to keep to the agreement. However, Norwegian courts might be willing to reduce to some extent the requirement of cause and effect in these cases.[57]

One might also ask if B may claim the *expectation interest*. In the present case this constitutes €1m (€3m less €2m). Whether it is possible to claim this loss as resulting from an unlawful act during the precontractual period has yet to be determined in Norway. Within the legal regulations with respect to tenders, two cases are available, both of which tend to favour such liability.[58] If, in principle, B can claim such losses, the main problem is trying to demonstrate that he would have been awarded the contract if matters had been conducted according to the agreement. In the present case, we are informed that the parties had agreed on the purchase price. However, how strong is the likelihood that the remaining problems would be solved? And further, what is the likelihood of the business being sold at £1m below its real value? Does the agreement with respect to B's offer exclude consideration of C's offer?

Agreement to negotiate in good faith: if the parties had limited themselves to agreeing that A 'will negotiate with B in good faith and only break off the negotiations for a proper reason', it is far more uncertain whether A has broken his obligations towards B.

In such a case, there is no agreement to negotiate exclusively. The parties have in reality agreed on the usual obligation to act in good faith in precontractual situations. There is then no obligation that the

[57] In Rt 1997, 574, the *Lrlingeklausul* case, at 577, it was stated: 'Preventative measures, and the particular difficulties arising with respect to liability in such situations, indicate in my opinion that no strict requirements should be applied as to cause and effect in order to establish liability where obviously unlawful acts have been committed.'

[58] In Rt 1997, 574, the *Lrlingeklausul* case, at 578, the presiding judge added, but without influencing the judgment, that 'what is clear is that the parties, who would have been granted the business if the mistake had not occurred, can claim damages, presumably based on positive contractual liability'. In Rt 1998, 1398, the *Torghatten* case, legal obligations based on expectation interest were imposed on the municipal authorities. However, the case concerned compensation in a public administration situation, and therefore is not of major significance in resolving common disagreements with respect to tendering. Both cases concerned invitations to submit tenders which fell outside the EU/EEA regulations. For another argument that the expectation interest, circumstances allowing, should be awarded, see Simonsen, *Precontractual Liability*, p. 352ff.

negotiations be exclusive.[59] Furthermore, a breach of agreement as a result of a better offer from a third person would essentially be considered a valid reason from a business point of view for terminating the negotiations. Even if Norwegian courts would strongly emphasise the obligation to act in good faith when the parties have agreed to it, it is nonetheless doubtful whether A's conduct is wrongful.

However, two questions arise: first, whether A is free to disregard the agreement on the purchase price of €2m. One can assume that the price was the major reason for breaking off negotiations with B. Norwegian law has no cases to refer to in this respect. In certain situations it has to be assumed that so-called 'back trading' (returning to points on which one had formerly agreed) would be contrary to the parties' obligation to act in good faith. The main rule, however, is that partial agreement is not binding on the parties. In the present case, A presumably would have renegotiated the price. There are also grounds for him to withdraw for the same reason. The second question is whether B should have been given the opportunity to match C's offer. In other words, should A have had *a duty to warn* B? There is reason to expect that A in the current situation should have given B this opportunity.

In the event of a breach of the obligation to act in good faith, the damages would be assessed as in the case of the agreement to negotiate exclusively, above.

Portugal

B can claim compensation based either in contractual liability or pre-contractual liability, but only for the expenses of the lawyers' and accountants' fees.

A and B have entered into a lock-out agreement. This kind of agreement is not very common in Portugal and only some legal writers refer to it.[60] Our legal system would regard it as a contract establishing an obligation *non facere*. Therefore, B can claim losses and damages based only in the fact that A has failed to fulfil his obligation – contractual liability, established in article 798 of the Civil Code. As no penalty clause was stipulated, B would have to prove that he has suffered loss arising from A's breach. However, the fact of B being unable to buy the

[59] See the Norwegian report on case 4.

[60] See E.S. Júnior, 'Acordos intermédios: Entre o início e o termo das negociações para a formação do contrato' ROA 57 (1997), 565, 594–5 and L.M. Leitão, 'Negociações e responsabilidade pré-contratual nos contratos comerciais internacionais' ROA 60 (2000), 49, 65ff.

business for a price well below the market value cannot be seen as a loss arising from the breach of the contract because the sale was not yet concluded and therefore B had not acquired the right to purchase the business at that price (expectation interest). In Portuguese law a simple loss of the chance to purchase the business is not sufficient for a claim to expectation interest damages. Therefore B would be entitled to claim only compensation for his expenses, the accountants' and lawyers' fees.

The same solution arises from the rules of precontractual liability.[61] In fact, the agreement on the price and the promise not to accept other proposals would be seen as a situation of reliance, which cannot be harmed without a good reason. The acceptance of another proposal in this situation would be considered as a breach of the duty of loyalty which makes A liable for the reliance interest. Therefore he could be required to pay the expenses B has incurred. The fact that B cannot buy the business at the agreed price is not, however, a loss that can be covered by precontractual liability, according to the majority of legal writers.

If A had instead agreed 'that he will negotiate with B in good faith and only break off negotiations for a proper reason' it makes no difference to the solution of this case. In fact, this kind of 'agreement to negotiate' would be considered irrelevant under Portuguese law as statute[62] already establishes a duty to negotiate in good faith, from which can be established that no one should break off negotiations without a proper reason, and in this case A has a 'proper reason'.[63]

Scotland

The undertaking by A given to B not to negotiate with other parties may operate as a free-standing contract or unilateral promise, so-called 'lock-out' agreements being valid obligations in Scots law.[64] As consideration is not a requirement of Scots contract law, the lack of any consideration on A's part would not preclude the enforceability of such an obligation. It would seem from the facts given that this undertaking has been broken, which should entitle B to damages for breach of contract or breach of promise.

[61] Article 227 CC. [62] Article 227 CC.

[63] The Portuguese rules of interpretation require a contract to be interpreted by a normal person in the position of the party (art. 236 CC). Concepts such as 'proper reason' therefore give some margin for the judge's interpretation.

[64] *Dawson International plc v. Coats Paton plc* 1988 SLT 854, affd. 1989 SLT 854.

One possible measure for the quantification of a damages claim for breach of a lock-out agreement would be to calculate B's lost chance of concluding the deal, and use this as a multiplier in relation to the anticipated profit to be gained from the deal. It may, however, be impossible to assess the level of chance of such a deal being concluded successfully, in which case damages for the lost chance would not be awarded. As an alternative, wasted expenditure might be sought. In *Dawson International plc v. Coats Paton plc*,[65] the damages sought (some £8.3m) represented the costs of underwriting the proposed merger of the companies, printing and professional services related to the bid, and tax chargeable on recovery of these costs; in other words, wasted expenditure. These damages were sought under two alternative heads, namely breach of contract and the equitable recovery of wasted expenditure. While the case based upon the equitable remedy was dismissed by the judge, the claim based upon damages for breach of contract was thought relevant. Lord Prosser, considering the case at a further stage of procedure,[66] addressed the question of whether wasted expenditure was an appropriate quantum for assessing damages. He agreed that it might be if it were possible to show that such expenditure would have been recovered had the breach of contract not occurred. On the facts of the case, he thought this unlikely. The general point is more important, however: such a quantification is theoretically possible in Scots law, even if it may be hard to recover in practice. If damages are awarded for the loss of the chance of concluding the deal, then damages for wasted expenditure would not be awarded, and vice versa.

Would it make a difference if A had instead agreed that 'he will negotiate with B in good faith and only break off the negotiations for a proper reason'? It is unlikely that such an obligation would be enforced by the Scottish courts. A similar obligation was denied effect by the English courts in *Walford v. Miles*,[67] which may fairly be described as the apogee of good faith scepticism in English law. This case has not been directly commented upon in any reported Scottish decision. At first sight, however, the decision in *McCall's Entertainments (Ayr) Ltd v. South Ayrshire Council (No. 1)*,[68] in which *Walford* was cited to the court, appears

[65] 1988 SLT 854, affd. 1989 SLT 854. [66] 1993 SLT 77. [67] [1992] 2 AC 128.

[68] 1998 SLT 1403. See also, for full facts proved after trial of the case and suggestive of the landlord's bad faith, *McCall's Entertainments (Ayr) Ltd v. South Ayrshire Council (No. 2)* 1998 SLT 1423.

to adopt a more positive approach to the enforceability of obligations to negotiate in good faith. The case concerned a lease, in which an option to purchase the leased subjects had been granted to the tenants. The option clause obliged the landlords to '*enter negotiations* for the sale to the Tenants of the subjects and to so sell the subjects, at a price to be agreed between the parties and failing agreement within three weeks, at a price to be fixed by an Arbiter' (emphasis added). The landlords argued that this obligation lacked specification and certainty, being merely an agreement to agree. The Court of Session disagreed, however, and held the clause to be enforceable. To suggest, however, that this decision supports the view that agreements to negotiate in good faith will always be upheld by the Scottish courts would be going too far. In the judge's opinion in *McCall's*, the fact that negotiations might produce no agreement by the parties on price was not fatal to the certainty of the agreement, due to the provision allowing settlement by the arbiter. Many obligations to negotiate in good faith will contain no such third party reference, however, and for such obligations the approach of *Walford v. Miles* is likely to be adopted, with the obligation to negotiate in good faith being denied effect.

Spain

By seriously considering C's offer within the period of three months and at the end by contracting with C, A breaks his express (precontractual) promise to B. Even if the breach of this promise is not necessarily the origin of any damage, as it does not guarantee that a contract will be concluded between A and B, the promise does in fact provide a certain protection, giving the parties a three-month period to negotiate without having to compete with any third parties. Therefore it is necessary to clarify the legal consequences of the promise.

A contract concerning only the negotiation period can be valid and can itself have consequences, such as the obligation to compensate loss arising from its breach.[69] Such a contract, according to general principles of Spanish law, would be validly concluded by consent, object and cause.[70] All these elements can be assumed here (consent by tacit acceptance of the offer; a certain behaviour as the object of the contract and a valid 'cause', probably to encourage the other party to negotiate).

[69] STS, 3 June 1998, no. 516/1998, RJ 1998\3715. [70] Article 1261 CC.

Based on this contract, B can claim compensation for the expenses incurred during the negotiations as the 'negative interest' of the contract (he is to be put in the situation he would be in if he had not concluded the contract, before the negotiations).[71] The 'positive interest' does not entitle him to claim the difference of value and the price already agreed, as he will not be able to prove that, without C's intervention, the contract would have been concluded after two months.

There is here no elaborate contract to conclude the future contract (*precontrato*), under which the parties have the same rights as under the contract itself.[72] For such a pre-contract, the essential content of the 'real' contract would need to be agreed upon. But in our case, even if the price and the object are certain, other 'outstanding matters' are not yet clear, which means that the parties have not reached agreement on all important parts of their contract; they have not yet reached the end of their negotiations.[73] In other words, even if the objective characteristic parts of the contract are determined, the subjective characteristic parts are not yet clear, and both parties know about this uncertainty. They do not act as if a final agreement has already been reached: the negotiations are still ongoing, in their preparatory phase (*fase preparatoria*), as there has not been a final proposition for the whole contract to be concluded.[74]

It might, though, be possible to admit the existence of a pre-contract in its broader sense, a contract by which only the objective essential elements of the contract to be concluded are agreed, but not the further details. As price and object are defined, there seems to be a pre-contract in the sense of article 1451.2a of the Civil Code (promise of sale impossible to fulfil). But it is not certain whether the parties, by only agreeing on a price and object, did mean actually to conclude a pre-contract or whether they did not rather want to wait until all elements (including subjectively important elements) were certain. In the latter case – which appears more probable – there is no pre-contract, as the parties did not want to be bound yet by their mere agreement.[75]

If A had only promised to 'negotiate in good faith and break off the negotiations for a proper reason' there would probably be no liability if

[71] Article 1101 CC. [72] Cf. STS, 29 July 1996, no. 680/1996, RJ 1996\6408, CUARTO.

[73] Cf. STS, 31 Dec. 1998, no. 1234/1998, RJ 1998\9772, CUARTO.

[74] Cf. STS, 31 Dec. 1998, no. 1234/1998, RJ 1998\9772, CUARTO; STS, 3 June 1998, no. 516/1998, RJ 1998\3715.

[75] STS, 3 June 1998, no. 516/1998, RJ 1998\3715: '*Voluntad negocial*', cf. in German: '*fehlender Rechtsbindungswille*'.

we admit that there is no *precontrato*. It must generally be admitted that receiving a clearly better offer from a third party justifies the breaking-off of negotiations and is not contrary to good faith, as good faith does not impose an obligation to conclude the contract which is only being negotiated. B might prove that 'proper reason' in this context meant B causing the breaking-off of the negotiations, but this seems rather improbable.

Sweden

A is not liable to compensate B for the breach of contract.

A has, by considering the offer from C, breached the agreement not to consider offers from others than B. The agreed term does not impose a duty on A not to consider C's offer if it comes wholly 'out of the blue' and A has been totally passive. Nor does the term impose an obligation on A that he should continue negotiations with B if he knows about another, and better, offer and therefore will not sell the business to B for the sum already agreed.

The agreed term and the negotiations between A and B do not impose on A a duty to enter into a final agreement during or after the three-month negotiation period, which means that B negotiates at his own risk and cost. However, the agreed term does impose a duty on A to inform B of the other offer he has received in order to make it possible for B to mitigate his costs and other losses.

It might also impose on A a duty not to take initiatives actively to find other bidders. If A has actively tried to find other bidders and that activity resulted in the bid from C, A has acted contrary to the agreement and will probably be liable to compensate B for his negotiation costs. Under these circumstances, there are grounds to conclude that A from the beginning intended to find other bidders as well. By entering into the lock-out agreement A therefore acted contrary to good faith by giving B the impression that B had a certain period in which he could solely try to convince A about the advantages of entering into an agreement of sale. Although there is no legislation or case law supporting it, there are reasons to believe that B would be entitled to compensation for his reliance interest. If A failed to inform B about the other bidder as soon as he received the bid, he is liable to compensate B for the unnecessary costs B has incurred in the meantime.[76]

[76] NJA 1990.745.

Had the agreed term instead imposed a duty on A to negotiate with B in good faith and only break off negotiations for a proper reason, he would not have had the duty not actively to seek other bidders. Nor would he have had a duty to inform B of the other bid he received.

Switzerland

B is not entitled to a claim resulting from the contract of sale. The parties have not concluded a contract because they have not reached agreement with regard to all (subjective and objective) points. But there is a contract not to negotiate with third parties and not to sell the object of the negotiations to third parties during a fixed period. A broke this lock-out agreement (*Vorfeldvereinbarung* or *Exklusivvereinbarung*)[77] when he started negotiations with C. The non-performance of this contract cannot be excused. A is liable and has to put B into the position he would be in if the lock-out agreement had been performed. A therefore has to compensate B's expectation interest in the lock-out agreement.

But in general this does not mean that B can claim compensation for the lost profit from the purchase of the business. The lock-out agreement gives no right to conclude a sales contract.[78] A was free to sell his business to a third party after the lock-out period. B can only claim the difference between the agreed price (€2m) and the market value (€3m) if he can prove that without A's breach of the lock-out agreement he would have concluded the sales contract and made the profit of €1m.

However, B can claim compensation for the (wasted) expenses he incurred after the violation of the lock-out agreement.[79] It is true that these expenses might have become wasted when A broke off the negotiations with B *after* the lock-out period. But in view of the violation of the agreement the expenses had already been wasted during the negotiations. As in the case of negotiations without any intention to conclude a contract,[80] A has to compensate B's expenses.

The lock-out agreement may be interpreted as containing the duty to disclose parallel negotiations with third parties. A has violated this duty. B can therefore claim compensation for the expenses he would not have incurred if he had known about the parallel negotiations. In

[77] BernerKommentar-Kramer, OR 18 n. 60ff.; Gauch, Schluep, Schmid and Rey, *Schweizerisches Obligationenrecht Allgemeiner Teil*, vol. I, n. 983ff.

[78] Cf. BernerKommentar-Kramer, OR 18 n. 62.

[79] Gauch, Schluep, Schmid and Rey, above n. 77, n. 985.

[80] See the Swiss report on case 1.

view of C's better offer, B might have terminated the negotiations and saved the cost of the accountants' and lawyers' fees.

A is not liable on the ground of *culpa in contrahendo* for the break-off of serious negotiations. According to the prevailing opinion, a party is free to break off serious negotiations even without a good reason before a binding offer. Only in exceptional circumstances (especially if he made the other party believe a contract would certainly come about) might the party be liable.[81] In the present case there are no such exceptional circumstances.

The contractual duty to negotiate in good faith would not add anything to the general duty to negotiate in good faith on the ground of *culpa in contrahendo*. A has not violated this duty when he started parallel negotiations. However, it might be material if A agreed to break off negotiations only for a proper reason because in general a party is free to break off the negotiations without a material reason. The liability (for the expenses) depends on whether C's higher offer was such a proper reason. The contractual term is not clear and has to be interpreted. By interpreting a contract the judge is not restricted to the general sense of the wording. He must consider the entire context of the contract, especially the parties' behaviour before and after the contract was concluded. The judge must also consider the parties' interests, custom and the general principle of good faith.[82]

Editors' comparative observations

This case contains two separate forms of precontractual agreement: (1) a 'lock-out' agreement, under which A agrees not to negotiate with a third party for a fixed period; and (2) an agreement under which A is to negotiate in good faith and only break off negotiations for a proper reason. When A receives a better offer from a third party, C, and breaks of the negotiations with B, almost all jurisdictions give B a remedy in the first case; but most do not give a remedy in the second case. The reasoning in the several reports is often very similar, but the case points up some interesting differences of approach even where there is on the surface a similarity of reasoning.

[81] See the Swiss report on case 4.

[82] Cf. ZürcherKommentar-Jäggi/Gauch, OR 18 n. 329ff.; BernerKommentar-Kramer, OR 18 n. 16ff.

Lock-out agreement: in almost all jurisdictions this is analysed as a case of contract, rather than of precontractual liability, even if it is a *precontractual* contract. Most reporters have little difficulty in seeing that A's agreement with B, that he will not negotiate with third parties, constitutes a contract within their jurisdiction. England and Ireland are more cautious, because their rules of contract law require that A's promise not to negotiate be supported by consideration, and these two reports contain an interesting contrast, the English courts apparently being more inclined than the Irish courts to try to find consideration in a case between commercial parties. But this is a matter of general contract law rather than of precontractual liability and need not be pursued in detail here[83] (although it should be noted that Scotland, which has no requirement of consideration for the validity of a contract, is aligned with the other ('civil law') jurisdictions on this point).

Of the jurisdictions that analyse this as a case of contractual liability, almost all then hold A liable in contract, although there are some differences in the analysis of the remedy. Some (England, France, the Netherlands, Norway and Scotland) will allow expectation damages calculated not by reference to the simple value of the intended contract (at the price of €2m, yielding a loss of €1m against the true value of €3m) but only as the lost *chance* of this because there was not yet any binding promise by A to sell at €2m. These reporters are all rather hesitant, however, particularly over the question of whether there can be proof of such expectation loss, given that the market value of the business is €3m and therefore the realistic chances of a sale having been concluded at only €2m must be very low. Most will allow recovery of B's wasted expenditure, some making clear that wasted expenditure is the only possible calculation of loss for a contract of this type, and some using the expenditure as a measure of A's lost profit (in the absence of clearer evidence as to the actual value of the lost opportunity; several reporters note explicitly that the expenditure cannot be recovered in addition to the lost (chance of) profit). The accountants' and lawyers' fees incurred by A are recoverable (in contract) according to Denmark, England, Finland, France, Ireland (if there is a contract at all, which the reporter doubts), Italy, the Netherlands, Norway, Portugal, Scotland, Spain and Switzerland, although some reporters doubt

[83] For a further comparative exploration of the requirement of consideration, see the companion volume in this series, Gordley, *The Enforceability of Promises in European Contract Law*.

whether these losses were in fact caused by A's breach of contract. The strongest analysis of causation is in the case of Germany, which would hold that A has contractual liability but none of the losses are caused by his failure to perform his contractual duty, and therefore there is no remedy. Other jurisdictions, however, take a less strong view of causation, the most extreme being Norway, where the courts have been prepared explicitly to relax the causation requirement where the defendant's act is 'obviously unlawful'. One might ask whether a lock-out agreement can serve any useful purpose if in practice it is so difficult to attach a remedy to its breach. The solution is hinted at by both the German and Portuguese reporters: to provide in the agreement for the payment of a fixed sum (a penalty) for breach of the lock-out obligation.

Sweden analyses the case rather differently: it is a case of contract, but Swedish law would interpret A's contractual obligation ('for a period of three months he will not negotiate with any third party nor consider any proposal from a third party with a view to concluding a contract for the sale of the business') as requiring him only not *actively* to solicit third party bids, although if this was in fact what A had done his liability would then be (as most jurisdictions agree) for B's wasted expenditure. This case therefore shows that, although there can be a general approach to the basis of liability (contract) on facts such as this, the application of the detailed rules of each system (here, on the interpretation of the contractual obligation, the quantification of loss and the test for causation of damage) can result in a significant divergence of result.

Greece does not focus on possible contractual liability but treats this as a case of precontractual liability; and other jurisdictions (Austria, Finland, Italy, Norway and Portugal) consider precontractual liability as an alternative to contractual liability on these facts: but then the trigger for liability is not (as in contract) A's failure to fulfil his promise not to negotiate, but A's failure to inform B of the negotiations with C (Austria) or his breaking off the negotiations with B in bad faith. In all cases, the remedy would be reliance damages, to cover B's wasted expenditure (again, subject to the question of whether the loss was caused by A's wrongful act). Austria and Greece see the lock-out agreement as having modified the precontractual duty of good faith under their Civil Codes, and therefore although the claim is in precontractual liability rather than in contract, the agreement is still in substance the basis of the liability. France, following its strict rule of *non cumul*, has to apply the contractual duty in preference to the general precontractual liability (which is founded on tort),[84] but reaches the same result since it regards the content of the contractual duty as identical to the general tort duty.

Agreement to negotiate in good faith: only Austria and Italy are clear that A is liable; but Ireland, Norway and Switzerland keep open the possibility of liability. All other jurisdictions are clear that there is no liability. These differences of result mask some significant differences of reasoning.

England, Ireland and Scotland rest their primary analysis on contract: England is clear that there cannot be a contractual obligation to negotiate in good faith and not to break off only for a proper reason; Scotland is a little more open to this; Ireland might go so far as to contemplate a contract but the reporter's focus is on whether there is sufficient consideration to make the contract binding. This case therefore shows an interesting contrast amongst the jurisdictions which have so far not admitted a generalised duty of good faith in negotiations.

Most of the other jurisdictions apply their general rules of precontractual liability, and almost all of them consider that the express agreement by A simply reaffirms his general duty and therefore adds nothing. The difference of result therefore becomes an issue of whether on the facts here A was entitled under the general rules of precontractual good faith to break off negotiations. France, again following its rule of *non cumul*, will apply the contractual duty in preference to the general precontractual liability founded on tort; and the Netherlands, Spain and Sweden also apply a contractual analysis (but appear to consider that the contractual duty here is the same as the general duty of good faith). Switzerland, however, thinks that the express agreement takes the duty beyond the general obligation of its rules of *culpa in contrahendo* since A has undertaken not to break off except for a proper reason (which is a stronger obligation since the general duty would allow a party to break off without any reason until a binding offer had been made). Even when the agreed duty is analysed as being of similar content to the general duty of good faith, however, there is a difference of opinion as to A's conduct on the facts. Most consider that A is not liable, because receiving a better offer from a third party is a good reason to break off negotiations. But Austria and Italy consider that A has broken his (general) duty of good faith; and Norway thinks it arguable that he should at least have given B the opportunity to match C's price.

[84] See the French report on case 1.

Case 7: Breakdown of merger negotiations

Case 7

A and B, both major firms of accountants, negotiate with a view to the merger of their firms. A breaks off the negotiations.

There are three separate situations to consider:

1. A breaks off the negotiations *after three years of very intense negotiations* in which both parties have incurred considerable expenses, but where the parties recognise that they have not yet reached agreement on all major points and A has not made any statement to B that it is convinced that they will reach final agreement.
2. A breaks off the negotiations quite soon after their beginning, but after *the parties have reached agreement on all major points*, and only a few minor points remain to be settled. A has not made any statement to B that it is convinced that they will reach final agreement. B has already incurred legal expenses.
3. A breaks off the negotiations when the parties have not yet reached agreement on all major points but *A has more than once made statements to B that it is convinced that they will reach final agreement.* B has already incurred legal expenses.

What liability (in contract, tort, restitution, or any other form of liability), if any, does A have to B in each of these situations if A gives no reason for breaking off the negotiations? Would it make a difference if it (honestly) gives as the reason for breaking off the negotiations:

(i) it has received a better offer from C for a merger of A's firm with C's firm;

(ii) it has discovered that there is an insurmountable cultural difference between the firms;

(iii) it cannot afford the merger;
(iv) (in the case of lengthy negotiations, situation 1) during the negotiations there is a general recession and the merger is no longer as attractive for A as it was.

In the case where the negotiations had already lasted three years (situation 1), does it make a difference in any of these cases if A knew of the reason a year before it broke off the negotiations?

Discussions

Austria

Under the doctrine of *culpa in contrahendo* a party to negotiations is only liable for breaking-off if his conduct gave his partner legitimate reason to rely on the successful completion of the negotiation process. This requires, first of all, a meeting of minds on the major points of the intended agreement.[1] If no such meeting of minds occurred during the negotiations, there is no reason for B's reliance on the certainty of the conclusion of the envisaged contract to be reasonable and legitimate.

Therefore, in situation 1, notwithstanding the long duration of the negotiation process of three years and notwithstanding the considerable expenses the two parties incurred, no reasonable or legitimate reliance on B's part can be found on the facts, and the breaking-off of the negotiations by A appears to be nothing but a correct exercise of the rights granted to each negotiating party by the fundamental rule of freedom of contract. It does not matter to which justification for breaking off the negotiations A resorts. Nor could A be subjected to liability under any other theory of Austrian law for any loss B may have suffered. However, if A had knowledge of definite reasons for breaking off the negotiations one year before it actually broke them off, A is to blame for having acted against the duty of mutual care which is imposed on the parties to negotiations as soon as a 'lawful contact' has been established.[2] This duty of care requires a party to negotiations to inform its partner about all circumstances that may endanger or prevent a final agreement. Usually, such a duty exists whenever good faith and fair dealing so require, for example, in the

[1] OGH 28 May 1991, JBl 1992, 120; R. Reischauer in Rummel, *Kommentar zum ABGB* I, Vor §§918–933, N. 17. See further the Austrian report on case 6.
[2] OGH 8 Oct. 1975 SZ 48/102.

case of foreseeable expenses which are apparently of use only if the contract is concluded in the end.[3] Since B incurred considerable expenses during the negotiations which A could foresee, A owed it a duty of care, a duty to inform B of the undisclosed reasons for breaking off negotiations. A breached this duty for a period of one year. Therefore, A may be held liable under the doctrine of *culpa in contrahendo* for B's reliance loss.[4] The exact amount of damages depends on the loss that B has suffered since the time A knew the reasons that would lead to breaking off the negotiations, since only this loss has been caused by A's breach of its duty of inform.

If A continued to negotiate with the positive goal of causing damage to B, its unfair conduct could amount to a violation of good morals and entail delictual liability under §1295(2) ABGB. It would be very difficult for B, however, to show that A acted wilfully to cause damage to B. The facts indicate that A may rather be successful in convincing the judge that it was not entirely certain whether there was a reason for breaking off negotiations.

In situation 2, even though no statement that a final agreement will be reached has been made, agreement on the *essentialia negotii* has been reached. Furthermore, it must have been foreseeable to A that B would incur legal expenses. Consequently, as both requirements are met, A is liable under the doctrine of *culpa in contrahendo*[5] and B is awarded reliance damages to the extent of the legal expenses that B incurred. However, A could avoid this liability if its breaking-off is justified by a good cause. Such a justification would be any reason significant enough to allow the cancellation of a contract that has already been concluded (such as mistake or subsequent impossibility). According to the OGH, a good cause is sufficiently established if reaching a final agreement would be unreasonable in the circumstances of the case.[6] There is no proper reason when, as in variant (i), A has simply found a better opportunity elsewhere, since an agreement with B would still be reasonable. The same is the case in variant (iii): an agreement with B may no longer be acceptable for A for financial reasons, but as this reason only affects A and is a result of its conduct, it cannot constitute a proper reason either. Therefore, A would be liable in both cases, as the given reasons are not proper.[7] Reason (ii), however, may give a different solution, as it affects both A and B and makes an agreement unreasonable

[3] R. Reischauer in Rummel, *Kommentar zum ABGB* I, Vor §§918–933, N. 17. [4] Ibid.
[5] OGH 28 May 1991, JBl 1992, 118. [6] Ibid. [7] Ibid.

for A. Consequently, in this case – and only in this case – A would not be held liable under the doctrine of *culpa in contrahendo.*

If the agreement on the major points in situation 2 is in writing and was signed by all parties to the negotiations, then it constitutes a so-called *Punktation* (or draft) according to §885 ABGB. Such a draft document has to contain the essential terms of the agreement, whilst minor points may remain unsettled. It is a valid contract and its contents may be enforced. Usually, a *Punktation* should later be replaced by another agreement. A *Punktation* has the effect of an enforceable contract, whereas *culpa in contrahendo* focuses on the precontractual stage, that is, creates a duty to compensate reliance loss of a negotiating partner before a contract or a *Punktation* is reached. Therefore, a cumulation of the remedies is not possible. The same factual background may give rise only either to the enforcement of a *Punktation* or to damages under the doctrine of *culpa in contrahendo.*

As stated above, liability under the doctrine of *culpa in contrahendo* can, as a rule,[8] be imposed on a negotiating party only if the *essentialia negotii* have already been settled. Exceptionally, however, the fact that A has made more than one statement that it is convinced that a final agreement will be reached could be crucial for the imposition of liability on A. In fact, such conduct of A may give B legitimate reason to rely on the coming into existence of the envisaged merger, provided that A created the assured impression that a final agreement will be reached.[9] In situation 3, therefore, the question of A's liability to B depends on the judge's evaluation of whether A, by its statements, induced an assured reliance in B that was reasonable and justified in the circumstances. This is doubtful on the facts, however. Since a variety of views exist in Austrian law about the range of precontractual liability, it is again difficult to predict with absolute certainty whether a claim by B based on *culpa in contrahendo* would be successful. All depends on whether B could be reasonably and legitimately confident, from A's statements and from the progress of the negotiations, that the contract would be concluded. If the judge finds that A has created a reasonable and justified reliance in B that a final agreement will be reached (this may be unlikely, but is not absolutely impossible), liability for reliance loss would be imposed on A if it fails to give a

[8] The use of the word '*grundsätzlich*' by R. Reischauer, in Rummel, *Kommentar zum ABGB* I, Vor §§918–933, N. 17, indicates that no clear and unequivocal answer can be given.

[9] The court uses the phrase '*in Sicherheit wiegen*' which means 'to lull somebody into a false sense of security': OGH 28 May 1991, JBl 1992, 118; see also OGH 30 May 1979, SZ 52/90 = JBl 1980, 33.

sound reason for breaking off. In that case, B would have a good chance to be compensated for those legal expenses it would not have incurred had it not relied on A's statements. Since A's contradictory behaviour caused B to incur expenses, A cannot excuse itself by resorting to excuses (i) to (iii): in the circumstances A would have no reasonable and legitimate reason for breaking off the negotiations. It is much more likely, however, that A will not be held liable for any of B's loss. Notwithstanding A's statements that it is convinced that a final agreement will be reached, B acted at its own risk when it incurred legal expenses at a time when the negotiations had not created a common position of the parties on the major points of the deal.

Denmark

In situation 1, each of the reasons is a good reason for breaking off the negotiations. If A knew the reason a year before, it is difficult to see a reasonable motive for keeping them secret and therefore reasons (i) and (ii) are not very likely. In situations (iii) and (iv) the only motive may be that A hopes that the situation may change in which case it can hardly be said to have known the reason.

In situations 2 and 3, A is probably not liable. If a party has not expressly or impliedly promised the other party that it will not conduct negotiations with others it has no duty to abstain from doing so. And A's statements (about being convinced that they will reach agreement) which are not promises make no difference. It is therefore doubtful whether A will be liable when it relies on reason (i). As for (ii) one can question whether this is not a major point which separates the parties. As for reason (iii) there may be liability if A negligently had not checked in time whether it could afford the merger.

England

In all these situations A has no liability unless B can show that any of A's statements were made fraudulently.

In situation 1, there is certainly no liability where A breaks off the negotiations at the time when it first formulates its reason for breaking off. B has no claim to damages for breach of contract since the parties acknowledge that there is no contract for the merger, nor is there any evidence of any other form of contract on the facts; and no representation has been made which could found a claim in tort based on a misrepresentation nor any estoppel. The length of the negotiations, and the reason for A's breaking them off, are irrelevant.

If, however, A had known the reason for a year before it broke off the negotiations a court will look carefully into the facts to see whether, during that period, it made any statement which can found a claim in the tort of deceit. If by its words or its conduct it communicated to B its intention to pursue the negotiations to a successful conclusion when it had already decided that it would not do so, it might have made a fraudulent misrepresentation: such a case would then be similar to case 1.

Situation 2 is indistinguishable from situation 1. There is not yet any concluded contract for the merger: the fact that the parties have agreed all the major points does not mean that there is yet a contract for the merger since the contract will (as the parties acknowledge) only be finalised when the 'few minor points' have also been settled. Nor is there any other form of contract. And A has not made any representation which could give rise to any claim by B in tort based on a misrepresentation nor any estoppel. The fact that the negotiations are almost complete, and the reason for A's breaking them off, are irrelevant.

In situation 3 again A has no liability unless it did not honestly believe its statement that it was convinced that the parties would reach final agreement. As long as A was honest in making that statement, this case is indistinguishable from situation 1. There is not yet any concluded contract for the merger: the fact that A has made statements that it is convinced that they will reach final agreement is not a promise to continue with the negotiations (and such a promise would not, in any case, generally be binding for the reasons given in relation to case 6). Nor is there any other form of contract. And A has not made any representation which could give rise to an estoppel. The only possible argument would be if A was lying when it made the statement that it was convinced that they would reach final agreement: this would then be a fraudulent misrepresentation of its opinion which would give rise to a claim by B for damages in the tort of deceit. However, in the absence of proof of fraud B has no claim, and the reason for A's breaking off the negotiations is irrelevant. Fraud is a serious allegation and therefore the courts require clear evidence to establish it.[10]

This case highlights each party's freedom to withdraw from negotiations, regardless of its reason, and regardless of how long the negotiations have been continuing and the loss that the breakdown of the negotiations will cause to the other party, as long it makes no false

[10] *Smith New Court Securities Ltd v. Scrimgeour Vickers (Asset Management) Ltd* [1997] AC 254, 274 (Lord Steyn).

statement which could found a claim based on misrepresentation. In English law, each party is generally free to withdraw from the negotiations even up to the moment immediately before the contract is finally concluded. In many commercial transactions it is common for the parties expressly to reserve such a right, by stating that their negotiations are 'subject to contract', that is, that they acknowledge that there is no binding agreement until a formal contract is entered into. But though such an express reservation assists a court by dispelling any doubt about whether the negotiations had yet culminated in a concluded agreement, it is not necessary, and as long as it is sufficiently clear on the facts that the parties have not yet reached a binding agreement, either party may still withdraw.

Finland

In situation 1, where the parties recognise that they have not yet reached agreement on all major points and A has not made any statement that it is convinced that the final agreement will be reached, the principle of freedom of contract negotiations prevails. It includes freedom to break off negotiations with no need to give good reasons. So A is not liable for breaking off the negotiations in any of the alternative circumstances (i) to (iv), even if it does not give any reason for its withdrawal. But if A knew of its reason to withdraw a year in advance, then it should have informed B about it without delay. If it has neglected to do this, it would very likely be held to have acted contrary to good practice, and thus shown *culpa in contrahendo*. This is a basis for the compensation of B's costs insofar as they have accrued during the period of A's omission to inform B of its reasons to withdraw.

In situation 2, the parties have reached agreement, which they acknowledge, on all major points and only a few minor points remain to be settled. A has, however, made no statement that it is convinced that the final agreement will be reached. In this case, too, the principle of freedom of contract negotiations prevails, as a starting point. It means freedom to break off negotiations with no need to give good reasons. So A would perhaps not be held liable for breaking off the negotiations in any of the alternative circumstances (i) to (iii), even if it does not give any reason for its withdrawal. But this case is a bit more complicated than situation 1. If both parties acknowledge that agreement has been reached on all major points, we should perhaps refer to aspects of reliance protection discussed in relation to case 2. If a party has very good grounds to believe that the conclusion of the contract is at hand, lacking no more than just the formal confirmation, his reliance may be worth protecting. In order to impose reliance-based liability on the other party, it must have been at fault in giving some basis to the other party's reliance. Withdrawing from negotiations should under these circumstances be sanctioned with liability covering at least the costs of the other party. Too little information about the facts is given, however, to decide upon A's possible liability on this basis. Further limits to the freedom of negotiations are derived from the fact that a party is not entitled to enter into negotiations with no true intention to conclude a contract. But none of the circumstances (i) to (iii) given in the facts indicate such motives on A's part. So A's possible liability should be judged on the basis of the protection of B's reliance.

Situation 3 is similar to situation 1 (the parties have not yet reached agreement on all major points) but here A has more than once made statements to B that it is convinced that the final agreement will be reached. In this case there could be some scope for the application of the principle of reliance protection, discussed above. B can have well-founded reasons to believe that the conclusion of the contract is at hand, lacking no more than just the formal confirmation. A has also given some basis to B's reliance. Withdrawing from negotiations should under these circumstances be sanctioned with liability covering the costs of the other party. So in this case A may be liable for B's costs.

France

A is free to break off negotiations until a real agreement on all the points to be discussed has been reached (that is, until a contract has been concluded) and as long as it does not do so wrongfully.[11] In order to obtain damages, B must prove that A is liable under articles 1382 or 1383 of the Civil Code, therefore needing to establish harm suffered because of A's wrongful conduct (fault).

To establish A's fault, B must show that the breaking-off occurred suddenly while an agreement seemed to be close. The fault is assessed with regard to the circumstances of the breaking-off.[12]

In situation 1, on the one hand, as the negotiations lasted three years – a long time – one might think that the condition of fault is satisfied. On the other hand, the two parties had not yet reached a

[11] Civ 1, 12 Apr. 1976, Bull Civ I, no. 122. See the French report on case 1.
[12] Com 20 Mar. 1972, Bull Civ IV, no. 93.

complete agreement, and A never made any statement to B that they would reach a final agreement. Furthermore, they have not agreed on all major points about the merger. As a result, it is not likely that A would be held liable for the breaking-off of the negotiations about the merger, because the breaking-off does not appear wrongful.[13] However unlikely the evidence of fault might be, it remains possible because it depends on the judges' assessment of the facts. If so, A would have to give a 'legitimate reason' to escape its liability.[14] If A does not justify the breaking-off, and if its behaviour is considered wrongful by the judges, it will be held liable for it.[15]

If A gives a reason for the breaking-off, the judge will determine whether the reason is 'legitimate' or not. Reasons (i), (ii) and (iv) may be considered as legitimate, whereas reason (iii) is not likely to be so considered. Reason (i) is a good reason because the purpose of A, as well as B, is to obtain the most profitable merger. However, A may have to inform B of C's offer before breaking off the negotiations, in order to respect the duty of good faith in negotiations, according to article 1134 alinea 3 of the Civil Code.[16] Otherwise, it could be held liable for not having allowed B to make a counter-offer. Reason (ii) is acceptable as well, as it is probably revealed by the difficulty of the negotiations, which lasted a very long time without an agreement on all major points of the merger. Reason (iii) is unlikely to appear legitimate because three years of negotiations are surely long enough for A to calculate the probable cost of the merger. Reason (iv) may be considered as a legitimate reason, as a recession is not due to one of the parties, and

[13] Com 18 Dec. 1990, Jurisdata no. 003753, where the termination of negotiations appeared to be 'inevitable' because of the deep disagreement between the parties.

[14] On this, see the French report on case 1. It is quite difficult to determine whether the burden of proof lies on A, or if it is only in its interest to establish a legitimate reason, because case law is unclear on this point.

[15] Com 7 Jan. 1997, D. 1998, J, 45; Com 20 Mar. 1972, Bull Civ IV, no. 93.

[16] Versailles, 1 Mar. 1991, JurisData no. 043489. The question of a duty of good faith in negotiations is debated among academic writers, because art. 1134 C.civ. only applies to contractual situations and not before the conclusion of the contract. Some authors think that the article applies to the formation of contract as well as to its performance (see J. Schmidt-Szalewski, 'La sanction de la faute précontractuelle', RTDCiv 1974, 52), and some explain that the duty of good faith is an integral part of the '*normes générales de comportement*', breach of which leads to liability under arts. 1382 and 1383 of the Civil Code (see P. Chauvel, note on Com 7 Jan. 1997, D. 1998, J, 45, no. 9; P. Mousseron, 'Négociations contractuelles et responsabilité civile délictuelle', RTDCom 1998, 253; J. Mestre, RTDCiv 1997, 651).

because we can assume that each party could foresee this recession[17] to a certain extent.

If A knew the reason one year before it broke off the negotiations, none of the reasons given should be considered as legitimate, because of the duty of good faith in negotiations imposed on each party.[18]

If A's fault is established, B would have to prove both harm and causation. These two last conditions do not raise difficulties. As far as the harm is concerned, three years of negotiations definitely represent 'considerable expenses' incurred in negotiations, as well as a long time during which B did not take advantage of the opportunity to conclude a contract with a third party. Each of these should be included in the damages awarded to B if A is liable. Finally, it is clear that a chain of causation between the fault and harm is established, because the breaking-off directly caused the harm suffered.

In situation 2, the negotiations have been carried out quickly, and though the parties have reached an agreement on all the major points of the merger, such an operation is complex enough to say without doubt that even a disagreement on minor points may cause a failure in the negotiations. Thus, A's withdrawal is not in itself a fault, even if the agreement seemed very close. Furthermore, A never made B believe that they would reach an agreement. Therefore, it is not likely that fault can be proved. However, if we assume that A's behaviour has been wrongful, it will need a legitimate reason in order to escape liability, and the analysis will be as discussed above in relation to situation 1, except that here reason (ii) can be considered as 'legitimate' because the negotiations did not take place over a long period of time and in consequence we can assume that the parties did not know each other very well; which is confirmed by the fact that A never made any statement about the fact it was convinced that they would reach final agreement. And here reason (iii) does not seem to be legitimate because one can assume that the price of the merger is one of the major points of the negotiations. That is why, as an agreement

[17] Paris 4 Dec. 1996, JurisData no. 024388; Rennes 3 Nov. 1998, JurisData no. 049142. The recession is not foreseeable in itself, but it does not correspond to what French law calls *force majeure*. That is why judges prefer to consider that, because a recession is always possible when negotiations are long-lasting, there is no fault of either of the parties when one of them breaks off the negotiations. *Force majeure* is a technical tool used to paralyse the effect of an existing fault, whereas in our case the recession impedes the judges in recognising the existence of a fault.

[18] See above n. 16. See Com 20 Mar. 1972, Bull Civ IV, no. 93.

has already been reached on all major points, the price is considered to have been accepted by A, which means it thought that it could afford the merger.

In situation 3, even if the parties had not yet reached an agreement on all major points of the merger, B 'legitimately' believed,[19] because of A's repeated statements about the future success of the negotiations, that they would reach final agreement. By breaking off the negotiations, A has not acted consistently with its repeated statements, therefore breaching its duty of good faith in negotiations. A's action in breaking off the negotiations is therefore likely to be held wrongful by the judge, if B is able to justify its reliance on A's statements. As discussed above, A can, however, escape liability by giving a legitimate reason justifying the breaking-off. As in situation 1, reason (i) is certainly a 'legitimate reason', although A may have to inform B of C's offer before breaking off the negotiations. Reason (ii) is, on the contrary, less likely in this situation to be considered as 'legitimate', for it appears inconsistent, on the one hand, to repeat several times that an agreement can be reached, which means that the present difficulties of the negotiations are likely to be solved, and, on the other hand, to find out finally that cultural differences justify the breaking off. The last justification (iii) might be 'legitimate', because the parties have not yet reached an agreement on all major points, that is, including the price of the merger. But on the other hand, A made statements to B several times that the negotiations would succeed. Therefore, one might think that, as A certainly knows very well how much it could pay for the merger, and never told B that it might have difficulties in affording the price, it has behaved inconsistently and

[19] The concept of 'legitimate belief' (*croyance légitime*) has been proposed as a criterion for precontractual fault by some authors. This criterion focuses on the victim: as soon as the victim had good reasons to believe the contract was to be concluded, because of the behaviour of the other party, the breaking-off should be considered wrongful. See J. Schmidt-Szalewski, 'La sanction de la faute précontractuelle', RTDCiv 1974, 46, no. 11. Courts have to a certain extent recognised the influence of this 'legitimate belief' on the fulfilment of the condition of fault in precontractual liability: Paris, 16 Oct. 1998, JurisData no. 024108; Riom, 10 June 1992, RJDA 1992, 732; Com 31 Mar. 1992, Bull Civ IV, no. 145. However, this criterion is just one among others in revealing the fault of the author of the breaking-off. See P. Chauvel, note on Com 7 Jan. 1997, D. 1998, J, 45, no. 11; P. Mousseron, 'Négociations contractuelles et responsabilité civile délictuelle', RTDCom 1998, 258. The concept of 'legitimate belief' may be related to a certain extent to the common law concept of *reliance*: see H. Muir-Watt, 'Reliance et définition du contrat' in *Mélanges Jeantin* (Paris, 1999), p. 57.

frivolously,[20] which constitutes a breach of its duty of good faith towards B. The effect of this last reason is therefore not very easy to evaluate, and should be left to the judges to assess.

Germany

As discussed in relation to case 1, a party is liable on the ground of *culpa in contrahendo* if it led the other party legitimately to believe that a contract would (almost) certainly be concluded, but then without good reason or from ulterior motives refuses to go ahead.[21]

In situation 1, A is not liable. A has not made B legitimately believe that a contract would (almost) certainly be concluded, as the parties had recognised that they had not yet agreed on all points and A had not made any statement to B that it was convinced that they would reach final agreement. In keeping with the principle of freedom of contract, A may therefore terminate contractual negotiations without indicating a reason, and it is irrelevant whether or not A justifies the termination of the negotiations by one of the reasons listed under (i) to (iv). In all of these cases, however, the situation is different if A already knew of the terminating reason a year before it broke off contractual negotiations. Under these circumstances, A is in breach of its duty to bargain in good faith. The law will not allow contractual negotiations as a sham. In that case, A is liable on the ground of §§280(1), 311(2) No. 1 BGB (*culpa in contrahendo*) and, if it intended to cause damage to B, in tort (§826 BGB). It then must compensate B's reliance interest, that is, it is liable for B's expenses from the moment B would have been informed by a partner negotiating honestly that it no longer intended a final agreement.

In situation 2, A is also not liable. B is not entitled to a contractual claim. Although A and B have reached agreement on all major points, as both parties agree that some minor points remain to be settled, a contract has not been concluded.[22] Nor is B liable on the ground of *culpa in contrahendo* for breaking off contractual negotiations. A did not enter into or continue the negotiating process without any intention to conclude a contract, nor did it make B believe that a contract would

[20] Rennes, 3 Nov. 1998, JurisData no. 049142; Aix-en-Provence, 16 Sep. 1993, JurisData no. 045651. In this case the defendant won on the grounds that he could not afford the contract price since he clearly behaved cautiously in relation to the price proposed by the plaintiff.

[21] Cf. BGH, decision of 22 Feb. 1989, NJW-RR 1989, 627.

[22] §154(1) BGB; and see the German report on case 6.

almost certainly come about. It is therefore immaterial which reasons A adduced to terminate the negotiations.

The test whether the other party could legitimately believe that a contract would (almost) certainly be concluded is both objective and subjective.[23] Hence, if there are no objective reasons for the other party's belief (for example, if the negotiations are not yet so far advanced that at least agreement on the essential terms of the future contract has been reached) a party cannot legitimately assume that a contract is very likely to be concluded. At this stage the other party's expression of its conviction that an agreement would finally be reached is nothing other than the mere confirmation of its offer, its willingness to enter into a contract on *its* terms. On the facts given it seems, therefore, that in situation 3 A is not liable on the ground of *culpa in contrahendo*. If one assumes, however, that B could legitimately rely on A' s statements, the crucial question is whether the reasons asserted by A for breaking off the negotiations are well-founded, the onus of proof for that lying with the terminating party. According to the predominant view, the termination is well-founded if, for the terminating party, the conclusion of a contract in the circumstances would be unconscionable. This will be the case if the reason asserted by the terminating party would also frustrate an already concluded contract.[24] The reasons listed under (i) and (iii) definitely fail that test. In the case of (ii) one might think of a frustrating event,[25] although the facts are not detailed enough to permit a definite conclusion. If A is held liable on the ground of *culpa in contrahendo*, it must compensate B's reliance interest.

Greece

The Greek Civil Code provides in article 197 that the parties must conduct negotiations in a manner which is consistent with good faith and business usage, whereas in article 198 it provides that a party who, in the course of negotiations, through his fault causes damage to the other party must compensate him for that damage. Fault in the course of negotiations is considered to be behaviour that is contrary to good faith, a general statement that is further concretised in a set of specific obligations. The degree of fault as regards the culpability of the

[23] §§133, 157, 242 BGB; and see the German report on case 1.

[24] Cf. MünchKomm-Emmerich, Vor §275 para. 163; H. Stoll, in *Festschrift für Werner Flume*, vol. I, 741, 755ff.; Gottwald, JuS 1982, 877, 879; Grunewald, JZ 1984, 708.

[25] §313 BGB (*Wegfall der Geschäftsgrundlage*).

negotiating party corresponds to the general fault requirement – intention and negligence – in contractual relationships.[26] Still, it is accepted that the degree of fault required in precontractual liability must be analogous to the degree of fault required in the formation and performance of the type of contract which the negotiations are aiming at; otherwise, in terms of the degree of fault, a party may be more liable in the case of negotiations than for not performing a contract.[27]

Thus, A and B negotiate with the intention of forming a merger of their firms. A merger is a formation of a new entity.[28] In Greek law, the fault of the partners is measured by the degree of fault they demonstrate in conducting their own affairs, which means that fault is assessed not by an objective standard but rather a subjective one: the personal abilities of the partners.[29] Accordingly, A's precontractual fault will be measured subjectively as regards the care it is expected to exercise in its own affairs. We should not forget that in this case the parties are major accounting firms and one may reasonably assume that they have the professional experience to assess certain issues before they engage in costly and lengthy negotiations.

The parties to negotiations are in principle free to break off negotiations.[30] Conducting negotiations in good faith does not amount to an obligation to conclude the contract. Having said that, it is also true that the further negotiations advance, the more the obligations of the parties to protect the interests of the other party increase. Where negotiations are lengthy, costly and advanced, it can be claimed that the parties may break off negotiations on condition that they provide a proper reason and that walking away from the negotiations for no reason can amount to precontractual bad faith.[31]

In situation 1, the parties, despite the costly and protracted negotiations, have still not reached an agreement on all the major points and A has not made any statement to B that it is convinced that they will reach a final agreement. In these circumstances it is not clear whether A is precontractually liable when it terminates negotiations without

[26] Article 330 GCC.

[27] See, e.g., the contracts where a party is only liable for gross negligence, such as a donation contract or a non-remunerated deposit: M. Karasis in Georgiadis and Stathopoulos, *Commentary on the Greek Civil Code*, vol I, p. 321.

[28] As regards precontractual liability in this case, there is no case law in Greece to distinguish between the particular nuances of each separate situation.

[29] Article 746 GCC. [30] See Court of Appeals of Athens 2403/1962 NoV 12, 101.

[31] Kambitsis, *Precontractual Liability*, p. 84ff.

giving a proper reason: it may or may not be, depending on the more specific aspects of the case and the importance that is to be attributed to the fact that negotiations have been costly and protracted but not complete. One may assume that A can break off negotiations without liability because time and cost alone are not considered of the essence: agreement must have been reached and the parties must have exchanged reassurances. Despite an indication that there is no liability, yet in view of all the specific circumstances a proper reason is the safest way to terminate negotiations. A would certainly have been liable if agreement had been reached on all points, it was reassuring B about the imminent conclusion, increasing the latter's justified reliance, and it still walked away.

If A genuinely invokes any of the four reasons then it is absolved from any hint of precontractual liability. However, we must make a reservation as regards reason (iii), that is, that A cannot afford the merger. In the circumstances of the case and taking into account the specific features of A's expertise, it may not constitute a proper reason for termination; instead, it may indicate fault on the part of A. Perhaps A was in a position to have known of its inability to afford the merger beforehand, which would indicate that A acted in bad faith and misled B into fruitless negotiations. In any case, if A is not liable, then B's expenses for the lengthy and costly negotiations cannot be recovered from A, even if the reason for breaking off negotiations only concerns A. This is the risk inherent in participating in economic life and the danger or sacrifice such participation entails. To conclude otherwise, A would have to have engaged in something more than negotiations and would not really be free to engage in and to terminate them. In addition, one further point must be made with regard to the first reason invoked by A. It is most probable that A did not act in precontractual bad faith by not telling B about the third party offer and giving it the chance of meeting that offer. In general, the parties to negotiations are not under such a good faith duty; however, we must make some allowance for the particularities of the commercial context in question.

The situation would be different if A knew of the reasons a year before it broke off negotiations, as long as one of the four reasons in A's belief formed a ground for breaking off negotiations and prolonging the negotiations had no chance of success. We note that because of the specific circumstances, the negotiations for the conclusion of a contract for the formation of a merged firm give rise to increased obligations on the part of the parties, such as obligations of trust, confidentiality and to provide information to the other party. In that case, A's behaviour is contrary to good faith, as it should have informed B that it had genuine reasons to break off negotiations at the time these reasons became apparent. It would probably have to inform B even if A believed that it could overcome these obstacles. Thus, if A is liable for precontractual bad faith, then it must compensate B for the expenses which the latter incurred for the period of one year, that is from the time A became aware of the reason for breaking off negotiations until it actually did so.

In situation 2, the fact that an agreement has been reached on all major points and only a few minor points remain to be settled is a factor indicating that the negotiations have reached an advanced stage (despite the fact that the negotiations have not been lengthy in time), which increases the obligations of the parties. If A breaks off negotiations without giving a proper reason, then it is probably acting against precontractual good faith and will have to compensate B for the expenses it has incurred. That its expenses have been moderate is not a factor relevant to liability. Nevertheless, A can still break off the negotiations without being liable if it honestly invokes a proper reason. What amounts to a proper reason depends heavily on the circumstances and the whole context. As already stated, whether A behaves in a manner which is consistent with good faith and trade usage and whether it is at fault, will be measured against its own capabilities and the care it demonstrates in conducting its own affairs. However, in view of the lack of guidance from the case law, it is debatable whether any of the reasons is proper. More precisely, it is not clear whether a better offer constitutes a proper reason for breaking off the negotiations, when there is an agreement on all major points but the parties do not produce statements confirming the expectation that the contract will be concluded.[32] The same is true for the insurmountable cultural difference,

[32] Case law indicates that when an agreement has been reached between the negotiating parties and one party reassures the other that the signing of the contract is imminent and all that remains is a formality, then a better offer is not a proper reason for breaking off the negotiations: First Instance Court of Thessaloniki 1278/1998 Arm 1998, 543. See also Gazis, *Legal Consultations 1956–1999*, p. 297ff., regarding the breaking-off of negotiations after agreement had been reached on all major points and the party breaking off negotiations (a public authority) had made statements in the press declaring that an agreement had been reached; the author argues that breaking off negotiations at such an advanced stage due to a better offer constituted conduct which was contrary to precontractual good faith. In that case, the author advised that compensation must amount to the *expectation interest* (p. 303). The factual and legal issues under examination by the late Prof. Gazis somewhat resemble those

which most probably seems to be a minor reason. That it cannot afford a merger is not a proper reason in view of the fault requirements in the case of A. If A breaks off negotiations in a manner which is contrary to good faith, it will be liable to compensate B on the basis of article 198 GCC for the expenses it has incurred.

In situation 3, the negotiations have not resulted in an agreement on all major points, though A has repeatedly stated to B that it is convinced that a final agreement will be reached. Apparently the negotiations have not reached the advanced stage where the precontractual obligations of the parties actually increase. However, in order to obtain the complete picture one must assess the statements made by A to B. And this is precisely the interesting point here, namely, what the effect of such a statement may be as regards the negotiation process. We should keep in mind that this is not a binding statement but rather a mere expression of hope and that an agreement has still not been reached. Thus, one may claim that with these statements A committed itself to the negotiations and gave B a reasonable expectation that it would exert all its efforts to attain an agreement. Therefore, it would probably be against precontractual good faith for A to break off negotiations without providing a proper reason.[33] In that case A will have to compensate B on the basis of articles 197 and 198 GCC. However, the case would be different if A invoked a genuine reason. Any of the reasons (i) to (iii) can be deemed to be proper given the fact that negotiations per se have not resulted in an agreement on all major points. Having said that, one cannot ignore the fact that with regard to the second and third reasons, an objection may be raised. One may claim that these are reasons A could and should have taken into account before making the statements; therefore breaking off negotiations after invoking these reasons leans slightly towards conduct which is contrary to good faith.[34]

in the case of the First Instance Court of the European Union in T-203/96 *Embassy Limousines v. European Parliament* [1998] ECR II-4239.

[33] M. Karasis, in Georgiadis and Stathopoulos, *Commentary on the Greek Civil Code*, vol I, p. 320.

[34] AP 969/1977 NoV 26, 895 concerned the sale of an apartment. Though an agreement had been reached and the seller reassured the buyer that the completion of the sale contract after compliance with the formalities was imminent, the seller broke off negotiations when the costs of the construction had risen considerably and the sale was no longer such an attractive proposition. The court decided that the seller's conduct was consistent with precontractual good faith; a small minority held otherwise. Compare AP 1565/2000 Chronika Idiotikou Dikaiou 2001, 220.

Ireland

There is no general concept of precontractual liability in Irish law. No liability attaches to either party for the failure to complete a contract and the expenses incurred are borne by the parties.[35] Whether or not there is a reason for the failure to complete the contract does not affect the question of liability. In situation 1, therefore, B has no remedy. However, where a person continues to engage in negotiations to complete a contract despite the fact that there is no intention to enter the contract, liability may arise in tort in accordance with the concept of deceit, discussed fully in the report on case 1. In such a situation, the damages payable would probably be confined to reliance loss, that is the expenditure incurred from the point in time when the defendant had decided not to enter the contract. In very rare cases, an award of punitive or exemplary damages may be claimed.

It is a question of fact as to whether the parties have actually concluded an agreement. Very often a court may find that the parties have concluded a complete contract despite the clear contention of one of the parties that this is not the case.[36] In fact, where the parties have settled on the principal issues involved a court is most likely to find the existence of an enforceable contract.[37] However, it remains an issue of fact to be determined in each individual case. If, in situation 2, the court finds that there is a completed contract, B may seek a number of remedies. First, an action for specific performance of the contract may be pursued. This would force both parties to implement the agreement. Secondly, damages may be available for breach of contract.

In situation 3, A has no liability to B or vice versa. The failure to conclude a contract does not, as a rule, create any liability between the parties.

Italy

In situation 1, since the negotiations had been long[38] (three years) and both parties had incurred considerable expenses, B's reliance on the merger could seem reasonable. On the other hand, both the parties

[35] Although, as we have seen, there may be liability where one party has made precontractual promises: see the Irish report on case 6.

[36] In particular, see Friel, *The Law of Contract*, pp. 44–5.

[37] For a striking example, see *Wettern Electric Ltd v. Welsh Development Agency* [1983] QB 796.

[38] For the Italian Supreme Court the length of negotiations is not relevant when it is short: Cass, sez. II, 12 Nov. 1986, no. 6629.

had made statements that they had not reached agreement on all major points. For A's precontractual liability, there are questions of evidence as to whether the parties' statements could exclude B's reasonable reliance, and whether A had a good reason for breaking off the negotiations.

Reason (i) would be a good reason if A informed B about the better offer. 'Insurmountable cultural difference' (reason (ii)) is a possible reasonable defence for A's conduct. The accountants' 'code of ethics', Italian doctrine and Italian case law[39] do not consider such a case: it will be a matter of fact whether during the negotiations such an insurmountable gap had been indicated as a major problem. Reason (iii) depends on why A cannot afford the merger. In particular, if it does not arise from external situations (circumstances beyond A's control, such as '*forza maggiore*', or because of new and more onerous laws), it would be easier for B to prove A's bad faith, where there is no objective reason to break off negotiations. Italian case law has recognised liability for unreasonable withdrawal only where 'co-operation of the parties did not depend upon excessively difficult or impossible conduct'.[40] On the other hand, basing the defence on the internal reasons of A's firm would give the judge freedom to assess the reasonableness of its justification for breaking off. Moreover, the Supreme Court has recognised the parties' freedom to keep secret their own economic situation during negotiations[41] (unless law or contract expressly provide a specific duty of disclosure). Finally, reason (iv) is similar to reason (iii) where the reasons rest on circumstances beyond A's own control. Since the Italian system recognises the principle of freedom to trade, A would be considered to be free to withdraw in the face of circumstances worsening. The change of circumstances has been held by case law to be 'a reasonable reason for withdrawal'.[42]

In any case, if B could prove that A knew of any of these reasons one year before its withdrawal, it would be difficult for A to avoid liability. Its conduct seems then to be clearly contrary to the duty of good faith during negotiations.[43] In the case of a malicious breaking-off of

[39] See in particular TRIB-T. Napoli, 22 June 1996.

[40] On the point see TRIB-T. Verona, 30 May 1981.

[41] Cass, 11 Oct. 1994, n. 8295.

[42] TRIB-T. Cremona, 6 June 1991. It seems that the general principle of *rebus sic stantibus* finds application also during negotiations: Silvestrini, *Il principio 'pacta sunt servanda' e la regola 'rebus sic stantibus'*, p. 19.

[43] For further discussion, see the Italian report on case 1.

negotiations it would be for the judge to decide whether to assess damages for the whole period of negotiations or just for the period of the wrongful failure to disclose. If the former, the judge would be likely to adopt a solution similar to the common law practice of punitive damages,[44] but there is no existing case law on this.

In situation 2, agreement has been reached on all major points. The relevant provision of the Civil Code is article 1337 (precontractual liability): case law within the last ten years has been generally committed to finding precontractual liability and assessing damages for the negative interest[45] if a reasonable justification is not provided.[46] In this case, B's legal expenses might be recovered. If A had openly stated that it would have informed B about the possibility of concluding the negotiations, no liability could have been found; such a statement is read by some judges as a signal of keeping the negotiations open and does not give rise to *culpa in contrahendo*.[47]

In situation 3, it seems difficult to talk about precontractual liability. Italian case law does not provide similar examples, but it generally considers businessmen's *pourparlers* as not implying *culpa in contrahendo*.[48]

In relation to all these cases, it should be noted that the duration of the negotiations is not as relevant in order to determine liability for breaking off negotiations as their intensity and conclusiveness.

Netherlands

The crucial question under Dutch law in all these situations is whether the 'third stage' in negotiations was reached. As explained in relation to case 1, in that stage a party is no longer free to break off negotiations, and if she nevertheless does so she may be liable to compensate the expectation interest.

In situation 1, it is most likely that a Dutch court would conclude that the 'third stage' was not reached. Although the parties had been involved in lengthy (three years) and, it seems, intense negotiations, where they both incurred considerable expenses, at no point was B justified in relying on the imminent conclusion of the contract (nor indeed does it seem to have done so). Rather, A has been careful never

[44] Article 96 c.p.c. [45] See further the Italian report on case 1.
[46] Trib. Nuoro, 9 Sep. 1986, Riv. Giur. Sarda, 1988, 85.
[47] Trib. Milano, 5 May 1997, *Foro It*, 1998, I, 601.
[48] Trib. Milano, 5 May 1997, Soc. Carneval de Venise C. Soc. Balmain, *Foro It*, 1998, I, 601.

to have made any statement to B that it is convinced that they will reach final agreement. Moreover, in spite of the lengthy negotiations no agreement had been reached yet on all major points which also means that there was no reason which would have justified B relying on the imminent conclusion of the contract. Rather, the fact that the negotiations had already lasted for three years should have made B cautious (and may actually have made it cautious since the statement of facts nowhere says that B thought that agreement would soon be reached). Under these circumstances, A's reason for breaking off does not make much difference. Some of these reasons might be of relevance as justifications for breaking off negotiations after the 'third stage' had been reached,[49] if this had been the case.

As discussed in relation to case 1, even if a party was still entitled to break off negotiations (breaking-off was neither contrary to good faith nor a tort), she may still be liable to compensate the other party's expenses. However, under what circumstances such liability may occur – when parties were in the 'second stage' in negotiations – is not clear. In this case the statement of facts says that both parties have incurred considerable expenses. However, this mere fact does not in itself mean that the party who breaks off negotiations has to compensate the other's expenses. Indeed, in this case there does not seem to be any reason to hold A liable to compensate B's expenses.

Does it make a difference if A knew of the reason a year before it broke off negotiations? If this means that during the last year A actually no longer had a serious intent to conclude a contract, the question arises whether this fact in itself may make A liable. This has been discussed in relation to cases 1 and 2, where it was argued that a party who negotiates while having no serious intent to conclude a contract may be liable (in tort) to compensate the other party's expenses made from the moment the first party (here, A) no longer had a serious intent to conclude a contract.

In situation 2, the difference is that the parties have reached agreement on all major points and only a few minor points remain to be settled, and that both parties acknowledge this. Under Dutch law, this may make a crucial difference because a Dutch court might conclude that the negotiations were in such an advanced stage that B was justified in expecting that a contract would be concluded. Under these

[49] Especially reason (iv), general recession, which may be regarded as a change of circumstances in the sense of *De Ruiterij/Ruiters*, HR, 14 June 1996, NJ 1997, 481.

circumstances, A might be liable for breaking off and B might even be able to recover the expectation interest.[50] On the other hand, the statement of facts explicitly states that A has not made any statement to B that it is convinced that they will reach final agreement. This means that if A has induced B's reliance this must have been by its mere conduct which is difficult to prove and which should not be too easily accepted, especially in the case of negotiations between professionals who, in addition, were also assisted by their lawyers. Therefore, A will probably not be liable.

Whether A should compensate (some of) B's expenses is unclear under Dutch law, as explained above. However, in this case there does not seem to be any reason to accept such liability.

Does the reason for breaking off make a difference under Dutch law in situation 2? Not when there was no justified reliance (in other words, when the third stage was not reached). However, if the third stage was reached, it may actually make a difference. In *De Ruiterij/Ruiters* (1996),[51] the Hoge Raad said that in determining whether a party who breaks off negotiations in the 'third stage' of negotiations is liable, the interests of the party who breaks off must also be taken into account. Such considerations might be interpreted as being open to allowing a 'good reason' to justify breaking off even when the other party was justified in expecting that a contract would be concluded.[52] If so, it must be established what reasons may be regarded as good reasons (and which, in the words of the Hoge Raad, should be taken into account when establishing whether that party should be liable). It seems that the reasons mentioned in the statement of facts (i) and (ii) should be accepted as good reasons for breaking off negotiations even when they are in a very advanced stage.

In situation 3, by his statements A may have induced B to expect that final agreement would be reached. However, in the light of the objective circumstances of the case (as the parties both recognise, they have not yet reached agreement on all major points), was B justified in relying on these statements (if it did)? The *Plas/Valburg* test for determining whether the third stage was reached requires not mere subjective reliance but also that it was justified (objectively, in the light of the circumstances of the case). Therefore, it seems, in this situation the

[50] See the Dutch report on case 1. [51] Above n. 49.

[52] See M.W. Hesselink, De schadevergoedingsplicht bij afgebroken onderhandelingen in het licht van het Europese privaatrecht, WPNR 6248–9 (1996).

third stage was not reached, and A was not liable to compensate the expectation interest.

However, as discussed above, even before the third stage was reached a party may have to compensate the other party's expenses when it breaks off negotiations. It is not at all clear under what circumstances negotiations reach this 'third stage'. In this case, one could argue that if A had not made these reckless statements B would not have incurred all the expenses. Therefore, if B can prove this, one could argue that A should compensate B's reliance interest. The argument that the parties were professionals could go either way: as a professional, A should not make such reckless statements; as a professional, B should not rely on mere statements of personal expectations. If A is indeed liable for the reliance interest, the question arises whether this would be different if it (honestly) gave as the reason for his breaking off the negotiations one of the circumstances which are mentioned in the statement of facts. Reasons (i) and (ii) seem to provide a good justification whereas (iii) is a reason which A probably should have thought of before starting negotiations.

Norway

As a rule, there is no requirement imposed on a party during the precontractual period to specify the reasons for breaking off negotiations: there does not exist a procedural requirement for providing a reason. However, there is reason to expect that the cause of the breach should not be irrelevant or unreasonable; there does exist a minimum material requirement as to the underlying reason for the break-off of negotiations. This is the case whether the cause of the break-off has been disclosed to the other party or not.[53]

In situation 1, there are also two aspects to the significance of the length of time of the negotiations. If, throughout the three years the negotiations have been carried on, reasonable progress has been made, such extensive negotiations might indicate that these are now in the

[53] See Rt 1995, 543, the *Selsbakkhøgda housing cooperative* case, at 552: 'The presumption with respect to this type of agreement [letter of intent] is that the parties are not forced to enter into the intended agreement; however, in some situations, there might be certain considerations which should prevent the parties from withdrawing from the agreement too easily.' This is supported in Simonsen, *Precontractual Liability*. This was discussed by the Supreme Court in Rt 1998, 761, the *Kina Hansen* case, at 772, though without a position being taken on the matter.

final phase, which should further strengthen the need for the parties to demonstrate good faith. If, on the other hand, the length of the negotiations is a result of the parties not being able to reach agreement (a deadlocked situation), the argument will be entirely the opposite. The parties would have done all that could be expected of them, and they should then be at liberty to discontinue the negotiations. The principle of good faith does not make presumptions other than that A 'through negotiations contributes to the solution of unresolved questions'.[54] The facts say that 'the parties recognise that they have not yet reached agreement on all major points'. Since negotiations have lasted for three years, this might indicate that one is approaching a deadlocked situation. Considering the possible reasons for breaking off:

(i) 'Received a better offer': usually, participants in a negotiation process must be prepared for competitive offers throughout the precontractual period. They might protect themselves against this by agreeing to exclusive negotiations. In the present case, this was not done. Consequently, a competitive offer establishes a legitimate reason for withdrawing from the negotiations. If, however, the parties are in the final negotiating phase – they are about to enter into a binding agreement – the result might be different. It would then be timely to impose a duty to inform the other party, who would then have the opportunity to match the offer from the third party or even to operate for a limited time during which negotiations with others are prohibited.

(ii) 'Insurmountable cultural difference': a successful merger of professional business firms presupposes a mutual compatibility of the parties. This is an assumption familiar to negotiating parties, and the absence of this is an ever-present risk in this type of negotiations. If differences in the attitudes and preferences of the parties repeatedly emerge throughout the negotiation period, this is a valid reason to discontinue negotiations. Neither party can be held responsible.

(iii) 'He cannot afford the merger': with respect to not having sufficient financial means for merger negotiations to succeed, the *Lrlingeklausul* case is a key example:[55] 'A different situation in which damages regarding the reliance interest of all parties will be recovered is where – without exceptions – invitations to submit tenders have been called for a project for which the owner knows financing has not been approved and hence its realisation is uncertain. In such a case, uncertainty is present unbeknown to the parties submitting tenders which could

[54] Rt 1992, 1110, the *Stiansen* case, at 1115. [55] Rt 1997, 574, at 578.

lead to a liability for wasted expenditure if unsuccessful financing causes the project to be abandoned.' In such a case, the requirements would presumably be more stringent with respect to tendering for a project which appears as a definite possibility, rather than negotiating a merger. But at least where the negotiations imply the use of greater resources, which seems to be the case in the present situation, the point of view expressed in the judgment is very significant.

(iv) 'A general recession': unfavourable economic fluctuations are part of the general risk which both parties in the negotiation process have to take.[56] Consequently, no one can be liable in situations where negotiations break down owing to such conditions.

Knowledge of the reasons for the discontinuation of negotiations imposes an obligation on A to inform the other party. In the Swedish courts, this was stated in NJA 1990.745, the *Super-V Pump* case:[57]

> From the discussion it appears that an agreement between the business firm and Gösta Svensson was not reached until 16 February 1982, and that the board consequently determined that Bertil L. should no longer be considered eligible for obtaining a resale agreement with exclusive rights. It was the duty of the firm to inform Bertil L. of its decision as early as possible.

Similar conditions would also hold under Norwegian law. On this basis, it is apparent that if A fails to provide information about the reasons for discontinuing negotiations at the earliest possible moment, it will be held liable. Losses which could be claimed by B are expenses which could have been avoided if information had been given in due time.

Situation 2 is different insofar as the negotiations after *a brief period of time* have led to agreement *on all major points* of the contract, and that only 'a few minor points remain' to be settled, at which time A decides to break off the negotiations. Even in this case A does not have a procedural duty to give B a reason for discontinuing the negotiations, although good business practice would require that an explanation be provided. (Further, it would be difficult to determine the consequences a failure to inform might have.) It must, however, *have* a good reason for breaking off.[58]

With respect to the material requirements for not breaking off negotiations on irrelevant or unreasonable grounds, the requirement of good faith is more rigorous when the parties are in the final stages of negotiation. Whether the parties have spent considerable time or little

[56] Simonsen, *Precontractual Liability*, p. 199ff. [57] At 760.

[58] There are, however, no Norwegian Supreme Court cases determining the duty to have a good reason for terminating the negotiations in their final stage.

time to reach this stage is, however, of little consequence. The only difference here in relation to the possible reasons for breaking off is in reason (i). Since the parties now are at the very end of the negotiating process – they are about to enter into a binding contract – it would be timely to impose a duty to inform the other party, so as to enable that party to match an offer from a third party. Whether one for a short period may still operate under a prohibition to negotiate with others is more doubtful. Furthermore, a prohibition against entertaining other offers is out of the question unless such a limitation has already been agreed to.

In situation 3, where A on several occasions has announced that their goals would be reached, the requirement as to what constitutes a valid reason for breaking off becomes more rigorous. Statements such as this contribute to strengthening the belief that an agreement would be achieved. This holds even if the parties are not yet in the final stages of the negotiations. A well-founded assumption of entering into an agreement would provide greater legal protection than less definite assumptions. The discussion in relation to situation 2 of the possible reasons for breaking off would equally apply in situation 3.

Portugal

In situation 1, B is entitled to compensation based in precontractual liability for the expenses it has incurred if A breaks off the negotiations which have lasted three years without giving any reason at all. Article 227 of the Civil Code establishes a duty to negotiate in good faith, from which it can be derived that no one should break off negotiations without a proper reason. The fact that A has not made any statement to B that it is convinced that they will reach final agreement does not prevent precontractual liability, because the fact that the negotiations lasted for so long and were so intense created a situation of trust.

If A (honestly) gives a reason for breaking off negotiations, the situation would be different. However, the reason must be very strong to justify that breach of trust. If the reason (i) is the fact that it has received a better offer from C for a merger of A's firm with C's firm, it is a fair reason to break off negotiations because there was no lock-out agreement, so a better proposal is always a ground to break off negotiations.[59] The fact that A has discovered (ii) that there is an

[59] See M.J. de A. Costa, *Responsabilidade civil pela ruptura das negociações preparatórias de um contrato*, p. 63.

insurmountable cultural difference between the firms could also be a fair reason to break off negotiations, but A should have investigated the cultural differences and so it does not necessarily exclude A's precontractual liability unless B had kept it a secret from A. The fact that A (iii) cannot afford the merger is certainly not a ground to break off long-term negotiations because A should have known about it earlier. Finally, the fact (iv) that the recession has made the merger less attractive is certainly not a valid ground to break off long-term negotiations. Only a strong economic reason against the merger would be sufficient.[60]

If A knew of the reason a year before it broke off negotiations it can no longer invoke it, because it is against good faith not to disclose a fair reason to break off negotiations as soon as it is known.[61] The remedy would be the expenses B incurred during the year.

In situation 2, B is entitled to compensation for the expenses it incurred, based in precontractual liability,[62] if, without giving any reason at all, A breaks off the negotiations which have already come to an agreement on all major points. Here we have also a situation of reliance, because the fact that the parties easily reached agreement on all major points creates in B the impression that the negotiations would continue and a final agreement would be reached. This is similar to situation 1, with only the difference that the negotiations were at the beginning when they were broken off. However, the fact that the negotiations were at the beginning does not necessarily exclude precontractual liability if a situation of trust was created by A. The fact that A has not made any statement that it is convinced that the parties would reach final agreement is not a sufficient reason to exclude any situation of trust, because the fact that an agreement was immediately reached on all major points can also be considered as a situation of trust.

As in situation 1, if A (honestly) gives a reason for breaking off negotiations the situation would be different. However, as in this case the negotiations were at the beginning the reason does not have to be as strong to justify the breach of trust. Reason (i) is a fair reason to break

[60] Portuguese law refers to change of circumstances after the completion of a contract in art. 437° and only considers it relevant if the change is 'abnormal' and 'not covered by the normal risks of the contract'.

[61] As regards to the duties of disclosure imposed by the rule of good faith, see A.M. Cordeiro, *Da Boa Fé no Direito Civil*, p. 549ff.

[62] Article 227 CC.

off negotiations because there was no lock-out agreement, so a better proposal is always a ground to break off negotiations. Reason (ii) would also be considered a fair reason to break off negotiations because the negotiations were still at a period in which that kind of discovery is a valid ground to break off negotiations without any compensation. The fact (iii) that A cannot afford the merger can also be a ground to break off short-term negotiations, unless it had prior knowledge as to what the economic conditions would be.

In situation 3, B is also entitled to compensation for the expenses it has incurred, based in precontractual liability,[63] due to the fact that A has made a statement that a final agreement could be reached and therefore created in B a situation of trust, which cannot be broken without a fair reason. This is similar to situations 1 and 2, with the difference that the situation of trust arises from A's statement. This makes it perfectly clear that a situation of trust was created by A, which makes breaking off the negotiations against the principles of good faith and involving precontractual liability. Here again, if A (honestly) gives a reason to break off negotiations the situation would be different. However, as in this case A made such a statement, the reason has to be stronger than in the earlier cases to justify the breach of trust. Reason (i) is still a fair reason to break off negotiations, because there was no lock-out agreement, so a better proposal is always a ground to break off negotiations. The fact (ii) that A has discovered that there is an insurmountable cultural difference between the firms would not be considered in this case a fair reason to break off negotiations because the statement issued by A excludes the relevance of such a discovery as a valid ground for that breach. The fact (iii) that A cannot afford the merger would also not be in this case a ground to break off negotiations because the statement issued by A involves a guarantee that it can in fact afford the merger.

Scotland

The basic facts of this case disclose no evident remedy in Scots law.

In situation 1 there seems little ground to argue that a contract has been concluded given that 'the parties recognise that they have not yet reached agreement on all major points'. As discussed in relation to case 4, parties are free to enter into and break off negotiations, and each must in general accept the risks and financial consequences of

[63] Article 227 CC.

such a process. If a transfer of value occurs between the parties, then recovery may be allowed. Alternatively, if one party has led the other to believe that there is a binding contract in force between them but, due to failure to comply with an essential formality, there is no such binding contract, a common law remedy may lie for wasted preliminary expenditure.[64] As the facts given in this scenario state that 'the parties recognise that they have not yet reached agreement on all major points', such equitable remedy would be unavailable. A is not required to give any reason for the breaking-off of negotiations. Of the four possible reasons (i) to (iv) for breaking off negotiations, it is unlikely that (i), (ii) or (iv) would make any difference to the foregoing answer. Regarding reason (iii), it might be argued that having entered into negotiations for the sale, A had impliedly represented that it had the financial ability to complete the contract. If at the time negotiations were begun this was not so, this implied representation may be argued to have been made negligently or fraudulently. If either of these grounds was successful, a claim would lie for damages in delict. There is no clear authority, however, that such an implied representation would be held to have been made.

If A knew of any of these reasons one year before breaking off the negotiations, this might suggest that it was continuing to negotiate in bad faith, with no real intention to conclude a merger. Whilst there is no specific obligation in Scots law not to negotiate in bad faith, to do so where one knows that the other party is incurring expenditure in the belief that a merger may occur might be held to give rise to a duty of care in delict. Damages would be for pure economic loss, and while these are in general more difficult to recover, the direct negotiations which have occurred here would create sufficient proximity between the parties to found such a claim. A damages claim in delict for pure economic loss would be designed to place B in the position it would have been in had the wrongful action or omission not occurred. Thus, any wasted expenditure incurred after the point of the wrongful behaviour and which was deemed not to be too remote from it[65] could be claimed by B.

In situation 2, despite the agreement on major points, it is unlikely that a contract has yet been concluded. If there are various outstanding

[64] Based upon the *Walker v. Milne* (1823) 2 S 379 line of cases as interpreted in *Dawson International plc v. Coats Paton plc* 1988 SLT 854, affd. 1989 SLT 854. See also *Karoulias SA v. Drambuie Liqueur Co. Ltd* 2004 GWD 31–638.

[65] As to which see Lord Kinloch's dictum in *Allan v. Barclay* (1864) 2 M 873.

matters which have been the subject of negotiation between the parties, that would indicate that *locus poenitentiae* (the opportunity to withdraw from negotiations) still exists, and that *consensus in idem* has yet to be reached. In some contracts where price is the only matter outstanding between the parties and performance has occurred, the courts may be willing to imply a reasonable price (a *quantum meruit*) and conclude that a contract does exist between the parties.[66] This is not the case on the facts given, however. Alteration of the facts, by the disclosure of any of the reasons (i) to (iii), does not alter the legal position. It might be argued that B had led A to believe that a contract was concluded, and that, therefore, the common law remedy based upon *Walker v. Milne*[67] might apply. This seems unlikely however, as the parties still appear to be in negotiation. The same point made in relation to situation 1 as to a possible implied misrepresentation as to financial ability applies *mutatis mutandis*.

In relation to situation 3, a statement by a party that it is convinced that it will reach agreement with a negotiating party does not create any liability in Scots law, unless it can be classified as a misrepresentation. This is unlikely, as a statement of intention is not considered to be relevant for these purposes (unless the intention was dishonestly represented). This is the case regardless of whether any of the reasons (i) to (iii) for negotiations being broken off are disclosed. However, again the point made in relation to situation 1 as to a possible implied misrepresentation as to financial ability applies *mutatis mutandis* here.

Spain

Breaking off negotiations does not in itself constitute an act contrary to good faith. The mere fact of negotiating does not impose any obligation to conclude the contract nor to continue negotiations: this is the essential characteristic of the precontractual stage. Good faith might impose a duty to justify breaking off negotiations, even if there is no such case in Spanish case law. But if there is a valid reason to break off negotiations, it seems just and fair that each party bears its own costs of the negotiations. The expenses are incurred because of efforts made to convince the other party to conclude the contract and to facilitate the conclusion of the contract. In situation 1, as A does negotiate in good faith, willing to enter into the merger or at least

[66] *Avintair Ltd v. Ryder Airline Services* 1994 SC 270.
[67] See above n. 64, and the Scots report on case 4.

to negotiate in order to find out whether a merger would be possible and profitable, the expenses B incurs serve their purpose and both parties know that they cannot count on finally concluding the merger. Only in exceptional circumstances could A be held liable.

Reasons (i) and (ii) seem valid and acceptable, both being unplanned circumstances which happened either due to things found out during (and maybe even because of) the negotiations or due to a normal (not unforeseeable) fact. The breaking-off of the negotiations because of these reasons is not contrary to good faith, but must be accepted. Reason (iii) is rather different, as A is supposed to know the financial capacity of its own firm. If it was supposed to know from the beginning that any merger would be too expensive, it in fact negotiated in bad faith. This seems rather improbable, though, as A itself had to bear considerable costs. It is much more probable that A found out during the negotiations that this particular merger would be too expensive. Breaking off negotiations after this discovery is again behaviour in good faith and does not create any liability. Reason (iv) is very similar to reason (iii): probably A found out or realised only after three years that with this development the merger was not attractive. Only if it should have foreseen the development and the lack of profitability, which seems rather improbable, might liability be justified.

Good faith being the basis for any precontractual liability, A could have an obligation to compensate B's loss if A knew the reason for breaking off the negotiations one year before actually breaking them off. It may have negotiated for a certain period of time in bad faith, which would impose on it liability for B's expenses during this period. Good faith requires it to inform the other party about circumstances which are essential. Reason (i) is such a circumstance, considering the long period of the negotiations and the considerable expenses incurred by both parties. From the moment at which A knows that C has made a *better* offer, which makes it very unlikely that it will actually conclude a contract with B, it negotiates in bad faith and therefore is liable to compensate the expenses incurred by B from that time.[68] Also reason (ii) has to be communicated to C as soon as discovered (at least, as soon as A is clear about the insurmountable character of the cultural difference) as this fact makes any further

[68] For further consideration of the relation of confidence, see STS, 14 June 1999, no. 527/1999, RJ 1999/4105.

negotiation useless. The same duty to inform arises in (iii). Reason (iv), on the other hand, is not a fact which makes any negotiation useless. A is entitled to continue negotiations, hoping to compensate the loss of attractiveness caused by the economic situation by better terms in the merger agreement. But also in that case, as soon as A considers (or decides for itself) that it is not willing to conclude the merger, it acts in bad faith if it continues negotiating.

In situation 2, even if A and B did not reach final agreement on all points, there seems to be consent on the major (objectively essential) points of the future contract. According to general principles of contract law[69] and case law, there might be a pre-contract, the parties postponing the actual conclusion of the contract until complete agreement on all minor points of the future contract are reached. There would have to be consent, though, also on the binding nature of this agreement, otherwise a pre-contract would *always* be concluded in negotiations as soon as agreement on major points is reached, something that the parties do not necessarily intend.[70] This consent is difficult to prove. But proof of the agreement on the major points might help to prove the binding nature of the agreement, and also the fact that negotiations on the minor points are continued afterwards in good faith can imply that such consent exists.[71] If we admit the existence of a pre-contract, the break-off of negotiations and, in consequence, the non-execution of the pre-contract can give rise to contractual liability. As not all terms of the future contract are clear yet, it is obvious that there is no possibility of concluding the future contract. But an action on the basis of article 1101 CC (contractual liability) would be possible. The different cases have to be examined more closely to decide whether there is liability or not.

If no reason is given for breaking off negotiations, A is liable. It culpably (as it does not show any reason) did not fulfil its contractual obligations (to conclude the contract). A would be liable for the 'reliance' interest, although it is not completely clear whether this reliance interest is supposed to put B in the same situation as it was before concluding the pre-contract (which means that only the expenses of negotiations from that moment on would be reimbursable) or in the

[69] Article 1261 CC.

[70] Cf. STS, 3 June 1998, no. 516/1998, RJ 1998\3715: '*voluntad negocial*'. Compare the German: '*Rechtsbindungswille*'.

[71] In that sense (even if different in that case): STS, 3 June 1998, above n. 70, SEGUNDO (B).

situation it would be without having negotiated at all (that is, reimbursement of all the expenses of the negotiations). Seeing the pre-contract as a kind of guarantee to conclude the future contract, it seems more appropriate to the special nature of this contract to consider all the expenses as loss caused by the breach of the contract. On a contractual basis, B could on the other hand (in the alternative) claim expectation damages, although in this case it seems rather difficult to prove them.

Receiving a better offer from someone else (reason (i)) does not change A's liability, as by accepting the offer it consciously breaks the pre-contract and intentionally causes damage to B. The extent of the damage is the same as discussed above. The discovery of an insurmountable cultural difference between the two firms (reason (ii)) constitutes a new circumstance which would justify the break-off of negotiations. But occurring after the conclusion of the pre-contract, it is not a circumstance which justifies the breach of a *contract*. A should have known or made sure that a merger was 'culturally possible' before concluding a pre-contract. Afterwards he will not be able to annul the contract based on 'error', even if the cultural competence of two firms is an essential condition or motive for the merger,[72] because A was supposed to know this circumstance (the error is inexcusable). For this reason, the pre-contract is valid and its rupture not justified, which makes A liable in the same terms as above. The fact of not having enough money (reason (iii)) is a similar circumstance. Furthermore, according to a general principle of law, a lack of money is not a valid excuse for breaking a contract.

In situation 3, as there is no agreement on any points, there is no pre-contract in the above-mentioned sense. Nor can A's statement of being convinced they he will conclude the contract with B be qualified as any kind of precontractual offer. Therefore we have to examine whether A is liable in tort. A's mentioning being convinced that they would reach a final agreement can probably not be qualified as a binding promise. It is just an expression of its optimism which, anyway, is inherent in conducting negotiations in good faith. It is, though, arguable that being convinced that an agreement would be reached does express a promise not to consider any offers from third parties. In that case, A would be liable for damages suffered by B in case (ii) (insurmountable cultural difference) but in the other two cases ((i) and (iii)) the circumstances

[72] Article 1266 CC.

which occurred are most probably new elements which justify a breaking-off of negotiations even after it has expressed confidence in the conclusion of the contract.

Sweden

A is not liable to compensate B in any of the given situations except that in situation 1, if A had definitely decided not to conclude any contract with B one year before it discontinued the negotiations, it is liable to compensate B for the unnecessary costs incurred during the last year.

In situation 1 the parties have not reached an agreement (either explicitly or implicitly), and so there is no basis for any contractual responsibility. The main rule is that the parties negotiate at their own risk and expense. The parties have not made any agreement about compensation and in this branch of business there does not exist any trade custom constituting an obligation to pay for the other party's costs. Therefore, A could break off the negotiations without having or giving any good reasons or reasons at all and B would not be entitled to any compensation. In the case of reasons (i) to (iv), breaking off negotiations does not constitute any liability for A to compensate B. If, however, A knew about any of reasons (i) to (iv) one year before breaking off the negotiations, it may be liable to compensate B since A could be considered to have acted in bad faith by not informing B about the risk that the merger might not take place (*culpa in contrahendo*). However, this result is dependent upon whether A was aware that the circumstances (i) to (iv) threatened the conclusion of the contract. Most probably A would not be liable to compensate B, as there is no duty to inform the other party of uncertainty about the outcome of the negotiations.[73]

In situation 2, it is unclear from the circumstances whether the parties have reached an agreement while agreeing upon all major terms. It is possible to conclude a contract even if the parties have not agreed on all terms. In practice, however, a contract such as this is usually presumed not to have been concluded until both parties have signed a written contract. If a contract has been concluded and A breaks off the negotiations, A is liable to compensate B according to the expectation interest. However, it is more likely that no contract has been concluded. Since A has not acted in bad faith in the negotiations

[73] Cf. NJA 1990.745, discussed in the Swedish report on case 1; Adlercreutz, *Avtalsrätt* I; Hellner, *Kommersiell avtalsrätt*; Ramberg and Ramberg, *Allmän avtalsrätt*.

with B or when breaking off the negotiations, there is no basis for liability even if A does not give any reasons for breaking off the negotiations. Consequently, there is no liability where A also gives reasons (i) to (iii) for its decision.

In situation 3, it is evident from the circumstances that no contract has been concluded. A generally has no obligation to conclude a contract even if it has initiated the negotiations. Therefore, A could break off the negotiations without any liability. If A acted in bad faith it could be liable for *culpa in contrahendo*. A could not be regarded as having acted in bad faith merely by stating that it is convinced that a contract will be concluded even if this in fact is not its conviction, nor could its statement be regarded as a binding promise to continue negotiations. There is no support for liability even if A knew that its statement was false, as long as the statement does not, in itself or together with other circumstances, constitute a binding promise. If, for instance, it made the statement after C had given its offer (in the case of reason (i)) or after its knowledge about not being able to afford the merger (reason (iii)), it could still have reasons to believe that further negotiations or changed circumstances could make a contract with B the best option. Nothing in the question indicates that A has acted contrary to good faith. Hence, the conclusion is that A is not liable to compensate B.

Switzerland

In situation 1, A is not liable on the ground of *culpa in contrahendo* for the break-off of serious negotiations. According to the prevailing opinion, a party is free to break off serious negotiations even without a good reason before he has made a binding offer.[74] Freedom of contract has priority. The negotiating party should always reckon on the other party changing his mind. The expenses of the negotiations of each party are at his own risk. The mere fact that the negotiations have lasted a long time or that the defendant knew the expenses incurred by the plaintiff are not sufficient for liability.[75] Only in exceptional circumstances (especially if he made the other party believe a contract would certainly

[74] BernerKommentar-Kramer, OR 22 n. 13; Merz, *Vertrag und Vertragsschluss*, n. 132; Schwenzer, *Schweizerisches Obligationenrecht Allgemeiner Teil*, n. 47.08; Gauch, Schluep, Schmid and Rey, *Schweizerisches Obligationenrecht Allgemeiner Teil*, vol. I, n. 991ff.; Gauch, *Der Werkvertrag*, n. 452ff.

[75] BGE, 29 Oct. 2001 no. 4C.152/2001 (in SemJud 2002 I, 164ff.), E. 3.

come about)[76] might the party be liable. In view of the apparent differences B was not entitled to rely on the conclusion of the contract in good faith.

However, A is liable for negotiations in bad faith if it gives the reasons (ii) to (iv) for the break-off and knew of the reason a year before. All these circumstances were obstacles for the contract. Hence A has negotiated without serious intention to conclude a contract. B can claim the expenses it incurred after A violated his duties. The same rule applies for reason (i) if the merger with B was no longer an option after A received the better offer from C. If A intended to continue the negotiations with B in order to have a safety option, it would have had to inform B about the better offer from C.

In situation 2, A is liable on the basis of contract. Swiss law has a special provision[77] in favour of the validity of contracts (*favor contractus*). In opposition to the principle of the autonomy of the parties (*Privatautonomie*) the parties do not necessarily need to agree on all points of the contract; the judge is authorised to determine ancillary points (*Nebenpunkte*) reserved by the parties; and it is not necessary that the agreement on the essential points is in writing and signed by the parties.[78] According to an earlier opinion of academic writers the agreement must contain the subjective *and* the objective essential points of the contract in order to have the legal presumption of a binding nature.[79] However, in this opinion the presumption is of little or even no importance. Therefore, a growing number of writers hold that the parties need only agree with regard to the objective essential points, that is the core of the contract (*Geschäftskern*).[80] A party then has to prove that it did not want to be bound, and that the other party should have recognised this, without agreement on the objective inessential (ancillary) points. If the party fails to prove this reservation the contract is valid and the judge has to complete the agreement (*Vertragsergänzung*). According to the Federal Court a party must make clear that an ancillary point is a condition for the binding nature of the contract.[81] In the present case it seems that the parties have

[76] Discussed in relation to situation 3, below.

[77] OR 2. [78] So-called *Punktation*: cf. the Austrian report on this case.

[79] Cf. the references in BernerKommentar-Kramer, OR 2 n. 8ff.

[80] ZürcherKommentar-Schönenberger/Jäggi, OR 2 n. 39; BernerKommentar-Kramer, OR 2 n. 10ff.; Schwenzer, *Schweizerisches Obligationenrecht Allgemeiner Teil*, n. 29.04.

[81] BGE 118 II 32.

agreed on all essential points. In any case, A did not make clear that its agreement on the minor points is a prerequisite for the validity of the contract.

However, if A can prove that the agreement on the minor points was a condition, it is not bound by a contract. But it might be liable on the ground of *culpa in contrahendo* because it seemed certain that a contract would come about. A has to compensate B's negative interests (the legal expenses). Only the cultural difference (ii) seems to be a proper reason to break off the negotiations and to exclude the liability.

In situation 3, A is not liable on the basis of contract because the parties have apparently not agreed with regard to all essential points. According to the prevailing opinion a party is free to break off serious negotiations even without a good reason before it has made a binding offer. However, some authors propose a different solution under which a party breaking off the negotiations may be liable if it makes the other party believe that a contract would certainly come about.[82] This opinion is supported by a judgment of the Federal Court of 1995, which was discussed in the Swiss report on case 4.[83] In view of A's statements, B seems generally to be entitled to claim against A. But the liability is excluded if A had a good (material) reason for the break-off of the negotiations. Due to the lack of court decisions in Swiss law, the prerequisites for the exclusion of liability are not clear. Considering the high demands for liability for breaking-off of negotiations in general, a reason excluding the liability should be assumed only in exceptional situations. It seems appropriate to demand that the reason must be significant enough to allow the cancellation of a valid contract. It must be unreasonable to conclude the contract. Neither the better offer (as in reason (i)) nor the lack of money (as in reason (iii)) are good reasons that exclude the liability. A must compensate the legal expenses incurred by B. However, it is not reasonable for the firms to merge in case of an insurmountable cultural difference. Hence, in the case of reason (ii) there is no liability.

[82] Cf. Piotet, *Culpa in contrahendo et responsabilité précontractuelle en droit privé suisse*, 128; Koller, *Schweizerisches Obligationenrecht Allgemeiner Teil*, § 28 n. 10; ZürcherKommentar-Schönenberger/Jäggi, OR 1 n. 587 (break-off at an improper time); Gonzenbach, *Culpa in contrahendo im schweizerischen Vertragsrecht*, p. 96ff.; Widmer, *Umfang des Schadenersatzes bei nicht zur Perfektion gelangten Verträgen*, 155, 184; Loser, *Vertrauenshaftung im Schweizerischen Schuldrecht*, n. 642.

[83] BGE 121 III 330. See also BGE, 29 Oct. 2001 no. 4C.152/2001 (in SemJud 2002 I, 164ff.), E. 3; BGE, 17 Nov. 2005 no. 4C.247/2005 E.3.

Editors' comparative observations

This case, with a range of rather complex variables in the facts, is designed to compare jurisdictions' approaches to the breaking-off of negotiations at different stages, and for different reasons. It involves the breakdown of merger negotiations between commercial parties: (i) after lengthy (but still inconclusive) negotiations; or (ii) after the parties have reached agreement on all major points but not yet on all the detail; or (iii) when one party has made statements that it is convinced that there will be agreement. Reporters were also asked to consider whether, in each of these cases, it makes a difference whether (a) no reason is given, or (b) one of a range of particular reasons is (honestly) given. The resulting reports are very revealing about the different approaches to the pre-contractual stage. The starting point for every jurisdiction, made more or less explicit in each reporter's answer, is that a party is free to withdraw from negotiations. The case therefore turns into an enquiry for each reporter as to whether A, who withdraws from the negotiations, has crossed a line which takes it beyond the point at which it has freedom to withdraw: does the mere fact that the negotiations have been lengthy make a difference? Or the agreement on major points? Or A's statements about the future success of the negotiations?

Lengthy negotiations: some jurisdictions have a rather simple answer: in English, Irish and Scots law (as we have seen in all the cases in this study) there is no general principle of precontractual liability and therefore there is an almost absolute freedom to break off the negotiations as long as A has not made any binding contractual commitment, and (as here) does not commit a tort in the manner of the break-off. However, other systems are again more cautious, admitting that there *can* be a liability for breaking off negotiations, but the question is whether the liability is engaged on the facts.

Most jurisdictions hold that the mere length of the negotiations, even three years' negotiations, does not suffice to impose liability on the party who breaks off, and therefore the reason for breaking off is not relevant. Reporters have viewed the facts from slightly different perspectives but still generally reached the same conclusion. Some point to the fact that a lengthy period of complex negotiations (without necessarily a successful outcome) is not unsurprising in the case of a merger of firms of accountants, and so no conclusion could be drawn about the break-off after a period of three years. Others suggested that the length of the negotiations, without yet a satisfactory resolution of the differences between the parties, could itself point towards the break-off being almost expected; at least, that the party complaining of the break-off (B) could not claim to have relied on the likely conclusion of the contract given the time which had already passed without agreement.

However, in the view of some reporters (France, Italy, Norway, Portugal) the length of the negotiations might give rise to the requirement to justify the break-off. The difference of approach between these jurisdictions and the others might be more a question of interpretation of the facts: the three-year period points towards the negotiations being in an advanced stage towards the completion of the contract, and it is this fact, rather than the length of the negotiations themselves, that triggers the requirement that the party justify its breaking-off. Certainly, some of these reporters are hesitant about holding that there might be liability.

In the case, however, where A broke off the negotiations after knowing for a long period that it had a good reason, most reporters have no hesitation in holding it liable. The trigger for liability is A's failure to inform B that it would (or, at least, might) break off the negotiations; the liability is for the losses B incurred from the time when A *should* have informed it; and the basis of liability is the general basis of precontractual liability recognised by each jurisdiction which has been discussed in earlier cases (whether a specific statutory provision, autonomous *culpa in contrahendo* or the law of tort). The only substantial variation amongst reporters is in their assessment of when A had a duty to inform: some would say that merely knowing of a reason by which it *might* break off is not sufficient, if it was still reasonable for it to continue to negotiate through to the point when the failure of the negotiations became a certainty; others would say that the mere possibility might mean that continuing to negotiate without disclosing it was already a case of bad faith in the conduct of the negotiations. As usual England and Ireland, however, can only impose liability if A made a false *statement* that can give rise to a claim in tort during the period after A knew of the reason; Scotland is here a little more open to the possibility that a court might find A liable for continuing negotiations in bad faith where the reason is A's lack of means, without, apparently, limiting the liability to A's misrepresentations.

Agreement on major points: there is a greater divergence of opinion about this case. England, Ireland and Scotland start from their usual, strong position: there is not yet a contract and so A is free to break off without giving any reason; and the manner of its breaking-off probably does not involve a tort (although, as in the case of the lengthy negotiations, above, Scotland considers the possibility of a claim in the tort of negligence where the reason is A's lack of means to conclude the merger). But the other jurisdictions are divided. Germany and Sweden regard A as still free to withdraw without giving a reason. Denmark thinks it unlikely that A would be liable, except perhaps where it could not afford the merger. Spain and Switzerland solve the case by contract – a binding pre-contract, or an incomplete agreement that the judge has power to complete; and Austria would also contemplate a contractual solution if a formal (draft) pre-contract (*Punktation*) had been entered into. But other jurisdictions hold that A is precontractually liable unless it can justify breaking off the negotiations. It is generally the advanced stage of the negotiations that means that the parties have crossed the line and are no longer free to withdraw without reason, although again the reporters' interpretation of the facts affects their analysis: France, for example, highlights the complex commercial context which therefore makes it still reasonable for either party to withdraw even at the stage where all major matters have been settled. And reporters who require A to have a good reason to break off differ as to what counts as a good reason. Portugal thinks that all the given reasons are good; the Netherlands that the better offer from C or the insurmountable cultural difference are good. Norway would not allow the better offer (or, at least, might expect A to offer B the chance of meeting C's offer). Greece doubts whether any of the reasons are good, relying on the fact that the negotiations are already at a late stage to exclude most reasons as being sufficient. Austria thinks that the discovery of insurmountable cultural differences between the firms is the only good reason at this stage.

The remedy, in the case of those jurisdictions that would hold A liable, would be either reliance damages (for cases of precontractual liability) or contract remedies (for cases solved by finding a contract). In the Netherlands, this is a case of the 'third stage' of negotiations where the remedy in precontractual liability might be *expectation* measure damages.

A's statements: the variant here is that A has made a number of statements about its conviction that the contract will be concluded. Although England, Ireland and Scotland are often looking for a misrepresentation on which to base liability in the negotiation phase, it should be noted that these statements do not satisfy them: A's statements are not false statements of fact (at least, as long as they are made honestly by A), nor contractually binding undertakings, but merely expressions of belief in the future of the negotiations. Some other jurisdictions are equally sceptical about whether such statements can change A's liability towards B given that they do not in fact bring the concluded agreement any closer: Italy, for example, sees the statements as just '*pourparlers*'; Sweden thinks that the statements cannot give rise to A's liability (even, it should be noted, if it knew they were false). However, some would say that such statements by A *can* give B reasonable cause to rely on the conclusion of the contract and that, if a court holds that in the circumstances B was entitled so to rely, A's liability has been engaged unless it can show a good reason for breaking off the negotiations. Austria, Finland, France, Germany, Greece, the Netherlands, Norway, Portugal and Switzerland all contemplate the possibility of liability arising from A's statements, although with notable variations in the likelihood of such liability being found on the facts: for example, Austria and Germany doubt whether these statements are sufficient to entitle B to rely on the contract being concluded. And amongst jurisdictions that think that there might be liability, there is as much disagreement here about whether the given reasons are good as there was in the situation (above) of breaking-off of negotiations after the parties had reached agreement on major points.

Case 8: A shopping centre without a tenant

Case 8

A, the country's leading department store, is negotiating with B for B to build a new shopping centre in which A is to rent substantial premises for a new flagship store. During the negotiations, before the contract for A's lease is concluded, B begins the building of the shopping centre, including elements of design and construction which follow the indications which A has given of the layout it will wish to have. A knows that B has begun the building works. When the building work is far advanced, A breaks off negotiations because it has then done a survey of the likely client base, and has decided that a store in that location would not, in fact, be sufficiently profitable. B is left with a shopping centre which he would not have built without a tenant such as A to form the focus for the centre; and he now has a building which is so constructed and organised that he cannot find any alternative department store as the tenant. What liability (in contract, tort, restitution, or any other form of liability), if any, does A have to B?

Discussions

Austria

As mentioned in discussing earlier cases, the freedom to negotiate is a cornerstone of contract law, including the freedom to break off negotiations; but it may collide with the mutual reliance on the honesty of the negotiating parties. The decision as to how far the freedom to break off negotiations goes, and at what point the creation of the negotiating partner's confidence in the completion of the deal prevails, is a matter of case-by-case analysis.[1]

The crucial question is again whether A's conduct was such as to lull B into a false sense of security that the rental agreement would be concluded. Was it 'lulling B into a false sense of security' when A remained silent upon witnessing that B included in the construction work elements of the design and construction which it had proposed? Was it right for A to observe the building work advancing further before initiating a survey of the prospective client base, and was it right for A to break off the negotiations after the survey gave rise to a disappointing prognosis of the profitability of a department store in B's building?

A ought to have warned B as soon as it realised that B was adhering to the design A had proposed for the layout of the shopping centre.[2] A had a duty of care vis-à-vis B. The violation of this duty results in a liability under the established rules of *culpa in contrahendo*. A will have to compensate B's reliance loss: the difference in the construction costs, if adherence to A's design caused higher costs. It is doubtful whether A would have to pay the cost of reconstructing the building by removing the specific construction elements indicating it to be A's store and reshaping the building in a neutral design. It is certain, however, that B has no claim for the loss of rent from A.

Denmark

B, who is a professional, acts improvidently by building the shopping centre following A's concepts without having obtained any contractual commitments from A. A probably has no duty to warn B when B starts and continues to build even if A is uncertain whether it will use the building. A Danish court would probably be confirmed in this view by the decision in the Swedish Supreme Court decision in the *Abacus* case.[3] A has no liability to B.

England

A has no liability to B unless either B can show some statement by A on which to found a claim in the tort of deceit, or the English courts are

[1] See, e.g., OGH 8 Oct. 1975, SZ 48/102; 6 July 1976, SZ 49/94; 30 May 1979, SZ 52/90; 30 Jan. 1980, SZ 53/13.

[2] See, e.g., OGH 28 May 1991, JBl 1992, 118; 29 May 1995, SZ 68/105.

[3] NJA 1978.147; see the Swedish report below.

prepared to develop English law in a manner similar to developments already made by the High Court of Australia.

B has no claim in contract for A's failure to take the lease, because the negotiations for the lease are not yet concluded and, in any case, a contract to grant a lease of more than three years must be in writing, signed by both parties.[4] Nor does there appear on the facts to be any other contract. Although B undertakes building work in accordance with A's indications about the layout it wishes to have, there is no contract between them for the building work: B does the work in anticipation of the proposed lease. A commits no tort by breaking off the negotiations, unless it made a false statement about its intention to continue with the negotiations and take the lease, at a time when it had already no such intention or when it knew that there was a risk that it would not be able to take the lease. Such a statement would be fraudulent, and so would form the basis of a claim by B in the tort of deceit to recover the losses he has suffered by relying on it. This is not the lost profits which the actual shopping centre (with A as tenant) would have made: that would be the measure of damages in contract, not tort. But B could claim in the tort of deceit the sum by which his wealth is diminished by his reliance on A's fraudulent statement: this may be the costs wasted in building the shopping centre and the lost use of his capital in the meantime (that is, his capital could have been employed in *another* shopping centre, without A's involvement).[5] Although there is no evidence that A made such a statement, a court would be likely to examine very carefully its words and conduct to see whether it made a fraudulent misrepresentation. This liability arises only if B can identify a misrepresentation: A has no duty to inform B about the risks he runs by incurring the costs of building to A's layout – not even when A knows that it might not in fact proceed to a finalised contract.

B will argue that there might be a claim in restitution, under which he is entitled to be paid the value of the services (the building work) performed at A's request. However, such a claim is unlikely to succeed. A party to a contract which is not ultimately entered into may sometimes be able to recover in restitution for the value of services performed at the other party's request which go beyond the normal preparatory work for the intended contract. This is an area of English law which is not entirely settled. In principle a claim in restitution

[4] Law of Property (Miscellaneous Provisions) Act 1989, s. 2.

[5] *East v. Maurer* [1991] 1 WLR 461.

ought to be limited to the value of the benefit received by the defendant (which would here be nil, since the work is done on B's own property), but sometimes judges have held that the mere fact that the claimant performed services at the defendant's request was itself a benefit for which the defendant must pay; and the value of the benefit has been measured by the claimant's cost of providing the services.[6] However, the case here seems not even to fall within this principle, since it does not appear that there was a sufficiently clear request by A that B should begin the work in anticipation of the conclusion of the negotiations for the lease; and in a case where it is still not yet clear that the contract will be entered into, the normal rule is that precontractual expenditure is at the risk of the spending party.[7]

In a case similar to the facts given here, the High Court of Australia has extended the doctrine of promissory estoppel to impose liability on the party seeking to withdraw from negotiations. In *Waltons Stores (Interstate) Ltd v. Maher*,[8] there was not yet a concluded contract to grant the lease of the property but the prospective tenant, who had sought to withdraw, had encouraged the landowner to continue to build the property when he had already decided not to take the lease. The High Court held that the tenant was estopped from denying that he was bound to complete the lease, because it would be unconscionable for him to retreat from his implied promise to complete the contract. The remedy was not, however, specific enforcement of the undertaking to complete the contract, but damages. This analysis is not, however, possible in England below the level of the House of Lords since it has been authoritatively held by the Court of Appeal that promissory estoppel cannot be used to create new obligations; the doctrine generally applies only to prevent one party to a contract from going back on a promise to the other party that he will not enforce his existing rights under the contract.[9]

[6] *William Lacey (Hounslow) Ltd v. Davis* [1957] 1 WLR 932; *Brewer Street Investments Ltd v. Barclay Woollen Co Ltd* [1954] 1 QB 428 (Lord Denning: the other two judges decided the case on the basis that there was a *contract* for the work). For discussion of the controversial aspects of the valuation of the benefit for a claim in restitution, see Goff and Jones, *The Law of Restitution*, ch. 26; P. Birks in Burrows, *Essays on the Law of Restitution*; Burrows, *The Law of Restitution*, pp. 16–25, 372–81.

[7] *Regalian Properties plc v. London Docklands Development Corporation* [1995] 1 WLR 212; there, however, the negotiations were expressly 'subject to contract'.

[8] (1988) 164 CLR 387.

[9] *Combe v. Combe* [1951] 2 KB 215; *Baird Textile Holdings Ltd v. Marks & Spencer plc* [2002] 1 All ER (Com) 737. The facts in our case are, though, less strong than in *Waltons Stores*

This case shows the limited remedies in English law for the breakdown of negotiations. As long as A has not contracted to take the lease, nor made any other contract to pay for B's costs in fulfilling its requests if it fails to complete the lease, and as long as A has made no misrepresentation on which B has relied in doing the work, the costs B incurs are at his risk. The prudent course of action for a person in B's position is to obtain from A a contractually binding undertaking either to take the lease or at least to grant B an option to require it to take the lease, or to compensate B for his costs if the lease is not concluded. Failing such undertakings, English law regards the precontractual expenditure as generally at the risk of the spending party. The development in Australian law, discussed above, may well not be taken up in England where the courts have shown no sign of any willingness to reallocate the risk during negotiations.[10]

Finland

A might liable to B on the basis of *culpa in contrahendo*. The liability covers the expenses that B has incurred in reliance on the contract (construction costs), but not his lost profits from the contract of lease with A that was never concluded or from other contracts that cannot be concluded due to the poor marketability of the premises in the building. Lost profits from the contract being negotiated belong only to the positive interest and are not compensated by the negative interest that is applied in *culpa in contrahendo*. But B's lost profits from contracts that were not concluded because of his preparations to fulfil the contract with A are in principle included in the negative interest. The strict conditions of foreseeability,[11] however, have to be met.

A's fault constituting the *culpa in contrahendo* would lie in letting B begin and continue the building work, and perhaps handing design material to B when A's own plans are not yet mature, including even fundamental questions such as the final decision whether to build or

(Interstate) Ltd v. Maher: there the prospective tenant had given a stronger explicit indication that he would go ahead with the lease, but once he had decided not to proceed he deliberately did not communicate his decision to the landlord, and watched whilst the landlord completed the demolition of an existing building and completed about 40 per cent of the new building before he told him. On the facts in our case, it appears that A's decision to break off the negotiations is reached at a later stage, when it has surveyed its likely client base, and the decision is communicated promptly.

[10] For further discussion, see the Conclusions, pp. 461–8.

[11] See the Finnish report on case 6.

not. This could be a case of reliance protection, too. By his behaviour A may have given B good reason to believe that the contract will be concluded, and B's reliance could thus be protected. B's possible contributory negligence (in relying too much on the impression he had of A's intention) should, however, be considered as a possible ground for reducing A's liability or even relieving A totally of any liability.

France

B has built a tailor-made department store for A and now finds himself without a tenant and in great difficulty to find another.

These facts have given rise to a very similar case[12] in France, where a promoter of a store made modifications to the premises being sold in order to comply with the buyer's specifications. In this decision, where the Cour de Cassation overruled the judgment of the Cour d'Appel, the judges decided that even though there was no wrongful intention on the buyer's part, his behaviour in pursuing the negotiations was sufficient to hold him liable on the grounds of tortious liability under articles 1382 and 1383 of the Civil Code.[13]

In this case A necessarily knew about the construction going on, especially since it asked B to implement its specifications for the store. Therefore, even though it might appear that it broke off negotiations in good faith, it will probably be liable under articles 1382 and 1383 of the Civil Code, since breaking off the negotiations after they had been going on for a very long time, long enough to complete the construction of the store, would amount to a fault. The other conditions of liability (harm and causation) are also satisfied.

The most difficult part of this case is to determine the basis upon which the judge will calculate the damages: more specifically, whether B should be compensated for the entire construction of the store. Although it seems quite clear from the facts that B would not have built the store had he not expected A to be the tenant, it might be difficult to hold A liable for the entire loss for two reasons. First of all, B might have been somewhat negligent in not making sure that A intended to contract, especially if A was his only prospective tenant. This contributory negligence may relieve A from part or all of his liability. Secondly, the mere fact that B started to build the store whilst negotiating with A is

[12] See the *Monoprix* Case: Civ 3 Oct. 1972, Bull Civ III no. 491.

[13] A may be held liable *only* if its breaking off is wrongful. Any other event at the root of the cancellation of the project is of no effect on A.

not sufficient to prove the extent to which A realised and allowed B to build the store exclusively for it.

As far as the special elements installed just for A are concerned, the judge would certainly grant B the costs incurred in order to comply with A's specifications. Under the principle of total compensation, B will be compensated for eliminating and replacing those elements as well as reimbursement for the purchase price. Therefore, A will be liable to compensate B for the excess costs and to put the store back into a condition that will enable him to find another tenant. However, it is quite improbable that the judge will compensate B for all the losses incurred as a result of building the whole store. In any case the amount of damages cannot include the full expectation interest;[14] that is, B is not entitled to obtain compensation for the benefits he expected from the project.

Germany

A is not liable. A contract did not materialise. B is not entitled to a claim on the ground of §§280(1), 311(2) No. 2 BGB (*culpa in contrahendo*). A did not make B believe that a contract would (almost) certainly come about, nor did it prompt B to begin the building of the shopping centre. It is beyond doubt that A's mere indication of the desired layout of the shop is not tantamount to instigating B to start the construction works.[15] If the principle of freedom of contract is to be maintained, then the same must apply for A's bare knowledge of B investing into the premises in the hope of a future contract. Hence, as a rule, a party is under no duty arising from §§241(2), 311(2) BGB (*culpa in contrahendo*) to warn the other party that an agreement might finally fail. Otherwise the investing party would be put into the position of indirectly pressurising the other party into a contract.

A is not liable in tort or in restitution.[16]

Greece

A and B are negotiating for a lease on a substantial part of the premises that B is to build. B starts construction following the design and

[14] See recent case law in the French report on case 1, n. 33.

[15] BGH, decision of 18 Oct. 1974, NJW 1975, 43; BGH, decision of 13 Apr. 1972, WM 1972, 772; Staudinger-Löwisch, Vorbem. zu §275ff. para. 54; MünchKomm-Emmerich, Vor §275 para. 54.

[16] Cf. the German report on case 6.

construction indications according to A's wishes. When the building work is far advanced A breaks off the negotiations.[17] From the outset one must distinguish the case as regards the two opposites: first, when A knows nothing of the construction undertaken by B and, secondly, when A encourages B to initiate the work. If A knows nothing of the building work carried out by B, one cannot claim that breaking off negotiations constitutes precontractual conduct in bad faith nor that A is at fault. The negotiations are indeed advanced but A invokes a proper reason which allows it to terminate them. The opposite is true in the second case. Had A induced B to commence early construction, the rest of the facts being the same, a Greek court would in all probability find A's conduct to be contrary to precontractual good faith (*venire contra factum proprium*) and it would compensate B's loss.

However, on the basis of the facts of the case A is merely aware that B has begun the building work. The question is whether by failing to warn B it violated its precontractual good faith obligation. One cannot give a straightforward answer to this question, any approach being debatable and much depending on the more specific circumstances of the case. Of course, the construction being at an advanced stage means that negotiations were also advanced, and in that case the precontractual obligations of both parties increase in intensity. However, our view is that A should not be burdened with an obligation to warn B not to proceed with construction on the basis of its layout and its failure to give such a warning does not constitute precontractual bad faith. Not taking these steps was a matter of prudence for B alone. B may in good faith rely on the prospective conclusion of the contract, but he must be careful not to misjudge the real situation: a contract may with high probability come about but it is still not there. According to the facts, initiating the construction was not necessary for B to conduct the negotiations properly. A had only provided a layout from which B presumed A's wishes; and we must not forget that B is a professional in the construction business. B's high expectations are not fulfilled but he cannot hold A accountable because the latter did nothing according to the facts

[17] For a vaguely similar set of facts see AP 1126/1986 EEN 1987, 410: in that case the constructor claimed compensation on the basis of precontractual liability for adjusting and modifying the plans of the construction to accommodate the needs and wishes of the prospective buyer, with whom he was negotiating the sale of the biggest part of the building (the claim was finally dismissed as not having being sufficiently substantiated).

of the case to nourish B's expectations.[18] B undertook a step beyond that which was necessary in the preparation for the prospective contract and, if the contract does not come about, he alone must account for the loss. He cannot transfer this to A's risk. Perhaps A was morally wrong in doing nothing to prevent the construction, but by doing nothing it did nothing legally wrong. Thus, it is most likely that A was not acting in bad faith when breaking off negotiations, even if it knew that B had proceeded with the construction of the shopping centre.[19]

Ireland

A has no liability to B.

On the facts given, A has made no representation or promise or undertaken any action that can be construed as creating a reasonable belief in B as to A's future course of action with respect to the contract. Admittedly B, in the hope that A will complete the contract negotiations successfully, has altered his course of action. But there is nothing disclosed which indicates that this was anything other than B's own decision. The building was not done at A's request, nor does it appear that A in any way influenced B's actions. No action lies in contract, tort or restitution.

Italy

This is a case of withdrawal of a contractual proposal (*revoca della proposta*) as provided by article 1328, paragraph 1 of the Civil Code. When a contractual proposal is withdrawn in breach of the duty of good faith in negotiations, both Italian academic writing[20] and case law[21] recognise precontractual liability of the party who made the proposal. According to article 1328, the proponent (*proponente*) always has the right to withdraw his proposal until the contract is concluded. But when the recipient has begun his performance in good faith and before having

[18] Cf. T-203/96 *Embassy Limousines v. European Parliament* [1998] ECR II-4239, where, contrary to the facts under discussion here, preparations were requested and supported for the proper performance of the forthcoming contract.

[19] Cf. Gazis, *Legal Consultations 1956–1999*, pp. 300–1, who indicates that the initiation of performance by one party during the negotiation stage reinforced the impression that the contract would be concluded, which makes it significantly more difficult for a party to terminate the negotiations. He claims that this is *venire contra factum proprium* conduct which is prohibited by article 281 GCC on the abuse of a right.

[20] See F. Benatti, '*Culpa in contrahendo*' CI 1987.

[21] In particular see the position of Italian Supreme Court in Cass, 8 Mar. 1972, n. 664, which remains unchanged.

notice of the other party's withdrawal, the proponent has to pay all his expenses and his consequential losses.

Italian case law sees this as either a case of liability without fault (*responsabilità senza colpa*),[22] or a case of *culpa in contrahendo* because of the breach of the duty of good faith (the parties' duty of co-operation) during the negotiations.[23] In any case it is necessary for the claimant to prove his reasonable reliance. Academic writers, however, considered damages under article 1328, paragraph 1 as deriving from a 'damaging but licit conduct' (*atto lecito dannoso*),[24] giving rise only to 'reliance damages' (recovery of expenses incurred between the notice of withdrawal and the time agreed for the conclusion of the contract).

In this case, the judge will have to decide whether A acted in bad faith, or whether B unreasonably snapped up A's offer. It would be important for the judge to decide whether A was in breach of a duty to warn which was implied within its general duty of good faith in negotiations. On the other hand, B must give evidence of his own justified reliance. In this, it would be for the judge to decide whether the documents by which A indicated its requirements for the department store constituted sufficient evidence of its real intention to contract with B. There could always be a question of why B had not given A any survey before starting construction.

If B shows sufficient evidence about A's serious proposal to contract, according to article 1328, he will recover his losses and the expenses of building. Moreover, if it emerges that A was aware that B had begun the building works, it would be difficult to justify its delay in communicating to B its intention to withdraw. On the other hand, if A was not so aware, its conduct would still seem negligent given the length of time required for the construction of a department store.

If A's breach of good faith in negotiation is shown, the judge could then increase the damages payable according to A's fraudulent behaviour: B could ask for the recovery of all his loss, although limited to the *interesse negativo*, as discussed in relation to case 1.

In a case of withdrawal of a contractual proposal, article 1328 seems to extend protection beyond the general principles of precontractual liability.[25] The offeree is deemed liable not because of his misbehaviour,

[22] Cass, 7 May 1952, n. 1279. [23] Cass, 31 Jan 1969, n. 296.

[24] Mirabelli, *Dei contratti in generale*; Bianca, *Diritto civile*, vol. 3, *Il contratto*.

[25] Especially the duty of good faith under art. 1337 c.c., discussed in the Italian report on case 1. It should be noted that most of the decisions on art. 1328 have been about public bids (see App. Milano, 15 Mar. 1985), and particularly cases of public

but because his conduct has damaged the other party.[26] Damages are recovered independently of the promisor's fraud or negligence. On the other hand, article 1328 does not provide the same amount of damages as precontractual liability.[27] For example, the loss of the chance of another contract is not necessarily covered by the provision.[28]

Netherlands

Contract: A and B never actually reached agreement.[29] They did not conclude a full contract, nor does the statement of facts give any indication that they reached any kind of agreement in principle. Even in the absence of agreement a contract may be concluded if one party wanted it and was justified in assuming, as a result of the other party's statements or behaviour, that the other party agreed.[30] Was there justified detrimental reliance? Although B has undertaken actions which may be regarded as acts in performance of a contract, this does not mean that he thought that a contract had already been concluded. He may have relied on his expectation that agreement would soon be reached. Moreover, if he did think that a contract was concluded there is no reason to think that he was justified in doing so. A never seems to have given the impression that it meant already to be bound by a contract and there do not seem to be any other facts or circumstances that would justify such reliance. Thus, it seems, A is not liable for breach of contract. Therefore, B can claim neither damages nor specific performance on this ground.

Breaking off negotiations: if A broke off negotiations in a manner which is contrary to good faith it may be liable to compensate B's expectation interest (including loss of profit) and may be ordered to continue negotiations or even to conclude the contract.[31]

Was A's breaking off negotiations contrary to good faith? That would have been the case if A broke off at a moment when B was justified in expecting that a lease contract would be concluded. This may be the case. Although A does not seem to have made any statements during the negotiations that may have induced such justified reliance, the fact that B had, to A's knowledge, started building the shopping centre, including the elements of design and construction which followed the

administration engagements (see Cass, Sez. un., 29 Nov. 1986, n. 7081; Cass 10 Jan. 1986, n. 63).

[26] See Cendon, *Commentario codice civile*, vol. IV; G. Alpa, 'Appunti sulla responsabilità precontrattuale nella prospettiva della comparazione giuridica' RCP 1981, 535.

[27] See the Italian report on case 1. [28] Bianca, *Diritto civile*, vol. 3, *Il contratto*.

[29] Article 3:33 BW. [30] Article 3:35 BW. [31] See the Dutch report on case 1.

indications given by A, and A remained silent, may have induced B justifiably to believe that a contract would be concluded. A Dutch court may hold that A should have warned B that it was not yet certain that agreement would be reached and that by not doing so it has induced B to expect that a contract would be reached. Such a holding would not provide incentives for recklessly starting to perform contracts that have not yet been concluded, and thus for imposing the conclusion of a contract or extensive liability upon the other party, because A could easily have avoided liability by warning B. Since, however, it did not do so, it will probably be held liable for breaking off negotiations. B will then be entitled to compensation for loss of profit, or may even obtain a court order (with a private penalty: *dwangsom*) which forces A to continue negotiations or even to conclude the contract.

Norway

It is assumed that the contract for the entire project has not been entered into, and that B commences the construction work on *his own initiative*, that is, not in agreement with, or on the order of, A. Hence, there is no presumption by the parties that A is to cover B's wasted expenditure. However, the result in this case would to some extent still depend on how the facts are interpreted.

The fact that B on his own initiative *commences the construction* (on his own property) should not be of major significance with respect to the question of liability.[32] It would, however, have a certain influence on the question of good faith inasmuch as A was aware of the construction work, especially with regard to the duty to inform.

On the other hand, a *reason for discontinuation* would influence the result of the case. The facts state that A 'has then done a survey of the likely client base, and has decided that a store in the location would not, in fact, be sufficiently profitable'. Regarded separately, this is, of course, a valid reason for discontinuing the negotiations. The question remains, however, whether the possibility of reduced market value should have been clarified in advance. If changes occur in the external market situation causing A to drop the project, A has no liability. This is

[32] In Rt 1992, 1110, the *Stiansen* case, at 1115, the presiding judge states that 'however, Stiansen had here put himself into a difficult position, even before the finalisation of the contract, by commencing the construction work, and chose not to terminate the project at the time of OBOS's letter of 19 January 1988 [in which it was stated that the price of the construction was exceptionally high]'. In other words, this was a risk the construction company itself was responsible for.

part and parcel of the general risk facing businessmen when no binding agreement exists. But there is good reason to believe that a contrary point of view should be taken if there had not been any significant changes in the market situation. The parties should have made a proper evaluation and examination of the feasibility of the project in advance, even if it would obviously have been acceptable at a later date for them to analyse their needs in depth.

In NJA 1978.147, the *Abacus* case, the Swedish Supreme Court moved in the opposite direction. This case concerned negotiations with respect to the purchase of newly constructed premises. Since a supermarket was to be operated on the premises, the owner had refurbished them with this in mind. However, the potential buyer broke off the negotiations as a result of a market investigation he conducted. The claim made by the owner of the premises to be reimbursed for his wasted project and installation expenses did not succeed. The Supreme Court stated that:

> when the project agreement was entered into, it must have been evident to both parties that the possibility for a later discontinuation of the agreement depended on certain undetermined factors and that the cooperation of the parties consequently was subject to risk, which was particularly evident with respect to Abacus's planning and the refurbishing of the premises according to Tössberg's wishes.

It was further noted that 'the other party should himself have been able to protect his own interests without the necessity on Tössberg's part to indicate or suggest an intended discontinuation of the agreement'. The rationale for this judgment might have been that the owner of the premises had sufficient insight into the elements of risk. However, it is doubtful whether the result would be identical today.[33] Legal developments in this field in recent years have probably occasioned stricter requirements with respect to the good faith of the parties involved than was previously the case.

It is therefore likely that A would here be held responsible, particularly if it realises that the construction has commenced, since it should have warned B about the risk that the contract might not be concluded.

[33] This case is also discussed in the Swedish report on this case, below, but in Sweden it is thought still to apply, and not to have been superseded by changes in the courts' approach to the precontractual phase.

Portugal

B is entitled to compensation for the expenses he has incurred, based in precontractual liability,[34] but the compensation would not be for all the losses suffered. The damages would be for the reliance interest, including not only the expenses of construction but also the loss of the tenancy. However, damages would be reduced due to B's contributory negligence.

During the negotiations A must fulfil the duty of good faith, which includes not allowing the other party to incur expenses on the assumption that the agreement will be concluded if there is no solid intention to reach agreement. So A would be liable for not warning B that it was not sure of its intentions and that the final agreement would depend on the survey of the likely client base.

However, B's own negligence obviously contributes to his loss. B should not have included in the building works elements of design and construction related to A's department store without a solid agreement concluded with A. Therefore article 570 of the Civil Code would apply, which allows the court, in cases of contributory negligence, to reduce or even to exclude the compensation.

Scotland

In general it seems likely that A would not be liable in damages in this situation, although there is nineteenth-century case law which might seem to point in the direction of a claim. But these authorities have been narrowly interpreted now for well over 100 years, and the re-interpretation has placed such limits upon recovery as to take the scenario outside the scope of the present law.

The facts of the case have elements in them of *Walker v. Milne*,[35] where a landowner had undertaken alterations to a plan for land development in order to accommodate the construction by others of a monument which was eventually relocated elsewhere by those others. The landowner was held able to recover his losses from the others involved. *Walker v. Milne* was used in a number of subsequent cases in the nineteenth century. In *Bell v. Bell*,[36] a son erected a house on his father's land on the faith of the latter's verbal (and so unenforceable) promise to convey the land to him. The father broke the promise and conveyed to his daughter. The son recovered his expenditure, two

[34] Article. 227 CC. [35] (1823) 2 S 379. [36] (1841) 3 D 1201.

judges apparently finding for him on the basis of fraud, and a third on the basis of *Walker v. Milne*. In *Heddle v. Baikie*,[37] H possessed B's farm for six years without any formal lease (although it was understood that one was to be executed) and made improvements. He was then ejected. A claim for loss and expenditure was allowed. In *Dobie v. Lauder's Trustees*,[38] D undertook the care of certain children in return for an annual payment from the trustees. Because it was envisaged that this arrangement would last some years, D entered a seven-year lease of a house in Frederick Street, Edinburgh, and incurred other expenses. After a dispute about the amount of the annual payment, the children were withdrawn from D's charge. She claimed successfully against the trustees for reimbursement of her expenses. The Second Division was clear that there was no contract in this case but only a family arrangement. But, said Lord Justice-Clerk Moncreiff,[39] 'the arrangement necessarily included the condition that if the arrangement was terminated it should not be to the loss of one party'. Lord Neaves took a slightly different view:[40]

> I think that the legal principle applicable to the case is this: that when parties are engaged mutually in promoting an object of common interest, and the expenses entailed in furthering that object are thrown on one of the parties, then when that expenditure fails of obtaining the end aimed at the party-disburser must be recompensed, as being the disburser for a common object.

The last case in which recovery was allowed is *Hamilton v. Lochrane*,[41] where a party made alterations to his villa in reliance on a verbal (and so unenforceable) agreement for its sale. When the buyer withdrew, the selling party made a claim for reimbursement of his expenses. He was allowed a proof. Here it could not be said on any view that the defender had been enriched; the claim was purely one of reimbursement for the pursuer's reliance expenditure. Again, we have unilateral withdrawal from an arrangement the terms of which were substantially settled.

However, *Walker v. Milne* was said in 1875 to be not a case of general application[42] and the reimbursement remedy was available only if substantial loss was occasioned to one party by the representations *recklessly and unwarrantably* held out to him by the other party. The present facts do not suggest that there have been any reckless or unwarrantable misrepresentations made by A to B. In recent times,

[37] (1846) 8 D 376. [38] (1873) 11 M 749. [39] At 755. [40] Ibid. [41] (1899) 1 F 478.
[42] *Allan v. Gilchrist* (1875) 2 R 587, 590.

Walker v. Milne has been re-interpreted as one where there would have been a binding agreement were it not for formalities (requirements of writing) that had not been complied with.[43] The same cannot be said of this case; it seems that there has not yet been agreement on all major points of the lease. It seems unlikely that there could be said to be any element of partnership between A and B.[44]

Spain

A is liable to B in tort, in *culpa in contrahendo*. The four conditions established by the Supreme Court are probably established.[45] The fact, known by A, that B begins building during the negotiations is a very strong indicator that the relation between those two can be qualified as a reasonable situation of confidence concerning the conclusion of the contract. Concerning the second condition (the absence of justification for the break-off of negotiations), A does actually give a reason which explains why it lost interest in the contract. But good faith requires different behaviour. A, knowing that B is firmly counting on the conclusion of the contract, and has already started working on the basis of its layout, has a duty to inform B either about the uncertainty of its concluding the contract or about the fact that it is still waiting for the results of the survey – but at least about the fact that such a survey is being undertaken. If B knows about this fact, he consciously builds at his own risk. Otherwise A negotiates in bad faith and the abrupt break-off of negotiations is not justified. Concerning the third and the fourth conditions, B suffers loss by building in a way he would not have built, if he would have built at all (reliance damages), and by not being able to find any alternative department store as tenant (expectation damages). As the liability is based on tort, only reliance damages are covered. The causal link serves to decide on the amount of damages: it is necessary to establish how B would have acted knowing about the survey and its importance for A. Most probably he would not have started building before knowing its result.

Another possible approach would be to establish the existence of two contracts: on the one hand, a mandate to build in a certain way, on the

43 See the interpretation placed upon the case by Lord Cullen in *Dawson International plc v. Coats Paton plc* 1988 SLT 854, affd. 1989 SLT 854. A wider approach to the relevant authorities is suggested in MacQueen and Thomson, *Contract Law in Scotland*, paras. 2.95–2.96.

44 Cf. *CIN Properties Ltd v. Dollar Land (Cumbernauld) Ltd* 1992 SC (HL) 104.

45 STS, 14 June 1999, RJ 1999\4105. See also the Spanish report on case 1.

other hand, the rent. The conclusion of the second contract (rent) can be understood as 'price' for the first. In that case, the parties have concluded the first contract, but the terms of the second contract are not yet completely clear. But A has to conclude the second contract; otherwise, it has to pay damages.

Sweden

A is not liable to compensate B.

In NJA 1978.147[46] the circumstances were very similar to those in this case. During negotiations, the parties agreed that in the ongoing renovation of the building, premises should be reserved for the other party (T) and designed in a way that would suit a supermarket. According to the agreement, T had the intention to rent or buy the premises, but neither the rent and term for the lease nor the price were agreed upon. Later on, T discontinued the negotiations, the main reason being a market survey showing that an establishment might prove not to be profitable, especially considering the range for the rent or price for the premises indicated by the other party. According to the Supreme Court, the parties were under the obligations to co-operate with the intention to reach a final agreement and to take the other party's interest into consideration. Therefore T had to devote himself in good faith to the final decision regarding the establishment of the supermarket and keep the other party informed about the development. However, T had grounds to believe that the other party could take care of his interests in a commercial relationship of this type. As T had not acted contrary to these obligations, the Supreme Court found that T was not liable to compensate the other party for the costs incurred in the design of the premises. There is very little in the later development that shows that the law in this particular respect might have changed since the case was decided.

In the present case, no precontractual agreement was formed according to which A had an intention to conclude an agreement with B. The remaining issue is therefore whether A during the negotiations acted in a way that could be a ground for compensation due to *culpa in contrahendo*. There is no indication that A was late or careless when

[46] This case is also discussed in the Norwegian report on this case, above, although it is there said to be probably no longer of authority, in the light of the development of a stricter doctrine of precontractual good faith. The case NJA 1978.147 is also discussed in the Swedish report on case 4. See also Adlercreutz, *Avtalsrätt*.

performing the relevant investigations necessary to decide whether to lease or not, nor in informing B about the results of the survey. Being a party acting in a commercial setting, B ran the risk that the parties would not reach a final agreement. B therefore started the construction and made the adjustments according to A's wishes at his own risk and cost. As the result from the market survey showed that it would not be sufficiently profitable to establish the department store in that location and as A informed B of the results of the survey while discontinuing the negotiating, A is not liable to compensate B.

Switzerland

A is not liable on the ground of *culpa in contrahendo* for the break-off of the negotiations. It did not make B believe that a contract would certainly come about, nor did it ask B to start the building work; the indication of the desired design and construction does not constitute such a request. The mere knowledge of B's investments is not sufficient to protect B's expectations in a future contract.[47] Otherwise the investing party would be able to undermine the freedom of contract of the other party.

But A can be blamed for negotiating without a reservation although it could have recognised that it might not conclude the contract. The client base and the expected profit were facts with influence on A's decision to rent the premises. A could have done the survey and recognised the obstacle to the contract earlier, at the beginning of the negotiations. It has therefore negligently raised unjustified expectations in B about the future possibility of a contract and is liable for the violation of the duty to negotiate in good faith.[48]

A must compensate B's negative (reliance) interest. This generally comprises the higher costs of the building work due to the layout desired by A and the expenses of a reconstruction in a neutral way. But B is partly responsible for his own loss because the contract was not certain and B should always have realised that A might change its mind. The judge can reduce the compensation according to OR 44 because the expenses served not for the negotiations but for the performance of the contract under negotiation.[49]

[47] BGE, 29 Oct. 2001 no. 4C. 152/2001 (in SemJud 2002 I, 164 ff.), E. 3; BGE, 17 Nov. 2005 no. 4C. 247/2005 E. 3. Compare Loser, *Vertrauenshaftung im Schweizerischen Schuldrecht*, n. 642.

[48] See further the Swiss report on case 3.

[49] Cf. BernerKommentar-Becker, OR 26 n. 6ff.; ZürcherKommentar-Oser/Schönenberger, OR 39 n. 10ff. On OR 44, see further the Swiss report on case 3.

Editors' comparative observations

A striking feature of this case is the number of jurisdictions that can point to actual decisions which have involved facts very similar to those given here. France, Greece and Sweden have very similar cases (the Swedish case being given an interestingly different interpretation by the Swedish and Norwegian reporters as regards the current legal position in their respective systems); and the English reporter points to a similar Australian case. It may therefore be assumed that the commercial context which is described by the hypothetical facts of this case is a reality which might easily occur in any of the jurisdictions studied. This makes the rather different approach across the several jurisdictions of particular interest in assessing whether there is a common core of the legal principles applicable in the precontractual phase. There is a division of opinion as to the result. A majority of jurisdictions would give B a remedy, but a significant minority would not.

Most of the jurisdictions which would award a remedy would limit it to reliance damages, at least to compensate B for his costs of construction but also sometimes, but not always, awarding the cost of reinstating the building to a form suitable for another tenant, and his lost opportunities of other tenants. The only jurisdiction that might go further, and award B either the value of the loss of the particular tenancy with A, or even perhaps a court order that A continue the negotiations, is the Netherlands, which again can award stronger remedies within its principles of precontractual liability, linked to the expected (but not concluded) contract when the negotiations have proceeded to an advanced stage. The basis, however, of the liability varies amongst these jurisdictions. Finland and Switzerland see the trigger for liability as A's having started the negotiations without reservation, and let B begin and continue the building work; or having given B precise instructions about its desired layout for the store without yet being sufficiently certain about the likelihood of the negotiations reaching a successful conclusion (since it had not yet conducted the client survey); or, at least, in not informing B at the *outset* that there were some such risks which B might not appreciate. Austria, Italy, the Netherlands, Norway, Portugal and Spain focus on the fact that there came a point, *after* the start of the negotiations, when A knows that B has begun to build, and it is the failure to inform B at that stage that engages its liability. In some jurisdictions, however (France and the Netherlands) the focus is on the fact that, given that the building work is now far advanced, the break-off of the negotiations is at a late stage, and therefore requires a substantial justification, which A cannot provide, given that the reason is one that it could have discovered earlier by undertaking a more timely survey of the likely client base.

Some jurisdictions, however, will not award B any remedy. As so often in this study, England, Ireland and Scotland cannot find a remedy because they have no general principle of precontractual liability and damages cannot be awarded in the absence of a binding contractual promise or specific wrong, such as a tort committed by A having made a fraudulent misrepresentation (which they do not find evidenced by the facts given). It should be noted that Scotland has some older authorities in the case law which might give a hint of a remedy on these facts but the reporters take the view that today's courts would be reluctant to give a remedy. And the English reporter points to the fact that in another common law jurisdiction (Australia) the courts have developed the principles of promissory estoppel to cover cases involving similar facts (although even that extension would not cover the particular case here). There are other jurisdictions, however, which in other cases in this study would apply a general principle of precontractual liability, that might here deny a remedy. The reason given varies slightly but comes down to a core principle: that B, as a commercial (professional) party, has taken it upon himself to begin the building – he has therefore (given that A did not actually request that the work be begun) incurred the expenditure at his own risk. This reasoning underlies the Danish, German, Greek and Swedish reports.

The question of *risk* could, moreover, be said to be the principle that underlies many of the reports, both those that decide on the facts in A's favour, as well as those that decide in B's favour. The facts given raise something of a borderline case, which might be affected to some degree by how the reader interprets the facts, but where the basic question is whether the risk of precontractual expenditure, incurred by one party, can be shifted to the other party as a result of the fact that the latter knows about it being incurred, and could (perhaps) have discovered earlier the reason which it eventually uses to break off the negotiations. The borderline nature of this case is shown not only by the division of opinion amongst the jurisdictions, but also by the fact that some reporters are rather tentative about the result (see, for example, the Greek and Norwegian reports). Also, even some of the jurisdictions that would impose liability on B will consider that the damages might be reduced by B's contributory fault: there is a sense that, even if A's conduct is such as to take onto itself in principle the risk of B's expenditure on the building work, B should share the risk. Finland, France, Portugal and Switzerland consider that B might have been contributorily negligent.

Case 9: Breakdown of negotiations to build a house for a friend

Case 9

A tells his friend, B, that he wants a house built on his (A's) land, but he cannot see how he will be able to afford the normal, full costs of having the house built. B, who runs a building firm, tells A that he would be able to find the time to undertake the job, and would be able to do it for a price which is lower than a commercial building firm would charge. While A and B are still in negotiation as to the price and other details about the final scope of the works, B starts the building work. When the house is nearly complete, A breaks off the negotiations because he finds that he cannot afford even the (lower than commercial) price which B wants to charge. What liability (in contract, tort, restitution, or any other form of liability), if any, does A have to B?

Discussions

Austria

Under Austrian law the facts of this case will not lead to the application of the rules of civil liability, whether contractual or non-contractual, since there are specific provisions within the chapters of the ABGB on property law that deal with 'constructions on another person's land'.

The relevant provisions in the Austrian codification are §417, dealing with the construction of buildings on one's land with materials of another; §418, on the construction of buildings on the land of another with one's own materials; and §419, on the construction of buildings on the land of another with another person's materials. These provisions apply in the absence of a contractual agreement between landowner and builder. Since A and B were still in negotiations when the construction work began, and since these negotiations were broken off by A, there is no contract.

The general rule is *superficies solo cedit*: the owner of the land acquires ownership of the building and the *bona fide* constructor will be compensated for his expenses. However, there is an exception from this rule, stated in §418 ABGB:

> if . . . a person constructs a building on the [land] of another using his own materials but without the knowledge and consent of the owner, the building becomes the property of the owner of the [land]. The bona fide constructor can demand compensation for the necessary and [profitable] expenses; the mala fide constructor is to be treated as an unauthorised agent. If the owner knew of the construction, and did not immediately order the bona fide constructor to [stop] such construction, he can only demand the general price for the [land].

Thus §418 ABGB gives a precise answer to this case: since A knew of the construction works by B and did not intervene to stop the works, he loses ownership of his land. B becomes owner of the land on which the building has been constructed, but the market price of the land has to be paid by B to the original owner A.[1]

Denmark

A Danish court might find some basis of liability in the consideration that A, on whose land B builds the house, should have warned B not to start building until A was certain that he could afford it. On the other hand, if B starts the work without A's express consent and knowing that A is a poor person he must know that he takes a risk, and perhaps as a friendly turn he then assumes that risk. In that case a court (acting as an *amiable compositeur* – Danish courts sometimes do that, although they are unwilling to admit it) might award B what it finds that A can afford.

A Danish court would not give much thought to the question whether A's liability is in contract, tort or restitution.

The court may also conclude that A has no liability. It might hold that we are in the area of friendly turns where the law should abstain from interfering and on this ground find A not liable.

[1] There are a very few rather old cases on §418 ABGB; see, however, OGH 15 Mar. 1989, JBl 1989, 582, stating that it is the *mala fides* of the owner of the land that is sanctioned by the loss of his ownership and the acquisition of ownership by the constructor.

England

A may be liable to pay B the value of the benefit he has obtained by virtue of the (nearly complete) house having been built on his land: this is a claim in restitution.

B has no claim in contract, since there is not yet any concluded contract for the house. Nor does B have any claim in tort: A commits no tort by breaking off the negotiations, nor is there any evidence of any misrepresentation made during the negotiations which would give rise to such a claim; for example, it appears that A discovers only at a late stage that he cannot afford the building works, and so he does not make any fraudulent misrepresentation on which B relies in continuing the work.

However, B has commenced the building work in the anticipation that the contract would be concluded; and in doing the work he has conferred on A the benefit of the building in circumstances where it was intended by both parties that A would pay for it but on a basis which had not yet been finalised. Since the building is a fixture it becomes A's property, and insofar as it increases the value of his land A obtains a valuable benefit. If the breakdown of the negotiations was A's fault, he would be required make restitution in monetary terms.[2] B will claim on this basis, although it is not certain that he will succeed, since A may successfully argue that B knew that A's ability to agree a price was uncertain, and therefore B carried out the work at his own risk. More detail would be necessary of the facts surrounding B's decision to start work, such as whether A made any request for the work to be started, or gave any assurances about payment. If a restitutionary claim succeeds, the valuation of the benefit cannot be made by reference to the contract since there is not yet an agreed contract price for the value of B's services. The valuation must therefore either be by reference to a *reasonable* rate for the work done by B; or, more likely, by reference to the increased value of A's land with the house built on it.[3]

[2] *Brewer Street Investments Ltd v. Barclay Woollen Co Ltd* [1954] 1 QB 428, 431 (Romer LJ: 'Suppose that, whilst parties were in negotiation for a lease, the landlords allowed the prospective tenants to go on the land and spend money on it in anticipation of a lease. If the landlords subsequently broke off negotiations for no reason at all they could not get the benefit of the work without paying for it').

[3] *British Steel Corp v. Cleveland Bridge and Engineering Co. Ltd* [1984] 1 All ER 504 (reasonable price payable for work done in anticipation of a contract which was confidently expected to materialise, but in that case there was a specific request by the defendant for the claimant to begin work in anticipation of the contract).

Finland

As with case 8, this case would be decided on the basis of A's *culpa in contrahendo* on the one hand, and B's contributory negligence on the other. If A was at fault he is liable to B for his negative interest. It covers the costs that B incurred when he relied on the contract and consists mainly of the cost of the building works. If the strict conditions of foreseeability[4] are met, it is possible that B might be compensated even for his lost profits from contracts that were not concluded because of his preparations to fulfil the contract with A. B's possible contributory negligence, in turn, could reduce A's liability, in extreme cases even to zero.

The solution is therefore mainly a matter of comparison of the degrees of possible negligence on the side of each party. This is, of course, a question of fact. In this case, too, A's possible negligence is to be found in letting B begin and continue the building work when A has not sufficiently surveyed his resources to carry out the building project. B on his side has possibly shown contributory negligence in starting the work too hastily when there are not yet any guarantees that the contract will be concluded, or that the work can be afforded. He may also have given A too optimistic indications of the cost of his performance.

France

B has started to perform the contract even though the terms (price, details and scope of the work) have not been fully agreed by the parties.

If the agreement to conclude a construction contract (qualified as a *contrat d'ouvrage et d'industrie* under article 1779 of the Code civil) is considered to be a contract to negotiate, an *avant-contrat*, A's potential liability to B will obviously be contractual. However, this hypothesis is not convincing on the facts.

If there is no contract, B must pursue a claim under articles 1382–1383 of the Civil Code. Can it be argued that A brutally broke off the negotiations, and as such his behaviour constituted a fault? On the one hand, it could be argued that since A knew that B was already building on his (A's) land, B's belief that A would ultimately conclude the contract was legitimate (no builder would carry out building work without payment) and that A's breaking off the negotiations could therefore be qualified as a fault. On the other hand, the very reason why the parties

[4] See the Finnish report on case 6.

had not yet concluded the contract and had not yet settled the price was A's impecuniosity. Indeed, the very reason A asked B to do the work was because the building work was too expensive. This may indicate that A's breaking off the negotiations was not brutal but rather predictable, in which case there is no fault to give rise to tortious liability.

The remaining avenue for B is to make a claim *de in rem verso* on the basis of *enrichissement sans cause*. Such a claim is traditionally considered subsidiary[5] in French law and can thus only be made if all other legal grounds are excluded.

The legal foundation of *enrichissement sans cause* has developed as a result of case law following the Cour de cassation's decisions of 15 June 1892.[6] The five conditions of this action are: (i) there must be an enrichment; (ii) a correlative impoverishment; (iii) the enrichment must be unjust, without *cause*; (iv) the impoverished person must not have a personal interest; and (v) there must be no other cause of action. All these conditions have been developed by case law and academic writers. The fourth condition is also treated under the heading of the impoverished person's fault (*faute de l'appauvri*). This notion has been the subject of a recent development in case law which means that the answer to these facts is somewhat uncertain.

On the one hand, it is arguable that it is not necessary to discuss the fulfilment of all these conditions since in particular condition (iv) may well create an obstacle for B's claim. In the past, case law developed the idea that if the impoverished person acted at his own risk and peril, in view of gaining a personal advantage, he could not make a claim under this head.[7] This seems to be precisely the case here, since B ran the risk, in starting the building work without A's consent as to the terms of the contract, that A would not pay him or even be financially able to pay him for the work done.

On the other hand, recent developments have made this idea more flexible; in particular, a distinction is now drawn between the

[5] V.P. Drakidis, 'La subsidiarité, caractère spécifique et international de l'action d'enrichissement sans cause', RTDCiv 1969, 577. But the purely subsidiary nature of the action is in the process of evolving: see Civ 1, 15 Oct. 1996, RJDA 1997, no. 327, 207, RTDCiv 1997, 657, obs J. Mestre; Civ 1, 3 June 1997, JCP 1998.II.10102, note G. Viney.

[6] Cass Req, 15 June 1892, DP 1892.1.596, S. 1893.1.281, note J.-E. Labbé.

[7] See Terré, Simler and Lequette, *Les obligations*, no. 975, 4°, p. 901. See also Civ 28 Mar. 1939, Gaz Pal 1939.I, 879; G. Bonet, 'La condition d'intérêt personnel et de faute chez l'appauvri pour le succès de l'action "de in rem verso"' *Mélanges Hebraud* (1981), 59ff. See also Com 16 July 1985, obs J. Mestre, RTDCiv 1986, 110; Com 24 Feb. 1987, Bull Civ IV, no. 50, 36; Civ 1, 7 July 1987, obs J. Mestre, RTDCiv 1988, 132.

impoverished person's negligence or imprudence, and behaviour which constitutes a real fault, such as fraud (*dol*).[8] According to this line of interpretation, it is plausible to allege that B's conduct in starting the work amounts to mere negligence or imprudence which does not necessarily exclude his action for a *de in rem verso* claim. It is therefore possible that B has a chance of succeeding under the head of restitutionary liability. In that case, B would be entitled to recover the lower of his impoverishment and A's enrichment.

Germany

For the same reasons as in case 8, A is not liable in contract on the ground of *culpa in contrahendo* or in tort.

B is, however, entitled to a claim in restitution on the ground of unjust enrichment. Pursuant to §§93, 94(1) and 946 BGB, A, being the legal owner of the piece of land, also became owner of the nearly completed house by virtue of the law. Therefore, A's assets are increased by B's building work. This transfer of wealth is not supported by a valid cause (*causa, Rechtsgrund*), that is, A's enrichment is unjust. According to §812(1) BGB an enrichment is, *inter alia*, deemed unjust if a person obtained another's performance without a legal ground (*condictio indebiti, Leistungskondiktion*, §812(1) sent. 1, 1st alternative BGB) or the purpose of a performance was not put into effect (*condictio ob rem* or *condictio causa data causa non secuta, Zweckverfehlungskondiktion*), §812(1) sent. 2, 2nd alternative BGB).[9]

In the case of a party already performing a contemplated contract which subsequently does not materialise, the courts and writers are at variance whether this set of facts should be classified as *condictio indebiti* or *condictio ob rem*. The differentiation is pivotal because, if the claim has

[8] See the overruling by the Cour de cassation on the question of fault where a clear statement that fault does not automatically exclude the action *de in rem verso* was made: Civ 1, 11 Mar. 1987, Bull Civ I, no. 88, 57; confirmed Civ 1, 3 June 1997, Bull Civ I, no. 182, 122 and Civ 2, 2 Dec. 1998. For the qualification of behaviour constituting fraud, see Com 19 May 1998, note J. Mestre, RTDCiv 1999, 105–6; this decision is somewhat clouded by the position taken by the first chamber: see 15 Dec. 1998, note J. Mestre, RTDCiv 1999, 400–1.

[9] §812 BGB: '(1) A person who, through an act performed by another, or in any other manner, acquires something at the expense of the latter without any legal ground, is bound to return it to him. This obligation subsists even if the legal ground subsequently disappears or the result intended to be produced by an act to be performed pursuant to the legal transaction is not produced. (2) Recognition of the existence or non-existence of a debt, if made under a contract, is also deemed to be an act of performance.'

to be based on *condictio indebiti*, a claim in restitution is barred *ab initio* by §814 BGB,[10] if A knew that he was under no obligation to build the house. If, however, the case must be brought under the heading of *condictio ob rem*, B may only raise the defence of §815 BGB[11] which takes precedence over §814 BGB as the more special regulation and whose conditions are not met in our case.

The courts, by and large, tend to cover performance in anticipation of a contract which later does not come about by *condictio ob rem*.[12] It would seem that this approach is accurate, since a party knowingly accepting performance of an anticipated contract does at least concede to, if not even implicitly agree with, the performing party that the purpose of a future contract is the reason for the performance. In the present case A knew that the contract contemplated by both parties was the sole purpose of B's performance.

A party unjustly enriched must provide restitution, pursuant to §818 BGB:

(1) The obligation to return extends to emoluments derived, and to whatever the recipient acquires either by virtue of a right obtained by him, or as compensation for the destruction, damage or deprivation of the object obtained.
(2) If the return is impossible on account of the nature of the object obtained, or if the recipient for any other reason is not in a position to make the return, he or she shall make good the value.
(3) The obligation to return or to make good the value is excluded where the recipient is no longer enriched.
(4) After the date an action is pending, the recipient is liable under the general provisions.

Since in the case of the construction of a building the party enriched is generally not in the position to provide restitution in kind, A must, instead, provide compensation for the value of the enrichment under §818(2) BGB. As a rule, the valuation standard is objective: that is, the

[10] §814 BGB: 'What was done with the object of fulfilling an obligation may not be demanded back if the person performing knew that he was not bound to effect the performance, or if the performance was in compliance with a moral duty, or for the sake of common decency.'

[11] §815 BGB: 'The right to demand return on the grounds of non-occurrence of the result intended to be produced by what was done, is barred, if the production of the result was impossible from the beginning, and the person performing knew this, or if he has prevented the occurrence of the result in bad faith.'

[12] Cf. Markesinis, Lorenz and Dannemann, *The German Law of Obligations*, vol. I, *The Law of Contracts and Restitution: A Comparative Introduction*, p. 762.

value of an enrichment is to be measured by the increase in the recipient's assets caused by the enrichment. If, however, the increase was imposed upon the recipient against his will (*aufgedrängte Bereicherung*), he may plead subjective valuation as a defence.[13]

The Bundesgerichtshof, however, has not yet decided whether the defence of imposed enrichment is available in *condictio ob rem* cases. The question should be answered positively, as acquiescence in the performing party's purpose does not necessarily imply free acceptance of that performance as well. Therefore, if A did not freely accept A's performance and if, from his point of view, the enrichment is worth nothing or less than the objective increase, for example because he cannot afford to finish the building or he cannot put it to productive commercial use, then B's claim may be reduced or even disallowed.

Greece

A wants to build a house on his land and B offers to build that house. Notwithstanding the fact that A and B are friends, they enter into negotiations for a construction contract. This assumption is reinforced by the fact that B is a professional and he is willing to undertake the work against payment. Thus, negotiations between A and B started when A announced to his friend B that he cannot afford the normal commercial price to build a house and B offered to undertake the work for a price which is lower than the normal commercial price. Indeed, B proposed a lower than normal commercial price but A found that he could not afford that price either, there and then ending the negotiations with B. In fact, the price which B proposed for the work is lower than the commercial (usual) price and such a price should have been in A's contemplation from the outset of the negotiations. Undoubtedly, A could have abandoned the negotiations without precontractual liability had the facts of the case been limited to negotiations regarding the price. But A's right to withdraw from the negotiations becomes questionable given that in the meantime B had nearly completed the house on A's land. A is well aware that by breaking off negotiations at that stage he is left with a house which is almost complete.

There is little indication as to precisely under what circumstances B has initiated the construction of the house on A's land. But the very fact

[13] Cf. Staudinger-Lorenz, Vorbem. zu §§812ff Rn. 47 (with a comparative overview); Markesinis, Lorenz and Dannemann, *The German Law of Obligations*, vol. I, *The Law of Contracts and Restitution: A Comparative Introduction*, p. 762.

of construction taking place indicates not only that A was aware of the work carried out by B but, most importantly, that A had given his agreement to and facilitated that work. In other words, by providing access to his land A did not simply tolerate or allow construction but he actually facilitated it. Irrespective of whether A required the work to start during the negotiating stage, the latter knowingly encouraged the initiation and continuance of that work.[14]

Hence, it must be accepted that the longer A tolerates the building of the house on his land by B, the more A's good faith precontractual obligations towards B increase and terminating the negotiations accordingly becomes less easy.[15] In view of all the above, on the basis of articles 197 and 198 GCC, A, by breaking off negotiations after rejecting the reasonable price proposed by B when construction had significantly progressed, is liable for precontractual conduct which is contrary to good faith and he will have to compensate B. It is very probable that damages here will amount to a quasi-expectation interest; however, a strict application by the courts of the reliance interest theory in this case would result in A having to compensate only the negative (for example, labour and material) and positive (loss of profit) damage, whereas the added value represented by the house would remain with A.

Instead of precontractual liability, B may alternatively invoke the provisions on unjust enrichment.[16] Article 904 GCC provides that a person who has become richer without a lawful cause by means of or to the detriment of the patrimony of another shall be bound to refund the benefit. B can freely choose upon which legal basis he will substantiate his claim; the remedy of restitution may only be invoked in the context of unjust enrichment. The possibility that there might be an operative contract between A and B concluded by means of conduct is not further explored here.

Ireland

There are two possibilities with respect to this scenario: first, that the parties have concluded a contract but the quantum of consideration has

[14] Compare AP 1126/1986 EEN 1987, 410.

[15] Gazis, *Legal Consultations 1956–1999*, pp. 300–1, indicates that the initiation of performance by one party during the negotiation stage reinforces the impression that the contract will be concluded, which makes it considerably more difficult for a party to terminate the negotiations. He claims that this is *venire contra factum proprium* conduct which is also prohibited by art. 281 GCC on the abuse of a right.

[16] Article 904ff. GCC.

not been finalised; secondly, that there is no contract between A and B because it is not possible to match a clear acceptance with an offer. However, in practice the consequences are similar in both situations.

If there is a concluded contract between A and B, then A will be contractually bound to pay such quantum of consideration as the court sees as just and reasonable. In *Lampleigh v. Braithwait*,[17] the parties had agreed that the plaintiff would do all in his power to secure the release of the defendant from prison. When this had been completed, the defendant promised to pay a certain sum of money. The rest was silence. The plaintiff sued and was met with the rejoinder that the promise to pay constituted past consideration and was therefore unenforceable. The court held that the parties had always contemplated that consideration would be paid but that the quantum had been left for later agreement. The defendant's subsequent promise now quantified the amount of the consideration but even if the defendant had not done so, the court would have imposed what was reasonable. The case has been approved in modern case law in *Pao On v. Lau Yiu Long*.[18] In the Irish case of *Fanning v. Wicklow County Council*,[19] the court held that where the parties had concluded a contract but had not specified the consideration payable, an action would lie to recover the reasonable value of the work performed (quantum meruit).

If the court is of the view that there is no contract between the parties, for example, that there are essential terms other than consideration that the parties have not agreed upon, a claim in quantum meruit will still be well founded. In *William Lacy (Hounslow) Ltd v. Davis*,[20] the court made an award where work was done at the request of the defendant during negotiations which were expected to, but did not in fact lead to a concluded contract. In *British Steel Corporation v. Cleveland Bridge Engineering*,[21] during the course of negotiations the defendant indicated that he wished the plaintiff to commence performance pending the conclusion of contractual negotiations. The parties never concluded the contract. The court ordered that the plaintiff be compensated in quasi-contract for the reasonable value of the work undertaken. This view was approved, and extended, by the Irish courts in *Folens & Co. v. Minister for Education*.[22] In that case the plaintiff entered

[17] (1615) Hob 105, 80 ER 255.

[18] [1980] AC 614; see also *Bradford v. Roulston* (1858) 8 IRCL 468.

[19] (Unreported, High Court) 30 April 1984, 423.

[20] [1954] 1 QB 428.

[21] [1984] 1 All ER 504.

[22] [1984] ILRM 265.

into negotiations with the Department of Education for the production of a children's encyclopaedia in the Irish language. During these negotiations the plaintiff commenced preparatory work, with the full knowledge of the Department of Education. The Department subsequently decided not to proceed with the project. The plaintiff successfully sought compensation for the preparatory expenses. The court held that the plaintiff was entitled to an award of quantum meruit, even though the Department had not benefited from the work undertaken. It was sufficient that the work had been completed with the knowledge and approval of the Department.[23]

It is clear that the facts above fit into either of the above possibilities. B has undertaken work with A's full knowledge and acquiescence. The result will be that A will have to compensate B for the reasonable value of the work undertaken through an action for quantum meruit.

Italy

As in case 8, the present case involves the withdrawal from a contractual proposal, as governed by article 1328 of the Civil Code.

Since the negotiations occurred between friends it would be very difficult for the parties to give evidence of their care in negotiation. On the one hand, A could be considered as precontractually liable because of his lack of care in starting the negotiations for the construction of the house despite his economic trouble. On the other hand, B's conduct seems to point more to a case of his own negligence in beginning the construction than to a case of justifiable reliance on the conclusion of the contract. From the facts of the case the price seems to have been a fundamental element in order to decide whether to start the construction. In general,[24] reliance is considered to be reasonable when the party has not acted with negligence. B does not seem to have complied with his duty of normal care in ascertaining whether A could afford the new house.

Both parties therefore seem to have been at fault. It is probable that a judge would decide on an equitable amount, if B's justified reliance is proved. In any case B's damages will be limited to the *interesse negativo*.

[23] See also *Premier Dairies v. Jameson* (Unreported, High Court), 1 March 1983.

[24] See for academic discussion Monateri, *La responsabilità contrattuale e precontrattuale*, p. 415; and for case law Cass 12 June 1959, n. 789; Cass 28 Jan. 1972, n. 199; Cass 22 Oct. 1982, n. 5492; Cass 29 Jan. 1985, n. 5920; TRIB-T. Milano, 3 Apr. 1967.

Netherlands

Contract: the safest approach for a court which wants to decide for the plaintiff and which wants him to be fully compensated is to accept the conclusion of a contract of some kind (for example, an agreement in principle). However, it is submitted that evidence to that effect is not overwhelming. At no point did the parties reach agreement on the *essentialia*, nor did A induce B to believe that they had reached agreement. In particular, the price remained under discussion throughout the negotiations. Therefore, it seems unlikely that A will be held liable under Dutch law for non-performance of a contract with B.

Breaking off negotiations: A may, however, be liable for breaking off the negotiations, for reasons similar to those discussed in relation to case 8.

Unjustified enrichment: one of the classic cases[25] where the Hoge Raad explicitly rejected the adoption of a general action for unjustified enrichment was a case of performance of a contract which had not yet been concluded. In that case, *Katwijkse haven*, the city of Katwijk and a contractor had started negotiations on a contract for the removal of a large amount of clay and sand from land owned by that city. While the parties were still negotiating the contractor started the work, allegedly encouraged to do so by a civil servant (the city had an interest in having the job done as soon as possible) and under his supervision, but in any case to their knowledge. When the work was nearly completed the contract was given to a competing contractor. The first prospective contractor sought restitution of the unjustified benefit from the city on two grounds: *onverschuldigde betaling* (undue payment/*repetitio indebiti*) and *ongerechtvaardigde verrijking* (unjustified enrichment). Both claims were rejected, the former because the work done by the contractor could not be regarded as a payment; the latter because Dutch law at the time did not recognise a general unjustified enrichment action and the Hoge Raad in that case refused to adopt one, as it had done before in its decision *Quint/Te Poel*[26] but unlike the draft for the new Dutch Civil Code which at that time had already been published. The Hoge Raad's decisions in *Quint/Te Poel* and *Katwijkse haven* were severely criticised by academic writers. In his note on *HR Katwijkse haven* Scholten rightly argues that the city of Katwijk should either have stopped the contractor from starting the work or have warned the contractor that he

[25] HR 19 Apr. 1969, NJ 1969, note Scholten (*Katwijkse haven*).

[26] HR 30 Jan. 1959, NJ 1959, 548, note Veegens; AA VIII, 171, note Beekhuis (*Quint/Te Poel*).

was acting at his own risk and that a contract might ultimately not be concluded, or now compensate him for the amount by which the city was enriched at the expense of the contractor. Since then the legislator has introduced a general action into the new 1992 Dutch Civil Code, article 6:212 BW, which provides (section 1):

> A person who has been unjustifiably enriched at the expense of another must, to the extent this is reasonable, repair the damage up to the amount of his enrichment.

Scholten rightly said that application of the new article 6:212 to precontractual situations of this kind would be appropriate.

Indeed, in this case it seems appropriate to hold A liable to compensate B. He should either have stopped B from building or at least have warned him. Since he has done neither he now should compensate B for the enrichment he has gained at his (B's) expense. According to article 6:212, in a case of unjustified enrichment the defendant should 'repair the damage up to the amount of his enrichment'. Interestingly, in this case that amount may be higher than the price the parties might have agreed since they were negotiating on a price which was lower than the commercial price.

Under Dutch law, a claim based on unjustified enrichment is not a 'subsidiary claim'. Therefore, B has a free choice between the claims for breaking off negotiations and unjustified enrichment.

Norway

In this case Norwegian courts would most likely find in favour of B receiving compensatory damages for the construction work carried out, but it is not clear which rationale would be employed or how the compensation should be determined.

Contractual liability: it seems most appropriate to answer the question from a contractual point of view. Even if a final contract with respect to the construction of the whole house was not entered into, it must have been understood that B at least should be paid for the work carried out during the time up to the signing of the contract. After all, A permits the construction to take place on his property. If he had not been willing to pay for the work carried out, he should have made this clear to B. This can be seen as a 'partial agreement'.[27] Frequently such agreements might be implied. As this case concerns two friends, there is all the

[27] Simonsen, *Precontractual Liability*, p. 399ff.

more reason to apply a contractual point of view on an informal basis. If a contractual analysis is applied, a regular demand for payment can be made against A. B's statement that he would 'do it for a price which is lower than that charged by a commercial building firm' has to be the guideline for determining the price for the work already carried out. He was aware of A's financial problems and consequently the price should be set below the market value.

Unjust enrichment: whether one could base a claim for compensation on unjust enrichment in a case such as this is unclear, because no general theory with respect to unjust enrichment has been developed in Norwegian and Nordic law. The concept 'unjust enrichment' is more an indication of a problem than an established basis for a claim for compensation.[28] Since B in the present case wittingly contributes an asset to A, one can hardly claim that this transfer of property is 'unjust'. The presumption that B at least should receive compensatory damages for the work carried out is more readily dealt with from a contractual perspective (see above). If the claim is to be based on unjust enrichment, it is not clear how such unjust enrichment should be estimated in Norwegian law.

Precontractual liability: precontractual liability assumes that A has acted contrary to the general obligation of good faith during the contractual period. As stated in the *Kina Hansen* case,[29] 'blameworthy behaviour during contract negotiations must have been displayed – such as acting in bad faith, or in a dishonest or misleading manner'. The reason for A breaching the negotiations is that he 'cannot afford even the (lower than) commercial rate'. His financial problems were admittedly conveyed to B prior to the commencement of the construction work. The question is whether A during the negotiation period had adequately informed B about his declining ability to meet the payment for the work. If, for instance, the break-off was caused by A's failure to obtain external financing (such as a bank loan) for the building project, the question then is whether or not B was made aware of the risk of the loan application being turned down. Since the case concerns two friends, there is reason to demand fairly strict requirements as to the need for good faith. Precontractual liability would entitle B to receive reimbursement for expenses as he had trusted A's good faith.

[28] In the case of mistaken payments, however, a particular doctrine has been developed as to when the claimant can request the restitution of the money; cf. *condictio indebiti*.

[29] Rt 1998, 761, 772.

It is not clear whether B has a free choice between the available claims. In the relationship between invalidity and breach of contract sanctions, there is a tendency to give the latter prevalence. However, there is no theory with respect to the relationship between precontractual and contractual liability.

Portugal

B is only entitled to restitution based on A's enrichment, on the ground of *accessio*, and only if A decides to keep the building.

B is not entitled to compensation under the rules of precontractual liability, as A has fulfilled his duty to warn imposed by the good faith principle under article 227 of the Civil Code. In fact, A has made perfectly clear that he cannot see how he would be able to afford the normal, full costs of having the house built. Although he has proposed a better price, B should not have initiated the building work. If he does so, A can reject the construction and even ask for its demolition. However, if he intends to keep the building he would have to pay B the value of his enrichment.[30]

The claim for unjust enrichment is based on an objective valuation which has no relation to the proposed price of the construction, so the valuation can result in an amount higher or lower than the contract price.[31] However, A could invoke his subjective valuation as a defence.[32]

Scotland

A is liable to B in unjustified enrichment, the relevant Scots remedy being that of recompense. The measure would be *quantum lucratus est* A, that is to say the extent to which A has been enriched by the services provided to him. Although the building works have acceded to A's land and hence are owned by him, B has a personal claim for recompense against A. It might be arguable that A was not enriched by having a half-built house on his land which he cannot afford to complete. It is highly unlikely that a contract would be implied here, and there seem to be no grounds to argue for any delictual liability. Nevertheless, in the case of *Avintair Ltd v. Ryder Airline Services Ltd*,[33] a contract for the supply of

[30] Article 1341 CC. See Leitão, *O enriquecimento sem causa no Direito Civil*, p. 693ff.

[31] Article 473, no. 1 CC. [32] Article 473, no. 2 CC.

[33] 1994 SC 270. See also *Robertson Group (Construction) Ltd v. Amey-Miller (Edinburgh) Joint Venture* [2005] CSOH 60.

services was held to exist despite dissensus as to the price, the services in question having been completed despite the disagreement. The recipient was thereupon required to pay a reasonable price for the services received.

A's liability in enrichment law is the extent to which he was enriched; in the case of an implied contract, it is to the extent of a reasonable price (and there is no cumulation of these remedies). It is unlikely that B could obtain an order of specific implement requiring A to accept completion of the building work.

Spain

According to Spanish case law and academic writing, A is liable to B based either in precontractual liability (tort) or in restitution, but not in contract as there has not been any concluded contract yet, especially since the price has not been agreed.

But the four conditions for precontractual liability,[34] established by writers and case law, are satisfied. First, there is a special situation of confidence between A and B, not only because A and B are friends, but also because A does not protest against B's starting building after having offered a contract with special terms. The reason A gives for breaking off negotiations probably does not justify his behaviour as, acting according to good faith, he is supposed not only to know his personal financial possibilities and limits, but also to communicate this fact if B starts executing a contract, considering that the price offered is not completely beyond A's financial possibilities. The damages B suffers are his expenses and include probably a normal remuneration, being limited by the amount B expected to receive (*lucrum cessans*).

The other basis of A's liability would be restitution (*gestión de negocios ajenos*, article 1893 of the Civil Code; or *enriquecimiento injusto*, article 1887). According to case law, the conditions for liability based on unjust enrichment are benefits obtained by one party; losses suffered by the other party, either as positive loss or as a gain that has not been obtained; and the lack of a *causa justa* (valid legal justification). As it is not certain that A did obtain a benefit by having an almost finished (but not completely and therefore not usable) house built on his land, this doctrine seems not entirely suitable, although in a similar case it has

[34] Díez-Picazo, *Fundamentos del Derecho Civil Patrimonial*, pp. 278, 279; STS, 14 June 1999, RJ 1999\4105.

been applied by the Spanish courts.[35] As the existence of an almost finished house adds value to the land, it has to be admitted that A is richer than before. Therefore he is liable on the basis of article 1893 even if he did not explicitly ask for the house to be built, as he did not object to the building work. On the basis of this article, he is liable for the expenses B incurred, including the time B spent doing the building works.[36]

Sweden

It is highly probable that a contract has been concluded. A is then obliged to pay for the house at a price that should be determined by taking into consideration the usual market price and what has been stated by the parties regarding the price in the negotiations. If a contract is considered not to have been concluded, A's behaviour could be interpreted as an agreement to compensate B for his costs incurred during the period until the discontinuation of the negotiations. In any case, A's behaviour in not speedily making up his mind could be regarded as *culpa in contrahendo* and A must therefore compensate B for the costs B incurred during the delay.[37]

B is taking a risk if the parties do not reach an agreement. As A owns the land he is bound to know about B's work proceeding. Contracts are formed when the negotiating parties have reached consensus. Usually an agreement is reached when the parties' expressed intentions correspond. A contract might very well be formed in other ways, for example from the behaviour of the parties. Subsequent behaviour may retroactively shed some light on the intention of the parties at an earlier point of time. The failure to object when there is reason to believe that the other party by mistake believes that the contract has been or will be entered into may give rise to a valid contract either by interpreting the inactivity as an expression of intent or on the basis of

[35] Audiencia Provincial de Badajoz, 15 June 1999, no. 265/1999, AC 1999\1286; cf. STS, 31 Oct. 1986, RJ 1986\5824.

[36] There can be a problem with this liability if the expenses were higher than the price B suggested. In that case, A should only be liable for the amount suggested, as this was the value B estimated.

[37] Hellner, *Om obehörig vinst. Särskilt utanför kontraktsförhållanden*; Karlgren, *Obehörig vinst och värdeersättning*; J. Kleineman, 'Avtalsrättsliga formföreskrifter och allmänna skadeståndsrättsliga ansvarsprinciper', JT 1993–94, 433; J. Kleineman, 'Skadeståndsgrundande uppträdande vid avtalsförhandlingar', JT 1991–92, 125; J. Ramberg, 'Pre-contractual Liability according to Swedish Law' in Hondius, *Precontractual Liability*; Ramberg and Ramberg, *Allmän avtalsrätt*.

the inactivity as such.[38] A contract of sale could well arise, although there is no agreement at all on the price.[39]

A's passive behaviour in not protesting against the initiation of the construction work, and his consent to B's access to the land, are important factors when determining whether a binding agreement existed or not, which would probably lead to the conclusion that the parties had concluded a binding contract. In this case, the price has to be determined by considering the normal market price and B's expressed willingness to undertake the obligations on favourable terms.

If a contract was not concluded, A might be liable in damages for *culpa in contrahendo*. A was aware of B's efforts and he did not make it clear to B that no contract had yet been concluded. He also gave B access to the land. Even if no contract was concluded, A's behaviour could be interpreted as his consent to compensate B for the costs incurred until the decision to conclude a final agreement was reached. These circumstances might constitute liability according to which A has to compensate B for his incurred costs for the work undertaken until A informed B about his decision.[40] A party has an obligation to inform the other party without delay as soon as it is clear that a final agreement will not be concluded.[41] It is not clear from the facts in the case whether A is late when he breaks off the negotiations. If A was aware of his financial limitations already at an early stage of the negotiations and of the approximate price range for the construction, he should have acted without delay and in good faith to make up his mind about the agreement.[42] Yet he did not object until the house was almost finished. Therefore he might be liable for the costs incurred by B during his delay in making up his mind.

B might also base a claim on the principle of unjust enrichment. This principle is, however, very rarely applied as an independent ground in Swedish law.[43]

Switzerland

A is not liable on the basis of a contract because the parties have not agreed on the price. The price was apparently an essential condition for the agreement.

[38] Ramberg, 'Precontractual Liability according to Swedish Law', above n. 37.

[39] Sale of Goods Act 1990, s. 45.

[40] NJA 1978.147. [41] NJA 1990.745. [42] NJA 1978.147.

[43] Hellner, *Om obehörig vinst. Särskilt utanför kontraktsförhållanden*; Karlgren, *Obehörig vinst och värdeersättning*.

For the same reason as in case 8, A is not liable on the basis of *culpa in contrahendo* for the break-off of the negotiations. In addition, it is doubtful whether A is liable for negotiating in bad faith. He can hardly be blamed for not informing B in exact terms about the price limit although he could recognise the possible loss to B. On account of A's statements, B should have informed himself about the financial possibilities and the price limit. To decide otherwise would only be appropriate if A had so little money that the price must obviously have been outside of the wide range of a friend's offer.

However, A is liable under special provisions within the chapter on property law of the Swiss Civil Code.

Where one person builds with his materials on another person's land, the materials become an integral part of the land.[44] In the present case A becomes the owner of the half-finished building and therefore he is unjustly enriched. However, the general rules on restitution of unjust enrichment[45] are replaced by the special provisions on buildings on the land of another.[46] Under certain circumstances the (former) owner of the materials can require that they be removed at the builder's expense. In the present case B has no claim for removal because he has built the house himself, and therefore the materials have been used with his consent.

Where the materials are not removed from the land, the owner of the land is bound to pay reasonable compensation for them.[47] The extent of the compensation depends on the good or bad faith of the owner of the materials. If the owner of the materials has built in bad faith, he can claim only that amount of compensation which represents the minimum value of the building to the owner of the land. B has acted in good faith because A knew that B has started the building work on his land and did not protest against this work.[48] B can therefore claim reasonable compensation. This means – against the wording of the provision – that the judge has to consider not only the value of the materials but also the other costs of the building.[49] A has also to pay compensation for B's work, at least to the extent of the added value of the land.[50]

If the value of the building clearly exceeds that of the land,[51] the party who has acted *bona fide* can require that the ownership of the land

[44] ZGB 671 I. [45] OR 62ff. [46] ZGB 671ff. [47] ZGB 672 I, III.
[48] BernerKommentar-Meier-Hayoz, ZGB 672 n. 6.
[49] BaslerKommentar-Rey, ZGB 672 n. 7.
[50] BGE 95 II 228; BGE 82 II 290; BernerKommentar-Meier-Hayoz, ZGB 672 n. 9.
[51] The Federal Court has applied this rule in a case (in 1955) where the value of the land was CHF 600 and the value of the building was CHF 14,500 (BGE 81 II 274).

and building together shall be adjudicated to the owner of the materials in return for reasonable compensation.[52] In the present case, if the value of the nearly-completed house clearly exceeds the value of A's land, B can claim that the ownership of the land and house be transferred to him because B has acted *bona fide*. In such case B has to pay reasonable compensation for the land.

Editors' comparative observations

This case should be read with case 8. The link between them is that in both B undertakes building work for the benefit of A, before (or so it appears) the final contract for the works has been fully negotiated, and the negotiations are broken off without the contract ever being finalised. The difference between the cases, however, is that in case 8 the building was on B's land and B's losses include not only the costs of the work but also having an unsuitable building now that A has refused to complete the proposed lease of it; but in case 9, the building work was done on A's land. B's losses are the time and expense of having done the work, but here A appears to have received a benefit of a house (even if not a completed house) on his property.

This factual difference has a significant legal consequence for some jurisdictions. Whereas the focus in case 8 was on whether A should bear the risk of the contract not being concluded (a question often, but not in all jurisdictions, decided in the affirmative on the basis that A was in breach of his precontractual duty in having allowed B to continue to incur expenses when the likelihood of the final contract was, or had become, low) in case 9 the emphasis shifts to the benefit that A has clearly obtained by the increase in value of his land with the building work done on it. In consequence, the outcome of case 9 is more favourable to B than case 8. Unlike in the earlier case, every jurisdiction finds that A might be liable to B, although the basis of the remedy, and the likelihood of success of B's possible claims, varies very significantly. Some (Finland, Greece, Italy, the Netherlands, Norway, Spain and Sweden) still focus (also) on the general principles of precontractual liability and (at least as one basis of A's liability) answer this case on a similar analysis to case 8, although the facts of this case may give a different outcome to that in case 8 (see, for example, the Greek and Portuguese reports). But others shift their focus to the law of unjust

52 ZGB 673.

enrichment, although significant differences between the jurisdictions on the principles (or, in some case, the lack of them) for unjust enrichment then throw up different answers for this analysis (see, for example, the very different discussions of unjust enrichment in the English, French, Dutch, Scottish and Spanish reports). Some jurisdictions that could find no liability in case 8 are able to use unjust enrichment and hold A liable in case 9: England, Germany, Greece, Ireland and Scotland. But some jurisdictions do not have very clearly developed principles of unjust enrichment (in particular, see the Norwegian and Swedish reports).

Austrian and Swiss law take a quite different approach: they have in their codes special provisions which cover the case of building on the land of another, and which override the general rules of unjust enrichment.

A few reporters consider that in this case the most likely claim – or, at least, a possible claim (by contrast with case 8) – is in contract. They appear to be more favourably disposed to interpret the dealings between the parties, and in particular the fact that A has admitted B onto his land to begin the building works, as evidencing an agreement between them for the works to be done, and will fill by a reasonable implication the gap in the negotiations left by the disagreement over price. This approach is taken by the Irish, Norwegian and Swedish reporters, and is considered by the French, Dutch and Scots reporters but thought unlikely on the facts. The Danish reporter considers that the fact that this is a transaction between friends may negative liability.

Case 10: Public bidding

Case 10

A, a private company, wants to have a swimming pool built and organises a public bidding for the construction contract. A's published statements include the rules of the bidding process A proposes to follow for submission of bids, and its method of acceptance, and a statement that A will give the contract to the lowest bidder. B submits a bid which follows the rules of the bidding process, but A awards the contract to C. B had incurred expenses in preparing its bid. What liability (in contract, tort, restitution, or any other form of liability), if any, does A have to B if:

- (i) B's bid was the lowest, but either
  - (a) A failed properly to consider the bid, because an administrative error within A's organisation led to the bid not being considered by those within the company who were taking the decision; or
  - (b) A always intended to give the contract to C;
- (ii) B's bid was not the lowest, but A had failed properly to consider it because an administrative error within A's organisation led to the bid not being considered by those within the company who were taking the decision.

Are the answers different if A is a public authority?

Discussions

Austria

There are specific statutes for procedures on awarding contracts upon public tenders by the federation (Bund)[1] or states (Länder).[2] In addition

[1] Federal Procurement Act 2002 (Bundesvergabegesetz), BGBl I 2002/99.
[2] Each State has its own Landesvergabegesetz.

to this, there is a standard form in use in Austria, Ö-Norm A 2050, which has to be used by public authorities and is also often used by private entities such as non-profit-making housing enterprises for public bidding, which do not fall within the field of application of the respective statutes.

Since 1988, the OGH has rendered several decisions in public bidding proceedings and the court has resorted to the rules of *culpa in contrahendo* on violations of precontractual duties of care.[3] It has been criticised, however,[4] on the ground that in these cases liability must be based on a breach of a duty of the organiser to follow the rules it has publicly declared to be the basis of the bidding, rather than on a breach of a duty to keep a negotiating partner informed of all relevant circumstances that have a crucial impact on the negotiating partner's dispositions. It is nevertheless well established court practice that, if a contract is not awarded to the best respondent to the invitation to tender, liability is imposed on the organising party of the public bidding. The party having submitted the best bid (or, as in this case, the lowest bid, which need not always automatically be the best bid!) is in any case entitled to reliance damages. Thus, there can be no doubt that where its bid was the lowest B could successfully claim all the expenses it incurred in the preparation of the bid from A. The question, however, is whether B can claim also the expectation interest.

Indeed, the OGH has gone further in recent decisions.[5] Starting with cases concerning public bidding processes that were organised by public authorities, the court extended liability to the expectation interest when it was clear that the contract would have been concluded with the ignored bidding party whose offer was found to comply in an optimum way with the publicly announced conditions of the bidding process, if the procuring party had not violated its duties vis-à-vis the best (or lowest) bidder. Whether this causality test leads to a sound solution in every case is subject to criticism.[6] It appears that in a case of

[3] OGH 13 Apr. 1988, SZ 61/90; 29 Nov. 1989, JBl 1990, 520; 19 Oct. 1994, SZ 67/182; 22 Nov. 1994, ecolex 1995, 328; 12 Aug. 1998, ecolex 1999/30; 20 Aug. 1998, ecolex 1999/32; 3 Feb. 2000, JBl 2000, 524; 28 Mar. 2000, JBl 2000, 519; 29 Mar. 2000, ecolex 2000/205.

[4] St. Heid, 'Vergabeverstoß: Ersatz des Erfüllungsinteresses' ecolex 1995, 93.

[5] OGH 19 Oct. 1994, SZ 67/182; 12 Aug. 1998, ecolex 1999/30; 28 Mar. 2000, JBl 2000, 519; 29 March 2000, ecolex 2000/205.

[6] St. Heid, 'Vergabeverstoß: Ersatz des Erfüllungsinteresses' ecolex 1995, 93 and ecolex 1995, 329; R. Reischauer, in Rummel, *Kommentar zum ABGB I*, Vor §§918–933, N. 17a.

deceit, where the entire bidding process was organised with the intention to cheat the honest participants, as in variant (i)(b), the compensation should include the expectation interest, since in cases of gross negligence or intention liability goes beyond actual damage and extends to lost profits.

The answer is not really different if A is a public authority, the federation, a state (Land) or a community. Two specific aspects are worth mentioning. First, it has to be recognised that the rules of the respective federal and state statutes on public procurement apply[7] and that public authorities are bound to proceed according to the Ö-Norm A 2050. Secondly, it must not be forgotten that public authorities are bound by the principle of equal treatment. It is this fundamental principle that prohibits public authorities from ignoring the best or the lowest bidder and serves as an additional argument for imposing on such a public authority a liability that goes beyond the reliance interest.

Where B's bid was not the lowest there is no basis for holding A liable. There is no causal connection between A's negligence and the fact that B's bid was not accepted, because even if B's bid had been correctly considered by A, the contract would not have been awarded to B.

Denmark

We assume that C also made a bid under the public bidding. The Danish Tender Act provides that in case of a public invitation to tender the enterprise which invites tenders (the owner) must accept one of the tenders or reject them all. It follows from general contract law that an undertaking in the invitation to accept the lowest bid will entail liability upon the owner if it breaks it. But it will probably not make the invitation into an offer which is accepted by the lowest bid. The tender is the offer which has to be accepted by the owner.[8]

In the case where B's (lowest) bid was not considered because of the administrative error within A's organisation, A is liable to B under the rules on vicarious liability, but probably only for the reliance costs. The answer is the same where A always intended to give the contract to C. In general, Danish law does not impose a more severe sanction upon a party in bad faith than upon a merely negligent party.

[7] See, e.g., OGH 22 Nov. 1994, ecolex 1995, 328; 28 Mar. 2000, JBl 2000, 519; 29 Mar. 2000, ecolex 2000/205 (procurement by the federation).

[8] Andersen, Madsen and Nørgaard, *Aftaler og Mellemmænd*, p. 54.

In case (ii), B's chance of getting the contract was not very high since its bid was not the lowest. Danish law will in general not award damages for the loss of a chance.

The fact that A is a public authority should make no difference.

England

Where A is a private company: in situation (i)(a), A is liable to B for damages for breach of contract. An invitation to tender is normally not a contractual offer: it is the tenderer (bidder) who makes an offer which the person inviting tenders is free to consider and to decide which (if any) bid to accept.[9] However, A has here gone beyond such an obligation by expressly undertaking in the invitation to tender that it will give the contract to the lowest bidder. In such a case, the general rule that an invitation to tender is not a contractual offer is displaced, and the invitation forms an offer which will be accepted by the submission of the highest conforming tender.[10] Here, A has bound itself to accept B's bid, which was submitted in accordance with the rules of the bidding process and was the lowest bid. B can sue A for damages for breach of contract, calculated on its loss of expectation: the profit it will lose by not performing the contract to build the swimming pool (less any profit it is able to make, or should reasonably make,[11] by obtaining alternative contracts). As an alternative to this measure B may claim as its damages for breach of contract the expenses it has incurred in preparing the bid, but these are only recoverable as long as it is not clear that it would not have recouped the expenses even if it had obtained the contract and performed it.[12] B will not be able to obtain specific performance of A's promise to award the contract to the highest bidder, since the contract has now been awarded to C, and damages will be an adequate remedy.[13] B's claims are limited to damages for breach of contract: A commits no tort by failing to consider B's bid,[14] and there is no claim in restitution (A receives no benefit).

[9] *Spencer v. Harding* (1870) LR 5 CP 561.

[10] Ibid. 563; *Harvela Investments Ltd v. Royal Trust Company of Canada (CI) Ltd* [1986] AC 207.

[11] Even if it does not in fact obtain such other contracts, it will be unable to recover such part of the loss as it could have avoided by taking reasonable steps to obtain other contracts (the rule of mitigation of damage).

[12] *CCC Films (London) Ltd v. Impact Quadrant Films Ltd* [1985] QB 16.

[13] For discussion of the general principles of specific performance, see Burrows, *Remedies for Torts and Breach of Contract*, ch. 20.

[14] In *Blackpool and Fylde Aero Club Ltd v. Blackpool Borough Council* [1990] 1 WLR 1195, there was also a claim for damages for the defendant's negligence in failing to consider

In situation (i)(b), A is liable to B for damages for breach of contract and (alternatively) in the tort of deceit.

The claim for breach of contract is identical to case (a) above: A has expressly contracted to give the contract to the lowest bidder, and has broken that contract.

This case is, however, different from case (a) in that A always intended to give the contract to C, regardless of whether another bid (such as B's) should conform to the rules of the bidding process and be lower. The invitation to tender therefore contained fraudulent misrepresentations about its intentions; this will enable B to claim damages in the tort of deceit for losses it suffered by relying on the misrepresentations. In this case, the expenses it incurred in preparing the bid will be recoverable.

B cannot, however, claim its loss under more than one head; nor can it make inconsistent claims for its loss. So if it elects to claim its wasted expenditure in an action of deceit, it cannot simultaneously claim expectation damages for breach of contract based on the return it would have made from the contract to build the swimming pool, since those losses cannot co-exist: its claim to expectation loss is based on the assumption that it would have had to incur the expenditure to obtain the return.

In situation (ii), where B's bid was not the lowest, A may be liable to B for nominal damages for breach of contract, but not for substantial damages. Where tenders are solicited from selected parties, all of them known to the invitor, and where the invitation to tender prescribes a clear, orderly and familiar procedure, the invitation to tender is an offer to the extent that it promises to each tenderer that if it submits a conforming tender it will at least be considered, or at least will be considered if other tenders are.[15] The facts here do not quite fit this, since A's invitation to tender is public, rather than addressed to a limited class of bidders. But it is possible that a court might be prepared to extend the earlier decision to cover this case, since the invitation to tender does appear to give very specific

properly the claimant's tender. The Court of Appeal did not decide this finally, but Bingham LJ (at 1203) was 'tentatively of the opinion' that the invitor owed no duty of care to bidders in the tort of negligence, or at least that there was no duty in tort which went beyond the contractual duty, and therefore the contractual duty should be preferred.

[15] *Blackpool and Fylde Aero Club Ltd v. Blackpool Borough Council*, above n. 14.

undertakings about how A will deal with the conforming bids which are submitted.[16] Such an obligation is, however, only to consider tenders. It does not impose on the invitor any obligation as to how to formulate its decision in the light of the tenders received.

A may therefore have impliedly contracted to consider properly the conforming bids which it receives, and if so it is in breach of that contract because it did not consider B's bid. But even if it is in breach of such a contractual obligation, B cannot show any loss which flowed from it. Even if its bid had been considered properly, it would not have been accepted because it was not the lowest. B's claim for breach of contract would therefore be limited to nominal damages (typically a sum such as £10) to reflect the fact of breach, but no substantial damages can be awarded. Nor (for reasons similar to those discussed in relation to case (i)(a) above) does A commit any tort by failing to consider B's bid. The fact that A has also expressly contracted to give the contract to the lowest bidder is here irrelevant, since we do not know that it has broken the contract (was C's bid the lowest?); and anyway B again does not suffer any loss itself since its bid would not in any event have been accepted since it was not the lowest.[17]

Where A is a public authority: the above analysis applies without any change. There is no special body of law governing contracts made by public authorities, and unless there is some particular statute or other regulation under which the public authority is acting and which circumscribes its powers, the normal principles of contract law apply to determine its rights and liabilities.[18] Public authorities are subject to additional rules relating to public tenders for works contracts under the Public Contracts Regulations 2006,[19] but the

[16] But in *Blackpool and Fylde Aero Club*, above n. 14, both judges who gave reasons emphasised the small class of intended bidders as a significant feature: see Bingham LJ at 1202 and Stocker LJ at 1203. Any extension is therefore uncertain.

[17] In *Blackpool and Fylde Aero Club*, above n. 14, the Court of Appeal agreed with the trial judge that, in principle, damages were payable (at least in contract, see above n. 14) to the bidder whose bid was wrongly excluded. But neither the judge nor the Court of Appeal assessed the quantum of damages (nor did they decide whether there was any substantial loss on the facts which could be covered by the damages).

[18] In *Blackpool and Fylde Aero Club Ltd*, above n. 14, the person inviting bids was a local authority.

[19] SI 2006/5, implementing Directive 2004/18/EC, replacing Public Works Contracts Regulations 1991, SI 1991/2680, as amended (which implemented Council Directive 71/305/EEC, amended by Council Directive 89/440/EEC).

value of the contract for the swimming pool appears very unlikely to be high enough to fall within the scope of the Regulations.[20]

Finland

There is a document of self-regulation of the Finnish building industry that is of importance in this case, entitled *The Principles of Competitive Bidding on the Building Branch*, published in the Building Information Foundation series (RT 16–10182).[21] The purpose of the Principles is to define good building and construction practices in using competitive bidding, and they are meant to be binding both on the builder and on the contractor.[22] The Principles are based on negotiations between central organisations of the industry, representing both builders and contractors.

The Principles are not public legislation. However, they are considered to be an expression of good practice in building and construction, and as such they can have some degree of bindingness. Court practice confirms that they bind parties if the builder has published a statement that they will be followed in the competitive bidding.[23] In KKO 1998:48 the builder had committed itself to follow the Principles of Competitive Bidding RT 16–10182. After opening the bids it had, contrary to the Principles, negotiated with bidders and accepted a new lower bid made by another bidder. The original lowest bidder was entitled to compensation for the loss in losing the contract, measured by the so-called positive interest.

Of course, the Principles are not compulsory norms, and the parties may agree upon the application of different rules. In this case, A's published statements of the rules of the bidding process, on the one

[20] The Regulations do not apply to contracts where the estimated value of the contract (net of VAT) is less than a defined threshold, currently (for public works contracts) €5,150,000: reg. 8.

[21] The Building Information Foundation (RTS) is Finland's leading information service for the building and construction sector. Its mission is to foster and promote good planning and construction practices as well as sound property management procedures. It is a private foundation with representatives from 42 Finnish building organisations. It publishes the *RT Building Information File* (RT = building information), which is updated regularly.

[22] See s.1.

[23] Court decisions, even those issued by the Supreme Court, are not considered to be legally binding in Finland. But in fact they often have great authority, and especially important precedents with thorough reasoning are followed in court practice. On the status of precedents as a legal source in Finland, see e.g. Aarnio, *Laintulkinnan teoria* [*The Theory of the Interpretation of Statutes*], p. 230ff.

hand, and submission by contractors of bids following the rules, on the other hand, can be considered as making an agreement between the parties on the application of those rules in the competitive bidding. Very little is said in the case about the content of the applicable rules, apart from A's statement that the contract will be given to the lowest bidder. As no differences from the Finnish Principles are indicated in the case, the Principles may be worth citing as examples of how questions of good bidding practice are regulated in them.

According to the Principles, the equal treatment of bidders has to be ensured in dealing with the bids.[24] The builder must not negotiate with a bidder to alter the bid price. The most profitable bid has to be accepted. All bids can be rejected only if the most profitable bid price is too high or the building project has to be suspended for good reasons or there are other special reasons for it.[25] The profitability of bids should in general be assessed on the basis of contract price. According to section 7.4 the builder should choose among acceptable bids the most profitable taking into account economic, technical and functional criteria. A bid should be rejected[26] if (1) the bid price is ambiguous or the bid is otherwise defective or incorrect; or if (2) after the call for bids, it has become evident that the bidder is considered to lack technical, economic or other qualifications to carry out the contract. A bid should also be rejected if (3) the bidder has acted dishonestly or its behaviour is contrary to good construction practice in the competitive bidding. In addition, a bid can be rejected if the bid price compared with the estimated building costs is so low that it is evident that the work cannot be carried out at the price indicated.

The rules agreed upon between the parties and, secondarily, general rules of good practice in competitive bidding are standards for judging the parties' behaviour and their possible fault. Instead of *culpa in contrahendo*, we should perhaps speak about *culpa in contractu* as the applicable basis of liability. A breach of the agreed rules could be considered as a breach of contract between the parties. Accordingly, the standard of measuring the loss should be the positive interest rather than the negative interest. In the case from the Finnish Supreme Court, referred to above, it was the positive interest that was applied.

The positive interest aims to put the injured party into a position that is economically equal to the proper performance of the contract, meaning in this case the proper application of the agreed rules. The

[24] Section 7.1. [25] Section 7.3ff. [26] Section 7.3.

prima facie positive interest of the lowest bidder is the economic value to it of the contract on the basis of its bid because according to the rules it is entitled to be awarded the contract unless any of the contrary reasons mentioned above exists. The only item of loss that is mentioned in the case, however, is the expenses incurred in preparing the bid. These are in principle not included in the positive interest. But if the value of the contract exceeds (or at least equals) the bidding costs, as is usually the case, the lowest bidder should of course have these costs compensated on the basis of the positive as well as the negative interest.

The positive interest of a bidder other than the one who is entitled to the contract is usually zero in spite of any fault on the other side. This is because it would not have been awarded the contract and thus would not have its expenses covered even if its bid had been treated properly. The application of the negative interest would not give a different result because there is no loss that would have resulted from an act by the liable party.

A pivotal fact is that A has promised to give the contract to the lowest bidder. A breach of this promise is no doubt wrongful unless there are reasons to reject the lowest bid (for example, those mentioned in the Finnish Principles: see above). Choosing another bid could perhaps also be acceptable if it appears to be the most profitable taking into account, besides the price, all other economic, technical and functional criteria. However, the reasons mentioned in the case for not choosing B's bid indicate no proper grounds for either rejecting it or accepting another bid.

In situation (i), B's bid was the lowest one but either (a) it was not properly considered by A because of an administrative error or (b) A always intended to give the contract to C. The latter alternative (b) is a case of intentional breach of agreed rules. Also the former (a) falls within A's control and thus indicates its fault. So both are cases of fault and constitute a basis of A's liability. As the lowest bidder, B was in a position which, according to A's promise, entitled it to get the contract. Only if A can show that the contract should not have been given to B, for example for the reasons set out above, can A avoid liability to B.

In situation (ii), B's bid was not the lowest but it was not properly considered by A because of an administrative error. As discussed above, an administrative error is regarded as wrongful. However, this case is more complicated because B's bid was not the lowest one and so it had no *prima facie* right to the contract. Only if B can show that according to the applicable rules the contract should have been granted to it and not to the lowest bidder can it be considered to have a right to the contract. According to the Finnish Principles, in considering this question all economic, technical and functional criteria can be taken into account.

So, in all of cases (i)(a) and (b) and (ii) there is the fault required for A's liability. The liability is measured according to the positive interest. If B can be considered to have had the right to the contract, which is the case as a rule in situation (i) but not in situation (ii), its positive interest includes the value of the contract to it. If only the bidding expenses are claimed, in general they can be compensated on this basis (see above). If B did not have the right to the contract – this is the case probably in situation (ii) – then it would not be entitled to any compensation from A.

If A is a public authority the legislation on public procurement will be applied. The Finnish Act on Public Procurement (APP,1992) is applicable, amongst other things, to procurement by the state and the communes (local communities responsible for public administration). If the value of the procurement equals or exceeds the threshold value defined in a special decree,[27] more detailed rules based on EU legislation will apply. The purpose of the APP is to promote competition and ensure the equal and non-discriminatory treatment of those who take part in the competitive bidding. The exceptions to the scope of the APP are not relevant in this case. According to the APP,[28] a building project may not be carried out as own work without competitive bidding if state subsidy relating to a particular project is granted to the project and the cost estimate (including VAT) of the project equals or exceeds FIM5,000,000.[29] Exception may be made only for special reasons, such as the small value of the procurement.

The APP contains detailed provisions[30] on proper grounds for excluding a bidder from the procedure (such as lack of technical, economic or other qualifications or omission to pay taxes or social security fees). The bidders have to be treated equally and in a non-discriminatory manner in all phases of the procurement. According to section 7, the procurement has to be made as profitably as possible. The bid that is the most profitable in the light of all economic aspects, or the cheapest, should be accepted. There is also a special provision on damages liability.[31] Liability

[27] Decree on Public Procurement and Building Contracts Exceeding the Threshold Value, 1998. The threshold value expressed in ECUs (without VAT) is that corresponding to 5m special drawing rights.

[28] Section 5. [29] Around €850,000 or £575,000. [30] Section 6. [31] APP, s. 8.

is imposed upon anyone who causes loss to a bidder or a supplier by an act that is contrary to the APP or statutes or provisions issued by virtue of it, or contrary to EU legislation or a WTO agreement on public procurement. If the claim for damages concerns the costs that have been incurred in the procedure, it is sufficient for the bidder to prove the wrongful act and that it would have had a real chance to get the contract if the correct procedure had been followed.

The main significance of the APP for civil law liability is in establishing the conditions of liability precisely but the provisions contain nothing that would be radically different from the rules applicable to competitive bidding in the private sector. The correct procedure is defined in law, and acting contrary to the provisions evidently constitutes fault that is required for compensation. It is clear that the facts indicated in the case as reasons for not choosing B's bid constitute breaches of these legal provisions.

Moderating the plaintiff's burden of proof as mentioned above can help the bidder to get compensation, especially in situation (i). For this, it is sufficient that it proves the incorrect act and that it would have had a real chance to get the contract in a correct procedure. The incorrectness of the procedure is proved, and in situation (i) it seems easy for B as the lowest bidder to prove its real chance of getting the contract. Of course, A can bring counter-evidence to rebut B's right. But in situation (ii), the application of the APP does not seem to alter B's situation from that in private sector bidding, because it would in any case have to bring evidence that it had a real chance to get the contract.

The APP contains also administrative means of satisfying the bidder for incorrect acts in competitive bidding.[32] The Market Court (which deals with cases pertaining to competition or marketing law) may quash the decision of the procurement unit or issue an order to correct the procedure. If these measures would cause the other parties, third parties or the public interest harm that would exceed the benefits of the measure, the Market Court may order an indemnity to be paid to a party that would have had a real chance to win the competitive bidding if the procedure had been correct. The indemnity is not a civil law remedy but an administrative fee. It is not aimed at compensating the actual loss, nor do its preconditions correspond to those of compensation for loss. However, the quality of the fault in the procedure, the total value of the procurement and the

[32] Section 9.

costs and loss that the applicant has incurred are taken into account in ordering the indemnity.

France

The issue of bidding in French law is very complicated because it is quite difficult to determine the legal nature of a bidding.[33]

The main issue is to determine whether the bidding is an offer to contract or a mere offer to negotiate. In case of an offer to contract, it is possible that a contract has been validly formed, therefore entitling the aggrieved party to obtain its enforcement. If it is a mere offer to negotiate, the party would only be entitled to damages, supposing the liability of the other party is established.[34]

There is an offer to contract (i) if the offer is precise and (ii) if the offer is certain. An offer is precise when it contains all the essential elements of the envisaged contract.[35] An offer is certain when it is made without any conditions.[36] It is not likely that a public bidding can be considered as an offer to contract, because it does not fulfil the certainty requirement. Usually there are explicit conditions in the offer, such as the faculty for the offeror to choose with which candidate to contract.[37] That is why it is quite unlikely that the facts of this case would happen in real life. However, the facts seem to concern an offer without explicit conditions, since the contract is supposed to be formed automatically with the lowest bidder. Therefore, it might be difficult to deny the existence of a firm and precise offer to contract in this case. French academic writers are not very clear on this question. The majority simply seem to ignore the problem; others are not very precise. Some refuse to recognise the existence of an offer to contract when considering a public bidding, because a real offer must be made to a specific person: a public offer would always contain a tacit condition allowing the offeror to choose

[33] Both academic writers and case law have little to say about the problem of public bidding, at least in private law. On the whole, it seems that biddings are unlikely either to raise difficulties or to induce the parties to solve their dispute in court.

[34] Ghestin, *La formation du contrat*, no. 292ff.

[35] These elements depend on the nature of the contract. For example, a contract of sale is formed in French law when agreement has been reached over the price and the object of the sale (art. 1583 C.civ.).

[36] Such as the possibility for the author of the offer to change the price initially fixed. The term 'condition' is here used in its general meaning, without any reference to a legal mechanism of any sort.

[37] Collard-Dutilleul and Delebecque, *Contrats civils et commerciaux*, no. 720.

the offeree.[38] At least one author[39] adopts a more balanced opinion: on the one hand, affirming that it is usual to stipulate conditions in a public bidding, therefore considering that such a bidding is not usually an offer in the French legal sense; but accepting, on the other hand, that a public bidding might be formulated without any conditions, therefore constituting an offer of contract 'in an extreme case' – that is, a matter of theory rather than practice.

Since it is not certain that such a public bidding can be considered as an offer to contract, the bidding will be considered to be a mere offer to negotiate a contract, preventing B from relying on a contract between it and A. This means that the tortious liability rules of article 1382 of the Civil Code will apply, as far as A's behaviour is concerned.

Precontractual liability under article 1382 requires the fulfilment of three conditions: fault, harm (loss) and a chain of causation.[40] If B was the lowest bidder, the last two conditions are quite easily proved. The loss is directly linked to the fact that B has not been chosen to perform the construction contract, although it should have been. It is also quite obvious that the loss has been caused either by the administrative error, or A's intention not to give the contract to someone other than C. However, the requirement of fault is not so easy to establish, at least in the case of an administrative error. Such an error appears to be a mere negligence, which is theoretically subject to precontractual liability as well as an intentional fault.[41] But the fault appears here so slight that it might be possible that the judge will not consider the error serious enough to constitute a fault. However, the fault is obvious if A always intended to give the contract to C because it knowingly breached its duty of loyalty[42] during contractual negotiations.

If B was not the lowest bidder, it is much more difficult to find a real loss caused to it. One could say that B lost a chance to have no chance, because it would not have been chosen anyway. In addition, as discussed above, it is not likely that an administrative error can be

[38] Flour and Aubert, *Les obligations*, vol. 1, *L'acte juridique*, no. 146; Malaurie, Aynès and Stoffel-Munck, *Les obligations*, no. 383; Marty and Raynaud, *Les obligations*, vol. 1, no. 110.

[39] Huet, *Les principaux contrats spéciaux*, no. 32168.

[40] See the French report on case 1.

[41] Though this remains controversial among writers and the courts: see the French report on case 1, n. 24.

[42] Com 20 Mar. 1972, JCP 1973, II, 17543; P. Mousseron, 'Négociations précontractuelles et responsabilité civile délictuelle', RTDCom 1998, 248.

considered as a sufficient fault to found A's precontractual liability under article 1382.

If A is found liable (that is, most likely, in hypothesis (i)(b)), damages will be awarded in order to cover both B's bidding fees and the loss of opportunity[43] to be given the construction contract.

In public law, the rules applicable to biddings are very specific, and quite different from private law.[44] These rules are contained in a Code des marchés publics.[45] Two set of rules may correspond to the situation in this case.

The *adjudication*[46] consists in a bidding where the contract is given to the lowest bidder. Every candidate submits an irrevocable proposal, which must comply with the characteristics of the task described in the offer. After that, a jury examines each proposal and give the contract to the author of the lowest bid. The administration is free to reject any proposal until a competent authority has given its agreement (this authority depends on the administrative service that made the offer). This mode of bidding is not used very often because it does not take into account anything other than price.[47]

The *appel d'offres* resembles the *adjudication* in many ways. However, here the administration is totally free to choose the best candidate, following the criteria of its choice. It is important to make clear that the administration cannot bind itself to these criteria, which remain purely indicative: the administration retains its discretion in such situations.

Both modes require the fulfilment of several formal conditions, without which the bidding is void. These conditions relate mainly to advertising and the competition. The offer must be announced in specific publications,[48] and the announcement itself must provide precise information about the proposed contract such as the time schedule. 'Competition' supposes that all candidates must be on an equal footing with each other. Discrimination, as well as administrative errors preventing a candidate's offer from being taken into account, can

[43] The compensation for loss of opportunity cannot match the full expectation interest: see the French report on case 1, n. 33.

[44] In general, French law is divided into two main branches: private law and public law. Each branch has its specific rules and courts. On this *summa divisio*, see Ghestin, Goubeaux and Fabre-Magnan, *Traité de droit civil, Introduction générale*, p. 67ff.

[45] Which can be roughly translated as the 'Code of public bargains'.

[46] Article 378 of the Code.

[47] Collard-Dutilleul and Delebecque, *Contrats civils et commerciaux*, no. 719.

[48] Such as the *Bulletin officiel des annonces des marchés publics*.

therefore cause the cancellation of the bidding. In addition, discrimination may result in an award of damages to the candidate who has been the object of discrimination.[49]

In conclusion, in public law as well as in private law, the situation described in this case is not likely to happen in real life. Supposing it were, public law seems to give the rejected candidate more means than private law of suing the offeror – that is, the administration – as well as the means of cancelling the public bidding, regardless of the reason why it has been rejected, as long as it has been caused by administrative malfunctioning.

Germany

Where A is a private company: A is not liable in contract. Under German law a public bidding is not an offer *ad incertas personas* but an invitation to make offers (*invitatio ad offerendum*). An *invitatio* neither represents an offer nor creates any duty to conclude a contract, so B is not entitled to a contractual claim.

As far as A's liability on the ground of §§280(1), 311(2) No. 1 BGB (*culpa in contrahendo*) is concerned, the situation is more complicated.

The courts and legal writers agree that in the case of a public bidding, from the moment a bidder receives from the offeree the documents regulating the bidding process or makes an offer, a precontractual relationship is established by virtue of the law creating mutual duties to have regard to each other's interests, and of loyalty.[50] The cases decided by the courts all deal with the awarding of contracts by public authorities, but it is undisputed that the principles developed by this line of rulings apply to private persons as well. If the contract-awarding party is in breach of its duty of regard and loyalty towards the bidder, then it must compensate the loss suffered by the bidder relying on the rules of the bidding process set up by the contract-awarding party or the law.[51] So far, however, only the bidding process of public authorities has been regulated by statutes based on several European Union directives.

As a rule, a contract-awarding party in breach of duty must compensate the bidder's reliance interest; that is, it must compensate the bidder's expenses caused by the participation in the bidding process. If, however, the bidder is able to prove that it would have won the award if the rules of the bidding process had been met, then it is entitled to

[49] Chapus, *Droit administratif*, vol. 1, no. 1183.
[50] §§241(2), 311(2) BGB. [51] BGH, decision of 8 Sept. 1998, NJW 1998, 3636.

expectation damages: it may claim the profits lost from not obtaining the award.[52]

Therefore, in both alternatives of situation (i) A is in breach of its duty of regard and loyalty towards B because the company did not abide by the rules that it set for the bidding process. B is at least entitled to reliance damages, i.e. the expenses incurred in making its offer, since it would have won the award if A had observed the bidding rules. In situation (i)(b), B is entitled to reliance damages even if it would not have won the award, because B was denied the chance of winning the contract right from the start of the bidding process. The law will not allow A to enter into mock negotiations. Moreover, B is entitled to expectation damages if B by bidding publicly assumed the obligation to enter into a contract with the lowest bidder. This depends on the construction of the public bidding.[53] In general, a contract-awarding party is not deemed to incur such an obligation, but rather wants to preserve the right to decide whether or not to enter in a contract with any bidder at all.[54]

In situation (ii), A is not liable, there being no causal relationship between A's breach of duty and B's economic loss. B, not being the lowest bidder, would not have obtained the award even if A had complied with its own bidding rules: B would still have incurred the expenses if A had dealt with its bid correctly.

With the exception of case (i)(b), A is not liable in tort. German tort law, as a rule, does not cover pure economic loss, provided the defendant did not wilfully cause damage.[55] Not being enriched at the expense of B, A is not liable in restitution.

Where A is a public authority: with regard to the public bidding of public authorities, the legislator established in 1998 a special provision within the Act Against the Restraint of Competition (GWB), thereby transposing the requirements of several European Union directives into German law. §126 GWB provides:

> If the contract-awarding authority has violated a provision intending the protection of an enterprise and if, without this violation, the enterprise would have had a real chance of winning the award which has been impaired by the violation of the law, the enterprise is entitled to damages for the costs incurred

[52] BGH, decision of 8 Sept. 1998, NJW 1998, 3636.

[53] §§133, 157 BGB. [54] BGH, decision of 8 Sept. 1998, NJW 1998, 3636.

[55] §§823(1), 826 BGB.

in order to make an offer or to participate in the bidding process. Any other claims for damages remain unaffected.

This may be regarded as a case of *culpa in contrahendo* regulated by statutory provision.

In both alternatives of situation (i), A is liable for reliance damages on the ground of §126 GWB. A did not comply with the bidding rules set up by §97 GWB in order to protect bidders and thus impaired B's 'real chance' as the lowest bidder to win the award. In situation (ii), the requirements of §126 GWB are not met: even if A had acted within the law, B would not have had a 'real chance' to win the contract. §126 GWB expressly states that other claims for damages remain unaffected. Therefore, in addition, A is liable according to the same principles set out above.

If, however, A intends to make a binding conditional offer to contract with the lowest bidder, a contract is concluded by B's acceptance provided it is the lowest bidder.[56] In that case, A's liability is for B's expectation interest, regardless of its status as a private company or public authority.

Greece

Parties to a public tender are bound by the obligation to conduct negotiations in good faith according to article 197 GCC.[57] The negotiation phase begins with the submission of offers to the public tender initiated by A.[58]

According to the facts of the case, A had published statements setting out the terms of the tendering process, which also included a statement that A will award the contract to the lowest bidder. These statements become binding upon the parties because with each tender submitted, an agreement is formed between the parties that these rules will govern the tendering process, and they will therefore govern the negotiation stage.[59] Moreover, it is accepted that the parties to the negotiations may determine and complement the notions of good faith and business usage, in essence building their own framework of what amounts to conducting negotiations in good faith. Indeed, the statements made

[56] BGH, decision of 7 Nov. 2001, NJW 2002, 363 (concerning the inverse case of a sale to the highest bidder via Internet).

[57] The Greek Civil Code provides specific rules regarding the conclusion of a contract for public tender in article 199 1st sentence GCC: 'Unless otherwise indicated, in an auction the contract is formed with the allocation of the successful bidder.'

[58] See Court of Appeals of Thessaloniki 3/1994 Arm 1994, 1132.

[59] Gazis, *Legal Consultations 1956–1999*, pp. 313, 318.

by A and accepted by B specify the content of the good faith and business usage obligation that binds both parties to the negotiations. If A contravenes one of its statements (*venire contra factum proprium*), then it behaves in a manner which is inconsistent with good faith, and will therefore be liable towards the other party.

Concerning A's liability in the three situations described:

first, B's offer had been the lowest but A failed to take it into account because of an administrative error. A must take all bids into account and a failure to do so results in responsibility for negotiating in bad faith. A is responsible for the error of its administrative personnel according to article 334 GCC as if it was its own.[60] Thus, A negotiates in bad faith and against business usage and will have to compensate B on the basis of article 198 GCC for the expenses which it has incurred in preparing its bid.

Secondly, A did not consider B's offer because it always intended to give the contract to C. It is the essence of public tendering that the party organising it must consider all the bids which are submitted. A never intended to do this and thereby submitted all the bidders (apart from C) to unnecessary expense and effort. In addition, A contradicts its statement that it will give the contract to the lowest bidder, namely B. There is no doubt that A's conduct is contrary to precontractual good faith and that it should compensate B for its expenses. In the case of precontractual liability compensation is, in principle, limited to the reliance interest and does not extend to the expectation interest.[61] However, there has been some support in the legal literature for the view that in such cases (as also in situation (i)), where the lowest bidder who would otherwise be awarded the contract is disregarded in bad faith, the expectation interest must be compensated.[62] Further, in terms of the remedies available, we note that B cannot have the contract concluded with A. A reasonable alternative to the precontractual basis would be for B to pursue a claim on the basis of delict,[63] particularly article 919 GCC for damage caused *contra bonos mores*, in which case compensation for immaterial damage may also be awarded.[64]

[60] This is the prevalent view in case law and legal literature: see Pouliadis, *Culpa in contrahendo und Schutz Dritter*, p. 203; contrary D.B. Bosdas, 'Precontractual Liability' *Arxeion Nomologias* 1968, 337, 343.

[61] A. Georgiadis and P. Paulopoulos, 'Precontractual Liability in Administrative Contracts' NoV 1987, 701, 705.

[62] Gazis, *Legal Consultations 1956–1999*, p. 318.

[63] Article 914ff. GCC.

[64] Article 932 GCC. For concurrence between precontractual and delictual liability, see AP 10/1991 NoV 1991, 1203; Court of Appeals of Athens 5382/1988; Court of Appeals

Thirdly, B's bid was not the lowest but A still failed to consider it due to an administrative error. In all probability the solution here will be no precontractual liability for A, because of a lack of causal link between A's oversight and B's damage. Even if A had not been negligent in properly considering B's bid, the latter would have incurred the expenses related to the bid but it would not have been successful. One last thing needs to be added: even if a court found a causal link and held A precontractually liable towards B for not complying with the rules of the tendering process, damages in that case would never amount to the expectation interest (B's bid was not the lowest, unlike in the first and second scenarios) but would be limited to the reliance interest.

In principle, public authorities concluding private contracts are also bound by the provisions of the Civil Code regarding precontractual liability.[65] Nonetheless, special legislation applies to public tendering initiated by a public authority specifying the rights and obligations of the parties. In addition, administrative law dictates that public bodies abide by the principle of equal treatment, which is not necessarily so in the private sector. If A were a public authority, in practice the main difference would probably be in the remedies. In short, the most striking difference is that the court may annul public tendering that has not been properly conducted and also that a party with the lowest bid may request the court to find that the contract has been concluded with that party.[66]

Ireland

(a) Where B's bid was the lowest, A may be liable to B for failure to abide by its statement that it will award the contract to the lowest bidder. Remedies in the form of damages may be sought, or an order for specific performance.

Where it is stated that a contract will be awarded to the party who submits the lowest bid, then if the contract is awarded it must be awarded to the lowest bidder. The rules regarding tenders are identical to those which apply to auctions.[67] Thus, in an ordinary auction, or tender, there is no obligation to accept the lowest, or indeed any bid. However,

of Thessaloniki 550/1983. For immaterial damage see Court of Appeals of Peiraius 856/1993 EllD1994, 1694; Court of Appeals of Athens 12101/1989 EllD 1994, 448.

65 Georgiadis and Paulopoulos, above n. 61. See AP 1126/1986 EEN 1987, 410.

66 AP 566/1993 EllD 1994, 1097; AP 1126/1986 EEN 1987, 410; Georgiadis and Paulopoulos, above n. 61, pp. 703–4; Gazis, *Legal Consultations 1956–1999*, p. 317.

67 Friel, *The Law of Contract*, p. 30ff.

if the auction is advertised as being 'without reserve', or the invitation to tender states that the contract will be awarded to the lowest bid, then, if the auction or tender proceeds, the lowest bid must be accepted. This rule was clearly laid out in *Tulley v. Irish Land Commission.*[68] It does not matter whether the contract was not awarded to the lowest bidder either deliberately or through the negligence of the defendant.

Where the contract is not awarded to the lowest bidder, then the lowest bidder is entitled to either an order for specific performance or an award of damages. An order for specific performance is an equitable remedy and therefore discretionary. A court will only make the award under limited circumstances and where it is just to do so. A plaintiff is entitled to an award of damages as of right where the substantive claim is upheld. Where damages are sought, they may consist of either reliance damages with respect to the cost of preparation of the bid or expectation damages with respect to the loss of profit, but not both.

(b) Where the invitation to tender states that the contract will be awarded to the lowest bidder, it is not open to the defendant to award the contract to any other bidder. There is authority in *Blackpool and Fylde Aero Club Ltd v. Blackpool Borough Council*[69] that a collateral contract may permit a bidder to claim reliance losses incurred in preparing for the bid. In that case, due to the negligence of the defendant, the plaintiff's tender had not been considered by the defendant. The contract was awarded to a third party. The court awarded damages for expenses incurred by the plaintiff in preparation for the bid. However, in that case the plaintiff may have been awarded the contract if the defendant had considered it. In the present case, where its bid was not the lowest, B could not have been awarded the contract in any event. The situation is not therefore governed by the precedent in *Blackpool* and accordingly there is no liability between A and B. In effect, A's carelessness has caused no harm.

Italy

A public bid between private parties (or where the public administration is acting as a private party)[70] is generally[71] considered to be governed by article 1336 of the Civil Code (*offerta al pubblico*): 'if it contains the essential elements of a contract, it can be considered as a

[68] (1961) 97 ILTR 174. See also 1, *Corbin on Contracts*, s. 46. [69] [1990] 1 WLR 1195.
[70] Cass, sez. I, 6 May 1995, n. 4989; Cass, sez. I, 25 Aug. 1993, n. 8975.
[71] M. Martini, 'Offerta al pubblico', Dig. Priv., XIII, 9.

proposal to contract, unless usage or the circumstances otherwise provide'.[72] A distinction has been drawn between *offerta al pubblico* and the simple invitation to an offer (*invito a offrire*). The simple invitation differs from the *offerta* in the absence of the fundamental elements for a contract. As a consequence, a simple invitation is related only to the precontractual phase. It does not bind the inviting party (*invitante*) except for the duty of good faith generally required in negotiations.

This case requires first a consideration of whether the statements about the bidding rules could be deemed as an *offerta al pubblico* or as a simple invitation. If the former, A will be liable in contract according to Italian case law on the point,[73] because B's conduct constituted an acceptance of A's offer. A's liability would then be to compensate all B's loss consisting in the actual damage (expenses of the bid) plus the loss of profit from the bid.[74] On the other hand, if it was only a simple invitation, A would be liable under article 1337 of the Civil Code, and damages will be awarded only within the limit of the *interesse negativo*.

Italian case law usually considers a public bid as a case of *offerta* 'if it contains all the elements of the contract specified in the scope of the bid'.[75] Moreover, in the decisions concerning public bids for public[76] or private[77] employment, case law recognises a case of *offerta*

[72] Despite discussion on the point (Sbisà, *La promessa al pubblico*) most of Italian academic writing distinguishes the case of *offerta al pubblico* from the similar feature of promise (*promessa al pubblico*) provided by art. 1989 c.c.: Bianca, *Diritto civile*, vol. III, *Il contratto*; A. Di Majo, 'Offerta al pubblico (diritto privato)' Enc. Giur. XXIX (Milano, 1979); Forchelli, 'Offerta al pubblico', NN.D.I. XI (Torino, 1968), 763; Messineo, *Il contratto in genere, Tratt. Cicu e Messineo*; Mirabelli, *Delle obbligazioni. Dei contratti in generale*; Sconamiglio, *Dei contratti in generale, Comm. Scialoja Branca*; Sacco, *Il contratto*. Their main difference is the time a party could be deemed bound by its offer.

[73] Cass, sez. lav., 5 Nov. 1998, n. 11142; Cass, sez. lav., 11 June 1991, n. 6590; Cass, sez. lav., 13 June 1987, n. 5225.

[74] In general judges recognise an expectation measure damages remedy more than specific performance of the contract.

[75] PRET-P. Roma, 5 Oct. 1998. See also for public employment contrary to the next note Cass, sez. lav., 19 Feb. 1992, n. 2067.

[76] Usually for the employment into public administration subject to the rules of labour law. See Cass, sez. lav., 5 Nov. 1998, n. 11142; Cass, sez. lav., 26 Sep. 1998, n. 9670; Cass, sez. un., 29 Aug. 1998, n. 8595; Cass, sez. lav., 21 Feb. 1991, n. 1836; Cass, sez. lav., 11 June 1991, n. 6590; Cass, sez. lav., 14 Mar. 1990, n. 2057; Cass, sez. lav., 19 Feb. 1987, n. 1804.

[77] Cass, sez. lav., 6 Oct. 1995, n. 10500; Cass, sez. lav., 1 Dec. 1994, n. 10278; Cass, sez. lav. 12 Nov. 1993, n. 11158; Cass, sez. lav., 26 Feb. 1988, n. 2064; Cass, sez. lav., 7 Apr. 1987, n. 3397.

without requiring any particular contractual element. Italian academic writing[78] generally considers as a simple invitation any offer that, although it contains the required contractual elements, gives particular importance to the other party's qualities.[79] Moreover, it is not an *offerta al pubblico* if the party reserves the right to choose its preferred acceptance.[80]

The facts do not provide enough information to decide on this point. It would be for the parties to give evidence about the real meaning of the offer. In questions of interpretation of private statements Italian case law provides criteria only for public bids concerning public employment.[81] Once the judge has decided whether the case involves an *offerta al pubblico*, it has then to be decided whether A acted in breach of bidding rules.

Where B's bid was the lowest, A would be liable. Situation (i)(a) could lead to *culpa in eligendo* or *culpa in vigilando* by the executive officers for the wrongdoing by the employees.[82] In situation (i)(b), A would be contractually liable for having acted contrary to the duty of good faith provided in article 1375 of the Civil Code.[83] The *contractual* liability depends on the fact that A's behaviour is considered as an offer followed by B's tacit acceptance.

In the case where B's bid was not the lowest, case law is silent. The judge would probably not consider B as damaged in its contractual expectations.

Italian law provides special rules for public bids involving public authorities. In particular, the formation of a contract is generally subject to the so-called scheme of 'contract subject to transparency rules' (*contratto ad evidenza pubblica*).[84] A three-phase administrative procedure[85] is

78 See Forchielli, 'Offerta al pubblico', NN.D.I. XI, 765; Sconamiglio, *Dei contratti in generale, Comm. Scialoja Branca*, p. 192; A. Di Majo, 'Offerta al pubblico (diritto privato)', Enc. Giur. XXIX; Di Staso, *I contratti in generale, Giur. Sist.Bigiavi*, vol. I; Mirabelli, *Delle obbligazioni, Dei contratti in generale*.

79 As, e.g., agency, partnership, directorship or management or activities that require specific specialisation or professional qualities.

80 See Di Staso, *I contratti in generale, Giur. Sist.Bigiavi*, vol. I, 403.

81 TAR-T.a.r. Basilicata, 6 Feb. 1995, 5/1995.

82 See Cass, sez. lav., 19 Feb. 1987, n. 1804.

83 See Cass, sez. lav., 8 Feb. 1982, n. 755; TRIB-T. Roma, 17 July 1982.

84 See C. Cattaneo and E. Furno, 'Appalto di opere pubbliche', Enc. Giur. II; Giannini, *Corso di diritto amministrativo*, vol. III.

85 The procedure is divided into: (1) a decisional phase (*fase deliberativa*), related to the public authority's decision to contract contained in a project of contract; (2) the choice of the other private party of the contract (*aggiudicazione*); (3) an approval phase (*approvazione*) by a controlling authority about the legitimacy of the procedure and the legality of the contract.

necessary for the validity of contract. In general, public bidding rules are contained in documents (*capitolati d'oneri*) concerning the procedure for the award of the contract.[86] If general (*capitolati generali*), Italian case law considers such documents as having the force of law.[87] If specific documents (*capitolati speciali*) are concerned, they are deemed to have contractual force.[88]

There are four kind of public administration bids[89] which differ in their procedural rules and in the degree of discretion granted to the public administration in choosing the other party to the contract. In the present case, the public bid could consist in a case of *asta pubblica* or *pubblico incanto* because the bid seems to be open to every firm with the required qualities.[90] Italian doctrine is divided on whether to identify such a bid as a public bid[91] or as a simple invitation for an offer.[92] If it is a public bid, B could invoke contractual liability on the basis of breach of good faith only if it can prove that the public authority had established discriminatory rules. However, if the public authority has acted as a private party, the ordinary judges[93] can decide on the legitimacy of a participant's exclusion, and will assess damages according to article 1223 of the Civil Code. In particular, the judge must assess whether the conduct of the public authority has been in breach of the principle of good faith in competition.[94] On the other hand, Italian case law does not recognise that excluded participants have any specific right to become party to the contract.

[86] S. Cattaneo, 'I capitolati generali per l'appalto di opere pubbliche' in Sandulli, *Atti del congresso del centenario delle leggi amministrative di unificazione, I lavori pubblici*; V. Cianflone, 'Il capitolato' In Enc. Dir. VI; Terranova, *Capitolato generale di appalto e norme pubbliche*.

[87] In the case of a breach of such rules, case law recognises the possibility to appeal to the Supreme Court or to the competent public administration. See Cass 29 Sep. 1997, n. 9531; Cass 18 May 1994, n. 4869; Cass 18 June 1987, n. 5355; Cass 24 Feb. 1982, n. 1146.

[88] Cons. Stato a. gen., 24 Mar. 1994, n. 498; Corte Conti sez. contr., 15 July 1991, n. 78.

[89] *Asta pubblica* or *pubblico incanto*; *licitazione privata*; *appalto-concorso*; *trattativa privata*.

[90] *Licitazione privata* differs in the limited range of private participants to the public bid that have to be expressly invited by the public authority. *Appalto-concorso* and *trattativa privata* imply specific conditions not required by the present case.

[91] Giannini, *Corso di diritto amministrativo*, p. 700.

[92] As discussed above, *offerta al pubblico*. In this case, see Cianflone, 'Il capitolato' Enc. Dir. VI, 341.

[93] Cass, sez. un., 26 May 1997, n. 4673; Cass, sez. un., 29 July 1995, n. 8298; Cass, sez. un., 20 Sep. 1995, n. 10924.

[94] Articles 1175 and 1375 c.c. Cass, sez. lav., 5 Nov. 1998, n. 11142, Cass, sez. un., 29 Aug. 1998, n. 8595; TRIB-T. Cagliari, 7 Mar. 1996; Cass, sez. lav., 21 Feb. 1991, n. 1836.

According to some authors it is also possible for a public authority to be precontractually liable when the public authority has selected the private party to give effect to the contract but the contract does not take place.[95] There are, however, no cases concerning precontractual liability due to the annulment of a public bid.

Netherlands

Where B's bid was the lowest

Contract: whether a contract was concluded between A and B depends on whether A's published statement should be regarded as an offer which was accepted by B in its bid, or rather as an invitation to make an offer, in which case B's bid should be regarded as a mere offer. This is a matter of interpretation. The *Haviltex* test,[96] which is the well-established test for determining the content and effects of a contract,[97] is also the test for establishing whether a contract was concluded at all. Therefore, everything depends on whether B was entitled to regard A's published statement as an offer the acceptance of which would lead to the conclusion of a binding contract. If the rules of the bidding process were such that they could lead to the establishment of the lowest bid without any further need for evaluation of the bids or the bidders, A's statement may be regarded as an offer and B's bid as an acceptance of it. However, usually a party may be expected to have some justified concern for some subjective characteristics of the other party (for example, whether it seems reliable).[98] Moreover, what if two bidders make bids which (objectively) are the same? Therefore, in practice it seems unlikely that A's statement should be regarded as an offer.[99] However, if it is, then B will have the ordinary contract remedies: a right to specific performance or expectation damages. In that case, it does not matter whether the actual facts were as stated in (i)(a) or as in (i)(b).

Precontractual liability: although the parties were not technically involved in any proper negotiations, A would probably be liable for breaking off negotiations since the parties' 'negotiations' reached the

[95] Monateri, *La responsabilità contrattuale e precontrattuale*, p. 417.

[96] HR, 13 March 1981 (*Ermes/Haviltex*), NJ 1981, note Brunner, 635; AA 30 (1981), 355, note Van Schilfgaarde.

[97] HR, 17 Dec. 1976 (*Bunde/Erckens*), NJ 1977, note GJ Scholten, 241.

[98] See HR, 10 Apr. 1981 (*Hofland/Hennis*), NJ 1981, note Brunner, 532.

[99] Cf. Hartkamp, *Mr. C. Asser's handleiding tot de beoefening van het Nederlands burgerlijk recht; Verbintenissenrecht*, vol. II, *Algemene leer der overeenkomsten*, no. 141.

so-called 'third stage'.[100] When B had made a bid which turned out to have been, in objective terms, the lowest bid it was justified in expecting that a contract would be concluded. Or, to put it differently, even beforehand, B was justified in expecting that a contract between it and A would be concluded if it made the lowest bid. There was no reason why B should expect that A would not conclude a contract with it if it made the lowest bid (and if its bid was otherwise in conformity with the rules of the bidding process). Therefore, the 'negotiations' may be said to be in the third stage where not only the expectation interest in damages may be claimed but also further negotiations and, according to some writers, even the conclusion of the contract. If negotiations were in the third stage, some reasons may still justify breaking off the negotiations (such as a change of circumstances, and perhaps a better offer from a third party),[101] but the reasons mentioned under (i)(a) and (i)(b) certainly do not qualify as such. Reason (a) falls under A's own risk: it is responsible for its own organisation; and reason (b) rather shows that the whole bidding was a sham, and should not help A as a defence (*nemo auditur turpitudinem suam allegans*).

However, if a court was inclined to leave A some autonomy in determining which bid or bidder it preferred (as discussed above), then the same reasons may lead a court to accept that B could not reasonably expect that the mere fact that its bid would be the lowest would ensure that a contract would be concluded. Nevertheless, the statement of facts only states the facts mentioned under (a) and (b) as the reason why A did not award the contract to the lowest (that is, B's) bid.

Where B's bid was not the lowest

Under these circumstances there does not seem to be any reason to accept any liability for A towards B because B suffers no loss. Even if A had not failed properly to consider its bid, B would never have won the bidding since its bid was not the lowest. Therefore, B has neither lost a profit nor incurred expenses or lost opportunities that it would not have incurred or lost if its bid had been properly considered.

Public biddings have to respect certain public rules and principles. In case of biddings for economically important contracts, EC rules apply.

[100] See the Dutch report on case 1.

[101] See HR, *De Ruiterij/Ruiters* (1996), discussed in the report on case 1.

If A is a public authority, a special regulation would apply with regard to the procedure for the award of the public work contract of this case. However, this regulation, which is based on Directive 2004/18/EC, does not contain any special provisions on liability in damages. This means that regardless of whether A is a private company or a public authority, B is in principle left with the same remedies as discussed above.

However, a proposal for a new general statute on public tenders[102] is pending before the Dutch Parliament. This proposal, like Directive 2004/18/EC, regards equal treatment, non-discrimination and transparency as the leading principles in the process of a public bidding by a public authority. In this proposed statute, there are no special provisions on liability either. However, in the official comment on the proposal, the government states that the legal protection in case of disputes arising out of public tenders is the same as for disputes arising out of contract or tort in general.[103] Moreover, it is also stated that a business may have a claim in tort if a public authority has violated the rules on public tenders.[104]

This means that on the facts as stated in both situations (i)(a) and (i)(b), A would probably be liable in tort towards B for violation of the principles of equal treatment and non-discrimination. In these circumstances, the damages may extend to lost profits.[105] On the facts as stated in situation (ii), there does not seem to be any reason to accept liability for A towards B because B suffers no loss.

The official comments on the new statute emphasise that, in addition to these remedies, in an urgent situation B could ask the civil judge in summary proceedings for a temporary measure (injunction) in order to stop a tort being committed. Temporary measures available to B in this kind of proceedings might include an order by the court to consider B's offer properly, a prohibition on A contracting with a specified third party, or an order for a retender by A. These provisions are available to B whether or not A has concluded a contract with C. If A has already concluded a contract with C then it is possible that A has to terminate this contract or suspend its performance. Obviously, in the latter case A would become liable towards C.

[102] Kamerstukken II, 2005–2006, 30501, no. 2. [103] Ibid. no. 3.
[104] Article 6:162 BW. [105] Article 6:96 BW.

Norway

Where B's bid was the lowest, it would have the right to damages according to the expectation interest, under both alternative (a) and alternative (b).[106]

A might be required to select the lowest offer on two different grounds. According to Danish law, legal regulations (statute) require the company to accept the lowest offer in a restricted procedure with respect to a construction project.[107] Such legal obligation does not exist in Norway. But A has in the present case stated that it will give the contract to the lowest bidder. A statement such as this would probably be interpreted as a binding promise to the participants who have submitted competitive tenders.[108] Consequently the employer has, based on *contract law*, committed itself to choosing the lowest bid. It should nonetheless be added that the employer has the right to reject all the bids if none is sufficiently favourable.

Out of consideration for C, B is not likely to claim specific performance but rather is able to claim the loss of contract (compensation according to the expectation interest). This is valid whether (a) 'A failed properly to consider the bid', or (b) 'A always intended to give the contract to C'.

It should, however, be added that liability on these grounds has never been tested in the Supreme Court of Norway.

If B's bid was not the lowest, it would have no bearing on the result of a claim that its bid had not been 'properly considered'. Such an 'administrative error' does not seem to have caused B to suffer loss. If one could point to gross incompetence in the handling of the bids, this might be entertained if it were to claim that it constituted a subsequently failed contractual assumption with respect to its participation in the competition for tender. In such a case, it could claim reliance interest damages. If, on the other hand, the reason was that 'A always intended to give the contract to C', the solution is clear. B could claim that its reliance interest be covered since it had participated in a fictional competition for tender.[109]

106 T. Sandvik in Selmer, *Nordisk Gjenklang. Festskrift til Carl Jacob Arnholm*, p. 495.
107 Licitationsloven (Procurement of Works Act), s. B, para. 2.
108 Simonsen, *Precontractual Liability*, p. 709ff.
109 Rt 1997, 574 Lærlingklausul-dommen.

Where A is a public authority, it follows in accordance with the Works Directive[109a] implemented in public legal regulations in Norway that the contracting authorities, in this case, are obligated to choose the lowest bid.

Portugal

Where B's bid was the lowest, in both cases (a) and (b), B is entitled to compensation for its expenses, based on the rules of precontractual liability (article 227 of the Civil Code).

This is a situation of a public bidding for a contract. It is not a contract because there was no proposal but only an invitation to the public to make proposals (*invitatio ad offerendum*). In this situation the rules of good faith are applicable,[110] so if A has made a statement that the contract will be given to the lowest bidder, it must comply with that statement. In both cases (a) and (b), A would be liable for the loss suffered by B. Case (a) would be considered a situation of negligence, but that cannot exempt A from its liability although the court can establish the compensation in a lower value.[111] Case (b) would be considered a situation of intentional fraud, in which the compensation would be established in the full amount of loss.[112]

Where B's bid was not the lowest, A is still at fault in not considering B's bid. That still involves precontractual liability.[113] However, as B's bid was not the lowest, we must consider that it would have had no chance of winning the public bidding, so there was no loss in not considering its proposal.

If A is a public authority the answers would be different. In this case the construction contract would be considered an administrative contract, which is subject to the rules of Decreto-Lei 59/99 (2 March). Article 49º of this statute establishes that any irregularity in the proceedings allows the bidders to present a reclamation to the court, and if the case

[109a] Council Directive 2004/18/EC, implemented in Norway with effect from 1 January 2007, replacing Council Directive 71/305/EEC, amended by Council Directive 89/440/EEC. (Basically the rules apply both above and below the so-called threshold values of the Directive.)

[110] See M. Cordeiro, 'Da abertura de um concurso para a celebração de um contrato no Direito Privado' BMJ 369 (1987), 5–59.

[111] Article 494 CC.

[112] Which a minority of legal writers would allow to cover the expectation interest: see the Portuguese report on case 1.

[113] Article 227 CC.

is established the court cancels the subsequent process in order to allow the missing bid to be considered.

Scotland

Scots law would be likely to view tender conditions as unilateral promises made to each party to whom the invitation to tender was issued, provided that the conditions were expressed in such a way as to indicate objectively an intention to be bound,[114] although in the case of tender invitations stating that the tender will be awarded to the lowest bidder it might in the alternative be possible to view this as an offer capable of acceptance by the lowest tenderer only, where such tender would be seen as an acceptance concluding the contract.[115]

If B's bid was the lowest (situation (i)), there is no Scottish authority to suggest that B could obtain implement of any contractual obligation that A might owe towards B. Instead, A would be liable to B in damages for breach of promise/contract. In situation (i)(a), damages could be recoverable in the amount of the expectation interest.[116] In situation (i)(b), damages for breach of contract/promise would probably be restricted to the reliance interest (wasted expenditure) and would not extend to the full expectation interest. In situation (i)(b), fraud might also found an action for damages in delict.

If B's bid was not the lowest (situation (ii)), then, given that the conditions state that the contract will be awarded to the lowest bidder, although B has technically suffered a breach of contract or breach of promise there is no loss and any damages for breach of contract, breach of promise, or in delict, will be nominal only.

In principle the answer is no different if A is a public authority.[117] But if so, then A will also be subject to EC public procurement law, implemented in Scotland in the Public Contracts (Scotland) Regulations 2006, SSI 2006/1. Reference should be had to the details of such secondary legislation for restrictions upon public works and services tendering procedures.

[114] MacQueen and Thomson, *Contract Law in Scotland*, para. 2.95; McBryde, *The Law of Contract in Scotland*, para. 6.19.

[115] *Hunter v. General Accident Corp* 1909 SC (HL) 30.

[116] See *Cosar Ltd v. UPS Ltd* 1999 SLT 259.

[117] For details of an ongoing litigation arising from alleged breaches of public procurement rules during the tender competition for the new Scottish Parliament building in Edinburgh, see H.L. MacQueen, *Scots Law News*, http://www.law.ed.ac.uk/sln, nos 413, 428, 447.

Spain

If B's bid was the lowest, according to Spanish case law A is liable to B in contract. The rules of the bidding process are an offer, accepted by those who submit their bid.[118] In either of the two situations (a) and (b), A is liable, as it is responsible for its own organisation.[119] The only (but rather theoretical) difference between case (a), in which the breach of contract is committed negligently, and case (b), in which A acts contrary to good faith (*dolo*) is the extent of the damages awarded, as in the first case only foreseeable losses are within the liability.[120] This distinction is of no practical relevance in this case, however. The consequences of A's liability are either a right for B to conclude the contract or, if this is not possible (for instance, if C had already started to build), damages (reliance or expectation, including immaterial losses).[121]

If B's bid was not the lowest, B did not suffer any loss as it would not have been chosen according to the bidding criteria. If the only criterion for giving the contract really was the price, A is not liable to B as there was no loss. But if other criteria were decisive as well, B could claim damages for the loss of its chance to get the contract (*'pérdida de opordunidad'*).

A would also be liable to B as a public authority. The contract concluded with C would probably be null, as the legally established procedure has not been followed, or at least be annullable.[122] Based on article 66 of the Law on Contracts of Public Authorities, the public authority also has to pay damages deriving from the nullity of the contract, if it is culpable. This leads, as above, to liability in situation (i)(a),(b), but not in case (ii), as there is no proof of any loss caused by the failure to consider B's bid.[123]

Sweden

Where B's bid was the lowest, a binding contract has been concluded between A and B. B is entitled to damages according to the expectation

118 STS, 20 Nov. 1990, RJ 1990\8988; STS, 14 Oct. 1996, RJ 1996\7107.

119 Cf. art. 1903 CC e contrario.

120 Article 1107 CC.

121 STS, 20 Nov. 1990, RJ 1990\8988: the Supreme Court in those cases does not mention explicitly if there are reliance or expectation damages, but according to general principles B can choose between the two.

122 Articles 62ff. and 74ff. of Ley de Contratos de las Administraciones Públicas; art. 62 of Ley de Régimen Juridico de las Administraciones Públicas y del Procedimiento Administrativo Común.

123 Cf. STS, 8 Feb. 1999, no. 3866/1993, RJ 1999\1383.

interest. Where B's bid was not the lowest A is not liable. The results are the same if B is a public authority.

Invitations to participate in a public bidding are normally to be regarded as invitations to third parties to make binding offers. As A's procedure for the bidding process is aimed at a non-limited number of persons, the published statement does not constitute a binding offer.[124] A's statement that it 'will give the contract to the lowest bidder' has to be interpreted, for example, by using the standard in article 8 CISG where due regard is taken of A's intent if B could not have been unaware what this intent was and otherwise to the understandings that a reasonable person of the same kind as B would have had in the same circumstances. Such an interpretation could result in the conclusion that the statement is at least an obligation according to which B is entitled to compensation for its costs incurred in reliance on the statement, that is, its costs for having prepared the bid. However, in this case A's statements should most likely be regarded as a conditional offer according to which A has an obligation to accept the lowest bid. B's acceptance was the lowest one and therefore a contract has been concluded between A and B. A's mistake in not considering B's bid does not constitute a valid ground for not being bound to the contract. If A does not fulfil his obligations, B is entitled to specific performance or damages (expectation interest).

There might exist usages in the construction industry that lead to a different result. In a case where the offer is directed at an unlimited number of persons, it might normally be presumed that the offeror must also ascertain the quality and the reputation of the lowest bidder before accepting the lowest bid. If so, A is only liable to compensate B if A cannot show any qualitative reason for not accepting B's bid. In the absence of a good reason not to accept B's bid, A is liable to compensate B.

Where B's bid was not the lowest, A has breached its obligation to consider all bids. However, B is not entitled to damages since B's bid was not the lowest one and there is no causal link between B's reliance losses and A's breach. The case would be different if A in this case always intended to give the contract to someone else. In this case B would be entitled to damages according to the reliance interest, as this is a clear case of *culpa in contrahendo.*

[124] Article 14 CISG and Avtalslagen (1915:218), s. 9 (Contract Act, CA); Adlercreutz, *Avtalsrätt* I; Simonsen, *Prekontraktuelt ansvar*.

If A is a public authority, the consequences are regulated by the Procurement Act (PA).[125] The PA is based on the EU Directive on Public Procurement. However, Chapter 6 of the PA contains rules on procurements that do not exceed the financial thresholds given in the EU Directive. According to Chapter 6 §12 of the PA, a public authority must accept the most favourable or lowest bid. If no decision is made in the public statement between these two models, bidders cannot generally claim to have a bid accepted because it is the lowest. In this case, A has undertaken to accept the lowest bid. When failing to do so, B is entitled to damages if its bid should have been accepted. The damages in a case of this kind should normally amount to the expectation interest.[126]

Switzerland

Where B's bid was the lowest, A is liable.

The public bidding is normally not an offer but an invitation to make offers *(invitatio ad offerendum)*. The invitation does not restrict the freedom of contract.[127] Liability can arise if the party organising the bidding has from the beginning no intention to realise the construction or the intention to award the contract to a specific person. Then it has violated its duty to negotiate in good faith and hence has to compensate the participating party for the expenses it has incurred (negative interest).[128] The same liability applies if the party organising the bidding does not follow the rules of the bidding and the participating party had a real chance to get the contract.[129] But the organising party is not liable if it does not award any contract because it has changed its mind on the project.

The public bidding can also be organised as a competition (*Wettbewerb*) or a similar procedure that leads to an obligation to contract (*Kontrahierungszwang*).[130] The prerequisites of this exceptional legal

125 Lag om offentlig upphandling (1992:1528).

126 NJA 1998.873, where the expectation interest was awarded when a municipality did not follow the rules in Ch. 6 PA by not accepting the lowest bid. Cf. also prop. 1992/93:88, 46 and Nils Wahl, 'Offentlig upphandling och skadestånd – reparation, prevention eller ingendera?', JT 1997–98, 619–625. Cf. NJA 2000.712.

127 BernerKommentar-Schmidlin, OR 8 n. 64. Cf. Merz, *Vertrag und Vertragsschluss*, n. 213ff.

128 ZürcherKommentar-Schönenberger/Jäggi, OR 8 n. 29; BernerKommentar-Schmidlin, OR 8 n. 65; Gauch, *Der Werkvertrag*, n. 490.

129 Gauch, *Der Werkvertrag*, n. 492ff.

130 ZürcherKommentar-Schönenberger/Jäggi, OR 8 n. 31; Gauch, *Der Werkvertrag*, n. 495, n. 514.

situation are met in the present case. A has proposed to assess all bids according to specific rules and to give the contract to the lowest bidder. A has thus promised to follow the rules for the public bid. For this kind of competition or a similar procedure the special provisions for an offer of prizes apply.[131] The performance consists in making an offer. The compensation or the prize consists in accepting the offer of the winner and in awarding the contract.[132] If the person organising the competition does not follow the rules it is liable on the ground of a contract in respect of a legal transaction (*Rechtsgeschäft*).

In both alternatives of situation (i), A has not followed the rules. Hence, it must compensate B's expectation interest because B would have won the competition if A had not violated its duties.[133] However, B has no claim for specific performance because A can, in its capacity as principal, withdraw at any time from the contract as long as it pays compensation for the work already performed and gives a full indemnity to the contractor.[134]

Where B's bid was not the lowest, A is not liable. B would not have won the competition and would not have been awarded the contract even if A had performed its duties. Hence there is no causal link between the damage and the violation of A's duty. Liability can only arise if A had the intention to give the contract to C from the beginning. It then has to compensate B's negative interest, that is, the expenses incurred by B.

These rules apply also if a public authority organises the public bidding.[135] In addition, special statutes for procedures on awarding contracts upon public tenders apply.[136] Some of these statutes have rules for special legal remedies and for liability.[137]

[131] OR 8 I: 'Whoever offers a prize or a reward as compensation for a performance is obligated to pay such compensation in accordance with his announcement.' Cf. ZürcherKommentar-Schönenberger/Jäggi, OR 8 n. 31.
[132] ZürcherKommentar-Schönenberger/Jäggi, OR 8 n. 31; BernerKommentar-Schmidlin, OR 8 n. 40ff.
[133] ZürcherKommentar-Schönenberger/Jäggi, OR 8 n. 58, 60; Gauch, *Der Werkvertrag*, n. 496.
[134] OR 377. [135] See Gauch, *Der Werkvertrag*, n. 470ff.
[136] E.g. Federal Act on Public Procurement of 16 Dec. 1994 (Bundesgesetz über das öffentliche Beschaffungswesen); Federal Act on the Common Market of 6 Oct. 1995 (Binnenmarktgesetz).
[137] Cf. Gauch, *Der Werkvertrag*, n. 500ff.

Editors' comparative observations

This case raises a common situation: a general public invitation for tenders for a construction project, where a bidder (B), whose bid is not accepted, makes a claim based on defects in the conduct of the employer (A) in receiving and processing the bids. In order to simplify the case, it has been assumed that A has undertaken expressly to give the contract to the lowest bidder: as several reporters noted, this is perhaps not a usual situation since the concept of the 'lowest' bid is itself not straightforward, quite apart from the fact that in practice an employer may normally seek to reserve the right to select amongst the bidders. However, on that simplified set of facts, the jurisdictions are almost unanimous in giving B a remedy in the case where its bid was the lowest; and in rejecting its claim where its bid was not the lowest. However, the reasons (and the remedies, where granted) are not always identical. Reporters were asked also to consider whether it made a difference if A was a public authority; and again the results are not entirely the same.

Where A is a private company inviting the bids, and B's bid was in fact the lowest (but was not accepted) all jurisdictions except for France find A liable both in the case where A's fault is an administrative failure within its organisation, and in the case where A had always intended to give the contract to a third party (C). France just doubts whether B has a contractual right to have its bid accepted and (if not) whether A is sufficiently at fault to give rise to delict liability, where the fault is the administrative failure. The reasons given by the several jurisdictions vary, as too does the remedy (although these two variations amongst the jurisdictions are not necessarily linked). Some find that A's liability is in contract, the contract being formed by the invitation to submit bids together with the submission of the bid itself. The contractual analysis is applied by Denmark (which also has specific statutory rules for public tenders, requiring A to accept B's tender in these circumstances), England, Finland (which has detailed provisions resulting from self-regulation of the building industry directly relevant to this case), France, Ireland, Italy, the Netherlands, Norway, Scotland, Spain, Sweden and Switzerland. Amongst these, France, Italy, the Netherlands and Switzerland also analyse the case in the alternative as one of precontractual liability or delict (and England and Scotland consider that the fraudulent invitation of bids by A, knowing that it would always give the contract to C, also gives rise to a tort/delict claim); and all the other jurisdictions simply hold A liable in precontractual liability (*culpa in contrahendo*) or delict (Austria, Germany, Greece and Portugal). The remedy also varies. Ireland, the Netherlands, Norway, Spain and Sweden, which analyse the case as one of contractual liability, consider the possibility of B obtaining a court order for specific performance of A's promise to give it the contract. As usual, the Netherlands is alone able to contemplate this strongest remedy even if the claim is in precontractual liability ('third stage of negotiations') rather than contract. These, and some of the others which follow the contractual analysis, award expectation damages, to reflect not simply B's expenses of the bid but also its lost profit on the contract which should have been awarded to him. Others would award only damages to cover B's reliance losses. There is not, however, an exact correlation between the contract claim and expectation damages. For example, Austria, Germany and Greece consider that the expectation measure might be awarded in the claim based on *culpa in contrahendo*; whereas Denmark awards only reliance damages in the contract claim and Scotland awards expectation damages in situation 1(a), but reliance damages in situation 1(b). In deciding whether to award the loss of the profit on the contract (expectation measure) some jurisdictions are influenced by the degree of blameworthiness on A's part, in particular, in the situation where the bidding procedure was fraudulent from the start.

Where B's bid was not the lowest but its bid was not considered as a result of administrative failure, all agree that whatever A's responsibility (in contract, delict or precontractual liability) might have been for the administrative failure, its misconduct did not cause any loss to B whose expenditure would always have been wasted. As some reporters point out, this would have been otherwise if the facts on this point had included the situation where the bidding had always been fraudulent, since that would be sufficient to show that all B's expenditure was from the beginning wasted: whether or not the bid was the lowest, the size of its bid was always irrelevant.

In the case where A is a public authority, the situation is generally unchanged in result, although the reasoning varies. All jurisdictions (at least those in the European Union) have similar rules based on the EC Directive on public procurement, although it was perhaps unlikely that the project described in the case would fall under the minimum threshold value of the Directive.[138] However, some jurisdictions have extended the EC rules to cover also lower value projects. And some have other special rules governing public invitations to tender made by public authorities which provide other possible remedies for a party such as B, for example, to have the bidding annulled (France, Greece, Portugal, Spain). Some (Austria, France, Greece and Italy) note particularly that the status of A as a public authority introduces a requirement of equal treatment between bidders which therefore opens up a possibility of B's claiming discriminatory treatment as a ground of invoking annulment or other remedies.

[138] It should be noted that during the period of final drafting of the reports in this volume, the several Member States were in the course of implementing Directive 2004/18/EC; some reports therefore refer to the newly implemented Directive, others to the earlier Directives which it replaced. This detail is not, however, significant for the purposes of this work.

Case 11: A contract for the sale of a house which fails for lack of formality

Case 11

After negotiations, A and B reach agreement on the sale of A's house to B, but do not comply with the formality requirements necessary within their legal system to make the contract valid. B does not know of the formality requirements. Soon afterwards, A tells B that, because of the lack of formality, he (A) is not bound. B has already incurred expenses in coming to the agreement (such as estate agents' fees and travel expenses). B complains that this was the house of his dreams, and he will now only be able to find a less satisfactory property, given the properties available in the market. What liability (in contract, tort, restitution, or any other form of liability), if any, does A have to B? Does it make a difference if:

(i) A knew of the formality requirements?
(ii) A is a professional?
(iii) B raised the question of the formality requirements at the time the agreement was concluded, but A misled him about it?

Discussions

Austria

It is not entirely certain whether these facts would constitute a case of precontractual liability.

Under Austrian law a party is expected to know the law. §2 ABGB states that '[a]s soon as a law has been properly published, no one may be excused on the ground that he had no knowledge of it'. Even though the huge number of statutory enactments in recent years has caused the courts to apply this principle liberally, asking in each case whether it could reasonably be expected that a person knows the relevant law, it is clear that B has contributed by his own negligence to his losses resulting from wasted expenditure. Formal requirements for the validity of contracts for the sale of real property ought to be known by those entering such a contract. That may lead a judge to refuse any compensation of B's loss by A, especially if he finds that both negotiating parties are to blame for negligent disregard of statutory formality requirements. In this case the third sentence of case §878 ABGB may apply by way of analogy.[1]

Nevertheless, B may be awarded compensation for his wasted expenses if there are reasons for B not having had knowledge of the formal requirements for the contract, whilst A knew of them or ought to have known as a professional (for example, as an estate agent). In an early decision the OGH held[2] that a prospective party to a contract who, during precontractual negotiations, negligently and unlawfully caused the other party to make a mistake in his assessment of the circumstances that might form an obstacle to the valid conclusion of a contract, could be held liable for the other party's reliance loss. Therefore, misleading the other party with regard to formality requirements may entail a claim under *culpa in contrahendo* principles.[3]

If A and B did not know the formality requirement at the time of agreement, there is no liability because A and B are equally to blame for not having known the law.[4] In situation (i), a judge may find a duty on the more experienced party to instruct the less informed party of the formality requirement; and it is even more likely that a judge may find in situation (ii) that such a duty lies on a professional vis-à-vis a layman,[5] since experts are subject to a higher degree of care according to §1299 ABGB. Violation of this duty will entail liability for B's reliance loss: only his wasted expenses will be compensated. In situation (iii), A's conduct may qualify as a fraudulent inducement of an error by B. B's negligent ignorance of the formality requirement will not entail a

[1] 'A person who, when entering into the contract was or should have been aware of [the] impossibility [of its performance], is liable to the other innocent party for any damage suffered by him through his reliance upon the validity of the contract, [provided that the other party was not aware thereof himself].'

[2] OGH 8 Oct. 1975, SZ 48/102.

[3] P. Rummel in Rummel, *Kommentar zum ABGB*, vol. I, §866, N. 17. [4] §2 ABGB.

[5] It is unlikely that A will be held liable only for a part of B's wasted expenses because of B's contributory negligence: cf. P. Rummel in Rummel, *Kommentar zum ABGB*, vol. I, §878, N. 6.

reduction of the damages for which A is liable under *culpa in contrahendo* principles.

Denmark

The case is difficult to decide since Danish law has so few formal requirements, and none for the sale of land. However, in Denmark it is very difficult for a party who alleges that there was an agreement to sell real property to prove it, if it was only oral; in most cases, the plaintiff has not been able to prove that a contract was made,[6] but there has been at least one Supreme Court case in which the court held that a contract was made, and in this case the defendant was ordered to convey the property to the plaintiff.[7]

England

In the basic case given, A has no liability to B. The formality requirement for a contract for the sale of a house is that all the express terms of the contract must be in writing, signed by both parties. In the absence of such writing there is no contract for the sale of the property,[8] and B therefore can have no claim for damages for breach of contract. Nor on the primary facts is there any other contract. No tort is committed by A; there is no representation by A to B which might found an estoppel; and there is no claim in restitution (A does not receive any benefit from B).

In the variant cases:

In situations (i) and (ii), it does not make any difference if A knew of the formality requirements, or if A is a professional. The mere fact that A is knowingly taking advantage of a statutory formality, or is in a superior (professional) position does not assist B: in principle, this formality rule is absolute.

In situation (iii), it may, however, make a difference if A has misled B about the formality requirement. If B can show that A was fraudulent (that is, he did not honestly believe his statements to B about the formality requirement) he may have a claim in the tort of deceit for the losses he has suffered in reliance on A's false statement. The fact that A's misrepresentation is one of law (as to the statutory requirements) rather than of fact does not prevent B basing an action of deceit on it.[9]

[6] See Andersen, Madsen and Nørgaard, *Aftaler og Mellemmænd*, p. 89.

[7] See, e.g., U 1988 522 H.

[8] Law of Property (Miscellaneous Provisions) Act 1989, s. 2(1).

[9] Until recently a misrepresentation of law was held insufficient to give rise to certain claims, but this rule has now been reversed: *Kleinwort Benson Ltd v. Lincoln City Council* [1999]

The damages recoverable in an action of deceit would be calculated to compensate only B's out-of-pocket losses incurred in reliance on the representation, and not the expectation loss he suffers by failing to receive his 'dream house'. However, it is not clear that any of B's out-of-pocket losses are recoverable on the facts, since his estate agents' fees and travel expenses appear all to have been incurred before the representation, not in reliance on it.

Another possible remedy, but which appears not to be available on the facts here, is through the doctrine of proprietary estoppel.[10] Although the contract of sale does not come into existence in consequence of the failure to comply with the statutory formalities, if proprietary estoppel can be established the court might in awarding a remedy require A to confer on B the interest which the contract would have conferred had it complied with the formalities. In such a case the court is not enforcing the (void) contract itself but is giving effect to an equitable doctrine which operates outside the statutory rule for the formality of the contract.[11] However, on the facts it seems unlikely that proprietary estoppel can be established: the claim requires proof by B that he has acted to his detriment on A's representation that he will obtain a certain interest in property. Even if such a representation can be shown, B appears not to have relied on it since his expenditure appears to have been incurred before the representation.

Finland

This case is similar to case 3. In both cases there is a sales transaction that is subject to the formality requirements of land. According to the

2 AC 349 (restitution of money paid under a mistake of law); *Pankhania v. Hackney LBC* [2002] EWHC 2441 (Ch), [2002] All ER (D) 22 (Aug.) (misrepresentation of law), approved in *Brennan v. Bolt Burdon* [2005] QB 303 (mistake of law). Even before these cases, however, it appeared possible to obtain a remedy in damages for a *fraudulent* misrepresentation of law: Cartwright, *Misrepresentation, Mistake and Non-Disclosure*, para. 5.08.

[10] See the English report on case 2.

[11] *Yaxley v. Gotts* [2000] Ch 162. The Law Commission Report which proposed the Law of Property (Miscellaneous Provisions) Act 1989 contemplated that proprietary estoppel could be available as a means of giving effect to an agreement which did not comply with the formality requirements of the Act: Law Com. No. 164 *Formalities for Contracts for Sale etc of Land* (1987), pp. 18–20. However, in *Cobbe v. Yeoman's Row Management Ltd* [2008] 1 WLR 1752, Lord Scott at [29] cast doubt on whether it is possible to use the doctrine of proprietary estoppel in this context, although his Lordship did not discuss the Law Commission Report, *Yaxley v. Gotts* or other Court of Appeal decisions which had followed *Yaxley*: *Kinane v. Mackie-Conteh* [2005] EWCA Civ 45; *Oates v. Stimson* [2006] EWCA Civ 548. For further discussion, see pp. 463–4 below.

Finnish Code of Real Estate, this kind of contract has to be concluded in a written form, signed by both parties, and confirmed by a notary public. The provisions of the Code of Real Estate, prescribing the legal consequences of a contract not complying with the formality requirements, can be taken as the basis for the solution of this case, too.[12] There is also a question of the duties of disclosure under general contract law, which are not much modified by these provisions.

A would be liable according to the rules of *culpa in contrahendo*. The basic case and its variations (i), (ii) and (iii) illustrate different aspects that would be taken into account as affecting the degree of A's fault. No one may make use of legal rules in a speculative sense, to get an advantage from the other party's ignorance of them, even if a party's right to rely on his ignorance of law is limited (*ignorantia iuris nocet*).[13] Even in the basic version of the case there are some hints of A's speculative intention. A seems to make use of the formality requirements and B's ignorance of them in order to avoid the contract. This is considered wrongful conduct, and A would thus be liable on the basis of *culpa in contrahendo*.

The liability covers B's negative interest, mainly the costs he has incurred in coming to the agreement. According to section 8 of the Code of Real Estate, which defines the scope of damages arising out of withdrawal from making the final agreement, the compensation covers reasonable expenses from advertising, visiting the land and other necessary measures pertaining to the conclusion of the contract. So B's costs mentioned in the text (such as estate agents' fees and travel expenses) are compensated.

B's 'complaint' that 'this was the house of his dreams, and he will now only be able to find a less satisfactory property' may refer to some kind of non-pecuniary damage he claims to have suffered. The Finnish contract law rules do not add much to the tort law rules[14] on non-pecuniary damages. In this case they cannot be applied, and it

[12] According to their wording, the provisions deal only with the pre-contract but can be considered to express principles applicable also to final contracts not concluded in the legal form.

[13] Hemmo, *Sopimusoikeus*, vol. I, p. 147.

[14] VahL ch. 5, ss. 2 and 6. These rules concern the compensation of pain and suffering, or defect and other permanent handicap in connection with personal injuries, and mental suffering caused by criminal offences against personal freedom, honour or domiciliary peace.

seems that there is no scope for the compensation of non-pecuniary damage.[15]

Variants (i), (ii) and (iii), seen from the point of view of contract law, differ from each other mainly in the degree of fault shown by A. In all of them, A would be held liable for B's negative interest. In situation (i), if A knew of the formality requirements, it is a case of deliberate causation of damage. In this case, however, A's intention probably does not alter the preconditions of his liability for damages, nor is the extent of compensation different.[16] The same applies also to variants (ii) and (iii). Situation (ii) would perhaps be quite similar to (i) as concerns the liability in damages, because according to the stricter standard of care applied to a professional, A should have known of the formality requirements.

France

This question is easily answered by French law since the validity of a contract for the sale of a house is not subject to any particular formality requirement.

The agreement between A and B produces full effect from the moment it is reached and B, therefore, has to be considered as the owner of the house. The contract being enforceable, no damage is suffered by B and, thus, A could not be held liable. This traditional solution is given by article 1583 of the Civil Code, applicable to any sale. Among the conditions of validity mentioned in this article, there is no reference to formality. By an *a contrario* interpretation of the text, academic writers and courts have always considered[17] that the contract of sale needs no registration to produce effect. The contract of sale is purely consensual.

[15] On non-pecuniary damages in contract law, see Hemmo, *Sopimusoikeus*, vol. I, pp. 276–7. There are, however, some legal provisions, mainly in the field of consumer law, concerning the compensation of lost use value (see, e.g., Consumer Protection Act, ch. 5, s. 10, para. 3.3, ch. 8, s. 10, para. 3.3, and ch. 9, s. 11, para. 3.3). In one case (KKO 1969 II 40) the seller of anthracite was held liable for the smell caused by contamination in the anthracite (in heating, the smell had become embedded in the flue).

[16] In Finnish contract law, intention and gross negligence of the liable party affect mainly the application of agreed limitations of risk. They can also have some role in determining the 'adequate causality' of damage. See Hemmo, *Sopimusoikeus*, vol. II, p. 294ff. and Hemmo, *Vahingonkorvauksen määräytymisestä sopimussuhteissa* [*On the Determination of Damages in Contract Law*], p. 250ff.

[17] See e.g., Malaurie, Aynès and Gautier, *Contrats spéciaux*, no. 156.

Let us imagine therefore a slightly different situation. Under French law, if the owner of land agrees to sell it to a buyer, who has a certain time to give his answer, the agreement (*promesse unilatérale de vente*) has to be registered within 10 days of its conclusion.[18] Otherwise, it is null. Would A be found liable if such a contract were not registered on time? Clearly the answer is negative if none of the parties knew that the validity of the contract was submitted to registration. In fact it is for B to have the contract registered and he is supposed to know the legal conditions to which the validity of his contract is submitted.[19]

The solution might be different in situation (i). A, aware of the formality requirements, should probably have informed B that the contract had to be registered to become fully valid. The obligation to inform supposes that A knew B's ignorance and deliberately kept the information to himself. He would be liable under tort law,[20] if B brings evidence that (1) A knew of the existence of this requirement and (2) A knew B was ignorant of the requirement. The solution is the same in situation (ii) if A, a professional,[21] knew that B was ignorant of the existence of the requirement. *A fortiori*, the same solution has to be given to variant (iii) where A misled B about the formality requirement.

The harm is here linked to the fault by the chain of causation. In situations (i), (ii) and (iii) the compensable loss is of three types: the expenses incurred; the loss of the opportunity to conclude the contract;[22] and the non-financial harm suffered by B as a consequence of the aborted contract (*préjudice moral*).[23]

Germany

Under German law, where form is required its absence will typically make the transaction void:

§125 BGB: A legal transaction which is not in the form prescribed by the law is void. Lack of the form required by legal transaction results also, in case of doubt, in nullity.

[18] Article 1840A Code général des Impôts, which recently became art. 1589-2 of the Civil Code.

[19] *Nemo legem ignorare censetur.* [20] Articles 1382 or 1383 C.civ.

[21] Reading 'professional' as professional of the sale of land.

[22] Since the chance for the contract to be concluded (had the fault not been committed) is 100 per cent, the judge should give B damages representing the profit expected from the contract.

[23] The valuation of this harm is never explicitly discussed by the courts (supposing it really differs from the loss of the chance to conclude the contract).

The instances where the effects of the lack of form are mitigated by the Code itself are seen as rather exceptional derogations from the basic rule of nullity contained in §125 BGB. Neither the legislature nor the courts have departed from this position of principle, though a considerable body of case law has developed since the 1920s which has tried to alleviate the rigour of such a rule in truly deserving cases. The recent case law, however, has managed the problem of contracts' invalidity for formality reasons in a rather inconsistent way and can give rise to difficult demarcation problems. Most cases are concerned with the question whether, according to the principle of good faith (§242 BGB) a party is entitled to *specific performance* despite the absence of form, that is, whether the other party's assertion of the lack of form is contrary to good faith. The problem of an action for damages based upon *culpa in contrahendo*[24] is only dealt with subsidiarily.[25]

It should, however, be kept in mind that derogations from the basic rule of nullity can only be justified in very exceptional circumstances. The policy behind the formal requirement which, in the first place, is meant to prevent parties from hasty and inconsiderate decisions must not be circumvented by means of the principle of good faith or *culpa in contrahendo*.

In situation (i): B has no contractual claim; that is, he is not entitled to specific performance. It is the consistent practice of the Bundesgerichtshof that specific performance of the contract may only be ordered if the invalidity of an agreement but for formality requirements would create an 'absolutely unbearable result' (*schlechthin untragbares Ergebnis*) for the innocent party and not merely a 'harsh one' (*nicht bloß ein hartes Ergebnis*). This is the case only (1) if there is a very heavy breach of duty of regard and loyalty by the party asserting the defect of form of the contract – if his conduct must be regarded as particularly outrageous; if a party knows of, but does not wilfully deceive the other party about, the formality requirements, these conditions are generally not met; or (2) if the invalidity of the contract seriously imperils the innocent party's economic viability.[26] These conditions are obviously not met.

[24] §§280(1), 311(2) BGB.

[25] Cf. W. Lorenz, AcP 156 (1956), 381. For a short overview, see Markesinis, Lorenz and Dannemann, *The German Law of Obligations*, vol. I, p. 80ff.

[26] BGH, decision of 23 June 1994, DTZ 1994, 339; BGH, decision of 27 June 1988, NJW 1989, 166; BGH, decision of 19 Nov. 1982, BGHZ 85, 315, 319; BGH, decision of 27 Oct. 1967, BGHZ 48, 396, 398; BGH, decision of 3 Dec. 1958, BGHZ 29, 6, 10. It will be noticed that no clear borderline can be drawn between 'an absolutely unbearable

Nor is A liable on the ground of §§280(1), 311(2) No. 1 BGB (*culpa in contrahendo*). A party asserting the lack of form of an agreement may, it is true, be liable on the ground of *culpa in contrahendo* if the invalidity of the contract is in fact harsh but not unbearable for the other party. This action, however, only lies in exceptional circumstances. Each party should ensure that formality requirements are met. Therefore, liability on the ground of *culpa in contrahendo* only comes into being if the party asserting the lack of form was under a duty to take care of the other party's interests in the validity of the contract (*Betreuungspflicht*) and for this reason should have informed the other party of the formality requirements.[27] This duty may derive from the special relationship (*Sonderrechtsverhältnis*) created between the negotiating parties by virtue of the law. The Bundesgerichtshof, however, is rightly cautious in assuming such a duty, because a party held liable on the ground of *culpa in contrahendo* might be indirectly put under pressure to perform an invalid contract. Until now it has only been approved of if one party knows that the other party is commercially inexperienced and that, therefore, this party relies on his legal expertise in relation to the perfection of the contract.[28] Hence, the reason for liability is not to be found in the refusal to complete the contract (as in case 3) but in the fact that one party has made the other party legitimately believe that a valid contract has already been concluded. Therefore, in situation (i) the requirements for imposing a *Betreuungspflicht* on A are not satisfied, since such a duty cannot emanate from the single fact of his knowledge of the formality requirements.

Nor is A liable in tort or restitution.[29]

In situation (ii): A is not liable in contract, even if he is a professional. According to the principles discussed above this additional fact cannot translate the invalidity of the contract into an 'absolutely unbearable result' for B.

A is, however, liable on the ground of *culpa in contrahendo*. It is acknowledged that the *Betreuungspflicht* required for liability may result

result' and a result which is merely 'harsh but not unbearable'. A distinction of this kind is not apt to promote the certainty of the law. It is, therefore, disapproved of by most legal writers: cf. Markesinis, Lorenz and Dannemann, *The German Law of Obligations*, vol. I, p. 68; Larenz and Wolf, *Allgemeiner Teil des Bürgerlichen Rechts*, §27 para. 47.

[27] MünchKomm-Emmerich, Vor §275 Rn. 85.

[28] BGH, decision of 29 Jan. 1965, NJW 1965, 812, 814.

[29] Cf. the German report on case 6.

from a party's role as a professional. This is particularly true if a party advocates his professionalism. In this case it is *prima facie* assumed that the other party, as a result, legitimately placed reliance on his expert knowledge.[30] Consequently, as B could rely on A's professionalism, A's failure to inform B about the formality requirements led B to believe that a contract had already been validly concluded.

As a rule, a party liable on the ground of *culpa in contrahendo* must compensate the other party's reliance loss, that is, B must be put into the position he would be in if A had informed him about the formality requirements. If B can show that, if he had been informed in time, he could have bought an adequate property for a smaller sum than he now has to pay for a similar one, A must make good the difference. However, A is not liable for the expenses in coming to the invalid agreement (estate agents' fees, travel expenses), as these were made before the parties agreed on the sale: B would still have had to bear these costs if he had been informed about the formality requirement. If, however, B can prove that the parties would have complied with the formality requirements if A had informed him properly, he is entitled to expectation damages.[31]

In situation (iii): A is liable in contract: (1) B is entitled to specific performance.[32] It is an almost unanimous view that a party purposely misleading the other party about formality requirements is culpable of a heavy breach of his duty of regard and loyalty towards the other party. Therefore, in keeping with the principle of good faith,[33] A's assertion of lack of form must not be heard (*nemo auditur fraudem suam allegans*).[34] (2) If A refuses to perform the contract, B may demand expectation damages or rescind the contract, provided the conditions of §§437 Nos. 2 and 3, 281, 323 BGB are fulfilled.[35]

30 BGH, decision of 29 Jan. 1965, NJW 1965, 812.

31 BGH, decision of 29 Jan. 1965, NJW 1965, 812, 814.

32 §433(1) BGB. 33 §242 BGB.

34 Cf BGH, decision of 21 Mar. 1969, NJW 1969, 1167; RG, decision of 10 Oct. 1919, RGZ 96, 313, 315; Larenz and Wolf, *Allgemeiner Teil des Bürgerlichen Rechts*, §27 para. 47. This case must not be confused with the famous *Edelmann-Fall* (RGZ 117, 121) where both parties knew of the need to observe the formalities but, due to the defendant's assurance that it was unnecessary between the parties, abstained from the formal recording. The solution of this case was highly controversial; cf. BGH, decision of 27 Oct. 1967, BGHZ 48, 396; RG, decision of 21 May 1927, RGZ 117, 121; MünchKomm-Förschler §125 para. 49ff.

35 See the German report on case 13.

There being a contract, A's liability on the ground of *culpa in contrahendo* is consumed by his contractual liability.[36] He may, however, also be liable in tort pursuant to §826 BGB, if he intended not only to mislead B but to cause damage to him.

Greece

In Greek law the agreement transferring immovable property from the seller to the buyer must be authenticated by a notary public and must also be entered in a public register.[37] A contract not complying with the formality requirements set by the law is invalid.[38] A and B have reached an agreement for the sale of a house and they would have concluded a contract save for a lack of compliance with a formal requirement. When negotiations have reached such a stage, when an agreement has been reached on all points and all that is left is a formality for the valid conclusion of the contract, then the abandonment of negotiations is deemed to be contrary to precontractual good faith.[39] It would be a fair estimation to say that in Greek case law the bulk of precontractual liability cases concern exactly this type of facts (sale of immovable property, conclusion of negotiations, walking away from agreement before validation for reasons of better offer). And the position of the courts has been adamant in recognising the precontractual liability of the party who walks away from the negotiations.[40] Although case law

[36] Cf. Lorenz and Riehm, *Lehrbuch zum neuen Schuldrecht*, para. 575ff.

[37] Articles 369, 1033 GCC. [38] Article 159 GCC.

[39] Article 197 GCC. By way of an example, see First Instance Court of Thessaloniki 1278/1998 Arm 1998, 543, which concerned the sale of offices (professional premises) to a notary. In that case, an agreement had been reached between the negotiating parties, the seller reassured the buyer that the signing of the contract was imminent and all that was left was a formal requirement (authentication by a notary public), but at the very last moment the seller declined to proceed, invoking a pretext. Nevertheless, the court accepted that the real reason was that the seller had been lured by a better offer from a third party and chose to discard the first agreement. The court held that at that stage a better offer could not be a proper reason for breaking off negotiations and compensated the notary not only for the positive loss but also for the loss of opportunity, which he adequately substantiated. But see AP 1565/2000 Chronika Idiotikou Dikaiou 2001, 220.

[40] AP 309/1996 EllD 1997, 83; AP 764/1996 EllD 1997, 574; AP 628/1995 EEN 1996, 545; AP 1505/1988 EEN 1989, 740; AP 756/1981 EEN 1982, 491; AP 969/1977 NoV 26, 895; Court of Appeals of Athens 2698/1978 Arm 1978, 551; First Instance Court of Thessaloniki 1278/1998 Arm 1998, 543; First Instance Court of Arta 79/1995 Arm, 1996, 1319; First Instance Court of Thessaloniki 831/1977 NoV 26, 539 (note Spiridakis); see also Pouliadis, *Culpa in contrahendo und Schutz Dritter*, pp. 171–2, who

has typically limited compensation to the reliance interest, in such cases some legal writers have claimed that the expectation (or quasi-expectation) interest must be compensated.[41] In any case, in addition to the positive loss (estate agents' fees and travel expenses) the negative loss suffered by B in having to buy another inferior property or at a higher price will also be compensated in full. However, it is the prevalent view that in precontractual liability damages cannot be awarded for immaterial loss, because it is not explicitly provided by the legal provisions on precontractual liability.[42]

It is immaterial whether or not A knew of the formality requirements before declining to comply with the formality and abandoning negotiations. Nevertheless, if A knows of the formality requirement or he is a professional (which implies that A has been aware of the formality requirements all along), both these variations only strengthen the presumption that A behaves in a manner which is contrary to precontractual good faith. Evidently, A will also be liable for precontractual bad faith if B had raised the formality requirement but he was misled by A. Such conduct by A may also amount to a delict,[43] and in particular to damage caused *contra bonos mores* according to article 919 GCC.[44] The remedies in the law of delict present the advantage that B may be compensated for immaterial loss in not acquiring the house of his dreams, which A in the meantime sells to another buyer.[45] Another possibility is for B to invoke article 281 GCC on the abuse of a right and to request the remedy of specific performance, that is, for A to comply with the formality requirement. However, case law does not favour such an approach.[46]

reaches a similar conclusion after categorizing the bulk of Greek precontractual liability cases up to the end of the 1970s. The present author affirms that this has continued to be the case.

41 *Inter alios*, M. Karasis, 'Precontractual Liability', NoV 26, 592ff.

42 In Greek law compensation for immaterial damage can only be awarded if there is provision for such type of compensation in the relevant sources of liability (art. 299 GCC). For instance, art. 59 GCC regarding the protection of one's name and personality or art. 932 in the law of delict provide for immaterial damage.

43 Articles 914ff. GCC.

44 Areios Pagos 756/1981 Ephimeris Hellinon Nomikon 1982, 491.

45 Article 932 GCC.

46 (In full bench) 33/1987 NoV 1988, 324 (note Doris); AP 404/1987 NoV 1988, 907; AP 167/1998 EllD 1998, 856.

Ireland

A has no liability to B in any of the circumstances outlined, with the possible exception of an action for the tort of deceit in situation (iii). However, the calculation of damages for B would be nominal only.

Under the Statute of Frauds, any contract for the sale of land, or any interest therein, must be evidenced in writing and signed by the person against whom it is to be pleaded.[47] In the absence of such writing, there is no enforceable agreement. Whilst the courts have given considerable latitude with respect to the writing sufficient to satisfy the Statute, it has not been prepared to ignore the plain meaning of the legislation.[48] It is true that the law will intervene if the parties have undertaken sufficient acts of part performance of the contract and enforce such an agreement despite the absence of formalities,[49] but there is nothing in this case to disclose that any such acts of part performance have occurred. These acts of part performance might include, for example, B moving into possession of the property, or A cashing a cheque for the purchase price.[50]

Ignorantia iuris non excusat: ignorance of the law is no excuse. Therefore, B will be expected to be aware of the legal requirements as to formalities in contracts for the sale of land. Even if A has misled B as to the law with respect to formalities, this will not be sufficient to have the agreement enforced. However, it may, as a very remote possibility, be sufficient to ground a cause of action in deceit. The action for deceit was fully explained in the report on case 1. The damages payable would be an amount of money sufficient to put B into the position as if the event complained of had never happened. If A had not misled B about the requirements about formalities, B would still have had to incur the various costs described and therefore the deceit itself has caused no loss to B beyond that which he would have had to incur. B therefore is entitled to nominal damages only. B might seek an order for punitive or exemplary damages against A but this is unlikely to succeed.

[47] Statute of Frauds (Ir) 1695, s. 2.

[48] For a fuller discussion, see the Irish report on case 3.

[49] *Lowry v. Reid* [1927] NI 142; see generally, Delaney, *Equity and the Law of Trusts in Ireland*, 439ff.

[50] *Howlin v. Thomas F Power (Dublin) Ltd* (unreported, High Court) 5 May 1978, per McWilliam J, adopting *Steadman v. Steadman* [1976] AC 536.

Italy

Italian academic writing recognises a general duty to comply with contract formality flowing from article 1337 of the Civil Code. For example, a party who did not ask for the public authorisation necessary for the validity of a contract has been deemed precontractually liable. And parents have incurred precontractual liability for selling a minor's goods without having sought the required authorisation of a tutor judge (*giudice tutelare*).[51] In this case, it first has to be understood what formalities are required for A's sale of his house, and which party has to comply with them.

In general, Italian law requires written contracts for the valid sale of houses or immovable property. According to article 1350 of the Civil Code, any contract of sale of immovable property is deemed to be void unless made by public deed (*atto pubblico*) or written document (*scrittura privata*). Moreover, article 2643 requires such contracts to be registered in order to produce effects for parties outside the contract.

Italian case law also considers the written formality as necessary *ad substantiam* for both pre-contracts and contracts for the sale of immovable property.[52]

In this case A seems to breach the duty to communicate relevant circumstances for the conclusion of the contract, derived from article 1338 of the Civil Code.[53] However, Italian case law has expressly recognised that in case of a sale of immovable property, both contractual and precontractual liability are excluded if the contract fails to comply with the requirements for written form. Article 1338 imposes liability only where the other contracting party (in this case B) has not acted negligently. The counterpart is deemed not to have taken the required care if his reliance derived from ignorance of current law.[54] On the other hand, case law also recognises that the judge ought to balance both of the parties' actual conduct in evaluating their good faith during negotiations, even in the case of ignorance of the law.[55]

In situation (i), the fact that A was aware of the formalities required does not seem necessarily to give rise to his liability. B was himself required by law to know about them.

[51] See, for academic writing, Patti, *Responsabilità precontrattuale e contratti standard*; and for case law, Cass, 13 Jan. 1979, n. 273.

[52] Cass, sez. II, 11 Feb. 1997, n. 2174; Cass, sez. II, 29 Oct. 1994, n. 8937.

[53] This duty was expressly recognised by the Italian Supreme Court in Cass, sez. II, 29 May 1998, n. 5297.

[54] TRIB-T. Napoli, 30 Apr. 1984.

[55] TRIB-T. Pescara, 4 Mar. 1978.

In situation (ii), according to case law,[56] A's capacity as professional could lead the judge to a more severe evaluation of his conduct, despite B's apparent unjustifiable reliance. Insofar as we do not know which formalities were required to be complied with, it is not possible to predict whether A will incur precontractual liability. It seems that A would incur extra-contractual liability if B could prove A's duty to inform him, or A's bad faith.

In situation (iii), where A misled B about the formalities, A would probably incur precontractual liability under article 1337 of the Civil Code. A would have acted in breach of the general principle of good faith in negotiations and, according to the Italian Supreme Court, this could be a sufficient reason not to apply article 1338.[57] In this case the recoverable damages would consist in all the expenses proved by B, within the limit of the *interesse negativo*. There is no case law to help us in determining exactly the measure of damages. In any case, it would be unlikely that B would recover the expenses needed to find another house.

Netherlands

A sales contract under Dutch law is an 'obligatory' contract, that is, a contract which creates the obligation to transfer property; it does not itself transfer property. The transfer of property is a formal act which needs to be made by a notarial deed.

Until recently, under Dutch law there were no formalities for the conclusion of the 'obligatory' contract for the sale of a house. However, a recent law reform introduced (among other things) a form requirement: since 2003 a contract for the sale of a house to a consumer has to be made in writing.[58] As a result, the facts of this case are now likely to occur, especially in the early days of the reform being in force. It has been suggested that in such cases the buyer should be protected by the courts.[59] This could be done in two ways: either the courts could impose

[56] See in particular, PRET-P. Salerno, 28 Dec. 1993.

[57] Cass, sez. II, 25 Nov. 1997, n. 1181; Cass, 18 Jun. 1988, n. 5371.

[58] Article 7:2(1) BW.

[59] See M. Hesselink and H. van Kooten, 'De rechtspositie naar artikel 7:2 BW (nieuw) van de consument die bij mondelinge overeenkomst een woning heeft gekocht' in van Buren-Dee, Hondius and Kottenhagen-Edzes, *Consument zonder grenzen*; Hijma, *Mr. C. Asser's handleiding tot de beoefening van het Nederlands burgerlijk recht; Bijzondere overeenkomsten*, vol. I, *Koop en ruil*.

liability for the expectation interest since the 'third stage'[60] of negotiations has been reached (indeed, the parties have even reached agreement); or the effect of the form requirement could be limited in such a case on the basis of the general good faith clause.[61] In the latter case each of the facts mentioned under variants (i), (ii) and, especially, (iii) could be regarded as an argument in favour of protection of a consumer buyer.

Norway

Norwegian law has no requirements as to formality, such as conditions of validity, for the sale of real property.[62] If the sale is to be judicially registered, however, a written statement is required by the owner. But judicial registration applies with respect to third parties. The parties might, however, agree on particular requirements as to formality.

In Sweden, on the other hand, the sale of real property must be in writing and signed by both parties.[63] A difficulty in permitting the right to damages in cases of invalidity is that the claim for damages to a certain extent would cancel out the formality requirements. In Sweden, the courts have traditionally been very cautious in awarding damages in such situations.[64] Jan Kleineman maintains, however, that such an award should not be excluded, but that it would have to be based on obvious bad faith or fault on the part of the person who withdraws from a contract which is formally invalid.[65] Withdrawal from a formally valid contract is not in itself sufficient to constitute liability.

Since the law applicable to such a case is much more developed in Sweden than in Norway, Swedish law can be used as an analogy to indicate the likely answer in Norwegian law. In the present case, A would probably not be liable. The fact that B is unaware of the formality requirements is not significant. Nothing in the facts suggests that A has acted in bad faith. (It is presumed that the reason for A withdrawing from the contract emerges only after entering into the agreement. At the time of entering into the agreement A had intended to honour it.)

In the alternative situations:

(i) 'A knew of the formality requirement': when A is aware of the formality requirement, and hence knows that the agreement between himself

[60] See the Dutch report on case 1. [61] Article 6:248 BW.

[62] Sale of Property Act, ss. 1–3: 'Agreement in respect to the sale of property can be made in writing or orally.'

[63] Jordabalkan (Estate Act), ch. 4, s. 1. [64] NJA 1973.175.

[65] J. Kleineman, JT 1993–94, 433ff.; see the summary at 459.

and B is not binding, the question arises whether he should have informed B of this. If, as presumed above, A had it in mind to honour the agreement at the time he entered into it, it is doubtful whether he has a duty to inform. A would have had to inform B that there was a possibility that he might withdraw during the period in which invalidity could be claimed. Here, it is natural to presume that the sale was to be judicially registered and hence that the formality requirements would be met. The question would then be whether it was bad faith on A's part not to inform B that he was at liberty to withdraw from the agreement until it was judicially registered.

(ii) 'A is a professional': generally, more stringent demands would be imposed on a professional person, for instance a real estate dealer, than on two private parties entering into an agreement. The question is whether A, as a professional, should have ensured that B was aware that the agreement was not binding (for example, before it had been judicially registered). If B is a consumer, there are reasons for A having such an obligation. For instance, if he is a real estate agent putting together contracts on behalf of a third person, this would appear to be the answer.

(iii) 'B raised the question of the formality requirements at the time the agreement was concluded, but A misled him about it': in this case, A is clearly liable to B for compensatory damages. A misleads B into believing that the requirement is binding. Consequently, B would be able to claim compensation for losses he had suffered as a result.

In those cases where B can claim damages against A, the basis of liability would be breach of the precontractual duty of good faith, and the compensation would consist of expenses he had incurred by relying on the validity of the agreement with A (the reliance interest).[66]

Portugal

B is entitled to compensation, according to the rules of precontractual liability.[67] However, according to the dominant view, that compensation

[66] Costs relating to negotiations, such as the estate agents' fees and travel expenses, can hardly be considered incurred in the belief that the contract was valid; see discussion of this question in Brkhus, TfR 1947, 527ff. It is nonetheless not clear how strictly the court would consider the need for causation in these cases. If one of the parties realised that the contract would become invalid, there is precontractual liability which also includes expenses relating to the negotiations.

[67] Article 227 CC.

would be only for the reliance interest (estate agents' fees and travel expenses) and would not involve the damage of not buying the house itself, although it can include the additional cost of buying an alternative property.

There are formality requirements for such a contract. A transfer of the house itself has to be done by a public deed.[68] If it is only an agreement to sell the house, it has to be contained in a written document.[69] In this case, A and B reached an agreement and intended to perform a contract which is void for lack of formality. As the agreement was reached, A and B should afterwards perform the contract in a legal way and if A refuses to do so, his behaviour constitutes a breach of the agreement without due cause, which involves precontractual liability.

Situations (i), (ii) and (iii) refer to circumstances involving fraud by A (variant (ii) should not be distinguished, since if A is a professional in this business, he is required to know the formality requirements). However, the solution would not be different as B is entitled to compensation based on A's precontractual liability in any of the situations.

Scotland

If B was unaware of formality requirements, but has relied to his detriment upon the supposed obligation, and A was aware of such detrimental reliance, then B can plead that A is personally barred from denying the validity of the obligation. The requirements to be met for such a plea are found in the Requirements of Writing (Scotland) Act 1995, section 1(3), (4):

> 1(3) Where a contract, obligation or trust mentioned in subsection (2)(a) above is not constituted in a written document complying with section 2 of this Act, but one of the parties to the contract, a creditor in the obligation or a beneficiary under the trust ('the first person') has acted or refrained from acting in reliance on the contract, obligation or trust with the knowledge and acquiescence of the other party to the contract, the debtor in the obligation or the truster ('the second person'):
>
> (a) the second person shall not be entitled to withdraw from the contract, obligation or trust; and
>
> (b) the contract, obligation or trust shall not be regarded as invalid, on the ground that it is not so constituted, if the condition set out in subsection (4) below is satisfied.

[68] Article 875 CC. [69] Article 410, no. 2 CC.

1(4) The condition referred to in subsection (3) above is that the position of the first person:

(a) as a result of acting or refraining from acting as mentioned in that subsection has been affected to a material extent; and
(b) as a result of such a withdrawal as is mentioned in that subsection would be adversely affected to a material extent.

The effect would be that, if B's reliance is within the scope of section 1(3) and (4), then there is a contract of sale with A and damages (on the expectation measure) are recoverable by B for that breach of contract by A. B can also specifically enforce the contract. (B could claim damages for any incidental unnecessary expenditure as well as specific implement of the contract, but not specific implement and full expectation damages, unless delay in transfer cost B an opportunity of resale to C at a profit.)

However, it is not clear that B's loss here (estate agents' fees, travel expenses) is incurred so much in reliance on the agreement as in the hope of obtaining it. If so, then the conditions of section 1(3) are not met. Even if they are, under section 1(4) it has to be shown that B was affected to a material extent, i.e. the expenditure was more than trivial.[70]

In the variant situations:

(i) the above position applies whether or not A knew of the formality requirements;
(ii) the above position applies whether or not A is a professional;
(iii) if A misled B as to the requirements of writing, then not only would B be entitled to claim that A was personally barred from withdrawing from the obligation, but an action in delict for misrepresentation would also be available, allowing B to claim any consequential losses from the misrepresentation. As B would be entitled to force A to proceed with the transaction, however, if B were to choose so to do there would be likely to be no such losses.

If B cannot bring his position within the scope of the Requirements of Writing (Scotland) Act, the answer to this question is in general similar to that for case 10: that is, A is not liable in damages unless some of the earlier case law following *Walker v. Milne*[71] has survived the general restriction of that authority. Only the reliance interest is recoverable under *Walker v. Milne*.

[70] MacQueen and Thomson, *Contract Law in Scotland*, paras. 2.49–2.53.
[71] (1823) 2 S 379.

Spain

In Spanish law, there are no formality requirements for the validity of a contract for the sale of land.[72] Therefore, B can demand that the necessary formalities are entered into for the transfer of the property, that is, that the public document is written,[73] if he can prove the first agreement.

If A knew of the formality requirements, or (being a professional) was supposed to know them, or even misled B about them, he would be liable in tort (*culpa in contrahendo*), as he negotiated in bad faith if he consciously concluded an invalid contract. His behaviour can even be qualified as *abuso de un derecho*,[74] which would provide another ground for his liability.

Sweden

A is not liable to compensate B, probably not even if he knew of the formality requirements (situation (i)). A might be liable to compensate B if he misled him (situation (iii)), but this is uncertain. If A is a professional (situation (ii)) his responsibility could be regulated in special legislation or ethical norms and hence there might be liability.[75]

Due to the form requirements for sales of real estate (the agreement has to be in writing and contain, *inter alia*, a declaration by the seller that the ownership of the property is transferred to the buyer), there is some uncertainty as to whether *culpa in contrahendo* may constitute liability. Neither party is bound by an agreement for sale of real estate until it fulfils the form requirements. In NJA 1973.175, where the parties were negotiating a sale of real estate and where the owner incurred costs for changes of the property in accordance with the wishes of the prospective buyer, the Supreme Court found that the latter could not be liable 'only because of the promise to buy the property'. Due to the principle of *iuris ignorantia nocet*, B bears the risk of his lack of knowledge about the requirements as to form and therefore A is not liable for damages. It does not make any difference whether or not A, as in (i), knew about the formal requirements at the time when the parties

[72] STS, 16 May 1996, no. 401/1996, RJ 1996\4348.

[73] Article 1279 CC. [74] Article 7.2 CC.

[75] Grauers, *Fastighetsköp*; Hellner, *Kommersiell avtalsrätt*; J. Kleineman, 'Avtalsrättsliga formföreskrifter och allmänna skadeståndsrättsliga ansvarsprinciper' JT 1993–94, 433; J. Kleineman, 'Skadeståndsgrundande uppträdande vid avtalsförhandlingar' JT 1991–92, 125; Ramberg and Ramberg, *Allmän avtalsrätt*.

reached the agreement not complying to the requirements as to form. In situation (ii), where A is a professional and B is a non-professional (consumer), the result would be the same: no damages would be awarded. Everyone, even consumers, should know about the rules on form regarding sales of real estate. Therefore, A would not be considered to have been acting against the requirements of good faith by reaching an agreement without mentioning that the parties are not bound by the agreement until the form requirements have been fulfilled.

If B raised the question of the formality requirements and A misled him about them, A might be considered to have been acting negligently, as he thereby at least gave B reasonable grounds to act on the assumption that the contract was concluded and binding, regardless of the form requirements. If he therefore regarded the sale as completed and paid the estate agents' fees, he is entitled to compensation for these costs, as they were incurred in reliance on the statement made by A. B is also entitled to damages for any other costs incurred in reliance on the statement. In some instances, B would probably be entitled to damages also for losses he made by relying on A's statement in such a way that he did not buy another property which he could have bought at the time. However, B is not entitled to damages for the costs he will incur in the future in trying to find a new, alternative property.[76]

Switzerland

The lack of formality generally prevents a contractual claim for specific performance or the expectation interest. According to OR 11 II the contract is not valid. In Swiss law there is no provision that the lack of formality can be cured by special acts of performance (for example, the transfer of the property).

It depends on the circumstances whether A is liable on the ground of *culpa in contrahendo* in situation (i). If a party knows the lack of formality and does not inform the other party, he might be liable on the ground of *culpa in contrahendo*. Although there is no specific provision in Swiss law, the liability is acknowledged by academic writing and the courts.[77] The defendant has to compensate the negative (reliance) interest.

[76] Herre, *Ersättningar i köprätten. Särskilt om skadeståndsberäkning*, p. 304ff. and NJA 1963.105.

[77] ZürcherKommentar-Schönenberger/Jäggi, OR 11 n. 94ff.; BernerKommentar-Schmidlin, OR 11 n. 186ff.; BaslerKommentar-Schwenzer, OR 11 n. 28ff.; Loser, *Vertrauenshaftung im Schweizerischen Schuldrecht*, nn. 540ff.; BGE, 8 June 1998 no. 4C.447/1997 (in SemJud 1999, 113ff.), E. 3.

However, there is no general duty to disclose because each party has to inform himself about the prerequisites for a valid contract. Academic writers thus demand that the defendant knew or should have known the lack of formality *and* the error of the other party.[78] Moreover, the plaintiff must have relied on the validity in good faith. If he acted negligently the judge may reduce or exclude liability because of his concurrent responsibility.[79] If both parties have the same fault, liability is also excluded.[80]

It also depends on the circumstances whether A is liable on the ground of *culpa in contrahendo* in situation (ii). If a party is negotiating with a professional (a person concluding contracts on the sale of houses by profession), he is entitled to rely on the disclosure of formality requirements. A is hence liable on the ground of *culpa in contrahendo* if he knew the lack of formality. He has to compensate the expenses incurred by B. Moreover, the party can expect the professional to inform himself about the formality requirements. He is therefore liable for negligence even if he did not know the lack of formality.[81] Earlier court decisions have, however, denied a duty to inform oneself.[82] These days it is not clear whether the Federal Court would keep to the old ruling in view of the criticism by writers.

A is liable on the ground of *culpa in contrahendo* in situation (iii). In case of wilful deception about the formality requirements, the defendant is liable and has to compensate at least the negative interest. According to writers the party committing the wilful deception has to compensate even the expectation interest in two cases: if it is proved that the contract would have been concluded in case of due disclosure;[83] and if the fault of the defendant is serious and equity requires compensation of further loss.[84] Some authors are even more favourable to the plaintiff

78 BernerKommentar-Schmidlin, OR 11 n. 188; ZürcherKommentar-Schönenberger/Jäggi, OR 11 n. 96; A. Koller in Koller, *Der Grundstückkauf* (1st edn), no. 370; Gauch, Schluep, Schmid and Rey, *Schweizerisches Obligationenrecht Allgemeiner Teil*, vol. I, n. 583; Schmid, *Die öffentliche Beurkundung von Schuldverträgen*, n. 835ff.

79 BernerKommentar-Schmidlin, OR 11 n. 190. 80 BGE 106 II 42.

81 BernerKommentar-Schmidlin, OR 11 n. 189; BaslerKommentar-Schwenzer, OR 11 n. 28; Koller, above n. 78, n. 370 footnote 177.

82 Vgl. BGE 68 II 237; BGE 106 II 42.

83 BernerKommentar-Merz, ZGB 2 n. 498; BernerKommentar-Schmidlin, OR 11 n. 195; Loser, *Vertrauenshaftung im Schweizerischen Schuldrecht*, n. 542. *Contra*, Schwenzer, *Schweizerisches Obligationenrecht Allgemeiner Teil*, n. 31.43.

84 ZürcherKommentar-Schönenberger/Jäggi, OR 11 n. 96; Merz, *Vertrag und Vertragsschluss*, n. 449; Koller, above n. 78, n. 372f.; Loser, *Vertrauenshaftung im Schweizerischen Schuldrecht*, n. 543. Compensation for further loss is an express rule in

and award a claim for specific performance, that is, a claim for transfer of the property.[85] The Federal Court has so far refused specific performance as long as the contract has not been performed even in part.[86]

The courts, however, award specific performance (for the rest) if the contract has been performed for the most part.[87] In this situation it is not even necessary that the party has committed a wilful deception. And the plaintiff is entitled to compensation in the expectation interest even if he knew[88] the lack of formality.[89] There is a serious dispute about the ground for the liability. Courts and some academic writers mostly base the liability on the general principle of abuse of right (*Rechtsmissbrauch*),[90] other writers will not apply the formality rule at all,[91] and the Federal Court has recently used the concept of liability based on reliance.[92]

Editors' comparative observations

In this case, there is at first sight a significant difference between the jurisdictions, although much of this can be put down to their different approaches to the particular context (a contract for the sale of land) and its formality requirements. Some reporters have difficulty analysing this case because the starting point (a land contract which fails for lack of formality) does not hold for their country. For example, the Danish, French, Norwegian and Spanish reporters begin by observing that there is no formality requirement for such a contract, and therefore either dismiss the case as unreal, or vary the facts to imagine how their system would answer the case if there were a failure of formality, or, more simply, answer on the basis that there is, in fact, a simple liability here in contract.

The much more interesting aspect of the reports is the way in which the several systems analyse the responsibility of parties to a contract

other provisions of *culpa in contrahendo* liability (cf. the Swiss report on case 1); this rule is also applied by analogy if a party has wilfully been misled about the form requirements (cf. CommRomand-Guggenheim, OR 11 n. 29; Gauch, Schluep, Schmid and Rey, *Schweizerisches Obligationenrecht Allgemeiner Teil*, vol. I, n. 557).

85 A. Koller in Koller, *Der Grundstückkauf* (2nd edn), n. 35ff.; *contra*, BernerKommentar-Schmidlin, OR 11 n. 195.

86 BGE 104 II 101f. 87 BGE 116 II 702; BGE 112 II 112.

88 In many cases the parties declare a lower price for the house in the public deed in order to pay less tax.

89 See recently BGE, 7 Jan. 1999 no. 4C/299.1998 (in ZBGR 1999, 387ff.), contrary to the earlier decision BGE 104 II 101.

90 BGE 112 II 112. 91 Cf. BaslerKommentar-Schwenzer, OR 11 n. 23.

92 BGE, 7 Jan. 1999 no. 4C/299.1998 (in ZBGR 1999, 387ff.). Cf. Loser, *Vertrauenshaftung im Schweizerischen Schuldrecht*, n. 961 and the Swiss report on case 1.

which cannot be enforced because of the failure to comply with legal requirements. Some systems take a strong view of the formality requirement, and find that it is generally very difficult to go behind it and to impose a liability where the contractual requirements have not been met. In substance, such systems decline to displace the policy which underlies the formality requirement, although other systems appear to be more open to displacing the policy of the formality, and a consideration of the main case and, especially, the variants to the facts tests the strength of their position. For example, England and Ireland will not normally allow a contractual remedy in a case where the statute provides for a contractual formality which has not been fulfilled, although the English report notes that this stark position is sometimes mitigated by other doctrines: in addition to the law of tort, the doctrine of proprietary estoppel may also operate to avoid the consequences of non-compliance with the formality requirement for land contracts. Proprietary estoppel[93] is a doctrine of equity, which provides remedies where it would be unconscionable for the defendant to deny the claimant's rights where he has encouraged or acquiesced in the claimant's belief that he has or will have a right in property and where the claimant has acted to his detriment in that belief. This is part of a wider area of English law where the courts have developed remedies to protect those who fail to comply with formalities, and shows that sometimes a statutory formality rule is not as absolute as might appear.[94] A not dissimilar, but perhaps simpler, solution is offered by Scotland: a statutory exception to the requirements of writing in contracts for the sale of land, to allow the contract itself to be enforced (or expectation damages to be recovered) by a party who relied materially on the conclusion of the contract. And in Germany (and arguably the Netherlands) A is barred from relying on the lack of formality in the case where he purposely misled B about the requirements, an application of the principle of good faith that resembles the common lawyer's estoppel. The Netherlands, which, as earlier cases in this study have shown, is generally more open to allowing expectation-measure remedies for precontractual liability,[95] could also here award expectation interest damages because the negotiations, even if they were

[93] See also the English report on case 2.

[94] J. Cartwright, 'Formality and Informality in Property and Contract' in Getzler, *Rationalizing Property, Equity and Trusts*, p. 36.

[95] See the Dutch report on case 1.

assumed not to have reached a concluded, enforceable contract because of the predicated formality requirements, would have reached the 'third stage'.

Other jurisdictions, too, take contrasting approaches to the importance of the formality and B's own responsibility for knowing the requirements. Finland, Greece, the Netherlands and Portugal allow the application of the normal rules of *culpa in contrahendo*, focusing generally on the fact that the negotiations had proceeded to such a late stage before A sought to withdraw from finalising the contract. But Austria, France, Germany, Italy, Norway, Sweden and Switzerland will not allow B a remedy on the basis that A is not at fault, or B is himself equally at fault for not knowing the legal requirements. When, however, the variants are added, there are some changes to these groupings, showing that different jurisdictions are prepared more easily than others to allow their normal principles of precontractual liability to displace the policy behind the failure to fulfil the formality requirements. Austria, France, Finland and the Netherlands hold that A assumes liability in all three variant situations ((i) A's knowledge of the formality requirements; (ii) A being a professional; (iii) A misrepresenting the requirements), but Germany, Italy and Norway allow a claim only in situations (ii) and (iii), taking the view that it is not sufficient to change the basic position (non-liability) that A knew the requirements. Sweden and (with some hesitation) Switzerland limit the liability to situation (iii), where A has misled B.

Although England and Ireland would not give any remedy on the facts, they still regard variant (iii) as significantly different because the active misrepresentation by A opens up the possibility of a claim in tort (the problem on the facts being the lack of causation of substantial recoverable damage). This is also an additional ground of recovery for Scotland. So again we see that, in the case of the common law jurisdictions, it is a false statement made by A during the course of the negotiations that makes all the difference to the remedies that are available to B.

Case 12: Confidential design information given during negotiations

Case 12

A is a major manufacturer of computers. B, who has recently established his business of design and manufacture of computer components, approaches him and tells him that he has designed a new form of computer chip which will allow hand-held computers to be produced to run at twice the current speed. A tells B that he is interested in the details, because he may wish to introduce the chip into his new model of computers, and they begin negotiations with a view to contracting for B to manufacture the computer chips for A. During the negotiations A asks for, and B gives, information about the detail of the design of the computer chip which A says he needs in order to evaluate whether the chip will be suitable for his computers. The design is not yet protected by any intellectual property rights (such as patent). After some time, A says that the price B is proposing is too high, and breaks off the negotiations; he then approaches C, asking C to produce the same kind of computer chip at a lower price than B had been asking. A passes on to C the design information he had received from B. C agrees to produce the chips, and a contract is formed between A and C for their production. What liability (in contract, tort, restitution, or any other form of liability), if any, does A have to B? Would it make any difference if B, when giving the detail of the design of the computer chip, told A that he expected A to treat it as confidential?

Discussions

Austria

This is a characteristic case for the application of *culpa in contrahendo* principles. B would not have forwarded the information about the design of the computer chip had A not given the impression that he would conclude a contract with him. The negotiating parties are each protected in the precontractual stage against the other party's arbitrary and unexpected breaking-off of the negotiations, and the mutual duty to take care of each other's economic interests results in a claim for damages if a disloyal party exploits the other party's ideas that were disclosed during the negotiations in the expectation that the contract would be perfected.

From a recent case, where similar problems had to be resolved by the OGH,[1] it may be deduced that parties are bound in good faith to use information about crucial aspects of the contemplated contract, which could be economically exploited by others, only in the context of that contract. If a party decides to abstain from concluding a definite contract after having received such information from the original negotiating party, he is deemed to be contractually bound not to disseminate information on product design that would have remained undisclosed by the original negotiating party. According to the OGH, the original negotiating party may successfully resort to injunctive relief sounding in contract and to a claim for misappropriation of intellectual property (though not yet protected), according to §1041 ABGB:

> Where property has been used for the benefit of another, not in the management of a business, the owner can demand the return thereof in kind, or if such return can no longer be made, the value thereof at the time of its use, even though no advantage was received therefrom.

Thus, A is responsible for restitution that is based on a 'claim for misappropriation' (*Verwendungsanspruch*) falling under 'unjust enrichment'.[2] The value of the frustrated benefit that could have been derived from the misappropriated design determines the amount of compensation.

Another possible ground for a claim, especially in the variation of the facts, could again be §1295(2) ABGB.[3] If one, consciously and without a

1 OGH 22 Mar. 1994, WBl 1994, 279, ecolex 1994, 552: a slogan was developed as a key component of a comprehensive advertising concept for a chain of restaurants by an advertisement contractor, who was later released from the negotiations by the operator of the chain in favour of another advertisement contractor.

2 Cf P. Apathy in Schwimann, *Praxiskommentar ABGB*, vol. V, §1041 nos. 1, 2; H. Koziol, 'Der Verwendungsanspruch bei Ausnützung fremder Kenntnisse und schöpferischer Leistungen', JBl 1978, 239; OGH 17 Mar. 1982, SZ 55/37 (use of a negotiating party's customer list).

3 Cf. Koziol, *Österreichisches Haftpflichtrecht*, vol. II, p. 98. See also the Austrian report on case 1.

legal right, exploits the economic value that another has created by taking all necessary effort and incurring considerable cost, the exploiter is to blame for having wilfully caused damage in a way that amounts to a violation of good morals. This would certainly be the case under the variation to the facts: it is obvious that liability for all B's prospective losses should be imposed on A, when B has told A that he expected A to treat the information about the design of the computer chip as confidential.

In principle, B can choose between these different remedies and measures of recovery. Under *culpa in contrahendo* reliance loss is recoverable: B must be put into the position he would be in had he not given the information about the chips in reliance on A's seriousness in negotiating. It appears, however, that reliance loss and expectation loss may be identical on these facts. Under §1041 ABGB, B may claim restitution of the objective economic value of the profit that A draws from the contract with C by using B's information in an unjustified and unauthorised way. Under §1295(2) ABGB, the quantum of recovery would be the greatest, and would extend to the actual profits made by A in using the information, provided that the court finds that A's conduct amounts to a wilful causation of damage that amounts to a violation of good morals. Whether it would do so is difficult to predict with absolute certainty.

Denmark

Marketing Act §10 prohibits such behaviour as described in the case. In a case decided in 1978,[4] the Copenhagen Commercial Court awarded damages to the plaintiff in a situation somewhat similar to the one described here. The plaintiff, a pharmacist, had negotiated with a physician about developing and marketing together a vegetable fibre pill which the plaintiff had developed and which was not patented. However, the parties abandoned the plan to do it together. The plaintiff had not expressly told the defendant that the recipe for the pill he gave him was confidential. The defendant, who acted as an advisor in the medical industry, had then passed the information he received from the plaintiff on to a medical factory which brought the pill into the market before the plaintiff could do so. The damages awarded were the plaintiff's lost profit, of which the court (as usual) gave a rather modest estimate.

[4] Ugeskrift for Retsvæsen 1978, 305.

England

B may seek an injunction against A to restrain him from using the confidential information or (more likely) he may seek financial remedies against A, either damages for his loss in being unable to make profitable use himself of the information or an account of the profits A makes from the use of the information.

Such remedies are available where the defendant makes unauthorised use or disclosure of information which is confidential and where it was received by the defendant in circumstances which imported the obligation of confidence.[5] The design information here has the necessary quality of confidence: there are cases in which such technical and commercially valuable information has been held to be subject to the duty of confidentiality.[6] And even in the case where B does not expressly require confidentiality it is likely that a court would hold that A ought to have realised that he was expected to respect the confidentiality.[7] There is no doubt about this where B tells A that he expects A to treat the information as confidential. The remedy of injunction may be inappropriate here because the information has already been passed to C, and it is not clear from the facts that the obligations of confidence will necessarily extend to C if he did not know the background to A's obtaining the information. Moreover, where information was given in confidence with a view to monetary reward for it, as in many cases of the sharing of trade secrets in a commercial context, a court will be more likely to refuse an injunction and instead order monetary remedies.[8] A will be liable either to pay damages or to account for his profits.[9] Damages in such cases may be calculated either on the basis of the lost royalty payment which B could have charged for

[5] *Saltman Engineering Co. Ltd v. Campbell Engineering Co. Ltd* (1948) 65 RPC 203.

[6] E.g. *Seager v. Copydex Ltd* [1967] 1 WLR 923 (unpatented design for new form of carpet grip).

[7] Ibid. (parties negotiating towards contract for joint exploitation of invention); *James Industries Ltd's Patents* [1987] RPC 235 (duty of confidence presumed between commercial partners); *Coco v. AN Clark (Engineers) Ltd* [1968] FSR 415, 421 (information of commercial or industrial value given on a business-like basis and with some avowed common object in mind, such as a joint venture or the manufacture of articles by one party for the other, will generally give rise to an obligation of confidence).

[8] *Coco v. AN Clark (Engineers) Ltd*, above n. 7, 423.

[9] *Peter Pan Manufacturing Corporation v. Corsets Silhouette Ltd* [1964] 1 WLR 96. It is not entirely clear when an account of profits will be ordered; perhaps it is more likely where the defendant has acted deliberately: Goff and Jones, *The Law of Restitution*, para. 34.021.

the use of the information, or the price that B might have been able to charge for the outright transfer of the right to the information.[10] Where, as here, the negotiations were with a view to B producing the computer chips for A's computers, the natural remedy in damages seems to be a capital sum to reflect the losses flowing from B being unable to sell the chips to A. Although damages would be for out-of-pocket losses (and therefore have the appearance of a tort claim), and an account of profits would be restitutionary in nature, the proper categorisation of the basis of a claim for breach of confidence is unclear, although well-established in English law.[11]

The United Kingdom is signatory to the Agreement on Trade-Related Aspects of Intellectual Property Rights (TRIPS), which requires parties to provide remedies for disclosure of secret confidential information which has a commercial value;[12] but TRIPS does not provide individuals such as B with direct rights of action.[13]

Finland

A is liable to B according to *culpa in contrahendo* rules. Infringements of the rules on good business behaviour and protection of business secrets constitute the fault required for this liability. The costs B incurs in contract negotiations are items that can be compensated for *culpa in contrahendo*. If A acts against B's express statement on the confidentiality of the information his act is intentional, which makes A's liability even more evident but does not add new elements to it. In addition to this liability, B may have a right to compensation up to the positive interest on the basis of restitution of the profit made by A.

One question, however, has to be considered as concerns the scope of A's liability on the basis of *culpa in contrahendo*. A's fault is not in breaking off the negotiations with B as such, but rather in surreptitiously obtaining B's business secret. This may affect the scope of damages that can be compensated, because the damages in question must be causal consequences of A's fault. This aspect has to be kept in mind when considering, for example, B's costs incurred during the contract negotiations.

[10] *Seager v. Copydex Ltd (No. 2)* [1969] 1 WLR 809.

[11] It was said by Lord Denning MR in *Seager v. Copydex* [1967] 1 WLR 923, 931 to be based on 'the broad principle of equity that he who has received information in confidence shall not take unfair advantage of it'. For analysis of the claim as one in restitution, see generally Goff and Jones, *The Law of Restitution*, ch. 34.

[12] Article 39. [13] *Lenzing AG's European Patent* [1997] RPC 245.

If the intellectual property system is not applicable, the legal protection of anything related to intellectual property rights is based on the general regulation of business practices. According to the Act on Improper Business Practice (1978)[14] any action in business contrary to good business practice or otherwise improper from the point of view of another business firm is prohibited. The Act also contains more detailed regulation of business secrets. According to these provisions no one may obtain without authorisation a business secret or use or reveal any information so obtained. Anyone who has obtained information of a trade secret when performing a task for a business firm, or to whom a technical prototype or technical instructions have been entrusted for carrying out a task or for other business purposes, may not make unauthorised use of it or reveal it. And no one having obtained information of a trade secret, a technical business secret or technical instructions, knowing that the person who disclosed the information had obtained it unlawfully, may make use of or reveal it.[15] A court may issue an injunction against anyone acting in violation of these provisions in business.[16] Deliberate violations of these rules are also subject to criminal sanctions.[17]

There are no provisions concerning damages liability connected with these rules, so general rules of tort law apply. Application of these rules returns the case to the basis of *culpa in contrahendo*. The fault is embodied in infringements of the above rules on good business behaviour and protection of business secrets. So A is liable to B according to *culpa in contrahendo* rules. If B told A that he expected A to treat the information as confidential A's fault is even more evident, constituting an intentional act.

Culpa in contrahendo is designed mainly for the compensation of investments made and other costs incurred in reliance on the contract. Lost profit from the contract not concluded with the other contracting party or other items pertaining to the expectation interest cannot in general be compensated, because *culpa in contrahendo* is usually understood as being connected to the reliance interest only.[18] In this case, no losses are expressly mentioned. Of course, any costs B incurred during the contract negotiations can be compensated for *culpa in contrahendo*.

[14] *L sopimattomasta menettelystä elinkeinotoiminnassa*, s. 1. [15] Section 4.

[16] Section 6(3).

[17] Act on Improper Business Practice, s. 10; Penal Code, ch. 30, ss. 5 and 6.

[18] See, e.g., Hemmo, *Sopimus ja delikti*, p. 205.

However, in addition, B will wish to claim the lost profit from the intended but not concluded contract with A, and especially the profit A has made by using B's design information in making the contract with C. A's profit consists of the reduced contracting costs between A and C because there is no need to design the relevant computer chip once again. Also possibly the profit which A makes from the contract with C counts as B's lost profit to the extent that it can be traced back to the use of B's design: in fact, all the profit that A can make by using this information, including, for example, the sale of products manufactured on the basis of the information.

A party's lost profit from the intended but not concluded contract with the original contracting party cannot be compensated on the basis of the negative interest. As concerns B's right to the profit made by A by using the information, we have to seek a possible basis of compensation in other rules. Perhaps we can seek here analogous help from provisions on compensation for using an object protected by intellectual property rights, on the one hand, and from general rules of restitution, on the other. Finnish Patent Act (1967), section 58, provides that anyone who has infringed a patent intentionally or negligently has to pay compensation for the use of the invention as well as for all other damage caused by the infringement. If there is only slight negligence the compensation may be adjusted. In cases of infringements that are not intentional or negligent any compensation for the use of the invention will be imposed only as far as it can be considered reasonable.

A profit made by the tortfeasor in connection with the tortious act is in itself no basis for imposing tort (or contract) law liability on him towards the injured party.[19] However, the rules of unjust enrichment (*condictio sine causa*), corresponding in some aspects to common law restitution, entitle in some cases a person at whose expense another person has made a profit to have restitution of the profit. According to these rules, there has to be a profit of one person corresponding to a loss of another person, both arising from one and the same origin.[20] In this case, A's profit and B's loss may correspond as required in the rules of unjust enrichment. B may therefore have the right to restitution of the profit made by A. But the value of B's positive interest is in any case the upper limit of his right: the maximum loss he can have suffered for

[19] See the Finnish report on case 2.

[20] Aurejärvi and Hemmo, *Velvoiteoikeuden oppikirja*, p. 226.

not having concluded the contract with A. This means that, although the positive interest is not as such compensated, B can have a right to compensation amounting to the positive interest on the basis of restitution of the profit made by A.

The possibility of compensating pure economic loss (in addition to investment and contracting costs dealt with above) on the basis of *culpa in contrahendo* is somewhat unclear. Perhaps the additional preconditions of compensation applied in general tort law have to be taken into account here, too, in spite of the 'neighbourhood' of the contract law sphere.[21] But infringement of good practice, as in this case, is commonly considered to form some basis for compensating economic losses in tort law.[22] So the loss suffered by B, if any, can be compensated notwithstanding the rules in tort law on economic losses.

France

The first question is whether A is liable even though nothing was said during the negotiations about the confidentiality of the information. In the absence of a negotiation agreement (*avant-contrat*), tort law is applicable. As seen before,[23] three conditions have to be fulfilled: fault, harm and causation.

Has A committed a fault? In such a case, article 1382 of the Civil Code seems applicable. One commits a fault when using somebody else's information without permission. In the absence of a contractual obligation to keep the information secret, there is a debate amongst academic writers whether the information must be new and exclusive to deserve the law's protection.[24] The condition is here, however, fulfilled.

[21] Hemmo, *Sopimus ja delikti*, p. 206. On the preconditions for compensating pure economic loss in tort law, see the Finnish report on case 1.

[22] See, e.g., Routamo and Ståhlberg, *Suomen vahingonkorvausoikeus [Finnish Tort Law]*, p. 182ff. and Hemmo, *Vahingonkorvausoikeuden oppikirja [A Textbook on Tort Law]*, p. 118ff. On Finnish court practice, see, e.g., KKO 1991:79 (untruthful comparison with products of a competitor in advertising). Also the degree of fault, in cases of *culpa in contrahendo*, has been considered possibly to have some effect on compensation for economic loss (Hemmo, *Sopimus ja delikti*, p. 77). So if A has acted against B's express statement on the confidentiality of the information, A's liability could be based also on an intentional act.

[23] See the French report on case 1.

[24] For: J. Huet and F. Dupuis-Touboul, 'Violation de la confidentialité des négociations' ICC 1990, 239ff., reproduced in PA, 4 Apr. 1990, p. 9. Against: Com 3 Oct. 1978, D.1980, 55, note J. Schmidt.

This liability is not controversial and seems widely accepted by the courts[25] and by writers.[26]

The damages should cover the entire loss suffered by B. The harm here is undoubtedly caused by A's fault. It is hard, though, to go further in the description of how the damages should be evaluated since academic writing largely ignores this question. The judge plays here a major role because he is free to choose the remedy with very little control from the Cour de cassation. It is probable that B will be able to obtain an injunction to force C to stop the chip's illegal production. This remedy leaves very little place for damages because it covers the entire loss.[27] To a certain extent, the application of tort law here will fill in for the absence of protection of intellectual property rights and lead to the same result for B.[28]

Is the solution different if B stresses during the negotiations the confidentiality of the information given to A? The extent of A's liability is not affected in this hypothesis. The solution may, though, be a little different since French law could theoretically consider that a negotiation contract is concluded. This pre-contract (*avant-contrat*) includes a confidentiality clause which forbids A from using or giving the information to another. The existence of a contract here will not affect the extent of A's liability but will mean that contractual liability procedural rules (such as jurisdiction of the courts and time limits)[29] must be applied. Because it is difficult to prove the existence of such an oral contract, however, it is likely that B will sue under tort law.

[25] Rouen 13 Jan. 1981, D.1983, 53, note A. Lucas; Paris 8 July 1972, JCP 1973, II, no. 17509, note J.-M. Leloup; Com 3 Oct. 1978, Bull Civ IV, no. 208; Com 3 June 1986, Bull Civ IV, no. 110; Paris, 30 June 1997, Gaz Pal 7 Jan. 1998, somm.

[26] R. Saint-Halary, 'Le secret des affaires et le droit français' in *Travaux de l'Association H. Capitant*, vol. XXV, *Le secret et le droit* (Paris, 1976), p. 263ff., esp. p. 269; P. Mousseron, 'Conduite des négociations contractuelles et responsabilité civile délictuelle' RTDCom 1998, 243ff., esp. 256; Ph. Le Tourneau, 'La rupture des négotiations' RTDCom 1998, 479ff., esp. no. 18, p. 486; G. Forbin, 'Comment gérer les informations confidentielles en cours de pourparlers', *Rev. de droit des affaires internationales* 1998, no. 4/5, p. 477ff.

[27] No punitive damages are conceivable under French law: see the French report on case 1.

[28] On this point, see J. Passa, 'Propos dissidents sur la sanction du parasitisme économique' D.2000, Chron. 297.

[29] Mousseron *et al.*, *Technique contractuelle*, no. 200ff.; *Le contrat, actes du 94 ème congrès des notaires de France* (Lyon, 1998), no. 1062.

Germany

Since B's design has not yet been registered, he is not entitled to damages on the ground of an intellectual property right (such as patent, copyright, design or utility model). This, however, does not imply that the design may be used freely by anybody else. The courts and the majority of academic writers no longer regard intellectual property legislation as an all-conclusive regulation and there is a growing tendency in German law to make other legal instruments available for the protection of intellectual works.

A person's intellectual creativity, albeit not covered by an intellectual property right, may be protected by the Unfair Competition Act:[30]

> §1 UWG: Who, in the course of business, for the purpose of competition, acts in a manner contrary to public policy, may be subject to an injunction to refrain from this act or to a claim for damages.

It has been held that the imitation of another person's intellectual work is contrary to public policy as defined by this provision if a competitor slavishly imitates the work of a competitor, that is, if he deceives the market about the origin of the work, immediately appropriates the results of the work of a competitor, or abuses the confidence of a competitor in order to gain possession of his knowledge.[31] A, it is true, has abused B's confidence; the parties, however, are not competitors. This is only the case with C. Therefore, A can only be held liable if C is liable according to §1 UWG *and* A must be regarded as his accomplice.[32] C could be liable for immediately appropriating B's chip design, provided he knew or could easily have known that the design was not A's but nevertheless did not investigate A's title to pass it on. These conditions, it seems, are not met. If, however, C is liable, any form of A's participation in C's act will suffice. The measure of damages is discussed below.

A is liable on the ground of §§280(1) 311(2) No. 1 BGB (*culpa in contrahendo*). The special relationship (*Sonderrechtsverhältnis*) created between negotiating parties by virtue of the law (*gesetzliches Schuldverhältnis*) imposes on a party the (collateral) duty to pay regard to the whole of the other party's assets he comes into contact with during

[30] *Gesetz gegen den unlauteren Wettbewerb* (UWG).

[31] Baumbach and Hefermehl, *Wettbewerbsrecht*, §1 UWG para. 433ff.

[32] *Mittäter*: cf. §§830(2), 840(1) BGB.

the negotiations (*Obhuts- oder Erhaltungspflicht*).[33] Therefore, a party is obliged (i) to treat information sought from the other party in order to assert his bargaining position as confidential; and (ii) not to make use of such information to the disadvantage of the other party. A, therefore, was not allowed to pass on the design to C without B's consent. He must put B into the position he would be without his breach of confidence.

As a result, B is entitled to damages which he may calculate in a threefold manner.[34] A must either recompense the profits B would have made if he (B) had marketed the design himself; or pay the sum he would have had to pay to B for a licence of the design; or disgorge the profits made by his own dealing with the design.

A is also liable in tort. A may be liable on the ground of §823(1) BGB. This depends on whether the design comes within the term of an 'other right of another' (*sonstiges Recht*) as defined by this provision. It is the unanimous view nowadays that a *sonstiges Recht* requires a position which by law is allocated to the exclusive disposal of a certain person (position with *Zuweisungsgehalt und Ausschlußfunktion*). The Bundesgerichtshof has held that a computer chip design corresponds to this definition if it constitutes a business secret which comes very close to an intellectual property right.[35] It would seem, therefore, that B has a claim according to §823(1) BGB, but the facts of the case are not detailed enough to permit a definitive conclusion. A is, however, liable on the ground of §826 BGB, as the law will not tolerate the abuse of information gained confidentially and A well knew that the passing on of the design would cause economic loss to B. B is entitled to calculate the damages in the threefold manner mentioned above.

A's liability in restitution is dependent on whether B's design amounts to a position at his exclusive disposal (position with *Zuweisungsgehalt und Ausschlußfunktion*).[36] In this case, A is liable on the ground of illicit *gestio negotiorum*:

§687 BGB: . . . If a person treats the matter of another as his own, although knowing that he is not entitled to do so, the principal may enforce the claims based on §§677, 678, 681, 682. If he does enforce them, he is liable to the manager as provided for in §684 sent. 1.

33 Soergel-Wiedemann, vor §275 para. 175; MünchKomm-Emmerich, vor §275 para. 77.
34 BGH, decision of 18 Feb. 1977, NJW 1977, 1062, 1063.
35 BGH, decision of 18 Feb. 1977, NJW 1977, 1062, 1063.
36 Staudinger-Lorenz, §812 para. 23ff.

Hence, if B exercises the option granted by sentence 1, he is entitled, according to §§687(2), 681 sentence 2,[37] 667[38] BGB to claim anything A received by virtue of his management. Then, however, he must repay the outlays A inevitably had to incur in order to manage the affair.[39]

If the design represents a position at the exclusive disposal of B and provided B does not exercise the option granted by §687(2) BGB, then A is liable on the ground of unjust enrichment. According to §812 sentence 1, 2nd alternative BGB,[40] a party interfering with another party's position with *Zuweisungsgehalt* must, as a rule, make good the value of such a position. As A knew that he was not entitled to pass on the design, he is barred from the defence of change of position.[41]

It would not make any difference if B told A that he expected him to treat the details of the design as confidential. The parties thereby would only contractually confirm a precontractual duty already established by virtue of the law.

Greece

B has several remedies.

First, article 197 GCC provides that the parties to the negotiations for the conclusion of a contract must abide by the principle of pre-contractual good faith. Although the exact scope of this obligation becomes apparent on a case by case basis, several aspects of it form the core of its content. In general, after commencing negotiations the parties must not act in a manner which contravenes a reasonable bond of trust that develops between them. More specifically, each party must negotiate in earnest, safeguard the interests of the other party and provide the other party with the information which is necessary in order to decide whether or not to conclude a contract. Consistent with

37 §681 BGB: 'The agent shall notify the principal, as soon as practicable, of the undertaking of the management of the matter, and await his decision, unless there is danger in delay. For the rest the provisions of §§666 to 668, applicable to a mandatary, apply *mutatis mutandis* to the obligation of the manager.'

38 §667 BGB: 'A mandatary is bound to hand over to his mandator all that he receives for the execution of the mandate and all that he obtains from the charge of the matter.'

39 §684 BGB: 'If the conditions of §683 do not exist, the principal is bound to return to the manager all that he acquires through the management of the matter under the provisions relating to the return of unjust enrichment. If the principal ratifies the management of the affair, the claim specified in §683 belongs to the manager.'

40 See the German report on case 11.

41 §§818(2), (3), 819 BGB.

the obligation to provide information is the obligation to treat the information received from the other party as confidential. In particular, the sensitive information that relates to business secrets and other kinds of trade assets, irrespective of whether they are protected by other provisions of the law, must be treated as confidential. Accordingly, whether B had told A that he expected him to treat the information provided as confidential would not make any difference, because confidentiality is already part of the obligation to conduct negotiations in good faith. Therefore, A, by divulging to a third party sensitive information with obvious economic significance, which was entrusted to him by B in the course of negotiations, acts contrary to precontractual good faith. B can claim compensation from A on the basis of article 198 GCC. The compensation will comprise the reliance interest, which includes the positive and negative (loss of opportunity/profit) loss. In particular, in this case, B may recover from A the profit the latter made by selling B's secret trade asset to C. Clearly, the reliance interest includes the lost profit and B could claim that irrespective of the legal basis upon which he bases his claim.[42] Given these circumstances, the measure of the damages, as generally accepted in the legal literature and reaffirmed by case law, may be higher than the expectation interest.[43] In addition, it is also possible for B to base his claim against A on unjust enrichment,[44] although in terms of quantum of compensation he would not be better off.

In addition, B may base a claim for compensation on the Civil Code provisions on delict.[45] B will have to prove fault on the part of A in causing the damage, that is, that A was either negligent or intended to inflict damage on B's interests. Compensation in delict covers all damage causally linked to the unlawful behaviour; compensation for immaterial damage (such as damage to market credibility, prospects of growth or the loss of a cutting-edge in market innovation) may also be claimed.[46]

An alternative to the above remedies would be for B to invoke articles 16 to 19 of Law 146/1914 on unfair competition. These provisions provide civil and penal protection for commercial and business secrets. In particular, B may base a claim on articles 17 and 18 of that Act for compensation of the damage incurred. Under article 19,

[42] See below for delict and the Act on Unfair Competition.
[43] See the Greek report on case 1. [44] Article 904ff. GCC.
[45] Articles 914 and 919 GCC. [46] Article 932 GCC.

a different shorter limitation period applies to this remedy than the limitation of five years which applies to a claim in delict or pre-contractual liability.

Ireland

A is liable to B for breach of confidence. It makes no difference whether or not there was any express statement that the information should be treated as confidential.

A defendant who is proved to have used confidential information belonging to the plaintiff without his consent is guilty of an infringement of the plaintiff's rights.[47] There are three essential elements.[48] First, the information must have the necessary quality of confidence. Secondly, the information must have been imparted in circumstances imposing a duty of confidentiality. Finally, there must be unauthorised use of the information to the detriment of the plaintiff. Each of these elements will be dealt with in turn.

The information must have the necessary quality of confidence. In *House of Spring Gardens v. Point Blank Ltd*,[49] the court set down four criteria for confidentiality. First, the information must be that which the owner believes will, if released, cause him damage or gain advantage for his competitors; secondly, the owner must believe the information is confidential; thirdly, the owner's belief must be reasonable; and finally, the facts must be judged in light of the relevant industry standards. These criteria are satisfied by showing that the information concerned is inaccessible to the public. Simply put, this means that a member of the public would have to expend special labours to reproduce the information. In *Point Blank*, the fact that the design of bullet-proof vests was drawn from information that was publicly available did not remove the confidential nature of the information since it would have required special labours to assemble it. Similarly in *Aksjeselskapet Jotul v. Waterford Iron Founders Ltd*,[50] the defendant had been given the designs of a particular furnace. It used these designs to reproduce a furnace made by the plaintiff. The plaintiff sued, claiming that the defendant had breached the duty of confidentiality with respect to the design. The defendant argued that the furnace could have been purchased on the open market, dismantled and from that process a design could have

[47] *Saltman Engineering Co. Ltd v. Campbell Engineering Co. Ltd* (1948) 65 RPC 203.
[48] *Coco v. AN Clark (Engineers) Ltd* [1968] FSR 415. [49] [1984] IR 611.
[50] (Unreported, High Court) 8 November 1977, McWilliam J.

been obtained. Thus, it claimed that the design was effectively in the public domain. The court rejected the defendant's argument. The dismantling process would have involved special labours.

If the information is found to be confidential, the next step is to show that the receipt of the information is in circumstances where there is an obligation of confidentiality. This obligation of confidentiality depends on the nature of the relationship between the parties or the nature of the information and the circumstances by which the defendant obtained the information.[51] Certain relationships presuppose such an obligation. In precontractual situations, the true test is therefore the latter, sometimes called the 'limited purpose' rule. Under this rule, it is the acquisition of confidential information on the basis that it will be used for a limited purpose and kept secret that render it unconscionable to permit the defendant to use such information.[52] In *Winterthur Swiss Insurance Co. v. Insurance Corporation of Ireland*,[53] the court held that the right to photocopy documentation was limited by the fact that the photocopies could only be used for the limited purpose for which they were obtained.

Finally, the confidential information must be used in an unauthorised manner. Generally speaking, this poses no difficulty. However, it is not clear whether there is a requirement to show that the misuse was detrimental to the plaintiff. No mention was made of such a requirement in *Waterford Iron Founders* but in *Ryan v. Capital Leasing*,[54] the court appeared to impose a requirement that the plaintiff show loss or detriment. The point remains undecided, therefore, but the better view is that there is no requirement to show detriment, but without it, any award of damages would be nominal only.

Finally, the jurisdictional basis for confidentiality of commercial secrets has caused some concern. In the absence of a contract, there is some argument as to whether the action is one of equity or tort. The remedies available to a plaintiff do not render this problem any easier. A successful plaintiff may seek an injunction restraining the defendant, an account of profits made by the defendant, an order for delivery or destruction of any goods, a constructive trust or an award of damages. An award of damages is usually based on the lost opportunity to the plaintiff though the calculation cannot be exact.

[51] *Ansell Rubber Co. v. Allied Rubber Industries* [1967] VR 37.
[52] *Stephens v. Avery* [1988] 2 All ER 477. [53] [1989] ILRM 13.
[54] (Unreported, High Court) 2 April 1993, Lynch J.

Italy

This case mainly concerns the law on trade secrets (*segreto d'impresa*).

Since the case refers to a new product invented by B (a computer chip), but not yet protected under the usual intellectual property right rules, it would imply the application of the rules on industrial secrets (*segreto industriale*).[55] In general, Italian law provides protection for trade secrets on three levels.

First, protection derives from articles 41, 35 and 9 of the Italian Constitution, which protect the exploitation of business assets,[56] scientific and intellectual work,[57] and the promotion of scientific and technical research.[58]

Secondly, under criminal law, article 623 of the Penal Code provides a general protection for industrial secrets (*segreto industriale*). The interpretation by academic writers[59] about secrecy requirements seems to be more severe than current case law.[60] The Italian Supreme Court has even provided protection where an invention lacked the required patent because of the absence of innovation and originality.[61]

Finally, Italian law provides civil liability under article 2598 of the Civil Code concerning unfair competition. It is generally recognised that the article covers not only scientific or industrial inventions, but also fabrication processes, client lists, sale techniques, commercial know-how and inventions not covered by patent.[62] Moreover, a recent

[55] Italian law distinguishes between secrets concerning the invention of new products (*segreto industriale*) and inventions related to new operative and organisatory systems (*segreto commerciale*). See, e.g., arts. 623 and 622 c.p.

[56] Article 41 n.1. [57] Article 35.

[58] Article 9. See, in particular, V. Oppo, 'Creazione ed esclusiva nel diritto industriale' RDCo 1964, I, 203.

[59] In particular, requiring that (i) inventions should not concern notorious facts and elements; (ii) the secrecy duty be legally relevant; (iii) the party's conduct does not constitute a renunciation of the secret. For academic writing, see A. Frignani, 'Segreti d'impresa' Dig. Comm. 1996, XIII, 341; F. Petrone, 'Segreti (delitti contro l'inviolabilità dei)' Novissimo Dig., XVI, 952; F. Pisa, 'Segreto (tutela penale del)' Enc. Giur. Treccani 1992, XXVIII; G. Vigna Dubolino, 'Segreto (reati in materia di)' Enc. Dir. XLI, 1989, 1037.

[60] PRET-P. Cremona, 17 Jan. 1995; App. Milano, 10 Nov. 1992; PRET-P. Nocera Inferiore, 30 May 1992; PRET-P. Monza, 15 Oct. 1983.

[61] Cass pen., 7 Feb. 1973, G. Miglietta and others, *Foro it*, Rep. 1974; Cass pen., 3 June 1977, F. Uguzzoni, *Foro it*, 1979, II, 304.

[62] For academic writing, see A. Barbetta, 'La concorrenza dell'ex-dipendente', App. Milano, 1 Oct. 1963, RDI 1965, II, 207; P.G. Marchetti, 'Sull'idoneità al danno dell'atto di concorrenza sleale con particolare riferimento al cosiddetto tentativo di

decreto legislativo,[63] modifying Italian patent law,[64] has expressly recognised the protection of trade secrets. Despite the lack of case law concerning the rule, writers consider it as specifying the content of article 2598 of the Civil Code.[65] It must, however, be emphasised that the new modification[66] provides protection only when secret information has been subjected by its owner to reasonable measures of 'keeping secret'. In the present case it does not seem that B has adopted any measures in order to avoid the disclosure of his invention.

A duty of secrecy with regard to confidential information is sometimes deemed to be implied into the general principle of good faith during negotiations. However, Italian case law requires a specific agreement if there is an agreement about non-disclosure during negotiations.[67] Also, according to commercial practice, parties usually provide appropriate letters of intent about this duty of non-disclosure. The express provision of such a duty is considered a specific case of liability.[68]

It seems, then, that in the present case it would be very difficult for B to justify his behaviour. B seems to have acted carelessly, not only because he started negotiations without providing at least patent protection for his invention, but overall because of the lack of any statement concerning the duty of non-disclosure about confidential information.

Where there is liability, damages for unfair competition are generally related to the damage suffered by B rather than the restitution of A's illicit profit.

Netherlands

Was A free to use the information he had asked for and obtained from B for his own purposes as he did, or should he be held liable? There do not seem to be any specific authorities on this type of case under Dutch law.

Arguments against A's liability could be the following. First, an *a contrario* argument could be derived from the law of intellectual property and from economics. Whatever is not (yet) protected by that law

spionaggio' RDI 1969, II, 78; F. Scirè, *La concorrenza sleale nella giurisprudenza*; L. Sordelli, 'Sul know how' in *Studi in memoria di Biscardi*.

63 In particular art.14 D.Lgs. 19 Mar. 1996, n. 198.

64 By introducing art.6 bis in r.d. 29 June 1939, n. 1127 (*legge brevetti*).

65 See, in particular, A. Frignani, 'Segreti d'impresa' Dig. Comm. 1996, XIII, 341, 350.

66 Article 6 bis(c) *legge brevetti*, above n. 64.

67 TRIB-T. Milano, 13 Apr. 1995.

68 TRIB-T. Milano, 19 Nov. 1984.

(especially patent law) should be open to free use by any competitor in the market. In other words, it would be an undesirable interference with patent law if the same protection was provided without a patent. Secondly, B could have explicitly asked for confidentiality. If confidentiality was so important to him, why did he not stipulate that the information was confidential? These arguments are inspired by a strong concept of party autonomy.

Arguments for liability would lie in the idea that A should take B's interest into account and in the lack of justification (consideration) for the transfer of a benefit from B to A. On that ground, various dogmatic constructions could be developed in order to protect B. First, an implied agreement of confidentiality could be constructed.[69] Somewhat more straightforward (and less fictitious) would be the imposition of a legal precontractual duty of confidentiality,[70] if necessary based on the general duty of precontractual good faith which generally obliges each party to negotiations to take the other party's interests into account.[71] Yet another solution would be tort law (delictual liability): to appropriate other people's ideas and/or confidential information would be regarded as an 'act breaching a rule of unwritten law pertaining to proper social conduct'.[72] Finally, a claim could be based on unjustified enrichment.[73]

Whether A would actually be liable under Dutch law is difficult to say. However, on the facts restitution of the profit which A made with B's ideas seems appropriate.

It would make a crucial difference if B, when giving the detail of the design of the computer chip, told A that he expected A to treat it as confidential. In that case A, by accepting the information, should be held to have agreed, even without saying anything,[74] to a confidentiality agreement. Since he has not kept the information confidential he is liable for breach of contract which includes not only the expectation interest but also the restitution interest.[75]

Norway

A appears to have broken the obligation of secrecy with respect to the material he has had the opportunity to peruse, and also to have made

[69] Article 3:37 BW. [70] Similar to art. 2:302 PECL.
[71] *Baris/Riezenkamp* HR, 15 Nov. 1957, NJ 1958, 67; see the Dutch report on case 1.
[72] Article 6:162 BW. [73] Article 6:612 BW. [74] Article 3:37 BW.
[75] Article 6:104 BW.

unlawful use of this material. B, therefore, has the right to monetary compensation.

With respect to *making use* of the information from B, A violates both the Marketing Act, section 7, with respect to business secrecy, and section 8, with respect to technological aids. Both rules are assumed, *inter alia*, to concern situations in which information is passed on as part of an effort to obtain a contract.[76] It follows from section 17 of the Act that a breach of these regulations is subject to penalty. The question of damages, or compensation generally, is not regulated by statute. Nonetheless, it is a correct assumption that being subjected to a breach of these regulations entitles one to claim damages.[77]

The passing on of information about the data chip is not in itself subject to the Marketing Act, sections 7 and 8. On the other hand, the general clause of the Marketing Act, section 1, stating that one should not 'commit actions contrary to good business practice between business owners' would apply.[78] Most likely, this rule corresponds to the position one would have arrived at based on the legal principle of good faith in precontractual relationships. Breach of the Marketing Act, section 1, is not a criminal offence, but gives the right to compensation.

There is some lack of clarity in valuing B's claim. General liability principles can be applied. This means that B can claim damages for losses incurred as a result of A's unlawful action. Frequently, however, this might lead to an unsatisfactory result. It might be difficult for B to prove that he has suffered substantial losses, for instance the loss of market-share. For this reason, in practice it has been considered from the point of view of monetary compensation or enrichment.[79] The aggrieved party has the right to reasonable compensation for the use the other party has had of the material. It is, however, still unclear what is the legal right in this respect.

Where B requests secrecy, the answer is the same. But when B imposes on A an obligation of secrecy with respect to the information

[76] Simonsen, *Precontractual Liability*, p. 384ff.

[77] See recommendation by Konkurranselovkomiteen (Competition Law Commission) June 1966, pp. 83–4; Ot prp (Proposition to the Odelsting) no. 57 (1971–72) pp. 6, 57; Rt 1959, 712; Rt 1964, 238; Rt 1990, 607; Rt 1997, 199; Lunde, *God forretningsskikk næringsdrivande imellom*, p. 35; Grimstad and Løchen, *Markedsføringsloven*, p. 250; Monsen, *Berikelseskrav*, pp. 68–82; and Gaarder, NIR 1968, 245.

[78] Krüger, *Norsk kontraktsrett [Norwegian Contract Law]*, pp. 232 and 590, indicates this.

[79] For a discussion about how to assess compensation with respect to infringement of a trademark, see Lassen, *Oversikt over norsk varemerkerett [Overview of Norwegian Trademark Law]*, p. 399.

given about the data system, the claim for monetary compensation should be based on contract law. The amount of the claim is determined in the same way as discussed above.

If the computer chip is considered property, it could be protected according to the Protection of Integrated Circuits Design Act.[80] Breach of exclusive rights allows for economic compensation according to section 6 if the offence has been committed intentionally or through negligence. Reasonable compensation should be made as part of the settlement for compensatory damages.

Portugal

B is entitled to compensation under the rules of precontractual liability (article 227 of the Civil Code) for all the loss he suffered from the disclosure of the information.

Legal writers say that among the duties imposed by the good faith rules in the precontractual stage is a duty of loyalty,[81] which naturally forbids any party to disclose to anyone information belonging to the other party that was given with the intention of performing a future contract. The design of a computer chip that B has made and is now negotiating is certainly privileged information that cannot be disclosed without his consent. As A has given that information to C, he acted against the duty of good faith and he will be liable for the losses suffered by B in losing the possibility of negotiating the design information. It would not make any difference if B told A that he expected A to treat the information as confidential. That would only make into an express term that which is already established by the rules of good faith.

In Portuguese law, unfair competition is only regulated in article 260 of the Código da Propriedade Industrial as a criminal offence. However, legal writers accept that it also involves tort liability subject to the general rules,[82] which can also constitute a cause of action for damages.

The possibility of a claim for disgorgement in this situation is very controversial. According to Portuguese law, the unjust enrichment action does not involve disgorgement of profits but only restitution of value.[83] Unlike the codes of certain other countries, the Portuguese Civil Code does not make any references to illicit *negotiorum gestio* from

[80] *Lov om vern av kretsmønstre for integrerte kretser*, 15 June 1990, no. 27.

[81] Cordeiro, *Da Boa Fé no Direito Civil*, p. 551ff., *Tratado de Direito Civil Português*, I-1, p. 399ff. and Leitão, *Direito das Obrigações*, I, p. 316.

[82] Leitão, *Estudo de Direito Privado sobre a Cláusula Geral de Concorrência desleal*, p. 147ff.

[83] Article 479 CC.

which such a claim can arise, but only refers to the normal *negotiorum gestio*.[84] However, some legal writers accept that in Portuguese law a claim based on illicit *negotiorum gestio* is also possible by analogy, as an option to the unjust enrichment action.[85] Others are against this possibility.[86] There is no case law on this matter. For the legal writers who support this possibility, if B exercises that option he would be entitled to claim anything A received by virtue of his management,[87] but he would also have to pay the expenses which A incurred in his activity.[88]

Scotland

Even though the design of the computer chip is not the subject of any intellectual property rights, it may still be classified as confidential information. As such, an obligation will rest upon A not to use the information or to disclose it to any other party. This may be implied even in the absence of any statement by B that the information was confidential: if A knew or ought reasonably to have known that it was confidential, the obligation of confidence will be imposed upon A whether or not A has specifically agreed to respect its confidentiality. B's statement to A that he expected A to treat the information as confidential would support the imposition of an obligation of confidentiality, provided that the information had the necessary quality of confidence.[89] Such liability will be imposed in delict, breach of confidence being one of the nominate delicts in Scots law.[90] Such a delictual claim would entitle B to damages from A, although possibly only if the court is satisfied that A's breach of confidence was made with knowledge that the information was confidential.[91]

The measure of damages for breach of confidence in Scotland is a matter on which there is little authority.[92] In one case[93] it was held that the measure might be either the market value of the information as

[84] Article 464ff.

[85] Varela, *Das Obrigações em geral* I, p. 454, note (3) and Leitão, *Direito das Obrigações*, I, p. 472.

[86] Coelho, *O enriquecimento e o dano*, p. 88ff. and Mendes, *A gestão de negócios no Direito Civil Português*, p. 259ff.

[87] Article 465 e), by analogy. [88] Article 468 no. 1, by analogy.

[89] *The Laws of Scotland: Stair Memorial Encyclopaedia* (1993), vol. 18, paras. 1458–66.

[90] *Lord Advocate v. Scotsman Publications* 1989 SLT 705.

[91] *The Laws of Scotland: Stair Memorial Encyclopaedia* (1993), vol. 18, para. 1476; Thomson, *Delictual Liability*, p. 32.

[92] *The Laws of Scotland: Stair Memorial Encyclopaedia* (1993), vol. 18, para. 1489.

[93] *Levin v. Caledonian Produce (Holdings) Ltd* 1975 SLT (Notes) 69.

between a willing buyer and a willing seller, or a consultant's fee for the information, depending upon the nature and quality of the information. The judge expressed no concluded view on an alternative argument that the confider might recover what the confidant had saved in time and trouble in obtaining the information by its own efforts. If the information was confidential, then B may, in addition to a damages claim, have a claim for account of profits should A have profited from an intentional breach of confidence.[94] If it can be said that A has used the design for its profit, then there may be, in the alternative, a claim under recompense, on the basis that B has been enriched by A's work and that A did not intend to donate such enrichment.[95] Such a claim may, however, be met with the counter-argument that the information (the design) was provided *in suo* by B, that is, that the expenditure was made for B's own benefit. This counter-argument succeeded in *Site Preparations v. Secretary of State for Scotland*.[96] In this case, the pursuer had prepared plans in an attempt to win a contract with the defender. The pursuer was denied an action in recompense even although the defender had taken some benefit from the plans, as the court held that the plans had been prepared to enable the pursuer to win a valuable contract. Any benefit received by the defender was incidental to this *in suo* expenditure.

B would be able to interdict A against further use or disclosure of the information[97] and also C, provided that C knew or ought to have known that the information was confidential.[98] B may be able to obtain from the court an order for the delivery up and/or destruction of material in the hands of A and C containing the confidential information.[99] Interdict might be linked with claims for damages, account of profits/ recompense and delivery-up/destruction of infringing material.

Spain

A is liable to B on the grounds of articles 13 and 18.5[a] of the law on unfair competition.[100] Article 13 establishes that the use or disclosure of any kind of industrial secrets by one who obtained them licitly (but

[94] *The Laws of Scotland: Stair Memorial Encyclopaedia* (1993), vol. 18, para. 1490.
[95] *Levin v. Caledonian Produce (Holdings) Ltd* 1975 SLT (Notes) 69, 71.
[96] 1975 SLT (Notes) 41.
[97] *The Laws of Scotland: Stair Memorial Encyclopaedia* (1993), vol. 18, para. 1488.
[98] *Lord Advocate v. Scotsman Publications* 1989 SLT 705; see also *Quilty v. Windsor* 1999 SLT 346, 356.
[99] *The Laws of Scotland: Stair Memorial Encyclopaedia* (1993), vol. 18, para. 1491.
[100] Ley 3/1991, 10 Jan. 1991 de Competencia Desleal, BOE no. 10, 11 Jan. 1991.

with the duty of confidentiality) or illicitly is considered an act of unfair competition. In this case, A obtained the information about the computer chip during negotiations. Knowing that this chip was a considerable technological advance, A at least implicitly accepted a precontractual duty of confidentiality, imposed by good faith, even if this was not explicitly mentioned and even though it is not covered by any special legal rule.[101] Passing on the information to a third party and in that way using the secret also for himself is to be qualified without doubt as an act contrary to fair competition. In that case, on the basis of article 18 of the Law on Unfair Competition, B can probably demand, on the one hand, that the production of the chip be stopped[102] and, on the other hand, claim the losses suffered, as far as loss has been caused intentionally or negligently by violation of the Act.[103] A, by passing on the secret for his own use and profit, intentionally causes loss to B: the loss B suffers by not being able to obtain any or as much gain by selling and producing his invention (*lucrum cessans*).

Sweden

A is liable to compensate B for all loss caused to B by A's use of B's trade secret, and to pay punitive damages to B.

The negotiations have probably resulted in the parties having explicitly or implicitly reached an agreement on confidentiality. According to the *travaux préparatoires* of the Trade Secrets Act,[104] this is the textbook case of when to apply the Act.[105] The information given by B to A legally constitutes trade secrets as it concerns information about B's business that B keeps secret and it is of such nature that it is liable to cause B competitive loss.[106] A's use of these trade secrets is unauthorised by B.[107] As A has – negligently or intentionally – used trade secrets that he has received in connection with a business relationship, he is liable to compensate B for the loss B has incurred due to A's behaviour.[108] When calculating the damages, regard should be had to the non-violating party's interest that the trade secrets be not used without

[101] Audiencia Provincial de Navarra, 10 Jun. 1998, no. 133/1998, AC 1998\1455.

[102] Article 18.2ª. [103] Article 18.5ª.

[104] Lag om skydd för företagshemligheter (1990:409) (TSA).

[105] Proposition 1987/88:155 *med förslag till lag om företagshemligheter m.m.*, p. 43; SOU 1983:52 *Företagshemligheter. Betänkande av utredningen om skydd för företagshemligheter*, p. 385; Fahlbeck, Reinhold and Företagshemligheter, *Konmkurrensklausuler och yttrandefrihet. En kommentar*, p. 229.

[106] TSA, s. 1. [107] TSA, s. 2. [108] TSA, s. 6.

authorisation and to other circumstances not having a direct economic importance.[109]

Accordingly, B is entitled not only to compensation for the damage and the pure economic loss caused by A's use of the trade secrets, but also punitive damages of such an extent that will discourage a person from considering the possibility of using trade secrets without authorisation.[110] The Act does not provide any more detailed guidance as to how the damages should be calculated. However, according to the *travaux préparatoires*, due regard should be had to such things as the lost profits and costs of the non-breaching party, the profits and turnover of the party in breach, whether or not the party in breach acted intentionally, whether the non-breaching party was the weaker party, and the non-breaching party's interest in keeping the secret to himself.[111] Due to the legislation, it does not make any difference if B told A that he expected A to treat the information as confidential.

Switzerland

A is not entitled to damages on the ground of an intellectual property right. However, this does not exclude the protection of intellectual work on other grounds.

A is liable on the ground of *culpa in contrahendo*. Where a party gives information in the course of negotiations, the other party, according to the general principle of good faith, has a duty not to disclose that information or to use it improperly for its own purpose.[112] B therefore has a claim for compensation of the lost profits (the profits he would have realised if A had acted lawfully).

A is also liable in tort on the ground of unfair competition. The use of confidential information is an act of unfair competition under article 5 lit. a or the general clause[113] in article 2 of the Unfair Competition Act.[114] According to article 5 lit. a, person is acting unfairly if he improperly uses for his own purposes the result of work such as offers, calculations or designs given to him as confidential. This rule applies in

109 TSA, s. 9.

110 Fahlbeck, Reinhold and Företagshemligheter, *Konmkurrensklausuler och yttrandefrihet. En kommentar*, p. 255

111 Proposition 1987/88:15 (above n. 105), pp. 26 and 49–50.

112 BernerKommentar-Kramer, OR 22 n. 36; Tercier, *Le droit des obligations*, n. 581. Cf. ZürcherKommentar-Baumann, ZGB 2 n. 176; Loser, *Vertrauenshaftung im Schweizerischen Schuldrecht*, n. 889.

113 In BGE 113 II 319, the Federal Court applied the general clause in a similar case.

114 Bundesgesetz gegen den unlauteren Wettbewerb (UWG), 19 Dec. 1986.

particular to technical drawings which a party discloses to the other party during the course of negotiations for a contract of work.[115] The unfair competition is an unlawful act. B therefore has a claim for compensation of the lost profits on the ground of tort.[116]

A must disgorge the profits made by his own dealing with the design. A is conducting B's business without mandate but in his own interest.[117] There is a special provision in the Code of Obligations:[118] 'If the conduct of the business has not been made in the principal's interest,[119] the latter may nevertheless appropriate the benefits resulting from the other person's acts.' B is therefore entitled to claim the net profits A received by virtue of his management. It is immaterial whether B would have made the same profit if he had marketed the design himself.[120] According to academic writers and case law, B is, however, not entitled to claim A's profits in addition to the compensation in damages.[121]

B may also apply to the judge for an injunction against the improper use of the information.[122]

It makes no difference if B told A that he expected A to treat the information as confidential.[123] This may lead to a confidentiality agreement.[124] The contractual duty, however, would only confirm the duty based on the principle of good faith.

Editors' comparative observations

All the reporters agree in giving B a remedy for the misuse by A of confidential information provided to him by B during the negotiations for a commercial contract which failed to materialise. B's telling A that the information should be treated as confidential can in some jurisdictions strengthen the case for the remedy, or even add additional grounds of relief (sometimes giving rise to a *contractual* obligation of confidentiality), but all jurisdictions are able to impose liability without this addition of the express stipulation of confidentiality. The only exceptions to this are Italy, where the reporter considers that B's own

115 Pedrazzini and Pedrazzini, *Unlauterer Wettbewerb*, n. 9.10. 116 UWG 9 III.

117 Cf. BaslerKommentar-Weber, OR 423 n. 3 and 16; Schmid, *Die Geschäftsführung ohne Auftrag*, n. 1079ff.

118 OR 423 I. 119 OR 422. 120 BaslerKommentar-Weber, OR 423 n. 13f.

121 BGE 97 II 178, BaslerKommentar-Weber, OR 423 n. 14; recently and with differentiations, BGE 133 III 153, 159f. E. 2.5.

122 UWG 9 I.

123 Cf. BernerKommentar-Kramer, OR 22 n. 36.

124 See BernerKommentar-Kramer OR 22 n. 61.

failure properly to protect the confidentiality of his information might undermine his claim to remedy; and the Netherlands, where there is no evidence in the case law of such claims, although the reporter thinks it likely that there would be liability on general principles.

Whilst the imposition of liability is virtually unanimous, the basis of liability is not, and many reports offer various multiple bases of claim to protect B's interests. Austria, Denmark, Finland, Germany, Greece, Italy, Norway, Portugal, Spain, Sweden and Switzerland have legislative provisions which cover this situation, either directly or indirectly (by defining the wrongfulness for a claim brought under the general principles of *culpa in contrahendo* or tort). Many jurisdictions use their general provisions for precontractual liability/*culpa in contrahendo* (Austria, Finland, Germany, Greece, the Netherlands, Portugal, Switzerland) or tort (France, Germany, Greece, the Netherlands, Scotland). Breach of confidence is treated in English and Irish law as an area *sui generis*: remedies can be given in the law of contract (in the case of contractual duties of confidentiality) as well as in tort and equity.

The remedy, too, varies. Most commonly it is damages to compensate B for his loss of profit. But many jurisdictions (Austria, England, Finland, Germany, Greece, Ireland, the Netherlands, Scotland, Switzerland and possibly Portugal) also require A to pay to B either the actual profits he has made from the misuse of the information, or the value he could have made from it, although in some jurisdictions the recoverable profits are limited under the general principles of unjust enrichment. Sweden also allows *punitive* damages to discourage parties from misusing confidential information without authorisation. Some reporters (Austria, England, Finland, France, Ireland, Scotland, Switzerland) point out that an injunction could be obtained (at least against A and, in the view of some, perhaps even against C) to restrain misuse of the information that was obtained in confidence. Jurisdictions which identified more than one possible remedy all made clear that the claimant has the choice amongst them.

Case 13: Misrepresentation or silence about a harvester's capacity

Case 13

A contracts to sell a harvesting machine to B, a farmer, which B requires to enable him to harvest his asparagus crop. In the pre-contractual negotiations, A told B that the machine would be able to harvest one acre a day, but when B comes to use it he discovers that it can only harvest half an acre a day. B is unable to obtain an alternative machine in time to save the half of the crop that cannot be harvested before it is ruined. He now also has a machine which he knows will be inadequate for next year's harvest. What liability (in contract, tort, restitution, or any other form of liability), if any, does A have to B?

Would it make a difference if A had made no statements about the capacity of the machine, but instead during the negotiations B told A that he expected that the machine would be able to harvest one acre a day?

Discussions

Austria

Since a contract has been concluded, the rules on 'warranty' (*Gewährleistung*) apply. The fact that express stipulations were made in the precontractual negotiations does not affect the application of §§922ff. ABGB. These rules have been changed most recently by the Warranty Amendment Act BGBl I 2001/48, which came into effect on 1 January 2002. The person suffering from a breach of express warranty must first claim repair or replacement of the non-complying delivered good. Only if repair and replacement are not possible or are economically unsound may he rescind, with the result that the seller has to refund the payment and take back the delivered good. That means that B would have to claim that the harvesting machine be replaced. A claim for compensation of the loss of the harvest will be available, according to the new §933a ABGB, only if A is at fault, which he will be here since, as an expert,[1] he should know the correct capacity of the harvesting machine he sells to B.

It does not matter whether A made an express stipulation, or whether he remained silent when he was faced with B's expectations about the capacity of the machine during the negotiations. By not reacting to B's disclosure that he expects that the machine would be able to harvest one acre a day, A has violated his precontractual duty of care vis-à-vis B. He was under an obligation to disclose to the buyer B that the harvesting machine did not have the capacity B expected. Thus, A implicitly attributed that capacity to the harvesting machine. Since the machine does not comply with the contract, A is liable under warranty principles, with the same legal consequence as discussed above.

Denmark

This is a typical example of contractual liability for information given in precontractual negotiations, dealt with in the unwritten rules on liability for information and in the Danish Sale of Goods Act. The rule that statements which are made before the contract is concluded give rise to contractual obligations if they are important for the other party and if they are made by a party who, as here, must be presumed to be a professional, appears to be part of the common core of the European legal systems.[2]

In Danish law the result is the same, whether A made the statement or was silent in response to B's statement.

England

B has a range of remedies against A in contract, or in tort, or under statute for misrepresentation.

B has various possible claims in contract. If A is selling the harvesting machine in the course of a business, the contract of sale will by statute contain an implied condition that the machine will be fit for its purpose, since B has made clear the purpose for which he requires it.[3]

[1] §1299 ABGB.

[2] *Principles of European Contract Law* Part I and II (The Hague, 2000) art. 6.111, p. 299ff.

[3] Sale of Goods Act 1979, s. 14(3), which implies such terms into contracts of sale of goods entered into by sellers in the course of a business where the buyer has expressly or impliedly made known the purpose.

A's assurance that the machine will harvest one acre a day is likely also to be an express term of the contract, whether or not A is selling it in the course of a business.[4] Since the machine is not fit for its purpose, and cannot harvest one acre a day, A is in breach of contract. The breach of a condition of the contract entitles the innocent party either to reject the goods and claim damages for loss he suffers, or simply to claim damages whilst retaining the goods. But it is too late to reject the goods if he 'accepts' them, a term which includes not only intimating to the seller that he accepts them in spite of the breach, but also the lapse of a reasonable time during which he could have examined the goods and discovered the defect.[5] It appears from the facts that B has continued to use the machine after he has discovered the defect, in order to harvest as much of his crop as he can; he will therefore now not be able to reject the machine on this basis.

However, B is a 'consumer' for the purposes of the legislation which implemented in the United Kingdom the Consumer Sales Directive, and so he will have the right to require A to replace the harvesting machine with a machine which conforms with the seller's statutory implied obligation as to quality and fitness for purpose;[6] or, if the buyer fails to replace it within a reasonable time, rescission of the contract.[7]

[4] The test is whether the parties can be taken to have intended the promise to be incorporated into the contract: *Heilbut, Symons & Co. v. Buckleton* [1913] AC 30; but this will normally be inferred where, as here, it is a clear statement about a quality of the good on a matter which is within the seller's (but not the buyer's) knowledge, and which is intended by the seller to influence the purchaser's decision to enter into the contract: *Dick Bentley Productions Ltd v. Harold Smith (Motors) Ltd* [1965] 1 WLR 623.

[5] Sale of Goods Act 1979, s. 35, amended by Sale and Supply of Goods Act 1994, s. 2(1). The buyer is not deemed to have accepted the goods merely because he asks for, or agrees to their repair: s. 35(3); time taken to ascertain what would be necessary to modify or repair the defective goods, and in carrying out the repairs, is therefore not to be counted against the purchaser: *Clegg v. Andersson* [2003] 2 Lloyd's Rep 32 at [63]–[64].

[6] Sale of Goods Act 1979, Part 5A, inserted by Sale and Supply of Goods to Consumers Regulations 2002, SI 2002/3045, implementing Directive 99/44/EC. B is a 'consumer' within the UK implementing legislation even if he buys the harvester for his business, as long as he (a) is not in the business of entering into that type of contract (he is a farmer, not a dealer in harvesters); and (b) this is a type of contract that he enters into only occasionally, rather than with a degree of regularity to make it integral to his business (presumably, he buys a harvester only rarely): *R & B Customs Brokers Co. Ltd v. United Dominions Trust Ltd* [1988] 1 WLR 321.

[7] Sale of Goods Act 1979, s. 48C. Reimbursement to B of the price may be reduced to take account of the use he has made of the machine: s. 48C(3). In practice, B may simply prefer to claim damages (below), which will give him control over the selection of a satisfactory replacement machine, and enable him to charge to A the additional costs, as well as his consequential losses.

B could claim damages for breach of contract. Damages in contract are calculated so as to protect the injured party's expectations: in the case of a claim for breach of a contract for the sale of goods based on the defect in the quality of the goods, this generally means, broadly, such a sum of money as would allow the claimant to go into the market and obtain goods equivalent to those which the defendant has failed to deliver – here, therefore, the cost of obtaining an alternative machine (giving credit for the value of the machine he has, which he can sell).[8] In addition, B can recover such consequential losses as he can show flowed from the breach, as long as they are of such a kind as were in the defendant's contemplation at the time of the contract as the likely consequences of a breach: so, here, the value of the lost part of this year's crop (including the lost profit he would have made on that part of the crop) will be recoverable.

As an alternative to claiming damages for breach of contract, B has a claim against A for damages on the tort measure: but this will not enable him to obtain compensation to cover the cost of buying a suitable harvesting machine for next year (since that is his 'expectation' loss, which is recoverable only in contract), but will only cover his out-of-pocket losses as a result of relying on A's misrepresentation about the qualities of the machine. A claim for tort damages would most easily be brought under section 2(1) of the Misrepresentation Act 1967, which imposes a liability to pay damages, calculated on the same measure as in the tort of deceit but without the claimant's having to prove fraud, on a party who made a false statement to the other in the course of negotiations for a contract and where the contract was in due course concluded on the faith of the representation. Under the statute, the defendant has a defence if he can show that he believed his statement was true, and had reasonable grounds for that belief (the defendant has the burden of showing that he was not, in effect, negligent). However, since this remedy is not as helpful to B as the claim for breach of contract, he is unlikely to wish to pursue it.

Where A makes no statement but fails to respond to B's statement about his own expectation about the capacity of the machine, B still has the same claim against A for damages for breach of contract under the contract of sale, as long as A is selling the harvesting machine in the course of a business. As in the case (above) where A made a statement

[8] Sale of Goods Act 1979, s. 53(3), which sets the time of assessment, *prima facie*, as the date of delivery of the non-conforming goods.

about the capacity, the contract will by statute contain an implied condition that the machine will be fit for its purpose, since B has made clear the purpose for which he requires it. However, other remedies which were available to B based on A's misrepresentation about the harvester's capacity will not apply because A makes no statement unless the court, on investigation of the facts, discovers that A said or did something in response to B's own statement about the capacity which could be held to be a confirmatory misrepresentation by A on which B relied. So there would be no express promise about the machine's capacity in the contract to found a claim for damages for breach of contract, and no claim under Misrepresentation Act 1967, section 2(1), which requires proof that a misrepresentation has been 'made', and therefore silence is not sufficient. Even if A knows that B is mistaken as to the capacity of the harvesting machine, A has no liability based on that mistake unless either he realises that B intends the capacity to be guaranteed, or A has caused the misunderstanding:

> even if the vendor was aware that the purchaser thought that the article possessed that quality, and would not have entered into the contract unless he had so thought, still the purchaser is bound, unless the vendor was guilty of some fraud or deceit upon him, and that a mere abstinence from disabusing the purchaser of that impression is not fraud or deceit; for, whatever may be the case in a court of morals, there is no legal obligation on the vendor to inform the purchaser that he is under a mistake, not induced by the act of the vendor.[9]

Finland

A is liable to B in contract for B's positive interest. Under the Finnish Sale of Goods Act,[10] goods not conforming with the information given by the seller in precontractual negotiations are considered to be defective in terms of contract law. This means that all the losses B has suffered for the non-conformity of the goods have to be compensated, or he has to be put in the same economic position as if the contract had been properly performed.

[9] *Smith v. Hughes* (1871) LR 6 QB 597, 607 (Blackburn J); Cartwright, *Misrepresentation, Mistake, and Non-Disclosure*, Pt III.

[10] 1987, s. 18: '(1) The goods are also defective if (i) they do not conform with information relating to their properties or use which was given by the seller when marketing the goods or otherwise before the conclusion of the contract and (ii) the information can be presumed to have had an effect on the contract. . . (3) The provisions of paragraphs (1) and (2) shall not be applied if the information has been corrected clearly and in time'.

This is a case of breach of contractual duties of information by the seller. Of course, the buyer's duty of inspection can affect the legal result. Any omission by the buyer to examine the goods, as well as his awareness of the defect, can deprive the buyer of claims based on the defect.[11]

The result is the same where A makes no statement about the capacity of the machine. The seller's contractual duties of information result in the goods being considered to be defective in terms of contract law.[12] Here, the seller knew of the buyer's purpose at the time of the conclusion of the contract because B told A about his expectations concerning the harvesting capacity of the machine. The seller's failure to react is considered equal to a positive statement confirming the buyer's expression of his expectations.

France

Two different means of protection for B are theoretically conceivable under French law: either annulment of the contract or remedies for breach of contract. Whether B has an option between these two types of protection is hard to determine.

Annulment of the contract: B has contracted under the belief that the machine could fulfil his needs and thus makes a mistake. This mistaken belief can lead to the annulment of the contract for mistake[13] or fraud (*dol*).[14] B has an option between these two actions. Fraud is, however, regarded as more advantageous for B since annulment of the contract can then be combined with a claim for damages. These damages cover the entire harm suffered by B: loss of half of the crop, and loss of the opportunity to conclude a satisfactory contract with a third party earlier (assuming, for example, that the price of a suitable machine increased while the first contract of sale was on foot).

[11] Sale of Goods Act, s. 20: 'The buyer may not rely on a defect which he cannot have been unaware of at the time of the conclusion of the contract. If the buyer, before the conclusion of the contract, has examined the goods or, without acceptable reason, has failed to comply with the seller's exhortation to examine the goods, he may not rely on a defect that he ought to have discovered in the examination unless the seller's conduct was incompatible with honour and good faith.'

[12] Sale of Goods Act, s. 17: '(2) Except where the parties have agreed otherwise, the goods must: (1) be fit for the purpose for which similar goods are ordinarily used; (2) be fit for any particular purpose for which the goods were intended if the seller knew or must have known of this purpose at the time of the conclusion of the contract and it was reasonable for the buyer to rely on the seller's skill and judgement; . . . (3) If the goods do not conform with the provisions of paragraph (1) or (2), they are defective'.

[13] Article 1110 C.civ. [14] Article 1116 C.civ.

Remedies for breach of contract: it is also arguable that B contracted a perfectly valid contract which the seller has failed to perform correctly. Since the parties agreed on the capacity that the machine was supposed to have, the absence of such a quality can be seen as a breach of contract. On the facts, there would not be a guarantee against latent defects[15] (because the reduced harvesting capacity is not the consequence of a defect of the machine) but a breach of the obligation to deliver goods in conformity with the contractual terms (*obligation de délivrance conforme*) under article 1604 of the Civil Code.[16] There are two remedies offered to the buyer in such a case: *résolution*, which is a termination that has a retroactive effect under French law, and specific performance, as mentioned in article 1184 of the Civil Code. B has the choice between these two remedies.

Specific performance theoretically enables B to force A to provide him with a suitable machine at A's cost (replacement of the first machine or upgrade of the first machine). Is specific performance conceivable here? Not if A has no means of providing B with a suitable machine. Article 1144 of the Civil Code offers, however, an interesting possibility of indirect specific performance: the wronged party can be authorised by the judge to obtain performance himself at the other party's cost. This remedy, if given by the judge,[17] is combined with contractual liability when the party, as in our case, commits a fault (the mere fact that A has not fulfilled his contractual obligations), allowing B to be compensated for the loss suffered from the defective performance.

B can also ask for termination combined with damages. Termination has to be pronounced by the judge and will not be allowed if the judge finds that the weight of the incorrectly performed obligation is not sufficient to justify terminating the contract. Termination will entitle

[15] Article 1641: *la garantie contre les vices cachés*.

[16] The distinction between guarantee against latent defects and obligation to deliver goods that are in conformity with the terms of the contract could have disappeared with the implementation of Directive 1999/44/EC (25 May 1999), which imposes one single broad guarantee in the contracts of sale between professionals and consumers. But the French government decided to add the new guarantee to the existing law: Ordonnance 17 Feb. 2005, comment O. Tournafond, D.2005, 1557. Consequently, the old distinction remains.

[17] Courts let the dissatisfied party act without authorisation in two cases: emergency and contracts of a commercial nature. Since the contract under consideration appears to be concluded between two professionals for the purpose of their business, it seems theoretically possible for B to buy a new machine without judicial pre-approval and ask A to pay the price. On the question see, e.g., Ph. Simler, JCL-Civil, arts. 1136–1145, fasc. 10, no. 135ff.

B to give back the machine and recover its price, together with damages since A's fault is here shown (the mere fact that he has not fulfilled his contractual obligations). These damages will compensate B for the loss suffered from the breach of the contract, amounting here to the loss of half of the crop or to the loss of the chance to conclude a satisfactory contract earlier if, for example, the price of the machine has risen during performance of the first contract of sale. If B chooses this remedy, he will have to buy a new machine himself but will not automatically receive sufficient damages to cover the cost. There is, therefore, probably a slight difference between specific performance and termination with damages.

Choice between annulment and remedies for breach of contract: there is one further question: does B have a choice between the two remedies for annulment and breach of contract? In the absence of a legal text, French courts used to solve this conflict by giving the dissatisfied buyer the choice. But a recent decision of the Cour de cassation[18] contradicts the earlier case law. According to this decision, dealing with an overlap between annulment for mistake and guarantee against latent defects, the only remedy available to the buyer is for breach of contract. Does this mean that there is no longer a choice between remedies for breach and annulment? The answer might be negative. In fact, the particularity of the rules governing the guarantee against latent defects (especially the very short time limit)[19] certainly played an important role in the decision. The Cour de cassation did not want the buyer to bypass the legal time limit rules governing latent defects by bringing a claim under the head of annulment. This is why the choice between the remedies was rejected. Since the rules applicable to the two types of remedies under consideration in our case (annulment and breach of the obligation to deliver goods in conformity with the contract) are quite similar, the Cour de cassation might find it appropriate to maintain a choice in favour of the buyer. As a result, it seems that B will have the choice here to bring a claim under either head.

Where A is silent: in the case where A is silent but B states his expectation about the harvester's capacity, the result is the same. First, B made a mistake about what he was buying and can, thus, ask for annulment.

[18] Civ 1, 14 May 1996, JCP 1997, I, 4009; Ch. Radé, 'L'autonomie de l'action en garantie des vices cachés' D.1997, SC 345, obs O. Tournafond; D.1998, 305, note Jault-Seseke.

[19] Which has disappeared since the modification of art. 1648 of the Civil Code by art. 3 of the Ordonnance no. 2005-136.

One might even think that A's lack of loyalty amounts to fraud (*dol*). Although in relation to a contract between two professionals, the buyer has a duty to inform himself about what he is about to buy,[20] it is arguable that A's wrongful silence after he was told of the characteristics looked for by B is a fraudulent concealment.[21] Secondly, we can assume that B's view of the contract prevails (that the obligation was to deliver a machine which harvested one acre a day).[22] In that case, A did not comply with his obligation to deliver the machine he had sold to B in conformity with the contractual terms. As discussed above, it seems that B has a choice between annulment for mistake or fraud and the remedies for breach of contract.

Germany

It is necessary to discuss A's potential liability in contract, *culpa in contrahendo*, tort and restitution.

A's liability in contract: the German law of sale was comprehensively reformed in 2001. The German legislature complied with the duty to transpose Directive 1999/44/EC[23] by implementing most of the Directive's rules into the general provisions of the BGB regulating the contract of sale.[24] Simultaneously the law on warranties of quality (*Sachmängelgewährleistungsrecht*) was for the most part synchronised with the general rules as to the impairment of the performance of an obligation (*allgemeines Leistungsstörungsrecht*). Therefore, the new law which entered into force on 1 January 2002[25] dispenses with special warranty rules for the contract of sale and thus avoids most of the intricate demarcation problems which characterised the old law. A purchaser's contractual remedies for a defect of the thing sold are now set down in §437 (Rights of the buyer in case of defects):

§437 BGB: Subject to the following provisions and insofar as nothing else is laid down, the buyer of a defective thing may:

1. require the seller to remedy the lack of conformity according to §439,
2. terminate the contract according to §§440, 323, 326(5) or reduce the price according to §441, and

[20] P. Jourdain, 'Le devoir de "se" renseigner' D. 1983, C, 139.
[21] *Réticence dolosive*. See, e.g., Civ 3, 7 May 1974, Bull Civ III, no. 186.
[22] Article 1602 C.civ. states that, in case of ambiguity in a contract of sale, the clauses are to be interpreted in favour of the buyer; Civ. 1, 13 Apr. 1999, Bull Civ I, no. 139.
[23] 25 May 1999, on certain aspects of the sale of consumer goods and associated guarantees.
[24] §433ff. BGB. [25] BGBl. I no. 61, 2001, 3138ff.

3. claim compensation according to §§440, 280, 281, 283, 311a or reimbursement of wasted expenditure according to §284.

A's liability under §§437 No. 1, 439(1) BGB: the purchaser of a defective thing may require the seller either to repair the defect or deliver a thing free from defects.[26] A thing is defective if it does not correspond to the standard laid down in §434 BGB (Defects in the thing sold):

> (1) The thing is free from defects, if, at the time when the risk passes, it has the stipulated quality. Insofar as the quality has not been stipulated, the thing is free from defects,
>
> 1. if it is suitable for the use provided for in the contract, or else
> 2. if it is fit for its ordinary use and possesses the qualities which are usual in things of the same kind and which a buyer may expect in a thing of this kind.

Qualities within the meaning of sentence 2 No. 2 are also characteristics which the buyer, taking into account public statements made by the seller, by the producer,[27] or by one of his employees, is entitled to expect especially in regard to advertisements and the description of certain qualities of the thing, unless the seller neither knew of the statement nor ought to have known about it, or if at the time of contracting it had already been rectified, or the decision to buy could not have been influenced by it. Moreover, the thing is defective if its assembly by the seller or by his employees which had been agreed upon was improper. Furthermore, a thing which has been put together is regarded as defective if the instructions for its assembly are defective, unless it has been assembled free from defects. It is also equivalent to a defect in the thing if the seller delivers a different thing or a smaller quantity.

Since A told B in the precontractual negotiations that the machine would be able to harvest one acre a day and did not correct this statement before the parties agreed on its sale, A's statement became an implied term of the contract. Therefore, the actual quality of the machine delivered (*Ist-Beschaffenheit*) does not correspond to the quality the parties contractually agreed upon (*Soll-Beschaffenheit*), and so the machine is defective according to §434(1) sentence 1 BGB.[28] It seems,

[26] §439(1) BGB (*Nacherfüllung*). Cf. Lorenz and Riehm, *Lehrbuch zum neuen Schuldrecht*, para. 504ff.

[27] Law relating to Product Liability, §4(1) and (2).

[28] It is beyond doubt now that the test whether a thing is defective is primarily governed by the contract of sale and not by objective criteria, i.e the new law confirms the

however, impossible to transmute a harvesting machine capable of harvesting half an acre a day into one capable of harvesting one acre a day. But even if this were possible such an operation would produce excessive and unreasonable costs for the seller. Therefore, B's claim under §439(1), 1st alternative BGB, to require A to repair the machine (*Nachbesserung*) is barred by §§275(1), 439(3) BGB.[29]

Nevertheless, A is, according to §439(1), 2nd alternative BGB, obliged to deliver a harvesting machine with a harvesting capacity of one acre a day (*Nachlieferung*). A and B did not agree on the sale of specific harvesting machine (*Stückkauf*) but on a purchase by description (*Gattungskauf*).[30] As harvesting machines of this quality are still available on the market at ordinary prices, A must organise a second delivery.

B's right to terminate the contract or to reduce the purchase price and to reclaim the purchase price or the surplus already paid under §§437 No. 2, 323, 346(1), 441(4) BGB: a buyer with a claim under §439(1) BGB may grant the seller a reasonable period within which to perform this obligation, that is, to remedy his first performance. If the seller does not perform, or only partly performs, within this period, the buyer is entitled either to terminate the contract if the seller's neglect of duty is significant, or reduce the purchase price.[31] B may, therefore, fix a reasonable period within which A must deliver a machine with a harvesting capacity of one acre a day. Given that the defect of the machine already delivered is significant, if A does not then perform in time B may either cancel the contract or reduce the purchase price under §§323(1), 441(1) BGB. Both rights are at the disposal of B, no matter whether A is responsible or not for his non-(conforming) performance. If B has already paid the purchase price he may also, if he decides to cancel the contract, reclaim the full price[32] or, if he prefers to reduce the purchase price, reclaim the surplus.[33]

so-called *subjektiver Fehlerbegriff* already prevailing under the old law, cf. Staudinger-Honsell, §459 para. 18ff.

[29] Cf Lorenz and Riehm, *Lehrbuch zum neuen Schuldrecht*, paras. 297ff., 511.

[30] If A and B had agreed on the sale of a specific harvesting machine, A would not be liable under §439(1) BGB, the delivery of a machine with a harvesting capacity of half an acre as a machine with a capacity of one acre being impossible (so-called *qualitative Unmöglichkeit*; cf. Lorenz and Riehm, *Lehrbuch zum neuen Schuldrecht*, paras. 302, 327). B could, however, immediately terminate the contract according to §326(5) BGB. Furthermore, he would be entitled to claim compensation instead of (full) performance according to §311a(2) BGB and damages resulting from the ruined asparagus crop according to §§280(1), 311a(2) BGB.

[31] §§323, 441 BGB. [32] §346(1) BGB. [33] §441(4) BGB.

A's liability of the seller under §§437 No. 3, 280(1), (3), 281(1) BGB: if the seller who has delivered a defective thing does not fulfil (or only partly fulfils) his duty under §439(1) BGB within a reasonable period fixed by the buyer, the buyer may claim compensation instead of performance (*Schadensersatz statt der Leistung*). If the seller's neglect of duty is significant he is entitled to compensation instead of full performance (*Schadensersatz statt der ganzen Leistung*). The seller, however, is only liable if he is responsible for the non-(conforming) performance of his duty.[34] Hence, if A does not deliver a machine with a harvesting capacity of one acre a day within a reasonable period of grace fixed by B, B may then claim his full expectation interest (*Mangelschaden*) against the restitution of the machine (*Schadensersatz statt der ganzen Leistung*) or, if he wants to keep the machine, claim the difference between his expectation interest and the machine's value. A is responsible for his non-(conforming) performance. Being the seller of a thing by description, his liability is strict. According to §276(1) sentence 1, 4th alternative BGB, the debtor of an object described by class is responsible for his inability to procure the object, even though no fault may be imputed to him. B's damages resulting from the crop shortfall, however, are not covered by §§280(1), (3), 281(1) BGB. Compensation instead of performance as defined by §281(1) BGB only refers to the economic loss immediately resulting from the non-(conforming) performance (so-called *Äquivalenzinteresse)* but not to damages to rights, legally protected interests or other interests of the creditor (*Mangelfolgeschäden*) caused by the non-(conforming) performance (so called *Integritätsinteresse)*.

A's liability under §§437 No. 3, 280(1), 433(1) sentence 2 BGB: the seller of a defective thing may, however, be liable for damages caused by the defect to rights and legally protected interests or other interests of the buyer according to §§280(1), 433(1) sentence 2 BGB, provided he is responsible for the *defect*. B's asparagus would not have been ruined if A had delivered the machine contracted for, that is, if he had delivered a harvesting machine free from defects. A is responsible for the delivered machine's defect in three cases.

(1) He is responsible if he guaranteed the machine's harvesting capacity to B under §276(1) sentence 1, 3rd alternative BGB. The seller guarantees a quality in the thing sold if he specially warrants the contractual terms as to quality. Such a stipulated warranty requires the seller's intention to assume strict liability for all the consequences

[34] §280(1) sent. 2 BGB.

resulting from the lack of the warranted quality. The courts and legal writers, however, in view of the effects of strict liability, set a rather high standard to ascertain a promised quality. In case of doubt, this is a question of the construction of the contract.[35] The decisive factor, therefore, is neither the seller's true intention nor his use of specific vocabulary (such as the terms 'express warranty' or 'guarantee') but whether, according to the requirements of good faith, the purchaser, in the specific circumstances of the case, was entitled to take the seller as promising a certain quality.[36] Hence, mere puffs as well as pure product specifications do not amount to a contractual warranty. Particularly in relation to newly manufactured things, the Bundesgerichtshof takes a very cautious point of view. Until recently, the court has stressed that a pure product specification may be characterised as an agreement as to quality as defined by §434(1) sentence 1 BGB but, as a rule, does not represent a guarantee according to §276(1) sentence 1, 3rd alternative BGB.[37] As a result (it would seem), B did not contractually warrant the harvesting capacity of the machine sold.

(2) A is responsible for the defect of the machine delivered if he assumed the risk of procuring a defective machine under §276(1) sentence 1, 4th alternative BGB. Commentators disagree upon this question. It would seem that, in view of the effects of strict liability, it is inequitable to make the seller in the case of a purchase by description answerable for all the consequences of the defect of the object selected by him for fulfilment.[38] The problem may, however, be left undecided here, in the light of (3) below.

(3) A is responsible for the machine's defect under §276(1) sentence 1, 1st and 2nd alternative BGB. If A fraudulently concealed the defect of the delivered machine he is, of course, responsible for it.[39] If this is not the case, A negligently failed to know the machine's actual harvesting capacity.[40] A seller exercising ordinary care would have been aware of

[35] §§133, 157 BGB. [36] BGH, decision of 5 July 1972, BGHZ 59, 158, 160.

[37] BGH, decision of 4 June 1997, BGHZ 135, 393; BGH, decision of 23 Mar. 1996, NJW-RR 1996, 951; BGH, decision of 14 Feb. 1996, NJW 1996, 1465; BGH, decision of 13 Dec. 1995, NJW 1996, 836; BGH, decision of 28 Nov. 1994, BGHZ 128, 11.

[38] Cf. Canaris, DB 2001, 1815ff. and ZRP 2001, 329, 335 with further references. The seller is therefore strictly liable according to §276(1) sent. 1, 4th alt. BGB for his inability, for whatever reasons, to secure the thing sold by description but not for the procurement of a defective item.

[39] §276(1) sent. 1, 1st alternative BGB. [40] §276(1) sent. 1, 2nd alternative BGB.

the harvesting capacity of the machine delivered, that is, he would have avoided the delivery of a defective machine.

As a result, B may claim the value of the ruined crop as well as the profits lost by its ruin.

A's liability on the ground of culpa in contrahendo: it is accepted beyond doubt that the seller is not liable for *negligently* misrepresenting a fact referring to the thing sold if this fact may be incorporated into the contract as a quality agreed upon as defined by §434(1) BGB (*Beschaffenheitsvereinbarung*).[41] The specific sales law regulations must not be circumvented by establishing liability on the ground of *culpa in contrahendo*. The requirements set up by §437 No. 3 BGB as to a seller's liability for damages would be rendered ineffective if, in addition to that provision, the purchaser was entitled to a claim on the ground of *culpa in contrahendo*. If, however, the misrepresentation refers to a fact that cannot be the subject of a *Beschaffenheitsvereinbarung* (§434 BGB) the specific provisions of the law of sale do not preclude the seller's liability on the ground of *culpa in contrahendo*. This has occasionally given rise to the tendency to construe the ambit of the term 'quality' rather narrowly in order to expand the scope of liability based on *culpa in contrahendo*. It is, however, beyond doubt that the harvesting capacity of one acre a day of the machine can and, therefore, does in this case represent a 'quality' of the machine sold as required by §434 BGB.[42]

If, however, the seller has *fraudulently* misrepresented a quality of the thing sold, the Bundesgerichtshof takes the view that the provisions of the law of sale do not take precedence over liability on the ground of *culpa in contrahendo*.[43] The special relationship (*Sonderrechtsverhältnis*) created between the negotiating parties by virtue of the law (*gesetzliches Schuldverhältnis*) definitely imposes on the seller the duty not to make wilfully false statements about the envisaged object of sale. Therefore, if A has fraudulently misrepresented the harvesting capacity of the

[41] Lorenz and Riehm, *Lehrbuch zum neuen Schuldrecht*, para. 575ff. with further references.

[42] The Bundesgerichtshof allows an exception to the rule that a seller negligently representing a quality of the thing sold cannot be held liable on the ground of *culpa in contrahendo* if the seller is under a special 'precontractual duty to give information': BGH, decision of 23 June 1999, NJW 1999, 3192; BGH, decision of 6 June 1984, NJW 1984, 2938; BGH, decision of 13 July 1983, BGHZ 88, 130, 135; BGH, decision of 31 Jan. 1962, NJW 1962, 1196. This liability is one of the most controversial issues of the German law of sales. In the present case, such a special duty to inform the purchaser cannot be assumed.

[43] BGH, decision of 10 July 1987, NJW-RR 1988, 10, 11; disagreeing. Soergel-Huber, §459 paras. 220, 228.

machine sold, B may claim reliance damages, and so he must be put into the position he would be in if the misrepresentation had not occurred. As a result, B may at least cancel the contract. Furthermore, he may claim the loss created by the crop shortage if he can prove that he could have bought another machine with a harvesting capacity of one acre a day. If he can show that, without A's deceit, he would have bought such a machine for a lower price than he had to invest after the cancellation of the contract, he is also entitled to that price difference.

A's liability in tort: as a rule, simply by the delivery of a defective thing a seller does not interfere with the purchaser's property or any other of the legal interests protected by §823(1) BGB. However, by delivering the machine, A indirectly caused damage to B's asparagus crop. Therefore, A is liable for the loss caused by the crop shortage according to §823(1) BGB if he either knew or negligently failed to know that he was putting an *objectively defective* product into circulation.[44] However, although not fit for B's purpose, the machine, *from an objective point of view*, is a *proper item* of its kind. Therefore, A is not liable on the ground of §823(1) BGB.

However, if A knew that the machine delivered did not correspond to the quality contractually provided for and seriously took into account that B could suffer loss from this fact, he is liable on the ground of §826 BGB.

A's liability in restitution: if A fraudulently misrepresented the machine's harvesting capacity, B may cancel the contract according to §123(1) BGB and reclaim the purchase price on the ground of §812(1) sentence 1, 1st alternative BGB.

Conclusion: B, therefore, may:

(1) require A to deliver a machine with a harvesting capacity of one acre (§439(1), 2nd alternative BGB);
(2) fix a reasonable period for B to fulfil his duty under §439(1) BGB and, if A does not perform within this period:
    (a) terminate the contract (§323(1) BGB) or reduce the purchase price (§441(1) BGB) and reclaim the purchase price (§436(1) BGB) or the surplus already paid (§441(4) BGB); and/or (cf. §325 BGB)
    (b) demand compensation instead of full performance (§§437 No. 3, 280(1), (3), 281(1) BGB);
(3) claim the damages resulting from the ruined asparagus crop (§§437 No. 3, 280(1) BGB).

[44] BGH, decision of 16 Sep. 1987, BGHZ 101, 337.

B is not liable on the ground of *culpa in contrahendo*, in tort or in restitution unless he has fraudulently represented the machine's harvesting capacity.

In the variant situation, where A makes no statement, it would seem that A is not liable.

A is not liable in contract if the parties did not agree upon a certain harvesting capacity of the machine sold. As a rule, B's unilateral expectations do not become part of the contract. The crucial question, therefore, is whether the parties provided for the machine's use in the contract according to §434(1) sentence 2, No. 1 BGB. Although such an agreement may be implied,[45] it would seem that for the reasons given below the contract should not be construed in this way. A, therefore, is not liable on the ground of §437 BGB.[46] Liability on the ground of *culpa in contrahendo* for negligently not giving information to B is excluded by the same reasons mentioned in the main case, above. There being no duty of giving information, A is not liable in tort.

The courts and legal writers agree that, as a rule, a seller is under no duty to inform the buyer about the qualities of the object sold (*caveat emptor*). An exception to this rule is only conceded if the seller knows about qualities of the thing that are crucial for the buyer's purpose. In this case, according to the standard of good faith, the buyer is entitled to information without asking for it.[47] The details of this liability are, however, still debated.[48] In the present case this exception does not apply. It is true that the machine's harvesting capacity was crucial for B to enter into the contract. However, a buyer may only expect information about the qualities of the object sold if he is not in a position to gain the relevant information by asking the seller about it. B could easily have asked A about the machine's harvesting capacity. Then the parties either would not have reached agreement or A would be liable according to the rules set out in relation to the main case, above. Therefore, although A knew of B's purposes as to the machine, B's unilateral expectations do not entitle him to avoid the contract.

[45] §§133, 157 BGB. [46] Otherwise the same rules as in the main case, above, apply.

[47] BGH, decision of 8 Dec. 1988, NJW 1989, 1793; BGH, decision of 8 May 1980, NJW 1980, 2460; BGH, decision of 2 Mar. 1979, NJW 1979, 2243.

[48] For details see Lorenz, *Der Schutz vor dem unerwünschten Vertrag*, p. 416ff; Breidenbach, *Die Voraussetzungen von Informationspflichten beim Vertragsschluß*.

Greece

According to the law of sales,[49] the statement made by A in the course of negotiations regarding the specific characteristics of the harvesting machine is an agreed quality of the thing sold.[50] If upon performance of the seller's obligations, the buyer discovers that the agreed quality is lacking, then the seller is liable for mal-performance. Hence A is liable to B for mal-performance of his obligation under the contract of sale to deliver a harvesting machine complying with the standards set by his statements. B may exercise a number of remedies, such as having the contract of sale rescinded or requesting a reduction of the sale price;[51] B may also seek damages for mal-performance.[52] Damages may be combined with one of the above remedies. In principle, B will be entitled to full damages comprising of the expectation interest and the loss of profit.[53] Thus, after rescinding the sales contract B may return the harvesting machine to the seller and may also be compensated for the lost profit represented by the ruined crop.

Also, A's statement to B regarding the harvesting machine may be interpreted as an innocent or fraudulent misrepresentation, which induced B's declaration of will.[54] On that basis, B may have the sales contract declared void[55] and seek compensation.[56] Compensation in case of innocent misrepresentation (mistake) cannot exceed the expectation interest, whereas compensation for fraudulent misrepresentation may also include immaterial loss.

Both avenues of liability are in fact specific manifestations of precontractual liability for negotiations that resulted in a contract. The performance in the contract of sale suffers from a defect that can be traced back to the period of negotiations. Therefore, provisions such as that on non-conformity in the contract of sale or a defect in the formation of the declaration of the will are in effect special provisions on precontractual liability. In view of that, the question has arisen whether one may instead invoke the general provisions on precontractual

[49] This case is considered on the basis of Greek sales law as it stands during the summer of 2002 before the imminent implementation of the Consumer Sales Directive 1999/44/EC.

[50] Article 535 GCC. [51] Article 540 GCC. [52] Article 543 GCC. [53] Article 298 GCC.

[54] Articles 140ff. and 147ff. GCC. It is submitted that the sales provisions take precedence over the provisions on deceit and they apply exclusively. Nevertheless, mention is made here to cover any potential avenue of recourse.

[55] Articles 140, 147 GCC. [56] Articles 145, 149 GCC.

liability.[57] Here, we will not delve into the discussion of the systematic and substantive arguments whether the special provisions pre-empt the general provisions, or whether both sets of provisions may apply concurrently. The prevalent view seems to be that the sales provisions are specific compared to the general provisions on precontractual liability; therefore they apply exclusively.[58] Nonetheless, the opposite is equally forcefully supported, namely that both sets of provisions may complement each other and may be applied concurrently.[59] Last but not least, it should be remembered that article 198 GCC provides that a party may be liable for conduct during the negotiations which is inconsistent with good faith and business usage, even when the negotiations have resulted in a valid contract between the parties.

Where A made no statement, the result is the same. With regard to A's liability on the basis of the sale provisions, the requirement made known by the buyer to the seller regarding the specific characteristics of the harvesting machine constitutes an agreed quality between the parties. A does not object to B's statement and therefore the parties appear implicitly to have agreed that the harvesting machine should be able to harvest one acre per day.[60] Thus, A will be liable towards B for a lack of agreed quality[61] and B can invoke any of the remedies provided for in the sales provisions,[62] as indicated above. With regard to the application of the general provisions on precontractual liability,[63] A's conduct should still be deemed to be contrary to good faith and B could thereby claim compensation.

Ireland

If A's statement has become part of the contract, then A will be strictly liable to B for any loss arising.[64] If the statement has not become part of the contract, A may still be liable to B.

First, A may be liable under section 14 of the Sale of Goods and Supply of Services Act 1980 which requires that goods should be

[57] Articles 197, 198 GCC. [58] Kambitsis, *Precontractual Liability*, p. 82.

[59] F. Doris, in Georgiadis and Stathopoulos, *Commentary on the Greek Civil Code*, pp. 153, 134ff. Concurrency of the provisions on precontractual liability and sales provisions is supported de facto by case law in AP 344/1982 NoV 1982, 184, where the case was pleaded on both legal bases.

[60] Doris, above n. 59, p. 153. [61] Article 535 GCC.

[62] Articles 540, 543 GCC. [63] Articles 197, 198 GCC.

[64] See generally, Friel, *The Law of Contract*, p. 185ff.; see also *Bank of Ireland v. Smith* [1966] IR 646, per Kenny J, who states that such precontractual statements are increasingly likely to form part of the contract.

merchantable; that is, fit for the purposes intended and as durable as one would reasonably expect. If the relevant statement has become a term of the contract, it constitutes a breach of contract for which the defendant will be liable. In any event, since this is a contract for the sale of goods, A will be liable for breach of Sale of Goods and Supply of Services Act 1980, section 14, in that the harvester was not fit for the purposes intended. A clearly indicated that the harvester was capable of harvesting one acre per day. It was not so capable and accordingly A is in breach.

Secondly, A may be liable to B in either contract or tort for negligent misrepresentation. A precontractual statement, which has not become part of the subsequent contract, may give rise to liability under either contract or tort but only where the statement is found to be untrue. A precontractual statement, which has not formed part of the contract, is termed a misrepresentation. A misrepresentation is an untrue statement of fact which induced the plaintiff to enter into the contract. There is no liability attaching for statements which are true or which relate to opinion or intention.[65] Further, if liability is to arise, the misrepresentation must have induced the plaintiff to enter the contract. If the plaintiff was not motivated by the misrepresentation to enter the contract there is no liability.[66] It stands to reason that the defendant, or his employee or agent,[67] must have made the misrepresentation to the plaintiff.[68] Where these requirements are satisfied, the plaintiff must then show that the defendant was fraudulent or negligent in making the misrepresentation. It is difficult to demonstrate fraud in commercial transactions and, in light of the higher compensation available in the law of tort, an action for deceit would be more likely.[69] If the misrepresentation has been negligently made, liability may arise in contract law[70] as well as in the law of tort.[71] Traditionally at contract law,

[65] The difference between fact and opinion is not always clear; see *Esso v. Marden* [1976] QB 801; American Law Institute, *Restatement of the Law, Contracts, 2d* (St Paul, Minn., 1981), s. 168 (opinions based on knowledge versus opinions based on judgment, the former giving rise to liability the latter not).

[66] *Smyth v. Lynn* (1954) 85 ILTR 57 (a misrepresentation regarding a property for sale made by the original owner was repeated by the new owner on a resale of the property a few months later. Held that the plaintiff had relied on the first misrepresentation, and not the subsequent repetition of it by the defendant).

[67] *Lutton v. Saville Tractors Ltd* [1986] NI 327. [68] Although see *Smyth v. Lynn*, above n. 66.

[69] *Delaney v. Keogh* [1905] 2 IR 267. [70] *Bank of Ireland v. Smith* [1966] IR 646.

[71] *Hedley Byrne & Co. Ltd v. Heller & Partners Ltd* [1964] AC 465; approved in *Securities Trust Ltd v. Hugh Moore & Alexander Ltd* [1964] IR 417.

or in tort, there is no remedy for innocent misrepresentation, but equity might intervene and grant rescission in very limited situations.[72]

Finally, A may be liable to B for innocent misrepresentation under the Sale of Goods and Supply of Services Act 1980. In contracts for the sale of goods, section 45(1) of the Act applies. If the person making the misrepresentation would have been liable in damages had the misrepresentation been made fraudulently, then that person shall be so liable notwithstanding that the misrepresentation was not fraudulently made.[73] It is a defence if it can be shown that the person making the misrepresentation believed that the misrepresentation was true and had reasonable grounds for so believing. It is not clear whether such damages should be awarded under tortious or contractual principles. Under the statute, rescission can be granted in lieu of damages where the court thinks it just and fit.[74]

Damages in contract are calculated on the basis of restoring the defendant to the position that he would have been in if the contract had been performed correctly. The damages payable in this case can be divided into two distinct yet equally important elements. First, there is the loss of half of the crop due to the failure of the harvester to perform as expected, for which A will be liable. In addition, A is liable for a sum of money which would enable B to replace the harvester with one that could harvest one acre a day.

Where A made no statement about the harvester's capacity, the result is the same. In relation to the claim under Sale of Goods and Supply of Services Act 1980, section 14, where the seller is, or has been made aware of the purchaser's requirements, then the purchaser is entitled to rely upon the seller's skill and knowledge and the test becomes one of subjective expectation.[75] How did the purchaser expect the good to perform having relied upon the seller's skill and expertise? Failure to perform in accordance with that subjective expectation is a breach of the implied term.[76] In the current scenario, A is aware of B's

[72] But only where there was a special relationship between the parties, such as a fiduciary relationship: see *Nocton v. Lord Ashburton* [1914] AC 932.

[73] It does not create a new cause of action where none existed before; it merely widens the scope of remedies available to include innocent misrepresentation: see *O'Donnell v. Truck and Machinery Sales* [1997] 1 ILRM 466.

[74] Section 41.

[75] Section 14(4); *Stokes & McKiernan v. Lixnaw Co-operative Society* (1937) 71 ILTR 70.

[76] Even where the seller could not himself have discovered the unfitness for purpose: *Wallis v. Russell* [1902] 2 IR 585; but see *Draper v. Rubenstein* (1925) 59 ILTR 119.

requirements for the harvesting machine and therefore when the machine fails to live up to those requirements, A is liable for breach of section 14. A's failure to respond directly to B's demand that the harvester harvest one acre a day is of no consequence since liability hinges upon A's knowledge of the intended use, not on any statements made by A. A might also be liable for misrepresentation by silence in either contract, statute or tort. However, the remedy for the breach of section 14 is to be preferred to the more nebulous action of misrepresentation given the facts of this particular case.

Italy

This case concerns liability arising from misleading information obtained during the negotiations. Since a contract has been concluded, the case seems not (subject to what is said below) to give rise to precontractual liability under article 1337 c.c. (that is, extra-contractual liability), but can be considered a case of contractual liability where lack of information might give grounds for contractual remedies.

(1) Where the harvester's capacity has been explicitly represented by A to B, we shall again turn to *dolo* (fraud). Article 1439 c.c. states:

> Fraud is cause for the annulment of the contract when the deception employed by one of the contracting parties was such that, without it, the other contracting party would not have entered into the contact.

If the deception was not such as to compel consent, the contract is valid, even though without the deception it would have included different terms; however, the contracting party in bad faith is liable for damages. Italian academic writers[77] place the violation of the duty to inform within the will theory and link it to article 1439 of the Civil Code.

[77] Very many Italian authors have written on this subject, and liability for non-disclosure is always considered along with the precontractual obligations of good faith. See Caruso, *La culpa in contrahendo. L'esperienza statunitense e quella italiana*; Grisi, *L'obbligo precontrattuale di informazione*; Nanni, *La buona fede contrattuale*, pp. 1–143; F. Benatti, 'Culpa in contrahendo' CI 1987, 287ff.; Benatti, *La responsabilità precontrattuale*; V. Cuffaro, 'Responsabilità precontrattuale' in *Enciclopedia del diritto*, XXXIX (Milano, 1988), p. 1265ff.; M. Chiola, 'Informazione' in *Enciclopedia giuridica Treccani*; G. Ferrarini, 'Investment banking, prospetti falsi e culpa in contrahendo' Giur comm 1988, II, 585; A. Fusaro, 'Fondamenti e limiti della responsabilità precontrattuale' GI 1984, I, 1, 1199; Loi and Tessitore, *Buona fede e responsabilità precontrattuale*; V. Rasi, 'La responsabilità precontrattuale' RDC 1974, 496; Visintini, *La reticenza nella formazione dei contratti*; M. Bessone, 'Rapporto precontrattuale e doveri di correttezza' RTDPC 1955, I, 360. So far there is no equally significant case law to match this huge range of academic writing.

The available remedies for B are contract resolution (recovery of the price and expenses; it might be possible to obtain the difference between the price and the cost of a replacement machine if the price has risen in the meantime) and, if A was in bad faith (he knew about the real capacity of the harvester), B can obtain damages for his lost crops related to the impossibility (which he must demonstrate) of providing a second harvester or a better harvester in due time.

Misleading information has also been recognised by Italian case law as a case of the tortious violation of patrimonial integrity giving rise to extra-contractual liability under article 2043 c.c.,[78] but the contractual solution seems to be the most likely general approach.

(2) Where A makes no statement about the capacity of the harvester, it will be more difficult for B to recover damages.

Silence by itself does not constitute fraud,[79] unless there was a fraudulent concealment of true facts or the silence violated an explicit duty to speak enforced by the law.[80] Using the provisions of the Code on precontractual liability (article 1337 c.c.), B can try to argue that the duty to behave in good faith gives rise to an obligation on each party to inform the other when he discovers the other's mistake. The same article 1337 can be considered as a basis for *culpa aquiliana*; Italian case law and legal theorists have considered that the violation of precontractual duties gives rise to private liability, as in the French solution.[81] Article 1337 c.c. is thus considered a specific form of the *neminem laedere* principle used by article 2043 c.c. The Italian courts are open to create new forms of private liability as society evolves. It could be easier for a court to take an innovatory decision on the basis of the broad form of 'unjustified injury', than to create a new kind of fraud.

Some academic writers,[82] according to the principles set out above, base liability for non-disclosure of relevant information (*dolo omissivo*)

[78] TRIB-T. Monza, 15 Feb. 1996.

[79] This statement could be found in a decision of the Trib. Verona, 18 Nov. 1946, in Foro Pad. 1947, 199 (the sale of a truck, without disclosing that it belonged to the state, was considered fraudulent and avoided).

[80] The Civil Code contains an explicit duty to disclose in arts. 1892–1893 concerning insurance contracts.

[81] Sacco, in Sacco and De Nova, *Il contratto*, I, p. 255; Cass 4 Oct. 1948, n. 1667, in GI 1949, I,1, 29; and nine other decisions up to Cass 11 May 1990, n. 4051, in FI 1991, I, 184; the opposite solution similar to the German tradition, where the precontractual liability is considered as a breach of a contract, has been followed in Italy by Mengoni, in RDCo 1956, II, 365.

[82] Sacco and De Nova, *Obbligazioni e contratti*.

on a wide interpretation of article 1439 c.c., using together the concepts of *presupposizione*, *culpa in contrahendo* and *dolo* (fraud). Up to now, however, only a very few decisions have applied article 1337 c.c. in order to sanction a party's failure to disclose information; the courts traditionally use it only to sanction unjustified withdrawal from negotiations.

A contract may be rendered voidable (*anullabile*) under the doctrine of the 'basic contractual assumption'.[83] We can consider the contract based on an implied condition, as if the parties have negotiated on the basis that 'the contract will not stand if A's harvesting machine cannot harvest one acre a day'. The breach of this condition renders the contract voidable.[84] The Italian courts often find the *presupposizione* in contracts for the sale of land[85] and in relational contracts, and article 1467 c.c. on contracts for mutual counter-performance[86] has been seen by courts as the explicit adoption of the *presupposizione* principle by the legislature.[87] It would certainly be innovative if a court were to use this doctrine to render this contract voidable, but it is not impossible.

Italian courts sometimes use indifferently the doctrines of *presupposizione*, the sale of *aliud pro alio*[88] or mistake[89] according to particular

[83] The *presupposizione* doctrine has a German origin. For an extensive discussion, see A. Pontani, 'La presupposizione nella sua evoluzione, con particolare riferimento all'errore ed alla causa' *Quadrimestre* 1991, 833.

[84] Cass 17 Sep. 1970, n. 1512, FI 1971, I, 3028; Cass 7 Apr. 1971, n. 1025 FI 1971, I, 2574; Cass 22 Sep. 81, n. 5168, FI 1982, I, 104; Cass 31 Oct. 1989, n. 4554, RDC 1990, II, 350; Cass 11 Aug. 1990, n. 8200; Cass 3 Dec. 1991, n. 12921, GI 1992, I, 1, 2210, note Oddi: the last case involved a purchase of shares of a company annulled when the only immovable good in the company's asset was under an action to obtain revocation (art. 2901 c.c.); Cass 1995, n. 1040; Cass 1995, n. 8689.

[85] Cass 1983, n. 6933, Cass 1984, n. 5512.

[86] Article 1467: 'In contracts for continuous or periodic performance or for deferred performance, if extraordinary and unforeseeable events make the performance of one of the parties excessively onerous, the party who owes such performance can demand dissolution of the contract, with the effects set out in article 1458. Dissolution cannot be demanded if the supervening onerousness is part of the normal risk of the contract. A party against whom dissolution is demanded can avoid it by offering to modify equitably the conditions of the contract.'

[87] Cass 1995, n. 1040; Cass 31 Oct. 1989, n. 4554, RDC 1990, II, 350; Cass 1986, n. 20.

[88] Article 1497: 'When the thing sold lacks the qualities promised or those essential for the use for which it is intended, the buyer is entitled to obtain resolution of the contract according to the general provisions on the resolution for non-performance (art. 1453ff.), provided that the defect in quality exceeds the limits of tolerance established by usage. However, the right to obtain resolution is subject to the forfeiture (2964ff., 1495 co.1) and prescription (2946ff., 1495 co.3) established in art. 1495.'

[89] Trib. Napoli, 24 June 1970, in *Giurisprudenza di merito* I, 1972, 407, note Baldanzi; Cass 8 June 1948, n. 864, GI 1949, I, 1, 174.

facts. B's position will be stronger by arguing that A was in bad faith or did not fulfil a standard of fair dealing during the bargaining process. According to the Tribunale of Milan, '*presupposizione* and essential mistake are two different aspects of the same factual situation; the principle of good faith[90] adds strength to the argument in favour of the *presupposizione* when it is a practical criterion for the interpretation of the contract'.[91] The *presupposizione* can be considered as the stronger approach for B where A makes no statement about the harvester. The remedy available will be annulment of the contract[92] (recovery of only the price and expenses, not the lost crops). B is unlikely to demonstrate a *dolo omissivo* and recover damages for lost crops.

Netherlands

During negotiations A has made a false statement on which B relied when he concluded the contract. Therefore, B may in principle annul the contract for mistake[93] and, if the false statement was intentionally made, for fraud.[94] However, the mere annulment and, as its consequence, restitution of the machine and the contract price, would not take away or compensate all the loss that B has suffered from relying on A's untrue statement. It is disputed under Dutch law whether B can recover his additional loss under tort or under precontractual liability (good faith). Some scholars argue that he can, since all his loss should be compensated.[95] Others argue that in such a case the expectation interest should not be compensated.[96] Therefore, the outcome of this case under Dutch law is uncertain. However, if B manages to prove that he had a specific opportunity to buy a similar machine from a third party but gave up the opportunity to conclude a contract with that

[90] *Buona fede*; arts. 1337 and 1375 c.c.

[91] Trib. Milano, 11 Oct. 1948, in DL II, 1949, 17, where the mistake was on the essential quality of the counterpart, but the judges used the *presupposizione* doctrine instead of the essential mistake rule. In favour of a broad interpretation of *presupposizione*: Cass 3 Oct. 1972, n. 2828.

[92] Article 1441 c.c. [93] Article 6:228(1)(a) BW. [94] Article 3:44(1)(3) BW.

[95] See, e.g., Castermans, *De mededelingsplicht in de onderhandelingsfase*, p. 135; M.A.B. Chao-Duivis, 'Schadevergoeding bij dwaling: de veroorzaker betaalt' *Themis* no. 6, June 1990, 261; M.M. van Rossum, 'De schadevergoedingsplicht bij dwaling en negligent misrepresentation' WPNR 5928 (1989).

[96] Hartkamp, *Mr. C. Asser's handleiding tot de beoefening van het Nederlands burgerlijk recht; Verbintenissenrecht*, vol. II, *Algemene leer der overeenkomsten*, p. 513; M.W. Hesselink, 'De schadevergoedingsplicht bij afgebroken onderhandelingen in het licht van het Europese privaatrecht' WPNR 6248–6249 (1996).

third party because he concluded the contract with A, then part of his damage may be recoverable as part of the negative interest.

Where A makes no statement about the capacity of the harvester the answer is the same. It does not make a difference whether A's violation of precontractual good faith consists in making a false statement or in a violation of his duty to inform.

Obviously, in either case there is also a breach of contract, more specifically a non-conformity with the sales contract.[97] Therefore, in principle, B has the specific remedies for non-conformity (repair and replacement)[98] and the general remedies for breach of contract (termination and damages).[99]

Norway

If an agreement has been entered into, statements and actions of the parties during the precontractual period would as a rule be considered from a contractual point of view.

The present case is regulated by the Sale of Goods Act of 13 May 1988, no. 27. If the object for sale does not correspond to the information given during negotiations, a *defect* is present.[100] This is an objective regulation. Hence, the seller has the responsibility to ensure that the information being provided with respect to the object for sale is correct. The statement regarding the capacity of the harvesting machine is false, and consequently a defect is present. Because the defect must be considered a fundamental breach, B can choose to *terminate* the agreement.[101] While B can terminate the agreement, he can also claim *compensation* for losses incurred as a result of the defect.[102]

On the adoption of the Sale of Goods Act in Norwegian and Swedish law, a distinction between direct and indirect losses was made. With respect to direct losses, the basis of liability for compensatory damages is objective, with the exception of 'an impediment beyond his control'.[103] On the other hand, compensation for indirect losses presupposes either that a guarantee has been given or that the seller is at fault.[104] The distinction between direct and indirect losses is defined in Sale of Goods Act, section 67(2). The losses suffered by B by terminating the contract and having to purchase the machine elsewhere are direct

[97] Article 7:17 BW. [98] Articles 7:21 and 7:24 BW. [99] Articles 6:265 and 6:74 BW.

[100] Sale of Goods Act, ss. 17(i) and 18.

[101] Sale of Goods Act, s. 39(1): termination is a retrospective remedy, see s. 64, second sentence.

[102] Sale of Goods Act, s. 40. [103] Cf. art. 79 CISG. [104] Sale of Goods Act, s. 40(3).

losses. In the preliminary draft to the Norwegian Sale of Goods Act, it was stated that misleading information with respect to the object for sale always results in liability, because such information is assumed to be within the control of the seller.[105] In agreement with the Nordic tradition of interpretation, such statements in the draft legislation would be adhered to by the courts. The loss of half of B's asparagus crop is, on the other hand, a direct loss, according to Sale of Goods Act, section 67(2)(a): 'losses as a result of reduced or lost production or turnover'. Whether A's statement with respect to the capacity of the machine is to be regarded as a guarantee is doubtful, although a precise statement about such a significant feature of the machine would perhaps be considered a guarantee. If not, negligence must be shown. This would depend on the facts. For example, if A is the producer of the machine, he would have to give a detailed account of the method he has used for determining that the machine in fact has the capacity to harvest one acre a day. It seems that particularly difficult and unknown operating conditions at B's farm would have to be shown in order to relieve A of his liability. On the other hand, if A is a dealer only, the information from the manufacturer that the machine has the capacity 'to harvest one acre a day' would be sufficient to relieve A of liability. Nevertheless, it would be reasonable to assume that A makes inquiries of B with respect to the operating conditions at his farm.

In the variant situation, where A makes no statement about the harvester's capacity, the remedies are the same, but the reasoning is different. If A knew or could not have been unaware of the fact that the machine did not possess the capacity that B expected, A is in breach of his duty to inform,[106] and there is a defect in the object for sale. Sale of Goods Act, section 17(2)(b)[107] provides that the object for sale must be 'fit for any particular purpose that the seller knew or could not have been unaware of'. This regulation appears to apply on the facts given here.

Portugal

A is liable to B under the sale contract. According to article 913° of the Civil Code, if the thing sold does not have the qualities promised by the seller, the buyer has the right to annul the contract for mistake or fraud and recover all the money paid.[108] He can also ask for the reparation or

[105] Proposition to the Odelsting, no. 80 (1986–87), p. 92.
[106] Cf. Sale of Goods Act, s. 19(1)(b). [107] Cf. art. 35(2)b CISG.
[108] Articles 913 and 905 CC.

replacement of the thing sold, unless A had no prior knowledge of the defect.[109] If A fails to repair or replace the thing he would be liable for the losses suffered by B (the additional cost of a new machine).

In addition, if A was fraudulent,[110] B is entitled to a compensation for all the losses he suffered from the contract, including the lost crop.[111] If A was not fraudulent he would not be liable for B's consequential losses (the lost crop).

Where A did not make a statement, the specific rules of the sales contract discussed above are not applicable, because the seller has not made any specific statement about the qualities of the thing sold, and we cannot objectively speak of a defect in the harvesting machine. Therefore, only the rules of mistake and the general clause of precontractual liability is applicable. In this case, B would only be entitled to recover the money he has paid for the harvesting machine, and to return it to the seller. B makes a mistake in thinking that the machine would harvest one acre a day. The mistake about the qualities of the object is a ground for the annulment of the contract, if A knew the essentiality of that quality for B,[112] as is the case here. As A has not made any statement about the capacity of the machine he has not acted contrary to the rules of good faith, so he has no liability for damages. However, if A had prior knowledge that the machine was unable to harvest one acre, as B expected, the failure to disclose that information would be considered contrary to the rules of good faith which would make A also liable for the loss suffered by B.[113]

Scotland

A's statement is certainly a misrepresentation, most likely either negligent or (if intended to deceive) fraudulent. This alone gives grounds to seek damages for the consequential losses in the law of delict. The fact that the parties to the representation have since entered a contract makes no difference to this position.[114] There is no need to reduce the contract before making this claim.

If the statement was made with an intention to be bound (objectively determined), then it may be a contractual warranty about the

[109] Article 914 CC.

[110] In Portuguese law fraud can be found in certain cases of negligence because it does not necessarily require intention, but only the consciousness that the other party is being induced into a mistake as a result of the behaviour of the agent (art. 253).

[111] Articles 913 and 908 CC. [112] Articles 251 and 247 CC. [113] Article 227 CC.

[114] Law Reform (Miscellaneous Provisions) (Scotland) Act 1985, s. 10.

machine's capacity, and breach of contract damages are available for its falsity.[115]

The contract would fall within the remit of the Sale of Goods Act 1979, as amended, in particular by the Sale and Supply of Goods Act 1994. This Act requires that goods sold by description must correspond with the description[116] and that goods sold in the course of a business must be of satisfactory quality, that is, fit for their purpose,[117] with failure in either regard being a breach of contract giving rise, *inter alia*, to a claim for damages.[118] However, it seems unlikely that the representation about the capacity of the machine would be treated as part of its description – statements as to quality are not usually so considered.[119] The comment about the capacity of the machine might be a 'relevant circumstance' to be taken into account in assessing whether the goods are of satisfactory quality,[120] but this would only be necessary if the statement was not itself a contractual warranty (see above).

For the delictual claim, A must pay damages on the reliance interest, to put B in the position he would have been in if the statement had not been made (difference in value or cost of putting the incapacity right;[121] if the misrepresentation was fraudulent, even losses not reasonably foreseeable are recoverable); for the contractual claim, on the expectation interest, to put B in the position he would have been in had the statement been true (and so he can recover for the lost harvest this year and possibly next, bearing in mind the possibilities of mitigating loss that may intervene). The costs of purchase of a replacement machine (or of repairs to the one already acquired), less the proceeds of any resale of the faulty tractor, would also be claimable in contractual damages.

B has the option of avoiding the contract (reduction) on the grounds of misrepresentation, leading to return of the machine to A and return of the price to B (*restitutio in integrum*).

If the Sale of Goods Act implied terms are relevant, B would have the right to reject the goods if the breach was considered material and to require the price to be returned to him (section 15B). Since implementation of the EC Consumer Sales Directive 99/44/EC in UK law

[115] MacQueen and Thomson, *Contract Law in Scotland*, paras. 3.14–3.19.
[116] Section 13(1). [117] Section 14(2), (6). [118] Section 53A.
[119] *Border Harvesters Ltd v. Edwards Engineering (Perth) Ltd* 1985 SLT 128.
[120] Sale of Goods Act 1979, s. 14(2A). [121] Thomson, *Delictual Liability*, pp. 270–1.

through amendment of the Sale of Goods Act, B now also has the right to require repair or replacement of the goods.[122]

Where A made no statement, B may have a claim by way of the term implied into the contract under Sale of Goods Act 1979, section 14(3), on the basis that the goods purchased were not fit for a particular purpose of the buyer made known to the seller, expressly or by implication, in circumstances showing that the buyer is relying, or it is reasonable for him to rely, on the skill or judgment of the seller. In general, if the seller knows the buyer's purpose, the latter's reliance will be presumed.[123] Breach of this implied term will give the buyer a claim for damages based on the expectation interest[124] and the right to reject the goods if the breach is material,[125] provided that the buyer has not accepted the goods.[126] There is some authority in Scotland allowing a party, whose uninduced error about the subject matter of the contract has been known to and taken advantage of by the other party, to reduce that contract, making it void. The error must, however, be an error in transaction rather than an error of motive, which must be induced by the other party to be relevant. This appears to be an error in motive and so irrelevant, being uninduced.[127]

Spain

In Spanish law there is liability on several grounds. On the one hand, B can obtain annulment of the contract on the basis of mistake, on the other hand, he can use the remedies contained in the law of sales (*actio redhibitoria/quanti minoris*).

By telling B that the machine would be able to harvest double the quantity it was actually fit for, A acted fraudulently, since (as A knew) it was mainly this false information which made B conclude the contract.[128] Therefore, B can bring the claim for nullity under article 1265 CC.[129]

[122] Section 48B. [123] Atiyah, Adams and MacQueen, *Sale of Goods*, pp. 199–200.

[124] Sale of Goods Act 1979, s. 53A(1), as added by Sale and Supply of Goods Act 1994: 'The measure of damages for the seller's breach of contract is the estimated loss directly and naturally arising, in the ordinary course of events, from the breach.' See also s. 53A(2): 'Where the seller's breach consists of the delivery of goods which are not of the quality required by the contract and the buyer retains the goods, such loss as aforesaid [i.e. under s. 53A(1)] is prima facie the difference between the value of the goods at the time of delivery to the buyer and the value they would have had if they had fulfilled the contract.'

[125] Section 15B. [126] Sections 34–35A.

[127] See further on error, MacQueen and Thomson, *Contract Law in Scotland*, paras. 4.45–4.66.

[128] Article 1269 CC. [129] STS, 23 July 1998, no. 734/1998, RJ 1998\6199.

In addition, and alternatively, B may also bring a claim for redhibition or *quanti minoris*, based on the concluded contract of sale.[130] If A knew that the machine would not work as promised, he is also liable for damages.[131] Only in that case will B be able to claim expectation damages, probably including the ruined crop.

In the case where A made no statement, the result is the same. In letting B think that the machine would be able to harvest double that which it was actually fit for, A acted fraudulently. According to good faith, A should have informed B about the actual capacity of the machine. A knew that it was mainly this false information which made B conclude the contract.[132] Fraud is possible through active information, but also in staying passive when information should have been given.[133] Therefore, B can bring the claim for nullity under article 1265 CC, if he can prove the fraud. Otherwise, he can claim annulment of the contract within four years on the ground of mistake,[134] as the capacity of the machine was essential for his decision to buy it, and his mistake was excusable since his belief was based on A's failure to correct him. His claims for redhibition or *quanti minoris*, and expectation damages, are the same as discussed above.

Sweden

B can declare the contract avoided, claim restitution of the price paid to A and claim damages for the ruined crop.

The parties have entered into a binding contract of sale. Therefore the Sale of Goods Act[135] is applicable.[136] The SGA is in most respects the same as the CISG. The statement by A about the quality of the machine is part of the contract and therefore the discrepancy in the capacity constitutes a non-conformity.[137] In any case, the machine is in nonconformity as it does not conform with information given by A before the conclusion of the contract.[138]

The possible remedies for breach are cure, delivery of substitute goods, price reduction, avoidance and damages.[139] B is entitled to avoid the contract, as the breach is fundamental.[140] If he would like to avoid

[130] Articles 1484 and 1486 CC. [131] Article 1486.2° CC. [132] Article 1269 CC.

[133] STS, 23 July 1998, no. 734/1998, RJ 1998\6199. [134] Articles 1266 and 1301 CC.

[135] Köplagen (1990:931), Sale of Goods Act (SGA).

[136] Kihlman, *Fel. Särskilt vid köp av lös och fast egendom*, pp. 55ff., 74 ff.; Almén, *Om köp och byte av lös egendom*, p. 573ff.; Håstad, *Den nya köprätten*; Ramberg and Herre, *Köplagen*; Herre, *Ersättningar i köprätten. Särskilt om skadeståndsberäkning*.

[137] Article 17 SGA. [138] Article 18 SGA. [139] Article 30 SGA. [140] Article 39 SGA.

the contract, he must give notice within a reasonable time after he ought to have discovered the defect or within a reasonable time after the time required for substitute delivery or repair. According to article 66 of the SGA, the buyer loses his right to avoid the contract if it is impossible to make restitution of the good substantially in the condition in which he received it.[141] This requirement could cause some problems for B, as he has already used the machine. However, dependent upon the circumstances, B could argue in two different ways in order not to lose his right to avoid the contract. The first argument could be that the machine was put into normal use before he discovered the non-conformity and that he therefore still has a right to avoidance. The second argument could be that, according to article 66(3) (which does not have any corresponding rule in CISG), he has a right to avoid the contract even if he could not make restitution according to the main rule, as long as he compensates the seller for the loss in value caused by the use of the machine.

As A has specifically promised the capacity of the machine, this would probably be regarded as a guarantee according to article 40 of the SGA. This question is of importance as the SGA, contrary to CISG, make a distinction between direct and indirect losses. The direct losses are recoverable when the party in breach could not show that the breach was due to an impediment beyond his control. Indirect losses are recoverable, when the breach is non-conformity, if the party in breach has acted with fault or if the object of sale at the time of contracting did not conform with what the seller specifically had promised (more or less guaranteed). As A specifically promised the capacity, B is entitled to damages according to the expectation interest.[142] A is therefore liable to compensate B for the ruined harvest.

B has a duty to mitigate the loss.[143] B could mitigate his losses by avoiding the contract and making a cover purchase or hiring a harvesting machine to take care of next year's harvest. Thus, he is not entitled to damages for half of next year's harvest. Instead, he is entitled to damages for the difference between the contract price and the price of the substitute transaction.[144]

As a general rule, B could not use rules based on precontractual liability in this case, as the parties have entered into a binding agreement of sale. However, if B, contrary to the facts of the case, had suffered no

[141] Cf. art. 82 CISG. [142] Articles 40 and 67 SGA. [143] Article 70 SGA.
[144] Article 68 SGA; cf. art. 75 CISG.

losses according to the rules on the expectation interest, or if he could not prove such losses, there is some support in academic writing for the view that B could have a right to compensation for the reliance interest.

In the case where A does not make a statement about the harvester's capacity, the statement by B about the quality of the machine is part of the contract and therefore the discrepancy in the capacity constitutes a non-conformity.[145] The possible remedies for breach are as discussed above, except that A's failure to inform B about his mistaken assumption might not be held to constitute fault. In that case, B would not be entitled to damages for the ruined harvest, as it is regarded to be an indirect loss.

Switzerland

Specific performance and damages in contract: A is liable under the sale contract. The object sold is defective according to OR 197 if the quality of the object delivered does not correspond to the (express) representations made by the seller. Under Swiss law, the demands for an (express) representation are not very high. Each statement that concerns the qualities of the object of the purchase and that has, in a recognisable way, an influence on the decision of the other party to buy is a representation.[146]

The seller is liable according to the special provisions on the warranty against defects in the object of the purchase.[147] These provisions determine in detail the claims of the buyer in case of defects, including specific replacement of the defective object. If the buyer has sued for rescission (see below), he is entitled to claim for damages.[148] It is accepted by courts and academic writers that the seller is obliged to pay compensatory damages also in other cases according to the general provisions on non-performance.[149] The extent of the compensation depends on whether fault is attributable to the seller.

A is at fault if he knew that the express representation is not correct. Under certain circumstances the seller is at fault even if he had no knowledge of the defect but has violated his duty to examine the object of the purchase, for example, if the seller has acted as a professional.[150] If fault is attributable to A he has to compensate B's positive interest in the contract (expectation interest) according to OR 208 III. B can

145 Article 17 SGA. 146 BGE 102 II 100. 147 OR 197ff. 148 OR 208.

149 OR 97; BGE 108 II 104. Cf. BernerKommentar-Giger, OR vor 197–210 n. 24ff.; BaslerKommentar-Honsell, OR vor 197–210 n. 6.

150 BernerKommentar-Giger, OR 208 n. 49ff.; BaslerKommentar-Honsell, OR vor 197–210 n. 6.

therefore claim the difference from the profit he would have made if the machine had harvested one acre a day.

According to OR 208 II, the seller has to compensate the damage directly caused to the buyer even in case of no fault at all. Traditionally, writers and courts apply this no-fault liability if the defect causes damage to goods of the buyer other than the object of the purchase;[151] this opinion is criticised by a growing number of authors.[152] In the present case, however, it is doubtful whether the ruin of half of the crop is damage of that category. The value of the crop is rather a lost profit that B could have achieved with another machine. Lost profits are never compensated if no fault is attributable to the seller.[153]

B can only recover damages and demand specific replacement if he notified A of the defect[154] and sued him[155] in due time. If the buyer fails so to notify, the object purchased is deemed to have been accepted to the extent that there are no defects involved which were not recognisable in the course of a customary examination. If defects are discovered at a later date, notification must be given immediately upon their discovery. Otherwise the object of the purchase is deemed to have been accepted with respect to such defects. The time periods are quite short.[156] The duty to notify in time and the statute of limitations are applicable even if the seller is not a professional and even if the liability is based on the general provisions of non-performance.[157] But the short time periods do not apply if A has wilfully misled B about the qualities of the machine.[158]

Culpa in contrahendo: most authors reject a concurrent liability on the ground of *culpa in contrahendo.*[159]

Tort: the seller of an object with defects is liable in tort only if he has violated a duty in favour of others in general and not only a duty based on the contract. But a claim on tortious grounds is also restricted by the short period for the notification mentioned above.[160] In the present

151 '*Mangelfolgeschaden*'; cf. BernerKommentar-Giger, OR 208 n. 36ff. Recently the Federal Court has confirmed this approach: BGE 133 III 257.

152 See BaslerKommentar-Honsell, OR 208 n. 9.

153 BernerKommentar-Giger, OR 208 n. 35. 154 OR 201. 155 OR 210.

156 OR 210 I: 'Actions based on a warranty for defects in the object of the purchase shall be barred at the end of one year after delivery to the buyer of the object sold, even if the defect was only discovered by the buyer at a later date, unless the seller has assumed the liability for a longer period.'

157 BernerKommentar-Giger, OR vor 197–210 n. 24ff. 158 OR 203, OR 210 I.

159 Cf. BernerKommentar-Kramer, OR 22 n. 48.

160 67 II 137; not decided in BGE 90 II 89. The courts' decisions are contrary to the views of academic opinion: cf. BaslerKommentar-Honsell, OR vor 197–210 n. 7.

case, the machine is not useful for B's purposes but it has no objective defect. A, hence, is generally not liable in tort. A might only be liable in tort if he wilfully misled B about the qualities of the machine and if he obviously could have foreseen the loss that would be caused. In that case A must compensate B for the lost profits he would have achieved with another machine.

Rescission of the contract: B can rescind the contract. In the case of warranty against defects in the object of the purchase the buyer can sue for rescission of the purchase according to OR 205 (*Wandlung*). The claim for rescission is restricted by the short time periods of OR 201 and 210 mentioned above. After the expiration of the period, the buyer can still annul the contract (so-called *Anfechtung*) because of a defect of the contract's conclusion (error) according to OR 24 I section 4;[161] this opinion of the Swiss Federal Court is, however, criticised by the majority of legal writers.[162]

In the variant situation, where A makes no statement, the result is the same. Based on B's expressly communicated expectation it must be assumed that A has made a representation (*Zusicherung*) for the capacity of the harvesting machine according to OR 197. Representations can also be implied.[163] According to academic writers there is a representation if the buyer demands a special quality of the object sold and the seller after that concludes the contract without protest.[164] If there is no representation, the capacity of the machine is at least an assumed quality according to OR 197. Like the representation, the lack of an assumed quality is a defect of the object sold and in general gives rise to the same claims of the buyer.[165]

Editors' comparative observations

This case is different from the other cases in this study in one significant respect: it raises questions of liability in respect of the precontractual negotiations where the negotiating parties have in fact concluded the contract. The case was included to test whether and (if so) how the conclusion of the contract affected each jurisdiction's analysis of the precontractual stage. Within the facts there is also a variant, to test the difference in this context between a misrepresentation and silence during the negotiations.

[161] BGE 114 II 131. [162] Cf. BaslerKommentar-Honsell, OR vor art. 197–210 n. 9.
[163] BaslerKommentar-Honsell, OR 197 n. 14.
[164] BernerKommentar-Giger, OR 197 n. 27. [165] BernerKommentar-Giger, OR 197 n. 80.

All jurisdictions give a remedy to B in the case of A's precontractual misrepresentation; and all except Germany give a remedy for A's silence. There is, therefore, apparently a greater unanimity of result in this case, although there are still some significant differences between the jurisdictions, both on the basis of the liability and on the scope of the remedy.

In the case of A's misrepresentation, almost all jurisdictions identify his primary liability as being under the contract of sale: the existence of the concluded contract has therefore changed substantially the focus of the analysis. The basis of the contractual liability is generally a warranty as to the quality of the harvester or as to its fitness to fulfil the purposes for which B made clear he required it – the nature of the warranty varying according to the respective jurisdictions' theory of contractual obligation (and so, for example, England, Ireland and Scotland look to terms implied into the contract; other jurisdictions look to the obligations inherent in the special contract of sale). However, some reporters analyse the facts, in the alternative, in similar terms to the cases in which no contract was ultimately concluded, basing the liability on B's mistake as to the harvester's capacity (France, Spain) or A's misrepresentation (Denmark, England, Ireland, Scotland; and, if A was fraudulent, France), or *culpa in contrahendo* (Germany) or tort (Germany, Switzerland) if A wilfully misled B. Some reporters make clear that the existence here of the contractual liability will override some or all of the claims based on precontractual liability.

The remedy also varies. All jurisdictions that identify a contractual claim give B a remedy in contract to protect his failed expectation in relation to the harvester's capacity. Austria, England, France, Germany, Portugal, Scotland and Switzerland give B the right to specific replacement of the defective harvester with one that meets the contractual standard; others allow only damages to cover B's additional costs of obtaining a replacement harvester. The right to claim replacement has a different source in different systems: in many it results from the implementation of the Directive on Consumer Sales 99/44/EC; in France, however, it flows from general principles of contract law. Those jurisdictions that allow B's mistake or A's fraud to nullify the contract will allow B in consequence to recover the price paid.

There is also some variation in the scope of damages that A might be required to pay to cover B's consequential losses, and in particular the lost crop. Most jurisdictions again focus on the liability in contract, and the result therefore depends upon the general rules of each jurisdiction for the scope of damages recoverable in contract. Some impose liability on A, or liability in respect of all the losses suffered, only if he was at fault or, sometimes, gave a specific warranty about the qualities of the goods (Austria, Germany, Italy, Norway, Portugal, Spain, Sweden, Switzerland); others have a general rule allowing for recovery by B of all his losses on the expectation measure (including therefore the lost crop) once the contractual liability is established (England, Finland, France, Greece, Ireland, Italy, Scotland). Again, those jurisdictions which allow B a claim based not (or not only) on the contract but on precontractual liability will allow an award of *reliance* damages, which can include the lost crop, if they fall within the principles of the relevant ground of liability (such as the jurisdictions' varying rules for liability in *culpa in contrahendo* or in tort).

In the variant situation, where A made no misrepresentation about the harvester's capacity but remained silent in response to B's statement about it, the German reporters take the view that A had no duty in such circumstances to disclose that B had misunderstood the harvester's capacity, and therefore B has no remedy. All other jurisdictions, however, would give a remedy. Some reporters simply see no difference between the cases of misrepresentation and silence here. For others, the basis of claim changes in the case of silence, but the substantive result may not. Any remedy which hinged upon a false statement (such as the misrepresentation claim in English, Irish and Scots law; although Ireland considers that there might be representation by silence) now falls away; and in Portugal the contractual liability itself no longer covers the case but is replaced by precontractual liability based B's mistake. But in other jurisdictions the contractual liability still arises. It is particularly interesting to note the response of the common law jurisdictions to this case. Throughout the cases in this study, it is the English, Irish and Scots reporters who have most often emphasised that there is no liability for failure to disclose: misrepresentations and breaches of contractual promises give rise to liability, but silence generally does not. However, in this case, the fact that there is a contract between A and B makes all the difference, because it is now possible to *imply* terms into the contract based on A's silence in response to B's statement. There is no general duty of disclosure between negotiating parties, and the starting point of the common law is the principle *caveat emptor*. However, statute reverses this position in the case of contracts for the sale of goods, where the business seller is required to make implied promises as to the quality of the goods sold and their fitness for purpose.

3 From the common law to the civil law: the experience of Israel

NILI COHEN

The dilemma

Precontractual liability relates to liability from a specific temporal standpoint: the time before a contract has been created. Thus, the very definition of such liability is coupled with a dilemma: if a contract has not been created, why should precontractual liability be imposed? This liability apparently could not be based on contract, since a contract has not been created. On the other hand, if such liability is grounded, for example, either in torts or in restitution it might be incompatible with the contractual principle of no liability. The absence of contractual liability means that the parties are free not to deal. Liability based solely on negotiations might seem to override the negative freedom not to deal. This dilemma is well reflected in the different approaches adopted by the common law, on the one hand, and the civil or continental law, on the other hand.

Israeli law under the common law: no rule of precontractual liability

The common law does not recognise a general principle of good faith which might create a basis for precontractual liability.[1] This derives from a wide application of the principle of the freedom of contract and from what seems to be 'a respect for the contractual rules of the game'. It reflects adherence to the rule of law in the strict sense and to the

[1] S. Whittaker and R. Zimmermann, 'Good Faith in European Contract Law: Surveying the Legal Landscape' in Zimmermann and Whittaker, *Good Faith in European Contract Law*, pp. 39–41 (their discussion relates to the whole concept of good faith).

values of certainty and predictability in law. It gives preference to rules over standards.[2] It puts emphasis on a clear demarcation line between negotiations and contract. It encourages self-reliance.

Yet certain conduct, even though performed during negotiations, might be improper, and should give rise to liability. The mere fact that this conduct is performed during negotiations does not give immunity from liability. In sum: though the common law does not contain a principle of precontractual liability, it nevertheless employs several devices to monitor conduct during negotiations, in particular through the law of torts, restitution, estoppel and even contract.[3]

Before the enactment of the Contracts (General Part) Law in 1973,[4] Israeli contract law was largely dominated by common law rules, a heritage of the British mandate over the country. The cautious approach concerning liability imposed on activities during negotiations also characterised Israeli law. But following English law, and sometimes even preceding it,[5] Israeli law occasionally employed torts,

[2] On the much discussed distinction between rules and standards: K. Sullivan, 'The Justices of Rules and Standards' (1992) 106 *Harvard Law Review* 22; L. Kaplow, 'Rules versus Standards: an Economic Analysis' (1992) 42 *Duke Law Journal* 557.

[3] For the general qualifications in English law regarding the absence of the duty of good faith: Zimmermann and Whittaker, *Good Faith in European Contract Law*, pp. 41–8. For the use of mechanisms other than a general principle of precontractual liability in English law, see the Conclusions, below, pp. 462–5.

For a general survey of American law: E.A. Farnsworth, 'Precontractual Liability and Preliminary Agreements: Fair Dealing and Failed Negotiations' (1987) 87 *Columbia Law Review* 217, 233–5. See also G. Shell, 'Opportunism and Trust in the Negotiation of Commercial Contracts: Toward a New Cause of Action' (1991) 44 *Vanderbilt Law Review* 221 (suggesting a new cause of action in American law to guard against opportunism in negotiations). In the same vein: J. Kostritsky, 'Bargaining with Uncertainty, Moral Hazard, and Sunk Costs: a Default Rule for Precontractual Negotiations' (1993) 44 *Hastings Law Journal* 621; A. Schwartz and R.E. Scott, 'Precontractual Liability and Preliminary Agreements' (2007) 120 *Harvard Law Review* 662. For balancing freedom and liability in negotiations: O. Grosskopf and B. Medina, 'Regulating Contract Formation: Precontractual Reliance, Sunk Costs, and Market Structure' (2007) 39 *Connecticut Law Review* 1977.

For a comparative study relating to American and German Law: M. Auer, 'The Structure of Good Faith: a Comparative Study of Good Faith Arguments' (17 November 2006), available at SSRN: http://ssrn.com/abstract=945594. On the international level: J. Klein and C. Bachechi, 'Precontractual Liability and the Duty of Good Faith Negotiations in International Transactions' (1994) 17 *Houston Journal of International Law* 1.

[4] 27 LSI 117 (1973) (Contracts Law).

[5] Liability for negligent precontractual misrepresentation was first imposed in Israel in CA 76/86 *Amidar v. Aharon*, 32(2) PD 337 (Hebrew), preceding the English case of *Esso Petroleum Co. Ltd v. Mardon* [1976] QB 801.

restitution, estoppel or contract[6] to impose liability for improper conduct in negotiations.

Section 12 of the Contracts Law

Rule of precontractual liability

The 1973 Contracts Law introduced into Israeli law some novelties, one of which is the duty of good faith which has been applied not only to the stage of performance in section 39,[7] but also to the stage of the negotiations and the conclusion of the contract.

Section 12 of the Contracts Law, whose title is 'Negotiation in good faith', reads:

> (a) In negotiating a contract, a person shall act in customary manner and in good faith.
> (b) A party who does not act in customary manner and in good faith shall be liable to pay compensation to the other party for the damage caused to him in consequence of the negotiations or the making of the contract, and the provisions of sections 10, 13 and 14 of the Contracts (Remedies for Breach of Contract) Law, 1970 shall apply *mutatis mutandis*.[8]

This section, which embodies the principle of *culpa in contrahendo*, a direct device for imposing a precontractual liability, mirrors the switch to the continental system made by the Israeli legislator. This liability applies either when a contract has not been concluded, or when it has been concluded.

Civil law impact

The concept of *culpa in contrahendo* is continental. It originated in Germany and spread around continental Europe. In the various jurisdictions in which it applies it has different variations, but there is a single idea nurturing it. The contracting parties are not strangers. They rely on each other. They have to be considerate with each other. This is

[6] N. Cohen, 'Good Faith in Bargaining and Principles of Contract Law' (1990) 9 *Tel-Aviv University Studies in Law* 249, 256–63.

[7] Which reads: 'An obligation or right arising out of a contract shall be fulfilled or exercised in customary manner and in good faith.'

[8] Contracts (Remedies for Breach of Contract) Law, 1970 (25 LSI 11), s. 10, provides for the right to compensation; s. 13 grants the court discretion to impose compensation for non-pecuniary loss; and s. 14 provides for reduction of damages in the case where the injured party has not mitigated his loss.

translated into a legal duty imposing an obligation to compensate the party who was injured as a result of the wrongdoing of the other party in the negotiating process.[9]

The principle of good faith derives from a stricter application of the notion of freedom. The idea underlying it is that negotiation is not a liability-free zone. It reflects an emphasis on morality. It indicates a preference for standards and discretion over formal rules.[10] Israeli principle postulates an *a priori* assumption of limitation of freedom of action in the bargaining process, subject to excuses or justifications exempting from liability. It has thus rejected the opposite assumption of English law based on an *a priori* freedom in the bargaining process, subject to special rules imposing liability.

Section 12 and other grounds of precontractual liability

Section 12 serves naturally as the major vehicle for imposing precontractual liability. But section 12 is not exhaustive. The possibility of using tort law, restitution, estoppel and contract still exists, and indeed they are being used.[11] Section 12 could be simultaneously employed, provided that there is no double recovery.

Nature of liability under section 12

The Israeli Supreme Court has expressed some doubts as to the nature of liability under section 12 – whether it is grounded in tort or contract – and finally held that it is a liability *ex lege*.[12] It has been argued by

[9] F. Kessler and E. Fine, '"Culpa in Contrahendo", Bargaining in Good Faith, and Freedom of Contract: a Comparative Study' (1964) 77 *Harvard Law Review* 401; G. Kuehne, 'Reliance, Promissory Estoppel and Culpa in Contrahendo: a Comparative Analysis' (1990) 10 *Tel-Aviv University Studies in Law* 279; Hondius, *Precontractual Liability*; A.M. Rabello, 'The Theory concerning Culpa in Contrahendo (Precontractual Liability): from Roman Law to the German Legal System – a Hundred Years after the Death of Jhering' in Rabello, *European Legal Traditions and Israel*, p. 69; D. Snyder, 'Comparative Law in Action: Promissory Estoppel, the Civil Law, and the Mixed Jurisdiction' (1998) 15 *Arizona International and Comparative Law* 695.

[10] For the polar approaches of English and continental systems: H.K. Luecke, 'Good Faith and Contractual Performance' in Finn, *Essays on Contract Law*, pp. 155, 170–1. For a recommendation to include precontractual liability in a future European Code which as an open norm could be differently applied by each system: J. van Erp, 'The Pre-Contractual Stage' in Hartkamp *et al.*, *Towards a European Civil Code* (3rd edn), p. 363.

[11] The tort of negligence is commonly used: CA 783/83 *Kaplan v. Novogrotzky* 38 PD(3) 477 (Hebrew); CA 714/87 *Sher v. Cohen* 43 PD(3) 159, 163 (Hebrew). Estoppel is now considered to be embodied within section 12: Friedmann and Cohen, *Contracts A, B, C*, ss. 12.22–12.23 (Hebrew).

[12] Further Hearing 7/81 *Pnidar v. Castro*, 37 (4) PD 673, 701 (Hebrew).

academic writers, however, that the nature of liability is substantially tortious. The law does not specify that the breach of the duty to act in good faith is a tort, but the fact that it is a duty imposed by law, and that the remedy for its breach is reliance damages, makes it close to tort liability.[13] That means that, for example, punitive damages might be awarded,[14] in particular where the loss was intentionally caused.

The Israeli Supreme Court has interpreted section 12 far beyond its strict wording. Though the sole remedy referred to in section 12 is reliance damages, section 12 has been employed as the basis of an estoppel, in which case the remedy can lead to the enforcement of a non-contractual promise.[15] Also, in a controversial case the Supreme Court has decided that breach of the duty of good faith might lead to the imposition of performance (expectation) damages.[16] The result is that where enforcement or expectation damages are awarded, liability under section 12 becomes contractual.

Evaluation of section 12

The introduction of the duty to act in good faith, in particular in negotiations, has been praised as a major innovation of the Israeli Contracts Law.[17] Section 12 has received attention in the legal literature more than any other section of the Contracts Law.[18] Judicial decisions are saturated with its application. After more than 30 years of operation, one can say that the switch to the continental system is absolute. The cautiousness of English law regarding precontractual liability has been replaced by an expansionist approach resulting in a very wide

[13] Friedmann and Cohen, *Contracts A, B, C*, s. 12.26. Negligent misrepresentation or fraud entail reliance damages: ibid. s. 12.116. But in American law under the dominant approach, fraud entails performance damages: *Restatement Torts 2d* (St. Paul, 1965) s. 549(2) and comment g.

[14] CA 30/72 *Friedmann v. Segal*, 27(2) PD 225 (Hebrew); CA 354/76 *Sharf Estate v. Advisory Economic Services*, 35(2) PD 169 (Hebrew).

[15] CA 846/70 *Atiyah v. Ararat*, 31 (2) PD 780 (Hebrew); CA 829/80 *Shikun Ovdim v. Zepnik*, 37 (1) PD 579 (Hebrew); CTA 7561/01 *Hanit v. Minister of Construction*, 57(3) PD 611, 622 (Hebrew).

[16] CA 6370/00 *Kal-Binian v. A.R.M.*, 56(3) PD 289 (Hebrew); CA 8144/00 *Alrig v. Brender*, 57(1) PD 158 (Hebrew). For a critical note, see G. Shalev, 'More on the Principle of Good Faith' (2003) 3 *Kiryat Hamishpat* (Tel-Aviv) 121 (Hebrew).

[17] CA 800/75 *Kut v. Irgun Hadaiarim*, 31 PD(3) 813 (Hebrew).

[18] For a general survey, see N. Cohen, 'Good Faith in Bargaining and Principles of Contract Law' (1990) 9 *Tel-Aviv University Studies in Law* 249; A.M. Rabello, 'Culpa in Contrahendo and Good Faith in the Formation of Contract: Pre-Contractual Liability in Israeli Law' in Rabello, *Essays on European Law and Israel*, p. 245. For a detailed survey, see Friedmann and Cohen, *Contracts A, B, C*, ch. 12, pp. 511–648.

liability which almost ignores the zone of freedom once assured to the parties during the negotiation process. Israeli courts have applied the principle in the most extremist way possible, probably in a similar way to the Netherlands.[19] This will be evident in the analysis of the cases.

Analysis of cases

In this section a brief account is given of how Israeli law would answer each of the cases in this study: the current position under section 12 of the Contracts Law, but also drawing attention where appropriate to changes in the outcome under section 12 by comparison with the earlier Israeli law (governed mostly by the common law). This commentary has been written in the light of the other countries' reports, and will therefore also highlight comparisons and contrasts with the various European jurisdictions.

Case 1 Negotiations for premises for a bookshop

Cause of action: good faith requires fairness and honesty.[20] Starting negotiations implies an intention to conclude a contract.[21] A did not have such an intention. An Israeli court would impose liability on A by virtue of section 12 and the same result would have ensued before the enactment of the section. The fraudulent misrepresentation by A might well establish also a claim for fraud in torts,[22] as in England, Ireland and Scotland.

Loss and remedy: the regular rule of section 12 is that the injured party is entitled to reliance loss. The €0.5 m (the difference between what A offered and the price B received) reflects, however, the possible performance interest of a contract between A and B which has not been concluded. B is not entitled to claim the performance interest. This might be subject to an exception which applies when negotiations reached a stage of no retraction, for example, where the defendant gives an assurance that a contract is going to be concluded, there is an

[19] In particular with regard to the remedy which has been interpreted as including expectation damages: CA 6370/00 *Kal-Binian v. A.R.M.*, 56(3) PD 289 (Hebrew); CA 8144/00 *Alrig v. Brender*, 57(1) PD 158 (Hebrew).

[20] HC 59/80 *Beer Sheva Transportation Services v. Labour Tribunal* 35(1) PD 828, 834 (Hebrew) (in the context of good faith in the performance of a contract, but the same applies to the stage of negotiations).

[21] CA 800/75 *Kut v. Irgun Hadaiarim*, 31 PD(3) 813, 818 (Hebrew).

[22] Civil Wrongs Ordinance (New Version) 2 LSI New Version (1972) 5, s.56.

agreement on major points, the injured party substantially relies on it, and later the defendant retracts with no reasonable justification.[23] The regular measure of reliance damages should apply in this case.

Reliance losses could be composed of direct costs (attorney's fees, brokerage fees, etc.), but also of consequential loss such as lost opportunities. In our case, the culpable conduct of A resulted in the loss of the contract opportunity with C. B would be entitled to claim €0.2 m, the difference between the contract opportunity with C and the price he finally received. This result is in conformity with the majority of reports.

A, an intentional wrongdoer, might be subject also to punitive damages.[24]

Case 2 Negotiations for renewal of a lease

Cause of action: similarly to the previous case, A entered negotiations with no intention to conclude a contract. The analysis of the former case is applicable here. Alternatively, since the parties are already contractually connected they are subject to a *contractual* duty of good faith by section 39 of the Contracts Law.

Regarding the contractual duty of good faith, an Israeli court has stated that a party must not misrepresent to the other party his willingness to continue the contractual relations with that other party.[25] The duty of good faith implies that as soon as A became aware of B's wish to renew the lease (in July 1999) he should have told him that he was not interested in it. A broke the duty of good faith and also committed the tort of fraud. Tort liability would apply also under the previous law.

Loss and remedies: first, the loss of opportunity with X cannot be attributable to A since B decided that he was not interested in a contract with X before starting negotiations with A. But this can serve as proof of the measure of the actual loss B suffered.

Secondly, the additional costs of renting a temporary warehouse and the business losses which might flow from the disturbance to the distribution arrangement are the actual loss suffered by B. Had B known

[23] Minority view, CA 579/83 *Sonnenstein v. Gabaso*, PD 42(2) 278 (Hebrew), which has become the prevailing view: CA 6370/00 *Kal-Binian v. A.R.M.*, 56(3) PD 289 (Hebrew); CA 8144/00 *Alrig v. Brender*, 57(1) PD 158 (Hebrew), see below n. 56.

[24] Friedmann and Cohen, *Contracts A, B, C*, s. 12.131.

[25] In the context of an employment contract: HC 566/76 *Elco v. Labour Tribunal*, 31(2) PD 197, 209, 212 (Hebrew).

A's real intention he would have looked for another lease in a convenient area in due time before the expiration of the lease. The fact that prior to the negotiations with A, B was able to find a lease at a price similar to that which he was paying A, might show that the additional costs could have been avoided.

The losses resulting from the move to another location are losses which B might have suffered anyway due to the expiration of the lease, but the present lease is temporary. B might justifiably argue that, had he been notified before, he might have found a permanent place and avoided the temporary lease.

In the contractual measure, B is to be put in the position in which he would have been had the contract not been broken (performance interest). That means that B would probably have saved the costs of the temporary move, the higher rate of the lease and the commercial inconvenience resulting from that move. But the same would apply if the base is precontractual. B is put in the position before starting the negotiations for the renewal of the lease (reliance interest). In that case, B would have started in due time the search for a new lease. As a result, he would probably have saved the costs of the temporary move, the higher rate of the lease and the commercial inconvenience resulting from that move.

Restitution claim for the profits A gained: the misrepresentation made by A enabled him to receive a higher sale price for the property he sold to C. Section 1 of the Law of Unjust Enrichment, 1979[26] provides for a duty of restitution if a profit was obtained without legal cause at the expense of another.[27] The profit here derived from A's ownership and not from any interest B had in the property.[28] B would not be entitled to A's profit from the sale to C.

Case 3 Mistake about ownership of land to be sold

Context: A contract for the sale of land needs to be in writing by virtue of section 8 of the Land Law, 1969.[29] This section has been interpreted as imposing a substantive requirement,[30] without which no contract is formed.

[26] 33 LSI 669. [27] Friedmann, *The Law of Unjust Enrichment*, ss. 3.18–3.20 (Hebrew).

[28] See generally D. Friedmann, 'Restitution of Benefits Obtained through the Appropriation of Property or the Commission of a Wrong' (1980) 80 *Columbia Law Review* 504, 508.

[29] 23 LSI 283. [30] CA 726/71 *Grossman v. Biederman*, 26(2) PD 781 (Hebrew).

Cause of action: a buyer of an interest in land can presumably rely on the statement of an owner that he has the full ownership in the land and negotiate with him on that basis. A did not act fraudulently, but he was negligent. The standard of good faith in Israeli law is objective.[31] Hence, negligent conduct might give rise to precontractual liability. Alternatively, A might be liable in tort.

This case reflects the swift move Israeli law has made with the enactment of section 12. Though not all the continental states would hold A liable (Germany, for example) Israel would probably join the states which impose liability. Under the previous law, as reflected in the English report, it is doubtful whether liability for negligence would ensue. Liability for negligent misrepresentation was usually imposed in Israel (as in England) when a contract was eventually concluded.[32]

Loss and remedy: the losses which B incurred could be attributed to the negligent misrepresentation of A, except for the architect's fees. As long as a contract has not been concluded, expenses resulting from the conclusion of the contract are within the risk of B.

Contributory negligence: as a negotiating party, A owes a duty of care to B, but B ought to act reasonably and to take care of his own interests. B negligently contributed to his losses by not verifying the true ownership. A's liability might be reduced by the principle of contributory negligence whether A is liable in torts,[33] or under section 12. The liability of section 12 is conceived as a species of tort and contributory negligence should naturally apply to it.[34] But even if it is regarded as contractual, A's liability might be reduced: Israeli case law has applied contributory fault to contracts as well.[35]

Case 4 An architect's preparatory work for a contract which does not materialise; parallel negotiations

Cause of action: parallel negotiations: freedom in negotiations means that each of the contracting parties might engage in parallel negotiations. This rule, which is the starting point of all reports, was prevalent in Israel before the enactment of section 12. Nowadays it has been made

[31] CA 6339/97 *Roker v. Salomon*, 55(1) PD 199 (Hebrew); Friedmann and Cohen, *Contracts A, B, C*, ss. 12.44–12.45.
[32] See, e.g., CA 76/86 *Amidar v. Aharon*, 32(2) PD 337 (Hebrew); below n. 100.
[33] Friedmann and Cohen, *Contracts A, B, C*, s. 12.133.
[34] CA 590/88 *Abraham Rubinstein v. Fisher*, 44(1) PD 730 (Hebrew).
[35] CA 3912/90 *Eximin SA v. Textile and Shoes Ital Style Ferrari*, 47(4) PD 64 (Hebrew). For a thorough analysis, see Porat, *The Defense of Contributory Fault in Contract Law*.

subject to the following rule: if negotiations have reached an advanced stage, the existence of parallel negotiations should be disclosed to the other party.[36] Considering the length of the negotiations and their intensity, B might reasonably expect that the conclusion of the contract is likely. In these circumstances, A might be under a duty by virtue of section 12 to disclose to B in due time the existence of parallel negotiations. B's policy to undertake one commission at a time and not to take part in competitive tendering should not and cannot bind A (even if he knows about it). This conforms to the reports of Germany, Denmark, Norway and Portugal. But if we regard engaging in parallel negotiations as transforming the negotiations into a competitive tender, then by virtue of the duty of section 12 A should notify B about it.

Loss and remedy: if A is liable, B's loss is reflected in the value of his preparatory work to A, at least from the point at which A broke his duty to disclose the fact that he was negotiating with C. Alternatively, B could claim that he lost other contract opportunities. This has to be proved by B. Both possibilities reflect reliance loss. Since B is engaged in one commission at a time, it is doubtful whether he could claim for both the preparatory work done for A and the loss of another opportunity.

Cause of action: precontractual expenditure: the crucial point is what was the understanding between the parties and whether the starting point is contract (no liability absent a final contract) or restitution (liability for services rendered). Professional norms might clarify the matter, but they are not easy to prove and do not always exist.

Israeli case law is not unanimous. In one case, liability to pay (based on restitution and on an implied preliminary contract) for preparatory work made by an architect was imposed, though a final contract was not eventually concluded.[37] This is in line with the minority reports (Finland and the Netherlands). In another case liability was imposed by virtue of section 12: the duty of the party who received the work was to tell the architect that he was not willing to pay.[38] But in another case the presumption of remuneration did not apply, and no liability ensued, mainly because negotiations were in a preliminary stage, and

[36] Friedmann and Cohen, *Contracts A, B, C*, s. 12.83. See CA 144/87 *Ingeener Faber v. State of Israel*, 44(3) PD 769 (Hebrew), where such a duty of disclosure was imposed.

[37] CA 474/80 *Gruber v. Tel-Yossef*, 35(4) PD 45, 59 (Hebrew); Friedmann and Cohen, *Contracts A, B, C*, s. 12.83.

[38] CA (Haifa) 2547/82 *Almagor v. Achihood*, PM 1986(3) 430, 437 (Hebrew).

the parties were to be bound only by a formal agreement.[39] This reflects the majority of reports.

Loss and remedy: if liability for precontractual expenditure is grounded in restitution, A would have to restore the benefit he received, namely the value of the work done or the reasonable fees B would be entitled to. The same would apply if liability is grounded in contract or in section 12. Since B is engaged in one commission at a time, it is doubtful whether he could claim for both the preparatory work done for A and the loss of another opportunity.

Case 5 A broken engagement

Position of a promise of marriage or engagement: a promise of marriage is considered a contract and in that sense is not a ground of precontractual liability. But since it is a preparatory step preceding marriage itself (which is considered under Israeli law a contract) it might pertain to the precontractual stage.

Though it has a binding force, a promise of marriage is weaker than a regular contract. Obviously, it is not enforceable[40] and the damages for its breach are reliance and not performance damages.[41] For many years, Israeli case law treated the claim for breach of this promise as repulsive and called on the legislature to abolish it.[42] A recent Supreme Court case, *Plonit*, awarded damages for pain and suffering to a woman whose lover, a married man, broke his promise to divorce his wife and marry her.[43] This has changed the previous law under which a promise given by a married person was void as against public policy.[44] At a time when the actionability of such a promise is being abolished or limited (England, Ireland, Scotland, the Netherlands, Norway), the Israeli

39 CA 739/86 *Shem-Oor v. Municipality of Kiriat Gat*, 44(2) PD 562 (Hebrew).

40 Also for the purpose of the tort of inducing breach of contract in Civil Wrongs Ordinance (New Version), s. 62, a promise of marriage is not considered a contract: Motion 1380/72 (Jerusalem) *Rosenberg v. Chazan*, PM 1974(1) 469 (Hebrew).

41 CA 171 473/75 *Ron v. Chazan*, 31(1) PD 40 (Hebrew).

42 E.g. CA 647/89 *Shifberg v. Avtalion*, 46(2) PD 169 (Hebrew).

43 CA 5258/98 *Plonit v. Almoni*, 58(6) PD 209 (Hebrew).

44 CA 337/62 *Reisenfeld v. Yakobson*, 17 PD 1009 (Hebrew); CA 563/65 *Ieger v. Palevitz*, 20(3) PD 244 (Hebrew). This rule was subject to two exceptions. First, where the promisor concealed his/her marriage; the claim is based on fraud: CA 609/68 *Natan v. Abdalla*, 24(1) PD 455 (Hebrew); CA 386/74 *Plonit v. Almoni*, 30(1) PD 383 (Hebrew). Secondly, where it could be proved that at the time the promise was given the marriage had already broken down: CA 337/62 *Reisenfeld v. Yakobson*, 17 PD 1009 (Hebrew); CA 563/65 *Ieger v. Palevitz*, 20(3) PD 244 (Hebrew).

Supreme Court's expansion of its scope is dubious.[45] This is in line, however, with the expansion of precontractual liability in general.

Loss and remedy: expenses: A, who broke the engagement one day before the ceremony and seemingly with no justifiable ground, is liable under Israeli law for the breach. B is entitled to damages for the expenses he incurred and also to non-pecuniary damages for pain and suffering.

Engagement ring: the issue is covered by the law of restitution, influenced by the contractual surrounding. The ring was given at the beginning of the engagement. In the context of engagement gifts, the assumption (which can be rebutted) is that the gifts are conditional.[46] By its very definition the ring was given on the assumption that marriage is to follow. With the non-occurrence of the condition, A is bound to restore it to B.[47]

Case 6 An express lock-out agreement

Agreement regulating the negotiations: the principle of freedom of contract allows negotiating parties to conclude a contract regulating their negotiations.[48] Israeli case law has recognised the validity of a contract to negotiate even before the enactment of the Contracts Law,[49] at a time when such a contract was not recognised in England,[50] and where no general principle of good faith in negotiations existed in our system.

Express lock-out agreement: this is a definite lock-out agreement which is recognised even in England.[51] By negotiating with C after two months, A broke the contract with B. Prior to that, A and B reached an agreement regarding the price (€2 m) but no contract was concluded

45 For a detailed survey, see O. Groskop and S. Halabi, 'A Breach of a Promise of Marriage' in Ben-Naftali and Naveh, *Trials of Love*, p. 107 (Hebrew); N. Cohen, 'The Fall and the Rise of a Promise of Marriage' (2005) 11 *Hamishpat* 27.

46 Friedmann, *The Law of Unjust Enrichment*, s. 25.71 (Hebrew).

47 On the history of the duty to restore (or not) the engagement ring in American law, see R. Tushent, 'Rules of Engagement and Rings' (1998) 107 *Yale Law Journal* 2583; on the New York law providing for the return of the ring with the breaking of the engagement, see A. Glassman, 'I do! Or do I? A Practical Guide to Love, Courtship, and Heartbreak in New York: or Who Gets the Ring Back Following a Broken Engagement' (2003) 12 *Buffalo Women's Law Journal* 47.

48 Contracts Law, s. 24, provided the contract is not immoral, illegal or contrary to public policy (Contracts Law, s. 30).

49 CA 615/72 *Gelner v. Haifa Municipal Theater*, 28(1) PD 81 (Hebrew).

50 *Courtney & Fairbairn Ltd v. Tolaini Bros (Hotels) Ltd* [1975] 1 WLR 297, 301. This case rejected the approach in *Hillas v. Arcos* (1932) 147 LT 503, 515, which gave effect (in an obiter dictum) to such an agreement.

51 *Pitt v. PHH Asset Management Ltd* [1994] 1 WLR 327.

because of other outstanding matters. Israeli courts tend to anticipate contractual liability, in particular where there is an agreement on the price, even though only a preliminary agreement has been achieved. The missing points are filled in by reference to the contractual default rules.[52]

Loss and remedies: enforcement and injunction: if the court finds here an agreement, B might be awarded €1m: the difference between the agreed price (€2m) and the price A received from C. Assuming that no contract is found, B lost the contract opportunity with A. He also incurred expenses: accountants' and lawyers' fees. It seems unlikely that a contact to negotiate will be *enforced* because of its personal character. But an *injunction* might be issued against A to refrain from negotiating with C. This could lead to the 'annulment' of the breach and to enabling the parties to keep negotiating.[53] Negotiations might succeed if B is given the right to buy the business on the same conditions and at the same price that A was willing to sell to C[54] (similar to the Norwegian approach).

Damages: reliance losses, namely accountants' and lawyers' fees, would be allowed by most systems. But B might be awarded damages reflecting his chances of having the contract with A,[55] as in England, France, Italy, the Netherlands, Norway, Scotland and Switzerland.

An Israeli Supreme Court case which dealt with an agreement to negotiate between a director and a theatre went even further. The court awarded the director damages reflecting his future earnings and loss of other opportunities. This case, which predated section 12, treated the contract to negotiate as if it were fully binding (probably due to the contracts that had been entered into in the past between the parties). To this one should add the willingness of Israeli courts to grant performance damages to the injured party where the negotiations have reached

52 See generally Friedmann and Cohen, *Contracts A, B, C*, ch. 8, especially ss. 8.6–8.21 for cases where a preliminary agreement was regarded as binding and was completed by default rules. see CA 1049/94 *Dor Energy v. Hamdan*, 50(5) PD 820 (Hebrew); CA 3102/95 *Cohen v. Cohen*, 49(5) PD 739 (Hebrew); CA 3026/98 *Cohen v. Irmiahoo* (2001) (Hebrew) (not yet published).

53 N. Cohen, 'Pre-Contractual-Duties: Two Freedoms and the Contract to Negotiate' in Beatson and Friedmann, *Good Faith and Fault in Contract Law*, pp. 25, 48.

54 This approach of awarding the defaulting party the best option he could get, was applied in CA 1049/94 *Dor Energy v. Hamdan*, 50(5) PD 820 (Hebrew) following Friedmann and Cohen, *Contracts A, B, C*, s. 8.21.

55 Cohen, 'Pre-Contractual-Duties', above n. 53, p. 49.

an advanced stage and there has been an agreement on the price.[56] If this is applied, the court might use the sum agreed by the parties as the binding price, and B's damages would be €1m, the difference between €2m (his price) and €3m (the price that A received from C). This would be the most far-reaching result among all systems.

Restitution: was A enriched at the expense of B by breaking the contract with B and receiving €3m from C (which, but for the breach, B could have obtained)? B had merely a contractual expectancy not a full contractual right. As with the remedy of damages, also here one could rely on B's chances of obtaining the contract in the absence of A's breach.[57]

Agreement to negotiate in good faith: an agreement to negotiate in good faith is valid in Israeli law. It exemplifies the shift from the common law, where such a contract is not recognised,[58] to the civil law, where it is recognised. It reiterates the duty imposed *ex lege* by section 12, fortifies it (similarly to Swiss law) and transforms it into a contractual duty stemming from section 39 of the Contracts Law. Breaking off negotiations without reasonable cause might be a breach of the duty of section 12 as much as it can be a breach of the contractual duty which the parties voluntarily assumed. Following the tendency of Israeli courts to impose contractual liability, in particular where there is an agreement on the price, the result might be that A was in breach of a contract.

If no valid contract was concluded, a better offer seems to be a reasonable cause for breaking off negotiations. Good faith does not limit A's right to negotiate with others (case 4), provided that the contact between the parties did not reach the point of no retraction.[59]

As soon as the agreement is concluded with C, A should notify B about it. In the present case there is no mention of a delay by A. Therefore, A should not be liable for the expenses B incurred.

[56] CA 6370/00 *Kal-Binian v. A.R.M.*, 56 PD(3) 289 (Hebrew); CA 8144/00 *Alrig v. Brender*, 57(1) PD 158 (Hebrew). For a more cautious approach limiting the remedy to reliance damages, see CA 10385/02 *Machness v. Regency Investments*, 58(2) PD 53 (Hebrew).

[57] Cohen, 'Pre-Contractual-Duties', above n. 53, p. 50. A similar question arises with regard to C. If C were aware of the contract between A and B, he might be regarded as committing the tort of inducing breach of contract, and as benefiting from the wrong: ibid.

[58] *Walford v. Miles* [1992] 2 AC 128.

[59] CA 6370/00 *Kal-Binian v. A.R.M.*, 56 PD(3) 289 (Hebrew); CA 8144/00 *Alrig v. Brender*, 57(1) PD 158 (Hebrew).

Case 7 Breakdown of merger negotiations

Context: this case raises the proper limits of contractual, precontractual and non-liability rules. In the past, Israeli negotiating parties had the power to retract up to the point where the contract was concluded. Before that, no liability was imposed unless a tort had been committed. This approach, which characterises the common law (English, Irish, Scots reports), has been changed with the introduction of the duty of good faith to negotiations. Liability has expanded and starts at a point where, in the light of the intensity of the negotiations and the expectations that were created during it, retraction is in breach of good faith.[60]

Situation 1. Breaking off after three years with no agreement on major points: merger negotiations seem naturally to be lengthy and complicated. Three years of intense negotiations might not be exceptional. After three years where no agreement was made it does not seem unreasonable to put an end to the negotiations. A should not be liable either if it gives one of the three reasons, or if it does not give any reason at all. Both parties incurred expenses during this time. This is the natural risk of negotiations. The same holds true if the withdrawal is a result of a recession.

But if A knew of reasons for withdrawal a year before it actually broke off negotiations, it went on with the negotiations with no real intent to conclude a contract. This is a breach of the duty of good faith.[61] A should be liable for the reliance losses which B incurred from the time it should have notified B about the contract with C.

Situation 2. Breaking off after a short time of negotiations with agreement on all major points: under Israeli law, a preliminary agreement, even subject to contract, might create a binding contract, if the parties agreed on all major points,[62] unless the parties expressly stated that the contract is binding only if they agree on the missing minor points. If agreeing on the minor points were not a condition, retraction by A for whatever

[60] CA 6370/00 *Kal-Binian v. A.R.M.*, 56 PD(3) 289 (Hebrew). [61] See cases 1 and 2.

[62] For cases where a preliminary agreement was held to be a contract with default rules as gap-filler, see CA 1049/94 *Dor Energy v. Hamdan*, 50(5) PD 820 (Hebrew); CA 3102/95 *Cohen v. Cohen* 49(5) PD 739 (Hebrew); CA 3026/98 *Cohen v. Irmiahoo* (2001) (Hebrew) (not yet published). Most cases have related to a contract for the sale of land, but not all of them; e.g., *Dor Energy v. Hamdan* (operation of a gas station).

reason would be regarded a breach of contract (similarly to Spain and Switzerland).[63]

Alternatively, A might be subject to precontractual liability. When the parties agreed on all major points, the negotiations came to the point of no retraction, unless A had a reasonable ground for breaking them off.[64] A better offer from C might not be considered as a good reason if negotiations had reached the point of no retraction. In such a stage, parallel negotiations are beyond the risk of the parties.[65] An insurmountable cultural difference might be regarded as a good reason. If A cannot afford the merger because of an abrupt change, this might be regarded as a reasonable ground, but not if A could have known it earlier.

Situation 3. A assured B that an agreement would be reached: such assurances have an ambiguous character: they might be either a mere expression of hope in the success of negotiations (Italy, Sweden), or create a contract to negotiate in good faith under which A would not be liable only if it had a reasonable ground for breaking off negotiations, as discussed above. Israeli courts would tend to impose liability on that ground.

Loss and remedies: as pointed out earlier,[66] section 12 has been expanded to include performance damages and enforcement. Enforcement is unlikely due to the personal character of the contract. Where the negotiations have reached an advanced stage, and the contract was not concluded only due to the breach of good faith, performance damages might be awarded (similar to the strong remedy in the Netherlands).[67]

Case 8 A shopping centre without a tenant

Cause of action: this case demonstrates again the tension, reflected in the division of opinions in the reports, between the freedom not to be bound by an unwanted contract and the duty to act in good faith during negotiations. Following section 12, and the tendency of Israeli courts to expand liability, Israel is likely to join the jurisdictions that hold A liable.

A should have made the survey before B started the construction. At least, it should have notified B that his tenancy is subject to the survey. It did none of this. A's conduct amounted to a promissory representation that a contract was going to be concluded. A is liable for the loss B incurred in reliance on A.

[63] Claiming either reliance damages or performance damages is the option of the party injured by a breach of contract: CA 3666/90 *Hotel Zukim v. Municipality of Natania*, 46(4) PD 45 (Hebrew).

[64] Friedmann and Cohen, *Contracts A, B, C*, s. 8.42.

[65] See cases 1 and 4.

[66] See cases 1, 4 and 6.

[67] CA 6370/00 *Kal-Binian v. A.R.M.*, 56 PD(3) 289 (Hebrew).

Promissory estoppel was part of Israeli law before section 12, though its scope was not certain.[68] It was not clear whether it could be used as a sword or only as a shield.[69] Therefore, it is doubtful whether B's claim on the basis of promissory estoppel could succeed in the past (as indicated in the English report). After the enactment of section 12, promissory estoppel has been independently used not only as a shield but also as a sword.[70] Alternatively, it can be regarded as being incorporated in section 12.[71] In any case, A's denying the expectation it created is contrary to good faith: A broke off negotiations at the stage of no retraction with no reasonable excuse (France and Netherlands).

Loss and remedies: the regular remedy is reliance damages. If the shopping centre would not have been built but for the negotiations with A, A might be liable for the construction cost. But this is subject to the rule of mitigation. If B is able to find another flagship store or make another use of the building, his losses might accordingly be reduced.

If the loss results not from the very construction, but from the adaptation of the building to the needs of A, A is liable for the cost of re-adaptation to another potential tenant.

Although A is liable for the loss which B incurred, B, as a professional, might be regarded as negligently contributing to his loss.[72] He should have verified that A was indeed going to be his tenant (similarly to Finland, France, Portugal, Switzerland).

If A gave an assurance, B's case is stronger, and A might be fully liable.

Case 9 Breakdown of negotiations to build a house for a friend

Context: does the understanding between friends, where B supplies building services on A's land and A is to pay a price lower than the normal commercial price, amount to a fully binding contract? Are there

[68] N. Cohen, 'Good Faith in Bargaining and Principles of Contract Law' (1990) 9 *Tel-Aviv University Studies in Law* 261–3; Friedmann and Cohen, *Contracts A, B, C*, ss. 12.19–12.21.

[69] CA 285/75 *Singer v. Kimelman*, 30(1) PD 804 (Hebrew).

[70] Friedmann and Cohen, *Contracts A, B, C*, ss. 12.22–12.23, following s. 90 of the *Restatement Contracts 2d*. There is a vast literature on this section. See K. Teeven, 'The Advent of Recovery in a Market Transaction in the Absence of a Bargain' (2002) 39 *American Business Law Journal* 289; G. Duhl, 'Red Owl's Legacy' (2003) 87 *Marquette Law Review* 297 and references in n. 85 in that article.

[71] Friedmann and Cohen, *Contracts A, B, C*, ss. 12.22–12.23. Cf. CA 2071/99 *Panti v. Izhary*, 55(2) PD 721 (Hebrew) where precontractual liability was imposed on a seller who let the buyer make building plans regarding the parcel to be sold, and then retracted. See below n. 129.

[72] See case 3.

any alternative grounds of liability based on restitution or the principle of good faith in negotiations?[73]

Contractual liability: usually, the price is a decisive factor in a contract and its absence might indicate that no contract was ever concluded. Israeli legislation contains, however, a default rule regarding the price, whereby the appropriate price should be paid.[74] Our case seems to suit the application of this section. A was willing to receive the services of B. The services were supplied. A was aware that the services are not to be given free. Both parties agreed that the price is going to be below the commercial price. This is the basis for the completion of the contract and for A's liability (similar to the Irish, Norwegian, Swedish reports).[75]

Restitutionary liability: this is a borderline case between contract and restitution. An important category of unjust enrichment, which covers the case, is where a benefit was bestowed upon someone following his request.[76] The benefit was given to A - not gratuitously - following his request or at least his approval. Holding the benefit without paying for it establishes an unjust enrichment at the expense of B. In measuring the enrichment, the court should take into account the understanding between the parties that the fees are going to be below the market price. This renders A's restitutionary liability the same as his contractual liability.[77]

Precontractual liability: A's conduct might be regarded as acquiescence. By not stopping B, or by not notifying him immediately of his exact financial position, he broke his duty to act in good faith during negotiations.[78] A is liable to B for his reliance losses, namely for the expenses

[73] Land Law, 1969, s. 21, regulates the case of building on another's property, but the section applies where the building was made without an agreement with the owner of the property. Probably the consent of the owner to the building suffices for the purpose of this section.

[74] Contracts Law, s. 46, states that absent an agreement on the price, the appropriate price according to the circumstances at the time the contract was made should be paid. A frequent case where fees are awarded irrespective of the absence of an agreed price is in the context of attorney and client. The award is based either on contract or on restitution: CA 525/81 *Gazit v. Rozen*, 36(2) PD 337 (Hebrew); CA 136/92 *Beinish-Adiel v. Dania* 47(5) PD 114 (Hebrew); CA 499/89 *Ramat-Avivim v. Miron*, 46(4) PD 586 (Hebrew).

[75] Friedmann and Cohen, *Contracts A, B, C*, s. 8.18.

[76] Friedmann, *The Law of Unjust Enrichment*, ch. 8, ss. 8.1–8.18 (Hebrew).

[77] Friedmann and Cohen, *Contracts A, B, C*, s. 12.142.

[78] CA (Haifa) 2547/82 *Almagor v. Ahihud*, PM 1985(3) 430 (Hebrew) (in an architect's claim for fees for work done the court held that the client had to remove the vagueness regarding the relations with the architect); above n. 38; Friedmann and Cohen, *Contracts A, B, C*, s. 12.142.

B incurred taking into account the fact that A was ready to do the work for a reduced profit.

This result renders precontractual liability similar to both contractual and restitutionary liability. The same result would have ensued under the former law since liability might be grounded in contract or restitution. This is also evident in the reports where virtually all the states (with the possible exception of Denmark) would hold A liable.

Case 10 Public bidding

Bidding rules: the procedure for public bidding is a well-known application of the rules of offer and acceptance, which has also been adopted by Israeli case law. By the advertisement the employer (A) is making an invitation to the public to submit offers; the bidders are the offerors; the acceptance is made by the employer,[79] and it is up to it to determine the mode of acceptance.

It is quite common for the employer to state in the bidding conditions that it is not bound to accept any offer.[80] But A took upon itself the obligation to conclude a contract with the lowest bidder.

The bidding rules create relations between the employer and each bidder, and between the bidders *inter se*. Similarly to France, Italy, the Netherlands and Switzerland, they are based either on a contract which relates to the bidding procedure or on the duty of good faith in negotiations.[81]

B is the lowest offer but contract is given to C; A failed to consider B's bid: contractual liability is not based on fault. A's conduct amounts to a breach of a contractual duty. The precontractual liability by virtue of section 12 is based on fault. Presumably, A did not consider B's bid due to negligence. This amounts to a breach of the duty. Due to the fact that the basis of liability might be contractual, the same result would have ensued under the former law.

A always intended to give the contract to C: A maliciously broke the duty to consider B's and the other participants' offers seriously, grounded

[79] CA 207/79 *Raviv v. Bet Yules*, 37(1) PD 533, 542, 546 (Hebrew) (which was overruled in Further Hearing 22/82 *Beit Yules v. Raviv*, 43(1) PD 441(Hebrew), but not on this point); Friedmann and Cohen, *Contracts A, B, C*, s. 7.38.

[80] As was done in CA 207/79 *Raviv v. Bet Yules*, 37(1) PD 533 (Hebrew).

[81] CA 207/79 *Raviv v. Bet Yules*, 37(1) PD 533 (Hebrew); Further Hearing 22/82 *Beit Yules v. Raviv*, 43(1) PD 441 (Hebrew).

either in contract or in section 12.[82] A broke the contractual duty to award the contract to B. A might be liable also in torts, for committing fraud: it fraudulently induced the bidders to participate in a procedure which it did not intend to follow. The same result would have ensued under the law before section 12 was enacted.

Loss and remedies: B lost the bargain to which it was entitled. Enforcement (including injunction) is the primary remedy in Israel for breach of contract.[83] An injunction against A (and C) might lead to the annulment of the contract with C and the enforcement of B's contractual right.[84] Otherwise, B is entitled to performance damages for the loss of profits from the contract with A.[85] The same result ensues if the breach is of the duty of good faith. Though the usual remedy is reliance damages, B has the right to sue also for the loss of the bargain with A, to which it was entitled.

B, who was not the lowest bidder, was not considered due to an error: B had the right to be considered either under the collateral contract regulating the bidding or by the rules of good faith. A broke the contract or the duty of good faith. This applies also in the case where A is a public authority. But B, not being the lowest bidder, did not suffer any loss. Hence, at most B might be entitled to nominal damages.[86]

Public authority: a public authority is, as a rule subject to exceptions, bound by a statutory law to have a bidding procedure as a mechanism of concluding its contracts.[87] The rules applying to A as a private employer would *a fortiori* apply where A is a public authority. A public authority is under a duty to consider all the bidders seriously and to treat them

[82] Cf. cases 1 and 2. C might also be liable for breach of the duty of good faith or for inducing A to break the contract regulating the bid: CA 207/79 *Raviv v. Bet Yules*, 37(1) PD 533, 553 (obiter dictum) (Hebrew).

[83] Remedies Law, s. 3. [84] See case 6.

[85] B also has the option to sue for reliance damages: CA 3666/90 *Hotel Zukim v. Municipality of Natania*, 46(4) PD 45 (Hebrew).

[86] By virtue of s. 13, which grants the court discretion to impose compensation for non-pecuniary loss and which applies by s. 12(b) to the measure of damages for breach of s. 12(a); above n. 8.

[87] Mandatory Tenders Law, 1992 (no official translation exists) which provides in s. 2 that the state and any governmental corporation is under a duty to conclude a contract only by a public tender which gives an equal opportunity to any person to take part in it. But the Law also provides for many exceptions (ss. 3B and 4). By virtue of this law there is a detailed regulation in Regulations of the Mandatory Tenders, 1993; reg. 21 states that the committee in charge of the bidding has a power to select the most appropriate offer or to decide that it does not select any offer. This power not to select should be employed reasonably: AAA 8328/02 *B. Yair v. Arim*, 58(1) PD 145 (Hebrew).

equally.[88] It has to obey the legal and contractual rules which apply to the procedure. In our case, A was under a duty to consider B and to conclude the contract with it.[89]

Case 11 A contract for the sale of a house which fails for the lack of formality

Requirement of formality: a contract for the sale of land must be in writing by virtue of the Land Law.[90] This requirement has been interpreted as substantive.[91] This interpretation has led to a series of cases invalidating 'contracts' for the sale of land when the documents which accompanied the contracts did not include sufficient details.[92] The Supreme Court has since given a narrower interpretation to mitigate the harsh consequences of the substantive requirement. Thus, a receipt with scant elements of agreement has been regarded as a binding contract for the sale of land.[93] Also, a preliminary agreement, subject to contract, hand-written on a notebook and bearing no signatures, has been regarded as a binding contract for the sale of land.[94]

Conflict between formality and fairness: where no written document exists, Israeli courts have occasionally applied section 12 to mitigate the formal requirement, in particular where there was a substantial

[88] The principle of equality is not applied to a private bidding. That means that a private employer can decide not to conclude a contract with either bidder, and to start negotiating only with one of the bidders in order to conclude a contract with him. This was decided in Further Hearing 22/82 *Beit Yules v. Raviv*, 43(1) PD 441 (Hebrew). In that case the employer did not bind itself to conclude a contract following the bidding.

[89] CA 700/89 *Electricity Company v. Malibu*, 47(1) PD 667 (Hebrew), where in a public bidding the party who should have won the contract was awarded performance damages. It was held that the grounds of liability, apart from s. 12, are the following: an independent administrative cause of action; a collateral contract; and negligent misrepresentation.

[90] See case 3. [91] CA 726/71 *Grossman v. Biederman*, 26(2) PD 781 (Hebrew).

[92] E.g. CA 285/75 *Singer v. Kimelman*, 30(1) PD 804 (Hebrew), where the written agreement for the sale of an apartment consisted only of a receipt signed by the seller, confirming that he had received an advance payment and mentioning (not clearly) the price of the apartment. The seller allowed the buyer to enter the apartment and to prepare it for her occupancy. When the time came to pay the balance of the price, the seller refused acceptance, claiming that there was no binding agreement in writing. The Supreme Court held that the requirement of a substantive document was not fulfilled. See below n. 97.

[93] CA 235/75 *Kadri v. St Charles Convent*, 30(1) PD 800 (Hebrew).

[94] CA 692/86 *Botkovsky v. Gat*, 44(1) PD 57 (Hebrew). For a survey, see Cohen, 'Good Faith in Bargaining and Principles of Contract Law', above n. 68, pp. 279–87.

performance of the contract.[95] In a case where there was actually completed performance, the court enforced the contract against the seller, stating that the combination of fault and reliance might override the lack of formality.[96] Before the enactment of section 12, the court was more cautious and gave predominance to the formal requirement.[97]

Case under consideration: B did not rely on the existence of a contract. The parties did not perform the contract. The stage is preliminary, and the expenses B incurred (agent's fees and travel expenses) seem to be part of the negotiations and not of the performance. B did not know about the requirement, but it is likely that A did not know about it either, and only when he realised that the agreement was not final did he make use of the 'let-out' and reneged. On the face of it, neither party is at fault, and so each should bear his own expenses.

A knew of the formality requirements: if A did not know that B was unaware of the requirement, it is doubtful whether he should have informed B about it.[98] They both had the right to renege as long as a formal contract had not been concluded. If, however, A knew that B was unaware of the formal requirement and kept silent in order to be able to renege, A might be held to have breached the duty of good faith. Probably under the previous law, A would not have been liable. Tort law does not give a claim for failure to disclose[99] (see the English report).

A is a professional: being a professional (for example, in the construction business) imposes a duty upon A to take care to comply with the formal requirement. Not doing this might be considered as fault and breach of the duty of good faith. Under the previous law, it is not clear whether tort law would impose liability for a mere failure to disclose[100]

95 CA 651/82 *State of Israel v. Eilat Company*, 40(2) PD 785 (Hebrew).

96 CA 986/93 *Kalmar v. Guy*, 50(1) PD 185 (Hebrew).

97 In CA 285/75 *Singer v. Kimelman*, 30(1) PD 804 (Hebrew), above n. 92, the buyer claimed that the doctrine of promissory estoppel should apply, thereby forcing the seller to perform his promise. The Supreme Court held that since this doctrine stood in sharp contradiction to s. 8 of the Land Law (providing for a written document) it could not be applicable. But it ruled that the buyer was entitled to damages for the expenses she incurred, which were spent with the approval of the seller.

98 CA 838/75 *Spector v. Zarfati*, 32(1) PD 231 (Hebrew): no duty of disclosure when one party did not know about the mistake of the other party.

99 Friedmann and Cohen, *Contracts A, B, C*, ss. 12.63–12.66.

100 Cf. CA 76/86 *Amidar v. Aharon*, 32(2) PD 337 (Hebrew), where a new immigrant approached a public housing corporation to rent a space for operating a locksmith's store. The contract contained a clause to the effect that the store could only be used for such a purpose. It turned out that the municipality did not license the store for

(see the English report which does not differentiate between the two situations).

A misled B about the requirement of formality: the fault of A is clear. But for his conduct, the contract would have been duly concluded. This should make him liable towards B either in tort or on the basis of section 12. This would have been the result also under the former law (see the English report).

Loss and remedies: the usual remedy for breaching the duty of good faith in negotiations is reliance damages. But if conclusion of the contract was prevented only due to the bad faith of a party to the negotiations, the injured party might be awarded enforcement or performance damages.[101] In the case where A misled B, the remedy of enforcement or performance damages should be considered.[102]

The expansive liability in Israel is therefore evident again: A would be liable in the last two cases (as in Germany, Italy, Norway) with some probability of liability also in the first case (as in Austria and France).

Case 12 Confidential design information given during negotiations

Context: confidential information and trade secrets: confidential information is often referred to as a quasi-proprietary right.[103] It has long been protected by the rules of breach of confidence, rooted in equity, which were absorbed in our legal system.[104] Confidential information might be protected in the sphere of negotiations, but its ambit is much wider.

As in many other jurisdictions, in Israel this area is governed by a special statute: the Commercial Wrongs Law, 1999,[105] which gives remedies additional to those provided by the general law.

that purpose. Though the contract included an exemption clause to the effect that the corporation was not liable for failure to obtain the necessary licence, the court imposed on it liability for negligent misrepresentation. The court put emphasis on the inequality between the parties: the new immigrant and the professional corporation. But the case dealt with a misrepresentation, not with a mere failure to disclose.

101 CA 6370/00 *Kal-Binian v. A.R.M.*, 56 PD(3) 289 (Hebrew).

102 Cf. CA 481/81 *Tabulitzky v. Perelman*, 38(4) PD 421 (Hebrew), where a seller agreed to sell an apartment to the buyer. Before signing the contract the seller assured the buyer that a storage room was part of the apartment. In fact, the seller knew that it had already been sold to somebody else. Though not included in the written agreement, the court awarded the buyer the value of the storage room, thus giving a binding force to the oral promise. The basis of liability was tort law.

103 HC 1683/93 *Yavin Plast v. National Labor Tribunal*, 47(4) PD 702 (Hebrew).

104 CA 649/74 *Polistick v. Cegecol*, 29(2) PD 397 (Hebrew).

105 No official translation exists.

Application: disclosing essential information during negotiations is typical[106] and is often essential to the negotiations, but it is limited and is not coupled with a licence to use it if negotiations fail. Where the nature of the information is intrinsically secret, the owner need not expressly state that it is confidential. It should be regarded as part of the understanding between the parties. When A passed on to C the confidential information without B's consent, he committed a clear breach of the duty of confidentiality.

Causes of action: A clearly committed the tort of conversion under the Law of Commercial Wrongs, and is also liable by virtue of the general principles of law, in particular section 12. Similarly to the position described in many of the country reports, A's conduct amounts to a breach of the duty of good faith.

Loss and remedies: B is entitled to damages for the loss he incurred. Also, by virtue of section 13 of the Law of Commercial Wrongs, the court might impose on A damages at a certain sum specified by the law even without proving loss. An injunction might be issued against both A and C[107] (see the English, French and Scottish reports), and A might be liable in restitution (as in many other jurisdictions) for the profits he has made at B's expense.[108]

Case 13 Misrepresentation or silence about a harvester's capacity

Context: this is not a case of failed negotiations or of a failed preparatory contract.[109] Following the statement by A, a contract was concluded between A and B. The statement by A can be either a precontractual statement (a misrepresentation) or a contractual warranty. This might have an impact on the remedies to which B is entitled. Israeli courts tend to allow the plaintiff to claim alternatively, either on the misrepresentation or on the contract.[110]

[106] For references in American law dealing with information and ideas transferred during negotiations which failed, see 9 *American Law Reports* 3d 665 (New York, 1966). Cf. also the Canadian case of *LAC Minerals v. International Corona Resources* (1989) 61 DLR (4th) 14 (the owners of the information were entitled to a constructive trust on its use).

[107] C might be liable as well if he were aware of the breach. But even if he acquired it bona fide he might be held liable under Commercial Wrongs Law, s. 8.

[108] Which could be a quantum meruit for the use made by B's information: CA 649/74 *Polistick v. Cegecol*, 29(2) PD 397 (Hebrew).

[109] Cf. cases 5 and 10.

[110] For a distinction and an analysis of the whole issue: Friedmann and Cohen, *Contracts A, B, C*, ss. 15.78–15.91.

Causes of action: the statement that the machine would be able to harvest one acre a day is a precontractual misrepresentation by which the contract was induced. The contract was entered into by a mistake for which A was responsible, either fraudulently or negligently. This is a breach of good faith in negotiations.[111] Negligent or fraudulent misrepresentation also constitutes a tort. This obtained prior to the enactment of section 12.

Alternatively, A took upon himself an undertaking regarding the machine's quality. A contract of sale is subject, unless agreed otherwise, to the implied provisions of the Sale Law, 1968,[112] which states in section 11 that a seller does not fulfil his obligation if he has delivered 'property lacking the quality or characteristic necessary for its ordinary or commercial use or for a particular purpose appearing from the agreement'. Israeli case law tends to regard a statement by a seller as to the quality of the property as part of the obligations the seller takes upon herself.[113] This is in line with the majority of jurisdictions.

Expectation as to capacity made by B, A remains silent: the analysis does not change if B states that he wishes to buy a machine which would be able to harvest one acre a day, and A keeps silent. There is no general duty to disclose information during contractual negotiations, but this duty may arise in proper circumstances and it is clear that section 12 expanded liability for non-disclosure.[114]

When B stated his expectation as to the quality of the machine, it was A's duty to clarify that the machine did not have this capacity. His silence is close to concealment[115] and constitutes a breach of the duty of good faith. But it is doubtful whether this could constitute a tort.[116]

B's expectation as to the quality of the machine might also be considered as part of the contractual understanding between the two and as a contractual warranty which was broken.

Loss and remedies: if the statement is precontractual, B can claim damages which will put him in the position before the contract and the

[111] Misrepresentation as to the quality of the contract subject matter is a typical breach of the duty of good faith in negotiations: CA 86/76 *Amidar v. Aharon*, 32(2) PD 337 (Hebrew); CA 590/88 *Abraham Rubinstein v. Fisher*, 44(1) PD 730 (Hebrew); CA 790/81 *American Microsystems v. Elbit*, 39(2) PD 785 (Hebrew); CA 794/86 *The Central Society v. Fink*, 44(1) PD 226 (Hebrew).

[112] 22 LSI 107.

[113] CA 607/83 *Aharon v. Kresenti*, 42(1) PD 397 (Hebrew).

[114] For a duty to disclose by virtue of s. 12 in a contract between a builder and a customer, see Further Hearing 7/81 *Pnidar v Castro*, 37(4) PD 673 (Hebrew).

[115] Cf. *Restatement Contracts 2d* (St. Paul, 1981) s. 160.

[116] Friedmann and Cohen, *Contracts A, B, C*, ss. 12.63–12.66.

negotiations.[117] Had B known the actual capacity of the machine, he would have bought another one with the capacity he wished. B claims the opportunity lost due to the negotiations and contract with A. Lost opportunity as a measure of recovery representing reliance losses operates similarly to damages for performance interest.[118] A is thus liable for the losses B incurred due to his inability to harvest the whole crop. But A might be liable also for the losses B incurred in buying a new machine if B could have bought the machine for the same price he paid to A (but not otherwise). The same measure would apply in torts.

If the statement is part of the contract, B is entitled to enforcement, namely to the replacement of the harvester (not if it is a misrepresentation). Otherwise, B is entitled to damages for the immediate losses and for the losses of replacing this machine with a new one.

B might rescind the contract either for the defect in its formation[119] or for its breach.[120] Rescission both for defect[121] and for breach[122] entails a mutual duty of restitution.

From a standard to rules: two categories of bad faith

The duty of good faith in negotiations is a standard, easy to create, difficult to apply. The true meaning of good faith could be ascertained only by reference to cases which turn the standard of good faith into an operative system of rules.[123] The rules might eventually create a roadmap which could tell the commercial and legal community in advance what is considered bad faith in negotiations. That means that the doctrine of good faith is best understood by its negative implications.[124]

[117] Contracts Law, s. 12(b).

[118] D. Friedmann, 'The Performance Interest in Contract Damages' (1995) 111 LQR 628, 642–3. See also case 1.

[119] Contracts Law, s. 15. The official English translation is incorrect: s. 15 talks about mistake caused by *misrepresentation* whereas the translation talks about mistake caused by *deceit*. Deceit is narrower than misrepresentation. Deceit is grounded in intention. Misrepresentation could be made negligently or even in good faith.

[120] Remedies Law, ss. 6, 7. [121] Contracts Law, s. 21. [122] Remedies Law, s. 9.

[123] For the principle of good faith as an open norm which must be concretised in order to be applied, see M. Hesselink, 'The Concept of Good Faith' in Hartkamp *et al.*, *Towards a European Civil Code* (3rd edn), pp. 471, 474–5.

[124] For the doctrine of good faith as an 'excluder' (regarding contract performance), see R. Summers, 'The General Duty of Good Faith: Its Recognition and Conceptualization' (1982) 67 *Cornell Law Review* 810; S. Burton, 'More on Good Faith Performance of a Contract: a Reply to Professor Summers' (1984) 69 *Iowa Law Review* 497.

Good faith is a dynamic notion. Conduct once considered legitimate might become illegitimate and vice versa. Our road-map reflects the law as it is currently understood. In a more or less stable system, if conduct does not fall into one of the forbidden categories, it is likely to pertain – for the time being – to the zone of no liability, to the zone of freedom of action.

The 13 cases in this study present a myriad of situations from which one could induce two main bad faith categories. The first is predicated on misrepresentation; the second on broken promises. Broadly speaking, where liability for bad faith in negotiations is imposed, the unifying elements of the two categories are fault and reliance. But the two categories are different in nature from each other. The first covers cases where A is responsible for the distortion of B's consciousness during negotiations. The second deals with B's frustrations following A's breaking of his promises during negotiations. Though the factual division between the two categories is not clear-cut,[125] it has a core in which it does operate, and is useful in offering justifications for precontractual liability and in clarifying the problems concerning such liability.

The first category is a natural cause for imposing liability in a contractual environment where voluntary choice is to be guaranteed. Liability within this category is justified when it is coupled with fault of the party making the misrepresentation, and reliance by the other party. The second category is problematic: as long as the promise is not contractual, why should liability be imposed? Such liability is incompatible with the principle of freedom from contract and with the rules that constitute contractual liability. Indeed, the major difference between systems with no principle of precontractual liability (English, Irish and Scots law) and those which do have such a principle (civil law systems) is evident in particular with regard to liability for broken promises. English, Irish and Scots systems will not impose liability for mere breaking of a non-contractual promise. But also among civil systems, the question of when breaking a non-contractual promise is coupled with fault, is a core of controversy.

[125] E.g. a fraudulent promise is a misrepresentation as to the mental element of the promisor (cases 1, 2 and 10). In American law it is called 'promissory fraud': I. Ayers and G. Klass, 'Promissory Fraud without Breach' (2004) *Wisconsin Law Review* 507. On the other hand, a misrepresentation as to the quality of a property might be regarded as a promise about that property (case 13).

The 13 cases will be grouped following the division between the two categories. They reflect the difference between the common law and the civil law, the difference among the civil systems *inter se*, and also the change that Israeli law has undergone from the common law to the civil law since the introduction of the duty of good faith into its system.

Misrepresentation

This category applies to false statements (including fraudulent promises) made during negotiations. Such conduct stands in sharp contrast to the very conception of contract, which stems from a voluntary choice of action made on the basis of genuine data. No wonder that virtually all systems, regardless of whether they have a principle of good faith in negotiations, would not tolerate it.[126] Hence, no major change has been made in Israeli law regarding incorrect statements made fraudulently or negligently. In the past, tort liability would have been imposed. Nowadays, section 12 might serve as the principal ground of liability.

It follows that starting negotiations with no intent to make a contract (case 1), to renew it (case 2) or to give it to the one entitled to get it, for example to the lowest bidder (case 10), is bad faith conduct. Similarly, agreeing on the contractual terms and misleading the other party by telling him that no written document is needed, is bad faith conduct (case 11), as is telling the other party that the object sold has a capacity that is actually absent (case 13). In a similar vein, making use of trade secrets which were disclosed only for the purpose of negotiations is improper conduct irrespective of whether there is a principle of pre-contractual liability (case 12). It is, however, questionable whether presenting oneself (mistakenly) as an owner of a property and discovering the truth before the conclusion of the contract is bad faith conduct (case 3). Yet Israeli law, which has adopted a wide rule of pre-contractual liability, is likely to impose partial liability in such a case.

The issue of non-disclosure might reveal the differences between the various systems. There is a general duty not to present misstatements, but no general duty to disclose the truth. Tort law will not impose liability for not disclosing information during negotiations (case 11). But the existence of a duty of good faith might trigger a wider liability for non-disclosure, and indeed this is the tendency in Israel (cases 8, 11, 12, 13).

[126] For a thorough exposition: Cartwright, *Misrepresentation, Mistake and Non-Disclosure*, Pt I.

Broken promises and frustrated expectations

This category, which raises fundamental issues of contract liability, is not problematic if the promises concerned constitute a contract or are included in a contract. This is the case of a promise regarding the administration of negotiations, such as a lock-out agreement (case 6), or a promise relating to the administration of a tender, for example, a promise to give the contract to the lowest bidder (case 10). Contractual liability applies also in the case of a statement made during the negotiations. A statement, for example, as to the quality of the subject matter of the contract is often considered a contractual warranty (case 13).

The question arises as to what are the proper limits of contractual liability, an issue reflected in the legal status of a promise of marriage (case 5). Such a promise constitutes a special category, in between a contract and a non-contractual promise, and it has been regulated by various legislatures, some of which do not attach any binding force to it (English, Irish, Scots reports). In Israel, the trend leading to expansive liability is reflected with regard to this promise as well. Once it was regarded as contemptible or repulsive. Nowadays, it has gained respectability, and is considered valid even when the promisor is solidly married (case 5).

Another question concerning the proper limits of contractual liability relates to the force of a contract to negotiate in good faith (case 6). Jurisdictions missing the principle of good faith would find it impossible to attribute validity to such a contract.

The expansionist approach in Israel is evident not only with regard to liability for bad faith in negotiations, but also with regard to the very existence of contractual liability. In the past, a memorandum subject to contract was not regarded as binding unless a formal contract was concluded (case 4). Nowadays, such a memorandum is usually considered binding. Retraction from it is a breach of contract. Indefinite contracts which the parties intend to complete have been often regarded as binding and are being filled in with the relevant default rules (cases 6 and 7). Hence, contractual liability often overrides precontractual liability.

On the verge of contractual liability, in a middle ground between contracts and restitution, are cases concerning benefits received during the negotiation process. Benefits that were transferred during negotiations were generally regarded in the past as absolute transfers entailing no liability. Such transfers were within the risk of negotiations. Only if they were given on the condition that a final contract is concluded might a cause in restitution have ensued. Though the distinction between absolute and conditional transfers is still valid (case 5, engagement ring), nowadays benefits given on request during negotiations tend to trigger liability (case 4). This might be more forceful when the benefits consist of the very performance of the contract (case 9). Receiving the benefit without protest, keeping it and not paying for it might be regarded as a breach of an implied promise, as bad faith conduct or as a ground for restitutionary liability. This does not differ from previous law.

The most difficult cases are those where negotiations were in an advanced stage not far from conclusion and one party breaks them off. Should the expectations of the other party be protected? Should any force be attached to promises given during failed negotiations? Is retraction bad faith conduct (case 7)? Do advanced negotiations impose a duty not to engage in parallel negotiations (case 4)? Could advanced negotiations substitute for the absence of a formal document (cases 3 and 11)? Is it bad faith conduct to stick to the rules which provide the conditions for the creation of a valid contract (cases 3, 4, 7, 8 and 11)? This is where the schism between the common law and the civil law is most conspicuous and this is where the change in Israeli law is the most radical.

In the past, the demarcation line in Israel between contract and negotiations was quite clear. Negotiations meant freedom: freedom to deal with others (case 4) or to make non-binding promises. Currently under the precontractual regime, liability progresses with the progress in negotiations. That means that even before a contract is made, negotiations can reach the point of no retraction where no justifiable excuse exists[127] (cases 7 and 8). This might limit the power of parallel

[127] The mark of the change could be found in CA 579/83 *Sonnenstein v. Gabaso*, 42(2) PD 278 (Hebrew), above note 23, where the parties signed a memorandum for the sale of an apartment and decided to agree further on the issue of instalment payments. The buyer argued that the parties actually reached an agreement on that point, but that the seller had insisted that a smaller sum than the agreed purchase price be written in the contract. The buyer rejected that, and the seller refused to sign the contract. The Supreme Court was divided: the majority held that no contract was concluded without the signatures of the parties. Therefore, each of them could withdraw at any point for any reason. This is the classical approach endorsed by English law. However, the minority judge, Barak, held that if the buyer's version was correct, then the seller by his illegitimate requirement prior to the conclusion of the contract broke his duty to act in good faith. The court might regard the contract as if it were

negotiations at that stage (Case 4). Statements and promises made during negotiations might occasionally constitute grounds of liability, even though a contract has not been eventually concluded (case 3). The expansive interpretation of section 12 is reflected where formal requirements for the conclusion of a contract were not met. In the past, there was hesitance in Israeli law whether to ignore the formal requirements. Nowadays, they are more easily ignored depending on the interplay between the fault of the party insisting on the formal requirements and the reliance by the other party (case 11).

Instead of the once binary system of contract (liability) – no contract (no liability), we have now a trinary system, consisting of three zones: no liability zone; precontractual liability zone; contractual liability zone. The no liability zone has been reduced in comparison with the one that preceded section 12. The precontractual zone has been largely extended and it could practically lead to a zone of contract liability because of the possibility of awarding the remedies of enforcement or performance damages. This interpretation, which deviates from the language of section 12, according to which the sole remedy it offers is reliance damages, deviates also from the approach of the vast majority of civil law jurisdictions, and is similar to that obtaining in the Netherlands.

Was there a price to be paid for the move?

The principle of good faith in section 12 is a flexible standard imposing a regime of liability during negotiations. Under this regime, the values of co-operation and solidarity, regarded as the core of modern contract law, have become part and parcel of the negotiation process. As shown in the various cases, good faith might occasionally clash with formal rules. This conflict reveals the advantages and disadvantages of rules versus standards. Rules are more difficult to create, more easy to apply. Standards are easier to create, more difficult to apply. Rules might be under- or over-inclusive, but easy to predict. Standards frequently serve as a corrective to over- or under-inclusiveness, but their application is

actually concluded. The content of the contract would be comprised of the memorandum and the oral agreement reached by the parties on the issue of the instalment payments. Ten years ago, Justice Barak became the president of the Supreme Court and his expansive approach, which once was in the minority, has since become the dominant one in Israeli law.

difficult to predict. Standards give ample discretion to the court, thus creating a potential for an incoherent, uneven application. Standards enlarge the grey area and may encourage non-compliance with the rules: just as rules create expectations regarding their application, so does deviation. Standards create uncertainty both on the part of the judiciary and on the part of the contracting parties.

The experience of Israeli law demonstrates that a price must be paid for the desire to enhance the standard of moral behaviour in the contractual arena. To the uncertainty as to the question whether a contract has been created at all, another certainty has been now added, namely whether even in the absence of a contract the negotiations involve a breach of the duty of good faith, and if so, what is the proper remedy. It follows that almost any negotiation is susceptible to future litigation, the results of which are hardly predictable.

The Supreme Court case of *Kal-Binian v. A.R.M.*[128] might serve as a good example. In a bidding case, the District Court ruled that no contract was concluded, and no breach of the duty of good faith occurred. The majority of the Supreme Court reversed the decision and held that, though no contract was concluded, there was a breach of the duty of good faith in negotiations. The minority judge held that a contract was concluded. The District Court to which the case was referred again for ruling on the issue of remedies awarded reliance damages, but on appeal the Supreme Court reversed the decision and ruled that the proper remedy is performance damages. All this litigation took about ten years.

This case (it is not the only one)[129] attests not only to the instability, to the absence of demarcation lines between contract and negotiations, and to the vagueness regarding bad faith conduct, but also to the embarrassment shared by both litigants and judges resulting from the plethora of causes of action and remedies in this sphere. Apart from the problems of uncertainty and unpredictability in this field, such a case

[128] CA 6370/00, 56 PD(3) 289 (Hebrew).

[129] See also CA 2071/99 *Panti v. Izhary*, 55(2) PD 721 (Hebrew), above n. 71: the District Court decided that the memorandum was a binding contract. About three years later, the Supreme Court reversed the decision but held that the seller acted in a manner contrary to the duty of good faith in negotiations. The Supreme Court referred the case back to the District Court to consider the proper remedy which might be reliance damages, restitution or even performance damages.

clearly exemplifies the intensive investment in energy and time both of litigants and of the judiciary. It is to be hoped that, during the years to come, the standard of good faith will gradually turn into a set of workable, definite rules.[130]

[130] N. Cohen, 'The Effect of the Duty of Good Faith on a Previously Common Law System: the Experience of Israeli Law' in Brownsword, Hird and Howells, *Good Faith in Contract*, pp. 189, 209–12.

4 A law and economics perspective on precontractual liability

ELEONORA MELATO AND FRANCESCO PARISI

The problem

Negotiations are the natural prelude to a binding agreement. During negotiations, parties evaluate contractual opportunities and define the terms of a mutually profitable transaction with an informal exchange. They speak with each other and communicate their respective interests and expectations regarding the potential transaction. During these interactions, the parties often preserve a certain degree of 'freedom of negotiation'.[1] Before entering into a binding contract, parties retain some freedom to change their mind, to negotiate with other prospective parties, to acquire information to verify the profitability of the proposed transaction, and to hold out if changes in the circumstances or some other aspect of the transaction make it unprofitable. A necessary consequence of the parties' freedom of negotiation is the lack of binding force of their manifestations of intent. Expressions of intent during the negotiation phase do not bind the parties and generally cannot be used to obtain performance before a contract is finalised. Negotiations enable parties to test the feasibility of a mutually beneficial transaction.

During negotiations, as information is gathered and the prospective contract begins to take shape, it may become reasonable for parties to make some reliance investments. From an economic perspective, these reliance investments may indeed be beneficial (for one party or for both) because they can increase the value of the contract, if the parties enter into one.[2] While potentially increasing the net private surplus

[1] E.A. Farnsworth, 'Precontractual Liability and Preliminary Agreements: Fair Dealing and Failed Negotiations' (1987) 87 *Columbia Law Review* 217, 221.

[2] R. Craswell, 'Offer, Acceptance, and Efficient Reliance' (1996) 48 *Stanford Law Review* 481, 495.

from the transaction, these 'relation-specific investments', however, always involve some risk. Reliance investments increase the private loss of the investing party when the negotiations fail and do not yield to a binding contract. Furthermore, reliance investments create an opportunity for opportunistic bargaining by the other party.[3] For example, it is possible that one party, having observed the investment of the other, may try to appropriate part of the surplus by asking for a greater price.

For each party, a reliance investment increases both the expected benefits and the expected costs of the transaction. Absent precontractual liability, the parties are free to retreat from negotiations, without legal consequence, at any time before entering into a contract. A regime of no precontractual liability puts the entire risk of losing reliance investments on the parties, thus creating an incentive to under-invest in reliance.

On the other hand, imposing strict precontractual liability, imposing liability on a party whenever that party retreats from an initiated negotiation, will probably lead to a moral hazard problem, because the other party, fully insured against the risk of unsuccessful bargaining, will not have any incentive to restrain its reliance investment. This may lead to an excessive reliance.[4] Legal rules for precontractual liability should balance the need for parties' freedom during the contract negotiation and the creation of incentives for optimal levels of reliance.

Economists may conceptualise the reliance investment decision as a cost-benefit analysis. The level of optimal investment can be determined by applying something analogous to the 'Learned Hand' test, generally used by law and economics writers for defining the efficient level of precautions in a negligence action. Briefly, investing is efficient whenever the potential benefit (weighted by the probability that the contract will be formed) exceeds the potential loss (weighted by the probability that the contract will not be formed).[5]

[3] Ibid. p. 490.

[4] This distortion will occur no matter what is the measure of damages required by the rule. Both expectation damages and reliance damages will create suboptimal incentives for investment, because the party will internalise the benefit of the investment but not the costs, which are fully borne by the retreating party.

[5] Hence, optimal reliance occurs where $pB = (1-p)L$. The opportunity of using a Learned Hand type test in this context is generally recognised by law and economics scholars. See, e.g., Craswell, above n. 2, p. 491; A. Katz, 'When Should an Offer Stick? The Economics of Promissory Estoppel in Preliminary Negotiations' (1996) 105 *Yale Law Journal* 1249, 1271.

From an economic point of view, the primary problem is therefore identifying a legal rule that would create incentives for optimal reliance, avoiding both under-investment (inefficient because it prevents the maximisation of the total surplus obtainable from the transaction) and over-investment (inefficient because it leads to a waste of resources when negotiations are unsuccessful). The problem is complicated by the necessity to optimise simultaneously the reliance incentives for *both* parties. In fact, although legal scholars and earlier law and economics scholars generally believed that the under-investment problem, created by the traditional common law rule of no liability, existed only when just one party relies, later analysis shows that under-investment can still occur even if both parties rely on the successful formation of the contract (and make 'relation-specific investments' based on that reliance).[6]

As critics of precontractual liability have pointed out, moreover, the imposition of some kind of precontractual liability may deter parties from entering negotiations in the first place. Potential liability may increase transaction costs and discourage people from negotiating, even when the transaction, if successful, would have created a positive surplus.[7]

In the subsequent sections of this chapter, we briefly discuss the solutions proposed by the law and economics literature. We then try to apply these solutions to some of the hypothetical cases used in this study to verify how those cases should have been solved according to the results of law and economics analysis.

Law and economics models of precontractual liability

Legal solutions to the precontractual liability problem are quite diverse. Solutions range from the absence of a general principle of precontractual liability (which is the dominant position in common law jurisdictions)[8] to the acceptance of very strict rules imposing liability on the retreating party in most every case (such as the Dutch 'third-stage' rule, which holds the retreating party liable if negotiations are broken off in an advanced stage and imposes liability for expectation damages or

[6] For an explanation of this point, see below text to n. 21.

[7] See Farnsworth, above n. 1, pp. 221, 243.

[8] See the Editors' Conclusions, below pp. 449ff. and the particular discussion of English law at pp. 461–8.

even specific performance of the contract).[9] In between these two extremes are those jurisdictions that recognise a general duty to negotiate in good faith, imposing on the retreating party liability for the claimant's reliance damages (that is, liability limited to reasonable expenditures made relying on the prospective contract).

The so-called 'law and economics methodology' developed primarily in common law jurisdictions. Until recent years, the vast majority of law and economics scholars were trained in these jurisdictions. This influenced the approach followed by law and economics scholars on a number of legal issues, including precontractual liability. This influence is evident in two main ways. First, since common law is generally reluctant to impose liability on negotiating parties prior to the formation of a contract, the problems related to precontractual liability have been largely neglected in the economic analysis literature. Secondly, the existing law and economics literature on precontractual liability focuses essentially on the economic analysis of legal doctrines (such as the 'promissory estoppel' doctrine)[10] developed in common law jurisdictions and applied by common law courts to impose liability for precontractual conduct in some circumstances. Because of this narrow focus, little attention has been devoted to the economic analysis of broader general principles of precontractual liability, such as the general duty to negotiate in good faith and the concept of *culpa in contrahendo* followed by a number of civil law jurisdictions.[11] Nevertheless, the results of the existing studies provide a useful framework for analysing the problems related to precontractual liability from an economic perspective.

The first economic analysis of precontractual liability evaluated the efficiency of judicial doctrines that departed from the general rule of no liability, imposing liability on the retreating party before the formation of the contract when certain conditions were met. These judicial doctrines drew a new line between no liability and liability by distinguishing between mere negotiations and commitment. Frequently, these analyses linked liability to the existence of an implied 'promise' that could be drawn from the parties' conduct during negotiations.

[9] See the Dutch report on case 1, above p. 46, and the discussion of Dutch law in the Editors' Conclusions, below pp. 468–70.

[10] See the English report on cases 2 and 8, above pp. 68 and 236, but note the discussion there to the effect that the scope of the promissory estoppel doctrine varies amongst the different common law jurisdictions.

[11] See generally the Editors' Conclusions, below pp. 452–6.

The economic analyses of such doctrines focus on the conditions under which it is efficient for courts to recognise that such commitments or promises were in fact present. Although the general duty to negotiate in good faith usually does not require the existence of a binding commitment to impose liability, the factual situations in which common law courts acknowledge such promises are similar to those involving 'reasonable reliance' leading to liability for *culpa in contrahendo*. The analytical framework developed in the studies can therefore be applied more generally to the problems of precontractual liability.

Craswell's model: liability as an incentive for efficient reliance

Professor Craswell links the analysis of precontractual liability to the theory of incomplete contracts, focusing on the selection of an appropriate default rule to be applied when parties do not explicitly say whether they intend to be bound by their preliminary exchanges.[12] Craswell considers the case of unilateral reliance, defining optimal reliance as a relation-specific investment that is beneficial for both parties. Optimal investment maximises the expected value of the transaction: this creates potential benefits to both parties, inasmuch as both the relying and non-relying parties can benefit from the investment if they can capture even a small fraction of the increased contractual surplus. This is a reasonable assumption, as non-relying parties may appropriate some part of (but likely, not all) the increased contractual surplus by charging a higher price.[13] Hence, in these situations it would be in the interest of the non-relying party to make binding commitments during negotiations to induce the other party to invest in reliance, thereby increasing the joint value of the prospective contract. Building on this intuition, Craswell concludes that the optimal default rule would recognise the implied existence of a commitment in those cases in which the party who seeks to withdraw *ex post* would have had an *ex ante* interest in seeking commitment in order to induce efficient reliance. In other words, courts should impose liability only when an enforceable commitment would have been necessary to induce an efficient level of reliance.[14]

Craswell's rationale for precontractual liability thus follows the traditional logic: the default rule for precontractual liability should mimic the hypothetical solution that the parties would have reached if they had agreed. Although at times difficult to implement, the logic of

[12] Craswell, above n. 2, p. 485. [13] Ibid. p. 495. [14] Ibid. pp. 483–4.

hypothetical contracting could serve as a useful benchmark for the analysis of precontractual liability. Some limitations of this approach should be noted, however.

As pointed out above, reliance investments potentially increase the value of the contract. Each party wishes to appropriate the surplus created by such investment. It is thus in the interest of parties who undertake the reliance investment to conceal their reliance, to protect the surplus from the appropriation efforts of the other party. This leads to a problematic circularity. To avoid potential lack of co-ordination between the parties' levels of commitment and reliance, Craswell's hypothetical-contract rationale for precontractual liability requires some correction, ensuring that reliance investments be disclosed to, or otherwise observable by, the other party.

Katz's model: the efficiency of 'promissory estoppel'

Professor Katz reaches a different solution. He considers specifically the doctrine of promissory estoppel, used by courts to bind a party to promises made during negotiations in order to find such party liable towards the relying party.[15] Katz investigates the conditions under which this rule can be deemed to be more efficient than the traditional common law rule of no liability. An important assumption of Katz's model is that neither judges nor juries are in the position to make a substantive determination regarding optimal reliance, which is the ultimate goal of an efficient legal rule.[16] Accordingly, the Learned Hand test is inapplicable (as is any rule that conditions liability on the ability of a court to find an efficient level of reliance).

For Katz, the rule for precontractual liability should assign liability based on Calabresi's concept of 'least-cost-avoider'. The least-cost-avoider, in Katz's view, is usually the party with the greater bargaining

[15] See *Restatement (Second) of Contracts* § 90 (1979): 'A promise which the promisor should reasonably expect to induce action or forbearance on the part of the promisee or a third person and which does induce such action or forbearance is binding if injustice can be avoided only by enforcement of the promise. The remedy granted for breach may be limited as justice requires.'

See also G.B. Buechler Jr., 'The Recognition of Preliminary Agreements in Negotiated Corporate Acquisitions: an Empirical Analysis of the Disagreement Process' (1989) 22 *Creighton Law Review* 573, 574 (pointing out the difficulty for parties to reasonably predict court decisions on the basis of such doctrines); R.E. Scott, '*Hoffman v. Red Owl Stores* and the Myth of Precontractual Reliance' (2007) 68 *Ohio State Law Journal* 1 (arguing that precontractual liability in the United States does not exist beyond the narrow case of enforcement of preliminary agreements).

[16] Katz, above n. 5, pp. 1272–3.

power *ex post* (the party who has the power to modify the initial terms once reliance investments have occurred).[17] If the non-relying party has the greater bargaining power *ex post*, that party should be bound by preliminary promises, in order to prevent opportunistic behaviour (e.g., raising the price after the other party has made reliance investments). Conversely, if the relying party has the greater bargaining power *ex post*, the traditional common law rule of no liability should apply, inasmuch as the opportunistic behaviour of the non-relying party is likely to be constrained by the stronger bargaining power of the relying party.[18]

Bebchuk and Ben-Shahar's model: searching for an efficient 'intermediate' rule

The solutions discussed above show powerful intuitions. However, their scope is somewhat limited. Being rooted in traditional contract theory, they try to determine when a party should be bound by preliminary manifestations of intent, establishing a stark line when contractual liability should begin. This approach leads to a dichotomy: the parties' precontractual exchanges are either fully binding or have no legal consequences. Precontractual liability can avoid this dichotomy, however, finding its fundament on other grounds.

One of the most recent and most complete works on precontractual liability is a paper by Bebchuk and Ben-Shahar.[19] Their analysis differs in several respects from those in the previous section.

First, the authors point out that the reliance problem is often bilateral: each party relies on the other's promises during negotiations and invests accordingly. Bebchuk and Ben-Shahar address this problem in their paper, expressly introducing bilateral reliance in their model.

Secondly, the authors move away from the previous all-or-nothing approaches to precontractual liability, noting that the efforts to determine a clear point where non-binding negotiations should end and precontractual liability should begin are generally misguided. The major focus of their analysis is on 'intermediate' liability rules that allow partial liability if a party does not fulfil precontractual promises and the parties do not enter into a contract.

[17] Ibid. p. 1273. [18] Ibid. p. 1277.

[19] L.A. Bebchuk and O. Ben-Shahar, 'Precontractual Reliance' (2001) 20 *Journal of Legal Studies* 423.

Thirdly, Bebchuk and Ben-Shahar explicitly analyse the impact of precontractual liability rules on the parties' incentives to participate in negotiations in the first place.

As for standard tort law analysis, they begin by considering the two polar regimes of no liability and strict liability. Predictably, under a regime of no liability (like the traditional common law rule) each party will under-invest in reliance[20] because the rule does not allow parties to fully internalise the benefit of investment. Conversely, under a regime of strict liability (defined by the authors as a rule which requires each party to fully compensate the other party for reliance investments if the parties do not enter into a contract), each party will over-invest because the cost of reliance is shifted to the other party.[21]

After assessing these results, the authors explore three different possibilities for intermediate liability rules that could potentially produce optimal reliance decisions.

Rule 1: the first proposed rule imposes full liability for precontractual reliance on a party that bargains in an *ex post* opportunistic manner (i.e., by demanding a price that, taking into account the other party's reliance expenditures, would leave the other party with an overall loss from the transaction).[22] Under this regime, both parties make optimal investments because neither can totally shift the costs to the other, but must bear a fraction of the total cost that is equal to the fraction of the incremental surplus that party will extract from the investment.

Rule 2: the second proposed rule is a cost-sharing rule: each party bears part of the total reliance cost (that is, pays for part of the other

[20] Ibid. pp. 431–2. Intuitively, it may seem that when both parties invest in reliance, the problem of under-investment would diminish substantially. In fact, what causes under-investment is the risk that the other party will walk away from the negotiations. But if both parties rely, neither would want to walk away because both have something to lose (the precontractual investment that is wasted if the contract is not formed). However, Bebchuk and Ben-Shahar show that this common assumption is incorrect: under-investment is more related to the existence of a surplus from the transaction than with the risk of negotiation breakdown. The surplus depends on the investment of both parties. When the parties' investments are 'strategic substitutes' (the investment of one party reduces the marginal value of the other party's investment), one party will invest less when the other party also invests than when the other party invests nothing. Conversely, when the parties' investments are 'strategic complements' (the investment of one party increases the marginal value of the other party's investment), one party will invest more when the other party also invests. Finally, when the parties' investments are independent, the investment of one party does not depend on whether or how much the other party invests.

[21] Ibid. pp. 433–4. [22] Ibid. pp. 435–7.

party's cost and recovers part of its own cost).[23] In order to achieve efficiency, the sharing formula should be linked to the parties' respective bargaining power. The rule, therefore, imposes a great informational burden on courts. While conceding that it is implausible to assume that courts will be able accurately to evaluate the parties' bargaining power, the authors suggest that a cost-sharing formula that requires the parties to share reliance expenditures equally could nonetheless reduce distortions produced by polar regimes.

Rule 3: the third and final rule combines a strict liability standard with a 'capped' measure of damages.[24] When negotiations break down, each party will be liable regardless of conduct. But a party's recovery is limited to the optimal reliance investment. If courts can correctly determine the level of optimal reliance, this rule creates incentives for optimal reliance because each party must bear the cost of any reliance investment beyond that point.

Bebchuk and Ben-Shahar's interesting insights highlight the potentialities of 'intermediate' liability regimes in solving relevant incentive problems in the analysis of precontractual reliance. However, none of the proposed intermediate rules resemble existing legal rules. The analysis is eminently 'normative', suggesting new legal solutions rather than analysing the efficiency of existing rules. For this reason, Bebchuk and Ben-Shahir's model will not be much used in the analysis of the following hypothetical cases.

An economic perspective on eight hypothetical cases

The cases analysed in this section cover a variety of situations in which precontractual liability may arise. In some of the cases, most jurisdictions would probably reach similar solutions, though not necessarily on the same legal grounds. For other cases, the solutions will be less unanimous, showing the differences in the approaches to precontractual liability in various jurisdictions.[25] Our purpose in this section is to analyse the hypothetical cases from an economic perspective and to determine the outcomes of the various cases if the economic models exposed above had been applied. Also, we will try to determine,

[23] Ibid. pp. 438–9. [24] Ibid. pp. 439–41.

[25] The cases selected for discussion in this section are cases 1, 2, 3, 4, 5, 6, 8 and 9 above. The results for each of the jurisdictions covered within this study are summarised in the comparative conclusions on each case, and a more general comparative conclusion is drawn by the Editors of the study in the Conclusions, below.

for each case, whether the application of the specific legal rules in the different European jurisdictions leads to solutions consistent with the results and suggestions of the economic models.

Case 1 Negotiations for premises for a bookshop[26]

In this case, A began negotiations with B without any serious intention actually to enter into a contract. A's conduct was motivated exclusively by the desire to prevent B from selling his premises to C. It is therefore plausible that A would be held liable both under a general rule of precontractual liability imposing a duty to negotiate in good faith and in common law jurisdictions where, even in the absence of a general precontractual liability rule, liability may be imposed under tort law, for instance under the tort of fraudulent misrepresentation.

From a legal point of view, the solution seems rather clear: there is no doubt that A acted in bad faith and in fact, even in those jurisdictions where there is reluctance to recognise precontractual liability, A's conduct will be sanctioned on different grounds.

From an economic perspective, the question is whether it is economically efficient to hold A liable for B's reliance damages (the difference between the price he could have obtained from C and the final selling price of the premises). To put it in another way, we need to verify whether holding A liable will create optimal incentives for reliance.

We briefly discussed two economic approaches to this problem in B(1) and B(2) above. According to Craswell, liability should be imposed when doing so is necessary to stimulate an optimal level of reliance. Since Craswell assumes that reliance is beneficial for both parties, he concludes that in this situation even the withdrawing party (in this case A, the bookshop owner) would have wanted to be bound in order to induce efficient reliance and increase the value of the contract. Here, however, it is clear that A never wanted to be bound: he never intended to form a contract with B; his sole intent was to prevent a successful transaction between B and C. Nevertheless, the success of A's (fraudulent) strategy depends upon B's reliance on A's intention to buy at the proposed price. Had A's intentions been serious, both parties would have gained from the transaction (B would have obtained a greater price for his property and A would have had the opportunity

[26] For the full hypothetical, see case 1, above p. 21. In brief, A, a bookshop owner, entered into negotiations with B to buy property for the sole purpose of preventing B from selling the property to C, a large bookshop chain. A never intended to enter a binding contract with B.

to expand his business while at the same time eliminating a potential disruptive competition). Hence, according to Craswell's reasoning, it is efficient to impose liability on A and to make him compensate B for the damages he suffered in consequence of his reliance on A's offer.

At first glance, it appears that we reach the same conclusion by applying Katz's model discussed above. According to Katz, the costs of the failed negotiations should be borne by the least-cost-avoider. Remember, the least-cost-avoider is the party who has the greater bargaining power after negotiations. Here, it is easy to see that A is the party with the greater bargaining power: once B has relied on his offer, A has obtained his purpose (to prevent B's transaction with C) and, in absence of liability, he would lose nothing in deciding to withdraw. However, it is somewhat doubtful that A is actually the least-cost-avoider in this situation: A is the owner of a small bookshop and probably his financial position is less favourable than that of B, who owns a large piece of property. B may be able to bear the costs of his lost opportunity; while those costs may be disruptive for A if he is liable for them. In addition, the specific facts of this particular case evidence a more complicated situation. B's damages are not a direct consequence of his reliance on A's offer, but rather a consequence of C's withdrawal from negotiations initiated with B. Hence, had B never relied on A's offer, he would nonetheless have suffered a loss because of C's withdrawal, Considering this peculiarity, it may be better to base A's liability on other grounds than precontractual liability, such as the tort of fraudulent misrepresentation. In fact, neither Craswell's nor Katz's model fits perfectly in this case.

This imperfect fit is supported by courts' treatment of this type of case. All jurisdictions considered above provide B with a reliance remedy. However, since damages were not a direct result of B's reliance on A's promise but rather were a result of C's withdrawal, even jurisdictions that have a specific legislative rule of precontractual liability or a general principle of precontractual liability turn to other legal bases in order to impose liability. For instance, Austria, Germany and the Netherlands would impose liability on tort grounds. Spain, which also has a general principle of precontractual liability, would turn to the doctrine of abuse of rights. England, Ireland and Scotland, which do not accept a general principle of precontractual duty, regard A's action as fraudulent misrepresentation.[27]

[27] See comparative conclusions on case 1, above pp. 60–3.

These solutions are consistent with the economic analysis in that they provide a remedy to B, and a disincentive for A to engage in fraudulent behaviour, even in the case in which B's damage is not a direct consequence of B's reliance on A's representation.

Case 2 Negotiations for renewal of a lease[28]

This case is very similar in its essence to case 1. As in case 1, one of the parties has no serious intent to form a binding contract with the other (the renewal of the lease) but entered negotiations for the sole purpose of maximising his own profit (through obtaining a higher price from C). B relied on A's representation that the lease would be renewed and as a consequence he suffers losses associated with the need to rent a temporary warehouse at short notice and with the disturbance to his distribution arrangements.

The fact that this case involves a contract for a lease may control the solution of this case in most jurisdictions. Indeed, many jurisdictions have a specific statutory protection for tenants against the wrongful termination of a lease. The need to apply a general rule of precontractual liability may then appear limited to a situation in which the statutory protection cannot be applied. Regardless, in light of the general perspectives adopted by Craswell and Katz, liability should be imposed on A. In this case, A is in fact the least-cost-avoider: the greater profit he received from C puts him in the position to repay B without disruptive consequences. In addition, A's liability is necessary in order to create an efficient reliance incentive for B: if no liability is provided, B (or any tenant in a similar position) has the incentive to incur the cost of searching for a new location every time his lease is close to expiring, even if the landlord clearly indicates an intent to renew the contract.

In accordance with this conclusion, almost all jurisdictions provide B with a remedy.[29] The only exception is Ireland, which does not recognise any ground for liability because the elements for an action in deceit or for fraudulent misrepresentation are not considered to be

[28] For the full hypothetical, see case 2, above p. 64. In brief, B, who leases a warehouse from A, enters into negotiations with A for an extension of the lease. In reliance on these negotiations, B declines to lease a warehouse from X. A, never intending to extend B's lease, in fact uses the negotiations with B as evidence of the warehouse's value in A's negotiations to sell the warehouse to C. A sells the warehouse to C, forcing B to rent a temporary warehouse and incur other damages based on his reliance.

[29] See comparative conclusions on case 2, above pp. 90–2.

extant in this case. Ireland's solution is not consistent with the analysed economic models in that it would create suboptimal incentives for B's reliance.

Case 3 Mistake about ownership of land to be sold[30]

This case differs from the previous two cases because here there is no bad faith or knowing misconduct. A has been, at most, negligent in not having ensured that he has authority to sell the property before entering negotiations. The solutions to this problem may therefore be significantly different by jurisdiction, depending on whether A's simple negligence would be sufficient to impose liability.

From an economic perspective, however, imposing liability on A is efficient. Allowing B to rely on the fact that A took the necessary steps to verify his own authority to sell avoids a wasteful duplication of information costs. In addition, A may be seen as the party with the greater bargaining power *ex post*, because the selling party is generally in the position to act opportunistically after the buying party has made significant investments in reliance on the possible contract. Hence, notwithstanding A's good faith, he should compensate B for his reliance expenditures.

The solutions adopted in those jurisdictions which find A liable on the basis of his negligence (France, Greece, Italy, the Netherlands, Portugal and Switzerland) seem to be consistent with economic findings, while the solutions adopted by those jurisdictions which require an intent to inflict damage in order to find precontractual liability conflict with the economic goals of cost minimisation and efficient reliance.[31]

Case 4 An architect's preparatory work for a contract which does not materialise; parallel negotiations[32]

Generally, precontractual expenditures by a professional do not give rise to liability. Nevertheless, B's investment is wasted because the

[30] For the full hypothetical, see case 3, above p. 93. In brief, B negotiates with A about buying a piece of land. A thinks he is the sole owner of the land, but later in the negotiations discovers that he owns the land jointly with his two sisters who refuse to sell to B, and B and A do not enter into a contract. B incurs costs relying on A's assertions that he is the sole owner of the land.

[31] See comparative conclusions on case 3, above pp. 113–16.

[32] For the full hypothetical, see case 4, above p. 117. In brief, A, a manufacturer, enters into negotiations with B, an architect, for a potential contract for B to design a new facility for A. At the same time, but unbeknownst to B, A enters into negotiations with

contract did not materialise. Therefore, it may seem that, at least when A knew of B's particular custom (and so knew that his silence concerning parallel negotiations could cause B to lose more than the average expected loss for a professional in the same position), B's expenditures should be compensated.

A is probably the least-cost-avoider and B's investment in reliance would have been beneficial for A had the contract be formed. However, a rule imposing liability on A has an obvious side-effect: it may have prevented A from entering negotiations with B in the first place. In fact, under such a rule, A, knowing the particular custom adopted by B, will be liable if he decides to form a contract with a third party even if the third party is able to offer better terms. In this situation, B will lose the possibility of even competing for the contract. Imposing liability on A in this case would go to the detriment of B, who probably himself prefers a rule of no liability, and to bear his own costs, in exchange for the opportunity to compete with other professionals.

Consistent with the economic analysis, most jurisdictions take the position that, unless there is some other basis of liability, B's expenditure is at his own risk and therefore he is not entitled to a remedy, at least when A had no knowledge of B's custom. By contrast, the majority of jurisdictions hold A liable when he has knowledge of B's custom, although generally it seems that A's liability does not arise from the parallel negotiations themselves but rather from the failure to inform B about such negotiations.[33] This last solution may be economically efficient to the extent that the duty to inform could place B in a better position to decide how much to spend in reliance, thus avoiding waste when B thinks the contract is not likely to materialise. From an economic perspective, A should inform B of parallel negotiations even when A does not have knowledge of B's policy because such a disclosure would serve to induce optimal reliance by B.

Case 5 A broken engagement[34]

This case involves many social policies and considerations of a non-legal nature. It may therefore have a number of different solutions

a different architect as well. B begins work on designing the facility as is his custom, incurring significant expense. Though he knows of B's investment, A eventually contracts with the other architect rather than with B.

33 See comparative conclusions on case 4, above pp. 136–9.

34 For the full hypothetical, see case 5, above p. 140. In brief, A and B got engaged. B bought A a ring and made a number of other expenditures in consideration of the

based on different jurisdictions' approaches to such a delicate matter. From an economic point of view, however, an engagement may well be seen as any other negotiation in view of the conclusion of a contract (the marriage). A should compensate B for his expenditures: the investments made by B in preparation for the wedding are in fact beneficial for both A and B because they increase the total benefit obtainable from the transaction. Adopting Craswell's terminology, A's liability is necessary to induce B to exercise optimal reliance. In addition, A is the party with the greater bargaining power *ex post* (she is in the position to change her mind about the marriage without losing anything). A rule which imposes liability on A for B's reliance expenditures is consistent with both the examined economic models.

Many jurisdictions, however, tend to regard this case as substantially different from more traditional cases of precontractual liability. Social policy and ethics often play a lead role in deciding whether, and under what circumstances, to impose liability. Some jurisdictions have special rules about the return of gifts, many for engagement rings in particular. Regarding expenses, most jurisdictions that have a general principle of precontractual liability would apply this principle to give B a remedy but only when A's breaking of the engagement was unjustified. This seems consistent with economic principles as discussed above. On the other hand, jurisdictions that have not accepted a general principle of precontractual liability (namely England, Scotland and Ireland) impose no liability, with the partial exception of Ireland, which has a statutory provision mandating a remedy in specific circumstances.[35]

Case 6 An express lock-out agreement[36]

The presence of an express agreement, whether it has the effect of precluding one of the parties from negotiating with third persons for a specific period of time or just imposing a duty to negotiate in good

upcoming wedding and marriage. Shortly before they were to marry, A broke off the engagement.

35 See comparative conclusions on case 5, above pp. 160–1.

36 For the full hypothetical, see case 6, above p. 162. In brief, A and B are negotiating for the sale of A's business to B. A agrees that he will not enter into negotiations with third parties for the purchase of his business for three months. Before the three-month period expires, A gets an attractive offer for the sale of his business from a third party and contracts with that party for the sale. B has incurred significant costs in the negotiations with A and investigations into A's business. Also considered is the situation in which A and B had agreed to negotiate for three months in good faith.

faith, may be interpreted as imposing contractual, rather than precontractual, liability or, in those jurisdictions which have a general rule of precontractual liability, as simply strengthening the already existing duty of good faith. Hence, although this situation is quite common in business acquisitions, legal solutions vary greatly within jurisdictions. The unpredictability of courts' decisions in cases of breach of lock-out provisions has opened the debate about the enforceability of this kind of precontractual agreement and, more generally, of the letter of intent as an instrument to facilitate the negotiation of complex transactions. An analysis of the factual hypothetical from an economic perspective, however, demonstrates the grounds for a more straightforward solution.

Applying Craswell's model, it is easy to conclude that A should be held liable to B. In evaluating the opportunity to purchase A's business, B necessarily has to incur substantial expenses. Without the assurance that, at least for a while, he enjoys exclusive negotiations with A, B may not be willing to engage in expensive due diligence. Of course, the interest of the seller is exactly the opposite: he tries to maintain as much of his freedom to negotiate with others as possible. However, if the seller agrees to an express lock-out provision, he demonstrates the seriousness of his commitment to negotiate with the buyer and, implicitly, his positive valuation of the buyer's offer. Indeed, a lock-out provision is often necessary to stimulate optimal reliance investment in the business acquisition context. In such situations, Craswell's model would suggest the imposition of precontractual liability on the seller who violates the agreement by negotiating with a third party. The same solution applies when the parties have agreed, more generally, to a duty to negotiate in good faith. In that context, the agreement to negotiate in good faith has the same goal of an express lock-out agreement, which is to stimulate the buyer's optimal reliance investment by spreading the risk of failed negotiations.

The application of Katz's model suggests the same solution. Another purpose of a lock-out agreement is to prevent the seller's opportunistic behaviour, specifically the seller's opportunity to 'shop' the deal by using the existing negotiations as leverage to obtain better offers. From this perspective, A (the non-relying party) can be seen as the party with the greater bargaining power *ex post*. Thus, according to Katz, A should be held liable for the violation of the precontractual agreement.

Furthermore, since precontractual agreements (whether or not they are themselves contractual in nature) are intended to stimulate optimal reliance investment and to prevent opportunistic behaviour, their purpose is better satisfied by treating liability resulting from them as precontractual liability, requiring just the compensation of reliance interest, rather then treating them as contractual liability, which may create incentives for over-reliance.

In almost all jurisdictions, however, this situation (especially when an express lock-out agreement is involved) is analysed as a case of contractual liability.[37] The inefficiency this approach may cause is, in any case, somewhat balanced by the fact that many jurisdictions would allow B to recover just his reliance expenditures in this situation.

With respect to the breach of an agreement to negotiate in good faith, only Austria's and Italy's solutions seem to mesh with our economic models, imposing liability for reliance expenditures.

Case 8 A shopping centre without a tenant[38] *and Case 9 Breakdown of negotiations to build a house for a friend*[39]

From an economic perspective, these two cases can be analysed together. In fact, despite some relevant differences, the crucial point in both is the same: there is over-reliance by B. Since the goal of precontractual liability is primarily to create incentives for optimal reliance, the efficient solution in both cases would be no liability whatsoever for A. By imposing liability on A, B would only have greater incentive to over-rely.

A significant minority of jurisdictions would not award B any remedy in case 8. The majority, however would award him reliance damages.[40] Again, the potential inefficiency of this approach seems to be recognised by reporters: some of the jurisdictions that would

[37] See comparative conclusions on case 6, above pp. 188–91.

[38] For the full hypothetical, see case 8, above p. 233. In brief, A, a leading department store, negotiates with B for B to build a new shopping centre in which A plans to be the primary tenant. Relying on those negotiations B begins construction of the shopping centre, including many of A's design and construction elements desired by A. Before the building is complete or a lease has been signed, A decides the venture will not be profitable and withdraws from negotiations.

[39] For the full hypothetical, see case 9, above p. 254. In brief, A tells his friend, B, that he wants a house but that he cannot afford normal rates. B, a builder, tells A that he has time to build the house and will do so for less than the normal price. While A and B are still negotiating, B starts work on the house. When the house is nearly complete, A breaks off negotiations because he discovers he cannot afford the house even at the lower price B has offered.

[40] See comparative conclusions on case 8, above pp. 251–3.

impose liability on A (Finland, France, Portugal and Switzerland) would at least possibly reduce the damages by effect of B's contributory negligence.

With respect to case 9, all jurisdictions find that A may be liable to B, although the legal bases of the remedy vary.[41] Rules of unjust enrichment probably fit the case better than general principles of precontractual liability and may give B a proper remedy when B's reliance on his friend's representation has been 'rational' and not based on the nature of their relationship. However, this solution does not eliminate the problem of over-reliance.

Conclusion

In this chapter we have addressed the issue of precontractual liability from an economic perspective. We described the existing law and economics scholarship dealing with precontractual liability, and have attempted to apply the models developed in that scholarship to a series of hypothetical cases. As those cases illustrate, existing precontractual liability regimes sometimes further the economic goal of optimal reliance but in other cases undercut it. All in all, however, it seems clear that an economic perspective can be valuable in determining which precontractual liability regime to impose.

[41] See comparative conclusions on case 9, above pp. 273–4.

5 Conclusions

JOHN CARTWRIGHT AND MARTIJN HESSELINK

The problem of precontractual liability

Peculiarity of the precontractual phase

The precontractual phase is difficult to characterise and analyse, in both legal and practical terms.

The negotiating parties have entered into a relationship by virtue simply of their negotiations. So they have begun their journey together. But they are not yet in the relationship – the contract – which is their aim. And they may never reach it. The negotiations may fail; and a failure may come sooner or later. It may become clear very quickly to them both that they will never reach the agreement necessary to conclude the contract. But, equally, it may be only after a lengthy exploration of their respective positions as regards the likely terms of a contract, and perhaps only after further information becomes available from third party sources, or the facts surrounding their negotiations change, that one of them decides that the contract is hopeless; or that a better deal is to be done elsewhere with another party. By then, either party may well have incurred significant expenses, as well as having invested time and effort, towards the hoped-for contract. The break-off of the negotiations may seem inevitable to the parties as they together realise that the contract will never be concluded; or it may come as a shock to one party that the other calls off the negotiations when they were so far advanced, or at least where there was nothing to suggest that they were not likely to lead to their fruition in the contract. Such 'negotiations' may occur in the kind of commercial setting where the negotiating parties have similar bargaining strength and a similar awareness of the commercial difficulties involved in the negotiations. But they may also occur between commercial parties whose relative bargaining strength and awareness is not equal; in a less commercial context, between a commercial party and a consumer; between two non-commercial parties (friends – or, at least, they started out as friends when the 'negotiations' began); or even (the most non-commercial example that one might ever conceive) the 'negotiations' for the 'contract' may not be negotiations at all, but an engagement, leading to a hoped-for marriage which never takes place. In this volume we have drawn together cases which are designed to explore such situations, and a wide range of variations on the nature of 'negotiations' (including, in case 5, the example of a broken engagement) and the types of reason that might be invoked by one of the parties for breaking off the negotiations, with a view to exploring how the European legal systems characterise the precontractual phase. The results of this exploration are discussed below. But first it is useful to identify why the precontractual phase presents difficulties of legal analysis, and what fundamental issues have to be addressed by any legal system in devising principles of precontractual liability (or non-liability). In this, we can draw on the explanations given by our reporters in their analysis of their jurisdictions' answers to the cases within our study.

Imposing liability in the precontractual phase: balancing the arguments

The negotiations: a legally significant relationship?

One might begin by asking whether the relationship which is created between the parties by virtue of their negotiations is a relationship to which the law should attribute legal significance at all, in the sense that it should of itself attract the protection of the law for each of the parties vis-à-vis the other. One view would be that the negotiations are designed to lead towards a legally-protected relationship (the contract) and so the significant moment is the formation of the contract itself. The negotiations are purely preparatory and are not themselves of legal significance. This does not mean that one of the negotiating parties cannot commit a wrong during the course of the negotiations which will attract legal consequences, in the same way that he might commit a legal wrong in any other (extra-contractual) context. It just means that there is no significance as such to negotiations: the opening of discussions towards a possible contract does not yet cross the line into a legally protected relationship, which is delayed until the contract is formed.

At the other extreme would be the view that there is something special about the negotiations for a contract, even from the very beginning of the negotiations. Although the contract itself is not yet concluded, the fact that the parties have begun to work together towards it places them in a relationship which merits the protection of the law. Negotiations are in some sense a collaboration between the parties. The fact of that collaboration, or, at least, the fact that each party has led the other to believe that he is engaged in the collaborative process of negotiation, means that each is entitled to the protection of the law. The negotiations are not yet the contract, and so the form and scope of protection will not be the same as the form and scope of the legal protection given to contracting parties as against each other. But the negotiations are still a relationship which by its very nature can be given legal significance, and protection can and should be given accordingly to each of the negotiating parties.

The principal enquiry in this study is into this very question: what is the nature and scope of the duties owed by one party to the other during the negotiations, and how does each of the legal systems within the study draw the line between a party's freedom to break off negotiations, and those duties? We shall consider the detail later in these conclusions, but from the outset it is worth noting that the different extremes of viewpoint set out above are demonstrated by different jurisdictions within this project. The strongest view against the model of negotiations as constituting a legally protected relationship is found within the common law jurisdictions, where there is a marked reluctance to attribute legal significance to the precontractual phase.[1] In its strongest form, and in its strongest statement within English law, we find a rejection of the duty to negotiate in good faith based on a rejection of the idea that one party, by entering into negotiations, has given up the freedom to change his mind. The moment at which the freedom not to contract is lost is when the contract is formed. Until then each party is an independent actor, at arm's length from the other, and is entitled to withdraw freely:[2]

> the concept of a duty to carry on negotiations in good faith is inherently repugnant to the adversarial position of the parties when involved in negotiations.

[1] For further discussion of this, and a contrast between English law and Dutch law, see below pp. 460–70.

[2] *Walford v. Miles* [1992] 2 AC 128, 138 (Lord Ackner), discussed in the English report on case 6.

Each party to the negotiations is entitled to pursue his (or her) own interest, so long as he avoids making misrepresentations. To advance that interest he must be entitled, if he thinks it appropriate, to threaten to withdraw from further negotiations or to withdraw in fact, in the hope that the opposite party may seek to reopen the negotiations by offering him improved terms.

On the other hand, reporters from some other jurisdictions identify the beginning of the negotiations[3] as the key moment when a relationship is created which has a formal legal significance. This is put perhaps most clearly by the German reporters:

from the moment of entering into contractual negotiations a special relationship (*Sonderrechtsverhältnis*) is created between the negotiating parties by virtue of the law (*gesetzliches Schuldverhältnis*) imposing on both parties duties of protection and loyalty (*Schutzpflichten*).[4]

And the Dutch reporter:

In *Baris/Riezenkamp* (1957)[5] the Hoge Raad decided that parties starting negotiations enter into a legal relationship that is dominated by good faith, which requires them to take each other's interests into account.[6]

These different approaches demonstrate a stark difference of view about the very nature of precontractual negotiations. However, the true picture is rather more nuanced than this would suggest, although the starting-point of the different jurisdictions may indeed be very far apart. English law does not reject all liability during the negotiations, but can impose particular liabilities to cover particular events or actions of the parties during the precontractual period. Nor do German or Dutch law in practice impose liability from the beginning of the negotiations: even if the beginning of the negotiations creates a legally-protected relationship, that does not yet say much about the content of the duties which that relationship entails, or the circumstances in which liability can in fact arise. All legal systems recognise, in effect, that there is a balance to be struck in the analysis of the precontractual phase. A party should be free to decide whether to contract. But he should also in certain circumstances have to pay regard to the position

[3] 'Or even earlier, when they prepare the ground for the contract': see the Swiss report on case 1.

[4] Report on case 1.

[5] HR 15 Nov. 1957, NJ 1958, 67, note Rutten.

[6] Report on case 1.

of the other party to the negotiations. This is put very helpfully by the Austrian reporter in his answer to case 2:

> the major problem in cases of this type lies in the difficulty of drawing the line between freedom of contract and bargaining in good faith. Indeed, freedom to negotiate is a cornerstone of contract law and it includes the freedom to break off negotiations, but it may collide with the mutual reliance in the honesty of the negotiating parties that stems from the duty to bargain in good faith. It is a matter of discretion to decide, in a given factual situation, how far the freedom to break off negotiations goes and at which point the creation of the negotiating partner's confidence in the perfection of the deal attains dominance, so as to put the disappointed partner in the position of a victim under the judge-made rules of *culpa in contrahendo*.

The 'collision' between freedom of contract (freedom *from* contract) and the responsibility towards the other party to the negotiations is at the heart of our study. Whether one begins from the position that the other party to the negotiations is an *adversary*, or that he is a *partner*, one must go further and examine where, short of the contract itself being formed, one party crosses the line and incurs some form of liability towards the other.

Expectation, reliance and shifting the economic risk of the negotiations

Different criteria might be used to determine when, and why, one party can incur liability towards the other short of the formation of the contract itself.

In the first place, one might say that entering into negotiations, or, alternatively, one party's conduct during the negotiations, might create in the other party the *expectation* that the contract is to be formed. This is not, of course, the same as the expectation which a contract itself engenders. The contractual expectation arises from a promise or an agreement which is protected as such within the law of contract through the remedies provided by the law precisely to give effect to a contractually binding obligation. An undertaking given within the negotiations might be recognised within a legal system as having contractual binding force: different forms of 'pre-contract' are widely recognised within the legal systems within this study.[7] But we can put such (pre-)contracts on one side for the moment. If a more general form of extra-contractual liability during the negotiations is to be based

[7] See, e.g., case 6 (lock-out agreement).

on the claimant's 'expectation' of a completed contract, the notion of 'expectation' is different. It is in some sense weaker than a contractual expectation: the contract contains complete and definitive obligations which are to be performed and for which the law should provide remedies in the event of non-performance.[8] The precontractual expectation is of a future contract, a stage removed from the final contractual expectation and generally less definitive as regards the content of the other party's future obligations (except, perhaps, in the final stages of negotiations where the precontractual expectation might shade into the contractual expectation).[9] However, a legal system might say that the weaker, precontractual expectation is still deserving of protection, within a regime of precontractual responsibility.

Another way of justifying the imposition of precontractual liability might be based on the *reliance* by the claimant. The language of 'reliance' is used by a number of reporters in explaining their system's approach to precontractual liability. But it can be used in different contexts and in different senses. Where, for example, the defendant makes a false statement during the course of the negotiations, which the claimant believes and acts on, one can speak of the claimant's reliance on the defendant's statement; and one can identify the causal consequences of the false statement by reference to the acts undertaken by the claimant in reliance on it. This is a context in which some systems[10] would impose liability for misrepresentations made during the negotiations, and might also define the remedy by reference to the losses incurred by the claimant in consequence of his reliance on the misrepresentation. The 'reliance' is at the same time part of the test for the imposition of liability and a defining element of the scope of the liability (causation). Sometimes, however, reporters use the language of 'reliance' in a rather looser sense, to describe the claimant's

[8] The form of the remedies will, of course, depend upon the legal system's view of the nature and force of the contractual obligation and the underlying policy in relation to contracts and the remedies for non-performance. Whether the default remedy for non-performance of a contract is damages (as generally in the common law) or specific enforcement of the contract (as generally in civil law jurisdictions), this of itself does not define the basis of the imposition of liability during the *precontractual* phase, nor the remedies which should be available for breach of precontractual duties.

[9] For the impact of such an analysis on the remedies which can be awarded in some jurisdictions, such as Dutch law, for precontractual liability in the case of negotiations which are broken off at an advanced stage, see below pp. 468–70.

[10] See, e.g., the English and Irish reports on case 1.

belief that the contract was going to be concluded. Precontractual liability may arise in the case of 'reasonable and legitimate reliance of the one party that the partner will not break off the negotiation process';[11] or because:

From the moment when the parties start negotiations or, even earlier, when they prepare the ground for the contract, a relationship of reliance (*Vertrauensverhältnis*) exists between the parties that leads to a legal relationship (*Rechtsverhältnis*) with duties of protection and loyalty (*Schutz- und Loyalitätspflichten*) for both parties.[12]

However, this 'reliance' is inextricably linked to the 'expectation' which was discussed above. The defendant's precontractual liability arises because the claimant relied on a hope, or expectation, that the (future) contract would be concluded:

A party liable on the ground of *culpa in contrahendo* has to make up for the aggrieved party's reliance interest (*Vertrauensschaden*). The scope of liability mirrors its rationale which is not to be found in a party's refraining from a bargain but in his creation of legitimate expectations within the other party that a contract would be brought about.[13]

Here we see the fundamental issue. For the claimant to obtain a remedy where negotiations are broken off, it is not sufficient for him to say that he 'relied' on the future contract, otherwise from the beginning of the negotiations each party would be bound to the other as if the contract had already been concluded. Even if the remedy were not to be the same remedy as for the non-performance of a concluded contract, it would still be too much to impose liability simply because the negotiations for the hoped-for contract had failed. The point of the negotiations is to test the possibility of a (future) contract. Negotiations must be allowed to fail, without legal liability on either side:

B may in good faith rely on the prospective conclusion of the contract, but he must be careful not to misjudge the real situation: a contract may with high probability come about but it is still not there.[14]

So if we are to use the principle of 'reliance' to justify the imposition of precontractual liability, and to define its operation, it is not sufficient that the claimant 'in good faith' believed that the contract would be

[11] Austrian report on case 6. [12] Swiss report on case 1.
[13] German report on case 1. [14] Greek report on case 8.

concluded. In addition, this belief – his 'reliance' on the contract, if we call it such – must be *legitimate* or *reasonable*. And since the effect of giving a remedy to the claimant is inevitably to impose liability on the defendant, it is natural also to look for the source of the claimant's legitimate expectation in the defendant's own conduct. It might, therefore, be appropriate to impose liability on the defendant who has created or encouraged the claimant's belief that the contract would be concluded, as long as the claimant's belief and his actions in consequence of holding that belief (for example, the costs he goes on to incur during the negotiations) are reasonable.

But legal systems might take different views about how this should operate; how readily one should allow the claimant to be heard to say that he 'legitimately' or 'reasonably' relied on the future contract. One way of viewing the general question of the imposition of precontractual liability is to examine the point at which the *risk* shifts from one party to the other during the precontractual negotiations – the *economic* risk of the negotiations. The negotiations are not yet complete. So why should the claimant be entitled to charge any of the costs he incurs in advance of the concluded contract to the other party?[15] As already discussed above, a legal system can take a hard line here, and say that each party should retain the risk up to the moment of formation of the contract; and might do so on the basis that the hope, or expectation, of a future contract is simply not something on which a negotiating party should be entitled to rely. He 'relies' at his own peril. On the other hand, it might be possible to define the sort of conduct by one party which would allow the other to begin to say that he was reasonably entitled to rely on the future contract; but, equally, there can be a spectrum here, with legal systems taking more or less restrictive views about the circumstances in which one party can be entitled to rely on the future contract being formed.[16] Even where they use a common terminology (such as *culpa in contrahendo*, and 'good faith') the underlying application may differ. We shall see different systems' approaches to such issues below.

[15] For precontractual preparatory work, see, e.g., case 4.

[16] See, e.g., the Finnish report on case 2: 'In Finnish discussion on *culpa in contrahendo* views have been presented that freedom of negotiations should have its utmost limit where the reliance of the other party on the conclusion of the contract has become worth protecting. This point should be reached only in extreme (and very rare) cases, when the other party has very good grounds to believe that the formation of the contract is at hand, lacking no more than just the formal confirmation.'

Placing the liability: contract, tort or *tertium quid*?

A further complexity in imposing liability in the precontractual phase is to determine the form of liability. The contract is not yet concluded, and so it is not obvious that the regime for precontractual liability should be the contractual regime. On the other hand, the relationship between negotiating parties is in some sense a legal relationship; at least, that is the underlying rationale of some systems in imposing precontractual liability. And so if the law of tort is perceived as being aimed at the protection against loss inflicted outside the context of a pre-existing legal relationship, then the precontractual phase does not quite fit the model of tort either. So should it be regarded as somewhere in between the two – a *tertium quid*?

The obvious first question to ask is why this matters at all. Indeed, some systems do not appear to think that the borderline between contract and tort matters much: the most straightforward version of this position is seen in the Danish report on case 1:

> Danish courts would probably classify B's behaviour as a tort but do not attach great importance to the distinction between tort and contract. On the whole, Danish courts tend to be moderate in awarding damages. A court might award damages but probably less than €0.2m and certainly not €0.5m.

The context of this statement makes clear why the contract/tort borderline does not really matter in Danish law, but why it may indeed have crucial significance elsewhere: there is no formal demarcation in Danish law in the law of damages between contract and tort.[17] In some other systems, however, a distinction is drawn between the nature of contact and tort, which is reflected in a scientific analysis of the difference between the calculation of damages for breach of contract and for tort.[18]

But the quantification of damages is not the only difference between contract and tort; and, indeed, different systems have developed different distinctions between their regimes of contract and tort, which

[17] Cf. the Danish report on case 4: 'the court awarded the contractor compensation. . . Whether the compensation was awarded on a contract, tort or *quantum meruit* basis is difficult to say'.

[18] See, e.g., the Finnish, German and Swiss reports on case 1, distinguishing between 'expectation' or 'positive interest' damages (contract) and 'reliance' or 'negative interest' damages (tort). The Dutch Code, however, provides a single regime for all types of liability: Dutch report on case 1.

will therefore have varying significance when they are brought into the context of how to place precontractual liability in relation to the contract/tort borderline. This is made clear by the Austrian reporter, who identifies a number of features of the contractual regime which make it more attractive to a claimant than the tort regime:[19] in contract, vicarious liability (for example, for employees) is more generally available; the claimant has a more favourable burden of proof of fault; and there is a wider scope of liability (and in particular of economic loss). Similar accounts of the differences between the contractual and tortious regimes are given by the reporters for other jurisdictions, such as Finland[20] and Switzerland,[21] by way of context for their explanation of their systems' approaches to precontractual liability.

The policy issues which lie behind these distinctions between the regimes of contract and tort have led some of the jurisdictions to devise particular approaches to the placing of precontractual liability. Some legal systems have a rigid division between contract and tort which has not been developed to admit a middle ground; and this usually leads to the decision that, since precontractual liability does not arise under a contract, it must be tort. The rules of tort must therefore be applied, either without any significant amendment (as in French[22] or Spanish[23] law) or as a special regime within tort law (as in Finnish law).[24]

Other systems, however, have held that the special nature of the precontractual phase merits special treatment: a *tertium quid*, between contract and tort. This can be traced back to the thinking of German law in its development of the doctrine of *culpa in contrahendo*, which is placed within the contractual liability regime.[25] But the detail of such a doctrine, as it has been developed within other systems, has varied, and the Swiss reporter makes clear that the policy reasons for differentiating between the contractual and tortious regimes are assessed

[19] Austrian report on case 1, esp. n. 3.

[20] Finnish report on case 1: recovery of pure economic losses and the burden of proof of fault.

[21] Swiss report on case 1: vicarious liability, burden of proof and limitation periods.

[22] E.g. French report on case 1, esp. n. 22, showing that French academic writers have debated whether to place precontractual liability within contract or tort, but the settled view is that it must be tortious.

[23] Spanish report on case 1.

[24] See Finnish report on case 1: the doctrine of *culpa in contrahendo* derives from German contract law, but is applied in Finland as part of tort law.

[25] German report on case 1.

independently for their application to *culpa in contrahendo* for the precontractual liability regime:[26]

In accordance with an emerging opinion in academic writing the Swiss Federal Court holds that *culpa in contrahendo* is neither contractual nor tortious but a liability by virtue of law, a liability *sui generis* with its own rules. For each modality of the liability there has to be a pragmatic decision whether contractual rules or tortious rules should apply by analogy in order to find an appropriate solution. In the field of vicarious liability and of the proof of fault the contractual rules apply in favour of the victim. By contrast the Federal Court applies the short period of prescription of one year (which is criticized by the prevailing opinion of academic writers).

Moreover, even in jurisdictions where the legislature has identified precontractual liability as an independent source of liability, there can still be room for discussion about whether it should follow certain particular rules within the contractual regime or the tortious regime. In particular, in relation to the Greek Civil Code which makes specific provision in articles 197 and 198 regarding precontractual liability:[27]

The specific nature of precontractual liability in Greece is disputed. The prevalent approach considers precontractual liability to form a separate, third type of liability, alongside the other two types, namely contractual and delictual. Thus, under Greek law precontractual liability is considered to be a *sui generis* type of liability and this is supported by the autonomous regulation of precontractual liability in the GCC. Nevertheless, among those who acknowledge precontractual liability as a separate type of liability there are still divergences: some emphasize the contractual affinity of precontractual liability (quasi-contractual), others stress the delictual nuances (quasi-delictual), whereas still others stand indecisively somewhere in between.

One should not, however, assume that a legal system which has developed a special regime for precontractual liability will necessarily regard it as exclusive; there can be an overlap with the regimes of contract and tort which might on occasion give the claimant a choice. For example, in a number of cases within this study reporters have identified alternative sources of liability on the same facts (most commonly, finding liabilities both on the basis of tort and for the system's autonomous regime of precontractual liability).[28]

[26] Swiss report on case 1. [27] Greek report on case 1 (footnotes omitted).
[28] See, e.g., the Austrian and German reports on case 1 (tort and *culpa in contrahendo*); and, for the most extreme example, the Dutch report on case 2 (contact, tort, precontractual liability and restitution).

One context in which it will be important to identify the proper place for precontractual liability is in cross-border disputes: private international law. For issues which arise entirely within a single jurisdiction, whether the contractual or tortious liability regime (or a third, autonomous regime) is applied will be an internal matter of policy for that jurisdiction. But where the rules of private international law apply, it will be important to define the nature of the potential liability for the purposes of both jurisdiction and the choice of law rules to determine the substantive dispute. The European Court of Justice has held that for the purposes of the Brussels Convention[29] (that is, to determine which court has jurisdiction) a claim for damages for breach of the precontractual duty to negotiate in good faith is a claim in tort within article 5(3) rather than a claim in contract within article 5(1).[30] And the Rome I and Rome II Regulations[30a] make clear that, for the purposes of choice of law, obligations arising out of precontractual negotiations are covered by the Rome II Regulation (non-contractual obligations), rather than the Rome I Regulation (contractual obligations). Article 12(1) of the Rome II Regulation provides:

> The law applicable to a non-contractual obligation arising out of dealings prior to the conclusion of a contract, regardless of whether the contract was actully concluded or not, shall be the law that applies to the contract or that would have been applicable to it had it been entered into.

This is not necessarily the end of the matter, however, because it might be argued that for both jurisdiction and the substantive rules of liability, and the remedies to be awarded for breach of precontractual duties, it is not sufficient that the selection is limited to the established rules of private international law for either contract or tort, and that a *tertium quid* should be devised.[31]

[29] Convention of 27 September 1968 on Jurisdiction and the Enforcement of Judgments in Civil and Commercial Matters (OJ 1978 L304/36), as amended.

[30] C334/00 *Fonderie Officine Meccaniche Tacconi SpA v. Heinrich Wagner Sinto Maschinenfabrik GmbH (HWS)* [2002] ECR I-07357 (reference by the Corte suprema di cassazione in relation to a claim for damages under art. 1337 of the Italian Civil Code); note G. Afferni in (2005) 1 *European Review of Contract Law* 96.

[30a] Regulation (EC) 593/2008 (Rome I), recital 10; Regulation (EC) 864/2007 (Rome I), recital 30 and arts. 2(1), 12(1).

[31] C. Seraglini, 'Le droit international privé et la période précontractuelle' in O. Deshayes (ed.), *L'avant-contrat: Actualité et processus de formation des contrats* (2008), p. 77; B. Bourdelois, 'Réflexions sur le traitement des relations précontractuelles en droit international privé' in *Mélanges Philippe Malaurie* (Paris, 2005), p. 107.

Two (extreme?) illustrations: English law and Dutch law

Each legal system has its own response to the problems of the precontractual phase which have been outlined above, and each defines the scope of precontractual liability accordingly. From the outset it is worth contrasting two jurisdictions which appear to take notably different and contrasting approaches to the precontractual phase: England and the Netherlands.

English law: the most restrictive?

We have already noted that, within our study, English law appears to exhibit the strongest reluctance to impose precontractual liability, although this is shared by the other common law jurisdiction (Ireland) and largely[32] also by the mixed jurisdiction of Scotland. The position adopted by English law, and its context within the common law generally in this respect, deserves to be considered a little further. Is the approach taken by English law an inherent function of the common law approach to this area of private law, or is it a position of principle, a reflection of a view of the negotiating process which is simply different - socially, politically or economically - from the view taken in other systems within this study?[33]

One might start by thinking that the rejection of a general principle of precontractual liability in English law follows from the reluctance of the common law to develop broad and general principles, and the preference instead to focus on specific, identifiable wrongs (specific and separate torts, or breaches of contract) or other causes of action (estoppel; unjust enrichment).[34] On this basis, there has been no generalisation of precontractual duties and therefore no reification of the precontractual negotiations into a separately identifiable legally-protected relationship; and the techniques of the common law, by contrast with the techniques of the civil law, might be at the root of the different

[32] For a note about the position in Scotland, by contrast with England and Ireland, see below text to n. 70.

[33] On the political analysis of contract law, see M.W. Hesselink, 'The Politics of a European Civil Code' (2004) ELJ 675, where rule alternatives for questions of contract law (including precontractual liability, at 680) are placed on a continuum between autonomy and solidarity.

[34] For further discussion, see Cartwright, *Contract Law: an Introduction to the English Law of Contract for the Civil Lawyer*, chs. 2 and 4; J. Cartwright, 'Negotiation and Renegotiation: an English Perspective' in Cartwright, Vogenauer and Whittaker, *Reforming the French Law of Obligations*, ch. 3.

approach to the precontractual phase. The common law can, of course, use general standards, such as 'reasonableness'. But within private law there is no general duty of, or based on, reasonableness. The law of tort is not organised around such general principles; and although the most general of the torts, negligence, is based on the reasonable foreseeability of causation of harm to the claimant, reasonable foreseeability is not sufficient to impose a duty of care, nor is there even a general duty to take care in one's dealings with others.[35] English law identifies particular circumstances in which duties of care are imposed within the tort of negligence, categorised by such criteria as the kind of harm which is foreseeable (physical; economic), and the kind of action in which the defendant is engaged (a positive act; the making of a statement; or an omission to act or to speak). And torts other than negligence are defined in such a way as to protect particular interests, or to impose liability for loss caused by particular forms of wrongdoing.[36]

Does this mean that English law could not develop a general duty between negotiating parties? Some legal systems within our study have taken the view that the precontractual phase cannot be protected within the existing extra-contractual sources of obligation, and so a separate set of rules must be devised to protect the relationship which arises by virtue of precontractual negotiations, such as *culpa in contrahendo* in German law, given that the German law of tort is so constructed as to protect only particular interests, or to sanction harm inflicted wilfully in a manner contrary to public policy.[37] Other systems have held that the existing rules of private law can naturally cover the precontractual phase and so should be developed to do so, such as 'precontracual fault' as one form of the 'fault' required to impose liability in tort in French law.[38] Could English law follow either of these paths? We have seen in this study that there are plenty of situations within precontractual negotiations where

[35] The duty of care in negligence is based on the relationship of 'neighbourhood', which is itself based on foreseeability of consequences of one's acts or omissions: *Donoghue v. Stevenson* [1932] AC 562, 580–1 (Lord Atkin). But this does not mean that a duty is owed simply on the basis of foreseeability of harm: 'Foreseeability of harm is a necessary ingredient of such a relationship, but it is not the only one. Otherwise there would be liability in negligence on the part of one who sees another about to walk over a cliff with his head in the air, and forbears to shout a warning': *Yuen Kun Yeu v. Attorney-General of Hong Kong* [1988] 1 AC 175, 192 (Lord Keith of Kinkel).

[36] Dugdale, *Clerk and Lindsell on Torts*, para. 1–19; *OBG Ltd v. Allan* [2007] 2 WLR 920, at [32] (Lord Hoffmann, approving P. Cane, 'Mens Rea in Tort Law' (2000) 20 OJLS 533, 552).

[37] BGB §§ 823, 826:1; see the German report on case 1.

[38] French Civil Code, arts. 1382, 1383: see the French report on case 1.

English law will impose liability on one party towards the other. It is notable that English law looks to place such liabilities within the particular sources of obligation which are established within private law: one of the torts (such as deceit or negligence); contract (a pre-contract, such as an option or a lock-out contract); or restitution for unjust enrichment. And, within those contexts, no general position has been taken that the precontractual phase itself should be identified as deserving protection. Where the facts happen to arise during the negotiations which involve a tort or breach of contract, or an enrichment conferred which should not be retained, then remedies might follow. But the precontactual context does not generally enhance the claim. The nearest that English law has come to recognising the development of a new source of obligation within the precontractual phase is through the doctrine of estoppel, which has not yet fully matured in English law. In other common law jurisdictions[39] the creation of an expectation by one negotiating party in the other party that a contract will be concluded – or, at least, that the latter is entitled to rely on it – can lead to the first party being estopped from denying his obligation to complete the contract, or at least to compensate the other for losses he has incurred in reliance on the expectation. In English law, until the House of Lords decides otherwise,[40] such an approach can be taken only in the particular context of the creation by the defendant of an expectation that the claimant has or will obtain an interest in land, under the doctrine of *proprietary* estoppel.[41] In *Cobbe v. Yeoman's Row Management Ltd* the Court of Appeal pointed towards the use of proprietary estoppel as a doctrine to sanction precontractual misconduct:[42]

This case is set very close to contract territory. It arises in the context of precontractual negotiations for the sale, purchase and development of a block of flats in Knightsbridge. Under English law there is no general duty to negotiate in good faith, but there are plenty of other ways of dealing with particular problems of unacceptable conduct occurring in the course of negotiations

[39] This is well-established in American law: American Law Institute, *Restatement of the Law (2d), Contracts* (1981), para. 90; Farnsworth, *Contracts*, para. 2.19; and has more recently been accepted in Australian law: *Waltons Stores (Interstate) Ltd v. Maher* (1988) 164 CLR 387, discussed in the English report on case 8.

[40] The Court of Appeal is bound by the decision in *Combe v. Combe* [1951] 2 KB 215 to the effect that promissory estoppel cannot create new obligations: *Baird Textile Holdings Ltd v. Marks & Spencer plc* [2002] 1 All ER (Comm) 737, at [55] (Judge LJ).

[41] See the English report on case 2.

[42] *Cobbe v. Yeoman's Row Management Ltd* [2006] 1 WLR 2964, at [4]–[7] (Mummery LJ).

without unduly hampering the ability of the parties to negotiate their own bargains without the intervention of the courts.

The case is also set in the area of work done or services rendered by a claimant without having first secured a contract to protect his position. The work done by this claimant was not, according to the judge, merely in anticipation of a contract: it was done in the positive expectation of a promised contract to sell deliberately induced, encouraged and then ultimately defeated by the unconscionable conduct of the defendant . . .

This appeal requires the court to find a principled way of devising relief in a form that fits a case where the court below found an expectation by the claimant that the defendant would not withdraw from a promise of a contract to sell property on agreed terms, and the specific expectation has been raised and then disappointed by the unconscionable conduct of the defendant.

One might wonder whether an English court could develop a similar doctrine, outside the context of the negotiations for the sale of property, to impose liability where a 'specific expectation [of a future contract] has been raised and then disappointed by the unconscionable conduct of the defendant'. But how far this can be pressed is now in doubt. In *Cobbe*, the Court of Appeal held that the claimant was entitled to a share in the increase in the value of the property under the doctrine of proprietary estoppel. However, this was reversed by the House of Lords,[42a] on the basis that the doctrine applies only where the claimant had an expectation of a certain interest in land, and it was not sufficient that he expected that the parties would finalise the outstanding contractual terms, particularly since both parties knew that the deal had not yet been completed, and that the particular contract, for the disposition of an interest in land, could be concluded only in writing. Their Lordships appeared to doubt whether, because of the risk of uncertainty, estoppel (except in its well-established narrow form) should be introduced into commercial transactions;[42b] and whether the law should be developed 'to provide a remedy for disappointed expectation engendered by a representation made in the context of incomplete contractual negotiations'.[42c]

The other context in which the English courts might be free to make such a development already is within the tort of negligence. Under this

[42a] *Cobbe v. Yeoman's Row Management Ltd* [2008] 1 WLR 1752. The claimant did, however, obtain the award of a sum in unjust enrichment to reflect the value his work had added to the defendant's property through obtaining planning permission, and a *quantum meruit* for the value of his services which the defendant knew he was not providing gratuitously.

[42b] See especially at [85] (Lord Walker). [42c] At [38] (Lord Scott).

tort, the defendant is liable for foreseeable loss which he causes to the claimant as a result of his failure to fulfil his duty to take reasonable care. If the negotiations were to be characterised as a relationship which imposed on each of the parties a duty of care towards the other; and if the courts were to give content to that duty of care by reference to what it is reasonable for each party to expect of the other during negotiations, then the law of tort could cover the situation. The English courts have developed a category of duty in relation to the making of statements: giving information or advice. This step forward was taken by the House of Lords in 1963, in the leading decision of *Hedley Byrne & Co Ltd v. Heller & Partners Ltd*,[43] and can apply in relation to statements made during precontractual negotiations.[44] That decision has been further explored in later cases, and has formed the basis of a broader approach to the duty of care in negligence, based on the defendant's 'assumption of responsibility' to the defendant for the careful performance of a task, whether the task be the giving of information and advice, or the performance of another service.[45] Could entering into the negotiations form the basis of such an 'assumption of responsibility'? And could the content of the duty arising from the entering into negotiations include such things as the duty not to enter into or to continue with the negotiations once the defendant knows that there is no realistic chance that they will reach a successful conclusion, or at least the duty to warn the other party that he is incurring expenses which might well be wasted; or the duty to inform the other party of relevant information of which the defendant knows the claimant is unaware? We have seen that some legal systems have given content to such duties within the law of tort.[46] Typically, these duties are summed up within the broader test of *good faith*. But each of the systems which uses the language of good faith can articulate it in particular factual situations as constituting particular duties, particular requirements of conduct as between the negotiating parties. Even if English law resists the language of a general test of 'good faith', could it not use the duty of care within the law of tort to give effect to more particularised duties which would in substance cover the same ground?

[43] [1964] AC 465. [44] *Esso Petroleum Co. Ltd v. Mardon* [1976] QB 801.

[45] *Henderson v. Merrett Syndicates Ltd* [1995] 2 AC 145, 180; Dugdale, *Clerk and Lindsell on Torts*, paras. 8.84–8.88.

[46] E.g. French law: see the French report on case 1; Spanish law: see the Spanish report on case 1.

No attempt has been made within English law to do so. The use of the duty of care in negligence may well not be seen as a suitable tool to impose general rules of conduct between negotiating parties because such general duties *should not be imposed*. That is, it is not simply a matter of legal technique where the courts have not yet noticed that they do in fact have the tools available to generalise the duties between the parties during precontractual negotiations. It is because, as a matter of principle, the courts do not think that the entering into negotiations should trigger duties between the parties which the law should categorise and enforce. The Supreme Court of Canada has rejected explicitly the use of the tort of negligence to impose duties of disclosure between negotiating parties because it would undermine the proper risk allocation during the negotiations:[47]

> It would defeat the essence of negotiation and hobble the marketplace to extend a duty of care to the conduct of negotiations, and to label a party's failure to disclose its bottom line, its motives or its final position as negligent. Such a conclusion would of necessity force the disclosure of privately acquired information and the dissipation of any competitive advantage derived from it, all of which is incompatible with the activity of negotiating and bargaining.
>
> . . . [T]o impose a duty in the circumstances of this appeal could interject tort law as after-the-fact insurance against failures to act with due diligence or to hedge the risk of failed negotiations through the pursuit of alternative strategies or opportunities.

We move, therefore, to a very different position: the real reluctance of the common law to impose precontractual liability is based on a principled view of the nature of the negotiating process. We have already noted that this found its most extreme articulation in the speech of Lord Ackner in *Walford v. Miles*:[48] 'the concept of a duty to carry on negotiations in good faith is inherently repugnant to the adversarial position of the parties when involved in negotiations'. Lord Ackner had another reason for rejecting a general duty to negotiate in good faith: that it is inherently *uncertain*, and he linked this uncertainty to the view that there should be no restriction on the parties' freedom to withdraw from negotiations:[49]

[47] *Martel Building Ltd v. Canada* (2000) 193 DLR (4th) 1, at [67]–[68].

[48] [1992] 2 AC 128, 138; above n. 2.

[49] Ibid. For an earlier view that the obligation to negotiate is uncertain, and therefore there can be no certain *remedy* in the event of breach of such an obligation, see *Courtney & Fairbairn Ltd v. Tolaini Brothers (Hotels) Ltd* [1975] 1 WLR 297, 301 (Lord Denning MR): 'If the law does not recognise a contract to enter into a contract (when there is a fundamental term yet to be agreed) it seems to me it cannot recognise a

> The reason why an agreement to negotiate, like an agreement to agree, is unenforceable, is simply because it lacks the necessary certainty . . . How can a court be expected to decide whether, *subjectively*, a proper reason existed for the termination of negotiations? The answer suggested depends upon whether the negotiations have been determined 'in good faith'. However the concept of a duty to carry on negotiations in good faith is inherently repugnant to the adversarial position of the parties when involved in negotiations. Each party to the negotiations is entitled to pursue his (or her) own interest, so long as he avoids making misrepresentations. To advance that interest he must be entitled, if he thinks it appropriate, to threaten to withdraw from further negotiations or to withdraw in fact, in the hope that the opposite party may seek to reopen the negotiations by offering him improved terms. [Counsel arguing that liability should be imposed in the case], of course, accepts that the agreement upon which he relies does not contain a duty to complete the negotiations. But that still leaves the vital question – how is a vendor ever to know that he is entitled to withdraw from further negotiations? How is the court to police such an 'agreement?' A duty to negotiate in good faith is as unworkable in practice as it is inherently inconsistent with the position of a negotiating party. It is here that the uncertainty lies. In my judgment, while negotiations are in existence either party is entitled to withdraw from those negotiations, at any time and for any reason. There can be thus no obligation to continue to negotiate until there is a 'proper reason' to withdraw.

This is the strongest statement which has been made in the English courts;[50] but it is part of the reasoning for the decision, and therefore binding on courts below the House of Lords. There have been signs in the Court of Appeal recently of a dissatisfaction with this apparently absolute rejection of a duty to negotiate in good faith, at least in cases where the parties have expressly agreed to negotiate.[51] However, even if the courts were to relax the strictness of the decision in *Walford v. Miles* and allow the parties to agree expressly to negotiate in good faith (which would, of course, mean an acceptance that such a duty could be defined in such a way as to enable the courts to police it and to impose remedies for breach) it seems hardly conceivable that they would take

contract to negotiate. The reason is because it is too uncertain to have any binding force. No court could estimate the damages because no one can tell whether the negotiations would be successful or would fall through: or if successful, what the result would be. It seems to me that a contract to negotiate, like a contract to enter into a contract, is not a contract known to the law.'

50 The 'apogee of good faith scepticism in English law', according to the Scots reporters: see the Scots report on case 6.

51 *Petromec Inc v. Petroleo Brasilieiro SA* [2006] 1 Lloyd's Rep 121 at [121]. For further discussion see Cartwright, 'Negotiation and Renegotiation: an English Perspective', above n. 34.

the further step and say that the entering into negotiations carries an *implied* duty to negotiate in good faith. Finding a way round the problem of definition of the duty – giving it content – is one thing. But accepting a general normative obligation between negotiating parties would involve a reversal of a well-established view of the proper risk allocation during the negotiations. As long as the defendant has not made (and broken) a binding contractual promise; has not committed an established tort (such as by intentionally or negligently making a false statement); has not received a benefit from the other in circumstances in which the established principles of the law of unjust enrichment would require him to disgorge it if the contract is not concluded; and perhaps (if English law were to be developed along the lines which American and Australian law have already developed) as long as the defendant has not encouraged the claimant to believe that the contract would be concluded and thereby to act in reliance within the doctrine of promissory estoppel; then the defendant should be free to withdraw from the negotiations, without giving any reason, and even at a late stage. The claimant incurs precontractual expenditure at his own risk.

Dutch law: the most expansive?

By contrast, Dutch law is not only open to the general notion of a duty to negotiate in good faith, but takes the view that the very nature of the negotiations creates a relationship which the law should protect; and sees that relationship as one which develops during the course of the negotiations and in its final stages almost merges into the contract itself. According to the *Plas/Valburg* case[52] the 'third stage' of negotiations[53] is one in which the parties are no longer free to break off, in the sense that if one party does break off he may be required not only to compensate the claimant's out-of-pocket losses but even to compensate the expectation which he had from the contract; or even that the court will require the defendant not to break off at all, but to conclude the contract – specific enforcement. In this, Dutch law goes even further than most of the other civil law systems in our study, which will impose liability for breaking off negotiations (for example, at a late stage and without justification) but will normally limit the damages to wasted

[52] HR 18 June 1982 (*Plas/Valburg*), NJ 1983, 723, note Brunner; AA 32 (1983) 758, note Van Schilfgaarde.

[53] For a general discussion of the three 'stages' of negotiations in Dutch law, see the Dutch report on case 1.

expenditure: the reliance interest.[54] The reasoning behind limiting the remedy to the reliance interest is that there is still a fundamental line between the negotiations and the contract. Until the contract has been formed, the contractual expectation has not yet been created, and the court cannot impose a remedy for breach of the negotiations which indirectly protects the future contract. This is put, for example, by the German reporters:[55]

> A party liable on the ground of *culpa in contrahendo* has to make up for the aggrieved party's reliance interest (*Vertrauensschaden*). The scope of liability mirrors its rationale which is not to be found in a party's refraining from a bargain but in his creation of legitimate expectations within the other party that a contract would be brought about. The aggrieved party has to be put into the position he would have been in if he had known the other party's unwillingness to make a commitment. This means there must be compensation for the necessary expenses incurred by the party legitimately expecting the conclusion of a contract.

In Dutch law, however, the reasoning begins from a similar position but ends rather differently. The 'third stage' of negotiations starts when the claimant could reasonably expect that the contract would be concluded. Having created that expectation, the defendant has limited his own right to withdraw. The wrong is therefore the breaking-off of the negotiations, and so the loss caused is the loss of the contract, because if the defendant had not committed the wrong, he would have concluded the contract and thereby fulfilled, rather than disappointed, the claimant's expectations:

> It is not impossible that negotiations concerning a contract may reach such an advanced stage that the act of breaking them off must in itself be regarded, in the prevailing circumstances, as a breach of good faith, on the basis that the parties may be assumed mutually to have relied on the expectation that some sort of contract would in any event result from the negotiations. In such a situation, it may also be legitimate to find that an obligation exists to pay compensation for lost profits.[56]

It must be added that, although English law and Dutch law might appear to be at opposite extremes of the approaches to the liabilities

[54] There are exceptions, where the reporters for other jurisdictions indicate that there are some minority academic views in favour of expectation damages for breach at a late stage of the duty to negotiate in good faith: see the Greek and Portuguese reports on case 1.

[55] German report on case 1.

[56] *Plas/Valburg*, above n. 52, 3.4.

arising from the breaking-off of contractual negotiations, they may in fact end up rather closer than one might expect. If English law were to take the step of accepting a development of the doctrine of promissory estoppel to cover contractual negotiations generally, rather than being limited (within the doctrine of proprietary estoppel) to promises relating to interests in land, both the rationale and the result of the liabilities might resemble the Dutch position. A party who has created in the other the expectation that he would receive the benefits of a contract, where the latter has acted in reliance on the belief that the contract would be concluded, might be estopped from denying that he is bound to complete the contract. That is, it would be open to the courts, in developing the doctrine of promissory estoppel, to allow the remedy to be based not simply on the value of the claimant's reliance on his belief that the contract would be formed, but on his *expectation* from the contract. The claimant's reliance is the trigger for the estoppel, but need not be the measure of his remedy under it.[57]

Moreover, a word of caution (and an element of legal realism) might be in place here as well. Today, *Plas/Valburg* is still the leading case on the subject. However, in the more than 25 years that have passed since the Hoge Raad took its bold decision in 1982, hardly ever have expectation damages been awarded by a court in the Netherlands; the remedy is available in theory but is very difficult to obtain in practice. Moreover, the *Plas/Valburg* doctrine is also under increasing pressure from legal scholars who have criticised it. In more recent cases, the Hoge Raad has limited the scope of the *Plas/Valburg* rule. Some observers have taken this as an indication of the Hoge Raad's own increasing dissatisfaction with its revolutionary decision of 1982.[58]

[57] In American law, the measure of the remedy awarded for promissory estoppel is more commonly the reliance interest, but may be the expectation: Farnsworth, *Contracts*, para. 2.19. In the Australian case which introduced a broader general principle of promissory estoppel, *Waltons Stores (Interstate) Ltd v. Maher* (1988) 164 CLR 387, the High Court of Australia awarded damages in place of specific enforcement of the contract. In the context of proprietary estoppel, the English courts will award the remedy which is the minimum necessary to satisfy the 'equity' which arises from the claimant's reliance on the belief or expectation created by the defendant that he had, or was to have, an interest in the defendant's land; but in recent years the courts have tended to award a remedy which protects the claimant's expectation, unless to do so would be disproportionate to the reliance which he has incurred, or the expectation is not clearly identifiable or quantifiable: *Jennings v. Rice* [2003] 1 P & CR 8. However, for uncertainty as to whether estoppel will be expanded beyond its existing limits, see *Cobbe v. Yeoman's Row Management Ltd* [2008] 1 WLR 1752, above n. 42a.

[58] See the Dutch report on case 1 and the references cited there.

The range of solutions: similarity and difference in particular cases

We saw above the detailed answers given by each jurisdiction to the 13 cases of our study, and the comparative conclusions which can be drawn for each of those cases separately. And in the earlier sections of this Part we have reflected on some of the problems of the precontractual phase which give rise to differences of approach in the different jurisdictions. We should now draw the study together with a general overview of the cases, to see where there are similarities and differences amongst the different jurisdictions' answers, and approaches, to the cases, with a view to considering in the final section of these Conclusions some wider lessons which can be learnt from this study.

Similarities of result?

In around half of the cases there is, at first sight, at least, unanimity or near-unanimity in outcome for each of the jurisdictions. This is so for case 1 (negotiations for premises for a bookshop: all jurisdictions would award damages based on the 'reliance' interest); case 2 (negotiations for renewal of a lease: with one possible exception, all award a remedy, mostly damages, but sometimes special forms of remedial protection for tenants); case 6 (the 'lock-out', although there is far from unanimity about the variant case, the 'lock-in'); case 9 (breakdown of negotiations to build a house for a friend: all hold that A might be liable to B for the half-built house which he now has on his land); case 10 (public bidding: almost all give a remedy where the bid was the lowest, and all refuse a remedy where the bid was not the lowest); case 12 (confidential design information: almost all would give B a remedy for A's misuse of the information) and case 13 (misrepresentation or silence about a harvester's capacity: all jurisdictions agree on a remedy for misrepresentation, and all but one give a remedy for silence on these facts).

These similarities are, however, often superficial. The reasoning employed by different jurisdictions can be very different, even if they appear to result in a similar remedy. And even where the remedy appears to be essentially the same, it may in fact have significant differences.

For example, in case 9 there is a consensus that A is liable to B, but some jurisdictions rest their analysis on the general principles of precontractual liability, whereas others apply their rules of unjust enrichment or the law of contract, or even (in the case of Austria and Switzerland) special legislative provisions which cover the case of building on another's land. These two jurisdictions have therefore identified this sort of situation as deserving of special treatment, whereas other systems respond within their regular legal principles. But the response depends on, and can be limited by, the tools available within each legal system. In the case A has a (half-built) house on his land; and B has incurred the costs of building. Some systems have both gain-based and loss-based remedies at their disposal, and so can consider both the possibility of a claim for the disgorgement of A's benefit (a restitutionary claim for unjust enrichment) and a claim to allow B to be compensated for the (reliance) losses he has incurred (generally a claim either in tort or for autonomous *culpa in contrahendo*). Some systems, however, have not developed restitutionary remedies significantly, and so are limited to claims in contract or for precontractual liability. The restricted development of the law of restitution is noted by the Norwegian and Swedish reporters. And France recognises a claim for unjust enrichment but it is a subsidiary claim, being available only if all other legal grounds are excluded; and even when it is available it does not allow A's enrichment to be claimed if it would exceed B's loss, a restriction which is not present in other jurisdictions, which therefore generally allow a greater freedom of choice to the claimant by way of remedies.

Even where the remedy appears to be the same, the reason for the remedy being invoked often differs amongst the jurisdictions; and the detail of the remedy (typically, the quantification of the recoverable loss) also varies. Case 1 is a good illustration of this. All jurisdictions award 'reliance' damages. But the reason for this award, in terms both of the category of law which applies (the cause of action), and the reason on the facts for their being an award of damages (the factual 'trigger' for liability), varies significantly. And there are significant differences in the quantification of the damages.

The cause of action differs in case 1 in a way which is typical of the different approaches of the systems to a range of cases of precontractual liability in this study. England, Ireland and Scotland stand apart as not recognising a general principle of precontactual responsibility: no general duty between parties negotiating a contract, so no general liability during the precontractual phase. They therefore have to look for a specific tort, breach of contract or ground of liability for unjust enrichment; and in case 1 they find it in A's fraudulent misrepresentation (the tort of deceit in England and Ireland; the delict of fraudulent misrepresentation in Scotland). All other systems within the study have recognised that there is a place for a generalised duty between negotiating parties, sometimes (for reasons related to the structure of obligations within the legal system) identified as a particular illustration of a broader liability in the law of tort (such as France and Spain); sometimes developed by the courts as an independent source of obligation, often in response to the defects of the existing categories of contract, tort and unjust enrichment (such as Germany's original development of *culpa in contrahendo*, as well as Austria and Switzerland); sometimes a hybrid (such as Finland, drawing on the Germanic *culpa in contrahendo* but placing it with the general law of tort); sometimes a specific statutory rule (such as Greece, Italy and Portugal, and, since the 2001 reforms of the Civil Code, Germany). Although there are some superficial similarities between the approaches of England, Ireland and Scotland, on the one hand, and some of the other jurisdictions on the other hand, in that liability in case 1 is based on tort, there is a fundamental difference. The language of 'precontractual liability', or 'duty to negotiate [in good faith]' is not used in the three former jurisdictions. It happens that, in case 1, A commits a recognised tort by making a fraudulent misrepresentation. In England, Ireland and Scotland, the law of tort has not been developed generally to protect the parties as against each other during precontractual negotiations, and tort will be the source of liability between negotiating parties only in cases where there is a false statement (misrepresentation), made either fraudulently (as here) or, if there was a duty to take care, negligently. This contrasts with jurisdictions such as France and Spain, where precontractual fault is recognised as a much broader concept within the law of tort allowing for the development of a generalised principle of precontractual liability. It even contrasts with jurisdictions such as Austria, Germany and Switzerland which have developed *culpa in contrahendo* because their law of tort cannot embrace a general principle of precontractual fault, but which do at least have a scope of recovery in tort which allows economic loss to be recovered if it is caused wilfully and *contra bonos mores*, which is still a more generalised principle of tortious liability for intentional harm than is accepted in England, Ireland and Scotland.

The factual 'trigger' for liability in case 1 also differs amongst the jurisdictions, which is more telling for our study than the different legal categorisation of causes of action. The Common Core method seeks to identify common (or different) solutions to legal problems grounded in particular facts. Here, the solution (reliance damages) appears to be a common solution. But the *factual* reason which is identified by the separate legal systems for this solution varies. We have already seen that England, Ireland and Scotland find A liable only because of his fraudulent misrepresentation. Other systems, however, have a different focus. Some use the fact that A intended to cause harm as justifying a cause of action in tort (Austria, Germany) or as demonstrating the breach of the duty to negotiate in good faith (Greece). This correlates with the *fraud* which is seen as significant by England, Ireland and Scotland, although as mentioned above the approach taken in these jurisdictions is narrower; it is not the fraud, but the fraudulent *misrepresentation* which constitutes the essential trigger. However, most jurisdictions in their analysis of the case saw A's breach of duty arising at the very beginning, in *opening* negotiations in bad faith. Other reporters focused (alternatively, or cumulatively in their reasoning, to demonstrate A's breach of duty to negotiate in good faith) on his bad faith *conduct* of the negotiations; or on his bad faith *breaking-off*. As we have noted on occasion in the conclusion to particular cases in the study, it can sometimes be difficult to see whether there are substantive differences between jurisdictions. Some reporters (as the courts in their countries might do) take a more global approach to the question of whether A was in breach of his duty to negotiate in good faith; others focus very precisely on whether the wrongdoing was comprised in A's acts (or omissions) at the beginning of the negotiations, at particular points during the negotiations, or at the point when he broke them off. But there are certainly significant differences between jurisdictions in this respect in analysing some of the cases.

We can also see from the various reports on case 1 that the approach of the systems to apparently similar concepts and legal tests (at least, concepts and legal tests which are articulated in similar language) can be very different. A number of jurisdictions apply a test of whether the defendant's conduct (whether in beginning, continuing or breaking off the negotiations) was contrary to *good faith*. But the application of this can then vary significantly. The content of the duty is apparently quite fluid in the view of some reporters,[59] whereas others are very precise about the particular duties which are encompassed by the generalised duty to negotiate in good faith.[60] There is not a unanimous view about whether the criteria for the assessment of good faith are objective or

[59] E.g. Austrian law (the 'still-expanding judge-made doctrine of *culpa in contrahendo*' makes an answer uncertain). See also the Austrian report on case 4 (difficult to confirm or deny whether a duty to inform has been violated).

[60] E.g. Greece; for further details, cf. the Greek report on case 3: including duties to conduct negotiations in earnest, to protect the interests of the other party, and to provide information.

subjective.[61] And, as we see in discussion of other cases, jurisdictions differ on such fundamental matters as the burden of proof of good faith.[62]

And when we look not just at the cause of action, or the factual trigger for the liability to pay damages in case 1, we see that the quantification of the damages can also differ significantly between the jurisdictions. This means that the actual result - the remedy - which would be obtained by B differs. Some jurisdictions are more scientific and rule-based than others in the quantification of loss; a reflection of the general approach to quantification of damages by the courts, rather than a specific response to the precontractual phase. Some reporters[63] emphasise the discretion which their courts have in the calculation of damages, which therefore inevitably leads them to be rather uncertain about the actual likely award on the facts of this case. French law allows damages to cover intangible losses;[64] others are reluctant to do so.[65] Some focus on whether B has proved his loss in absolute terms, others allow him to recover on the basis of a proof of his lost *chance*.[66] Some take a more rigid approach than others to proof of the causal link between A's breach of duty and B's recoverable loss.[67] There is even a

[61] Cf. Greece (objective: 'the expected sincerity . . . of a reasonable man; . . . fair and usual conduct of the relevant business'); Italy (academic views differ, but Supreme Court consistently applies objective test based on 'fair play, reliability and co-operation between the parties'); Germany: a 'party breaches his duty to bargain in good faith by the mere fact of entering into contractual negotiations if he starts negotiations without any reasonable chance for the opposite party to make a bargain (objective test) or without any intention at all to contract with the other party (subjective test)'.

[62] Cf. the Italian report on case 2 (different opinions within the Italian Supreme Court) and the Spanish report on case 2 (good faith is presumed).

[63] Denmark, France, Italy. Cf. also the French report on case 3 (assessment of damages is global), and the Danish report on case 9 (Danish court might award what A can afford, acting as an *amiable compositeur*).

[64] *Préjudice morale*; cf. also the French report on case 11 (noting that damages to compensate *préjudice morale* are awarded, but their valuation is never outwardly discussed by the courts; and speculating that *préjudice morale* suffered as a consequence of an aborted contract may be indistinguishable from damages for the loss of chance to conclude the contract).

[65] Cf. the Greek report on case 4 (non-material damage can only be compensated in delict).

[66] E.g. French law (damages for the lost opportunity; but see also the possible link to *préjudice morale* on the facts of case 1: above n. 64). The Scots reporters also contemplate an award of damages for loss of chance in case 1.

[67] The Danish reporter notes in case 10 that Danish law will not generally award damages for the loss of a chance The strict causal link is emphasised by, e.g., the German reporters in their report on case 1. For more flexible approaches, see the Norwegian report on case 6 ('the Norwegian courts might be willing to reduce to some

different approach to whether the appropriate measure of recovery for precontractual liability is 'reliance' damages or 'expectation' damages. Although most reporters are clear that the cause of action for expectation damages can only be a claim in contract, some note that there are arguments in favour of expectation damages as the remedy for precontractual liability (the clearest such case being the Netherlands,[68] although this is not the likely solution in Dutch law on the facts of case 1). It should be noted that in many civil law systems[69] the quantification of damages is a matter of fact for the trial judge, which affects the extent to which reporters can predict the outcome of cases with certainty.

Differences of result

By contrast with the group of cases mentioned in the last section, there are significant differences of result in the other half of the cases in our study. This is so for case 3 (mistake about ownership of land to be sold: a minority give no remedy, and amongst those which do the remedy is sometimes contractual, sometimes based on precontractual liability); case 4 (an architect's preparatory work: although there is agreement that parallel negotiations do not as such give rise to precontractual liability, there is a difference as to whether A's knowledge of B's policy on tendering would give rise to a remedy at all); case 5 (a broken engagement: a range of different answers to whether and what remedies are available); case 6 (on the question about whether breach of a 'lock-in' undertaking should give rise to a remedy); case 7 (the breakdown of merger negotiations: a range of different answers to each of the variants in the case); case 8 (a shopping centre without a tenant: a majority of jurisdictions give a remedy in damages, but a significant minority do not); case 11 (a contract for the sale of a house which fails for lack of formality: a mixture of answers as to whether B has any, and if so what, remedy).

The lessons to be drawn from these cases where the results show greater differences between the jurisdictions are partly the same as

extent the requirement of cause and effect in these cases') and the Dutch report on case 3 ('Dutch law contains a very open and normative causation test').

68 The Greek and Portuguese reporters in case 1 note that academic writers have argued for an award of damages on the expectation interest for precontractual liability, but that these arguments have not been followed by their courts. In the Netherlands, however, the Hoge Raad has itself contemplated expectation damages as a remedy, although this has also been criticised: see above p. 470.

69 Perhaps the clearest example is France: see the French report on case 1. The same point is, however, made also by the Italian reporter in the same case.

those which were noted in relation to the cases of similar result. There, the differences were hidden behind the apparent similarity of result; here they become more overt. In addition, these cases illustrate some particular reasons for the differences between jurisdictions, often based on different approaches to particular factual situations for reasons of legal or social policy.

A case which illustrates very well the different approaches to the precontractual phase is case 7, which was drafted with a range of variations for this very purpose, to ensure that the reporters focused particularly on whether the existence or scope of A's liability for breaking off negotiations hinged on the length of negotiations, the advanced stage of the negotiations or A's statements of its conviction that the contract will be concluded, as well as its reasons for breaking them off or the fact that it delayed for a lengthy period after knowing that the negotiations would not be successful. These facts teased out some significant differences between the jurisdictions, both in the result and in their explanation of the reasons. They confirmed the relative isolation of England, Ireland and Scotland, which find no tort committed: there is no misrepresentation to give rise to liability in the torts of deceit or negligence; and no action in contract; and so there can be no liability. There are some signs of a softer approach by Scotland to the facts here, but not enough to move from the 'common law' camp to the 'civil law' camp. Although a mixed jurisdiction, and although the historical bases of the Scots law of contract are different, and more rooted in the civilian tradition,[70] Scotland in almost all cases aligns with the restrictive English and Irish approaches to precontractual liability.[71]

The other jurisdictions all (as usual) start from the point that there is a generalised duty between negotiating parties, but disagree on the significance of the factors triggering the liability. For example, most do not think that the length of negotiations itself imposes any duty, but some say that this might give rise to a duty to justify the breaking-off of negotiations; that is, whilst (as all jurisdictions agree) in principle the starting-point is that both parties are free to withdraw from negotiations without giving any reason, in the view of some the length of

[70] R. Zimmermann, 'Double Cross: Comparing Scots and South African Law' in Zimmermann, Visser and Reid, *Mixed Legal Systems in Comparative Perspective*, pp. 8–12.

[71] The notable exception is where there is a promise which can be given contractual force in Scotland but where there might be no consideration to make it binding in England; e.g., Scotland finds it easier to classify the lock-out agreement as contractual (case 6).

negotiations can change this. This may link to the variant in the case under which A has made statements about its conviction that the contract will be concluded. Many jurisdictions hold that a key feature of the imposition of precontractual liability is that the claimant was reasonably entitled to believe that the contract would be concluded (or, at least, that there was no obstacle to this). The length of the negotiations, as well as A's statements, can foster such a belief. However, even here we see that there is a significant variation between the jurisdictions as to whether the particular statements by A should be sufficient to *entitle* B to believe that the contract will be concluded. The most restrictive in this case are Austria and Germany, and this links to other approaches within those legal systems, since the significance of the offer as the moment at which one party enters into a potential commitment means that the other party is not so easily held to be entitled to rely on the (future) contract before an offer has been made, or the parties have come to an agreement on all the essential elements.[72]

Similarly, there is a variation in the approach of the various jurisdictions to the situation where the parties have already reached agreement on major points, but not quite yet on outstanding minor points. England, Scotland and Ireland are again restrictive here: a contract requires agreement on all points, and if there is not yet agreement there is no contract. The court has no general power to complete the contract for the parties. But the fact that the contract is almost complete is sufficient for many jurisdictions to hold that it becomes wrongful to break off without good reason. Some jurisdictions would even allow their courts to complete the contract. No doubt this reflects a more generally applicable view of the role of the courts in relation to the contract which is different from that in other legal systems.

Some jurisdictions modify their approach to precontractual liability in relation to negotiations for particular types of contract, revealing differences of legal and social policy in relation to those types of contract. The two cases which illustrate this most clearly are cases 3 and 5.

Case 3 involves negotiations for the sale of land.[73] For some jurisdictions this is almost irrelevant: the normal rules of precontractual

[72] See the German report on case 1. Cf. also the Austrian report on case 6: reliance is reasonable only if the *essentialia negotii* are already agreed, and the reliance is foreseeable by the other party. However, for the Dutch reporter (report on case 2) it is not easy to predict whether the claimant's reliance was justified, because it is a question of fact for the lower courts to decide.

[73] For the detail, see the Editors' comparative conclusions on case 3.

liability apply, without any particular concession being made to the subject matter of the transaction. But for others, the context is crucial, not simply because there are statutory provisions directed specifically at land contracts, but because for some jurisdictions the policy which lies behind those statutory provisions displaces or at least colours the application of the normal rules of precontractual liability. The question of whether the legislative policy relating to land transactions would be undermined by allowing a remedy under the general rules of precontractual liability provokes a discussion in a number of reports, with different results.

Case 5 is the case in which one might perhaps most expect a difference to be based on differing social views of the nature of the transaction: the broken engagement. The difference of view extends to whether the engagement is to be seen as contractual; whether marriage is itself a contract (and therefore whether the engagement is a case of precontractual liability); the extent to which the particular, personal relationship involved in an engagement should be treated differently from other cases of precontractual liability (for example, the relevance of the parties' fault in triggering liabilities); and whether there should be special rules for standard questions which will inevitably arise on the breaking-off of an engagement (such as the ownership of the engagement ring, and the liability for expenses incurred in anticipation of the marriage). The particular social context is emphasised by those jurisdictions which have made provision for remedies not only for the disappointed fiancé(e), but also for his or her relatives who have in fact incurred costs associated with the planned marriage. There is also a historical context: the changing view of marriage has in some jurisdictions resulted in changes to the particular rules in this area to reflect changes in social reality. There is a limit to the general conclusions that can be drawn for a study on precontractual liability from such differences.

Drawing together the threads

A number of lessons can be learnt from this study; of course, they are all related to the particular context of the study, precontractual liability, but they can also illustrate or inform broader issues of comparative law, particularly when the basis of comparison is the fact-based study of cases, as in the Common Core methodology. Here, we draw together quite briefly the threads of the more detailed discussion in the earlier sections of this study.

Different techniques in dealing with the precontractual phase

We have seen that the European legal systems have developed different general techniques of dealing with the problems arising in the precontractual phase.

Most of our jurisdictions have recognised some generalised form of precontractual liability, although the techniques vary. Some have developed the law of tort to cover the situation; others have created a separate doctrine of precontractual liability for fault (*culpa in contrahendo*): some have done so judicially, whereas in others there has been a specific legislative enactment of a general duty. But all these jurisdictions would say that the relationship between the parties during precontractual negotiations is a relationship, regulated and protected by the law.

England, Ireland and Scotland, on the other hand, have not developed a general doctrine of precontractual liability, and do not even see the precontractual phase as having legal relational significance in the same way as all the other jurisdictions within our study have done. Their approach is therefore to deal with precontractual issues within the discrete sources of obligation within private law - tort, contract, unjust enrichment[74] - and to be more restrictive as to when there will be precontractual liability at all. It is not simply a different technique, a patchwork of duties rather than a single generalised duty, but a fundamentally different starting-point which does not see negotiations as a collaborative relationship. In consequence, it is these jurisdictions which more commonly stand out not only as reasoning differently, but also in finding no liability in the cases in our study. But, as we have seen, there are many cases where this fundamentally different theoretical view of precontractual negotiations does not in fact result in a different outcome, because many of the typical situations which occur during negotiations and give rise to liability under a generalised doctrine of precontractual liability happen in English, Irish or Scots law to involve the commission of a tort (if there is an express or implied misrepresentation),[75] or a breach of a contractually

[74] The use of estoppel in this context is limited in English law: see the English report on cases 2, 8 and 11, and the discussion above pp. 463–4. For the doctrine of personal bar in Scottish law, see the Scots report on case 3. In case 12, English and Irish law rest the liability on the *sui generis* obligation to respect confidence in relation to information, although this falls within delict in Scots law.

[75] Especially cases 1, 2 (but perhaps no remedy in Irish law), 3 (but no claim in Irish law), 7, 8 and 11.

binding undertaking,[76] or a breach of a duty of confidence,[77] or give rise to a claim in unjust enrichment for a benefit conferred during the negotiations.[78] Indeed, in almost no case do England, Ireland and Scotland stand completely alone in the result. This is discussed further below in relation to so-called legal 'families'.[79]

Influence of other legal practices and policies

We have also seen that, although legal systems use apparently similar language and concepts to describe and implement their doctrines of precontractual liability, there can be some differences which flow from the operation of other practices or policies within their system.

We have noted that different systems can view the type of contract differently, such as the policies relating to land contracts, or an engagement to be married. The difference in other general approaches to private law, and the role of the courts in dispute resolution, can also impact on the outcome of cases in the context of a breakdown of precontractual negotiations. Some legal systems have particular views about the scope of damages which can be awarded - how they should be calculated, and the interests that they can protect - which then operate as a limiting factor in a claim for precontractual liability. And the different views of the role of the courts in relation to the contract (such as whether it is thought appropriate for the courts to intervene and complete a nearly-complete contract for the parties) and in relation to which issues are treated as questions of fact and which as questions of law (issues of fact being often subject to a wider discretionary judicial power in the view of several reporters) can make the outcome of a similar case in different jurisdictions quite different.

Commercial context and risk allocation

It would not be surprising, perhaps, to find that a commercial (or in other respects 'stronger') party negotiating with a consumer (or 'weaker' party) might have more extensive duties during the negotiations. But we have not focused on cases of inequality but on cases where the parties are, broadly speaking, more equal, whether both acting socially (the engagement) or as friends (the builder who loses the contract to build for his friend) or at arm's length, on purely commercial terms. What we have discovered in this study is that even in such cases of

[76] Cases 6 and 10. [77] Case 12 (England and Ireland).
[78] Case 9. [79] Below pp. 485–8.

apparent equality most jurisdictions contemplate mutual duties between the parties during the negotiations. Precontractual duties of good faith are not designed simply to protect inherently weaker parties. On the other hand, the starting-point of English law is to see the very nature of negotiations as at arm's length, negativing duties of good faith, apparently without considering that a stronger party should have a positive altruistic duty, or that a party with special and relevant information might have to disclose it. We have seen, of course, that the cases are not quite as polarised as this when one considers particular facts, not only because there can sometimes (or, even, often) be a form of precontractual liability in English law based on tort, contract, unjust enrichment or breach of confidence, but also because some of the systems which accept a general duty of good faith during negotiations can also be cautious in its operation. For example, in case 4 both the German and Greek reporters emphasise that the operation of the doctrine of precontractual liability (*culpa in contrahendo*) must not be allowed to undermine the freedom of contract; the proper economics of the negotiating process should be preserved. The argument is not that there is no duty of good faith in the negotiations, but that the *operation* of the doctrine of good faith does not require of one party action which contravenes the proper functioning of the market. That said, however, there is no single view amongst the jurisdictions as to how restrictive and cautious they should be in this respect in the operation of the general doctrine of precontractual liability. Here, as elsewhere, we see differences in the operation of what might at first sight seem to be a similar general test.

Superficiality of similarity and difference in results

We have seen throughout the study that there are apparent similarities and differences of reasoning and result. Cases which appear to involve applications of a similar test, or to have similar results amongst a wide range of jurisdictions, turn out to differ in such things as the operation of the essential test for liability (whether there is a breach of the duty of good faith on the facts; whether the claimant was justified in anticipating the contract; or whether the burden of proof lies on one party or the other), or the applicable rules for the remedy (such as different approaches to causation or to the rules for calculation of damages). Whilst we have often emphasised the (hidden or overt) differences of reasoning and result amongst the different jurisdictions, it should also be noted that sometimes the appearance of differences is also misleading because there can be an underlying (hidden) similarity between the approach taken by jurisdictions. At the source of the duty of good faith during the negotiations lies (according to many of our reporters) a general test of whether the claimant was reasonably entitled to rely on the contract going to be formed. And although at first sight English law does not appear to recognise either such a general principle, or a particular test which would give effect to it, it is not far from the general approach taken in property cases under the doctrine of proprietary estoppel, and which could perhaps be extended into the general context of precontactual negotiations under the doctrine of promissory estoppel, as has already been done in other common law jurisdictions.[80]

A common core?

In the previous subsections we pointed out some more general tendencies that we found in the responses by our national reporters concerning the different cases. The obvious final question, which must be addressed now, is whether there is a common core of precontractual liability in Europe. This question is especially interesting from a policy perspective. Those involved in the political and academic debates concerning the desirability of (further) harmonising the law of contract in Europe will be keen to know whether a common core actually exists today and how difficult it would be in the future to reach further or even total unity, for example, in the shape of a European Civil Code.

Interesting as this general question may seem, in spite of the title of the project which suggests otherwise, we do not think that the method adopted in the Common Core Project can lead to any such broad general conclusion, at least not with regard to the present subject. The Common Core method is first and foremost a case-based method. It consists of the comparative analysis of specific cases. Of course, these cases are selected by the general reporters because they are expected to raise issues concerning a common subject, in the present case precontractual liability. However, it seems far-fetched, on the basis of the comparison of national reports concerning these cases, to reach a general overall conclusion with regard to the state of precontractual liability in Europe. The detailed case comparison that is possible as a result of the case method, and the impossibility of drawing very general conclusions, are two sides of the same coin.

[80] Above text to n. 57.

In another research project (with some personal links to the present one)[81] researchers recently formulated, not a 'common core', but a first academic 'Draft Common Frame of Reference' (DCFR).[82] Concerning precontractual liability, the DCFR contains the following provision:

II.–3:301: Negotiations contrary to good faith and fair dealing

(1) A person is free to negotiate and is not liable for failure to reach an agreement.
(2) A person who is engaged in negotiations has a duty to negotiate in accordance with good faith and fair dealing. This duty may not be excluded or limited by contract.
(3) A person who has negotiated or broken off negotiations contrary to good faith and fair dealing is liable for any loss caused to the other party to the negotiations.
(4) It is contrary to good faith and fair dealing, in particular, for a person to enter into or continue negotiations with no real intention of reaching an agreement with the other party.

How does this draft Article fit the cases which we have analysed in our project? First, the Article, which is very broadly formulated, would certainly apply to, and therefore provide a result for, most of the cases analysed in this project.[83] Moreover, the language of the Article is of a similar level of generality to that which was stated by many of the national reporters as their general rule of precontractual liability and which (when applied as interpreted by the case law in each jurisdiction) was able to resolve particular cases with a sufficient degree of certainty; and so the outcome following from the Article, especially when read in connection with the official commentary and the illustrations which will accompany it, would probably not be much less certain than the results found by most of our national reporters for most of our cases. Would *the result* also be similar to the majority position for most of the

[81] Ole Lando, Johnny Herre, Christina Ramberg, Hector MacQueen, Martijn Hesselink and George Arnokouros were involved in the Study Group on a European Civil Code which produced the academic Draft Common Frame of Reference. Ole Lando chaired the original Commission on European Contract Law (which produced the Principles of European Contract Law) and Hector MacQueen and Willibald Posch were members of the Commission.

[82] von Bar, Clive, Schulte-Nölke *et al.*, *Principles, Definitions and Model Rules of European Private Law: Draft Common Frame of Reference.*

[83] The DCFR contains another, more specific provision (II.–3:302: Breach of confidentiality) which would be directly relevant to our case 12.

cases? In broad terms, it probably would.[84] Under the DCFR the answer to most of the questions would be determined by a general duty of precontractual good faith, in the same way as in most of the systems which were under consideration here. Moreover, liability, if any, would be limited to the reliance interest, as in the vast majority of the systems. However, again it would be a step too far, we think, to conclude that the Draft Common Frame of Reference represents the common core of precontractual liability in Europe. There are many more possible cases than the 13 which we analysed in this project; there are many more European legal systems than the 16 we discussed;[85] and, in particular, as we have seen, on a lower level of generality than that on which the DCFR operates there are many important differences concerning the remedies and the facts which trigger them. The fact that a project such as ours and national legislation (together with statements of principles like the DCFR) operate on very different levels of generality is both a strength and a weakness of the Common Core methodology. Having said this, it is only fair to add that both in terms of underlying ideology, legal technique and outcome, Article II.–3:301 of the DCFR seems to represent the common core of the European *civil law* tradition, although not a broader European common core.

This brings us to another very general issue: the so-called common law/civil law divide. Does our project suggest anything with regard to the (continued) existence of such a major divide in Europe? Some other projects within the general Common Core Project have reached general conclusions in this respect, in particular three projects which are in some sense related to our own project: those on good faith,[86] on the enforceability of promises,[87] and on mistake, fraud and duties to inform,[88] which all cover aspects of the formation of the contact. It is

[84] These provisions of the DCFR are developed from the original text of the PECL: see Lando and Beale, *Principles of European Contract Law, Parts I and II*, arts. 2:301 and 2:302. Our Danish reporter, Ole Lando, in his original report for our project was able to draw similarities in the result of many of the cases between Danish law and the likely outcome under the PECL.

[85] Our project was constituted before the recent expansions of the European Union. Our reports cover all the then-existing EU jurisdictions except for Belgium and Luxembourg, and also include Norway and Switzerland.

[86] Zimmermann and Whittaker, *Good Faith in European Contract Law*, which includes the issue of *precontractual* good faith, as well as good faith more generally in the performance of the contract.

[87] Gordley, *The Enforceability of Promises in European Contract Law*.

[88] Sefton-Green, *Mistake, Fraud and Duties to Inform in European Contract Law*.

interesting to note that all three found that the differences in answers to their questionnaires did not coincide simply with the classical division - the caricature - between common law and civil law systems. Simon Whittaker and Reinhard Zimmermann, with regard to good faith,[89] and James Gordley, with regard to the enforceability of promises,[90] noted the varied range of doctrines amongst the different jurisdictions, and the equally varied understandings of the jurisdictions as to the application (and, therefore, the specific outcome) of these doctrines in particular cases. But they drew attention to similarities of outcome and even of underlying philosophy which blurred the distinctions, and which certainly did not draw firm lines along the common law/civil law divide. Such findings seem to confirm recent claims by comparative lawyers that the common law and the civil law traditions in Europe are converging or even have never been very far apart.[91] Ruth Sefton-Green's study on mistake, fraud and duties to inform, however, was more nuanced. In her conclusion she found that the frontiers between the jurisdictions in her study in relation to both the outcome and reasoning of her cases did not generally lie in terms of legal traditions or legal families but rather there were different clusters of cases which reflected different considerations.[92] And in discussing a number of particular cases she drew attention to the fact that the result of the study was inconsistent with the normally preconceived dividing line between civil law and common law countries.[93] However, she began her study with a recognition that the common law and civil law systems do divide over the precontractual obligation to provide information.[94]

We should emphasise that any general conclusions concerning 'the' difference between 'the' common law and 'the' civil law cannot be

[89] Above n. 86, pp. 676–8, 698–701.

[90] Above n. 87, pp. 371–8. See esp. p. 378: 'common law courts reach many of the same results as those in civil law systems, in part, because of the exceptions that they have recognized. If one wishes, one can speak of the carving out of these exceptions as "convergence". But, in this area of law, the doctrinal structure has not converged.'

[91] See, e.g., J. Gordley, 'Common Law und Civil Law: eine überholte Unterscheidung' (1993) ZeuP 498; Hesselink, *The New European Legal Culture*, pp. 21–2; Markesinis, *The Gradual Convergence: Foreign Ideas, Foreign Influences, and English Law on the Eve of 21st Century*; E. McKendrick, 'Traditional Concepts and Contemporary Values' (2001) 10 ERPL 95; Mattei, *Comparative Law and Economics*, p. 69ff.; R. Zimmermann, 'Roman Law and European Legal Unity' in Hartkamp *et al.*, *Towards a European Civil Code* (3rd edn), p. 21ff.; S. Vogenauer, 'Eine gemeineuropäische Methodenlehre des Rechts - Plädoyer und Programm' (2005) ZEuP 234.

[92] Above n. 88, pp. 369–71. [93] Ibid. pp. 372, 374, 379. [94] Ibid. p. 24.

based on a limited and specific study like the present one. However, with regard to the cases under consideration in the present project it seems fair to say that we have detected a fundamental difference in approach between the countries which are usually considered to be part of the civil law tradition and those which are said to be part of the common law. Indeed, throughout these Conclusions we have pointed to this difference on several occasions. Unlike English, Irish and Scots[95] law, all the other systems contain some general doctrine of precontractual liability, usually based on good faith. English, Irish and Scots law were the systems that most often offered no remedy and never were they the system that provided the most extensive liability. There was therefore both a doctrinal difference between the 'common law' systems and the 'civil law' systems and a corresponding difference in the outcome of cases. England, Scotland and Ireland not only rejected the general duty between negotiating parties to take each other's interests into account, but even characterised the period of negotiations as being one in which the parties *should* generally have no such duty; and this was then translated into a significantly more limited range of liabilities between negotiating parties where the negotiations failed to result in a concluded contract. However, having said that we also saw, when it comes to the details of the remedies available and the facts which actually trigger the remedies, that both the differences between common law and civil law and the similarities within the civil law turned out to be much less important than they seemed to be at first sight. The common law was able to impose liability in particular situations, because what passed between the parties during the negotiations, which in many of the civil law systems would have constituted a breach of the precontractual duty of 'good faith', or precontractual 'fault' for the purposes of liability in tort, would also happen to fall

[95] For the purposes of our study Scots law, whilst being a mixed system rather than a system of purely common law origin, is generally aligned with English and Irish law: see above text to n. 70. James Gordley's study on the enforceability of promises treated Scotland as a civil law system, although noted that 'its doctrinal structure is much different, one might almost say *sui generis*': above n. 87, p. 374. It is perhaps not surprising that Scotland should be aligned with the civil law jurisdictions for the purpose of that study, since Scots law lacks the key doctrine of the common law in relation to the legal enforceability of promises: the doctrine of consideration. In our study, however, we have found that in other respects Scots law follows the same general approach as English and Irish law to the scope of liabilities to be imposed on parties negotiating a contract.

within a specific tort (delict) in English, Irish or Scots law, or would give rise to another claim such as for unjust enrichment. Nevertheless, it would go too far to conclude, with regard to the subject of precontractual liability, that the factual approach has uncovered underlying pervasive substantive unity (a 'common core') which was disguised by merely conceptual differences.

Bibliography

1. GENERAL BIBLIOGRAPHY, INTRODUCTION AND CONCLUSIONS

C. von Bar, *Principles of European Law: Benevolent Intervention in Another's Affairs* (Bern, Brussels, Munich, Oxford, 2006)

C. von Bar, E. Clive, H. Schulte-Nölke and others, *Principles, Definitions and Model Rules of European Private Law: Draft Common Frame of Reference (DCFR), Interim Outline Edition* (Munich, 2008)

M. Barendrecht, C. Jansen, M. Loos, A. Pinna, R. Cascao and S. van Gulijk, *Principles of European Law: Service Contracts* (Bern, Brussels, Munich, Oxford, 2006)

H. Beale, A. Hartkamp, H. Kötz and D. Tallon (eds.), *Cases, Materials and Text on Contract Law* (Oxford, Portland, 2002)

M. Bussani and U. Mattei (eds.), *Making European Law: Essays on the 'Common Core' Project* (Trento, 2000)

The Common Core of European Private Law (The Hague, London, New York, 2002)

M. Bussani and V.V. Palmer, *Pure Economic Loss in Europe* (Cambridge, 2003)

J. Cartwright, *Contract Law: an Introduction to the English Law of Contract for the Civil Lawyer* (Oxford, 2007)

J. Cartwright, S. Vogenauer and S.J. Whittaker (eds.), *Reforming the French Law of Obligations: Comparative Observations on the Avant-projet de réforme du droit des obligations et de la prescription* (Oxford, 2008)

R. David and C. Jauffret-Spinosi, *Les grands systèmes de droit contemporain* (19th edn, Paris, 1988)

J. Derrida, *L'Université sans condition* (Paris, 2001)

U. Drobnig, *Principles of European Law: Personal Security* (Bern, Brussels, Munich, Oxford, 2007)

A.M. Dugdale (ed.), *Clerk and Lindsell on Torts* (19th edn, London, 2006)

E.A. Farnsworth, *Contracts* (4th edn, New York, 2004)

P. Feyerabend, *Against Method* (3rd edn, London, New York, 1993)

G. Gandolfi (ed.), *Code Européen des contrats: avant-projet* (Milan, 2001)

J. Gordley, *The Enforceability of Promises in European Contract Law* (Cambridge, 2001)

M. Graziadei, U. Mattei and L. Smith, *Commercial Trusts in European Private Law* (Cambridge, 2005)

A. S. Hartkamp, M. W. Hesselink, E. H. Hondius, C. E. du Perron and J.B.M. Vranken (eds.), *Towards a European Civil Code* (1st edn, Dordrecht, Boston, London, 1994)

A. S. Hartkamp, M. W. Hesselink, E. H. Hondius, C. A. Joustra and M. Veldman (eds.), *Towards a European Civil Code* (3rd edn, The Hague, London, New York, 2004)

M. W. Hesselink, *The New European Legal Culture* (Deventer, 2001)

M. W. Hesselink (ed.), *The Politics of a European Civil Code* (The Hague, 2006)

M. W. Hesselink, J. W. Rutgers, O. Bueno Díaz, M. Scotton and M. Veldman, *Principles of European Law: Commercial Agency, Franchise and Distribution Contracts* (Bern, Brussels, Munich, Oxford, 2006).

E. Hondius (ed.), *Precontractual Liability: Reports to the XIIIth Congress, International Academy of Comparative Law* (Deventer, 1991)

D. Kennedy, *A Critique of Adjudication (fin de siècle)* (Cambridge, Mass., London, 1997)

E.-M. Kieninger, *Security Rights in Movable Property in European Private Law* (Cambridge, 2004)

H. Kötz, *European Contract Law*, Part I (Tony Weir (trans.), Oxford, 1997)

O. Lando and H. Beale (eds.), *Principles of European Contract Law, Parts I and II, prepared by the Commission on European Contract Law* (The Hague, 2000)

O. Lando, E. Clive, A. Prüm and R. Zimmerman (eds.), *Principles of European Contract Law, Part III, prepared by the Commission on European Contract Law* (The Hague, 2003)

B. Latour, *Science in Action* (Cambridge, Mass., 1987)

P. Legrand, *Fragments on Law-as-Culture* (Deventer, 1999)

Que sais-je? Le droit comparé (Paris, 1999)

B. Markesinis (ed.), *The Gradual Convergence: Foreign Ideas, Foreign Influences, and English Law on the Eve of 21st Century* (Oxford, 1994)

U. Mattei, *Comparative Law and Economics* (Ann Arbor, 1997)

T.M.J. Möllers and A. Heinemann, *The Enforcement of Competition Law in Europe* (Cambridge, 2007)

B. Pozzo, *Property and Environment: Old and New Remedies to Protect Natural Resources in the European Context* (Bern, 2007)

Research Group on the Existing EC Private Law (Acquis Group), *Principles of the Existing EC Contract Law (Acquis Principles), Contract I (Pre-contractual Obligations, Conclusion of Contract, Unfair Terms)* (Munich, 2007)

R. Rorty, *Philosophy and the Mirror of Nature* (Oxford, 1980)

R. Sacco, *Introduzione al diritto comparato* (5th edn, Torino, 1997)

E. Said, *Orientalism* (London, 1978)

R. B. Schlesinger (ed.), *Formation of Contracts: a Study of the Common Core of Legal Systems* (New York, 1968)

R. Sefton-Green, *Mistake, Fraud and Duties to Inform in European Contract Law* (Cambridge, 2005)

S. Shapin, *The Scientific Revolution* (Chicago, London, 1996)
F. Werro and V. V. Palmer, *The Boundaries of Strict Liability in European Tort Law* (Bruxelles, 2004)
R. Zimmermann, D. Visser and K. Reid (eds.), *Mixed Legal Systems in Comparative Perspective* (Oxford, 2004)
R. Zimmermann and S. Whittaker, *Good Faith in European Contract Law* (Cambridge, 2000)
K. Zweigert and H. Kötz, *Introduction to Comparative Law* (3rd edn, Oxford, 1998)

2. CASE STUDIES: BIBLIOGRAPHY BY COUNTRY

Austria

C. Faistenberger and H. Mayrhofer, *Gedenkschrift Franz Gschnitzer* (Innsbruck, 1969)
H. Koziol, *Österreichisches Haftpflichtrecht* (vol. 1, 3rd edn, vol. II, 2nd edn, Vienna, 1997, 1984)
H. Koziol and R. Welser, *Bürgerliches Recht* (12th edn, Vienna, 2002)
P. Rummel (ed.), *Kommentar zum ABGB* (3rd edn, Vienna, 2000)
M. Schwimann, *Praxiskommentar ABGB* (2nd edn, Vienna, 1997)
R. Welser, *Vertretung ohne Vollmacht – Zugleich ein Beitrag zur Lehre von der culpa in contrahendo* (Vienna, 1970)

Denmark

L. L. Andersen, P. B. Madsen and J. Nørgaard, *Aftaler og Mellemmænd* (4th edn, Copenhagen, 2001)
L. Simonsen, *Prækontraktuelt Ansvar [Precontractual liability]* (Oslo, 1997)

England

E. H. Burn and J. Cartwright, *Cheshire and Burn's Modern Law of Real Property* (17th edn, Oxford, 2006)
A. Burrows, *The Law of Restitution* (2nd edn, London, 2002)
Remedies for Torts and Breach of Contract (3rd edn, Oxford, 2005)
A. Burrows (ed.) *Essays on the Law of Restitution* (Oxford, 1991)
J. Cartwright, *Misrepresentation, Mistake and Non-Disclosure* (2nd edn, London, 2006)
J. Getzler (ed.), *Rationalizing Property, Equity and Trusts* (London, 2003)
Lord Goff of Chieveley and G. Jones, *The Law of Restitution* (7th edn, London, 2006)
Spencer Bower, *Estoppel by Representation* (P. Feltham, D. Hochberg and T. Leech (eds.), 4th edn, London, 2004)

Finland

A. Aarnio, *Laintulkinnan teoria [The Theory of the Interpretation of Statutes]* (Helsinki, 1989)

A. Aarnio and M. Helin, *Avioliittolain muutetut säännökset [The Revised Provisions of the Marriage Act]* (Tampere, 1987)

E. Aurejärvi and M. Hemmo, *Velvoiteoikeuden oppikirja [Law of Obligations]* (2nd edn, Helsinki, 1998)

M. Hemmo, *Vahingonkorvauksen määräytymisestä sopimussuhteissa [On the Determination of Damages in Contract Law]* (Helsinki, 1994)

Sopimusoikeus [Contract Law] (Helsinki, 1997)

Sopimus ja delikti [Contract and Tort] (Helsinki, 1998)

Vahingonkorvausoikeuden oppikirja [A Textbook on Tort Law] (Helsinki, 2002)

H. von Hertzen, *Sopimusneuvottelut [Contract Negotiations]* (Vammala, 1983)

E. Routamo and P. Ståhlberg, *Suomen vahingonkorvausoikeus [Finnish Tort Law]* (Helsinki, 2000)

France

F. Accad, *Les pourparlers* (thesis, Paris, 1996)

A. Bénabent, *Droit de la famille* (11th edn, Paris, 2003)

Contrats spéciaux (6th edn, Paris, 2004)

J.-L. Bergel, M. Bruschi and S. Cimamonti, *Traité de droit civil: Les biens* (Paris, 2000)

R. Chapus, *Droit administratif* (15th edn, Paris, 2001)

A. Cohérier, *Des obligations naissant des pourparlers préalables à la formation des contrats* (thesis, Paris, 1939)

F. Collard-Dutilleul and Ph. Delebecque, *Contrats civils et commerciaux* (6th edn, Paris, 2002)

J. Duclos, *L'opposabilité, essai d'une théorie générale* (thesis, Paris, 1984)

M. Fabre-Magnan, *De l'obligation d'information dans les contrats: essai d'une théorie* (thesis, Paris, 1992)

B. Fages *et al.* (eds.), *Lamy droit du contrat* (Paris, 1999)

J. Flour and J.-L. Aubert, *Les obligations* (vol. 1, *L'acte juridique* (Paris, 2004); vol. 2, *Le fait juridique* (Paris, 2003); vol. 3, *Le rapport d'obligation* (Paris, 2004)

J. Ghestin, *Traité de droit civil: la formation du contrat* (3rd edn, Paris, 1993)

J. Ghestin, M. Billiau and C. Jamin, *Traité de droit civil: les effets du contrat* (3rd edn, Paris, 2001)

J. Ghestin, G. Goubeaux and M. Fabre-Magnan, *Traité de droit civil, Introduction générale* (4th edn, Paris, 1994)

J. Huet, *Les principaux contrats spéciaux* (2nd edn, Paris, 2001)

A. Laude, *La reconnaissance par le juge de l'existence d'un contrat* (thesis, Aix-Marseille, 1992)

Ph. Le Tourneau and L. Cadiet, *Droit de la responsabilité et des contrats* (Paris, 2004)

L. Leveneur, *Situations de fait et droit privé* (thesis, Paris, 1990)

Ph. Malaurie, L. Aynès and P.-Y. Gautier, *Contrats spéciaux* (Paris, 2003)
Ph. Malaurie, L. Aynès and Ph. Stoffel-Munck, *Les Obligations* (Paris, 2004)
G. Marty and P. Raynaud, *Droit civil, les obligations* (2nd edn, Paris, 1988), vol. I
J.-M. Mousseron, M. Guibal and D. Mainguy, *L'avant-contrat* (Paris, 2001)
J.-M. Mousseron, P. Mousseron, P. Raynard and J-B. Seube, *Technique contractuelle* (3rd edn, Paris, 2005)
M. Pédamon, *Droit commercial: commerçants et fonds de commerce* (2nd edn, Paris, 2000)
G. Ripert and R. Roblot, *Droit commercial* (17th edn, Paris, 1998), vol. I, *Actes de commerce, baux commerciaux, propriété industrielle, concurrence, sociétés commerciales* (M. Germain and L. Vogel)
P. Roubier, *Essai sur la responsabilité précontractuelle* (thesis, Lyon, 1911)
J. Schmidt-Szalewski, French report in *Formation of Contracts and Precontractual Liability* (Paris, 1990), p. 89
F. Terré, Ph. Simler and Y. Lequette, *Les obligations* (8th edn, Paris, 2001)
G. Viney, *Traité de droit civil: introduction à la responsabilité* (2nd edn, Paris, 1995)
G. Viney and P. Jourdain, *Traité de droit civil: les conditions de la responsabilité* (2nd edn, Paris, 1998)
Traité de droit civil : Les effets de la responsabilité (2nd edn, Paris, 2001)

Germany

A. Baumbach and W. Hefermehl, *Wettbewerbsrecht* (20th edn, München, 1998)
S. Breidenbach, *Die Voraussetzungen von Informationspflichten beim Vertragsschluß* (München, 1989)
J. Gernhuber and D. Coester-Waltjen, *Lehrbuch des Familienrechts* (4th edn, München, 1994)
K. Larenz, *Lehrbuch des Schuldrechts*, Bd. I, *Allgemeiner Teil* (14th edn, München, 1987)
K. Larenz and M. Wolf, *Allgemeiner Teil des Bürgerlichen Rechts* (8th edn, München, 1997)
S. Lorenz, *Der Schutz vor dem unerwünschten Vertrag* (München, 1997)
S. Lorenz and T. Riehm, *Lehrbuch zum neuen Schuldrecht* (München, 2002)
B. Markesinis, W. Lorenz and G. Dannemann, *The German Law of Obligations*, vol. I, *The Law of Contracts and Restitution: A Comparative Introduction* (Oxford, 1997)
D. Medicus, *Schuldrecht, Allgemeiner Teil* (10th edn, München, 1998)
O. Palandt, *Bürgerliches Gesetzbuch* (64th edn, München, 2005)
K. Rebmann and J. Säcker (eds.), *Münchener Kommentar zum Bürgerlichen Gesetzbuch* (4th edn, München, 2001)
T. Soergel, *Bürgerliches Gesetzbuch mit Einführungsgesetz und Nebengesetzen* (12th edn, Stuttgart, 1991)
J. von Staudinger, *Kommentar zum Bürgerlichen Gesetzbuch mit Einführungsgesetz und Nebengesetzen* (13th edn, Berlin, 1993)
H. Stoll, *Festschrift für Werner Flume* (Köln, 1978), vol. I

Greece

I. Androulidaki-Dimitriadi, Greek reports, in R. Zimmermann and S. Whittaker (eds.), *Good Faith in European Contract Law* (Cambridge, 2000)

I. Androulidaki-Dimitriadi, *Obligations arising from Good Faith in the Law of Contract [Υποχρεώσεις συναλλακτικής πίστεως]* (Athens, 1972)

I. Deligiannis, *Legal Consultations 1960–1966 [Γνωμοδοτήσεις]* (Thessaloniki, 1967)

P. Filios, *Law of Obligations, General Part [Ενοχικό Δίκαιο, Γενικό Μέρος]* (Athens, 1996)

General Principles [Γενικές Αρχές] (Athens, 2001)

A. Gazis, *Legal Consultations 1956–1999 [Γνωμοδοτήσεις]* (Athens, 1995)

A. Georgiadis, *Law of Obligations [Ενοχικό Δίκαιο]* (Thessaloniki, 2000)

A. Georgiadis and M. Stathopoulos, *Commentary on the Greek Civil Code [Αστικός Κώδιξ]*, vol. I (Athens, 1979); vol. II (Athens, 1979, repr. 1997); vol. III (Athens, 1980, repr. 1997)

A. Kambitsis, *Precontractual Liability [Περί της προσυμβατικής ευθύνης]* (Athens, 1960)

K. Kerameus and P.J. Koziris (eds.), *Introduction to Greek Law* (2nd rev. edn, Deventer, Boston, 1993)

P. Papanikolaou, *Methodology of Private law and Interpretation of Contracts [Μεθοδολογία του ιδιωτικού δικαίου και ερμηνεία των δικαιοπραξιών]* (Athens, 2000)

A. Pouliadis, *Culpa in contrahendo und Schutz Dritter* (Berlin, 1982)

M. Stathopoulos, *General Contract Law [Γενικό Ενοχικό Δίκαιο]* (2nd edn, Athens, 1993), vol. A1

Contract Law in Hellas (The Hague, London, Boston, Athens, 1995)

Ireland

H. Delaney, *Equity and the Law of Trusts in Ireland* (2nd edn, Dublin, 1999)

R. Friel, *The Law of Contract* (2nd edn, Dublin, 2000)

B.M.E. McMahon and W. Binchy, *Irish Law of Torts* (3rd edn, Dublin, 2000)

J. Perillo (ed.), *Corbin on Contracts* (rev. edn, St Paul, Minn., 1993)

E. Quill, *Torts in Ireland* (2nd edn, Dublin, 2004)

A.J. Shatter *Family Law* (4th edn, Dublin, 1997)

Italy

F. Benatti, *La responsabilità precontrattuale* (Milano, 1963)

M.C. Bianca, *Diritto civile*, vol. III, *Il contratto* (Milano, 1987)

D. Caruso, *La culpa in contrahendo. L'esperienza statunitense e quella italiana* (Milano, 1993)

P. Cendon, *Commentario codice civile* (Torino, 1995), vol. IV

M. Di Staso, *I contratti in generale, Giur. Sist. Bigiavi* (Torino, 1980), vol. I

G. Faggella, *I periodi precontrattuali e la responsabilità precontrattuale* (Palermo, 1918)
M. S. Giannini, *Corso di diritto amministrativo* (Milano, 1967), vol. III
G. Grisi, *L'obbligo precontrattuale di informazione* (Napoli, 1990)
M. L. Loi and F. Tessitore, *Buona fede e responsabilità precontrattuale* (Milano, 1975)
A. Luminoso, *La lesione dell'interesse negativo* (Milano, 1972)
F. Messineo, *Il contratto in genere, Tratt. Cicu e Messineo* (Milano, 1974)
G. Mirabelli, *Delle obbligazione. Dei contratti in generale* (Torino, 1980)
P. G. Monateri, *La responsabilità contrattuale e precontrattuale* (Torino, 1998)
A. Musy, *Il dovere d'informazione* (Trento, 1999)
L. Nanni, *La buona fede contrattuale* (Padova, 1988)
D. Palmieri, *La responsabilità precontrattuale nella giurisprudenza* (Milano, 1999)
G. Patti, *Responsabilità precontrattuale e contratti standard* (Milano, 1993)
S. Richter, *La responsabilità precontrattuale* (Torino, 1996)
R. Sacco, 'Il contratto' in F. Vassalli (ed.), *Trattato di diritto civile italiano* (Torino, 1975)
R. Sacco and G. De Nova, 'Obbligazioni e contratti', in *Trattato rescigno* (Milano, 1992)
'Il contratto' in R. Sacco (ed.), *Trattato di diritto civile* (Torino, 1993)
A. M. Sandulli (ed.), *Atti del congresso del centenario delle leggi amministrative di unificazione. I lavori pubblici* (Vicenza, 1967)
G. Sbisà, *La promessa al pubblico* (Milano, 1974)
F. Scirè, *La concorrenza sleale nella giurisprudenza* (Padova, 1975)
R. Scognamiglio, *Dei contratti in generale, Comm. Scialoja-Branca* (Bologna, Roma, 1970) arts. 1321–1352
E. Silvestrini, *Il principio 'pacta sunt servanda' e la regola 'rebus sic stantibus'* (1982)
F. Terranova, *Capitolato generale di appalto e norme pubbliche* (Roma, 1982)
A. Trabucchi, *Promessa di matrimonio* (Torino, 1986)
P. Trimarchi, *Rischio e responsabilità* (Milano, 1991)
C. Turco, *Interesse negativo e responsabilità precontrattuale* (Torino, 1990)
G. Visintini, *La reticenza nella formazione dei contratti* (Padova, 1972)

Netherlands

J. M. van Buren-Dee, E. H. Hondius and P.A. Kottenhagen-Edzes (eds.), *Consument zonder grenzen* (Deventer, 1996)
A. G. Castermans, *De mededelingsplicht in de onderhandelingsfase* (diss. RU Leiden, Deventer, 1992)
A. S. Hartkamp, *Mr. C. Asser's handleiding tot de beoefening van het Nederlands burgerlijk recht; Verbintenissenrech*, vol. II *Algemene leer der overeenkomsten* (12th edn, Deventer, 2005)
J. Hijma, *Mr. C. Asser's handleiding tot de beoefening van het Nederlands burgerlijk recht; Bijzondere overeenkomsten*, vol. I, *Koop en ruil* (6th edn, Deventer, 2001)
H. J. van Kooten and H. M. Wattendorff (eds.), *Hartkampvariaties* (Deventer, 2006)

Norway

C. J. Arnholm, *Privatrett IV* (Oslo, 1969)
A. Grimstad and T. Løchen, *Markedsføringsloven* (Oslo, 2003)
K. Krüger, *Norsk kontraktsrett [Norwegian Contract Law]* (Bergen, 1989)
B. S. Lassen, *Oversikt over norsk varemerkerett [Overview of Norwegian Trademark Law]* (2nd edn, Oslo, 1996)
T. Lunde, *God forretningsskikk næringsdrivande imellom* (Bergen, 2001)
E. Monsen, *Berikelseskrav* (Oslo, 2007)
K. S. Selmer (ed.), *Nordisk Gjenklang, Festskrift til Carl Jacob Arnholm [Nordic Echo, In Honour of Carl Jacob Arnholm]* (Oslo, 1969)
L. Simonsen, *Precontractual Liability* (Oslo, 1997)
G. Woxholth, *Avtaleinngåelse, ugyldighet og tolkning* (4th edn, Oslo, 2001)

Portugal

F. P. Coelho, *O enriquecimento e o dano* (Coimbra, 1973)
Direito da Família (Coimbra, 1987)
A. M. Cordeiro, *Da Boa Fé no Direito Civil* (Coimbra, 1984)
Tratado de Direito Civil Português (2nd edn, Coimbra, 2000), I-1
M. J. de A. Costa, *Responsabilidade civil pela ruptura das negociações preparatórias de um contrato* (Coimbra, 1984)
F. P. Jorge, *Direito das Obrigações* (Lisboa, 1976)
A. M. Leitão, *Estudo de Direito Privado sobre a Cláusula Geral de Concorrência desleal* (Coimbra, 2000)
L. M. Leitão, *O enriquecimento sem causa no Direito Civil* (Lisboa, 1996)
Direito das Obrigações (Coimbra, 2000), I
F. P. De Lima and J. A. Varela, *Código Civil Anotado* (2nd edn, Coimbra, 1992), IV
A. R. Mendes, *A gestão de negócios no Direito Civil Português* (Lisboa, 1971)
J. C. Da Silva, *Estudos de Direito e Processo Civil (Pareceres)* (Coimbra, 1996)
I. G. Telles, *Direito das Obrigações* (7th edn, Coimbra, 1997)
J. A. Varela, *Das Obrigações em geral* (10th edn, Coimbra, 2000), I

Scotland

P. S. Atiyah, J. N. Adams and H. MacQueen, *Sale of Goods* (11th edn, Harlow, 2005)
J. Erskine, *An Institute of the Law of Scotland* (Edinburgh, 1871)
A. D. M. Forte (ed.), *Good Faith in Contract and Property* (Oxford, Portland, 1999)
H. L. MacQueen and J. Thomson, *Contract Law in Scotland* (Edinburgh, 2000)
W. W. McBryde, *The Law of Contract in Scotland* (2nd edn, Edinburgh, 2001)
J. Thomson, *Family Law in Scotland* (4th edn, Edinburgh, 2002)
Delictual Liability (3rd edn, Edinburgh, 2004)
Sir T.B. Smith and R. Black (eds.), *The Laws of Scotland: Stair Memorial Encyclopaedia* (25 vols, 1987–1996, and subsequent updates)

Spain

L. Díez-Picazo, *Fundamentos del Derecho Civil Patrimonial* (Madrid, 1993)

L. Díez-Picazo and A. Gullón, *Sistema de Derecho Civil* (Madrid, 1992), Vol. II

Sweden

A. Adlercreutz, *Avtalsrätt* (12th edn, Lund, 2002), I

A. Agell, *Äktenskap, samboende, partnerskap* (Uppsala, 2004)

T. Almén, *Om köp och byte av lös egendom* (R. Eklund (ed.), 4th edn, Stockholm, 1960)

R. Fahlbeck, Reinhold and Företagshemligheter, *Konkurrensklausuler och yttrandefrihet. En kommentar* (Stockholm, 1992)

F. Grauers, *Nyttjanderätt* (Lund, 1998)

Fastighetsköp (16th edn, Lund, 2005)

J. Hellner, *Om obehörig vinst. Särskilt utanför kontraktsförhållanden* (Stockholm, 1950)

Kommersiell avtalsrätt (4th edn, Stockholm, 1993)

J. Herre, *Ersättningar i köprätten. Särskilt om skadeståndsberäkning* (Stockholm, 1996)

L. Holmqvist, *Hyreslagen. En kommentar* (7th edn, Stockholm, 2003)

T. Håstad, *Den nya köprätten* (5th edn, 2003)

H. Karlgren, *Obehörig vinst och värdeersättning* (Stockholm, 1982)

J. Kihlman, *Fel. Särskilt vid köp av lös och fast egendom* (Stockholm, 1999)

J. Ramberg 'Pre-contractual Liability according to Swedish Law' in E. Hondius (ed.) *Precontractual Liability* (Montreal, 1990)

J. Ramberg and J. Herre, *Köplagen* (Stockholm, 1995)

J. Ramberg and C. Ramberg, *Allmän avtalsrätt* (6th edn, Stockholm, 2003)

L. Simonsen, *Prekontraktuelt ansvar. Det alminnelige prekontraktuelle ansvar. Ansvar ved gjennomføring av anbudskonkurrenser* (Oslo, 1997)

Switzerland

C. Chappuis and B. Winiger (eds.), *La responsabilité fondée sur la confiance – Vertrauenshaftung* (Zürich, 2001)

P. Gauch, *Der Werkvertrag* (4th edn, Zürich, 1996)

P. Gauch, W. Schluep, J. Schmid and H. Rey, *Schweizerisches Obligationenrecht Allgemeiner Teil* (8th edn, Zürich, 2003)

R. Gonzenbach, *Culpa in contrahendo im schweizerischen Vertragsrecht* (Bern, 1987)

C. Hegnauer and P. Breitschmid, *Grundriss des Eherechts* (4th edn, Bern, 2000)

H. Honsell, N.P. Vogt and W. Wiegand (eds.), *Kommentar zum Schweizerischen Privatrecht, Obligationenrecht I, Art. 1–529 OR* (3rd edn, Basel, 2003)

A. Koller, *Schweizerisches Obligationenrecht Allgemeiner Teil* (vol. I Bern, 2006)

A. Koller (ed.), *Der Grundstückkauf* (St. Gallen, 1989; 2nd edn, Bern, 2001)

P. Loser, *Die Vertrauenshaftung im Schweizerischen Schuldrecht* (Bern, 2006)
H. Merz, *Vertrag und Vertragsschluss* (2nd edn, Fribourg, 1992)
M. Pedrazzini and F. Pedrazzini, *Unlauterer Wettbewerb* (2nd edn, Bern, 2002)
P. Piotet, *Culpa in contrahendo et responsabilité précontractuelle en droit privé suisse* (Bern, 1963)
J. Schmid, *Die öffentliche Beurkundung von Schuldverträgen* (Fribourg, 1988)
Die Geschäftsführung ohne Auftrag (Fribourg, 1992)
I. Schwenzer, *Schweizerisches Obligationenrecht Allgemeiner Teil* (4th edn, Bern, 2006)
P. Tercier, *Le droit des obligations* (3rd edn, Zürich, 2004)
L. Thévenoz and F. Werro (eds.), *Commentaire Romand, Code des Obligations I* (Basel, 2003)
F. Werro, *Concubinage, mariage et démariage* (5th edn, Bern, 2000)
La responsabilité civile (Bern, 2005)
C. Widmer, *Umfang des Schadenersatzes bei nicht zur Perfektion gelangten Verträgen* (Basel, 2003)

3. From the common law to the civil law: the experience of Israel

J. Beatson and D. Friedmann (eds.), *Good Faith and Fault in Contract Law* (Oxford, 1995)
O. Ben-Naftali and H. Naveh (eds.), *Trials of Love* (Tel-Aviv, 2005)
R. Brownsword, N. Hird and G. Howells (eds.), *Good Faith in Contract* (Suffolk, 1998)
J. Cartwright, *Misrepresentation, Mistake and Non-Disclosure* (2nd edn, London, 2006)
P. D. Finn (ed.), *Essays on Contract Law* (Sydney, 1987)
D. Friedmann, *The Law of Unjust Enrichment* (2nd edn, Tel-Aviv, 1998)
D. Friedmann and N. Cohen, *Contracts A, B, C* (Tel-Aviv, 1991, 1992, 2003)
A. Porat, *The Defense of Contributory Fault in Contract Law* (Jerusalem, 1997) (Hebrew)
A. M. Rabello (ed.), *Essays on European Law and Israel* (Jerusalem, 1996)
European Legal Traditions and Israel (Jerusalem, 1994)

Index

For EU product safety concerns, contact us at Calle de José Abascal, 56–1°, 28003 Madrid, Spain or eugpsr@cambridge.org.

www.ingramcontent.com/pod-product-compliance
Lightning Source LLC
LaVergne TN
LVHW052211200926
848481LV00001B/81
9780521183949